Nethered Regions – An Anatomy of Mina Loy

For Val Raworth (1936–2023)

Nethered Regions – An Anatomy of Mina Loy

Sara Crangle

EDINBURGH
University Press

Edinburgh University Press is one of the leading university presses in the UK. We publish academic books and journals in our selected subject areas across the humanities and social sciences, combining cutting-edge scholarship with high editorial and production values to produce academic works of lasting importance. For more information visit our website: edinburghuniversitypress.com

Edinburgh University Press Ltd
13 Infirmary Street
Edinburgh EH1 1LT

First published in hardback by Edinburgh University Press 2024

Typeset in 11/13pt Adobe Sabon
by Cheshire Typesetting Ltd, Cuddington, Cheshire, and
printed and bound by CPI Group (UK) Ltd, Croydon, CR0 4YY

A CIP record for this book is available from the British Library

ISBN 978 0 7486 8938 5 (hardback)
ISBN 978 1 3995 2429 2 (paperback)
ISBN 978 1 3995 2430 8 (webready PDF)
ISBN 978 1 3995 2431 5 (epub)

Contents

Acknowledgements

Over fifteen years ago, I decided that Mina Loy's poems should become the subject of a chapter in a monograph I have yet to write. On this basis, I was given money by the Weil Fund at Queens' College, Cambridge to travel to the Beinecke Rare Book and Manuscript Library and have a rummage through Loy's papers. Three Loy books later, I remain an advocate for small but transformative sums that permit open-ended research, that enable thinking selves to wander intellectually without clear destination. I'm painfully aware that these sums are increasingly hard to come by.

I returned to Yale in April 2015 with funding gratefully received through a Leverhulme Trust Research Fellowship entitled "Mina Loy and the Avant-Gardist, Feminist Rejuvenation of Satire". Over the course of that fellowship year, I drafted chapters of this ever-expanding *Anatomy*, and as a director for the Centre for Modernist Studies at Sussex, co-hosted a Loy conference with New York University. Entitled "Mina Loy: Radium of the Word", its organisers included Peter Nicholls, Patrick Deer, and the ebullient David B. Hobbs. Roger Conover sent his enthused regards.

For a Loy scholar, this event was the stuff of dreams: Janet Lyon, Jonathan Eburne, Mary Ann Caws, Suzanne W. Churchill, and Bob Perelman were among a surfeit of terrific presenters. The inimitable Carolyn Burke closed the event with a swingeingly gorgeous recounting of her discovery and restoration of Loy's assemblage "Househunting" (c. 1950), which left her audience in floods of happy tears. Quite a conference.

Over the past decade, many modernist scholars have been generous in allowing me space and time to trial balloon the ideas contained in these volumes. Fellow Loyalista Sarah Hayden graciously hosted me at University College Cork, where I first articulated my thoughts on Loy, satire, and punctuation. Whenever I teach *Insel*, Sarah's wonderful *Curious Disciplines* is the rather forcefully recommended reading. Sandeep Parmar brought me to Liverpool for a Loy round table, where I recall offering fledgling ideas about Loy's blind back to an audience tolerant and amiable. Throughout the drafting of this *Anatomy*, Sandeep's razor-sharp clarity about Loy's messy, intertwined romans à clef has repeatedly grounded me in moments of overwhelm.

I have spoken on Loy at numerous Modernist Studies Association conferences, and on Loy, laughter, and satire at the Universities of Edinburgh and Galway. The latter event occurred through the auspices of a Moore Institute Visiting Research Fellowship kindly granted by the University of Ireland in 2018. Queen Mary University lavishly hosted me twice: once to discuss philosophical Loy and a second time, archival Loy. Alongside colleagues from Columbia University, Lorraine Sim invited me to the University of Western Sydney to speak about Loy and sentimentality. On that same trip, Sean Pryor – himself an exquisitely erudite reader of Loy's "Anglo-Mongrels and the Rose" – made it possible for me to run a master-class at the University of New South Wales on Loy's multivalent "Pazzarella".

I presented the final chapter of the present volume at the University of Notre Dame courtesy of an invitation from Joseph Rosenberg, an irreplaceable friend whose original, witty readings of modernist literature have inspired me since we were undergraduates together. Bringing my Loy journeys full circle, I joined Peter Nicholls at Università degli Studi di Torino in 2022 to present more of this work. To Peter I owe more than can be adequately expressed: in my experience, his perceptive reading and generous mentorship remain unparalleled. Most recently, the brilliant, lion-hearted Sascha Bru brought me to the Modernism Research Seminar at the University of Leuven to discuss Loy's esotericism. The considered responses of that group were matched by those who appeared a week later for a talk on Loy's queer pleasures delivered for the University of Glasgow. All of these audiences have indubitably shaped my thinking.

I am also grateful to Lee Jenkins and Alex Davis, who invited me to write on Mina Loy for their *History of Modernist Poetry* (2015), a chapter that allowed me to scratch some long-standing Loy itches. I am similarly beholden to the gracious Doug Mao, who gave me an opportunity to consider feminist archives – Loy's and Anna Mendelssohn's inclusive – for *The New Modernist Studies* (2021), a volume filled with contributors whom I admire, envy, emulate.

When I started working on Loy, the relatively small group of scholars devoted to her work was as ardent as it was welcoming; it has been tremendous to see it grow year on year. For at least a decade, I have been in regular and supportive correspondence with Linda Kinnahan, Susan W. Churchill, and Susan Rosenbaum, discussing Loy publications, events, and approaches. It was a complete privilege to be invited to sit on the advisory board for their award-winning digital platform, "Mina Loy: Navigating the Avant-Garde".

Similar camaraderie and much-appreciated intellectual enthusiasm has come from many individuals as I've completed this *Anatomy*, a list that includes Rebecca Barr, Christopher Bush, Muireann O'Cinneide, Debra Rae Cohen, Patricia Dailey, Maud Ellmann, Edgar Garcia, Alex Goody, Edward Holberton, Benjamin Kahan, Heather Love, Cristanne Miller, Zakir Paul, Adam Piette, Sophie Read, Luke Roberts, Paul Saint-Amour, Rebecca Stott, and John Wilkinson. To Eric White I am expressly obliged for help in locating Laurence Vail's "Cannibalistic Love Songs" (1922), a poem referenced reverentially in Loy's "Modern Poetry" (1925). That the poem embodies so many of the concerns of these volumes made that discovery all the more serendipitous.

My colleagues at Sussex have also supported me through this lengthy undertaking: Hope Wolf stands out in this regard, as do Sara Jane Bailes, Peter Boxall, Natalia Cecire, Sue Currell, Alistair Davies, Andrew Hadfield, Daniel Kane, Sam Solomon, Helen Tyson, and Carol Watts. Catherine Packham's work on vitalism was crucial reading for this volume. My turn to Loy's esotericism in the second book necessitated a replete, satisfying immersion in Pam Thurschwell's and Nicholas Royle's rigorous publications on the spectral and telepathic.

Inevitably, Sussex students have influenced these books. Undergraduate enthusiasm for Loy's "Songs to Joannes" shows no sign of flagging. On one memorable occasion, Loy's famous poetic sequence inspired a performance by our drama students to which I was invited. Predictably, I was thrilled to attend. A number of my doctoral students have similarly sparked my thinking. I hold Byron Heffer personally responsible for my reluctant engagement with the labyrinthine texts of Madame Blavatsky; his keenness for my proposal of this Loy link proved as inescapable as it was cogent.

To Roger Conover I will always be indebted for his faith in a postdoctoral scholar who he magnanimously encouraged to compile *Stories and Essays of Mina Loy* (2011). My indebtedness now extends to his generous permission for my use of Loy images and archival materials in these volumes. Carolyn Burke has been similarly unstinting in allowing me to use her generative Loy archive at the Beinecke, itself a testimony to the depth of her pioneering feminist scholarship.

I am grateful to Beinecke librarians and archivists – Nancy Kuhl in particular – for their permission and assistance in replicating parts of Loy's archive. For images in these volumes, I extend my thanks for the prompt and informed assistance of staff at the Isabella Stewart Gardner Museum in Boston, the National Gallery of Modern and Contemporary Art of Rome, and the Metropolitan Museum of Art and the Naumann Gallery in New York.

Jackie Jones: thanks so much for sussing that this was not a one-book project. Your benevolent incursion made sense of a decade-long endeavour that I am pleased and privileged to be producing with Edinburgh University Press, an ideal home for modernist literary scholarship. My fastidious and helpful copyeditor, Jane Burkowski, significantly improved the legibility of these pages.

Lastly because most importantly, readers of these volumes include Sandeep Parmar, Peter Nicholls, Alistair Davies, and Sam Ladkin. Academia is increasingly squeezed by an economy of scarcity, and time remains our most valuable resource. As such, the munificence required to read through lengthy, nascent tomes cannot be underestimated. To all four: your patience and intelligence have improved this *Anatomy* immeasurably. My heartfelt thanks.

Abbreviations

Mina Loy

B 6: 12	*Brontolivido* (c. 1913–20)
	Folders 1–9; pagination as prescribed by Beinecke PDFs
CP 19: 6	*The Child and the Parent* (c. 1932–6)
	Folders 10–20; Loy's pagination where extant
EP 21, EP 23: 2	*Esau Penfold* (c. 1910s/20s)
	Folders 21–6; only 23 is paginated
G32 7	*Goy Israels: A Play of Consciousness* or *Goy 32* (1932)
	Pages 1–39
GI 28: 127	*Goy Israels* (1925–30+)
	Folders 27–9
I	*Insel* (1933–6)
IA 69: 142	*Islands in the Air* (c. 1940s–50s)
	Folders 58–71; Loy's pagination
LaLB	*The Last Lunar Baedeker*
LoLB	*The Lost Lunar Baedeker*
SE	*Stories and Essays of Mina Loy*

Georges Bataille

AS1	*The Accursed Share* Vol. 1
AS2	*The Accursed Share* Vol. 2
AS3	*The Accursed Share* Vol. 3
BR	*Bataille Reader*
E	*Erotism*
G	*Guilty*
IE	*Inner Experience*
LE	*Literature and Evil*
TR	*Theory of Religion*

Henri Bergson
CE   *Creative Evolution*

Carolyn Burke
BM   *Becoming Modern*

"Of the Cuttings a Garden of Ecstasy": Anatomising Mina Loy

On 19 November 1916, the New York *Morning Telegraph* featured an article offering guidance on the accoutrements requisite to creating an ideal bohemian residence in Greenwich Village. The checklist included a gold screen, a silver curtain, a carelessly tossed tapestry contrasted with a spot of black carpet, and "'a copy of *Rogue* [magazine] on a low table open at Mina Loy's poem'" (*BM* 6). Only two years into her literary career, London-born Mina Loy – then living in Florence – was already an international byword for poetry transgressive, licentious, and cutting edge. The article in question was written by Djuna Barnes, who would soon embark on a lifelong friendship with Loy. Loy featured as the token heterosexual in Barnes's *Ladies Almanack* (1928), a Rabelaisian romp based on the Parisian salon run over six decades by Natalie Clifford Barney, a wealthy American writer popularly known as the Amazon. Typically, almanacs forecast the year ahead – meteorologically, astronomically – or tally recent facts and figures of interest to a specific audience. Barnes's tome postures at the genre: divided into months, it includes taxonomies of lesbian desire, arguments about gender and sexuality, character sketches, and bits of repartee laced with private, often opaque humour. *Ladies Almanack* centres on the tireless conquests of Dame Evangeline Musset, aka Barney, whose birth we revisit, and who, now 50, is anticipated to die at 99, much mourned by legions of women, her tongue alone surviving to provide cunnilingual pleasure for eternity. In many regards, *Ladies Almanack* mirrors Loy's own authorial practice: Barnes's satire presciently, often brutally, dissects the desiring female body by way of excavating foundational, feminist intimacies.[1] En route, Barnes uncovers longings for an uninhibited, ecstatic transcendence that encompasses and exceeds corporeality. Given Barnes's deep, sustained knowledge of Loy as person and writer, the *Almanack* is a fascinating, cogent introduction to Loy's preoccupations and positioning.

Loy arrives early on the scene of *Ladies Almanack* as Patience Scalpel, her surname alluding to Marianne Moore's 1917 "Those Various Scalpels", a poem focused on a simmeringly aggressive, regal sophisticate presumed to be Loy. Born 27 December 1882, Loy was a Capricorn, and Barnes has her represent January and its barren winter season. "[I]n this month", Barnes tells us, Woman tends to question her generativity, becoming "a little pitiful for what she has made of man" (11). Unhappily, egregiously accountable for Mankind, Patience nevertheless remains wedded to her defining heteronormativity, as is indicated by her introductory soliloquy:

> 'I am of my Time my Time's best argument, and who am I that I must die in my Time, and never know what it is in the Whorls and Crevices of my Sisters so prolongs them to the bitter End? Do they not have Organs exactly alike as two Peas, or twin Griefs; and are they not eclipsed ever so often with the galling Check-rein of feminine Tides? So what to better Purpose than to sit the Dears on a Stack of Blotters, and let it go at that, giving them in their meantime a Bible and a Bobbin, and say with all Pessimism—they have come to a blind Alley; there will be no Children born for a Season, and what matter it?' (11–12)

Guileless though Patience appears, there is cunning in Barnes's presentation of "her Voice . . . heard throughout the Year, as cutting in its derision as a surgical Instrument" (12). While the tautologous "I am of my Time my Time's best argument" hardly affirms Scalpel's discursive exactitude, its resemblance to the argument of another revered *salonnière* and friend to Loy, Gertrude Stein, cannot go unremarked. This is Stein in "Composition as Explanation", a lecture published by the Woolfs' Hogarth Press in 1926: "No one is ahead of his time, it is only that the particular variety of creating his time is the one that his contemporaries who also are creating their own time refuse to accept" (454). For Stein, to be "ahead of one's time" is to be an outlaw before converting "almost without a pause" into a classic. The achievement of canonicity is a volte-face. Cultural assessment changes quickly, near-inexplicably moving from derision to acceptance and laudation of the "wonderfully beautiful" in the blink of an eye (454–5). Emphatically of her time, Patience may not have long to wait for recognition.

But Stein's arguments about vanguardism sit uneasily beside the traditionalism exhibited in Patience Scalpel's soliloquy. Perplexed by lesbianism, Patience emphasises women's reproductive capacities, comparing them to domesticated animals inseparable from nature, and in thrall to "the galling Check-rein of feminine Tides". By check-reins horses are tied to one another and disabled from easy movement of the head, the site of intellection and autonomy. Patience's metaphor sustains the belief purported by post-Enlightenment, Western medicine that because women menstruate, they are brain addled, needing blotters for menstrual blood only, rather than to absorb the overflowing ink of written erudition. Finally, Patience avers that her peers should be attuned to a Hebraic-Christian deity and confine themselves to weaving and sewing, sacrificing their individual desires. Narrative hyperbole insists that Patience is confounded by gender and sexuality: she "could not understand Women and their Ways as they were about her, above her and before her" (11). Is this conservative Patience a Socrates, feigning bewilderment about what is most familiar with a view to gaining fresh philosophical insight? Patience vows that her own "'Daughters shall go amarrying'", and this is no empty diktat, as Loy's oldest daughter, Joella Haweis, is wed to the New York art dealer and gallerist Julien Levy just as *Ladies Almanack* is written (13). This match was enthusiastically designed, encouraged, and then closely monitored by Loy, even at the level of sexual pleasure and technique, a truth exposed by wincingly explicit archived correspondence.[2] Throughout *Ladies Almanack*, Patience is rarely without a glass in hand, evidently requiring a perspective-blurring intoxicant to sustain the resolute singularity of her position. Despite this mollitive, Patience can prove exasperated – *im*patient – with Dame Musset's coterie, as when she exclaims whilst "draining her Glass": "'God help us! . . . not one good hammer-throwing, discus-casting, coxy Prepuce among you!'" (67).

If we take her conventionalism at face value, Patience's statement "'I am of my Time my Time's best argument'" is simply apt: Patience *is* status quo foil to the rebellious women who define the *Almanack*. Mina Loy was certainly familiar with perching on the edges of coteries: as an artist, she was repeatedly the non-member of avant-gardes who defined themselves by their collective outsider status, meaning that throughout her lifetime, Loy was a marginal notation in the annals of the obstreperously marginalised. Loy kept vigil at the borders of Italian Futurism, New York Dada, Parisian Surrealism, and ultimately, of modernist cultural networks *tout court*. Yet, in her later years, Loy found herself elided from criticism that came to define the epoch and the canon proper, an experience she shared with Barney and many of their female peers. Even when she is fictionalised, Loy's peripheralisation is foregrounded: critics roundly tout Patience Scalpel as the melancholic naysayer of Barnes's otherwise captivatingly contrary, pleasure-filled tome. This reading is not inaccurate: Barnes precisely crafts Patience as a sulky, sceptical, self-justifying striver amidst a group of exuberant, comfortably upper-class women convinced of their superiority as sexually satiated, erotic transgressors.[3] Published in the same year as Virginia Woolf's *Orlando* and Radclyffe Hall's *The Well of Loneliness* (the latter novel also references Barney's salon), Barnes's *Ladies Almanack* is a like equation of lesbianism with literal and ideological aristocracy, taking its place in a textual triad that affirms how inherited wealth facilitates liberated queerness (Snaider Lanser 41). Lacking neither furs nor cognac, Patience nevertheless represents anxious heteronormativity and signals the sexual binary from which Musset's coterie seeks liberation. Against this binary, as Patience herself observes, they are forced to define themselves: "'Were it not for [men]'", she tells one Lady Buck-and-Balk, "'you would not be half so pleased with things as they are'" (24). At her worst, Patience serves as an irritating reminder that "there is no 'beyond' that does not hold vestiges of what it seeks to supersede" (A. Jones 13).

To be patient is to endure, to withstand, to sacrifice one's immediate needs for a long-term goal. Nominally speaking, Loy's character is an antidote to Italian Futurist rush: she counsels the platitude "'Time passes'" in response to Musset's protracted, vociferous unease about ageing into a too-predictable sex life; at another juncture, she intones "'Still and nevertheless!'", an oxymoronically static oppositional phrase (68, 50). Sacrifice is what transgender protagonist Stephen Gordon undertakes in *The Well of Loneliness*, renouncing her one true beloved and encouraging her into a heterosexual marriage that she believes will save her from a life of homophobic aspersion and social isolation. Given the close links between women and self-effacing sacrifice, this disavowal may well be Stephen's most feminine act. By contrast, the ecstatic pleasure of Barnes's *Ladies Almanack* rests in its refusal to have women compromised or immolated (Taylor 154). As enduring heteronormate, Patience is crucial to Barnes's agenda: she is the unhappy, illustrative correlate to women who demand and receive precisely what their hearts, minds, and bodies desire. But this is not a story of over-simple binaries: close examination of Patience's dialogue reveals its explicitness, its dissent from female sufferance, and its advocacy of alterity as a generative combativeness that promotes intimacy. In other words, Patience's supposed witlessness offers a microscopic diagnosis of the ideological fascinations that drive Loy's erudite art, and Barnes mocks her preoccupations only to exculpate their complex truths.

Barnes's is a bawdy text, and Patience's articulation of genital whorls and crevices, and her affectionate denunciation of lesbians as "'Sluts!'" is consistent with its tenor (13). A potential deviance emerges in Patience's anatomies: the coxy prepuce she believes might round out this group of women-loving-women most obviously refers to an arrogant prick, but etymologically speaking, could as legitimately suggest a brash clitoris. The ease of my first phrase over the clunkiness of my second speaks to the gendered expectations we bring to self-important impudence, but Barnes's queer text demands that we reassess these very assumptions. Patience's pursuit of male company annoys Musset's crew, but she proves unfazed by confrontation with the opposite sex, liking the balance male difference brings to a rigidly gendered world. And where some of Musset's women continue to advocate on behalf of women's gentle refinement, sentimentality, and fear of maiming another, Patience is aligned with their revered Musset in equating happiness with wounding. As Patience asserts: "'Delight is always a little running of the Blood in Channels astray!'" (24). In a late work, Loy offers a variation on this theme: "There may be something redemptive about a fabulous blood" (*IA* 61: 20). Ritualistic pleasures call for ceremonial bloodletting, and intimacy, for Patience as for Loy, cannot exist without cruelty, unintentional or otherwise. Patience knows that the body transgressed and maimed can lead to a porousness, a dissolution that portends transcendence, *jouissance*. She suggests as much from the outset of *Ladies Almanack*, surveying the lushness of women's supposedly partial or incomplete love for one another, which she describes as a "Tree so cut of Life, that the Branch turned to the Branch, and made of the Cuttings a Garden of Ecstasy" (12). Loy's via Barnes, this image encapsulates the primary argument of this *Anatomy of Mina Loy*. Affectionate proximity strengthened by fragmentation is the goal of Loy's satirical, anatomical method, one continually aspiring toward a transcendent Eros that is as physical as a tree and its branches, as metaphysical as an enchanted, transportive oasis.

Patience's respect for the violence love portends is not totalising; it has limits. On hearing that Musset, "'a Child of ten, was deflowered by the hand of a surgeon'", Patience is as incensed as any

Musset devotee, vowing: "'That Man's Hand . . . must drip more Agony and Regret than the Hand of Lady Macbeth, and must burn hotter than a Serpent's Tongue!'" (26). While we presume Musset is a victim of sexual assault, a parallel emerges here with Loy's "Feminist Manifesto" (1914), a tract matching Barnes's *Ladies Almanack* in its historicised, extreme satirical nous, disreputably advocating on behalf of "the <u>unconditional</u> surgical <u>destruction of virginity</u> through-out the female population at puberty —" (*LoLB* 155). Where Swift's "A Modest Proposal" (1729) recommends eating Irish babies to resolve mass starvation directly attributable to English colonial policy, Loy advises that if women are valued by the patriarchy for their intact hymens alone, a quick preliminary incision will render void the strictures of the marriage market. With Musset's non-consensual surgical defloration, Barnes may test Loy's commitment to genital harm as a means of feminist embodiedness.

It remains uncertain whether Barnes read Loy's manifesto, given that it was part of a letter Loy wrote at least two years before they met and remained unpublished in Loy's lifetime. Nevertheless, Barnes clearly grasped the pith of Loy's feminism, her adamant criticism of the heterosexuality to which she adhered, her genuine curiosity about what divides and unites the sexes. What's more, Barnes is unfailingly accurate in attributing to Patience a "Voice . . . as cutting in its Derision as a surgical instrument" even as she is considered "so curing to the Wound" (12, 50). So curing is Loy's voice that after cutting away to the heart of the matter, Loy-as-Patience imagines her way into an "Amateur" lesbianism, no doubt "all Thumbs at the business" but keen to persist regardless (50). As her biographer Carolyn Burke reports, Loy loved teasing and being teased in turn by the women of Natalie Barney's salon. On one occasion, with Barney's approval, Loy enthusiastically reported to those assembled that she was preparing to live with Barnes and her lover Thelma Wood in a *ménage à trois* (*BM* 362). The inquiring gaze Patience Scalpel turns on lesbianism is apposite to the probing gaze Loy turns on heterosexuality. In its honed, radical challenge to sexual presumptions, Loy's gaze queers, and Barnes is an early perceiver of this association.[4] In turn, Loy's feelings toward *Ladies Almanack* are encapsulated by the image Burke offers of Loy in Barnes's Paris flat in 1927, attended by her youngest child, then aged 8. Both parties assisted Barnes with the hand-tinting of the illustrations of a book so self-evidently prey to censorship that Barnes refrained from identifying herself as its author (*BM* 368).

The conversation between Mina Loy and Djuna Barnes lasted fifty years, culminating in eye-wateringly expensive long-distance phone calls from Aspen, Colorado, where Loy spent the end of her life, to Barnes, who was leading a comparably reclusive existence in New York City (*BM* 435). While undated, Loy's typed playlet "Rosa" – attributed at its outset to a spoonerised Bjuna Darnes, if emphatically signed "MINA LOY" at its end – appears to be a riposte to the in-jokes and occlusions of *Ladies Almanack*. Secrecy is intimated by the name Loy gives Barnes's character, Rosa Trinklestein: referring to strict confidence, the Latinate "*sub rosa*" is a favoured Loy phrase, and "Trinkle" means underhanded, undisclosed, intriguing, or provoking.[5] The setting of this brief drama is lavish salon meets bordello; the characters are a desultory triumvirate of sparring adults surrounded by illegitimate children; the prime action, Rosa's wielding of weapons verbal and literal. Loy may go too far in this spoof, presenting Rosa with a man attracted to her because she was sexually molested as a child (Barnes was known to have been similarly abused), and saddling her heroine with unacknowledged, unintelligent offspring and infanticidal tendencies (raised in an incestuous, bigamous family, and having taken care of half a dozen intergenerational siblings, Barnes swore off child-bearing).[6]

Homosexuality is hinted at in the lilac boots of Rosa's potential lover, but where the diction of *Ladies Almanack* is excessively "dripping", "lavender", "mid-mauve", "honeyed", "downpouring", "saccharine", and "dragging in the Gum of Love", Loy's "Rosa" exhibits a dearth of sentimental or desirous language; attentiveness to what the neighbours think overtakes pleasure (45–6). Against the small surgical knives for which Patience Scalpel is named, Rosa Trinklestein is a pistol- and sword-juggler always *en garde*, poised even to impale the eye of a replica of Raphael's *Madonna* (c. 1513–14) – possibly another allusion to Barnes's reproductive resistance. The playlet concludes with Rosa creating a bed of swords and inviting the man she despises to lie on it with her as she extols the value of "a divine hatred" (*SE* 187). Were this the equally punchy *Ladies Almanack*, Barnes might have had Patience complicate this all-determining sexualised aggression. But the pendulum between combat and intimacy swings variously in Loy, and in "Rosa", an oblique creation that may never yield every one of its internal references to the reader, it journeys protractedly toward the sadistic. While the scales of Loy's judgement – satiric or otherwise – are not always in balance, Loy leans consistently toward venerating the agential, powerful female, incisive weaponry at the ready.

As Barnes writes in another homage, Loy actively provoked this potency through displays of "ferocity toward women", who she "handled … roughly, yet gladly" ("Dusie" 75). In turn, "Rosa" reconfirms how Loy repeatedly directs our attention to the incessant immolation of the marginalised whilst insisting that the privileged share in this vulnerability, taking up their own prone place on a collective bed of swords.

Barnes and Moore were far from the only modernists to deploy Mina Loy as a literary subject: Loy is quoted in *Peter Whiffle* (1922), a roman à clef by the American writer and photographer Carl Van Vechten, Loy's friend and erstwhile agent. As Gusta Rolph, a widowed, grieving Loy appears alongside a version of Barnes in Robert McAlmon's fictionalised account of life in Greenwich Village, *Post-Adolescence* (1923). Fascinatingly renamed after the first female prophet in the Bible, Loy is Miriam in Laurence Vail's *Murder! Murder!* (1931) and reappears as Rita in American author and publisher Bob Brown's *You Gotta Live* (1932). And as Loy's biographer Carolyn Burke attests, Loy was an integral presence in key modernist memoirs, appearing in the autobiographies of writer and publisher Alfred Kreymborg, poet William Carlos Williams, gallerist Julien Levy, and art patrons Peggy Guggenheim and Mabel Dodge.[7] This list is not comprehensive. These subjective but resonant accounts demonstrate Loy's hold over her talented peers, reflect her memorable wit, nous, and participation in the avant-garde circles that defined the first half of the twentieth century. In this preface, I delineate Loy's trajectory as an author, her biographical coordinates as an artistic individual, and her concerted attempts – compelling, satirical, philosophical, mystical, feminist, incomplete – at becoming an autobiographer. Loy was all but lost to literary circulation in the middle of the twentieth century, but the two volumes of this *Anatomy of Mina Loy* build upon a resurrection of her work and reputation that began in earnest in the 1980s and has since generatively, spectacularly reaffirmed Loy's central position within the modernist canon.

Author

Urbane, vanguard, the writer and artist Mina Loy possessed a voracious intellectual curiosity. Highly attuned to injustices of gender, class, race, and ability, she was equally enamoured of the revolutionary and the self-evidently archaic. Her birth coincided with the outset of *fin-de-siècle* Victorianism, and as an adolescent Loy gravitated toward the Pre-Raphaelites and Decadents. In turn, her artistry was part flights of fancy and fits of soulfulness, part scabrous, transgressive wit evincing an ingenious consciousness brilliantly humorous, well-timed, and discerning. Loy established herself as a visual artist in her twenties. From 1914, at the age of 32, she began publishing her writing, and in the decades that followed, she turned her hand to poetry, satirical plays, manifestos, essays, short fictions, and a series of romans à clef. Despite this noteworthy output, Loy's description of her first day as an author is awash in ambivalence. In a letter Carolyn Burke dates at 1930, Loy describes her nascent attempts at writing "'poetry'". Her sceptical punctuation is portentous:

> This is what happened – Before the war – somebody said at a tea party – one should write as one <u>feels</u> – & the next morning – at breakfast in bed – I tried to forget that I had ever in my life <u>read</u> anything & see if I could <u>let</u> <u>out</u> that natural expression that must be innate to all mankind – I found my natural rhythm of expression – & wrote many things – [. . .] However what I wish to point out is that this was <u>never</u> <u>supposed</u> <u>to</u> <u>be poetry</u> —— if it was anything it was <u>prose</u> – it was as though I had taken the <u>pulse</u> of my impressionistic memory – Naturally as I have rhythm —— it had a good rhythm – [. . .] However and nevertheless Carlo Van Vechten took the stuff to America – where they had heard of *vers libre* – & they evidently thought I know <u>the</u> way to write *vers libre*
>
> ("Loy, Mina to Joella and Assorted Others")

There is an extraordinary lack of agency in this passage: before she rises to start her day, Loy evacuates her brain in an idle attempt to write prose, attends to the outstanding bodily rhythms that are, evidently, her singular birthright, and ends up writing poetry that proves definitive of a relatively new genre, thereby receiving unsought international acclaim. (Perhaps augmenting any readerly incredulity, Loy's "However and nevertheless" notably echoes her satirical alter ego Patience Scalpel's "'Still and nevertheless!'") By Loy's terms, she is a genius commensurate with the thinking of her age, alert to her innate subliminal uprushes of visionary proportions. But as resonantly, Loy's recollection collates the thinking of some of her damning critics. According to critic-poet John Collier, Loy produced work so awful that only "'by some monstrous exertion of faith, or self-hypnotism'" could its creator consider it poetry; according to *Poetry* editor Harriet Monroe, not even an act of "prestidigitatorial magic" – purest conjury – could turn Loy's "descriptive, explanatory, philosophical" *prose* into poetry (Collier qtd. in Conover, "(Re)Introducing" 250; Monroe, "Guide" 102–3). Proudly claiming both tendencies as her own, quinquagenarian Loy positions herself as a natural, if fortuitous, poetic savant.

Loy's ambivalence defines many aspects of a legacy by which she has become defined as a poet first and foremost, even as she laid strong claim throughout her life to her identity as a visual artist. Loy published a not very grand total of two books in her lifetime, the first being *Lunar Baedecker* (*sic*), a poetry collection produced by Robert McAlmon's Contact Editions in 1923. Playing on the popular, global *Baedeker* travel guides originating in Germany in 1827, Loy's lamentably misspelt title promised to map out a moon provocatively equated with female biological cycles and Symbolist nyctophilia. Predominantly a reissue of past publications, Loy's next book, *Lunar Baedeker and Time-Tables* (1958), appeared thirty-five years later with Jonathan Williams's Jargon Press. Loy's title juxtaposed cosmic cartography with the objective, spatialised clock and calendar time that the French modernist philosopher Henri Bergson countered with *durée*, his phenomenological model of subjective temporality.[8] In an interview given in August 1965, a year before she died, Loy expressed some desire that this already hard-to-obtain book be reissued; another book of poems was clearly not on the horizon. But the books were never the mainstay of Loy's reputation, which rested instead upon what one of her publishers, Alfred Kreymborg, considered her "nudity of emotion and thought [that] roused the worst disturbance" as well as an "utter nonchalance in revealing the secrets of sex" for which she "was denounced as nothing less than lewd" (*Singing* 488). While Loy published in journals that came to define modernism – among them *Camera Work*, *The Trend*, *The Blind Man*, *Rogue*, *Contact*, *The Dial*, *The Little Review*, and the *transatlantic review* – it was her contributions to Kreymborg's *Others* that catalysed her scandalous renown.

First appearing in four parts in 1915, Loy's replete, thirty-four-part poem "Songs to Joannes" was the substance of an entire issue of *Others* in 1917. A work of self-conscious abjectification twinned with an insistently fierce arousal written from a female perspective, Loy's poems were, according to her, "*the* best since Sappho" (Loy, "Series 1"). Many disagreed: Imagist poet Amy Lowell considered "Songs to Joannes" proximate to the pornographic, while the American poet Louis Untermeyer denounced the series as "nephritic", diseased of kidney, an organ associated with the emotions, moral discernment, and inspiration (*BM* 190–1; 311).

Both were correct: "Songs to Joannes" is salacious and anatomically fixated, a continuation of the base body parts and intelligent, uneasy innards that are mainstays of Loy's work. "Songs to Joannes" earned Loy comparisons with the American birth-control advocate Margaret Sanger and the Lithuanian-American anarchist Emma Goldman, both notorious feminist proponents of sex education and free love (Kinnahan, *Poetics* 53). Countering the denunciations, in 1918 Ezra Pound praised Loy for generating "logopoeia", or poetry "which is a dance of the intelligence among words and ideas" ("'Others'" 57). For other critics, Loy was woefully impassioned and troublingly abstract. "[W]e can pass over lightly . . . the tentacular quivering of Mina Loy", wrote the Pulitzer prize-winning American poet Conrad Aiken in 1919 (*Scepticisms* 162). Echoing Pound, but with added vitriol, T. S. Eliot believed Loy capable of occasional flashes of brilliance, if far too inclined to sever word from referent ("Observations" 70). As discussed above, critics interpret Loy corporeally and metaphysically, and though diametrically opposed, each is a sustainable response to her intelligent dissections of viscerally affective bodies rendered in dictions archaic, scientific, philosophical, and audacious.

Loy's second major poetic work was the autobiographical, satirical masterpiece "Anglo-Mongrels and the Rose", fragments of which would be published in *The Little Review* in 1923, McAlmon's *Contact Collection of Contemporary Writers* in 1925, and as "The Anglo-Mystics of the Rose" in *Lunar Baedeker and Time-Tables* (1958). As yet, "Anglo-Mongrels and the Rose" has only once been assembled in full, in Roger Conover's discontinued *The Last Lunar Baedeker* (1982). The sixty-plus pages of "Anglo-Mongrels" are divided into twenty-one sections devoted to significant figures and events in Loy's life: her parents, her lovers, her burgeoning consciousness. As for "Songs to Joannes", critical responses are contrary. Where Burke deems "Anglo-Mongrels" a work that "uses logopoeia as a battering ram", Jerome Rothenberg considers it "'one of the lost master-poems of the twentieth century'" (*BM* 353; qtd. in *LoLB* 171). Marjorie Perloff celebrates "Anglo-Mongrels" as a cabinet of curiosities displaying *fin-de-siècle* mores and language replete with neologisms, solecisms, foreign and explicit phrasing, all offering "a rupture with lyric tradition that parallels Gertrude Stein's [earlier] break with conventional narrative" (*BM* 353; Perloff n.p.). Critics continue to regard "Anglo-Mongrels" as a key representation of the modernist valorisation of form and language, one perpetually teetering on disillusionment (Pryor). Due to spatial constraints,

"Anglo-Mongrels" was not reproduced in Conover's 1997 reissue and reworking of his 1982 Loy edition, newly retitled *The Lost Lunar Baedeker*.[9] The collection included Loy's earliest feminist satirical poems, "Songs to Joannes", post-World War I homages to modernist geniuses Wyndham Lewis, James Joyce, and Gertrude Stein, among others, and writings of the 1940s and 1950s, often elegiac, often focusing on those poverty-stricken, disabled, or aged. Although reclusive, Loy continued to seek publication late in life, contributing new poems to the journals *Accent*, *Between Worlds*, and *New Directions*.

In 2011, I edited *Stories and Essays of Mina Loy*, a book collating previously uncollected short fictions, dramas, and essays. Much of this work existed in partial or unpublished drafts housed with the mainstay of Loy's literary archive in the Beinecke Rare Book and Manuscript Library at Yale University, where it was donated by Loy's eldest daughter between 1974 and 1975. A prospective table of contents surfaces in the manuscript of Loy's short story, "In Maine: Green's Colony" (c. 1920s–30s). This list suggests that Loy aspired to make a single collection of ten short fictions and/or long narrative poems, most of which are either included in *Stories* ("Hush Money", "The Stomach", "Transfiguration") or, as for Loy's "Songge Byrde", a long poem about the modernist dancer Isadora Duncan, can be accessed through her Yale archive (*SE* 326). A volume of Loy's one complete roman à clef, *Insel* (c. 1932–6), was published posthumously in 1991, edited by Elizabeth Arnold. *Insel* was reissued in paperback in 2016, with a newly discovered draft episode located at Yale by its second editor, Sarah Hayden. Loy's remaining seven romans à clef are *Brontolivido* (c. 1913–20), *Esau Penfold* (c. 1910s/20s), *Colossus* (c. 1920s), *Goy Israels* (1925–30+), *Goy Israels: A Play of Consciousness* (1932), *The Child and the Parent* (c. 1932–6), and *Islands in the Air* (c. 1940s–50s). Including *Insel*, four of these works examine Loy's intimate, protracted relationships with male vanguardists. The last four are künstlerromans, or Loy's delineations of her coming into being as an artist; each of these is grounded in the pragmatics of her upbringing and her always central esotericism. While only part of *Colossus* has been published, all of Loy's remaining romans à clef, and the vast majority of her Yale-based literary archive entire, are publicly available through the Beinecke's Digital Collections. Through this invaluable resource, Loy's audience can encounter the full extent of a wide-ranging, prescient oeuvre generated over five decades, one central to our understanding of twentieth-century avant-gardism, satire, feminism, embodiedness, and esotericism.

Individual

Mina Gertrude Löwy was born in London in 1882. Her mother, Julia Bryan, was an aspirational English Rose, resolutely proper and unyieldingly feminine. Her father Sigmund Löwy was a Hungarian, Jewish migrant whose success was measured by his marriage to Loy's Protestant mother and his progression from tailor to wealthy sartorial entrepreneur. The historical truth that Jewishness was a highly racialised category in the late nineteenth and early twentieth centuries, or the period of Loy's coming of age, cannot be overstated. In an England awash in anti-Semitism, Loy's family was perceived as mixed race, and in her adulthood, her origins were continually foregrounded, so that she was described by supposedly progressive artistic peers as "the exotic and beautiful . . . . English Jewess, Mina Loy" (Kreymborg, *Singing* 488). Loy's Jewishness was a crucial component of her early and ongoing reception as an author, a fact initially neglected by contemporary critics (Feinstein 336). Adding to this identificatory unease, Loy was made aware that she was conceived out of wedlock, meaning convention superseded love in prompting her parents to marry. From these fractious, controversial origins, the Löwy family staggered along in a state of perpetual discord, with the soft-hearted, culturally aspirational father often standing reticently by as the mother embraced the role of domineering-to-abusive matriarch. The family resided in a series of escalatingly well-turned-out homes in North London with a succession of governesses on hand to provide an early education for Loy and her two sisters, the musically accomplished Dora and the evidently unremarkable (because unartistic) Hilda. Siblings feature infrequently in Loy's extensive accounts of her earliest years. Loy proved exceptionally precocious where reading and writing were concerned, a capacity matched by her evident skill at drawing. Like many women in the Euro-American avant-garde circles in which she moved as an adult, Loy attended a series of international art schools: St John's Wood in London from 1897 to 1899 (she wanted to go to the more cutting-edge Slade, at whose daring reputation her parents balked); the Society of Female Artists' School, an outpost of the Munich Academy of Fine Arts in 1900; the Académie Colarossi in Montparnasse at the outset of the twentieth century, where she enjoyed free access to anatomy lessons at the renowned École des Beaux-Arts. Loy is also believed to have been tutored by Augustus John in London's Chelsea district, and in 1922, she took drawing classes with the Ukrainian cubist Alexander Archipenko in his newly opened Berlin art school (*BM* 70, 316).

In Paris in 1903, Loy inadvertently followed in her mother's footsteps, conceiving out of wedlock with an ambitious man she found both fascinating and despicable. The child of well-connected Victorian stock, Stephen Haweis gave Loy good reasons to loathe him: her impregnation was an assault, and as its consequence, she was pressured to marry a man who proved increasingly threatened by her superior talents and beauty, a known philanderer whose controlling behaviours included a spate of wielding a gun at Loy over breakfast.[10] Loy's father promised to support his daughter financially only if she remained committed to Haweis. The couple's first child, Oda Janet, died in 1905 of meningitis, aged 1 year. Loy's second child was the result of an affair with a Parisian doctor who was treating the neurasthenia Loy experienced as a consequence of this loss, an abuse of authority that remains curiously undiscussed by Loy critics. Haweis was motivated to present this second child as his own to keep up appearances, to maintain his in-laws' stipend, and because his awareness of its biological parentage furthered his hold over Loy. In Paris, Haweis developed his reputation as an artist and a photographer, associating with key cultural figures: the French sculptor Auguste Rodin, the English painter Walter Sickert, and the terror of the British Isles, the occultist magician Aleister Crowley.

Throughout her early adulthood, Loy devoted herself to painting and drawing, earning increasing recognition for the same: she had her artwork accepted by the annual Salon d'Automne from 1903 (an honour she would earn regularly into the 1920s), and was invited to be a member come 1906. In 1905, her work was accepted by the prestigious Salon des Beaux-Arts. These accolades were among the first in a lifetime of artistic achievement that included exhibiting at the First Free Futurist International Exhibition in Rome in 1914 and contributing to the now-legendary Society of Independent Artists Show in 1917. In the early 1920s, Loy's designs and drawings were exhibited in New York department stores and galleries under the heading "Jaded Blossoms"; in this same period, a Long Island gallery showcased her portraits (*BM* 339). Loy garnered three solo exhibitions: in London's Carfax Gallery in 1912, and in New York at the Julien Levy Art Gallery in 1933 and the Bodley Gallery in 1958 respectively. In 1959, Loy received the Copley Foundation Award for Outstanding Achievement in Art. It was with her first exhibition that Loy chose the name by which she would be known forevermore: Mina Loy. Rejecting patrilineages familial and marital – Löwy,

Haweis – the name homophonically resonates with the French *loi*; by it, as Burke convincingly argues, Loy became a law unto herself (*BM* 97). It is fitting that Loy's autonomy came into existence alongside artistic recognition which, in turn, fed her literary nous. "'[W]riting and painting,'" she asserted, "'go together with me'"; ease or inhibition in one medium facilitated the same in the other (Letter dated 28 November 1932, Loy to Julien and Joella Levy, Box 30, Folder 12, 1932).[11] This important claim notwithstanding, Loy's artwork has been difficult to access, as much of it was lost or damaged, and what remains is primarily held in private collections. The first retrospective exhibition of Loy's art and design took place at Bowdoin College Museum of Art in Maine in 2023. Incredibly well received, the exhibition was accompanied by a long-awaited book devoted to reproducing Loy's visual art in relation to her writing, *Mina Loy: Strangeness is Inevitable.*

In 1907, Loy and Haweis moved to Florence, where Joella Sinara was born in July of that year, followed in February 1909 by her brother Giles, Loy's and Haweis's biological child.[12] As she had in France, in Italy Loy associated with a migrant community of major modernist figures, among them Gertrude Stein and Mabel Dodge Luhan. Although initially dispirited by Florence, Loy was ultimately transformed by this period of her life. Continuing to paint and submit work to European exhibitions, reading the esotericist intellectuals Henri Bergson and Frederic Myers, it was in Florence that Loy converted to Christian Science and committed fully to her defining literary avant-gardism. Stein was a foundational influence: in 1929, Loy wrote an homage to Stein praising her ability to make words new, and to encapsulate the "flux of Being" with writing that effects an "aesthetic analysis of the habits of consciousness in its lair" (*LaLB* 290, 297). In 1933, Stein returned this favour, praising Loy's literary nous in *The Autobiography of Alice B. Toklas* (297). Where Stein embodied the pith of modernist philosophy and art, Futurism instructed Loy in vanguard performativity. In Florence, Loy became immersed in artistic and intimate infatuations with the two rival, iconoclastic leaders of the then-burgeoning Italian Futurist movement, Giovanni Papini and F. T. Marinetti. Both were showstopping polemicists who offered a bewildered public hyperbolically confident presentations and publications praising violent combat and novelty whilst resisting semantics, grammar, and other "outdated" traditions. Following her exposure to this politically suspect if trailblazing and often highly comical bravado, Loy began to write in earnest, publishing her first poems and "Aphorisms on Futurism" in 1914.

With the onset of World War I, Loy volunteered as a nurse in an Italian hospital, boasting about her endurance for watching soldiers operated on without anaesthetic. Having undertaken a trial separation in their Paris years, Loy and her first husband were already cognisant of the incompatibility that contributed to Haweis's desire to set sail for Australia in 1913. Much to Loy's relief, Haweis finally consented to a legal divorce in 1917, or the same year that Loy's father died, his will guaranteeing her a small annual income for life. This was not the end of the threat that Haweis posed, however: in 1920, without consulting Loy, he returned to Florence and took their son with him to the Caribbean. Giles would die in 1923 of a rare cancer, aged only 14. The death of this second child was complicated by an acrimony that meant Loy had been in precious little contact with Giles from 1916 onward, or the year she left him and Joella with their devoted Italian nurse in Florence to set sail for New York, aiming to establish herself in what was then recognised as the new capital of the avant-garde. With this decision, the 11-year-old Joella was prematurely catapulted to a position of responsibility for the family finances, bureaucracy, and ethos that she retained for the rest of her life. While her love for Loy was never in doubt, Joella identified throughout her life as a Cinderella.[13]

New York welcomed Mina Loy. In 1917, the *Evening Sun* presented Loy to the American public as the emblematic modern woman. A cosmopolitan speaker of English, French, Italian, and German, Loy was a well-connected artist and satisfyingly scandalous poet who associated with the outrageous Italian Futurists, thereby residing "'half-way through the door into Tomorrow'" (qtd. in *BM* 8–9). After her 1916 arrival, Loy immediately ensconced herself in the salon established by the art collectors Louise and Walter Arensberg, thereby coming into regular contact with major figures of the period including the photographer Man Ray, writers Wallace Stevens, William Carlos Williams, and Baroness Elsa von Freytag-Loringhoven, and the epoch-defining artist Marcel Duchamp. At New York's recently opened Provincetown Playhouse, Loy acted witless, newly wedded wife to Williams's tempestuous husband, a man who takes great satisfaction in cursing her in the name of the marriage god Hymen for failing to cook their play's titular "Lima Beans" for the fifteenth night running of their brief marriage.[14] Through the Arensbergs, Loy also met her real-life second husband, Arthur Cravan, at first resisting his advances before yielding wholly to his outsized handsomeness and unpredictable charms.

A Swiss national who resided extensively in England and France in his youth, Cravan was born Fabian Avenarius Lloyd in 1887; like Loy, he changed his birth name in adulthood. When Loy met Cravan, he was a provocative figure known for having founded, written, edited, and distributed the furious, ribald anti-art art journal *Maintenant* in Paris between 1913 and 1915; for having been knocked out in the embarrassingly early stages of a well-publicised fight with the world heavyweight champion Jack Johnson in Barcelona on 23 April 1916; and for offering to deliver a lecture on abstract art for the Society of Independent Artists on 19 April 1917, at which he arrived drunk, dishevelled, and overheated, uttering only a few sentences before doing his utmost to strip before the startled audience gathered at New York's Grand Central Palace (Jones 229). His arrest brought the event to an abrupt end. At the Arensberg's that evening, Duchamp roundly praised Cravan's "lecture" (Buffet-Picabia 16). Loy and Cravan were separated when Cravan, ideologically opposed to conscription, went to Canada as the United States entered World War I. They were briefly reunited in New York in 1917, and again in revolution-torn Mexico in January 1918, following an impassioned correspondence in which Cravan asserted that his very sanity and will to live hung upon Loy's reciprocation of his love. Cravan begged Loy to come to Mexico and become his wife; this Loy duly did (Jones 260).

Now newlyweds as the First World War dragged on, the Lloyds nearly starved as Cravan tried his hand at running a boxing school and planned more farcically doomed boxing matches. The couple determined to travel to neutral Argentina with the understanding that from there, they would return to Europe to retrieve Loy's children in Florence. Cravan's repeatedly falsified papers meant that the risk involved in crossing national boundaries remained high. While Loy had proper documentation, her ease of travel was complicated by the realisation in July 1918 that she was pregnant. With the American author and publisher Bob Brown and his wife, Rose Johnson, the Lloyds moved to Salina Cruz, a major seaport in the Mexican state of Oaxaca. A novice sailor, Cravan bought a small, damaged boat, intending to fix it up and trade it for a larger watercraft upon which he and some companions would voyage to South America. According to the plan, Loy would travel overland with the Browns, and everyone would reunite in Buenos Aires. From here, unresolved variants enter the narrative.

According to Carolyn Burke, Cravan determined to gauge his vessel's seaworthiness, and was waved off the shore of Salina Cruz by an exuberant Loy.[15] Loy waited on the beach, wrapped in Cravan's coat. When he did not return, Loy had to be dragged to her room by the Browns, who were exceptionally alarmed when, days later, still in shock, she began knocking on the bedframe to send Cravan a message through the universal ether (*BM* 264). According to Dafydd Jones, Loy departed in a Japanese ship with the Browns before Cravan tested his boat and, come November 1918, was "safely ensconced in Buenos Aires awaiting news of her husband" (273). Less romantic versions of the story suggest that Cravan was imprisoned en route to South America, or that he was terrified of his weighty commitment to Loy and their unborn child, and abandoned them for a life of permanent hiding, only emerging from time to time, true to his love of hoaxes and audience, to publish pseudonymous literature.[16] Alternate, emphatically authoritative versions of Cravan's death exist: the editor of Natalie Barney's writings, for instance, asserts the following in an endnote: "After unsuccessfully searching for her husband in Europe and America, Loy eventually learned from the U.S. State Department that Cravan's body had been found beaten and robbed in the Mexican desert" (Spalding Gatton 251). No body ever materialised. To Cravan's incredulous mother, Loy wrote as late as 1921: "'There is not the slightest possibility of his disappearing on purpose'" (Jones 273). Loy assuredly travelled to Buenos Aires in 1918, either before or after Cravan set sail, remaining there with members of the Arensberg circle until 1919, among them the ubiquitous Duchamp.[17] She then determined to have her fourth and final child in England. Jemima Fabienne Cravan Lloyd was born in London in April 1919. When Loy returned to New York in 1920 and 1921, she would tread the boards again at Provincetown Playhouse. Five years earlier, on the verge of falling in love with Cravan, Loy had played newlywed wife to William Carlos Williams; this time round, art imitated life again: a grieving woman in real time, Loy played a "'drab'" spinster in Laurence Vail's play, *What D'You Want?* (*BM* 296).

Cravan was and remained central to the Loy landscape. In a questionnaire of era-defining literati conducted for the final issue of *The Little Review* in May 1929, Loy was asked to identify the happiest moments of her life, and answered: "Every moment I spent with Arthur Cravan." The unhappiest, by this same account, were "The rest of the time", a response that understandably distressed at least one of her children (*LaLB* 306).[18] Cravan embodied the outlandish insouciance Loy loved in twentieth-century avant-gardism, and his brashness was matched by an astute critical consciousness, absorbed attentiveness to minute, unusual detail, and raging originality. Like Loy, Cravan believed in the power of corporeality, both as desire and intellection. Claiming that art was more the work of guts than brain, Cravan insisted that "genius is nothing but an extraordinary manifestation of the body" (7). In turn, Loy considered him a "biological mystic" who "traced his poetic sensibility to his power of 'thinking' with any part of his body" (Undated sheet, Loy to Julien and Joella Levy, Box 30, Folder 8, 1928). Like Loy, Cravan adored dissection. His ideal artistic portraits revealed not only a well-turned head, but the legs, spleen, and liver of the subject in question. He insisted that good artists should train by taking purgatives, engaging in extreme physical exercise, and doing "a lot of fucking" (7). Loy similarly conflated sex and writing, presenting herself as "the mongrel-girl / of Noman's land" who "coerce[d] the shy / Spirit of Beauty / from excrements and physic" (*LaLB* 143). Both Loy and Cravan turned to art for its sublime resistance; both disparaged civilisationary proprieties that mask the outdated and overdone.

But while Loy paid direct and indirect authorial homage to Cravan after 1917, it is mistaken to argue that his "refractory presence is discernible through all her writings produced subsequent to their romance" (Januzzi, "Mongrel Rose" 584). Loy's artistic style and direction were well in hand before she met Cravan, and theirs was a meeting of mature minds, established aesthetic proclivities, and longing bodies. Loy remained protective of Cravan's legacy, resisting, for instance, André Breton's eagerness to co-opt Cravan as a proto-Dada-cum-Surrealist at one with Breton's own enigmatic, transgressive, and self-aggrandising vanguardism. But in 1942, Loy succumbed to Breton's legendary pressure, giving him some of Cravan's unpublished work to reproduce in the Surrealist journal *VVV*. These tracts were introduced by a Loy-approved, Breton-authored introduction that proclaimed Cravan's genius, compared him to Rimbaud, and unequivocally confirmed that he was murdered in Mexico in 1918, even as friends and associates recall clearly that Loy never ceased hoping that Cravan might yet be alive, might yet reappear (*BM* 401–2, 285).[19]

Loy's life and work continued apace in the near fifty years following Cravan's death. In 1919, she spent a summer in Switzerland, regularly visiting the Women's International League for Peace and Freedom, newly stationed in Geneva. She then journeyed to Florence to see her children Joella and Giles for the first time in three years, leaving baby Fabienne with the ever-loyal Italian nurse before returning to New York in 1920. Burke speculates that Loy may have returned to Mexico in this period to look for Cravan (*BM* 285). In 1921, Loy headed back to a Florence absent of Giles, taking Joella and Fabienne to Vienna, where she met Freud, and then onward to Berlin, where the family briefly resided, associating with "Red Emma" Goldman, as well as a series of renowned American modernists – Barnes once more, Marsden Hartley, Isadora Duncan, and Duncan's then-partner, the Russian poet Sergei Esenin. Loy moved again, to Paris, in 1923, the same year that she published *Lunar Baedecker*. Loy was 40, still struggling to make ends meet, still full of well-intentioned if patchily executed plans for her two surviving children, still buoyed up by her artistic associates. Ezra Pound, James Joyce, Alice Prin, Tristan Tzara, Constantin Brâncuși, Gertrude Stein, and Loy herself were integral participants in the Paris-based group of predominantly expatriate geniuses who Joyce's publisher Sylvia Beach affectionately dubbed "'The Crowd'" (*BM* 330). Loy would stay in Paris until 1936, surviving through the 1920s by starting a lamp-making business located off the Champs Élysées. Backed by American art collector and patron Peggy Guggenheim, at the height of her success, Loy managed a group of assistants and produced prize-winning designs featured in *Art et Industrie* and *Arts and Decoration*.[20] The business sold for a healthy sum in 1929. In the early 1930s, Loy became the European agent of her son-in-law Julien Levy's New York gallery, now remembered as the US gateway to Surrealism. In this role, Loy exerted considerable influence on the North American reception of that landmark vanguard movement, one toward which she maintained her ambivalence. In 1936, Loy moved to New York City to join Joella, who had been residing there since her marriage in 1927; Fabienne had already been sent to live with her sister, brother-in-law, and nephews in 1935. Loy continued living with Joella and Fabienne in turn before moving to boarding houses in New York's Bowery District in 1948.

Loy become an American citizen in 1946, but her origins were always on show; responding to her persistent English accent and her no doubt middle-class mien, the people with whom she socialised in her last years in New York City called her The Duchess (*BM* 410). When Loy criticism resumed in greater earnest with the recovery work of the second wave of feminism, Loy was appropriated as an American just as anglophile American T. S. Eliot has so often been presented as a token Englishman. The first monograph on Loy was Virginia M. Kouidis's *Mina Loy: American Modernist Poet* (1980), bravely published by Louisiana University Press at a time when none of Loy's poetry was readily available. Kouidis's subtitle insists that Loy belongs to the United States, and it is true that Loy compared her first sighting of New York to an "arriv[al] in Paradise" (Loy, "Alda's" 8). But aged 39, Loy proudly proclaimed herself a European in the pages of *The Little Review* (Postscript, "To Mina Loy" 45). As Cristanne Miller aptly observes, however enthusiastically Loy embraced Americanness, before the age of 54, she had spent fewer than three years in the self-styled Land of Opportunity (11). Through her late years in her adopted country, Loy continued to write poems and fictionalised memoirs whilst making art from detritus. She was preoccupied by her inventions, constantly creating new products that she hoped might sustain her financially: alphabet assembly games for children, a powder compact, domestic utensils, support devices for ageing female backs, and contributions to the war effort (a dress emblazoned with a "V" for victory, for instance). While none garnered the hoped-for windfall, these inventions are not a curious add-on to Loy's archive, but an extension of her 1920s successes in generating "cutting-edge plastics designs" (E. White 109).[21] As Eric B. White compellingly argues, Loy is an exceptional, distinctly feminist example of the modernist avant-garde's tendency to challenge the sublimity associated with technology by becoming "artist-engineers" who bathetically parody or competently exceed the technical apprehension and servility of their contemporaries (109–10).

Loy admirers persisted: in the 1940s, Loy became remarkably close with the brilliantly whimsical collagist, fellow New York resident and Christian Science practitioner Joseph Cornell; the American poet Kenneth Rexroth strove to republish Loy's verse; Henry Miller took her out to dinner; and proponents of Black Mountain College, Robert Creeley among them, read and respected her work (Burke, "Introduction" 205). Never fully recovered from her losses – daughter Oda, son Giles, husband Cravan – from the 1930s, Loy threatened suicide so often that her children came to perceive hers as an empty provocation. By the early 1950s, Loy had become absent-minded to the point that her daughters feared for her well-being. In January 1953, Fabienne came to New York to move Loy to Aspen, Colorado, where she and her sister Joella were then living, both in second marriages. At this point, Aspen was an up-and-coming mining town where Loy stood out for her unusual dress, diet, and apartment full of canvas and eggshells, the literally raw materials of her unceasing art making. Familial relationships were often fractious, but Loy's children remained remarkably loyal, supporting their parent financially for three and a half decades, visiting her regularly in Aspen, and assisting Jonathan Williams and Jargon Press by cohering Loy's disorganised personal archive to produce her second book, *Lunar Baedeker and Time-Tables* (*BM* 390).[22] Loy died of pneumonia, aged 83, in 1966.

Autobiographer

"Mina Loy", writes William Carlos Williams, "was endowed from birth with a first rate intelligence and a sensibility which has plagued her all her life facing a shoddy world." Loy's close friend for nearly five decades, Williams recognised that Loy lived through difficult historical and personal times. He praises her for not succumbing to personal loss, for maintaining "[t]he essence of her style" in the face of adversity, and for championing a "directness in which she is exceeded by no one" ("Mina Loy" n.p.). Interspersing impassioned emotion with distanced critique, Loy continuously articulates the coordinates from which she sprang, returning, often, to the biographical truths she found generative because appealingly unorthodox or worthy of protracted rejection. Much critical ink has been spilt defining the content and nature of the autobiographical impulses of Loy's writing. A parent gendered female infamous for writing visceral poetry about sexuality is bound to generate a readership keen to locate the links between her life and literature, an appetite whetted by Loy's well-publicised affairs with renowned artists. Loy's subject matter furthers these associations: she focuses upon the constrained, domesticated lives of middle-class women like herself, born in nineteenth-century Europe; whilst living in Italy or France, Loy writes poems about their citizens and localities; during World War I, she devotes poems to the injured, hospitalised, and dead of that global conflict; diagnosed neurasthenic, her work includes women perceived to be on the edge of mental breakdown; associating with modernists, she publishes homages to those she admires and self-reflexive treatises about her era's aesthetic challenges to convention; witness to rampant anti-Semitism in London, New York, and Berlin, Loy develops a poetics fiercely, proudly attuned to the complexities of her "mongrel" background; inhabiting New York as an ageing recluse, Loy's poems linger over that city's outcasts, destitute figures with "features, / verging on a shriek / reviling age" (*LoLB* 119).[23]

But to make too-easy equations between Loy the person and Loy's writings raises problematic assumptions that have dogged women's creativity for centuries: uneducated and inexperienced by social and cultural design, women's inspiration has long been dismissed or considered suspect, presumed necessarily imitative or parasitic. In the 1980s, as the extensive research for Carolyn Burke's Loy biography was under way, feminist criticism expressly grappled with the historic difficulties encountered by women autobiographers (N. Miller, 132). Alert to this lineage, Burke observes in 1985 that modernist women like Loy wrote "in part to bring into question the very notion of the self" (133). For Burke, Loy is more expressly gender-attentive than many of her peers – Marianne Moore and Laura Riding are given as alternate examples – and as such, Loy actively explores the "tension between a fixed female identity and a fluctuating, shifting subjectivity" ("Supposed" 135, 146). Alex Goody offers this adroit encapsulation of Loy's self-reflexivity: "Loy is not a confessional poet, but her ambiguous and mobile selves do bear witness, in particular to her position as a woman poet, writing against a tradition that disavows her presence" ("Empire" 64).[24] Resisting paternalistic authority, Loy collectivises and politicises her experience, foregrounding how the supposed universality of the white male subject has excluded gendered and racialised subjectivities like her own.

Burke and Goody point to the truth that Loy explores both the biological and cultural repercussions of what it means to be designated female, and what it meant to resent, challenge, perform, and celebrate that designation throughout a lifetime. By extension, Loy's subject matter can be acutely personal, a potential vulnerability she counters with first-person pronouns that actively pronounce: hold forth, resonate. Without ambivalence or apology, Loy's "I" asserts, contradicts itself, exposes its innards, and arbitrates. "Mother I am / Identical / With infinite Maternity", she proclaims; as readily, she insists elsewhere, her words directed at a needy child: "I cannot be your mother / There are already / So many ignorances / I am not guilty of" (*LoLB* 7, 26). "I am the jealous store-house of the candle-ends / That lit your adolescent learning", she tells a lover, adding ominously: "I store up nights against you" (*LoLB* 56, 61). Loy's "I" judges unhesitatingly: "I cannot imagine anything / Less disputably respectable / Than prolonged invalidism in Italy" (*LoLB* 9). Her pronoun embodies sacred authority: "I christen you", Loy intones, preparing to mock another whilst rejecting the patriarchal constraints of a Christianity that forbade the female "I" from performing this very initiatory rite (*LoLB* 85). Bringing creatures into folds human and spiritual, Loy is equally godlike in pronouncing herself dead: "the one I was with you", she writes to Arthur Cravan three decades after he disappeared, is "inhumed in chasms" (*LoLB* 131).

Consistent with this deific perspective, Loy gives herself a poetic headstone in the late, undated poem "An Aged Woman", which concludes: "Mina Loy / July 12th / 1984" (*LoLB* 145). Trickster autobiographer, Loy performs an impossible feat: telling a replete life story from the vantage of her own death at 102. More than men, women are said to experience the self in relation to others; in their autobiographical writing, they tend toward the mythology of the self-sacrificing woman (Marcus 219–21). In Loy's oeuvre, relationality tests the self's mettle, and female immolation is observed only to be trounced. Of autonomies linguistic, creative, subjective, and gendered, Loy is an unabashed fan, an adherent to and professor of what Janet Lyon terms a "radical individualist feminism" (382). These proclivities are echoed by her recognised aesthetic singularity: Kenneth Rexroth wrote of Loy's "extreme exceptionalism", while Barbara Guest celebrated her outsiderness, her "originality . . . [that] does not align itself with Imagism or Eliotism" ("Les Lauriers"; Guest 497). As Jed Rasula attests, Loy's poems "attain a technical perfection so unique [they] can only be regarded as the test site of a new aesthetic", the work of "a breed of one" (164, 166).

The urge to seek biographical coordinates in Loy's writing is compounded by the fact that she wrote eight autobiographical fictions that I am calling, throughout the two volumes of this Loy anatomy, her romans à clef. My definitional phrasing muddies water bound to get muddier, as autobiographical coordinates are renownedly complicated. "[O]ften defined as the literature of the first person", autobiography is recognised as "both test and limit-case for the parameters of subjectivity and literature", a genre unearthing human consciousness whilst exposing what Nietzsche recognised as the impossibility of self-presence (Marcus 190, 180). For French autobiographical theorist Philippe Lejeune, an autobiography is "[r]*etrospective prose narrative written by a real person concerning his own existence, where the focus is his individual life, in particular the story of his own personality*" (4). So far, so Loy. But for Lejeune, the autobiographer establishes what he calls an "autobiographical pact" with the reader by ensuring that author and storyteller are self-evidently identical, that the name on the cover of the published text is commensurate with that of the narrator. While Lejeune's formulation leaves style and content provocatively undefined, the specifics of his pact never arise in Loy's lifelong retrospective attempts to delineate her existence, and nor did she ever intend to bring them to fruition. In 1933, Loy insisted that her late prose work would never "be published under [her] name" as she feared becoming "defendant in a libel case brought by the world against the author—" (Letter dated Easter Eve, Loy to Julien and Joella Levy, Box 30, Folder 13, 1933). Riddled with anxiety about these writings, Loy perceives the world entire as prosecutor, even as she longs to publish the work and feels that if she fails to finish it, she "shall be finished [her]self".[25] Incomplete, fragmented, and unpublished, Loy's romans à clef importantly fail to achieve another key autobiographical goal: a narrative of coherent selfhood. Longing for this cohesion, Loy found herself unable to bring it into being, remaining perpetually torn between the "dire disorder" of life and the "visionary Distance" she believed the replete autobiographical exercise required (*IA* 58: 2).

In Loy's oeuvre, there exist two distinct if interconnected autobiographical lineages, the dialogic and the künstlerroman. Beginning in 1913, the dialogic is Loy's earlier preoccupation. Loy is living in Italy, a period in which biography and autobiography were that nation's "most fundamental modes of literary reception" (Scuriatti 164). In correspondence with American writer and photographer Carl Van Vechten in 1915, Loy told him that she was drafting a novel "'absolutely personal and entirely *im*personal—It tries to analyse moods—newly—it *never* gets away from fact—& is tremendously imaginative—brutally impartial & *never* unkind.'" This quotation has been identified as Loy's dialectical theory of autobiography, one emphasising artistic expression and inspiration as much as the science of impersonality and factuality (Feinstein 335). The specific text to which Loy's letter refers is assuredly *Brontolivido* (c. 1913–20), a series of dialogues between a Loy character (alternately named Sophia and Jemima) and variants on the Futurists F. T. Marinetti (alternately Mafarka, the Martinet, Brontolurido, and Brontolivido) and Giovanni Papini (aka Johannes or Geronimo). Wryly, scabrously, in *Brontolivido* Loy duels verbally, and often successfully, with Futurists who are combatants for leadership of their movement and her sexual attention alike. Both men are so caught up in their self-promoting aesthetics that they fail to understand that they are skilfully usurped by a creature they deem adorable but weak, a dismissal consistent with the infamous Futurist scorn for women. *Brontolivido* tests the tenability and consistency of Futurist principles, becoming a vehicle by which Loy reveals the hypocrisies of this vanguard movement's unexamined ties to traditions ideological and aesthetic. Regrettably, *Brontolivido* remains incomplete and in places illegible, some of its pages gnawed away at by time, rodents, or both.[26] *Brontolivido* is clearly the gestational text for Loy's short fiction "Pazzarella" and her play "The Sacred

Prostitute"; now included in *Stories and Essays of Mina Loy*, neither of these narratives was published in Loy's lifetime.

Brontolivido is the prototype for Loy's subsequent dialogic autobiographical endeavours: consisting largely of series of dyadic conversations, this lineage involves dialectical fictions in which Loy positions her protagonist as a feminist character who slowly asserts her formidability over creatively successful, hopelessly misogynist, and self-absorbed male members of the European avant-garde. With satire subdued by weary despair, this narrative frame repeats itself in Loy's incomplete *Esau Penfold* (c. 1910s/20s), a manuscript and typescript text focusing on Loy's early, difficult years with the artist and photographer Stephen Haweis, alternately named Esau Penfold, Esau Ambrose, or Paddy. In *Esau Penfold*, Loy appears as Sophia, Ova, Linda, and Dinah. She details her experiences in art school in Paris, the rape and subsequent abuse she experienced at Haweis's hands, her earliest years as a parent, and her first meeting with Papini/Geronimo. Evidence suggests that Loy intended to situate Sophia and Esau within a larger narrative about an artist's community named Palms, Loy's fictional name for Florence. Within this expanded story, Mabel Dodge Luhan appears as Gloria Gammage, a character who first surfaces in *Brontolivido*, and is the eponymous protagonist of a self-enclosed anecdote – quite possibly a draft chapter – in *Stories and Essays*. *Esau Penfold* is overpowered by Loy's all-encompassing loathing for her first husband. Given his aggressions, this resentment is justifiable, but it manifests itself in the very prejudice Loy more typically stands against. Loy's racism surfaces in her fixation upon a distant South Asian Haweis relative whose stereotyped features she seeks out in her husband; she also proves homophobic toward Haweis's self-styled androgyny, his embrace of femininity that initially fascinates the young Loy, then repulses.

Interspersed with references and individuals that recur in "Anglo-Mongrels and the Rose", *Esau Penfold* includes the occasional draft sheet of another Loy autobiography, *Colossus* (c. 1920s), Loy's name for Arthur Cravan. An extract from this predominantly unarchived text was published by Loy's executor and editor Roger Conover in a 1985 issue of the journal *Dada/Surrealism*. In *Colossus*, Loy returns to the satirical affinities of *Brontolivido*, holding her lover in affectionate and erudite disdain whilst betraying her attraction at every turn. *Colossus* is unique to Loy's oeuvre: while the remainder of Loy's romans à clef detail a deep relational unhappiness, a "one-sided intimacy" either romantic, familial, or platonic, *Colossus* reveals Loy fully under the spell of Eros, enacting "[t]he formal dream of [her] life, a marriage of love" (*B* 3: 17; 2: 2; "Colossus" 117–18). Throughout, Loy is "I", "'*cherie*'", "'little angel'", and "'*ma mignonne*'", a unique being showered with dears and darlings, an individual entranced by having met her match, "an utterly unprecedented biographical and psychological enigma" ("Colossus" 110, 118, 112). Her relationship with Cravan curtailed by disaster, in 1930s Paris Loy would meet a far less appealing unprecedented being in the German anti-Surrealist painter Richard Oelze (1900–80), who Loy dubs Insel, the German word for "island". Where Loy and Cravan connected on every plane of consciousness, Loy and Oelze fare poorly at the material, embodied, or pragmatic, excelling at supernatural intimacy alone. Protagonist Mrs Jones and Insel dialogue comically and gnomically throughout *Insel*, each taking turns at mystifying the other as the eponymous protagonist is cajoled into creating paintings for exhibition at a New York gallery run by Jones's son-in-law. World War II looms; Papini makes an appearance as Geronimo; Cravan's photograph is discussed. *Insel* is Loy at her esoteric best, embedding her discursive autobiographical impulses in the very cosmos. From these stratospheric heights Loy never returned: *Insel* is Loy's last known dialogic autobiographical text, her final pairing of self with male vanguard artists, personality with impersonality, impartiality with imagination, brute force with compassion, self-effacement with assertion. In Loy's forays in this genre, we witness her thriving on the fringes of Italian Futurism, Cravan's Dadaism, and Insel's anti-Surrealism in turn, strategically drawing from their originalities, energies, and contradictions. Positioning herself as underestimated foil to the male artists whose names alone determine her titles – *Brontolivido*, *Esau Penfold*, *Colossus*, *Insel* – Loy challenges, controls, and experiments with their legacies to foreground her skills as a thinker and writer, her own superlative creativity.

Through most of her dialogic romans à clef, Loy is at sophisticated ease, her wit perpetually at the ready. Not so her second lineage, the künstlerroman that is a return to origins in which Loy palpably struggles to maintain balance, consistency, and motivation.[27] Loy considered these disparate texts part of a large, singular project that she labelled her "psychology novel"; her youngest daughter called it "her book about her Dimension", a space in which Loy strove to demarcate her singular, alternate realm (Undated letter, Loy to Julien and Joella Levy, Box 30, Folder 11, 1931; Letter dated 24 April 1930, Fabienne Lloyd to Julien and Joella Levy, Box 30, Folder 6, 1929–74). The last of these incomplete texts, begun in the 1940s, is *Islands in the Air*, a title that turns the metaphysical "Insel" into an archipelago of isolated yet interconnected subjectivities. *Islands* begins with a chapter ironically titled "Hurry", in which Loy delineates her reticence to return to this never-complete autobiographical lineage; although she feels "impelled to write" this expansive text, it is now in its fourth or fifth manifestation, its "piles of ivory paper" taunting her (*IA* 58: 3). The story of Loy's entry into worlds material, familial, and spiritual, this roman à clef strand – one which includes *Goy Israels*, *Goy Israels: A Play of Consciousness*, *The Child and the Parent*, and *Islands in the Air* – articulates Loy's development as an artist and as a feminist theorist of a sex-positive, esoteric love or Eros, or the inseparable facets of Loy's being. Awash in an ambivalence predicated on a "panic of postponement", "a sense of enterprise", and "an exhausted body", Loy finds herself writing occasionally and without resolution, perceiving the work that results as an extension of her "inhibition" (*IA* 58: 2–3).

Gesturing to the Western autobiographical landscape emergent from Augustine's pioneering, fourth-century CE *Confessions* and monumentalised in the modern era by Jean-Jacques Rousseau's 1782 variation on the same, Loy is galled by the generic need for "unconditional confession", pronouncing herself "a woman anxious, under the onus of revealing her whole absurdity, to preserve her incognito" (*IA* 58: 3). Where in 1915 Loy assertively lays claim to writing a new brand of subjectively impersonal, fictionalised fact, she is now overwhelmed by the knowledge that in writing an account of her life, she will be judged differently than men who partake in the same process, deemed insufficiently cultured or philosophical, for instance, perhaps unworthy of the moniker "author", certainly unable to "provide the bases from which the laws of human nature will be drawn" (Marcus 269, 230). Loy considers the female consciousness, like the child's, "volant" – expansively highflying, if also uncertainly hovering – and "dilator[y]", an ego fallen behind in "settl[ing] upon itself" (*CP* 15: 38). In her künstlerromans, Loy struggles to settle upon her goals, to expose her longing for recognition as an artist worth memorialising. Loy's desire aligns her with other autobiographers of the twentieth century, a period in which the genre was increasingly used to venerate the spectacular self as salve and counter to ubiquitous mass culture (Marcus 5–6). About her ideological and aesthetic exceptionality, Loy is resolutely assured and palpably hesitant. A marginal note in *Child* identifies this work as the "attempts of a woman constantly interrupted to begin a book she is too <u>shy</u> to write" (*CP* 15: 35).

Paradoxically, as Loy grew reclusive, withdrawn from the cosmopolitan vanguard movements and coteries against which she defined herself artistically, her desire increased to write her own modernist künstlerroman à la Lawrence's *Sons and Lovers* (1913), Joyce's *A Portrait of the Artist as a Young Man* (1916), Woolf's *To the Lighthouse* (1927), or Wright's *Black Boy* (1945). Within Loy's oeuvre, the most replete manifestation of this urge remains "Anglo-Mongrels and the Rose" (1923–5), in which poetic form and caricature occlude and cushion the autobiographical impulse at stake. With its satirical self-dissection, "Anglo-Mongrels" is an arguably magisterial instance "in which 'experience'" is to a large degree overpowered by "'experiment'" (Marcus 209). Yet Loy clearly felt that "Anglo-Mongrels" was insufficient to her cause: following the publication of its final instalment in 1925, she began writing *Goy Israels* (1925–30+).[28] The gentile-Jewish name given to the eponymous protagonist – the first instance in which Loy as character takes the titular stage – betrays how this archived, fragmented typescript continues the multi-racial narrative of "Anglo-Mongrels". Delving into far greater detail about the abuses, privations, and injustices Loy suffered as a child, *Goy Israels* gestures toward experiences that will recur in later variants of this autobiographical lineage: the histrionics of the imperialist, über-English Mrs Israels, Loy's mother; the pain Mrs Israels inflicts on her family in voice and action; the anxious business ambitions of Loy's father; the body and home as highly gendered sites of entrapment; and the contradictions of English and Jewish culture. Most significantly, *Goy Israels* depicts Loy's attempts to come into consciousness – *creative* consciousness, no less – in a world where she is expected to behave herself, marry, and reproduce. As Loy asks: "What becomes of our individuality if it is only a confection of broken straws blown from the big hay-rick?" Her answer is speculative, indeterminate: humanity might be "disclosed as vehicles of a general drift of an instinct we have not invented towards a satisfaction that has not been determined by ourselves" (*GI* 28: 106). Seeking purpose in an increasingly alienated, untraditional world, Loy's narrator is in many regards a typically restless modernist.

Like *Esau Penfold*, *Goy Israels* often devolves into turgid polemic. Loy is no doubt as justified in resenting her abusive mother as she was her abusive first husband, but because every infraction is rendered hyperbolically – however explicable, minor, or at odds with countering statement or event – the reader often loses hold of clear perspective or sustaining righteousness. Levity is in short supply. Experimentalism, on the other hand, is not: where Sandeep Parmar considers Loy's late autobiographies something of "an aesthetic and thematic break from the poetry that shaped her early reputation", the reader shouldn't anticipate realist prose (*Reading* 13). Loy's poetic distortions of traditional syntax, grammar, and diction persevere in these autobiographical works: she remains fond of elliptical phrasing that prevents easy recognition of everyday events or otherwise familiar material objects. Furthermore, she writes astonishingly dense, highly stylised, clause-laden sentences rivalling Wyndham Lewis's most involved, collagelike units of expression.[29] And come her second attempt at *Goy Israels*, a short work entitled *Goy Israels: A Play of Consciousness* (1932), Loy's famously difficult register is married to a mysticism that precludes ready penetrability for readers not well versed in nineteenth- and early twentieth-century occultism and philosophy. Abstruse though it is, the second *Goy Israels*, which for ease of reference I follow Parmar in calling *Goy 32*, is a magnificently concise bridge between its text of origin and that which follows, *The Child and the Parent* (c. 1932–6).

Goy 32 is the metaphysical pith of Loy's künstlerromans. By its terms, the child's arrival on the planet is a flight from the cosmos, and the ensuing acclimatisation to three dimensions is a confused pain mitigated only by the infant's continued ease of access to the universal ether. Consistent with the subject matter, Loy's language is abstract; the second and third person proliferate, and Loy's life – emblematising the lived experience of all geniuses – marks the beginning of *the* (not *a*) world. While the phenomenal realm constrains, Loy is artistic, and therefore more attached to the metaphysical than most because of her creative, individualising will; one of the very short chapters of *Goy 32* is devoted to her pronounced, exceptional volitionality. By Loy's gestational account, the child supersedes all adults, particularly her parents, who function as a chance backdrop against which she strains every fibre of her being in order to facilitate an eventual liberation from their hold and her past. Similar thematics define *The Child and the Parent* and *Islands in the Air*. The first of these latter Loy künstlerromans, *Child* uniquely devotes its final chapters to a disquisition on gender and Victorianism, focusing on educational and marriage systems that prevent women from knowing or enjoying their bodies for life, a situation Loy considers criminal. As archived, *Child* concludes with "Being Alive", a spectacularly philosophical chapter in which Loy considers the genius and love that underpin her romans à clef, effectively generating her own ontology. *Child* and *Islands* can form an echo chamber of near-identically rendered character, incident, chapter title, or turns of phrase; as in Parmar's *Reading Mina Loy's Autobiographies*, I treat the second and third chapters of *Islands* as the first and second of *Child*. But while *Islands* opens with a theoretically oriented discussion of Loy's relationship to autobiography, it loses the ideological or metaphysical thrusts of the earlier künstlerromans. Instead, *Islands* continues in a more traditionally realist vein, offering verifiable anecdotes and experiences from Loy's life, including unique, extensive accounts of a first boyfriend and her year in Munich studying art. In *Child*, Loy oscillates from first to third person; in *Islands*, Loy is both "I", and in one or two fleeting instances, the character Linda Gore.[30]

To label Loy's autobiographical self unstable is an understatement. While the romans à clef are grounded in established coordinates of Loy's life, their historicity is complicated by style, by the incursion of polemic, theory, and proselytising, and by the various, overlapping, repeat names she gives herself and her characters, names that rather incredibly extend, in life, to Loy's own children.[31] Loy recognised that she blurred beings. A telling note that Loy pencils in the margin of one page of *Islands* reads: "'None of the people in this book have ever really existed—although if you look into them deep enough—they are all the same person'" (qtd. in Parmar, *Reading* 7). With this claim, we appear to witness the return of Loy's autobiographical trickster. Is Loy even aiming at truths historical, collective, or personal? Written over two decades, Carolyn Burke's biography is a landmark of Loy studies and will deservedly retain this status; every Loy scholar is indebted to Burke's incisive, beautifully articulated research. Throughout *Becoming Modern: The Life of Mina Loy* (1996), Burke treats Loy's romans à clef as factual, interweaving the anecdotes they contain with the actualities of Loy's existence. Yet when Loy's autobiographical writings were discussed in interviews with her eldest daughter, Joella denied their existence. Burke understandably persisted, pointing out that Loy's archive is full of memoirs, to which Joella replied bluntly: "They're not all about her life" (Bayer, "Interview, Burke and Bayer" 3).

Joella is correct: as I've detailed, Loy's romans à clef include feminist ideology, aesthetic methodologies, ontologies, mysticism, and affect theories. Yet, on occasion, we discern Loy reaching for a precision that suggests she is striving to accurately narrate her existence. For example, next to an anecdote in which Loy, then a young adult on a London street, asked a woman working in the sex trade for the hour, autobiographer Loy pens a marginal question mark above a note asking herself if the time given is accurate. It is important to her that it really was 5.30 pm (*IA* 69: 142). And Loy's edits reveal a desire to relinquish the feint of fictionalisation, as when she writes:

"He turned to ~~Sophia~~ me, bracing himself" (*B* 3: 1). Furthermore, in her romans à clef, Loy's self-characterisation is discernibly consistent: smart, funny, critical, feminist; she persistently seeks creative outlet, recognition, love. Giving herself a panoply of names, Loy augments the truth that by its very nature, autobiography others and objectifies the self. Through thin self-disguise, Loy seeks to increase the "[p]sychological long-distance" requisite to human understanding; as she argues in *Goy Israels*, in order to grasp our subject matter, we have to position ourselves "as far back as possible" from what we want to comprehend (*GI* 28: 75). This *Anatomy of Mina Loy* concurs with Loy's position, arguing that through the repulsive–attractive nexus of satirical attack, Loy seeks greater proximities. So it is that while I believe that Burke might have productively exposed her reliance upon Loy writings that blend fact, fiction, and contemplation, I follow Burke's lead in referring to the female protagonists of Loy's romans à clef as Mina Loy. My kinship with Burke goes further: I share her recognition of Loy's romans à clef as vital attempts to cohere a self who created a staggeringly original, revolutionary legacy of artistic prowess and intimate association by which I, too, have been entirely beguiled, as the two volumes of this *Anatomy of Mina Loy*, a decade in the writing, all too amply attest.

About These Volumes

What does this *Anatomy* set out to achieve? First and foremost, these books – *Nethered Regions* and *Elevated Realms* respectively – are an in-depth exploration of Loy's relationship to the human body, a relationship inextricable from her esoteric understanding of the human soul. While Loy has always been considered a writer who insists on the primacy of the corporeal, and women's corporeality in particular, my criticism does not take that assertion as read, but anatomises Loy's theoretical, lived, and creatively rendered approaches to limbs, organs, and a highly sensualised spirit. Part I of the first volume involves two interrelated chapters that begin with Loy's interrogation of the baseline of existence: sentience, the capacity to feel that has long determined the very substance of being, and by which the denigrated are, often reluctantly, granted a scant subjectivity. A woman of Jewish origins, Loy reclaims her degraded sentience with palpable pride, erudite flourish, and intellectual curiosity: she is fascinated by how life itself has been interpreted and gauged through history. Exploring ontologies, primitivism, evolution, vitalism, and sensibility – all topics I address – Loy gave herself the requisite tools to dismantle social hierarchies, and with them, the post-Enlightenment illusion that ours is a rational and ordered world. When origins, bodies, minds, and animating principles are bestial, ungendered, deracialised, or inexplicable, distinctions between individuals must be earned and justified, the presumptions of entitlement and knowledge abandoned. These interests make Loy a perpetually backward-looking iconoclast; hence this first chapter is titled "Loy's Atavistic Avant-Gardism".

In Chapter 2 of Part I, "Bodies Sacrificial and Intimate", I delve into Loy's embrace of the emotional self and her express challenge to the modernist sentimental economy – one espoused from Baudelaire to Joyce to Benjamin – whereby the admirable individual *pays* for emotion, for exercising their sentient capacity to feel. Loy resists this jarringly capitalist affectivity through her atavistic fascination with a sacrificial model of intimacy, one that sidesteps positivism and utility. Sacrifice is an ancient ritual I conflate with satire, a similarly ancient practice; as I argue, both immolate to restore or reassert the status quo. For Loy, as for her contemporary, the French philosopher Georges Bataille (1897–1962), cruelty is integral to loving abandon. Only in welcoming aggression do bodies become porous enough to embrace dissolution, thereby relinquishing sovereignty and the desire to hold oneself distinct from the beloved. By asserting the need to yield wholly, Loy and Bataille retheorise intimacy, restoring irrational excesses to a censorious civilisation defined by loss and lack.

But what Loy foregrounds as Bataille does not is that those who are marginalised bear more than their fair share of self-sacrifice, and that these enforced obligations and constraints preclude the possibility of transcendences ecstatic or subjective. Rather than ridding us of an originary human ritual, Loy aims to democratise sacrificial methodologies by extending them to the privileged, a move Bataille, so genuinely keen for his own ritualised decimation, might well applaud. These same sacrificial coordinates motivate Loy's satire. Aware that satire began with male and female performing maledictions against one another, Loy's literature deploys feminism as a weapon to undermine her male peers. Unlike traditional satirists, however, Loy attacks what angers or repulses her not to generate distance between herself and her enemy, but to establish a greater proximity, an accord that might flourish into an affection or love free of inequity. Consequently, these two volumes are underpinned by the claim that Loy's Thanatos is driven by her specific and highly theorised Eros. Chapter 2 concludes by considering how Loy's sacrificial model impacts on her original renderings of female cruci-fixion, resurrection, and virginity.

Chapter 3 of *Nethered Regions*, "Feet, Legs, Genitals: The Pornographies of Loy's Punctuation", takes us to specificities corpo-real and textual. Punctuation has long been feminised, seen as super-fluous helpmeet to the integral, intellectual script proper. Against these suppositions, Loy centralises punctuation as a cartography of the feeling, longing, rhythmic body, its movements and transit. Loy hyperpunctuates, conflating diacritical marks with beings, body parts, and affect: her asterisk is queering asshole, her rows of dashes desire lines; both challenge the censorious, heteronormative presumptions of sexed humanity. As the comma lies low upon and crosses the line, so does this chapter consider a base corporeality, reflecting on how toes, feet, legs, and genitals are the limbs and organs Loy uses to interrogate gendered desire, and in particular, the dead-ended perceptions of women's sexuality, which reach their nadir in condemnations of the fallen woman and streetwalker. Here the modernist affective economy resurfaces as the distinctly unsenti-mental economy of prostitution, one that, in Loy's hands, calls into question the misogynist reckonings of the masculinist avant-garde. Following her feminist Victorian peers, Loy defends the forced woman, but with a sex-positive difference: Loy champions a non-censorious approach to women's sexuality, a wilfully open-ended wandering through the intimacies of self and other. In sum, Loy envisions a sexuality that is sacrificially risky for men and women alike, positioning everyone as a potentially fallen being, bathetically yet generatively prone upon civilisational and textual horizon lines.

Chapter 4, "'Upon Bossed Bellies': Loy and the Accursed Muse", considers the female torso, its necessarily ruminative stomach and potentially fertile womb. The focus is Loy's story "The Stomach" (1921), in which the positioning of a midriff determines the course of a female muse's life; by her outswung stomach she becomes famous, a celebrity that extends to the artist who painted her first, and whose reputation rests on his repeat replications of her body. Based on notes made in Loy's archive, I explore how the substance of "The Stomach" is attributable to the career of John Singer Sargent (1856–1925), the American artist whose reputation was made and nearly broken on three controversial paintings that foregrounded his subjects' torsos. This history offers important context for the gestation of "The Stomach", a story that is emblematic of Loy's preoccupation with the objectifying male gaze and with what I label the accursed muse, a neologism that names the unrecognised counter to Verlaine's famous *fin-de-siècle* account of the accursed poet. While both figures are damned – poor, undervalued, working against artistic and social tradition – the *poète maudit* martyrs himself to a deferred legacy in which he has genuine faith, while the accursed muse is condemned to a life of ignominy and an afterlife of anonymity. Of her sacrificial status the muse is profoundly aware. Against this tradition, Loy repeatedly centralises the model in her writings, demonstrating how she is central to the creative inspiration for which the artist is singularly celebrated. Come *The Child and the Parent*, Loy triumphantly attributes to women's wombs the capacity for an authoritative cognition implicit in Loy's repeat portraits of the torso-centric muse.

The second volume of this *Anatomy*, *Elevated Realms*, offers three chapters focused on Loy's presentation of the heart – or more precisely, the etherealised heartscape that drives her esoteric proclivities – as well as the spine, its brain centre or nerves, and the eyes. These realms are elevated in originating above the waist, and because Loy uses these body parts as the rationale for her pursuit of a transcendental mysticism, one that is never far from the orgasmic ecstasy or abjection of the nethered regions discussed in the first volume. In brief, this second book drills to the core of Loy's numerous heterodox influences, which include, but are not limited to, mesmerism, telepathy, and spiritualism; Freudian and post-Freudian psychoanalysis; philosophies Platonic and phenomenological; Theosophy and Christian Science; atomic physics and fourth dimensionality. Loy's spiritual quest is, in her own terms, "infinitarian" – she longs for a sense of her lived self that is deeply material, yet can exceed the same – and consumed by a longing to establish her own uniqueness as a creator ("Street" 41). In typical Loy style, this quest is grounded in the soma, its positions and parts. Loy seeks a coherence of self and legacy that may evade any mere mortal, but was still more frustratingly inaccessible due to her inability to complete her autobiographical project. Along the way, Loy develops and articulates a pronounced, embodied feminist vision, one that counters the overlooking of female desire and satiation by religion and science. Central to this second volume is the argument that the pain, trauma, and loss Loy experienced throughout her life motivates her satirical and authorial strategies, her identification with women's constrained experience, and her gravitation toward liberating esoteric beliefs.

Mina Loy was a feminist attuned to the fact that "the first patriarch has not yet loosened his grip" on humanity, well aware that even at her abusive worst, her own mother was drawing upon what little power Victorian culture offered those circumscribed by femininity: "woman becomes more magnified in the nursery to exactly the inverse of the inconsiderable proportions she attained in the world where she was only in evidence as a picture" (*CP* 14: 34). What those Victorians called the "sex war" was the mainstay of Loy's satire, a battle that took place in the Western entrenchment of male and female, each relegated to traditional heteronormative roles by which men retained legal, financial, and political power over women, whilst women fought for access to education, the vote, and public life. This battle emerges in one of Loy's first poems, "Parturition" (1914), where amidst the all-consuming pangs of labour, Loy's speaker locates sufficient energy to observe that "The irresponsibility of the male / Leaves woman her superior Inferiority" (*LoLB* 5). It permeates the draft version of a late, undated Loy story, where two women discuss "'men' . . . . like [an] iceber[g] scanning the horizon for something to collide with" (*SE*: 303). By the terms of Loy's simile, supposedly passive, inert womankind harbours submerged perceptions, aggressions, and longings for meaningful contact. But as the sex war tallies its victims and victors, necessitating more bloodletting and injury with a democratised good in view, why does Loy further anatomise already riven bodies?

Fragmented, the feminised body that is Loy's focus becomes still more vulnerable. Intellectual histories of anatomy have never been kind to women: Plato believed women too close to the body at the expense of their souls; Aristotle considered the female a deformed or mutilated male, a verdict by which women's cyclical physiologies continue to be associated with disability or pathology.[32] And the founder of modern anatomy, sixteenth-century European Andreas Vesalius, the first to separate organs from bodily or social context, perceived the clitoris as a useless "'sport of nature'" found only in unhealthy women (Birke 51–2). In combination, the eighteenth-century gendering of even the most universally shared human body parts and the nineteenth-century professionalisation of medicine saw the rise of hysteria diagnoses, and the further subordination of women based on "enervating" hormones and reproductive systems (Birke 36). As such, it is little wonder that contemporary Western feminism has been infected with what Elizabeth Spelman labels "'somatophobia'" (qtd. in Birke 25).[33] Since the post-Fordist period, feminists have repeatedly documented their hard-earned fear of the material body, prioritising malleable, agential "nurture" over the fixity continually ascribed to "nature" or biology.

Loy exposes the social constructivism made famous by Simone de Beauvoir's assertion that "[o]ne is not born, but rather becomes, a woman", a maxim furthered by Judith Butler's insistence in *Gender Trouble* (1990) that gender is imposed, learned, and regulated performance, not a birthright inextricable from biology.[34] In Loy's "Feminist Manifesto" (1914), we witness her unmasking the "pet illusions" that sustain the divide between male and female, the recognised binary of her day. Loy understands that the enactment of masculinity or femininity affects all human beings, and maintains, with evident relish, that it will require "<u>Absolute Demolition</u>" of eminently destructible "social code[s]" to change "the lies of centuries" (*LoLB* 153). Loy actively works against the Freudian precept that anatomy is destiny, encouraging women to engage in Gayatri Spivak's strategic essentialism – "Woman for her happiness must retain her deceptive fragility of appearance, combined with indomitable will, irreducible courage, & abundant health" – whilst striving to imagine a womankind more satiated, more diversely embedded in her own society (*LoLB* 156). Increasingly, feminists recognise that idealised gender norms transcend lived experience, can never be sufficiently embodied.[35] As Butler tells us: replete categorical identifications are politically and socially posited and enforced in part because the sustained inhabitation of any gender "is open to splittings, self-parody, self-criticism, and those hyperbolic extensions of 'the natural' that, in their very exaggeration, reveal its fundamentally phantasmic status" (200). Loy exhibits a like exaggeration in her "Feminist Manifesto", arguing that woman does not need to be mistress, mother, or whore – the roles society imposes – because "Nature has endowed the complete woman with a faculty for expressing herself through <u>all</u> her functions—there are <u>no</u> <u>restrictions</u>" (*LoLB* 154). *Contra* Loy, nature does endow specific, if expansive, functions: at present, woman cannot, for instance, fly, spontaneously grow new limbs, or gestate a foetus in her leg. That said, she can dramatically reform herself by stepping outside of the circumscribed boxes into which she has been parcelled.

The canyon demarcating the nature/nurture divide is riven with myriad crevices, and these fissures speak to Loy's exploration of the body in bits. By this exploration, Loy self-consciously holds up fragments for our inspection before reintegrating the same into social narratives of flux and conditioning, always with a view to cohering the body, however ephemerally, however impossibly. As Goody writes, Loy wants to highlight the corpus, not disown it, and she moves perpetually toward a "celebrat[ion] of the de-objectified body" ("Ladies" 280). In short, Loy is as much anti-anatomist as she is anatomist. Loy is aware that women are determined by their biology: by stature, strength, and endurance; by the decades-long preparations for reproduction; by moods affected by cyclical hormonal change. All bodies are in flux, developing and changing through time, moving from the disability of infancy to that of old age, both periods over which Loy dwelt with exacting phenomenological, ontological, and aesthetic precision. Loy attends to the non-normate body, the corporeality that for Butler as for Rosemarie Garland-Thomson, reveals "the limits of constructivism" or "the boundaries of bodily life where abjected or delegitimated bodies fail to count as 'bodies'" (Garland-Thomson 15).[36] Loy's anatomies purposively call into question the closed, smooth classical body; at times, they supersede the contemporary privileging of bodily surface, lending autonomy to organs and innards (Wolff 84).[37]

Loy precedes the cautious, considered feminist return to corporeality by some six or seven decades, aiming to encapsulate the body in its aleatory transitions as an ever-changing, interactive being. While she predominantly adheres to the limited and limiting gender binaries of the pre-Fordist era, and can espouse troublingly essentialist views about race and sex, Loy is an atavistic vanguardist who anticipates contemporary calls for a contingent, non-linear view of embodied experience, one that combines sexed selves with gender identities, as well as social relations and recognition (Lane 148). She challenges heteronormativity, she asserts her right to create, she dissects and assaults strategically. Loy knew what we continue to relearn: that Western humanism is productively challenged by the knowledge bodies offer, and that it persists only through recognising diverse bodies, their coordinates and interactions (Weigman 118). Furthermore, Loy was aware that the rational self espoused by that humanism was a misnomer, that there was no core, autonomous self, free of identities of race, class, or gender (Alcoff 22). Instead, Loy perceived her own sets of identifications – female, "mongrel", middle-class, English cosmopolitan, artist – as "horizons from which certain layers of reality can be made visible" (Alcoff 43). Paradoxically, her very need to taxonomise these relational layers made it impossible for Loy to finish her autobiographies. Striving for a completist coherence, she became ensnared in the unique, interlocking facets of her own identificatory anatomy, a process that reinforced and echoed the fragmented feminist corporeality that defines so much of her writing.

With the above in view, you have before you two books wilfully divided into body parts, but also aiming at a cohesion as impossible as finalised identity. While there exists a welcome and growing collection of Loy monographs, this paired *Anatomy of Mina Loy* is the first critical study to comprehensively consider Loy's literary oeuvre in its entirety, examining her poetry, fiction, essays, and all of the romans à clef, as well as archived correspondence in Philadelphia and New Haven, manuscript drafts, and the parts of her Yale papers that elude ready classification.[38] Via Loy, each chapter delineates a distinct, innovative theory in relation to Loy or modernism: Chapter 1 of the first volume, *Nethered Regions*, establishes the ontology subtending Loy's aesthetics, the sentience or "being alive" that is the baseline to which marginalised individuals remain tethered. From these foundations, this chapter explores the atavism Loy and Darwin celebrate, delves into Loy's underdiscussed primitivism, and establishes how her Freudian ambivalence pushes her toward older, heterodox models such as vitalism. Chapter 2 articulates a relationship between modernist satire and the sacrificial. It then puts Loy's satire into conversation with a systematic, novel consideration of what I label the modernist sentimental economy, a lineage antedating Stephen Dedalus's much-quoted claim that "the sentimentalist is he who would enjoy without incurring the immense debtorship for a thing done" (Joyce, *Ulysses* 550–1). Chapter 3 posits new modes of thinking about punctuation as corporeality and affective cartography, showing how Loy uses pictorial marks as feminist critique and as a means of mapping a transcendent, as-yet-unrecognised female desire, a theory jointly drawn from treatises on stigmeology and urban planning, and applicable to Loy's poetic peers from Emily Dickinson to Baroness Elsa von Freytag-Loringhoven. Chapter 4 introduces the accursed muse, establishing this figure as the overlooked counter to the near-colloquial, reverential understanding of the *poète maudit*. With her self-reflexive elevation of the accursed muse, Loy foresees second-wave feminist art in which creator and model are increasingly seen as inextricable.

In *Elevated Realms*, I uncover Loy's theory of esoteric Eros, one that lays significant ground in comprehending a complex web of heterodox referents from her earliest writings to the latest works, many of which have been treated generically or altogether overlooked. Loy's esoteric Eros importantly coalesces her feminist revisioning of a united self and spirit. The second chapter of the volume analyses how Loy – ever the atavistic vanguardist – possesses an intensive understanding of occult practice (mesmerism, spiritualism, telepathy) from the eighteenth century forward. Loy draws on occult postulations and literal posturing to critique the phallocentrism of avant-gardism (Decadence, Futurism, Surrealism) and psychoanalysis, schools of thought that replicate models of female mediumship and dorsal supinity. While Freud's relationship to this occult history is better known, Loy's anatomies cannily dissect vanguard esotericisms, particularly within Futurism, that remain underexamined. From Loy's attentiveness to a strategic, mystical proneness, I turn in the final chapter to the first fulsome discussion of Loy's oeuvre-long articulation of the "blind back". Through this anatomical incursion, Loy presents the dorsal region as a threshold to transcendence or full-blown regression. The only intensive examination of Loy's relationship to Theosophy, a sect that shares Loy's fascinations with pineality and the returns of reincarnation, this last chapter also defines and situates Loy's place within the modernist preoccupation with fourth dimensionality.

Bataille has become a mainstay of this work because he and Loy dovetail in their valuing of sentience over rationality; in their unabashed embrace of sexual excess and the abject; in their shared understanding of the inextricability of love and cruelty; and most importantly, in their fascinated veneration for the sacrificial and maledict. Misogynist, homophobic Bataille often becomes a useful foil to feminist Loy's more inclusive considerations of gender and sex. That said, Bataille and Loy are aligned in recognising the dual importance of the body and of the gnomic, and in their belief that things can and must transgress and transcend human comprehension for life to have significant meaning. This emphatically embodied mystical focus is central to the second volume, *Elevated Realms*, where transcendences ecstatic and spiritual emerge as the zenith of Loy's feminist vision. In this first volume, *Nethered Regions*, I attend to the ideologies, science, and politics that literally ground Loy's resolute focus on the base body: atavisms and primordialities resident in the toes, legs, genitals, reproductive organs, and digestive tracts. From these slighted portions of the self – literally and figuratively lower, nether and nethered in the eyes of proudly intellectual, erect *Homo sapiens* – Loy generates her philosophical, affective, and spiritual challenge to Western patriarchal culture.

Notes

1. Teresa de Lauretis includes *Ladies Almanack* in a celebration of feminist literary attempts "to escape gender, to deny it, transcend it,

or perform it in excess, and to inscribe the erotic in cryptic, allegorical, realistic, camp, or other modes of representation, pursuing diverse strategies of writing and of reading the intransitive and yet obdurate relation of reference to meaning, of flesh to language" (53).

2. Highly affectionate letters sent between mother and daughter between 1926 and 1936 track out an implicit, uncomfortable love triangle between Loy, Joella, and Loy's son-in-law Julien Levy. Of this relationship only Joella appears ignorant, responding in replete earnest to direct questions from Loy about positioning and technique during lovemaking with her new husband, listing the likenesses shared between mother and son-in-law, and admitting to calling Levy "little Mina". Joella informs her mother that Levy keeps Loy's letters at his office, meaning Joella reads them only once; in addition, he becomes upset when Joella doesn't report to Loy about their sex life (Bayer, "Bayer, Joella to Mina Loy, 1926–1936").

   Levy's letters to Loy includes boastfulness about his lovemaking techniques, affirmations of his capacity to "surprise" his wife, and statements such as: "We are apprehending the true meaning of that phrase 'the romantic phallusy'" (Letter dated May 28, Julien Levy to Loy, Box 31, Folder 11, 1928–1954). In *Becoming Modern*, Burke repeatedly points out that Levy was unusually enamoured of his mother-in-law, and that Loy failed to support her daughter when her first marriage encountered the difficulties that would end in divorce. Levy and Loy can be discerned performing amorously for each other in correspondence dating into the 1950s.

3. Susan Snaider Lanser's description is typical: Patience is "the stubbornly heterosexual damper on lesbian heat" (42). As Jaime Hovey aptly points out, the comedy of Barnes's project is enhanced by Patience. Where satire generally lampoons the perverse or immoral, in *Ladies Almanack*, it is über-normal Patience who is the butt of Barnes's joke (86). For Hannah Roche, *Ladies Almanack* presciently presents heterosexuality as performance some seventy years before Judith Butler's landmark *Gender Trouble* (1990), and Patience's ostensibly intractable desire for the masculine is key to that portrayal (153). In her wonderful article on *Ladies Almanack*, Daniela Caselli also discusses how Patience acts as an outsider and a figure who signals belatedness (476, 478).

4. In *Queer Poetics: Five Women Writers* (1999), Mary E. Galvin references Adrienne Rich's "Compulsory Heterosexuality and the Continuum of Lesbian Existence" (1978), which suggests that lesbianism might be broadened to include a range of woman-identified experience beyond sexual desire between women (3). With this expansiveness in view, Galvin devotes a chapter to Loy's presentation of love and intimacy as a call to a radical restructuring of sexuality. Galvin considers Loy's interrogation of heterosexuality so thorough as to undermine

its pervasive gendering and concomitant stereotyping, thereby refuting, and queering, heteronormative dominance.

5. For examples of Loy's use of the phrase *sub rosa*, see "Agony of the Partition" and "History of Religion and Eros" (*SE* 11, 249). The German for alcoholic is *Trinker*, suggesting that with Rosa's surname, Loy offers a riposte to Patience's constant tippling, a proclivity extended by the first name of Rosa's erstwhile lover, Jeroboam (a term referring to a double-magnum or three-litre bottle of wine), and his surname, Winered. Both Loy and Barnes spoke fluent German.

6. The trauma of her family of origin is widely referenced in Barnes criticism, but a concise, considered overview is provided by Margot Norris's 1996 essay-review of Philip Herring's *Djuna: The Life and Work of Djuna Barnes* (1996).

7. The volumes to which I refer are Kreymborg's *The Troubadour: An Autobiography* (1925); Williams's *The Autobiography of William Carlos Williams* (1951); Levy's *Memoir of an Art Gallery* (1977); Guggenheim's *Out of This Century* (1980); and Mabel Dodge Luhan's *Intimate Memories*, specifically volume 3, *Movers and Shakers* (1936).

   To this list we might add similar memoirs by American artist Beatrice Wood (1893–1998); American writer Natalie Clifford Barney (1876–1972); the American journalist Matthew Josephson (1899–1978); and, as will be referenced in what follows, Gertrude Stein (1874–1946).

8. I have located only one other significant reference to "time-tables" in Loy's work. In her first roman à clef, *Brontolivido* (c. 1913–20), Loy envisions having a slighted lover return to her, thereby "turn[ing] the (Times)-tables" on the man he recognises as his rival (*B* 6: 13–14). In this instance, "times-tables" refers to foundational logic of mathematical equation, but the bracketing of "Times" suggests that lover one might engage in table-turning. Also known as table-tapping or -tipping, this was a popular occult practice by which a table became a medium through which the spirit world was believed to communicate with the individuals gathered round its perimeter.

   As is discussed in the second volume of this *Anatomy of Mina Loy*, there are many such occultist references in *Brontolivido* (see Chapter 2 in particular). In combination, Loy's curious phrasing conflates the love of scientific principle central to the thinking espoused by her lovers – both are Italian Futurists who pride themselves on their hyper-rationality – whilst dabbling in the late-Victorian occultist practice that Bergson himself was known to endorse. Of course, we can't verify if this phrasing was on Loy's mind four decades later as she titled her second volume of poems; that said, the *Brontolivido* passage occurs during a memorably climactic moment in the plot.

9. The 1997 collection is condensed and contains fewer of Loy's poems, as it excises a considerable number of the previously unpublished drafts that were included in 1982. Poem order in 1997 differs in being more

chronological than thematic, and Loy's two Futurist playlets go by the wayside, as do some prose pieces drawn from various parts of Loy's archive. In 1997, Conover includes Loy's prose works "Aphorisms on Futurism" and "Feminist Manifesto" (both 1914), "Modern Poetry" (1925), and "Auto-Facial Construction" (1919). Absent from the 1997 volume are Loy's essays on Stein (1929) and Joseph Cornell (1949), as well as her post-war rallying cry, "International Psycho-Democracy" (1918), all of which appear in 1982.

10. Haweis's mother was a respected author of guides to decor and fashion, as well as a writer of literary adaptations; his father was a reverend with a large following. Haweis's extramarital affairs are discussed by Burke in *Becoming Modern*; that his adulteries were well known by the community he shared with Loy is clear from the frank discussion of one of his mistresses in *The Confessions of Aleister Crowley: An Autohagiography* (1979), as is discussed in the second chapter of *Elevated Realms*.

11. A year before she died, Loy observed that while "[s]he no longer had it in her to write poetry [she] felt that she could still paint: her fondest wish was to send one more canvas to the *Salon d'Automne*, where she first achieved artistic recognition" (Burke, "Introduction" 207). This anecdote speaks to the lingering sense that Loy believed that her artistic drive eclipsed her authorial drive, even as her legacy continues to direct her audience first and foremost to her literature.

12. Chosen by Haweis, Joella's name was a private barb; her biological father was Dr Henri Jöel Le Savoureux.

13. Loy expected a great deal from Joella: in an early, indicative letter to her first husband, Joella tells him that she is not wretched because her mother sees to it that she has no time to be so (Letter dated 28 July 1927, Joella Levy to Julien Levy, Box 29, Folder 8, 1926–1980). Joella appears to have first expressly identified with Cinderella around 1928, as Loy's demands on her daughter continued after Joella's marriage to Julien Levy took her from her Paris home to New York. During a solo visit to Paris a year or so after their wedding, Levy reports to Joella that Loy takes serious umbrage with this figuration (Letter dated 2 May, Julien Levy to Joella Levy, Box 29, Folder 7, 1928).

    Over twenty years later, Joella will return incredulously to this self-descriptor after a particularly aggressive letter from Loy, writing to Levy to say that incessant parental demands are, in her opinion, worsened by Loy's creative inactivity in her later years, as "[i]t would be less bitter to support a brilliant poetess" (Letter dated 3 April 1951, Joella Levy to Julien Levy, Box 29, Folder 8, 1926–1980).

    The above truths notwithstanding, evidence of family affection is everywhere: Loy and her daughters are genuinely interested in each other, corresponding often to express support, pride, and concern; Fabienne and Loy are immensely excited when each of Joella's three sons is born. When Julien travels alone to Paris (likely in the 1930s), Joella writes with typical sincerity: "I'm so happy about Mina and Fabi looking so well and happy . . .. I'm feeling very heartbroken about not being with them" (Undated letter, Joella Levy to Julien Levy, Box 29, Folder 9).

14. The playlet "Lima Beans" was written by Alfred Kreymborg, and reads as a plausible precursor to Loy's "The Effectual Marriage, or the Insipid Narrative of Gina and Miovanni" (1917). Loy's character, "She", is absurdly domestic and vacuously committed to the love of a "He" who champions his work as their salvation whilst haranguing "She" for not foreseeing his unarticulated desires. Seizing the bowl that contains the string beans "She" purchased for dinner, "He" chants a malediction likening her to lowly creatures, then dramatically recants his love, throws the legumes out the window, and stages a brief departure, only to return, abject and abashed, to interrogate for the second time her adherence to a love "She" cannot coherently defend.

    While Kreymborg writes that "'the super-sophisticated Loy sniff[ed] a little at the commonplaceness of the marriage theme'", the entirety sends up gender relations that lie at the heart of Loy's own satirical literature, including the connection between immolation and intimacy that is central to this *Anatomy* (qtd. in Conover, "Introduction", *LaLB* xlii).

15. Burke's account is drawn primarily from Bob Brown's *You Gotta Live* (1932).

16. Roger Conover details these variants on Cravan's demise in his introduction to *The Last Lunar Baedeker* (1982), noting that Loy's second husband had written a much-publicised article pronouncing his uncle Oscar Wilde still alive, one taken up by the American press and widely believed. With this infamous proclivity for stunt-making in view, many refused to accept Cravan had died. To an "A. Cravan" has been attributed the Mexican-based novels of one B. Traven, for instance, as well as forged Wilde documents sold in Dublin in 1921 (Conover, "Introduction" liv–lv).

    Gabrielle Buffet-Picabia speculated on the likelihood of Cravan's imprisonment in "Arthur Cravan and American Dada", adding that after Armistice, Loy was understood to have looked for him in previously warring nations that he might have travelled through en route to South America (17). To add to the interpretive complications of Cravan's legacy, it has been memorialised in fantastical novels including Albert Guerard's *Hotel in the Jungle* (1996) and in Antonia Logue's *Shadow-Box* (1999) (Quartermain, "Value"). See also endnote 19.

17. Incredible as it may seem, according to Burke, Loy and Duchamp did not meet when they both resided in Buenos Aires, even as many members of their shared circle were in the city at the same time (*BM* 270).

18. To her husband Julien Levy, Loy's daughter Joella noted that this statement in *The Little Review* effectively eradicated any happiness

experienced with her own children; cynically, Levy told Loy not to worry about this response as it would make Joella work still harder to please (Undated letter, c. 1929, Julien Levy to Mina Loy, Box 31, Folder 11, 1928–1954).

19. In an interview in 1965, when Loy was 82, she discussed Cravan's death, and affirmed that she had heard, through a fellow Christian Scientist, about a man who had met someone just like Cravan in Mexico, and was certain that Cravan had been murdered. Loy expresses relief at this confirmation, stating that it meant "that he hadn't tried to shove me off, I didn't think he had, because we were the only people who could talk to each other" (Loy, "Mina: Interview" 211). When Loy tells this version of the story, it appears that Cravan was going to Buenos Aires *after* she set off for the same destination. These details notwithstanding, the interview indicates that until the end of her life, Loy sought proof that Cravan was a victim of homicide by way of calming her fears about his commitment to her and the as-yet-unborn Fabienne. See also endnote 16.

20. Carolyn Burke's Loy archive at Yale includes clippings from March 1927 and February 1928 issues of *Art et industrie* and the July 1927 issue of *Arts and Decoration* featuring images of Loy's designs, which garnered prizes in 1927 at a Paris exhibition of interior design (Burke, "Paris in the 1920s" and "Loy, Mina: Lampshades"). In his autobiography, Robert McAlmon recalls Loy's business as fairly prosperous, noting how she worked daily alongside a dozen female employees (163–4).

21. As Eric B. White details for the first time, Loy appears to have discovered "a new method of processing cellulose acetate" that she named "verrovoile" or "glass fabric", a key ingredient of her celebrated ethereal lamps (106–7). White's evidence is drawn from a newly unearthed article in England's *Daily Telegraph* dated 11 October 1929; accredited to a "Paris Fashion Expert", this publication uses Loy-esque turns of phrase and includes well-known and novel images of her lamps (106).

22. For both Fabienne and Joella, the cost of taking care of Loy was extensive and multi-faceted. Letters from Fabienne to Joella and Julien Levy illustrate her constantly assessing Loy's emotional and physical well-being. When Loy was creating work that pleased her, the family appears to draw a collective sigh of relief. In June 1930, aged only 11, Fabienne writes, anxiety in evidence: "Mina is drawing and writing and everything is all right"; from Aspen, where Loy moved in 1953, Fabienne – now in her thirties or forties – repeats this refrain: "Mina is well – wants to work, and have another show" (Fabienne Lloyd to Julien and Joella Levy, Box 30, Folder 6, 1929–1974).

Loy received emotional and material filial support. Her letters to Joella and Julien Levy in the late 1920s and 1930s are full of requests for cheques, clothing, travel fares, and assistance with Fabienne's school fees. Joella attended to concerns large and small, taking on paid work expressly to cover Loy's living costs, and come the 1950s, freezing meals in advance for her when she had to leave Loy alone in Aspen (Letters dated 22 November 1948 and 28 January 1959, Joella Levy to Julien Levy, Box 29, Folder 8, 1926–1980). "She's been an expensive mother!" Joella writes as Loy entered an increasingly disoriented senescence and required a "constant care" that both daughters faithfully supplied (Undated letter, Joella Levy to Julien Levy, Box 29, Folder 8, 1926–1980; Letter dated 2 February, Joella Levy to Julian Levy, Box 29, Folder 9).

23. Elisabeth A. Frost has made a strong case for the influence of British anti-Semitism on Loy's thinking and language use, or her wilfully "mongrel" poetics ("'Mongrel'"). Similarly, the anti-Semitism Loy encountered in Germany and the USA is posited as a catalyst for her return to the Jewish roots she shared with her father (Goody, "Empire" 64).

24. A like claim to self-reflexive presentations of constructed selfhood arises in *Mina Loy's Critical Modernism* (2019), where Laura Scuriatti explores how "Loy's texts call up both 'autobiography' and 'the autobiographical,' and play them against one another" (143).

25. In correspondence, Loy repeatedly approaches Julien Levy for editorial advice and, on at least one occasion, asks him for names of publishers she should approach with these writings; her letter about needing to complete the text is dated February 1932 (Loy to Julien and Joella Levy, Box 30, Folder 12, 1932).

26. At the outset of her final roman à clef, *Islands in the Air*, Loy appears to acknowledge the damage done to *Brontolivido* in a description of her accumulated autobiographical writings: "Ghosts of manuscripts written at odd whiles they had waned to inconclusion on subversive interruptions [. . .]. Half one volume had gone to the mice ... they leave a pleasing debris of a flaky somehow oriental substance, fretted to the measure of a nibble" (*IA* 58: 3).

27. My claim to Loy's turn to the künstlerroman is shored up by Parmar, who argues that from 1929, Loy moves toward autobiographical writings focused on the question of how creativity begins and "an ongoing and unresolved search for her own aesthetic origins" (*Reading* 29, 169, 86).

28. Parmar dates *Goy Israels* as composed between 1925 and 1930. For the most part, I agree with this supposition, but I cautiously add this "+" because, in one instance in this text, Loy writes about France in 1930 in the past tense, suggesting that she is looking retrospectively on this year (*GI* 28: 89). That said, on an alternate occasion in the same text she writes about 1930 as if it were the present year; the sentence in question reads: "~~Already~~ In 1930 half the World is forever off to the sea-side" (*GI* 28: 117).

29. In "Mina Loy and Lexicophilia" (2019), Peter Nicholls offers a tremendous close reading of Loy and Lewis on these very grounds.

30. This tentatively used name is fantastic evidence of the cross-pollination of Loy's writings and characterisations: Loy identifies as Linda in *Esau Penfold*, a manuscript drafted two or three decades before *Islands*. "Gore" is a surname Loy ascribes to what appears to be a fictionalised account of Arthur Cravan in the undated "The Three Wishes", a text in which Loy attributes to one Ian Gore specific incidents that she experienced in art school, all detailed in *Esau Penfold*. See also subsequent endnote.

31. As if the fictionalised nominal appropriations were not sufficiently complex, the legal first name of Loy's fourth and last child, Fabienne, is Jemima, and Fabienne is dubbed Sophia in "Visitation of Insel", the addendum to the 2016 variant of *Insel*. Jemima and Sophia are the same names Loy gives herself in *Brontolivido*. See also previous endnote.

32. See Wolff 86–7; Garland-Thomson 19–20; Birke 43–4.

33. On the subject of fearing or rejecting the material, itself a gateway to reinforcing the dualities of culture/nature, mind/body, human/animal, sane/hysterical by which women have been subordinated, see Alaimo 237; Birke 69–70; Wilson 3–8; Lane 146; Pitts-Taylor 6–7.

34. Butler writes: "Gender is the repeated stylization of the body, a set of repeated acts within a highly rigid regulatory frame that congeal over time to produce the appearance of substance, of a natural sort of being" (43–4).

35. For the feminine and feminised, the body is a problem to be solved, a project requiring tireless labour with no discernible finishing point. As Chrisler and Johnson-Robledo attest, a study of girls' diaries from 1830 to 1990 showed that self-improvement was a consistent theme: in the nineteenth century, the melioration was aimed at spiritual purity, in the twentieth, at physical perfection (5). In addition to this incessant, internalised gauging of self-worth, women remain persistently aware that they are more harshly scrutinised regarding their behaviour and appearance than their male-identified peers.

36. In her portrayals of people with disabilities, Loy's motivations are not consistently respectful. While she highlights the marginalisation of those with non-normate bodies, she also yields to what Garland-Thomson delineates as the uncomplicating of these individuals, speaking readily and reductively on their behalf or presenting them as "exotic aliens" or "spectacles" (Garland-Thomson 9).

37. Many feminist critics note that when it is acknowledged, the human body is reduced to its surface: this failure to address the complexity of internal anatomy is at the heart of Lynda Birke's *Feminism and the Biological Body* (1999) and can be observed in Karen Barad's new materialist critique of Butler (see Alaimo 249).

38. Caveats invariably attend all such absolutist statements, or, as in this case, are embedded within them. Firstly, there are Loy writings that are not archived, as in the instance already mentioned above, the incompletely available manuscript of Loy's *Colossus*. Secondly, while Loy's artworks are included in these volumes, they are not a sustained focus. As discussed above, until *Mina Loy: Strangeness is Inevitable* (2023) only occasional, scattered reproductions were available to Loy scholars and admirers.

Part I

"About to be a Body": Loy's Corporeality

Shuttle-cock and battle-door
A little pink-love
And feathers are strewn (*LoLB* 56)

At first pink-blush, combative play marks the "pink-love" of Mina Loy's jesting haiku. The proximate but separate words of "Shuttle-cock and battle-door" elucidate intimate conflict; as in the game Loy references, bodies collide to stay aloft. A precursor to modern badminton and tennis, this ancient sport is best known as "battledore and shuttlecock": no hyphens, battles before shuttles. Loy's inversion foregrounds the feminine trope of the shuttle, the instrument of Penelope's fidelity to Odysseus. Shuttles synthesise, weaving through an extant framework or warp; shuttles are carriers, transporting threads, facilitating journeys less epic than local, pragmatic. Loy's "shuttle-cock" draws on a verbal lineage that incorporates the spindles of "shuttle-prick" and "weather-cock".[1] This cock crows, fights for autonomy with fortitude, is a veritable battle-cock, hence its provocative pairing with "battle-door". ("I thought of cock-fighting", Loy writes, years later, about seeing Arthur Cravan naked for the first time, "how the swelling of blood vessels and the conceit of conquest turn the victor's pace into a strut and give him an air of cruel surety.") Loy's "battle-door" gestures to the processual; it conjures battering rams, phallic aggression at close quarters. But this conflict is not one-sexed: "battledore" also speaks to the constrained, fervent banalities of domestication, as its etymology includes animal pasturing and cleaning clothes by beating them with a paddle. The "shuttle" of "shuttle-cock" anticipates the door that closes this first line. A shuttle can bolt, firmly close, and open the floodgates; the sexologist Havelock Ellis, whom Loy admired, tells of a sex-trade worker's admission that once "'broken in'" a door can be "'difficult to keep . . . closed'" (*Studies* IV 293). Battle-door, like shuttle-cock, evokes presumptions masculine and feminine, and Loy's resolute pairs – and pairs within pairs – affirm likeness and difference.[2] (Her desire palpable, Loy recalls how the ruthless, magnificent, statuesque Cravan "camped his gorgeous head backwards" and revealed himself by allowing his inadequate woman's bathrobe – borrowed from Loy – to fall open ["Colossus" 110].)

In "the little love-tale" of Loy's haiku, the moveable barrier satiates, opens to a little pink-love (*LoLB* 35). But we shouldn't be deceived by the diminution, or its suggestion of roseate health. To be "in the pink" is to be at one's best, but pink is also combative, as in the navy vessel "pink", the coat worn for foxhunting, or meat lightly underdone with its all-too-recently circulating blood on show. To add to this antagonism, Loy's "pink" may be a satirical reference, in that the Italian Futurist F. T. Marinetti – widely considered one of the potential addressees of this poem – was nicknamed "Poeta Pink", and, further, Loy will use this colour to denigrate the "surgical exhibit" that is "pinked up and painted" womankind, reserving a special animosity for the insidious, paralysing "ideological pink" of those typed "English Roses."[3] For one of Loy's characters, shocking pink signals an equally fearsome libido (*I* 143). But to suggest that love contains animosity, that it is not just "a fond eros of knowing possession", is not to undermine the reciprocity of this exchange (Blau Duplessis 57). As Georges Bataille writes:

> union comes at the end of a tournament at which death is the stake [. . .]. If love is sometimes pink, pink goes well with black, without which it would be a sign of insipidity. Without black, pink would surely lose that quality which affects the senses. (*LE* 121)

Bataille refers to Baudelaire, the master of hyperbolic juxtapositions, who admired a "Lola de Valence" as an exceptional commodity, "a jewel of black and rose" (*Flowers* 311).[4] For Bataille, as for Loy, sex is a competition involving brutality and harmony, extreme contrasts that awaken vital awareness and feeling (*LE* 121). In a text Loy assuredly read, Henri Bergson extends this analogy beyond the sexual, arguing that all "sensible reality . . . is a perpetual oscillation from one side to the other" of "the theoretical equilibrium of Being" (*CE* 177). The Bergsonian subject is in constant transition and motion, swinging to and fro between the conscious and the sensory, "on the wing, like a shuttlecock between two battledores" (*CE* 128).

Loy returned repeatedly to the metaphorical use of battledore and shuttlecock from 1914 to 1962, or the half century in which she actively sought out opportunities to publish her work.[5] In her groundbreaking Loy biography, Carolyn Burke upholds Loy's sporting agility – her hiking and tennis – as evidence of her modernity, her willingness to embrace newfound feminine freedoms. Adolescent, petit bourgeois Loy favoured romanticised, inert images of women in Pre-Raphaelite painting, but she was not passive in life, excepting at social gatherings where she stooped to languid feminine stereotypes.[6] It was on school tennis courts that Loy first fell in love (*BM* 46–9). Near comically, this conflation of "pink-love" with playful physical combat proves prophetic. In Loy's authorial hands, tennis becomes a means of questioning gender roles and asserting aesthetic style.[7] In her story "Hush Money" (c. 1922), Loy depicts the game as wearily played between a servile husband and his unwilling wife:

> Conversation between husband and wife was like a game of tennis in which the husband served the ball gallantly to his wife—the wife retaliating with a lump of coal or a potato. Eventually as each ball had rolled away the balls became exhausted. (*SE* 33)

In Loy's "imaginary game of tennis", male and female rally with the tools at their disposal. The woman's equipment echoes the domestic quarters to which she is relegated; the husband's is properly sporting; even proudly, punningly anatomical. The ensuing fatigue is ascribed not to the players but, absurdly, to the man's unreturned and unreturning balls. For Loy, an "unruffled catch & return" signifies a romance lacking spark (*IA* 69: 152). But in the above quotation, Loy's critique is ultimately not directed at heteronormative skirmishes but at an enervated patriarchy, one less and less able to dismiss the dissatisfactions of traditional femininity or uphold the outdated mores of gallant masculinity. Without irony, Loy's feminist peer Olive Schreiner uses a similar metaphor:

> that higher and more socialised human race we dream of can only come into existence, [if] the sex forms have evolved together, now this sex and then that, so to speak, catching up the ball of life and throwing it back to the other, slightly if imperceptibly enlarging it and beautifying it as it passes through their hands. (132)

Where Loy assaults patriarchal missiles to diminish the status quo, Schreiner idealises and inflates the same.

Familiar from birth with playing the part of unwilling projectile in paternalistic economies, rapidly acquainting herself with the curiosity and wilfulness that will define her as an artist, child-Loy determines, whilst "falling after a rubber ball" that she will "conquer the world" (*IA* 65: 57; 62: 28). Loy will not succumb to trajectories perfunctory or collapsing. This decision becomes poetics. In "Modern Poetry" (1925), Loy asks us to "[i]magine a tennis champion who became inspired to write poetry" whose "verse [would] embody the rhythmic transit of skimming balls" (*LoLB* 158). This workaday example relates Bergson's "sensible reality" to contemporary poetic creativity. (In a later, undated story, Loy will reverse this view, creating a rebellious vanguard artist – a figure resembling Cravan – who rejects sportsmanship, "defin[ing] the ball as the nincompoop's microcosm" [*SE* 113].) In later life, Loy describes a need to gather the "erratic parts" of her "<u>communication</u>." Amidst the considerable notes she generated toward an esoteric, feminist, autobiographical novel, Loy envisions her writing as missive and transcendent missile: "how light it would grow", she anticipates blissfully, "describing an arc, in transit" (*IA* 58: 5). Imaginative sporting volleys relieve Loy of the burden of self-definition, the stasis of writer's block, the deeply feminised frustration of going unseen and unrecognised. While this arc never transpires, rallies recur in Loy's mid-1930s ballet "Crystal Pantomime", where an aggressive, hyperbolic match of shuttlecock and battledore ensues as further evidence of the interdependent economies of sentiment and hostility, culminating in the ritual sacrifice of the female. To this telling instance we will return.

Processual pairings physical and intellectual, combative and proximate, are mirrored in modernist ontological catchphrases: Bergson's *élan vital*, Gertrude Stein's "being existing". Influenced by both, Loy chooses "being alive".[8] (On reuniting with Cravan after months apart, Loy writes: "Longing had aroused our emotions to such crescendo it crashed the senses . . .. When all that is left of being alive is a ferocious longing to unlock the centre of oneself with the centre of someone else . . . exquisite flood" ["Colossus" 117].[9]) Loy's foundational intimacy is twinned with violence; her pink presupposes red, which she characteristically describes as "a warm colour on the battle-field" (*LoLB* 60). Almost too obviously, in the "Shuttle-cock and battle-door" haiku, Loy's "pink-love" gains no points, but scatters feathers: "strews" refers to spreading one's limbs, as in sexual abandon, but can be a post-storm levelling, a lived (if brief) equilibrium, a long-sought "shoreless lake of sentient calm" (*CP* 17: 56). As ours is a cock-and-hen story, a mutual ruffling, plucking, and tossing between birdies is implied.[10] Loy's brief tale exposes gender as a narrative: shuttles and cocks keep time, tell enduring stories about dissembling, weaving and unweaving, cock and bull, poppy-cock. Similarly literary, "battledore" is not only a game, but signi-fies a hornbook, or primer for study, just as feathers connote pens. Likening love to a "preeminent litterateur", Loy the satirist never-theless treads heavily over romantic fictions in this minute, potent lampoon (*LoLB* 68). These lovers are linked by a humanity that is fundamental, bestial, conflicted.

This poem is part ten of the thirty-four-part "Songs to Joannes" (1917), the definitive variant of Loy's reputation-making series. A scabrous, intimate lyric collection, "Songs to Joannes" is exceeded in poetic scale and satiric nous only by Loy's "Anglo-Mongrels and the Rose" (1923–5), a phenomenal desecration of outdated, formative moralities and values, among them the sexism and racism that defined her Victorian, inter-racial family of origin. "Songs to Joannes" shocked Loy's modernist peers and American customs officers alike.[11] It is a collage of provocative juxtapositions – of body parts and effluvia, of complex and unrequited feeling – glued together by passion, loss, punctuation. Hyphens are thresholds visual and semantic, echoing Loy's fondness for the doorway as a metaphoric site of intimate struggle, one dating from her earli-est memories.[12] In the second poem of "Songs to Joannes" the speaker's "finger-tips are numb from fretting" the beloved's hair, which she considers "A God's door-mat / On the threshold of [his] mind" (*LoLB* 54). Tactility and anxiety suffuse the lover's pursuit of physical and intellectual closeness, and hyphenations under-score the liminality of what Loy describes elsewhere as a search "for the little love-tale / That never came true / At the door of the house" (*LoLB* 35).[13] Fairy tales elude Loy's speakers time and again, but "pink-love" effects what she champions in her "Feminist Manifesto" (1914) as the only means of uniting disparate gendered motivations: "the sexual embrace" (*LoLB* 154). Sex offers access to social, existential, and mystic transcendence; it is physical and esoteric experience, "[a] flash of attainment to infinite sentience" (*SE* 250). As do the feminist thinkers who follow in her wake, Loy articulates "the body as the threshold or borderline concept that hovers perilously and undecidedly at the pivotal point of binary pairs" – an entity that challenges dichotomies of female and male, private and public, natural and unnatural, spiritual and lived (Grosz, *Volatile Bodies* 23). In turn, Loy's elliptical verse generated criticism defined by unusual affective pairings: "furious despair" for "passionate, clinical" writing that generated a "violent sensation" (Kreymborg 488–9).

Loy's bodies flout convention, offering maligned, trampled bridges over decency and propriety, the inhabitants of Loy's inverted netherworld. In its full thirty-four-part glory, "Songs to Joannes" first appeared in the April 1917 issue of *Others* magazine, which was wholly dedicated to Loy's sequence. In June of that same year, Marianne Moore published "Those Various Scalpels", a poem widely believed to be about Loy, one that likens its female subject's coiffure to "the tails of two fighting-cocks head to head in stone" and her cheeks to "rosettes / of blood on the stone floors of French châteaux". Moore's is an adamantly one-sided assault on the symbiotic gendering and "pink-love" of Loy's songs. But Moore recognises the satiric legacy to which her opponent belongs, likening Loy's very hand to "a bundle of lances all alike", no matter how ornamentally bejewelled. "[A]re they weapons or scalpels?", Moore asks knowingly. Loy's digits are both, and in Moore's opinion, are overwrought instruments, too specialist for the "destiny" they "dissect" and experiment upon. Moore's attack on Loy's "hard majesty" exposes her own rectitude, even as it affirms the corporeality that so consciously informs Loy's satirical vanguardism (116). By extension, Moore identifies Loy's place in a long history of satirical anatomists and surgeons. In embryo, "Songs to Joannes" was "Love Songs", a sequence of four, in the 1915 inaugural issue of *Others*. In 1923, "Songs to Joannes" was edited and published for a third time in the censored *Lunar Baedecker* (*sic*), the first of two books Loy published in her lifetime; it would reappear in a similar format in the second, *Lunar Baedeker and Time-Tables: Selected Poems* (1958). In the latter versions, the sequence was reunited with its original title, "Love Songs", but chopped down into thirteen parts. Between 1917 and 1958, Loy shuffled poem order and excised phrases, lines, stanzas. Lineation shifts, hyphenation changes, a series of dashes is taken away.[14] An ephemeral fragmentariness thus marks the gestation and anatomy of Loy's most notorious poem, one consistent with a poet who liked to think about "[b]its of bodies" and "sailing, flailing limbs", a poet who reduces even the idealised infant to a "composite" self (*LoLB* 12, 135, 17).

Pretending at a cure, the prolix anatomist's dissection thinly veils punitive exposure; as a genre, anatomies are diffuse, disorganised, and various, and are nearly indistinguishable from Menippean satire (Frye 312; Blanchard 118–36). No work survives of the third-century CE Greek cynic Menippus, whose legacy exists through discernible lines of literary influence. Menippean satires parody literary form, intersperse prose and verse, and address abstractions and ideologies. Character is supplanted by figures who represent stereotypes and ideologies. Living beings become corpses or ventriloquist's dummies, and this deadening of individuality facilitates the dissection that anatomies betoken. Hence Robert Burton's *Anatomy of Melancholy* (1621–51) begins not only with a nod to Menippus, but also with a venerative story about the pre-Socratic philosopher Democritus, who determined to unearth the cause of melancholy by sitting in his garden with books and "the carcasses of many several beasts, newly by him cut up and anatomised" (19–20). In turn, one of Burton's hundreds of digressions details human body parts and the faculties of the soul in a pursuit of robust health. While this anatomy primly skirts "[m]embers of generation" in an un-Loy-like manner, it does valorise the heart as the "fountain of life . . . the king and sole commander of [the body], the seat and organ of all passions and affections" (152–3). In "Anglo-Mongrels and the Rose", Loy's character Exodus is archetypal émigré, a Hungarian Jew "undone!" at the first recognition of "the primary / throb of the animate", his "cardiac cataracts." "How should he know / he has a heart?", Loy's speaker asks, a question that will repeat itself in many guises throughout an oeuvre devoted to formulating an esoteric Eros. The speaker answers by affirming the need for a replete understanding of the corporeal: "The Danube / gives no instruction in anatomy." As the poem details, instructions in anatomy prevent the individual from being at the mercy of his own body, from preparing for "involuntary sacrifice" by his own foreign, powerful heartbeat (*LaLB* 113–14). This immolation by infatuation foreshadows Exodus's spiritual death by a pink love that quickly fades. A little anatomical knowledge goes a long way, a truth still greater for womankind at the mercy of "[j]ig-saw gestures of living" that "disintegrate her and put her together again in more pleasant patterns", thereby masking female self and desires (*CP* 19: 10).

Burton's text remains the emblematic encyclopaedic anatomy, a form that will resurface in the modernist works of Robert Musil and Gertrude Stein, as well as James Joyce, whose *Ulysses* (1922) is a lengthy disquisition on love structured by staggering, severed body parts, the limping heart among them. Loy is not an immediately obvious anatomical contender, perhaps because the majority of her decades-long, interconnected draft variants toward an extended roman à clef remained unpublished in her lifetime and beyond. This fragmentary, unfinished state is another notable feature of the anatomy (Frye 234). Unlike her satiric peer Wyndham Lewis, who virulently took against "the repulsive turbidness of the intestine" and refused to be identified as "an anatomist", Loy is perpetually preoccupied with "esoteric anatomical science", ceaselessly fascinated by innards and corporeal disjecta (*Blasting* 9; *LoLB* 166). In one roman à clef, Loy theorises a relationship between human organs and volition, insisting that each has its "own particular consciousness to drive us or serve us", a consciousness-cum-genius that is heritable from one generation to the next (*CP* 19: 2). But autonomous corporeality arises in Loy's earliest works. As she writes in 1914: "So much flesh in the world / Wanders at will" (*LoLB* 22).[15] And in her poems and prose, Loy repurposes the function of one body part only to find it lacking in another. In Loy, hands are "[i]naudible", eyelids "silent", eyelashes "virgin", and fingers touch most sensitively with their "lips" (*LoLB* 24, 37; *SE* 165; *EP* 25). These collaged incongruities, a catachresis of body part and purpose, are a noted feature of Joycean prose, where arms are "elocutionary" and eyes "beth[ink]" (*Ulysses* 108, 116). Often, Joyce's and Loy's subjects are in thrall to anatomies presiding over the illusion of unified subjectivity. The oxymoronic truth behind this stylistic trope is well expressed by Loy: "We splinter into Wholes" (*LoLB* 72).[16] This figurative diminution of individuality has its materialist antipode: Loy calls our attention to the corporeal potentiality of the inanimate, so that her streets contain "earless gutters" and "breastless slab[s]" (*LoLB* 135, 144). These interminglings elevate and denigrate the body simultaneously, speaking to what is possible when part overtakes whole, or self meshes with world.

Loy's anatomical fixation is not fetishisation. Instead, it is a chopping up of bodies that makes a strategic, politicised claim about those considered incoherent, marginal, abject, or "degenerate". Loy's bodily fragments are a synecdoche of disenfranchisement, and of her belief in a universal, irrevocably divided self, one torn between body and soul, self and world. A feminist, Loy dissects and amputates in conscious opposition to the impossibly ideal "composed contours of the virtuous female body", or the non-alienated, unfragmented "eternalised" feminine that is at one with the external world, lacking the male "capacity for detachment" (Januzzi, "Dada" 592–3; Felski, *Gender* 37, 46). The self-sufficient, impermeable, "normate" body is another favoured target.[17] Modernism is said to be the period "where the body invades the text", a claim that encompasses the centralisation of corporeality as well as the merging of form into content, leading to a proliferation of montage, seriality, citation, reproduction, and collage in modernist literature, film, and drama (Weiss 140–2). Loy's own wilful play with bodies and genres alike has provided ample fuel for her greatest detractors. "[H]er work as a whole is perhaps somewhat less than its parts suggest", writes Reno Odlin in 1984, but Clement Wood arrived at a similar destination five decades previous, describing Loy's poetry as "insane fragments" that are less lyric than "prose on its way to becoming a hamburger" (Odlin 62; Wood 621).[18] Vestiges of these critiques recur in more contemporary criticism: "Original as she was, Loy was interested in familiar anatomies", writes Jessica Burstein, noting that one Loy manifesto combines the discourse "of the late Victorian bourgeois" with "the quasi-medical, bred through a Wittgensteinian species of French symbolism" (186). According to Northrup Frye, the word *satura*, the etymological foundation of the satire that comprises the anatomy as genre, means "hash" (233). More precisely, *lanx satura* refers to a medley or a full, mixed dish. Were she lacking deliberation, Loy's literary miscellanies might deserve relegation to mere critical fodder. Instead, Loy attacks her enemies by way of shoring up the ruins of disenfranchised subjectivities, most often women's. But where satirists traditionally attack with a view to keeping a repulsive, unjust, or infuriating enemy at bay, Loy unusually and originally assaults with the express goal of generating intimacy between her opponents. This intimacy is bipartite: in exposing her enemies as more like those they oppress or overlook than they understand, Loy creates a level playing field meant to enable the trust requisite to proximity, even love, between historically warring factions of gender, sexuality, class, race, ability, or age.

As Bataille writes, wilful enucleation – a term usually referring to surgical extractions – is potentially generative: "The rupture of personal homogeneity, and the projection *outside of the self* of a part of oneself" can be an act of initiation, a resolution of mourning, a purge facilitating individual liberation ("Sacrificial" 69). Bodily mutilation is "humble speech": an immolating plea to the powers that be – gods literal or figurative – with limitless appetites for sentient flesh (Mizruchi 339). By tearing apart the living entity we reduce it to "a bodiless category", a baseline of bones and innards, or the very subject of Loy's *Untitled (Surreal Scene)* (c. 1935), a painting of outsized ribcages, floating limbs, exposed organs, and bodily hybrids of machine and human, human and divine (Hughes 203). Potentially decimating the powerless, mutilation can also be a spectre that haunts the empowered: "Societies . . . have an almost essential tendency to dismember their leaders" (Hughes 93). Loy's anatomies

examine both sides of this sacrificial coin, revel in immolative oppositions of divine and human, loss and regeneration, fear and hope,
powerlessness and control, brute violence and civilisation, abjection
and purification, myth and history, imagination and reality. As Ezra
Pound reminds us in "The Serious Artist" (1913), satire gives and
takes away; it "is surgery, insertions and amputations." But Loy
assaults surgically with a feeling that surpasses the obviousness or
singularity of aggression. Loy's songs are maximally, wonderfully,
and affectively vicious in one of their most replete manifestations, the
1917 "Songs to Joannes". Not *for* but *to*: where "for" pays tribute,
Loy's "to" is mobile and driven, expressing position, contact, possession, attack. Though furious at self and others, these self-same
poems dare to sentimentalise about beauty, and arguably contain the
sort of content Pound denounces as "slither", as well as direct references to mucous membrane ("Serious Artist" 45). And we can never
lose sight of how Loy's 1917 version remains bracketed on either
side by the title that speaks to her amorous preoccupations and aspirations: "Love Songs". In Loy's satiric universe, slither and surgery
openly cohabitate. Every volley begs a return.

> (Starving in 1918 in Mexico with Cravan, Loy is witness to a sacri-
> ficial remainder:
>
> I found the sill of our small window had been made an altar for a
> flayed red dot, the bloody jumble of a mangled mouse .... [T]he
> height of the funereal slab from the ground equalled the towering
> Aztec altars where feline priests – with sacrificial flourish [–] gouged
> out beating human hearts to steam oracularly against the sky – –
>
> "A little while after" she and Cravan are miraculously saved from
> certain death:
>
> I could see, for the window was lateral to our bed, paper parcels sail
> miraculously onto that high altar .... these offerings were the size
> of houses – Within their loose wrappings they held a considerable
> amount of food: one, a ruddy chunk of raw flesh beef, whereas the
> mouse had been useless. [*EP* 25])

The title given to this Introduction, "About to be a Body", is
drawn from "Incident", an undated recounting of a "petty accident"
that took place when Loy was crossing a square in Geneva with a
friend in 1919. By Loy's recollection, an emphatic nod prompted
the temporary dislocation of her cranium from her spinal column,
the literal separation of mind and body. Loy became conscious

without coordinates, and internally debated whether she wanted to remain transcendentally "serene in an empty universe" or return to the corporeality she normally inhabited, now reduced to an alien form approaching her from within the otherwise bereft cosmos into which she had accidentally fallen (*SE* 37–8). For a brief instant, before becoming "telescoped" into "the intervening space", Loy was aware that her body had experienced something her mind could not compute, about which she was profoundly interested, even as she realised that "'this time'" she would not gain access to that knowledge (*SE* 38). Vestiges of a universal energy running through her reanimated self gave her a sense of an alternate "measure of time" (*SE* 39). "So this was Life", Loy concludes, "being a sort of magnet to a sort of universal electricity, while in some deeper stratum of consciousness there lies embedded a familiarity with eternal existence withheld from our everyday consciousness" (*SE* 39). "Incident" encapsulates the inextricability of Loy's embodied dualities, be they human brain and soma, or universe and sentient animal. As its title reads, this section of this *Anatomy* is literally *about* Loy's bodies: how they are figured, the intellectual lineages upon which she draws to orient her limbs, organs, senses, and affects. But it is also about the body *as process*, always en route to becoming, always incomplete. To further her own corporeal understanding, Loy reached for prehistories, taking backward journeys to what precedes our contemporary bodily consciousness, the period before the modern human corpus, perpetually in flux, was first realised. By these remote, partial ancestries – bestial, primitive, evolutionary, mystic, sacrificial – Loy defined her vanguardism. Drawing on historical intimations, Loy developed living, changing, forward-looking theories of somatic and affective intimacy.

Chapter 1, "Loy's Atavistic Avant-Gardism", begins with Loy's baseline: a "being alive" or sentience that bears resemblance to Georges Bataille's "inner experience", a feeling of self that exceeds and evades full consciousness, a recognition as base and basic as the abjection with which Loy – a female of Jewish heritage – was herself equated. Sentience anchors Loy in the bestial and in the cosmos alike. Having established this sentient ground, I turn to Loy and primitivism. In writing archived and published, Loy discernibly conforms to the appropriations and racisms of that modernist discourse, but also challenges its moral prurience and othering. Ultimately, as her story "In Maine: Green's Colony" indicates, Loy demonstrates awareness of the potential residing in the "primitive" challenge to post-Enlightenment reason. From primitivism

I consider Loy and evolution. Revering the creative power of the human intellect, Loy nevertheless revels in the evolutionary equation of animal and human, and particularly the shared exposure to what Darwin labelled the principle of reversion, or the atavism by which evolution can pull us backwards as well as forwards. Challenging positivist and misogynist evolutionary interpretations, Loy invests heavily in the possibility that geniuses like herself can hone their individual development, a thesis she gleans from contemporaries Henri Bergson and Frederic W. H. Myers, among others. I then turn to Loy and vitalism, or the universal animating force that takes numerous guises through her work. Bergson is again a key influence for Loy in this regard, given that her first discussions of vitalism work with and against the Italian Futurist bombast about the need to harness and exploit Bergsonian intuitional intelligence at every turn. Again, Loy's interpretation of vitalism is importantly feminist: she proves deeply and presciently suspicious of how her male peers co-opt this ancient discourse, presenting themselves as at one with "life's original, animating, and fertile voice" (Colebrook, "Joys" 283). That said, Loy finds in vitalism, as she does in esotericism writ large, a reassuring harmony absent from psychoanalysis. Cognisant of the deep links between vitalist thought and the eighteenth-century Cult of Sensibility, Loy deploys terms used by that period's feminist writers. Like them, she strives to counter the underestimation of women's sensibility, drawing upon discourses of compassion and recognition as she articulates the perspectives of those derided as throwbacks or outcasts, individuals like herself who were reducible and reduced to mere "sentients".

Alert to the discourses that define and predate human intellection, Loy asks questions about the nature of existence, primordialism, the origins and interconnections of species development, and the possibility of a universal, cosmic force. Paradoxically, these very anteriorities catalyse her avant-gardism. For Loy, the way forward is always backward, and the body is the vehicle for all journeys, be they biological, affective, or spiritual. "[A] conjuncture of the atavistic and the avant-garde, the very old and the very new, is characteristic of modernism as a whole", writes Terry Eagleton in 2021 ("Foreword" xxv). Assuredly. But this conjuncture plays itself out differently for modernists such as Loy, modernists who were perpetually perceived through lenses sexual and racial, for whom turns to the primordial risked further entrenching already intractable stereotype. From her deep, wilfully extremist awareness of her own vexed social positioning, Loy strategises an alternate modernist paradigm, one that toys with, but ultimately refuses, the distantiation of the white male artist, a figure recognisable by his vociferous claims to impersonality and unacknowledged appropriations of the othered.

In considering Loy's sentience, primitivism, evolution, and vitalism, I lay the ground for the second chapter, "Bodies Sacrificial and Intimate", which considers how Loy deploys the equally ancient ritual of sacrifice as a challenge to contemporaneous, masculinist economies of the feeling, effeminised, and disempowered body. Equating sacrificial with satiric practice, this chapter argues that in playing her part in the sex war, Loy wounds with language, expressly aiming to call attention to the unrecognised harm done to the marginalised. In a brilliant reversal of traditional satire, Loy immolates by way of drawing her enemies closer: her version of Eros is inextricable from cruelty and mockery, and in this association, she anticipates a key modernist theorist of sacrifice, Georges Bataille. Both Loy and Bataille powerfully argue that in disrupting subjectivity, aggression and violence can generatively produce a long-sought intimacy integral to all humankind. But quite unlike Bataille, the feminist Loy realises this is a lesson women have learned too one-sidedly, one she hopes to fruitfully transpose to the more privileged.

Notes

1. In addition, to "shuttle-kiss" is to suck the weft through the eye of a shuttle, a term that insists on the intimacy of shuttle-doings.
2. Or, as Thom Gunn puts it: "The battle of the sexes in 'Love Songs' is between 'shuttle-cock and battle-door', a phrase compact with contemporary daring and undated wit" (Gunn 47). My reading works with and broadens Rachel Blau Duplessis's argument that Loy's "'battle-door' . . . suggest[s the] site of penetration" (56). By extending "shuttle" to "door" and emphasising the hyphenation of the masculinised and feminised terms at stake, the phrasing becomes more mutual, and arguably less specifically genital.
3. In his editorial introduction to F. T. Marinetti's "The Foundation of Futurism" (1909), Günther Berghaus writes that as the Futurists became a known entity in Italian society,

> Marinetti gladly accepted the epithets *Caffeina d'Europa* and *Poeta Pink*, the latter echoing the name of a popular medicine that was advertised thus: 'The Pink Pill is to the weak organism what water is to the withering flower. The Pink Pill gives rich and pure blood and slams the door shut on illness. It immediately restores vitality to the exhausted organs and is the best remedy for anemia, sclerosis, general fatigue, and nervous exhaustion.' (10)

In *The Child and the Parent* (c. 1932–6), Loy likens women to "pinked up . . . bon-bon[s]" (*CP* 19: 9). In "Anglo-Mongrels and the Rose" (1923–5), Loy's roseate critique is racial and gendered: she despises the "World-Blush" emanating from the "never-setting-sun" of the British Empire, which reveres its English Roses, or pink-and-white complexioned women (*LaLB* 122). Replicating the conflictual "Shuttle-cock and battle-door", Loy describes these pinknesses as irresistibly attractive for her male, Jewish protagonist, whilst noting that this symbolism bars the English Rose from conscious selfhood, as "an impenetrable pink curtain / hangs between it and itself" (*LaLB* 128). Pink thus stands for intimate battles objective and subjective.

4. The contrast of black and pink permeates Bataille's work. His allusion to Baudelaire is detailed by Susan Rubin Suleiman (81–2).

5. I include in my calculations the 1917, 1923, and 1958 versions of Loy's "Songs", the undated prose works "Hush Money", "Crystal Pantomime", and "The Three Wishes" (all in *SE*). In this category we can also include Loy's essay "Modern Poetry" (1925) and the archived, undated, and unpublished first draft of "Ceiling at Dawn", where Loy uses the regrettable phrase "passionate air ball".

6. In her youth, Loy's favourite painting was Edward Burne-Jones's "Love Among the Ruins" (1894), a title that reflects her mature approach to intimacy, in which she reveres the decimated, Eros-laden subject (*BM* 41).

7. With reference to Loy's "The Sacred Prostitute" – a love story infamously culminating in a boxing match – Tim Armstrong asserts that Loy takes part in a modernist trend whereby "[t]he confluence of writing and sporting metaphors . . . enables an aesthetic which celebrates the 'hard' and clinical", thereby "cod[ing] itself as 'masculine'" (123).

8. *Élan vital* or vital force is the subject matter of Bergson's *Creative Evolution* (1907), which will be discussed in greater detail in the section of Chapter 1 entitled "'[C]osmic Force': Vitalism". Stein's uses of "being existing" are too extensive to enumerate, but it is a key phrase in the "Poetry and Grammar" essay of her 1935 *Lectures in America* and in "Two: Gertrude Stein and her Brother". In "Gertrude Stein" (1929), Loy describes reading a passage from Stein's "Galeries Lafayette" as follows: "This was when Bergson was in the air, and his beads of Time strung on the continuous flux of Being, seemed to have found a literary conclusion in the austere verity of Gertrude Stein's theme—'Being' as the absolute occupation" (*LaLB* 289).

9. This precise phrasing recurs in a chapter entitled "Interlude: Being Alive" in Loy's *The Child and the Parent*: "being alive is a soft ferocious longing to unlock the center of one's self with the center of someone else" (*CP* 20: 14). In a manuscript variant of *Colossus*, the resolution of this desire is less satisfactory, as Loy and Cravan find that

the time they have spent apart takes on a spectral, embodied quality, inserting itself between them; in lieu of an "exquisite flood", they resort to sleep to appease their "over-driven feelings" (*EP* 25).

10. As evidence of the conflicted interpretations the sequence engenders, Rachel Blau Duplessis attributes the generation of intimacy in "Songs to Joannes" to its "abundan[t use] of I-you pronouns" (55); by contrast, Peter Quartermain suggests that the repetition of the same "amplifies the tensions" (82).

11. When not vexed, responses to Loy's work could be outright damning: the American Imagist Amy Lowell threatened to withdraw support for the little magazine *Others* after it published Loy's "Songs"; Loy's first book, *Lunar Baedecker* (*sic*) (1923), was confiscated on the grounds of lewdness at US customs (*BM* 191).

12. Drawing from Loy's romans à clef, Loy's biographer Carolyn Burke tells us that a doorway topped by unattainably beautiful colours features as Loy's earliest memory; when Loy became conscious of books, she perceived covers as little doors (*BM* 13, 26).

13. Thresholds are key Loy locales: in poem 5 of "Songs to Joannes" (1917), an angelic boy, alone on the street at midnight, "Pull[s] doorbells to remind / Those that are snug"; as in poem 2, the threshold anxiously signals the pursuit of care and closeness (*LoLB* 55). Thresholds demarcate hyperbolic sexual and social constraint in Loy's "Virgins Plus Curtains Minus Dots" (1915) and a mockably banal liberation in "The Effectual Marriage" (1917), which begins with a couple passing "quotidienly" through an absurd door (*LoLB* 21–3, 36).

14. Burke describes the editing of this book as a patchwork process that included Jargon Press's Jonathan Williams, Loy, and Loy's daughters Fabienne and Joella at a time when Loy herself was no longer in possession of her 1923 *Lunar Baedecker* (*BM* 431–2).

    The excised dashes are easy to spot and are particularly dramatic in poems 3 and 10 of the 1923/58 sequence (poems 21 and 30 of the 1917 "Songs to Joannes"). Subtler changes in hyphenation include the "mucous-membrane" of the first poem in 1917, which becomes "mucous membrane" in 1923; similarly, the "daily news" of 1917 poem 3 becomes "daily-news" in poem 9 of the 1923/58 variant.

15. Loy's volitional body parts may be rooted in contemporaneous science: Darwin ascribes sentience and elective capacities to all corporeal systems, insisting that autonomy can occur at the microscopic level of the cell. He asserts: "Each living creature must be looked at as a microcosm – a little universe, formed of self-propagating organisms, inconceivably minute and as numerous as the stars in heaven" (*Variation of Animals* II 404).

16. "Splinter" is a favoured Loy term. In this instance, it describes the decimated bodies of soldiers and the need for a societal post-war healing: "To your dissolution / We splinter into Wholes" (*LoLB* 72).

"With what courageous self-discipline she attends to the soldiers' splintered bodies", writes Loy in "Pazzarella" (c. 1914–16), referring to the eponymous protagonist's volunteer work in a World War I hospital, a post Loy herself took up whilst residing in Italy during that conflict (*SE* 77). See also "The Mediterranean Sea" (c. 1928), where Venice "[s]plinters on the opal angle of the sun" (*LoLB* 101).

17. I take my cue here from *Extraordinary Bodies* (1997), where Rosemarie Garland-Thomson coins the term "normate" to refer to a composite identity unmarked by social stigma.

18. In a less critical spirit, Loy's use of fragmentation as a way of constructing poetic collages often merits mention, as when Susan E. Dunn points out that "Loy's consolation for the working poor is patched from the fabric of refuse", or when Virginia M. Kouidis argues that Loy foresees "the composition by field proposed in Charles Olson's 'Projective Verse'" (113; *Mina Loy* 186).

Chapter 1

Loy's Atavistic Avant-Gardism

"Being Alive": Sentience

"The struggle for life", writes Mina Loy, takes place between the "opposite poles of sentience", namely pleasure, or "the attraction of the body towards the soul" and pain, or "the attraction of the body away from the soul" ("Miscellaneous"). "[P]leasure confirms our most tenacious intuition, pain is the major opposition to our will, and being submitted to by all humanity alike, it arouses a certain sympathy that is never extended to the pleasure-seeker." Consciousness devotes more energy to pleasure, Loy acknowledges, even as culture is prohibitive of the same. But the social sympathy for pain does not extend to women giving birth or procuring illicit abortions, or, for that matter, to "our really rollicking sisters and brothers" who suffer from sexually transmitted disease (*CP* 16: 52). We all oscillate between joy and distress, but some types of pain isolate more than others. Suffering is foundational for Loy: in pain, we humans realise the accident of our birth, our chance but all-determining ties to a specific corner of the material world by which some individuals become proportionately larger in relation to their original environment, whilst others shrink against its immensity (*CP* 20: 3). Loy's acute sensitivity to that initial accident of being and its subsequent discomforts is the basis of a lifelong attunement to immolation and injustice, to disproportionalities crucial to satire. Maligned existences incite Loy's ire. On more than one occasion, Loy describes herself as hyperaesthetic, or excessively sentient.[1] And in her unfinished romans à clef, Loy devotes many pages to showing her reader how suffering is the fertile ground that yields her artistry in general and her embattled satiric spirit in particular, as will be discussed in greater depth in the first and third chapters of *Elevated*

Realms. Loy affirms Bataille's proposition that the need to convey information and be heard in turn is akin to a fault line, or "a coincidence of two lacerations, in myself and in the other": for Bataille, communication requires pain, "[i]ncompletion, the wound" (*G* 26).

According to Loy, the most primary wound is the truth that by the norms of European, patriarchal culture, "man will convert time itself into achievement so that the centuries condense to flashes of his genius" whilst "the inconclusiveness of woman is of the very nature of duration in its aspect or mere <u>being</u>" (*CP* 18: 66). Woman is sentience, a taxonomic subspecies of the "being alive" that evokes and unites the foundational determinants of life, sensations instinctual and grounding. "Being alive" moves through time, "[o]ur every advance shed[ding] trails of vanishing sheathes of us, instant reoccupations of our evacuated space" like "[a] dissolving diagram of fading arms and hollow legs" (*CP* 20: 11). This self-anatomisation is a collective temporal experience with spatial ramifications: "being alive" is a means of measuring ourselves against the mass of humanity, even as we strive to understand "[t]he unreal distance between" ourselves and our reflection in the glass, the whole truth of our embodiedness, or the impression we make upon others (*CP* 20: 10). And because Loy is an esotericist who believes in a metaphysical beyond, being alive "gives us the sensation of using an infinitesimal amount of an infinite potentiality", affirming our humble if ambitious place in the cosmos (*CP* 20: 1). For womankind, this infinitesimal potential is still more constrained.

As women are reduced to sentience – a categorisation they share with infants, Jews, those without homes or with disabilities – Loy gives greater credence to that very experience. Sentience is a term regularly deployed and interrogated within Loy's oeuvre. Rather than considering consciousness that prioritises feeling the lowest gauge of intellection, Loy describes *insentience* as the worst conceivable state. For Loy, affective failure is notably exhibited by the privileged. The English – often depicted by Loy as imperialists – she considers prone to "organic insentience"; a loathsome male is critiqued for his failure to "impress [his wife's body] with his sentience" (*EP* 24). Sentience may be base, but it corresponds with the intoxicant Loy makes of abjection, a treatment she shares with Bataille, who is equally interested in the lowest filth, equally consumed by a desire to sully inviolate intellectual and spiritual entireties.[2] Loy and Bataille both know that a flicker of life must be present – and recognised – for sacrifice to do its most healing and intimate work.[3] Life scarcely operant is closest to death, is fodder for a cleansing revulsion and rejection, a lucid site of understanding. In league with Bataille, channelling Darwin, and echoing Bergson, Loy turns to the carrion-eating fly as a life-long affirmation of the rudiments of our existence.[4] "[T]he insect", Bergson tells us, "has already something of our intellect" (*CE* 203). The "adamic insec[t]", Loy concurs (*LoLB* 140). Bataille writes:

> You and I exist inside ourselves. But so does a dog, and in that case so do insects and creatures smaller still. However far we may go down the scale of organisms from complex to primitive we cannot draw a line between those which exist inside themselves and those which do not. This inside existence cannot be a result of greater complexity. (*E* 14–15)

Bataille's lineage links us to a universal, self-reflexive animacy, an "inside existence" that levels, elevating some creatures, lowering others. Nevertheless, Bataille believes that there exists a great "distance between these diminutive creatures and ourselves", one best characterised by our "yearn[ing] for a lost continuity" that surfaces in eroticisms religious, physical, and emotional (*E* 15). Loy will similarly turn to an esoterically defined Eros to resolve the sense of diminishment being alive can portend. And like Bataille, Loy delineates an integral, aware sensation fundamental to consciousness, one that links us to all life forms.

For Bataille, this is "existence for-itself" or "inner experience". He writes:

> I cannot fail to know that this inner experience which I can neither undergo myself nor picture in my imagination implies by definition *a feeling of self*. This elementary feeling is not *consciousness of self* . . . . feeling of self varies according to the degree of isolation. Sexual activity is a critical moment in the isolation of the individual. We know it from without, but we know that it weakens and calls into question the feeling of self. We use the word crisis: that is, the inner effect of an event known objectively. As an objective fact of knowledge the crisis is none the less responsible for a basic phenomenon. (*E* 99–100)

Inner, outer; pleasure, pain. Bataille's "basic phenomenon" is the interrelationship of the world that calls into question a sensation affirming our own existence, its continuities and inevitable discontinuities. Selves feel, and are aware of their limitations. When these limits are called into question, we are threatened, "and this attack is critical for a being having consciousness of itself" (*E* 101–2).

Bataille's inner experience is constricting and affirming, isolating and uniting; it is an awareness by which we measure both our susceptibility and our expansivity. Loy juxtaposes our "restricted and utilitarian consciousness" against our "potential consciousness" (*CP* 20: 5). Utility is equally worrying for Bataille, who believes that we are instrumentalised beings, full of distracting conscious purpose, but more primarily, that we attain to sovereignty, a state that "evades the grasp of our aware intelligence" yet is responsive to chaos, obscurity, overwhelming awareness, and, pivotally, violence (*E* 193). To be conscious of violence is "to bring men back to an awareness of something they have almost completely turned their backs on", activity repulsive to civilisation, intolerable, destructive, unpredictable, but also integral, because "those things which repel us most violently are part of our own nature" (*E* 194–6). Acclimatised to violence through the cruelties of her Victorian upbringing and her subsequent immersion in Futurism, Loy joins Bataille in a race to the bottom, a site of strategic disarray from which to reposition consciousness against the pervading rationality of the European Enlightenment. This is the cultural tradition in which they are both schooled, one that persistently demands honour and placation, one that passes judgement on those deemed lesser, mere animates, even as science "acknowledges its limits . . . admits its powerlessness to arrive at *self-consciousness*" (*AS1* 134). Alongside abjection, denigrated sentience – that which links us to the bestial limits of consciousness – resists the positivism Bataille and Loy loathe for its co-optation of passion and excess, for its reduction of individuals to exploitable, constrained objects.

As base, Loy's sentience is idealisable, free from the constraints of civilisation and its relentless discontents, a place of shared origins: "in close-up of inferno face / a nobler origin / than practicality's elite" (*LoLB* 139). Sentience can withstand its own apocalypse, can challenge the judgement wreaked upon it. "Can one who still has being / be inexistent?", asks Loy. And as riposte, she discovers a "sub-cerebral surprise": "life's intemperance" lies just under the surface of even the most "lenient coma" (*LoLB* 131–2). Just so does she return us to sordid palliatives imbibed in common. A woman of mixed ethnic origins, Loy reclaims her degraded sentience with pride, exhibiting the most primal urges and actions – sexual desire, cruelty, bodily leakage, avid disgust – with erudite flourish. For Loy is not immune to Western intellectual ambition: where her mentor Gertrude Stein effects sentience through complex "hypnotic rhythms" and deceptively simple diction, Loy's feeling body is rarefied, studiedly arcane: she places gesture, sense, and emotion under a lens so sharply crystalline she waters the reader's eye (McGann 3).[5] Loy's sweat is cymophanous, her hiccups homophonous, her soul impossibly cuirassed, her body alarmingly etiolate.[6] "Sentience" belongs within this archaic, aspirational adjectival litany.

Loy's is a body intuitively felt, but it is also one we are forced to interrogate intellectually; consciousness, she shows us, can be honed, elevated.[7] Hers is an "amplifying tendency" typical of satiric discourse, revelling in "elaborate periphrasis, macrology, pleonasm—in short, the prolix style" (Kernan 38).[8] This prolixity contains a drive for betterment that resists traditional progress narratives, yet cultivates righteousness. Reconditely condemning those who damn others to a disposable sentience, Loy demands recognition. Not by proxy, but by proximity. Stand next to sentience, she insists, and consider its relationship to yourself, your own limited, needy place in the evolution – such as it is – of universal consciousness. Loy's wilfully alienating language and bare-fisted polemics, in other words, are a call to a deep-seated need for the intimacy of recognition. For Loy, as for Bataille, "*self-consciousness* is essentially the full possession of intimacy", a prospect acknowledged as impossible, given that, in order to thrive, sentient proximity must be without goal, without achievement of a target or completion, an uncircumscribable ecstasy (*AS1* 189–90). It is because an overdetermined consciousness irrevocably alters the relationship between inner experience and outer world that Loy and Bataille theorise alternate, uncorrupted forms of awareness. Their sentience is reliant on twentieth-century prohibition and novelty, even as it is keenly alert to what has been lost due to civilisation and its myriad discontents. In very different ways, both long for an unattainable, integrated whole from the world of thought and that which exceeds it: Loy aims at an intimate, mystical Eros; Bataille, at an eroticism reliant on the transgression it opposes (*AS2* 23–4).

Modernism gorged itself on self-reflexive consciousness, a preoccupation that chimed with its fascination regarding, and foregrounding of, the present moment, as in the Joycean epiphany or Woolfian moments of being (Derrida, *Margins* 17). Where consciousness begins, where it ends, how expansive it might be, how well it can be known or rendered, its relation to its inextricable body: modernists are obsessed with feeling and perception, and with cognisance that so often eludes intellection, yet remains palpably central to lived existence. Darwin's *The Expression of the Emotions in Man and Animals* (1872) examines involuntary responses to "emotions and sensation", equating "the wagging of a dog's tail, the drawing back of a horse's ears, [with] the shrugging of a man's shoulders" (33–4). Nietzsche posited the ever-shifting ground of perspectivism, itself determined by an active, unknowable unconscious; phenomenologist Edmund Husserl studied structures of consciousness, lending subjective understanding constitutive powers. In "The Metropolis and Mental Life" (1903), sociologist Georg Simmel expressed alarm at urban overstimulation that leads to a deadening of human senses; in *A Foray into the Worlds of Animals and Humans* (1934), biologist Jakob von Uexküll coins the term *Umwelt* to refer to the lived, felt, and perceived animal environment. William James popularises the stream of consciousness in whose immersive waters countless authors are said to have bathed, including his brother Henry.[9] "It appears that there is a perfect continuity between the mind of the animal and the mind of man", asserts Rebecca West, who likened the author's articulation of experience to Pavlov's recordings of canine reflex, placing "body-consciousness" on a par with "mind-consciousness" (82, 99, 175). Sergei Eisenstein's emphasis upon expressivity in film takes its place on this roster: in addition to "the highest explicit steps of consciousness", Eisenstein's ideal artworks must convey "the never dormant armoury of sensual thinking", a category comprised of pre-logical conceptualisations, or the unuttered, inner speech of sentient beings (143–4). No wonder there is a widespread belief that modernism represents an inward turn, a collective dive into the depths of individual psychology.[10] Drawing on similar modernist legacies, philosopher Eugene T. Gendlin works with and against Merleau-Ponty's *The Primacy of Perception* (1945) in articulating a lived, aware body that precedes language. For Gendlin, we are not only a body, we are an interacting body-sense, a "self-sentience" ("Primacy" 345). Bodily sentience is never removed from consciousness; it guides our every moment, even as we have no word to designate this felt, understood, defining experience; in this vocabular absence, Gendlin labels it ". . ." (348). Modernist consciousnesses continue to beguile and instruct.

Gendlin's theories intriguingly unite Loy's love of expressive punctuation with her anatomisation of the lived, sentient body; in Chapter 3 of this volume, this link will be further examined. And as both of these Loy volumes unfold, we will turn and return to the question of how Loy's lauded intellectual embodiedness reflects and counters that of her peers. In Loy's writing, mentality lumbers along, consciousness relies on concreteness, and sentience incorporates the experiential and the experimental.[11] A visual as well as a literary artist, Loy extensively and imaginatively references our exalted capacity to see and perceive, but she also often turns to that which cannot be verified by sight alone, staking claims for herself as a feminist visionary on the receiving end of prophetic revelations. At the other end of the spectrum, Loy continually validates touch, long the least regarded sense. Tactility makes the abstract palpable, even bestial, as when protagonist Insel's "tempo of thought and sentience" generates currents that "ran out of him . . . as if he were growing a soft invisible fur" (*I* 32).[12] As this example alone indicates, Loy's sentience is informed by contemporaneous discourses on primitivism – themselves the product of anthropology, ethnography, sociology, and fine art – as well as evolutionary theory and its countering corollary, Bergsonian vitalism. Loy's sentience looks forward, but also reaches over an expansive shoulder to the origins of modernity, and still further, to the primordial, or the beginning of life itself. While this sentience arguably resembles what Eagleton considers the "phenomenological time" of modernism – the inward, subjective time that bypasses the exigencies of history – Loy is resolutely fearless about the historical, so that her vanguard retrogressions are juxtaposed against "pre-modern, prelapsarian paradise[s]", but also the reclamation of more immediate pasts ("Foreword" xxiii, xxv). Loy is astonishingly unique among her peers for her prescient, steadfast understanding that the nineteenth century was too formative to modernist consciousness to be rejected outright.

A wilful, all-encompassing backwardness defines what I am calling here Loy's atavistic avant-gardism, one discussed in countless ways by her critics, though never, to the best of my knowledge, so named.[13] With her robust turn to atavisms of immediate and distant pasts, we observe Loy navigate the choppy waters between the Scylla of Italian Futurist anti-passéism and the Charybdis of Eliotic tradition. The Futurists famously rejected what they perceived as a too-sentimental aesthetic past – the nostalgic Symbolists with their love for beauty, their "passion for things eternal, the desire for the immortal, imperishable masterpiece" – as well as cultural hierarchies ranging from "the traditional authority of [art] Academies" to "the calculated, usurious concept of the Christian paradise" (Marinetti, "We Renounce" 43–4; Marinetti and Nevinson 197). As Marinetti writes: "History, in our eyes, can be nothing but a falsifier . . . . The past is necessarily inferior to the future" ("We Renounce" 43–4). The Europeanised "primitivism" of Futurism – its strategic aggression, outlandishness, celebrations of "obscene" sexualities, refusals of rationality – Loy eagerly retains. Recognising the fierce Futurist allergy to the nineteenth century, Loy satirically, repeatedly juxtaposes their aesthetics with decadence and symbolism, their morality against Victorianism, their revered hierarchies and magnetism with religiosity and superstition. The substance of this mockery regularly defines Loy's preoccupations, as *fin-de-siècle* content and form are components of her own work. In her expansive historicity, Loy finds a peer in Eliot. In "Tradition and the Individual Talent" (1919), Eliot delivers his famous injunction that poets must develop, by dint of great labour, a "historical sense" that "involves a perception, not only of the pastness of the past, but of its presence", one that "compels a man to write not merely with his own generation in his bones, but with a feeling that the whole of the literature of Europe from Homer and within the whole of the literature of his own country has a simultaneous existence and composes a simultaneous order" (49). Reverentially Eurocentric, Eliot's consciousness of an aesthetic past is nevertheless aggregate over the *longue durée* of human evolution, "abandon[ing] nothing *en route* . . . [It] does not superannuate either Shakespeare . . . or the rock drawing of the Magdalenian draughtsmen" ("Tradition" 51). Lacking his elitism, and overtly valuing, as Eliot does not, the base and abject, Loy nevertheless shares Eliot's high estimation of the full breadth of art history.

Where the Futurist past is integral by negation, Eliot's by necessity, both approaches profess that the authentic artist is immolated to cultural history. Marinetti writes: "We have sacrificed everything for the success of this Futurist concept of life" ("We Renounce" 43). More famously, Eliot insists: "The progress of an artist is a continual self-sacrifice, a continual extinction of personality." The artist yields to legacies that exceed him, to the "living whole of all the poetry that has ever been written" ("Tradition" 53). These creative sacrifices are heroic, era-defining. Loy is not immune to the appeal of this position: her late romans à clef are an extended exercise in retrospection by which she maps out her life, from birth, via the coordinates of the exceptional malediction that is the all-consuming artistic desire to express. But Loy's feminism will not let this heroic performance stand unquestioned. By her feminism, Loy is alert to the truth that women's lives are often a litany of sacrifice that goes unrecognised and unrepresented, a relentless, quotidian diminution that facilitates the grand narratives of cultural history that Marinetti and Eliot unabashedly claim as their own. For Loy, female sacrifice is an anonymised martyrdom traceable to the Neolithic dawn of civilisation. Loy's perspective foresees Heather Love's assertion that modernity cannot exist without backwardness, that "[t]he association of progress and regress is a function not only of the failure of so many of modernity's key projects but also of the reliance of the concept of modernity on excluded, denigrated, or superseded others" (5–6). The sacrificable others Love charts can include people of colour, the non-heteronormative, those with disabilities or accused of crimes. The overwhelmingly white and male Futurists ignored or exoticised these supposed "deviant" or "underdeveloped" groups; by affiliating himself with learned European culture, American upstart Eliot distanced himself from the same. But Loy's consciousness of her positioning as laggard because female makes her particularly willing to confront vexatious pasts, "embrac[e] loss, ris[k] abjection" (Love 30).[14] These are qualities writ large throughout Loy's oeuvre, which repeatedly calls our attention to the unexamined and internalised backwardness of the avant-garde whilst aiming to restore the sacrificial as the requisite ground for all intimacy, regardless of any individual identity.

Loy began her artistic career by associating with an avant-garde who insisted – bellowed, even – that they were defined by an imminence she provocatively labelled *passéiste*. As Loy enters senescence, artists openly fascinated by retrogression became her mainstay. The German painter Richard Oelze (1900–80), the model for Loy's *Insel* (1932–6), was an artist she associated with in the mid-1930s who developed lines of creation that reach into a primordial past, his aesthetic processes "rich in postponement." "'I have existed before my time'", Loy's avatar, Mrs Jones, tells Insel (*I* 151). This claim to originary rear-guardedness explains Loy's attraction to the American artist Joseph Cornell (1903–72), with whom she formed a lasting friendship on her return to New York at the end of the 1930s. A neo-decadent, Cornell drew on youthful snapshots, the homes of his family of origin, dreams, "incessantly recycle[ing] his childhood experiences . . . to 'catch up' with them, as he used to phrase it" (Caws 23). For Cornell, artistic creation is neither forward-looking nor linear, but is a set of unfurling overlaps, an "unfoldment".[15] These associations confirm Loy's ease with histories long gone and recent, with the constitutional interlinking of avant- and arrière-garde.[16] Loy's exclusion from modernist privilege on gendered and racialised grounds was an incontrovertible loss that she did her utmost to turn to gain: by it, she proves capable of feelingly, consciously occupying both halves of the avant-garde and arrière-garde binary. Loy's writings can encapsulate Natalie Adamson and Toby Norris's complex depiction of the arrière-garde, which is not merely "kitsch", "retrograde", or "reactionary" but "bears within it a telling ideological inflection . . . referring to the defence of a cause that one already knows to be lost" (18–19). But in the main, aware that "the first patriarch has not loosened his grip" on humanity, Loy refuses to accept this knowledge: instead, she is a cultural archaeologist seeking evidence that might foster present-day revolution (*CP* 14: 12).

In *Goy Israels* (c. 1925–30), Loy reaffirms the complexities and significances of the long "lost" battles of her own upbringing. Mrs Goy's English, imperialistic heritage is transposed onto the psyche of her children, who "received the mortal wound before the battle of life has begun", and her household entire, who are forced into "a retreat from which it is impossible for them to issue" (*GI* 28: 39, 63).[17] Yet this very impossibility feeds a vision for Loy's protagonist-self by which "the lovers of humanity" will deploy the "leaden cannon" and "tin armies advancing from behind" to blow up convention, and "inherit a place in the sun" (*GI* 28: 80). Loy's arrière-garde will triumph, and this thematic informs her oeuvre from her reworked, primordial sentience – that elusive baseline of human existence – to her complex spirituality, her pursuit of a metaphysics informed by bodily intimacies.

From her earliest writings, Loy deploys her genius to turn the outmoded, the "'reminiscent'", into art, beauty, Eros, thereby "evoking the aesthetic from the ridiculous" (*B* 8: 23). This conversion of pasts immeasurable and personal is the basis of Loy's satiric method. But while its processes may be wittily scabrous, Loy's goal is serious, both abjectly finite and ambitiously infinite. Loy believes in reincarnation as destiny, as a process by which we are indelibly imprinted by past knowledge: "The lasting ideas of brains that die are refleshed through the generations, until our very emotions reflect the sequent ideas of the past." For her, evolution is the product of a "cosmic will" with which we, mere mortals, remain most gloriously associated in infancy, the developmental period that best exhibits the "atavistic tendencies" Loy considers sublime, transcendental (*CP* 14: 33). At our most undeveloped, our most feral and dependent, defined solely by nascent sentience, we approximate the most spiritual. As we move toward a consciousness utilitarian and material, we long to return to that initial interweaving with a universal past. Working against surfeits of pain, we seek out pleasure because it is the "biological illumination in which the body perceives its origin in cosmic sentience" (*CP* 18: 60). Constrained by workaday consciousness, Loy's sentience is the arrière-garde that affirms her esotericism and propels her toward aesthetic, feminist avant-gardes.

"Primeval Recognitions": Primitivism

Mina Loy was surrounded by modernist instantiations of the primitive. She returned to live in Paris in 1923 at the height of *négro-philie*, shortly before Josephine Baker took to the stage in her banana skirt (Sweeney 1–37). Around 1925, Loy lauds Picasso's "disruptive aesthetic" in an essay celebrating modernists who broke with classical form (*SE* 230). Picasso's innovations are never far from appropriations of African and "primitive" cultures, as indicated by his era-defining *Les Demoiselles d'Avignon* (1907) alone. Come the late 1920s, Loy's friend and one-time muse Nancy Cunard begins to compile *Negro: An Anthology* (1934), a transatlantic exploration of race that includes Zora Neale Hurston's anthropological readings of contemporary African-American culture. And while Loy was never fully convinced by Surrealism, through the 1930s she was the European agent for the Julien Levy Gallery in New York, now recognised as the gateway by which that movement was introduced to the United States. As such, she could not have failed to perceive the Surrealist return to primitivist motifs, and writes with scepticism about their appropriation of "black magic" on more than one occasion, as will be explored further in the second volume of this *Anatomy*. Hal Foster argues that Surrealism was more strategic than earlier vanguards – Fauvism, Cubism – in deploying the primitive to disrupt Western rationality and order, an approach in which the transgressive Bataille, himself a "dissident surrealis[t]", was at the forefront ("Unconscious" 63–7). Yet examples of Loy's proximity to primitivist thinking and art proliferate as criticism on the same does not. This absence surprises, given that Loy's is an oeuvre self-reflexively "haunted by . . . primeval recognitions" (*SE* 141).

Loy's "primitive" is integral, messy, and defining. It is a locus of anxiety and an identification generatively and vexatiously complicated by Loy's status as a woman with a Jewish lineage widely perceived as "degenerate". Describing the primitive as "a compensatory form" that refers to a history that cannot be compensated, Foster argues that the term proposes "an imaginary resolution of a real contradiction", a literal and figurative masking of how Western "civilisation" is a sacrificial economy founded on the destruction and ostracisation of other cultures ("Unconscious" 61). The word's use coincides with the rise of modernity in the fifteenth and sixteenth centuries, and has always been "articulated by the West in deprivative or supplemental terms: as a spectacle of savagery or as a state of grace, as a *socius* without writing or the Word, without history or cultural complexity; or as a site of originary unity, symbolic plenitude, natural vitality" ("Unconscious" 58). In *Gone Primitive: Savage Intellects, Modern Lives* (1990), Marianna Torgovnik similarly highlights the links between the primitive and originality, purity, and simplicity, and notes that in its twentieth-century renascence, the discipline of anthropology strove to disrupt these narrow suppositions (8). Often, Loy is insufficiently averse to linking primitivism to the childlike, or related stereotypes of the untamed, violent, and illogical. Often, but not always. Primitivism is not, for Loy, a past or straightforward category. For instance, when examining authority in her family of origin, Loy ties the Victorian domestic "bogeyman" to "the phantasmic grimaces" of the "ceremonial masks" of "savages", claiming both as superstitions by which familial hierarchies are maintained. For Loy, the "respect for initiative" that permeates the Global North prompts "outrage" for the "prolonged convention[s]" of other cultures, yet she draws a line of continuity between primordial and modern, considering the exoteric God as irrational a "bully" as any esoteric deity (*CP* 14: 34–5). Loy's primitivism is the site of an unsimplifiable chaos both damning and liberating, a chaos radically explored in her reading of woman as the original creator; troublingly racist in her renderings of African Americans and "aborigines"; and compellingly critiqued through the "degenerate" wildness arising in her fiction "In Maine: Green's Colony" (c. 1920s/early 1930s).

Loy holds up the primitive as a mirror to modernity. In "New York Camelio" (c. late 1920s/early 1930s), a sloppily drunk, near-feral couple behaves badly in city streets.[18] His name evoking the capricious and reptilian, Camelio is in a state of continual supine collapse. His enervated saviour, a resolutely nameless woman with a badly made-up "horse's face", strives to raise Camelio to the status of *Homo erectus*, but neither he nor gravity complies (*SE* 63). Both audacious and bestial, this equine woman echoes Loy's 1921 design for a "Horse Ear Hat" complete with two "ear-like sprays at either side of the head"; by dressing women like animals, Loy aspires "to satisfy the most ambitious of those who seek to be different", women comfortable with positioning themselves outside and ahead of modernity (Loy, "Would You Be"). Having ascended at least and last to the interior of a taxi, the horse-faced woman gives Camelio her finger to suck, which he dutifully does, "like a young calf" (*SE* 64). Lacking language, this woman wails, moans, and, as Camelio nurses away, "meditate[s] primevally on how unconsciousness relapses to the tremendous suction of life that drew man out of chaos — — — —" (*SE* 64). This chaos is the primeval mire that precedes evolution, through which life gathers and develops. Loy repeatedly uses this terminology to speak of origins, as in "the primeval bog of protoplasmic slime" into which Lawrence plunges the reader in his 1920 *Women in Love* (not a compliment), or a need asserted in "History of Religion and Eros" (c. late 1940s) to measure how far human "mental capacity" has journeyed "since, sequent to chaos, a miniscule incipience of life first quivered in an ocean" (*SE* 255, 247). While the primeval is a gauge of lack, it can be an ideal: in Loy's *Insel* (1932–6) Mrs Jones stares into the "insane pupils" of the eponymous protagonist and locates "an 'entente' in the visionary lethargy of that primeval chaos we were able to share", an accord she deems "fundamental and secure" (*I* 114–15).[19]

Torgovnik tells us that the primitive represents a return to origins as appealing as it is frightening (245). In "Tuning in on the Atom Bomb" (c. 1940s) Loy presents the devastating apex of civilisation – nuclear weaponry – as a catalyst for just such a vexed return. Comparing threatened apocalypse to "an echo of some forgotten wisdom sunken in ancient time", Loy envisions this tumult returning her to a pre-evolved formlessness within "a glaucous continuity of evacuated space", thus exposing how she has always been "a dupe of molecular pretence" (*SE* 286–7). A similar juxtaposition of modern advancement and primordial persistence is at work in "New York Camelio". For the horse-faced woman's primeval meditation on a life force that yanks humanity from chaos is an echo of an earlier moment in this sketch where she strives and fails to pull Camelio out of a gutter to which he has crawled, "splash[ing] goldenly" as he descends. The comparison is precipitous. As a car nearly backs over Camelio, the woman fails to animate or rescue her companion from his abject state because "unconsciousness is heavy" (*SE* 63). Retaining his proximity to base, nethered regions – the ground, piss, irrationality, uncontrollability – Camelio does not rise, but somersaults out of harm's way in the nick of time. "New York Camelio" is an antiheroic parody of the strictures of civilisation and human evolution. Linking primordial ooze with urban effluent, this hapless, contemporary Eve and Adam illustrate how humanity is never far from its perversely desirable, unselfconscious genesis, its foundational sentience.

Woman, maternal originator, is forcibly bound to the primitive, as Loy knows too well. In *Insel*, Jones tells her fellow artist-protagonist the gestational history of a set of her paintings:

'I felt, if I were to go back, begin a universe all over again, forget all form I am familiar with, evoking a chaos from which I could draw forth incipient form, that at last the female brain might achieve an act of creation.'

I did not know this as yet, but the man seated before me holding a photo in his somewhat invalid hand had done this very thing—visualised the mists of chaos curdling into shape. But with a male difference. (*I* 20)

On the one hand, this passage positions Jones as part of the modernist vanguard circles that were deeply invested in a "transgression . . . underwritten by an impulse toward psychic regression that is perceived, by Picasso no less than Freud, as anticivilisational, that is, as 'primitive'" (Foster, "Scenes" 93). On the other hand, that transgression was rooted in the perception of marginalised groups – women, Jews, working classes, all non-white people – as inextricable from that very primitive. With this latter truth in view, we might mark how the primitive is not immediately available to Jones, but requires a difficult, incomplete journey: "'*if* I were to go back'", she postulates, as though she has not yet reached the primordial, or has wandered away from this supposed site of origin (emphasis added). Embedded in Jones's struggle is an implicit critique of the modernist perception of womankind as a "pure referent" or "organic wholeness" inextricable from unchanging nature: the belief that Woman is ahistoric being, near-infantile and unbesmirched by self-reflexivity or social change (Felski 37–9).[20] As Georg Simmel, a founder of modern sociology, writes, woman is "'at one with the basis of life itself'" (qtd. at Felski 46). Sentient, but only just. If woman *is* ooze, why must Jones travel to reach it? A third hand might be needed to read Jones's aesthetic testimony: perhaps Loy is telling us that woman, so unremittingly unselfconscious, cannot even come to terms with that by which she is defined; if so, Jones might heed or be heeding the directive of Loy's 1914 "Feminist Manifesto": "Leave off looking to men to find out what you are <u>not</u> —seek within yourselves to find out what you <u>are</u>" (*LoLB* 154). The precise nature of Insel's "male difference" in his rendering of primordial artifice goes unstated as if negligible or indefinable, a critique by omission.

The equation of femininity with the primitive is the catalyst for the "flicker of elements unconditionally primeval" of the two window-shopping cocottes in Loy's 1914 poem "Magasins du Louvre" (*LoLB* 18). This equation permeates Loy's late 1920s portrait of Nancy Cunard, whose prized "moonstone whiteness" and "chiffon voice" are disrupted by references to masks, carnival, and the oxymoronic "exotic snow" of her nomadically "drifting hands" (*LoLB* 103). It is the ground of Loy's claim that the women-only boarding house in her late, undated "The Agony of the Partition" is suffused with "the staccato chatter of the inmates, relayed like tom-tom messages" (*SE* 5). Further, the landlady of these "savage" communicants moves with the "prowling gait of a limp orangutan", a predatory ape from a potentially weak gene pool (*SE* 7). The simian woman is a curious Loy motif. In "Piero and Eliza." (1910s/20s), Eliza is drawn to "the fetishes of savage ancestry and the Christian devil" and is, at one juncture, draped in monkey fur by Piero's bachelor friends, his primal horde (*SE* 102, 100). In "Pazzarella" (c. 1914–16), our protagonist communes freely with nature, blithely identifies herself as an imbecile, and at the story's end, lies dying upon a bedspread ornamented with "a printed monkey" that "climbed toward her heart, while the grey mist of empire mirrors reflected her waning life" (*SE* 90). Pazzarella's threatened return to constitutive primordial chaos is underscored by a monkey who sees her heart as belonging to him, even as woman and primate alike are reflected within the constraining frame of Western imperialism. Approaching insentience, Pazzarella is equated with and threatened by this human ancestor, who, as it turns out, has a troop or tribe of his own. For when Pazzarella's brutish lover returns to her bedside to gaze at "the primitive monkey" on the spread, he observes that the animal "look[s] at [him] in quite brotherly fashion" (*SE* 93). Virgin and whore respectively, Eliza and Pazzarella are sacrificial figures, taking their place in a host of such women in Loy's oeuvre, and in the "primitive" sacrificial economy upon which Western civilisation is constructed, itself key to Loy's aesthetics and the focus of these volumes.

Loy is alert to the truth propounded by Gayle Rubin, namely, that our "'phallic' culture" affirms how "the palaeolithic relations of sexuality are still with us" ("Traffic" 191). Pazzarella's lover is as vicious as Futurism in "Sacred Prostitute" (c. 1914–16), or he whom the hypercivilised Tea Table Man dismisses as "disappointing—too primitive" whilst Love defends him as "one of the most amusing characters [she's] met" (*SE* 214). Between them, Futurism and Love reduce Eros to a fool's game defined by lust and violence underwritten by covert forays into "civilised", articulate affection. On reflection, Love describes this game as one that "takes you a long way back", as if gesturing to the Neolithic period from which Futurism takes his cues (*SE* 214). Less rapturously, Loy often equates bad sex with the primordial. In her "Feminist Manifesto" Loy argues that some of her female peers are "psychosexually primal", or "so incompletely evolved as to be un-self-conscious in sex" (Foster, "Scenes" 81; *LoLB* 154). To be unselfconscious in sex, as Bataille repeatedly insists, is a defining feature of animality, as only humans reflexively recognise the erotic as a disequilibrium, a permeation of the self and its foundational isolation (*E* 16–17, 29).[21] To be unselfconscious in sex portends a totalising symbiosis with what Loy considers "those steaming swamps of a yet unpopulated planet" (*SE* 50). Bataille concurs, wonderfully positing non-reflexive, bestial creatures as existing "in the World like Water is in Water" (*G* 24). For both Bataille and Loy, sexual consciousness facilitates our understanding of what is forbidden and sacred in intimacy, its transcendent potential (*E* 133). Where Loy welcomes the persistence and pervasiveness of originary lust, she insists that affect and intellect be part of sexual expression; for her, the primordial is too completely severed from anthropic intimacy.

Loy's explorations of women, sexuality, and primitivism move toward goals recognisably liberatory, but her presentations of race and the primitive can be less forward-thinking. In 1920, she writes Mabel Dodge about her voyage to Chile, admiring the "civilised" Japanese rice-pickers who shared her boat, and comparing the white people who occupied the first- and second-class compartments to "malformed indecencies". This experience prompts the exclamation: "I have come to look on the word <u>savage</u> as a synonym for 'European imbecility in applying it'" (Letter dated 1920, "Loy, Mina, 1913–1920, n.d." Mabel Dodge Luhan Papers). Similar insights run through her work, as when Loy castigates her homeland: "England has gained supremacy through the strategic process of depriving the other races of their reason ——— / Britain – as discouraging as her climate" (*EP* 24). And Susan E. Dunn argues convincingly on behalf of a late Loy poem draft "Gloria Populi" (c. 1942), where Loy struggles to demarcate – and ultimately resists articulating – the revolutionary possibilities and racialised complexities of the sweated labour of Jews and African Americans in the New York garment industry (106). These glimpses of awareness aside, Loy's primordial chaos is often inarguably racialised, her subconscious a "rubbish heap of race-tradition . . . coloured by the pigment of retrograde superstitions" (*LoLB* 152). Although these lines are drawn from her early "Aphorisms on Futurism" (1914), we can't consign this thinking to Loy's association with that culturally sanitising movement and its imbrication with Italian fascism. Resident in New York for three years, Loy describes the human "subconscious archives" as comprised of "our forebear's excrements". This is primitivism as abject otherness that cannot be reincorporated or assimilated, so must be buried under "unaffected flowers" (*LoLB* 71).

Similarly discomfiting are Loy's alignments of jazz with a sexualised primordialism; she oscillates in in this regard between a knowing satire and an unnervingly salacious veneration. In "Lady Asterisk." (c. 1920s), one of Loy's conversational collages, the propriety of the conversation at the table of social worthies – ladies, an ambassador, a king's mistress – is undercut by a proposed "solution" to the sex problem, one that is, on closer examination, a race problem:

> If we are to preserve our Civilisation we must avoid climax—
>   Keep 'em jumpin'—
> And jazz is such a stimulus to memory—
> right back to when you were nothing but steam in a coal forest—
> We can recapitulate our reproductive history—
> through the saxophone—
> without an effort! (*SE* 43)

These lines reach back, first, to the nineteenth century, as the phrase "Keep 'em jumpin'—" recalls "Jump Jim Crow", the popular American song that surfaced in the 1830s and catalysed the racist tradition of mocking African Americans in music and performance, one that would culminate with minstrelsy. This song popularised the name now indissociable from post-Civil War segregation laws which assuredly kept, as Loy's socialisers surmise, "freed" African Americans in a perpetual state of suspended, torturous unease. Loy's conflation of suppressed orgasm and the desire to maintain "Civilisation" with Jim Crow legislation suggests that a eugenic proposal is under discussion. Loy's speakers then reach back still further in time to a primordial era, to which we are transported by African-American music and a stereotypical reading of the libidinous "primitive" whose sexual satisfaction can be traced to, and ideally replaced by, artistic generativity. This conversation in "Lady Asterisk." might well satirise the unabashed malice of elite white conversationalists.

Or not: in "Lady Asterisk." the archaic and the repressed are intertwined in a reading of jazz as liberator of sexual desire and antediluvian memory, a combination that recurs in Loy's "The Widow's Jazz" (1931), where this musical genre transports the speaker to the past she shared with her dead husband via a "lethargic ecstasy of steps / backing into primeval goal" (*LoLB* 95). Loy's language becomes increasingly appropriative in this poem as she lingers over stereotypes, describing the musicians, for instance, as "black brute-angels / in their human gloves" (*LoLB* 96).[22] This idealised combination of beast and spirit recurs in Loy's undated "Negro Dancer", where the subject's face is "ape and angel", and "[t]he ancestral smoulder / of jungle ritual" excites. The speaker's experience of "these aboriginal innocencies" leads to their own "overwrought Eros", a lasciviousness that knowingly undoes the classical proportions typically requisite to this term, and implicitly reinforces the imperialist credo by which primitivism is permission to transgress (*LaLB* 216).[23] This same appropriation of racial stereotype is at work in one variant of Loy's "To You" (1916), where the presumably white speaker declaims on behalf of a "hybrid-negro" sullied by association and silenced, bearing a "mask of unborn ebony" and existing as an "aboriginal / In the levelling dirt" (*LaLB* 89–90). To be sure, none of these poems lack complexity: "The Widow's Jazz" is a melancholic, self-deprecating satire; the black dancer is expressly identified as a puppet performing a requisite role, and within "To You" exists a discernible critique of the unheard and marginalised. That said, these works incontrovertibly aestheticise the same primitivist tropes that are satirised in "Lady Asterisk." As Foster cogently reminds us, modernism itself is now an artefact requiring the same acknowledgement of difference that we hope archaeologists will apply to "primitivism" ("Unconscious" 55). But nor does Foster refrain from pointing out that "[t]he primitivist avant-garde was politically ambiguous at best" ("Scenes" 76).

Allegiance to this ambivalence enables Loy to occupy deeply opposed positions: she can equate Futurist innovation with a much-derided Native American primitivism (hence Pazzarella's Futurist lover is "Geronimo") whilst enthusiastically erasing the history of North America's first inhabitants in "America * A Miracle". Written in 1940, roughly eighteen months before the US entered World War II, this poem celebrates pilgrims, Thanksgiving, and the speed with which America obliterated its "scarecrow ancientry", whilst commending the country's "soaring architecture" that evidently "rose from the aboriginal grass / of a virgin continent" (*LaLB* 227–8).[24] The "virgin" terrain in this anxious illusion of American impenetrability housed at least 10,000 years of human civilisation before it saw skyscrapers, and this is a history Loy willingly sacrifices to privilege the supposed purity of her subject matter. The egregiousness of this elision is compounded by Loy's renowned cognisance of the misogynist lie that is glorified virginity (discussed in depth at the end of Chapter 2), and because the First Nations are referenced within the same exclusionary line of poetry, albeit kept in their marginalised place: underfoot, and as insentient as the uprooted grass from which they are, evidently, indistinguishable. This denigration is consistent with Loy's assertion, in "History of Religion and Eros", that "oriental" and "occidental" "intellection [soon] outgrew the aboriginal simplicities" (*SE* 237). Aboriginal complexities garner too little of Loy's attention.[25] Furthermore, an early typescript of "America * A Miracle" indicates that Loy was entirely cognisant that the birth of her chosen homeland was neither uncontested nor completed. Here, Loy asks America:

> Are you, so youthful in your splendour,
> In danger
> Of an internecine colonisation
> Of your atavisms?
>
> That you forget it is your heritage
> America;
> To amaze the world
> With the dimensions
> Of your achievements . (*EP* 24)[26]

In this variant, the destruction of its pre-European legacy threatens contemporary American culture. An atavistic avant-gardist, Loy generally values the disruptive power of long-forgotten or repressed inheritances, and these lines suggest that she believes the United States should reappraise the same. In this partial typescript, the ghosts of Loy's pilgrims offer "interrogations" of their legacy rather than the "laudations" of the final text.[27] In other words, Loy makes a conscious decision to edit out her uneasy awareness that America is built on the aggressive subduing of its foundational "primitive" past, no doubt due to her express hope that American might will conquer once more "on the allies' field of honour".[28]

Like their author, Loy's speakers alternately internalise and externalise the primitive, and in so doing, they participate in the long conflict between civilisation and savagery by which barbarism and wildness are first displaced from geographically demarcated spaces of shared human culture – city states, individual nations – to a growing recognition that the primitive is an incontrovertible aspect of the individual psyche, as in the Freudian unconscious. Between these two positions – one medieval, the other modernist – lies the nineteenth-century judgement of primitivism as an arrested form of humanity, "as that from which civilised man, thanks to science, industry, Christianity, and racial excellence, had finally (and definitively) raised himself" (H. White 178). Loy's "In Maine: Green's Colony" is a miniaturised account of this very history, one that illustrates how, as Hayden White argues, "[a] given culture is only as strong as its power to convince its least dedicated member that its fictions are truths" (153). For White, "savagery" and, to a lesser extent, "primitivism", are self-authenticating terms that are necessary to any culture that attempts to distinguish itself from nature. Loy's Maine, less state than small town, is in thrall to that very process: censorious, hard-working, God- and Devil-fearing, and priding itself on its cleanliness and rectitude. "They are always sweeping something away, they are always shaking something out, they trade, they bank, they 'ever' prosper in a modest way—" (*SE* 46). From the outset, Loy labours to make this proudly "civilised" culture indistinguishable from the "primitive" it so actively resists. Her unnamed first-person narrator cannot understand how anyone reproduces in Maine, yet another locale of unevolved intimacy: sex "lurks ... in the hot mud and primeval bottom of the Maine consciousness" (*SE* 50). An inhabitant to whom the speaker becomes close, John Straher, a husband, father, and landowner who "was about 50", is predicted to "blossom into that belated adolescence of the 100 per cent clean American" by his sixtieth birthday (*SE* 47). A former sword swallower with a circus, a man who freakishly flosses his nose with grass and is scarcely able to articulate his thoughts, John is presented to us as a childish imbecile. Though insisting on his pure intentions, John is beset by a love for a woman married to another; his idealised Lucy is a "complacent cow" and "brigh[t] ... robin" annually consigned to a sanatorium (*SE* 47–8). Madness, ferality, feeble-mindedness, sexual profligacy, and impropriety: these are terms that describe what White calls the "Wild Man" and the "Wild Woman", or the mythical creatures of yore banished from a tribe or civic centre. Yet, in Loy's story, these wild folk are at the centre of their community, and what is more, they consider themselves above a nearby community that they disdain as less civilised.

In his historical account of "wildness", White considers its Christian and Hebraic origins. "In Maine: Green's Colony" explores both systems. In the Christian doctrine of forgiveness, the loathed savage cannot be wholly cast out, but remains a plausible candidate for redemption. As evidence, White cites Augustine, who recounts the monstrous races encountered by ancient travellers, races who might bark like dogs, or have backward-turned feet, or, lacking heads, have eyes in their shoulders; these are the inexplicably atavistic beings who so frequently attract Loy's attention. While these individuals horrify and disgust, Augustine "insists that the[y] should not be denied possession of an essential humanity" because they have all emerged from "'the one protoplast'" (H. White 163). This enforced acceptance of every formulation of human sentience is identifiable in John Straher's account of local inhabitant Young Granger, a man credited with the spirit of a werewolf, who suffers from syphilis and rapes schoolgirls presumed perpetually "under the long straight eyes of the Maine mothers watching from their well scoured stoops" (*SE* 51). Christian propriety precludes indictment of Young Granger, who is an inextricable, always forgivable part of this devout community. Similarly, Bad Mary, the local prostitute and char, is accepted as Maine's resident Wild Woman, her glazed eyes and stick-like arms repugnant to behold even as her body is believed succour for every man in town, a duplicity consistent with her legendary origins. Unspeakably ugly – fur-covered, with breasts so long they had to be thrown over her shoulders when she walked – the medieval Wild Woman could evidently make herself appear beautiful when attracted to ordinary men, as she often was; during sex, she revealed her true appearance (H. White 167).

Maine's treatment of the residents of nearby Green's Colony falls under a Hebraic model, whereby those deemed wild or savage are said to have lost God's blessing, and are cast out because irredeemable; Cain, Ishmael, and Ham fall into this moral category (H. White 159). As John Straher tells Loy's narrator, so too do members of Green's Colony, who live down a path everyone fears to tread:

> These degenerates were a race sprung from an unnatural brother and sister and had in a few filthy hovels continued to breed prodigiously in the same biblical manner—
>
> They were dwarfed, they were hunched, some of them were web-footed and from the half demolished hedges of that ostracised domain—their microcephalus heads with bulging eyes would 'start out at you'. Their major impulse was murder then minor rape. They bred at deplorably infantile ages—their lives were spread in one long loathsome lust. In one infested lair, you could find . . . five generations, forming the seraglio of the same papa.
>
> They had their own fearsome language of signs and snarls. (*SE* 53–4)

Having listened to this deliberately off-putting account, Loy's speaker states: "A tremendous interest in this race of dithering imbeciles supporting, clothing, protecting themselves without a keeper sprang up in me" (*SE* 54). She determines to visit them, and does so, a stout walking stick in hand. But what she stumbles upon is an Eden populated by an old man with a long, white biblical beard, and his charming, cultured wife, inhabitants of "a beautiful house covered with honeysuckle." At their laden table, the "melodious tinkling of china" is akin to the "call home from Wonderland that ended Alice's dream" (*SE* 55). Rumoured to be a transgressive hellscape, Green's Colony is in fact a domestic oasis from the degenerate, inexplicable world of Maine proper, a Maine beset by a civilising mission that scarcely veils its defining "black magical quality" (*SE* 51). As the title of Loy's story suggests, inside Maine lies a pastoral utopia, one sorely needed by its depraved inhabitants, but blocked to access by prejudice. Within Green's Colony itself Loy deposits a small motif of the savage and base, allowing her Whitmanesque old man to converse with the narrator without his shoes and socks, "stretching his toes … out into the sunlight" by way of disrupting – or completing – this civilised rural idyll (*SE* 56). For as Loy writes satirically in "Giovanni Franchi" (1915): "the incandescent breath of civilisations" – a breath illuminating but ephemeral – merely facilitates the pursuit of "Philosopher's toes", or a transcendent wisdom grounded by the abject appendages of the feet (*LoLB* 31). Unhindered by a civilisation he has mastered and rejected, Loy's wise old outcast is atavistically vanguard.

"In Maine: Green's Colony" does not have its incredulity sufficiently in hand to permit its unhindered classification as a satire, but it is a judgement, an indictment of the assumed cultural need for the cohering effect of barbarians, outsiders. As such, Loy's story participates in a long tradition of challenging rationalism, one discernible in Erasmus's fools and Rabelais's grotesque giants. As White argues, these explorations of the category primitive radically expose the contradictions, repressions, and omissions that are constitutive of "civilisation" proper (172–3). Repeat, variegated returns to "primitive" chaos remain a key means by which Loy effects that radical challenge, returns that include her examination of the most basic components of life or sentience, discussed in the next section of this chapter. Through the lens of primitivism, Loy traces out women's conflation with an eternalised baseness, and participates – critically, but also thoughtlessly – in the modernist appropriation of that which precedes and exists alongside exalted European and Anglo-American cultures. Whilst Loy regularly foresees the feminist innovations of the second half of the twentieth century, where primitivism is concerned she is more often of than ahead of her time.[29] That said, Loy recognises that primitivism is a malleable, troubled concept, as well as the foundational half of any civilisational binary. As the next chapter will explore in depth, that recognition is evident in Loy's exposure of the sacrificial proclivities inherent to her beloved, aggressive satire.

Loy's understanding of woman as the reified site of a prehistoric sacrificiality, her recognition that the Palaeolithic is now, comes implicitly to the fore in her essay "Modern Poetry" (1925), where she praises the "primitive ideation" of Laurence Vail's "Cannibalistic Love Songs" (1922). A long-forgotten and hard-to-locate example of modernist primitivism, Vail's poem is praised by Loy as a "perfect" cohering of originary consciousness and new thinking (*LoLB* 160).[30] A three-page-long appropriation of a black male speaking voice, "Cannibalistic Love Songs" posits romance between the primitivised speaker and a white woman. After frolicking and reproducing in an idealised nature, their relationship concludes, as all good love evidently should, with the male sacrificing "his" female. This act is committed with the understanding that the speaker will be sacrificed in turn at the hands of Freud's primal horde, or the generation succeeding this couple. Celebrating interracial intimacy as a sharing of the same "red blood", Vail then has his speaker repeatedly fetishise his lover's "skin more white than cloud, / More white than swan, more white than milk", thereby exposing his acculturated need to appropriate the purity and strength associated with whiteness (34, 36). Vail's gendering is likewise emphatically stereotypical: man is warrior, woman is child-bearer and passive object of desire who must be killed when her skin toughens and her breasts droop. Or, as Vail articulates in the "primitive speak" that bludgeons its way through the poem: "You no good to give love fever to black man. / I do the best thing, little white girl, / I draw knife across soft trembling throat" (35). Vail's black man eats the woman's corpse with their "white" son, thereby restoring youthful prowess to the father whilst resurrecting the mother to a heaven over which he remains the presiding deity: "All day white girl waits in blue sky and thinks of black lover" (35). Woman is anatomised: Vail's poem is a blazon, cataloguing the body parts of its "white girl", her lips, fingers, legs, and the "[p]ink bells" of her toes (36). Woman is then literally sacrificed to restore male virility: the black man eats her to keep her close as he continues hunting, warring, and fathering more children with women who are not as reverentially white as his first, devoured love (36). While it is near-inconceivable that Loy genuinely adored the clunky form and tone of "Cannibalistic Love Songs", its content is a ringing endorsement of the feminist critiques integral to her oeuvre.

A swingeing exposure of white male sexual anxieties – potency and racial purity among them – the gender politics of Vail's poem encapsulate Loy's emphasis on the idealisation of an outdated female sacrifice that continued to thrive in the twentieth century. And as Darwin himself theorised, it is by these atavistic characteristics that we continue to be defined.

"Trailing the Rest of the Animal Behind": Evolution

Consciousness originates in protoplasm, the primordial substance that constitutes the living part of all cells, be they protozoic or human. Dying in the same year that Loy was born, Charles Darwin radically overturned the anthropocentrism that encouraged humans to see themselves as innately superior protoplasmic beings. "How inexplicable the similar pattern of the hand of a man, the foot of a dog, the wing of a bat, the flipper of a seal, on the doctrine of independent acts of creation!", Darwin enthuses in *The Variation of Animals and Plants under Domestication* (1868).[31] A single progenitor or prototype is implied, one that might explain why, in embryo, fish, mammals, birds, and reptiles are "barely distinguishable" (*Variation* 12). In "Songs to Joannes" Loy welcomes this scientific hypothesis for its democratisation, its elevation of the most atavistically "drivelling humanity", and its denigration of rhapsodic lovers to the status of "only human" animals, near indistinguishable from pigs, insects, and birds equally compelled to copulate and reproduce (*LoLB* 59). Evolution proves that sentience is shared condition and emancipatory principle. And Loy's humans are frequently zoomorphic, as in: "it was as if among moral humans, her heart craved curs and mongrels" or "they stole into the atmosphere . . . like soft cats, heavy with satisfaction" (*SE* 14, 101). Loy's "being alive" is often bestial, so that a coma has "the lucent opacity of an oyster" and Giovanni Franchi and the black priests of Loy's poetry "scuttl[e] winsomely" like Phoridae, winged insects who counterintuitively run hurriedly, rather than fly, when preyed upon (*SE* 95; *LoLB* 28, 42). This transvaluation of feral values includes Loy's much-quoted lines from "One O'Clock at Night" (1914): "Beautiful half-hour of being a mere woman / The animal woman". Loy's speaker is blissfully indifferent to the man she accompanies, a man who oscillates between resembling gods or children, yet possesses a leonine "roa[r]" commensurate with her self-identification as full-fledged beast (*LoLB* 15).[32] Animal woman equals animal man; the abject margins of society are as untamed as those who wield power. And Loy's early zoological egalitarianism continues into the 1930s and 1940s: in "Surfeit of Controversy" a notorious criminal, or wild outcast, is commended for an "ideal / honesty of purpose", whilst the press who hunt him down are castigated for "thrusting their teeth / lit with hyena laughter" (*LaLB* 232). Never negating the paramount importance of human intelligence, affect, consciousness, or wilfulness, Loy's evolutionary world view nevertheless celebrates our corporeality, presenting us as mere mammals scarcely at one remove from avian, reptilian, insectile, and molluscan lineages, our forward-facing bodies inevitably consigned to "[t]railing the rest of the animal behind" (*LoLB* 16). Or, as she puts in her archived notes: "If we would be saved we must see ourselves not as religion proposes, the original sinner – but as a scientific problem on the path of evolution" ("Miscellaneous"). To move forward, we must recognise and reclaim our bestial origins.

Commensurate with Loy's relation to the primitive, her evolutionary propulsion is tethered to an equal, opposed interest in how the past retains its hold on human psyches, bodies, and cultures. These forebears need not always be ancient or proto-human, as Loy is as compelled by the more immediate, verifiable logic of inter-generational inheritance, a logic Darwin extends to the specifics of human gait, gesture, behaviour, health, and intelligence. Whilst acknowledging that inheritance can be capricious, Darwin neverthe-less expresses an extraordinary faith in its capacities: "The wonder, indeed, in all cases is not that any character should be transmitted, but that the power of inheritance should ever fail" (*Variation* 27). So great is Darwin's amazement at the human capacity to transmit traits that he is, like Loy, a celebrant of the great Victorian bugbear, atavism. For Darwin, "The principle of Reversion is the most won-derful of all the attributes of Inheritance." Atavism compels because it can persist over generations, potentially (if unverifiably) hundreds of generations. Furthermore, atavism shows that evolution is not positivist, and that inheritance and development are at odds, thus compounding the miracle that is evolution itself, a miracle by which Darwin never ceases to be captivated (*Variation* 372). Evolution is marvel and mystery, in that we never know what traits lie hidden in any human being, which Darwin likens to characters "written on paper with invisible ink, all l[ying] ready to be evolved under certain known or unknown conditions" (*Variation* 61).

Darwin is absorbed Sherlock in this detective narrative, his informed enthrallment always on show. But the fact that evolutionary theory is "a system governed by chance" posed "a radical and intellectual moral problem" for Darwin's Victorian audience, a problem, as George Levine asserts, that no one took as seriously as Darwin himself (263). An avant-gardist working with and against a Victorian lineage, Loy has few such scruples, preferring atavism over the stock Victorian character Loy labels Tea Table Man, or he who pronounces himself so "easily adapt[ed] . . . to civilisation", that "accommodating contrivance that relieves us of all the onus of individual action." Tea Table Man is delimited by sentience: he can sit still and absorb, but cannot act upon his environment. Proudly declaring himself "born in an age when it is unnecessary . . . to live", it is only by his ability to state this depressing truth aloud that his base existence is confirmed (*SE* 193).[33] Loy and Darwin are united in their aspiration to change this sort of reductive, habitual thinking. For both, atavism is the body's welcome, rebellious response to ingrained, staid environmental acquiescence. Paradoxically, atavism validates the innateness of the unpredictable. Like Darwin, Loy perceives sex and sexual reproduction as fundamental, defining, and captivating counters to civilisational structures and strictures. But Loy is not in accord with all foundational Darwinian precepts: challenges to his views on crossbreeding and sexual selection can be discerned in her writings. Aligned with Darwinian pangenesis, Loy nevertheless counters evolutionary predictability with her belief that consciousness can be actively evolved through the individual will, and through the transmission of specific characteristics from one generation to the next. In these views, Loy follows in the wake of French naturalist Jean-Baptiste Lamarck (1744–1829), who cohered long-standing theories on the inheritance of acquired characteristics. And in this specific regard, Loy is often more in league with influential, contemporaneous intellectuals: the sociologist Leonard Hobhouse (1864–1929); the founder of the British Society for Psychical Research, Frederic W. H. Myers (1843–1901); and pivotally, with Henri Bergson, whose riposte to Darwinism influenced so many of Loy's peers. But Darwinian thinking is unquestionably the ground for Loy's fascination with what constitutes the very basis of consciousness, animacy, and humanity.

Breaks in the predicted evolutionary chain appeal to Loy, for whom "spontaneous evolutionary modification of the parental type" is "usual in the imaginative young" (*SE* 116).[34] This quotation comes from "The Three Wishes", Loy's narrative challenge to Victorian presumptions about heredity and class. All three male protagonists perceive their parents as lesser forms, "as animals who had learned to count", as "poor beasts" or inanimate objects (*SE* 125–6). Hyde Park Hinderman is born into a family of petty criminals, yet has a choirboy mien and a longing to make the world a better place. When Hyde's parents are sent to prison, "childless widow" Mrs Switheringham Bates finds him loitering round a local church (*SE* 118). She longs to adopt Hyde, but first interrogates the parson about the likelihood that he will inherit "'The Taint'". The parson reassures Mrs Bates that Hyde is "a pure throw-back" to a commendable ancestor (*SE* 120). Unassuaged, Bates consults a similarly encouraging criminologist, who affirms Loy's narrative viewpoint: "The impulse of the child is towards the negation of the parent" (*SE* 122). Implicitly confirming Bataille's supposition that "the ruling class [is] but a set of lucky thieves", this criminologist offers a critique of the theory of malign inheritance famously propagated by Cesare Lombroso (1835–1909): he celebrates adolescent rebellion, denies that crime is genetic (arguing instead that it is a condition of material want), and finally, distinguishes pathology from criminal behaviour.[35] On this last basis, he then astonishingly denounces his own field outright (*SE* 122).

Like this criminologist, Loy's story recognises genetic pathology – small heads and immoral behaviour can indicate heritable evil – but where these conditions are absent, she posits atavism as a recuperation of liberation. Ultimately, the gloriously atavistic Hyde is adopted, an act underscoring Loy's resistance to reproductive expectations.[36] And just as Darwin displays the miracle of evolution on the combative plinth of genetic transmission and development, Loy's "The Three Wishes" concludes by affirming this opposition as an ideal. Her final protagonist, Ian Gore, finds "no inoculation of sensuality among the animated furniture that so unaccountably stood for his parentage". Instead, he "instinctively conjectured that he might rather to have been conceived of some circumstance virile and intransigent, like a boxing match." Like Hyde, Ian is a creative youth regenerated by his "absence of conviction of continuity with anything antedating him" (*SE* 136). Not coincidentally, Ian is also an avant-garde genius, superior to Hyde in his refusal to conform to any standard, be it moral or aesthetic. This motif is writ large through *Insel*, where the eponymous artist, recognisably genius, is primordial in behaviour and physique, prone to "slump[ing] back into a larva" and possessed of a single "remaining tooth . . . so thin as to be atavistic in an adult" (*I* 89, 111). Insel is the culmination of Loy's supposition that reversion is not simply perversion, but possibility.

As with most characteristics close to Loy's heart, atavism is eminently satirisable, the target of a knowing mockery founded on Loy's conversance with evolutionary principles. In his discussion of inheritance, Darwin argues that "the protoplasm contained within the ovules and within the sperm-cells . . . act on each other by some law of special affinity" so that the female of the species inherits her mother's sex characteristics, and the male the father's (*Variations* 380). But within a given generation, dormant traits include sexual characteristics, which is why, for instance, a cow can produce a bull. For Darwin, this truth explains transgendered animals such as a hen who grows spurs and crows each morning like a cock: "Thus every character, even to the instinct and manner of fighting, must have lain dormant in this hen as long as her ovaria continued to act" (*Variations* 52). This argumentation potentially adds yet another layer to the blurred genders of the mutually pink love and strewn feathers of Loy's "Shuttle-cock and battle-door" haiku, a blurring arising still more forcefully in Loy's prose. In "Gloria Gammage" (c. 1910s), the protagonist and her cuckolded husband Antony endeavour to save their marriage by having a child. But as the months pass and their infertility is reconfirmed, Antony can be found "mooing around the[ir] golden bedroom—and any stray member of the house party is informed—that Antony is 'the cow mooing for its lost calf—'" (*SE* 29). Loy's adjectives and metaphors echo the Old Testament narrative condemning the worship of the golden calf in Exodus, suggesting that Antony may be in thrall to a long-denounced, unvital god. In another nod to the primitive, Loy reinforces Antony's atavistic and lamentable lowing for an offspring he literally cannot engender. In the nineteenth century, pregnancy was often prescribed as a cure for problems with the nervous systems of married women, as a means of anchoring and curing the wandering, hysterical womb. In "Gloria Gammage", Antony and Gloria are both high-strung, and the procreative failure at the heart of their tale prompts another Victorian nightmare: Antony's evolutionary regression to domesticated ungulate, one that chimes with his inability to exert the requisite patriarchal authority over his wife.

This satirical use of atavism recurs in Loy's "Anglo-Mongrels and the Rose", a poem that elaborates further upon paternalistic failures to control the angel in the house.[37] The family at the centre of "Anglo-Mongrels" has a combative dynamic credited to a racialised atavism commensurate with Darwin's repeat cautions against the likelihood of producing good offspring from mixed races. Darwin expressed disbelief "that a race could be obtained nearly intermediate between two extremely different races or species" (*Origin of Species* 18). Too conciliatory to his contemporaries, Darwin writes with complicity and caution on show: "we may perhaps infer that the degraded state of so many half-castes is in part due to reversion to a primitive and savage condition, induced by the act of crossing" (*Variation* 47). While Darwin considers this condition particularly prevalent among the so-called "lower races", Loy categorically extends this concern to the mixing of English citizen and Jew in "Anglo-Mongrels". She does so in a period that saw a heightened, prejudicial attentiveness to the "Jewish physique", given that Jews were increasingly integrated – and for anti-Semites, alarmingly invisible – within urban centres (Gilman 177). The poem is framed by our understanding that male protagonist Exodus brings to his marriage not only "[t]he arid gravid / intellect   of Jewish ancestors" but also "the senile juvenile / calculating prodigies of Jehovah / crushed by the Occident ox" (*LaLB* 112). In turn, the English Rose is comprised of a "pot-pourri / of dry dead men   making a sweetened smell / among a shrivelled collectivity" (*LaLB* 122). While they are not barbarians, the union of these two figures is primed to produce enervated offspring dominated by Rose's incestuously weak lineage, one replete with its history of "tactful terrorism" against the likes of Exodus – an unanswerable, eminently heritable violence that is scarcely held in check (*LaLB* 121). In turn, we are not surprised that daughter Ova's "emotions rise / from no beginning", "worn / with racial patience" (*LaLB* 138). It is Ova's struggle to outstrip this lineage, to cultivate her consciousness beyond its drear, inherited beginnings. Ova thus becomes another of Loy's rebellious artistic youths who endeavour to "coerce the shy / Spirit of Beauty" and triumphantly locate "indissoluble bliss" (*LaLB* 143, 164).

Atavism questions basic presumptions about human reproduction and development, a truth well encapsulated by a cartoon in an 1872 issue of *Harper's Weekly* entitled "The Darwinian Student's After-Dinner Dream", which illustrated a series of evolutionary stages by which said student's cutlery gradually metamorphose into the ideal marriageable woman. These sorts of satires were rife in Victorian popular culture, and include, as a further example, a barrel and a goose merging over time to become a man wearing tails, or a figure who represents the heady heights of paternalistic civilisation disturbingly produced by the coupling of object and beast.[38] These caricatures express anxiety about the limits of what might constitute sentient, living matter; they also prey upon fears of miscegenation, meaning the mixing of racial or ethnic backgrounds is lampooned to include any protoplasmic being and the inanimate. In combination with allusions to Darwinian evolution in newspapers, "freak" shows, agricultural contests, and music halls, these caricatures speak to the way Darwin's thought permeated the late Victorian psyche (Browne 497). Central to that theory was reproductive history, and Darwin's theory of sexual selection. Historians disagree on how well understood sexual selection was in Darwin's time. But even the greatest detractors of its influence acknowledge that public debates ensued about what has been touted as the most contentious aspect of this still-debated theory: that by Darwin's thinking, the female of the species has the autonomy to choose her mate, and that her decision ultimately determines inheritance. Carefully posited as a hypothesis, the very mention of female authority and discernment nevertheless riled Darwin's peers.[39]

Sexual selection continues to be viewed as an imposition of Western paternalism upon non-human animals, so that male bravado, aggression, and posturing remain valued ways of beguiling the supposedly more subdued, inconspicuous female sex. As Joan Roughgarden asks: "Does social life in animals consist of discreetly discerning damsels seeking horny, handsome, healthy warriors? Is the social dynamic between males limited to fighting over the possession of females?" And answers: "Darwin conceived his theory in a society that glamorized a colonial military and assigned dutiful, sexually passive roles to modern wives"; convincingly, Roughgarden argues that these values are still used to disregard female perspectives and justify the behaviour of predatory males (167–8). This fraught ideological legacy compounds John Holmes's assertion: "Since Darwin, sex has been at the very heart of biology" (185). Biology and body: Darwin's now discredited theory of pangenesis laid the ground for a contemporary understanding of DNA and genetics. To explain how human traits are passed through generations, Darwin argued that when dividing and proliferating, all cells of the human body "throw off minute granules or atoms" (*Variation* 374). These "cell-gemmules" are heritable, and can lie dormant for generations, resurfacing in subsequent generations. Pangenesis, in other words, identifies not just the reproductive organs, but all parts of the human body as the catalyst for human inheritance. Darwin's body is sexed from head to toe, skeleton to blood cell.

Within Loy's literary corpus, sex similarly dominates her anatomised bodies, as politicised sex war, as an esoteric Eros that incorporates intimacy and desires for beauty, and as a Darwinian evolutionary principle by which the very substance of the body's building blocks determines who we become: "Proto-plasm was raving mad / Evolving us – – –" (*LoLB* 67). In turn, consciousness is determined by "subliminal deposits of evolutionary processes" (*LoLB* 6). Loy's deposits recall Darwin's "cell-gemmules" that accumulate in the body from one generation to the next as a burgeoning material inheritance; as such, it is particularly apt that they are mentioned in Loy's "Parturition". And if, as Darwin asserts, "all the forms of reproduction depend on the aggregation of gemmules derived from the whole body", then asexual reproduction is no longer a surprising occurrence. "[I]n fact", Darwin writes, "the wonder is that it should not oftener occur" (*Variation* 383). This same view is proffered in Loy's "The Sacred Prostitute", which takes aim at the Futurist anticipation of a male-led human parthenogenesis that would exclude women from the reproductive process, thereby completing the patriarchal domination of "nature". Mocking Futurist anxiety about women's procreative power, Loy nevertheless posits exceptions to the presumptions of heteronormative reproduction. Echoing Victorian evolutionary caricatures coupling animal and object, Loy details an "esoteric union / of Mission and gin-mill" that breeds an "unlikely spill / of God's mysteriously / variously / retarded children" (*LoLB* 140). This developmentally delayed, abject offspring is Loy's critique of the atavism imposed upon the homeless of New York's Bowery district. Through no fault of their own, these people devolve into Darwin's "primitive" mixed breed, the weakened product of controlling parents, namely, Christian church and American bar.

A similar challenge to the assumptions of "good" evolutionary inheritance lies at the core of poem 29 of "Songs to Joannes". Tackling Darwinian misogyny, it begins: "Evolution   fall foul of / Sexual equality / Prettily miscalculate / Similitude" (*LoLB* 65). In *The Descent of Man* (1871) Darwin argues that in combination, natural selection – the struggle for life – and sexual selection further develop male energy, perseverance, courage, and genius (itself a combination of patience, rationality, and imagination). Throughout life, these qualities are "transmitted more fully to the male than the female", so that "man has ultimately become superior to woman" (*Descent* 328). Attributing male power to honed competitive capacities, Darwin's argument leaves a hopeful residuum: perhaps women could aspire to the same standard. This residuum Darwin acknowledges, then obliterates. For Darwin, eugenic cultivation of the very best and brightest women for countless generations could result in nothing but the transmission of these better qualities to their daughters alone. And in any case, as men would simultaneously continue to "undergo" their evidently singular and "severe struggle . . . to maintain themselves and their families", they would continue to out-develop even the most developed woman, a creature presumably languishing at home on a chaise longue with her bonbons (*Descent* 329). As for so many of his Victorian peers, Darwin maintains that women share with "the lower races" the "powers of intuition, of rapid perception, and perhaps of imitation", but as *just* sentient creatures, they will never ascend to genius (*Descent* 326). As the ferociously satiric opening lines of Loy's twenty-ninth poem clarify, Darwin's calculated underestimation of women is less dainty error than thunderous evisceration.

Poem 29 continues its hyperbolic refutation of Darwin's sexist principles, envisioning the reproduction of male with female as equal to the mixing of two distinct species, a distinctly, resolutely, and uniformly "[u]nnatural selection" of the diametrically opposed. This "clash" of irresolvable unlikeness produces boys and girls who can only "jibber" incomprehensibly at each other, bray like donkeys, or communicate through an uncontainable, unevolved body that speaks through gesture, hiccups, laughter, or tears. These children are stereotypical "savages" said to be well worth the "seismic orgasm" that engendered them. Far better, Loy wryly concludes, to continue this atavistic heteronormative crossbreeding than choose the easier alternative, which should be as simple as recognising the vast similitudes shared by differently sexed human animals (*LoLB* 65–6). Should be, but is not. In poem 29, Loy strategically makes a mountain of the molehill of sex difference. Deploying Darwin's methods and ideologies, she illustrates the gargantuan disbelief that must be willingly suspended in order to swallow Darwin's theories wholesale, theories that pretend to democratise all living creatures whilst reinforcing Darwin's male, white, educated middle-class status.

Darwin is questioned elsewhere in Loy's writing. "Pazzarella" houses an embedded critique of female-driven sexual selection: telling Geronimo that she has chosen him, Pazzarella points out that in reality, "'the confirmation of my choice is beyond my power'" (*SE* 68). Geronimo is and remains infuriated by Pazzarella's so carefully couched presumption, demanding that she "'let somebody choose [*her*]'" (*SE* 69). When she does, he is further incensed. "The Sacred Prostitute" enacts a similar challenge: sulking because Love does not seem to want him, Futurism asks if it is because of his appearance. She replies: "Oh, I don't mind *what* you look like— Let that confound the critics" (*SE* 211). In this case, the plumage of the peacock is not as important to the peahen as Darwin avows. But these critiques do not mitigate Loy's awareness of the radicalism of Darwin's thinking. For where natural selection pitched species development into arbitrary freefall, Darwin's theory of sexual selection recovered intention as a fundamental component of mate choice, with an inevitable impact on the next generation (Levine 176). Still more significantly, evolutionary intention is rooted in *female* choice, a decision Levine considers Darwin's "most daring and . . . least appreciated move", one Darwin never revoked, his detractors notwithstanding (177). While Loy questions interpretations and enactments of sexual selection, her satires show her thinking through the implications of its under-recognised subtending of female autonomy.

Loy's feminist evolutionary agenda has literary forebears, including late Victorian poet, satirist, and evolutionary theorist Constance Naden, who published works that challenged Darwin's antiquated, romanticised views on women, and whose poem series "Evolutional Erotics" (1887) lampooned the viability of female sex selection in a male-dominated world.[40] Along with George Meredith's *Modern Love* (1862) and Edna St. Vincent Millay's *Fatal Interview* (1931), Naden is part of a literary lineage devoted to and liberated by Darwinian evolution:

> Where a Cartesian divide between the mind or soul and the body can lead to an idea of love as essentially higher than and in conflict with desire, a Darwinian realisation that love and desire in all their forms are expressions of biological impulses and imperatives leads to a different [and more sympathetic] analysis of the tensions between them . . . . [T]he Darwinian poetry of the human animal yields a new and profound sense of our common condition. (Holmes 189)

This combination of the corporeal and spiritual elements of human Eros underpins Loy's lifelong attempts to theorise the same. By this account, "Darwinian poetry" focuses on the visceral, the somatic, and instinctual desires that can aggress, but also dispense with possession. On these grounds, "Songs to Joannes" might be added to the evolutionary poetic canon: throughout, Loy insists, repeatedly, that protoplasm evolves all living things, and is the basis of love in all its abject, cruel, compulsive, and euphoric glory.

Darwin's democratisation of species, trumpeting of atavism, and centralisation of sexuality and reproduction all appeal to Loy. Loy's writing foresees a feminist reclamation of Darwinian methods and theories evinced by Elizabeth Grosz, who speculates that the models propagated by the English scientist might well be applied to "prevailing structures of (patriarchal) power" ("Darwin and Feminism" 27). For Grosz, natural selection provocatively flourishes under maximal diversity and differentiation, propounds individual overcoming of past harm for the greater good of the species, and posits (feminised) nature and (masculinised) culture as interdependent – all goals to which we might aspire in our contemporary age ("Darwin and Feminism" 31, 41, 43). But *contra* Darwin, Loy was part of a generation that perceived evolution as potentially subject to the individual, who believed that they could use their own will to actively improve upon the inherited limitations of human consciousness. This belief is evident in the work of Loy's contemporary, the British political theorist and sociologist Leonard T. Hobhouse, whose *Mind in Evolution* (1901) is a user's guide to "orthogenic" or "aristogenic" evolution, which "consist[s] in the unfolding of all that there is of latent possibility of Mind, the awakening of its powers, the development of its scope" (5). Against the perceived passivity of Darwin's biological model, Hobhouse argues for a "'self-conscious evolution'" that will permit humanity's "mastery of the forces of nature" and lead it "towards whatever perfection it may be within its power to attain" (399, 397). A like theory permeates the work of Frederic Myers, for whom humanity is evolving toward a greater integration of its mental anatomy that will ultimately make the mystical and subconscious as transparent as our currently perceived "reality". Loy initially read Myers's *Human Personality and its Survival of Bodily Death* (1903) in 1913 and 1914, and continued to make detailed, specific reference to it in her late romans à clef (*BM* 144). In this text, Myers argues that geniuses and artists are more capable of advanced evolutionary change, and this is an opinion Loy clearly savours. This belief chimes with Loy's conversion to Christian Science in 1909, a religion focused upon consciousness-heightening, and underscores the Theosophical lineage to which she was attuned, links discussed more fulsomely in *Elevated Realms*.

The most famous proponent of individual evolution is Henri Bergson, an associate of Myers and Freud who was at the forefront of modernist thinking. Loy was among the many modernist devotees of Bergson's *Creative Evolution: An Alternate Explanation for Darwin's Mechanism of Evolution* (1907), which takes issue with Darwin's centralisation of the aleatory, foregrounding a Lamarckian intellectual line whereby evolution is directed by a cohering principle. Bergson felt that evolution could not be as mechanistic or contingent as Darwin claimed, but was instead guided by the *élan vital*, "an *original impetus*" or life consciousness, to which all living beings – plants, animals, humans – had differing access. Generating variation and inventiveness, the *élan vital* is inextricable from existence yet "transcends finality" (*CE* 129). By contrast, Darwin's "life" is too inert: where individual adaptation is treated as if it "were an effort of the organism to . . . tur[n] external circumstances to the best possible account", we speak of adaptation "*in general* as if it were the very impress of circumstances, passively received by an indifferent matter" (*CE* 39–40). Most deplorably, there is not enough creativity or autonomy in Darwin, whose species evolution develops slowly, painstakingly, and for the most part, beyond human control, while Bergson's creative evolution is dynamic, incessant, and encourages individuals to "'attain [an] absolute'" that "'is synonymous with perfection'" (Schuster 100). This striving is imperative, as Bergson's "consciousness is action unceasingly creating and enriching itself", an analogy he extends to the universe entire in *Creative Evolution* (Douglass 108; Burwick and Douglass 4). Where inanimate matter is used up or unmade, Bergson's conscious action labours "against a slump back into sentience" (Burwick and Douglass 4).

While Loy affirms that it is "[t]he aim of the artist to miss the Absolute", she does speculate on perfection as a goal in abstract, intellectual, and bodily terms (*SE* 228). In her undated philosophical dialogue "Mi & Lo", perfection is defined as "[t]he maximum reciprocity between conception and realisation". This is a "zone where it is possible to advance but not recede", one in which "the infinite dissimilarities are reconciled" (*SE* 281). Emphasising origins, progress, and accord, these qualities suggest the evolution of an ideal species; Hobhouse, for instance, also considers "the transmutation of rivalry into co-operation" a key phase toward well-socialised self-consciousness (396).[41] And as Loy's dialogue proceeds, it is clear that the mind is her perfectible focus: her interlocutors consider how "[i]n meditation the mind unbuilds itself for a divine re-edification" (*SE* 282). This process is intensively introspective, potentially neurotic. In a typical Loy turn to the atavistic, she has "mi" state: "Yet all the evolutionary 'odds' are on the neurotic for it would seem that it is in the yet unsown fields of consciousness that he loses himself." Reversion remains opportunity, yet "lo" counters: "And the genius finds himself" (*SE* 282). For the genius – a figure Darwin describes as a cultivator of patience, reason, and imagination – new planes of consciousness open upon an evolution self-reflexive and generative. Alternating between satire and veneration, Loy posits an individual, accelerated evolutionary consciousness in many of her works. Geronimo congratulates himself on affectionately prompting "an incredible evolution" in Pazzarella's face; so too does Loy's "Auto-Facial-Construction" (1919) assert the control of the "conscious will" over the countenance, "our most potent symbol of personality" (*SE* 72; *LoLB* 165–6). Loy admires Romanian artist Constantin Brâncuşi (1876–1957) for his access to a "certain *élan* of primary embodiment—" which she elaborates as a return to "an elemental form whose evolution is submitted to the process of the intellect—" (*SE* 221). Aware that human development is an incontrovertibly incomplete process, Loy insists that "the gamut of vibrations to which man, through his senses, responds" broadens "in the course of his evolution" (*SE* 247, 239). Our bodily sentience unites us with all living things, but it is also, for Loy, a tool responsive to calculated sharpening.

"Cosmic Force": Vitalism

For Darwin, evolutionary theory "led . . . to a thoroughly enchanting vision of the world in which everything is infused with a spirit recognisable to human consciousness" (Levine 170). A like spirit mattered to Loy, who was forever in pursuit of a substance, being, or power that might cohere the malleable, sentient self with the universe entire, be it "Deific Electricity", "INTELLIGENTIAL ETHER", or vitalism (*SE* 240–1). While a vast, various vitalist thinking has existed since Aristotelean entelechy, vitalism is a discourse united by "the theory that life is sustained through some form of non-mechanical force or power specific to and located in living bodies" (Packham 1). Vitalism rejects the possibility that life can be described in purely physical or deterministic terms. In its modernist guise, it was a popular strain of thought that privileged flux, intuition, creativity, affectivity, the sensory, unpredictability, open-endedness, alertness, and adaptability, rather than progress, reason, instrumentalisation, the habitual, and certain or scientific knowledge. The list of modernist thinkers and artists said to have ascribed to a vitalist viewpoint is long. With a universal *élan vital* by his side, Bergson stands at the head of a queue that includes Constantin Brâncuşi, Charles Darwin, T. S. Eliot, William Faulkner, Sigmund Freud, T. E. Hulme, William James, D. H. Lawrence, Wyndham Lewis, Friedrich Nietzsche, Pablo Picasso, Ezra Pound, George Bernard Shaw, Edith Sitwell, Alfred Stieglitz, Gertrude Stein, Walt Whitman, and Virginia Woolf, twelve of whom Loy knew personally or wrote about. Omri Moses argues that modernists found vitalism attractive because their period was defined by two deeply opposed social changes: a loss of the security once assumed in communal and intimate relations, coupled with the burgeoning of socially administered individual constraints (16). Divorce, proto-feminism, and urban migration were pitted against travel timetables and punch clocks committed to "the tightly regulated industrial discipline of time" that contributed to an increasingly alienated labour force (Esbester 163). With this upheaval in view, modernist writers took solace in the liberating naturalisation of change that vitalism promised, all premised on a revaluing of memory, the senses, and intensity. With caveats, Loy was among their number.

Loy's allegiances are immediately legible: vitalist values dovetail with vanguard values, not least because both discourses privilege experimentalism and incertitude. The esoteric Eros that Loy sought and theorised throughout her life also privileges a vitalist sensory and affective intensity. Loy replicated her inharmonious and occasionally cruel upbringing in a first marriage that she describes as "an immoral intimacy" wherein "bewilderment ousted the feeling of proximity" (*EP* 24 and 25). In the Italian Futurist F. T. Marinetti, Loy cherished an "exuberant vitality" that she credited with adding two decades to her own mortal span; from the disappearance of her second husband in 1918 Loy never fully recovered, and in the 1940s, she can still be seen contemplating "the paralysed vitality of loneliness" (Undated letter, "Loy, Mina, 1913–1920, n.d.", Mabel Dodge Luhan Papers; *SE* 292). Nevertheless, Loy resists aspects of vitalism due to its approaches to gender and the sexed body, which might give us pause: why, then, is Loy not as drawn to psychoanalysis as she is to vitalism? Further grist to this identificatory mill is provided by British philosopher George Henry Lewes's definition of psychology as "'the science and facts of Sentience'", a term he claimed embodied consciousness, the unconscious, affect, and conation (qtd. in Holland 34). Moses's arguments shed light on why Loy remained at one remove from these discourses: noting that the vitalist approach to the human is marked by the mutable and improvisatory, he points out that it differs importantly from psychoanalysis, which "is heir to a nineteenth-century view of character as a persevering structure and, mutatis mutandis, continues to insist on a sedimented, repetitive personality shaped by certain formative events in personal life" (24). Deeply respecting Freud's success in facilitating open conversations about sexuality, Loy nevertheless finds crucial aspects of his theories lacking, too in sync with our problematically fragmented, gendered, and repressed world, and too out of sync with the metaphysical cosmos in which Loy ardently believed.

Loy's resistances to the Freudian intellect and spirit are examined extensively in *Elevated Realms*, but I will relay them in embryo here. Positioning herself as the perpetually split and wounded offspring of a racially mixed marriage, Loy actively resists Freud's defining anatomisation of the psyche. Instead, she twins her significant understanding of psychoanalysis with occult discourses that promote harmony, that unite self and universe as Freud does not. In her earliest writings, Loy demonstrates her awareness that psychoanalysis emerges from the practices of mesmerism, followed by spiritualism and telepathy, practices that begin to exert their influences on European and North American culture at the end of the eighteenth century, retaining their hold well into the twentieth. In writings dated after Loy's own forging of these connections, Freud enunciates and repudiates these links, actively distinguishing psychoanalysis from its occult lineage and insisting upon its validity as a fledgling science. This is not an argument that beguiles Loy. "For what psychological close-up can reveal the Ego, in whose name no deed is ever done?", writes Loy in a telling fragment in her Yale archive. For Loy, should psychoanalysis succeed in deconstructing identity down to its "mainspring", it would find it is only a "magic spring" or "[t]he puissance of the wish." Loy reduces psychoanalytic discoveries to wish fulfilment, interpretations too subjective, too self-flattering and idealised, to be trusted. Psychology is magical thinking, and as Loy's notes go on to suggest, "'the whole show'" of human identity can only be realised by a deity, even as she observes that neither Buddha nor Christ was prepared to venture into this terrain ("Notes on Metaphysics"). Ultimately, Loy remains suspicious that empirical knowledge alone can offer a thoroughgoing account of the mind. By this reasoning, Freud yields to a "mechanised mysticism" implicitly rooted in "a scientific aegis" and its corollary, the rigid parameters of an exoteric Catholicism, minus the latter's mitigating spiritualism (*SE* 228, 252). Freud promises a freedom from positivist and paternalistic social mores that returns us to their very origins in Western culture.

As a corollary to her own interest in the gnomic and transcendent, Loy finds Freud suspect because his theories fail to attend sufficiently to the orgasmic bliss by which the corporeal and spiritual become indistinguishable. Loy maintains that Freud posits viable links between religion and intimacy that go problematically unresolved in his theories. In part, Loy develops her esoteric Eros as compensation for what is lacking in Freud. That this theory is feminist is also a response to the social mores that Freud reflects. From Loy's perspective, Freud's most significant failure is his representation of women's sexuality and reproduction. With this problem in view, she scabrously critiques the unexamined misogyny she locates at the heart of psychoanalysis: notably, Loy's "Pazzarella" (c. 1914–16) was written six decades before Luce Irigaray published her groundbreaking, witty riposte to psychoanalytic sexism, *Speculum of the Other Woman* (1974). In "Pazzarella", Loy not only tracks out the occult history upon which psychoanalysis relies, but also challenges Freud's inability to generate a psychology that sustainedly, impartially articulates an independent female consciousness. Hence Loy's tale concludes with a letter to Geronimo, wherein Pazzarella states that their story – a manuscript for which she claims authorship – is a "gigantic opus for the vindication of feminine psychology" (*SE* 97). These links are an in-depth focus of Chapter 2 of *Elevated Realms*.

Loy shared her complex relationship to psychoanalysis with many modernist peers and associates, among them D. H. Lawrence, Ezra Pound, and Wyndham Lewis.[42] Ironically, Loy's lifelong ambivalence regarding Freud is the very substance of his process. In 1922, Loy makes a point of meeting Freud, drawing his portrait, and asking for his analysis of "Hush Money", her story that is transparently about her own vexatious family of origin (*BM* 212). In her late work, Loy professes admiration for Freud's "semitic acumen" – a Hebraic heritage and intellectual keenness she shares – even as she writes that his "intelligible voice" barely supersedes the "throng of neurotic minnikins" that issue from his mouth (*CP* 19: 1). Resisting her own mother's equation of psychoanalysis with a "sinister atavis[m]" that fills the subconscious with otherwise non-extant desires, Loy nevertheless actively discouraged her own grandchildren from undertaking psychoanalytic treatment (*GI* 28: 102).[43] But from her first authorial forays, Loy deploys psychoanalytic terms and references methodologies that illustrate her awareness of this body of thought: Keith Tuma and Elizabeth Frost have written about the impact of Freudian theory on the child development delineated in Loy's "Anglo-Mongrels and the Rose", whilst Andrew Gaedtke convincingly discusses the relationship between the protagonists of *Insel* as one that mimics and claims to supersede psychoanalytic therapeutic practice (Tuma, "Loy at Last"; Frost, "Loy's 'Mongrel' Poetics"; Gaedtke, "Transmissions"). Yet Loy's direct evocations of Freud are never uncritical. Not coincidentally, the constitutive qualities of psychoanalysis that trouble Loy most – its deterministic subjectivity, scientism, and sermonising; its disregard for female intellection and pleasure – are countered by the vitalist flux, intuition, and relentlessly creative life consciousness that affirm Loy's own renderings of sentience and corporeality, or the bodily knowledge that is our focus in these first two chapters. As Tamara Beauchamp quotes from a late Loy roman à clef by way of cogently summing up her resistance to psychoanalysis: "'*Life* is fleeting and escape[s] us while we essa[y] to reason it out'" (emphasis added, 292–3; *CP* 20: 15). Vitalism importantly affirms life, rather than dissecting or rationalising it.

Like Loy, the neovitalist Bergson privileged the artistic, intuitive, and mystical over the limitations of intellection and scientific aspiration.[44] For Bergson, "we are [all] creating ourselves continually", but his vitalism expressly identifies artists proper as superior beings (*CE* 14). While numerous modernist theorists argued that the increasingly chaotic reality of modern life could not be understood by the intellect alone, Bergson maintains that artists are a privileged class uniquely capable of accessing intelligent intuition.[45] Loy upholds Bergson's hierarchy in her essay "Modern Poetry" (1925), arguing that "[t]he new poetry of the English language . . . . attains the aristocratic situation of vitality" (*LoLB* 157). Bergson's intelligent intuition is an ideal consciousness combining disinterest and reflexivity whilst facilitating fleeting, expansive access to the inner realm of subjective and universal being, "a consciousness as wide as life" itself (*CE* 8).[46] And how often Loy shouts versions of this very truth to reader or cosmos: "LIFE / A leap with nature"; "LIFE is only limited by our prejudices" (*LoLB* 6, 150). Women are encouraged to overcome their "inadequate apprehension of <u>Life</u>" whilst the "occasional men of precursive genius [who are] aware of Life as a Deific Electricity . . . conve[y] to us our animation, our intelligence, our intuition" (*LoLB* 154; *SE* 240). Loy's can be a highly animate vitalism, and this resistance to a soporific sentience often leaps at us from the page. It clearly matters to her: from her first writings until the end of her life, Loy never ceases to agree with Bergson that "it is consciousness, or rather supra-consciousness, that is at the origin of life", a consciousness that "is made manifest to us only where creation is possible" (*CE* 147).

Bergson's influence is pivotal, as he was "the most significant proponent of evolutionary vitalism at the turn of the [twentieth] century", but he was indebted to prominent predecessors with like fascinations: "the linkage between vitalism and evolution had already begun in the 1870s, and [Madame Helena] Blavatsky directly based much of her Theosophical critique of Darwin upon a kind of theological evolutionary vitalism" (Morrisson 84). Loy's underdiscussed relationship to Theosophy receives extended consideration in *Elevated Realms,* but in the short term, these two influences – Bergson, Blavatsky – indicate how embodied vitalism can be perceived as philosophical or esoteric, aspirationally theoretical or religiously mysterious. Abstraction, in other words, pervades its intuitively felt principles in ways that permeate Loy's first renderings of its terminology in *Brontolivido* (c. 1913–20), her draft roman à clef detailing her encounters with the Italian Futurists. Loy portrays F. T. Marinetti stumbling over his own rendering of vitalist principles à la Bergson, as if uncertain how to label its intrinsic nous. Of a chance, reluctant meeting with Marinetti at a party, Loy drafts the following elliptical thoughts:

> . . . no-body took anything but the noise of him —— —– – – – [. . .] he was much less atrocious among the uproar he persistently induced – till, dropping the inevitable "Woman" conversation [. . . he] posed himself for the attack – Intui – stinct – illectual, which he did, with a sharp turn – about face to the listener he sat along-side of – holding an ankle to a knee – with an indefinable air of indiscreet personal approach – Each one of us – he declaimed – has got a cemetery within ourselves – but that cemetery must be reduced to a minimum – to a minimum – he insisted, with imperative gesture – (*B* 3: 10)

In his 1913 manifesto "Destruction of Syntax—Untrammelled Imagination—Words-in-Freedom", Marinetti argues that when we find ourselves in situations where life is "intensified", we instinctively change the way we speak, "brutally destroying syntax", refusing to "waste time building sentences", abandoning "punctuation and . . . adjectives." Revolutions, war, earthquakes are situations that force us to speak with haste and fervour, breathless, vehement, determined "to convey all the vibrations of [our] being" (123). Bergson's influence on Marinetti's thought is evident: Bergson believed that "literature must confound thought to invoke intuition" (Douglass 121). In turn, Marinetti's challenging words-in-freedom were meant to encapsulate our vitality at its most extreme, its most excessive. "*[L]yricism*", Marinetti states, "is that most rare *capacity for inebriating oneself with life* and *inebriating life with our selves*" ("Destruction" 123). The charismatic whirlwind that was Marinetti was, arguably, Loy's revolution, war, and natural disaster, and her passage conveys the immediacy and disorder he values, even as Marinetti's "[i]ntui – stinct – illectual" may be more inebriate than strategic. Another variant of this episode shows Loy redacting Marinetti's spoken "intellectual" twice before settling upon the Bergsonian phrase "intuitional intellectual" (*B* 3: 12). Having at last located the correct terms for his own vitalism, Marinetti proves bombastically eager, in word and gesture, to murder vestiges of mortality within the self, the ubiquitous internal cemetery. By Futurist logic, a willingness to kill affirms life, an aggression that extends to performance, human interaction, and social proprieties.

Loy was never wholly convinced by the inextricability of Futurist vitalism and bellicose machismo. According to *Brontolivido*, Marinetti repeatedly insisted that Loy prioritise her intuition, putting its felt intelligence before over-conscious thinking; to this, Loy wittily ripostes that her intuition tells her to find something or someone other than Marinetti in which to entrust her own belief (*B* 5: 2, 12). Loy clearly admired Marinetti's "fructuous vitality" from which he "gather[ed] a lightning impulsiveness", thereby exercising an irrefutable attraction over what remains "primeval" in "woman" (*B* 9: 6, 8). But she was also suspicious of the same:

> As a man [he] just didn't seem to exist – as vitaliser he was dynamically conveyant – You might not think much of the vessel – simply – anyone whose instincts were alert enough for refreshing – was instantaneously aware – that he had the right stuff to give, & he flung it about this liveness of his careless of who picked it up; when he manipulated it with intention was where he became dangerous. (*B* 2: 16)

On reflection, Loy considers Marinetti a mere transmitter of vitalist energy, at his best when separate from a strategic intellection that leads him astray. What is more, her experience of "being lifted up, & let down – simultaneously" by this vital presence is, as far as Loy can surmise, the inevitable condition of extended proximity to any man (*B* 2: 16). Yet Loy was proud to have learned and internalised Marinetti's vitality, believing herself "'the only female who has reacted to it – exactly the way [she had] noticed men do'" (qtd. in Conover, *LaLB* lxviii). Loy certainly does not have the same unequivocal reaction as the Lithuanian-born Eva Kühn, whose contribution to a Futurist journal uncritically reiterated Futurist propaganda, claiming the movement was "in the first place, all about health, superior harmony, [and] vital energy aimed at creating *new values*".[47] Loy's reaction is playful, observant, questioning, fascinated, satiric; by this variegated response, she sidesteps the status of "primeval woman" led unwittingly astray by Marinetti's irrefutable charisma. From the Futurists she learns a hyperbolic vitalism that surfaces in her apostrophes to "Life!" But those self-same Futurists also inculcated her with a healthy scepticism about how vitalism could be manipulated, allowing male writers to unquestionably perceive themselves as godlike, the very origin and replicators of life itself.

This vitalist co-optation is central to Loy's Futurist and post-Futurist writings. It is the butt of Loy's satire, "The Pamperers" (1920), where newly inaugurated member of the avant-garde Houston Loony announces: "I am going to make *Life* out of cigar-ends / *Life* / I must have Life . . . more life . . . I am Life . . . my hair is full of life . . . my clothes are alive; but I am not satisfied. I will have more life".[48] Loony's breathless diatribe pants its way through a comparison of himself with God, to an avowal that the life he so venerates "is *amusing!*" (*SE* 170). Having belittled life to a plaything for his own deific amusement, Loony recites his poetry. His verse is resistant to comprehension and defined by "a broken chain of metaphors", thereby embodying the very stylistic and rhetorical devices Bergson and Marinetti admired. The Loony's poem is intrinsically vitalist, prompting his interlocutor, the renowned genius-handler Diana, to swoon: "The cosmic force of the idea behind it!" (*SE* 177). In Loy's "The Sacred Prostitute", Futurism commends Love for offering herself as "the unique pleasure the warm gulf of intoxication from which one emerges—vital" (*SE* 201). So too does the newly baptised "Houston Loon" emerge as "The great Vitalist" because of Diana's emotional and intellectual ministrations in "The Pamperers" (*SE* 181). And this motif recurs, so that the disruptive, admired "creative idiosyncrasy" that defines the subject of Loy's "Sketch of a Man on a Platform" (1915) is troubled by his adherence to a "vital" physicality that permits his denigration of others as insentient "THINGS" to be pushed about at his behest (*LoLB* 20). Vitalism often brings out the worst in the male artist.

If male artistic vitalism can overwhelm, its absence reduces men to the vehicular. Loy directs Bergson's argument that supra-consciousness "lies dormant when life is condemned to automatism" specifically toward men who fall prey to an all-encompassing mechanisation, a charge, we will recall, that Loy levied at the "mechanised mysticism" of psychoanalysis (*CE* 147; *SE* 228). Both ailing Mr Bundy of "Hush Money" and the male interlocutor of "Songs to Joannes" possess bodies likened to "a clock-work mechanism / Running down against time" (*LoLB* 54; *SE* 32). (Notably, the Bundy Manufacturing Company is believed to have been the first to mass-produce punch clocks.) Where Bundy is a worn-out automaton, his son Daniel possesses the "delicate feminine intuition of poets", signalling Loy's belief that a well-proportioned vitalist intuition belongs to those who uninhibitedly identify with femaleness (*SE* 33).

Recognising Geronimo's destructive desire, Pazzarella knows that she will make him happy when she tells him that her living body is depleted, has become nothing other than "'the continued functioning of the mere machine'" (*SE* 81). When a coma overtakes her, Geronimo anxiously watches her to confirm this decline, but infuriatingly (for him), he discerns a sputtering but persistent "vital rhythm" in her female spirit (*SE* 96).

This gendered divide continues in Loy's "Human Cylinders" (1917), a poem that rejects – as does Bergson – a mechanistic view of evolution. At its heart is a dispiritingly intellectual sexual exchange that is expressly anti-vitalist: it is enervating, Loy states twice; it drains both participants of energy. These two human cogs in the evolutionary machine have no desire to "form one opulent well-being". Lacking the reassuring, wholistic complexities of a reciprocated communication that encompasses brain, body, and senses, the speaker envisions alternatives lying dimly, faintly just beyond the reach of this lifeless interaction: a "pale trail of speculation" or an "elastic tentacle of intuition / To quiver among the stars". Sluggish remainders and feelers conflate, once again, Loy's human animals with primordial beast. Further, they suggest that even when reduced to tenuous longings, vitalistic mores exceed base reality as the certainty of scientific thinking cannot: the poem concludes by roundly rejecting "polemic" and "solution" as oversimplified, destructive teleologies (*LoLB* 40–1). As for the soulless intimacy on offer, completion does not satiate. Gendered pronouns are excised from "Human Cylinders", but the speaker condemns the "[s]implifications of men" and validates an intuition Loy satirises elsewhere as the essence of the domesticated female, or she who "'[i]ntui[ts the] quality of flour", thereby reconfirming her sexed vitalist/mechanistic binary (*LoLB* 40–1, 39).

If Loy's transcendent vitalism is more freely available to the feminised individual than the manly man, this association surely constitutes a sly, protracted dig at contemporaries such as Darwin who dismissed the likelihood that women could ever attain genius. In addition, Loy might critique Bergson's implicitly phallic discourse, which has been interpreted as re-marginalising femininity. As Claire Colebrook argues, vitalism imagines "[l]ife . . . as some fluid, oceanic, maternal plenitude from which the bounded form of a distinct and representing body would emerge" ("Joys" 285). Reliant on intuition, Bergson idealises what Colebrook critiques as a "mind camera" that cuts the world into contained, comprehensible images. In other words, Bergson's fluid, infinite creative vitalism "[is] set against a static norm of man" even as it "affirm[s] all those masculine figures of active, forceful, creative, incisive, penetrative, and productive life" ("Joys" 285). Colebrook's interrogation of vitalist gendering is furthered by Joshua Schuster's contention that while Loy may share Bergson's "cosmological outlook", she should not be perceived as swallowing his theories wholesale. Instead, via a brilliant reading of Loy's "Parturition" (1914), Schuster maintains that Loy critiques the philosopher "for having evacuated the body and sexuality from his theory of life" (95).

For Schuster, Loy's poem "combines birth and sexuality as moments of intensity that are mediated by the simultaneous ecstasy and abjection of the female body in a modernist world where masculinity is associated with the vitality of life in general" (95). Giving birth, Loy's speaker is acutely sensory, but not sentimental; her present "is full of sentience directed toward an ideal existence beyond conventional subjectivity" (Schuster 123). "Parturition" pays next to no attention to the forthcoming baby, who is reduced to a brief pressure on a thigh. Instead, the focus is the arduous, self-reflexive "'coming into being'" of the female speaker, whose labour pains, or by Loy's phrasing, "infinitely prolonged nerve-vibrations", are commandeered to "link sensation to cosmology" (Schuster 125–6; *LoLB* 4). Bergson writes that processual, constantly evolving beings are often regrettably treated as inert objects, barring "fleeting vision[s]" in which "the invisible breath that bears them is materialised before our eyes." He continues sentimentally: "We have this sudden illumination before certain forms of maternal love, so striking, and in most animals so touching" as it "shows us each generation leaning over" the next, proving "that the living being is above all a thoroughfare" (*CE* 78). But in her fiction, as in her critiques of Freud, Loy dismisses the supposedly innate maternal instinct as one that occurs "whenever it does" (*SE* 130). For Loy, Freud "offer[s] no escape from the post-natal womb of the Eternal Mother", who, by his terms, "invariably" eats her own young (*SE* 227). Consequently, in "Parturition" the speaker is not a thoroughfare for the next generation, but for a transformative, self-validating "cosmic reproductivity" (*LoLB* 7). As Schuster notes, it is no accident that in the closing lines "— Man and woman God made them— / Thank God" – "woman" is positioned next to "God" (130).[49] "Parturition" is satire resplendent with an apotheosis dogged by frankly embraced abjection, one that will "climax in" a palpably felt "sensibility" that drives Loy's uniquely feminist vitalism (*LoLB* 5).

"Sensibility" is a favoured Loy term, and her use of it is often, but not always, commensurate with its deployment in the eighteenth-century "Age of Sensibility", a period that dovetails with a resurgence of vitalist thought in Europe. This age roughly encompasses the post-Augustan, pre-Romantic period, c. 1740–90, when sensibility and sentiment – often used interchangeably – were considered key to morality and understanding. Emotion was said to elevate rationality, bringing us closer to truth; as the Scottish philosopher David Hume (1711–76) asserts repeatedly in *Enquiries Concerning Human Understanding* (1777), sensation facilitates knowledge. The dominance of this discourse is wryly and exuberantly encapsulated by the triumphant "climax" of Laurence Sterne's *A Sentimental Journey* (1768), where protagonist Yorick attributes all of his joys and cares to sensibility, that "great—great SENSORIUM of the world!" (111). As Janet Todd asserts: "the Newtonian sense of the omnipresent deity permeating all things parallels the way the sentient principle of humanity, sensibility, informs the bodies of individuals" (100). These bodies include what Hume delineates as all "classes of sensitive beings" – animals, children, "barbarous Indians", and women (107, 191). In tandem with the burgeoning science of human nature, writers directed readers to hone quick, direct sensations, emphasising benevolence, virtue, delicacy, tenderness, pity, and transport (Todd 5). Compassion – which Loy pronounced her weakest characteristic in a 1929 questionnaire published by *The Little Review* – was the foundation of sensibility (*LaLB* 306). But further, sensibility was informed by the growing predominance of vitalism, a truth readily evinced by thinkers associated with the Scottish Enlightenment.

As Catherine Packham details, at the Edinburgh Medical School, faculty members earnestly discussed the relationship between bodily "'nervous power'" and an animating life force that questioned mechanistic models of the body, Enlightenment reason, and the Cartesian mind/body divide whilst paving the way to the prospect of a subconscious or unconscious form of bodily regulation (6–7). Prominent amongst this group was Robert Whytt, who argued on behalf of an autonomous, all-pervasive "'sentient principle'" or "'animal œconomy'" that directed the ease, animation, integration, and preservation of all aspects of the human body from birth until death (qtd. in Packham 6, 105). In a clear foreshadowing of Bergson, Whytt and his peers hypothesised a vital force that emphasised the flux, animation, and fluidity of human subjectivity. That these theories soon extended the scientific confines is widely evident: the popular press discussed vitalism from 1780 forward; Adam Smith applied the notion of a vitalising, self-regulating principle to the economy, and the Cult of Sensibility borrowed from vitalism a somatic focus built upon precepts of generative, unrestrained feeling, and of instincts that exceed intellectual control (Packham 11, 183; 53–4). This latter combination proved particularly resonant for women writers – Eliza Fenwick, Mary Wollstonecraft – who wrote highly sensibilious narratives that interrogated "opposed tropes of deathliness and vitality, stagnation or suffocation and life, torpor and energy" as a challenge to the marginalisation experienced by female characters, and as a means of exploring "how women's own vital resources might provide some sort of solution" (Packham 183–4). Forerunning Loy's reworking of masculinised, modernist vitalism, some of these women posited the universal, unsexed vital principle as the potential foundation for overturning women's systematic discrimination. These terms repeat themselves in Loy's oeuvre. Consider Loy's rendering of the sexually frustrated bride: "the shock of unsatisfied intercourse is a form of murder that leaves her desire alive in the corpse of her sensibility" (*CP* 18: 60). If "[f]lesh is a cloud of matter enshrining the electric apparatus of our sensibility", Loy repeatedly registers dismay that that cloud is "kneaded, prodded, and fumbled" without attending to "the very finite" but vital "centres of communication" by which body and longing unite (*GI* 27: 35). For Loy, sexual pleasure – so rarely experienced by women that Loy likens it to the gnomic – ameliorates the incessant crucifixion of women's sensibility, be that sensibility experiential, developing, psychic, or imaginative (*GI* 28: 113; *IA* 67: 110).

These feminist-oriented authors aside, sensibility was not, in general, meant to be overtly political; in lieu of change, it advocated heightened sensitivity toward life's inevitable pleasures and ills. By extension, and again in tandem with vitalism, sensibility co-opted "feminine" feeling as the pre-eminent social virtue whilst maintaining women's lesser status. Speaking a corporeal language – blushes and swoons abound – sensibility accommodated sensuality, though the spate of free love that followed this passionate age was reserved for the man of feeling alone; the feeling woman was expected to be chaste (Todd 137). This partial, faintly condemning resurrection of femininity was doomed to a certain death. What was "exquisite" and "dear" in the 1760s became "mawkish" and "sickly" for Coleridge, Byron, Austen (Todd 7). But the feminine would become venerable again in *fin-de-siècle* decadence, and in this guise, sentimentality was targeted by modernists who may have had vitalist leanings, but, as Frank Kermode argues, could just as sincerely believe themselves resolutely double-minded, their brains operating independently of their feeling (172). Clearly, it was the very pervasiveness of weak and puling sentiment that necessitated this backlash. While Loy's own engagement with the modernist economy of sentimentality is the focus of the section that follows, she remains alert to its sensibilious origins. As Michael Bell demonstrates, these origins were the ground of the modernist cult of anti-sentimentality (7).

A swingeingly sincere sensibility motivates Loy's earliest authorial forays. In Loy's little-discussed first poems of 1914, her speaker is a charitable, maternal moraliser uniquely attuned to "sorrows" and "toil", spiritual and physical nourishment, religious humility and beneficence, and the dispossessed: "half-broken mother[s]" with sore-covered infants (*LoLB* 220–1). Sanctimonious, cloying, and aggressively self-effacing, Loy's speaker and tone present the "feminised heart" as the requisite standard for moral value (S. Clark 22). While this guise is quickly dropped, echoes of the Cult of Sensibility reverberate through Loy's work, which remains attuned to susceptibility and vulnerability, to "creatures who 'think' through their feelings", and particularly to those for whom this very capacity is underestimated or undermined: non-normate individuals, children with disabilities, women diagnosed lunatic, rural inhabitants labelled inbred and perverse, homeless men on the streets of New York, the aged (McGann 13). Further, Loy pursues and articulates the "'intelligence of the senses'" both via impassioned sensuality and as a form of morality.[50] A sensibility incorporating comprehension, control, and utility infuses Loy's drive to understand right from wrong, and these ideals are identifiably Humean: for Hume, the body must attune itself to the stamp or pressure of experience in order to acquire information, learn propriety, and be of use to society (78). Loy can be serious about sensibility: its confusion and intensification is genuinely rendered in "Parturition", and in "Anglo-Mongrels and the Rose" her speaker is sincerely distressed by the inculcated "ignorance" and the "involute / inhibitions [etched] / upon the sensibility" of her feminised, passive Jewish protagonist, Exodus (*LaLB* 113–14). As Loy's protagonist Mrs Jones chides the ever-needy Insel, authority figures must also be recognised in this regard: "'Even the least of philanthropists … has sensibilities'" (*I* 28). Linking intellect and body, Loy tells us: "Sensibility explores the nervous system and reports to the soul" (*SE* 274). More menacingly, child Loy finds that in response to constant parental berating, her sensibility habitually "twisted … to a drill boring the depths of [her] consciousness to locate 'what [she] had done'" (*IA* 65: 71–2). Experiencing suicidal ideation when adolescent, Loy hopes to drink herself to death in her room one evening, finding only that her body grows numb as her eyes remain awake, watching "the illimitable rictus of human sensibility" that is her face in the mirror (*IA* 69: 140–1). These are the struggles of womankind's highly "fragile sensibilities" that Loy respectfully acknowledges but also freely lampoons (*SE* 192). Wittily, wittingly, Loy extends these antiquated mores into the modernist avant-garde: the Futurist Geronimo promises to "extend the scope of [Pazzarella's] sensibility until it comprises a universe" comically indistinguishable from his narcissistic self (*SE* 84). Given Marinetti's desire to "[p]lunge ... the essential word into the waters of sensibility", Loy's is a cogent connection ("Destruction" 125).

Sensibility informs Bergson's vitalism. Where Hume argues for the interdependence of feeling and knowledge, Bergson maintains that knowledge is bereft without an attendant theory of life because the mental and the physical are inextricably intertwined (*CE* 9, 197). "Instinct is sympathy", writes Bergson, adding: "If this sympathy could extend its object and reflect upon itself, it would give us the key to vital operations" (*CE* 102). For Bergson, intelligence alone treats life as inert matter. Compassionate intuition, however, generates a "sympathetic communication ... between us and the rest of the living", a "reciprocal interpenetration" not unlike the benevolence at the heart of sensibility (*CE* 103). Bergson is concerned that the "metaphysic of the human mind" has too long held sway, and has never properly accounted for the language of the body, or "organic creation" (*CE* 20–1). He is aware that philosophers who set their sights on the spiritual alone fear and recognise the all-too-easy prospect that humanity might be "reintegrate[d] ... in animality" (*CE* 151). Darwin celebrates this reintegration as a humbling democratisation, and Bergson is similarly inclined to perceive human proximity to the bestial as further evidence of "the intimate connection in which [we] stand to the rest of the universe" (*CE* 156). Although equally fundamental, Bergson's pastness is more individual and immediate than Darwin's. Rejecting the view that lived time is simply one moment replacing another in our perception, Bergson articulates a temporality – *durée* – which "is the continuous progress of the past ... gnaw[ing] into the future" (*CE* 12). This pastness resides within the organism, "acting and actual" (*CE* 18). And this history is crucial to human development: "organic evolution resembles the evolution of a consciousness, in which the past presses against the present and causes the upspringing of a new form of consciousness" (*CE* 24). The will is required to bring this evolution to pass: the intellect tends to be backward-looking, while the intuitive gaze faces forward; thus, consciousness labours to "detach itself from the *already-made* and attach itself to the *being-made*." Where intellectual thought causes the body to twist upon itself, and does "violence to our nature", intuition frees the self-reflexive cramp of traditional consciousness. A dialectic encompassing both perceptual positions is required, "a continual coming and going . . . between nature and mind" (*CE* 136). The result is creative, vital activity, in which "*a reality which is making itself [works alongside] a reality which is unmaking itself*" (*CE* 141).

Bergson's dialectic development of consciousness is reflected in Loy's writing, which, to borrow a phrase from her poem "Lady Laura in Bohemia" (1931), "proceeds recedingly" (*LoLB* 98). In Loy's "Der Blinde Junge" (1922), a blind child-man, a poignant veteran, is seen on the streets of Vienna, and described as a "Pure purposeless eremite / of centripetal sentience" – an isolate revolving upon his own conscious sensations, his soul made extinct, extinguished, by the stasis to which he is consigned (*LoLB* 83). Recalling the vitalist "elastic tentacle of intuition" sought after by the speaker of Loy's "Human Cylinders", this poem continues: "Upon the carnose horologe of the ego / the vibrant tendon index moves not" (*LoLB* 83). As in *durée*, this body is a flesh-encased timekeeper, but one without the conscious flexibility needed to enact Bergson's vital dialectic. This being is likened to waste, impediment, object, and a single body part, a "snout" upon which the blind, like beasts, become increasingly reliant (*LoLB* 84). He is also virgin sacrificial victim. Everything about him intimates disposability: in keeping with her interest in primordial chaos, Loy describes him as "[v]oid and extinct", consumed by "dumbfounded instinct" (*LoLB* 83–4). Intuition has disproportionately overtaken intelligence, and this sentient being appears doomed to neglect and self-destruction. But Loy demands that he be heard, recounts for us his capacity to "blo[w] out damnation and concussive dark // Upon a mouth-organ" (*LoLB* 84).

Loy's oeuvre entire continually announces its refusal to move into a rectilinear future, continually delves into pasts primordial, evolutionary, regressive, and individual. Loy's bodies falter and flounder; are passive and indecisive; are knowingly subject to circumstances beyond their control. Yet they remain vitally sentient, and are recognised as such by their author. Loy's is a vitalist dialectic between subject and speaker. She applies the high intellection of her theoretical, abstracted language to abjectified, anatomised, yet importantly aware individuals, whose experience she lays out to our purview throughout her writing via her processual, experimental, difficult aesthetic, one that Bergson, and many avant-garde modernists after him, considered a key means of confounding habitual thought, as well as an invocation of the intuition requisite to an affirming life consciousness.

Bergson's dialectic returns us to the terms of Loy's atavistic avant-gardism. For, like Bergson, Loy recognises the importance of rear-guardedness, and continually moves from a significant if abandoned past to an intuitive, experimental "being-made." As early as 1967, Loy's work is described as cutting-edge, yet likened to symbolism, or the avant-garde movement of the generation that preceded hers (Fields 604). Her biographer Carolyn Burke notes her "blatant modernist ties" yet insists, not unreasonably, that "she remained a late Pre-Raphaelite whose artistic voyages were shaped in reaction to a *fin-de-siècle* aesthetic" (*BM* vii). The author of the first Loy monograph diagnosed Loy as a figure torn between a Wildean elitism and the rollicking jokiness of Dada (Kouidis, "Rediscovering" 114). The editors of the first collection of essays devoted to Loy ask: "What is this avant-gardism with its roots in Victorianism and Decadence?" (Shreiber and Tuma 12). Loy's link to decadence – a movement loathed by her immediate Futurist, Dada, and Surrealist peers – has been noted in passing again and again.[51] More recently, Sarah Hayden argues: "Mina Loy retained – throughout her engagements with the avant-garde – a residual adherence to . . . outmoded conceptions of artistic subjectivity", among them aesthetic autonomy and individuality (146). A compulsive fidelity to anteriority is viscerally and affectively described in a draft chapter of Loy's roman à clef *Esau Penfold* (1910s/20s). Immersed in artistic communities chosen by a peevish, abusive husband, Loy reflects:

> In those days, never going anywhere of my own volition, I felt like a casualty borne along by an army on the march and dumped on their successive halting places to ache all alone in the conflict of my psychological wounds.
>
> Try as I would, I could not divert my mental flux from flowing into the conflicting channels that had been hollowed out for it by the turbulent years.
>
> Assisting at the peculiarly unanalytic conversation of second-rate artists, I despised them with the instinct of blind loyalty to an inner conviction as yet—unformed!

> The Duty obsession stamped upon my brain with a hoof, cloven,
> of that ~~Jew's~~ 'free thinker's' exhortation for me to arise among the
> geniuses of Earth (whereas I succeeded in 'taking place' nowhere)
> and that Christian's digging me into the bottomless pit of inferior-
> ity. My confusion resulted in feeling sullen over the accident of my
> presence—anywhere. (*EP* 23: 3)

A commitment to moral and exoteric religious traditions – marriage, humility, constancy, as well as the summative, mimetic arts – does battle with Loy's burgeoning sense of alternatives: free thought, experiment, self-propagated genius. Loy's Judeo-Christian parentage conflicts with her fledgling attempts to carve a place for herself in the world: hence Loy replaces the anti-Semitic stereotype of the cloven-hoofed, devilish Jew with a contemporaneous embrace of Jewish progressivism (Gilman 39). Along the way, Loy describes an inner, thwarted avant-gardist ripe for the deployment of a fraught, sulky, but ultimately legendary martyrdom.[52] In short, in this portrait of an unhappily married young woman, Loy insists upon taking her place alongside the celebrated male protagonists of her age, among them Joyce's Dedalus, Eliot's Prufrock, and Lewis's Tarr.

Furthering her foundational, oppositional pastness, Loy engages in satire, a genre uniquely bound to imparting "regress in the form of a progress, a presentation in the form of a violation" (Seidel 23). To a greater degree than Bergson, Loy embraces a past that cannot be contained or controlled: hence she admires the untamed regression so problematically, if pervasively, attributed to primitivism, to the point that she shares the not untroubling modernist fascination with "idealiz[ing] *any group* as yet unbroken to civilisation" (H. White 154). Furthermore, she is as attuned as Darwin to the generative value of atavism, thereby making a strength of Max Nordau's dire prophecy that "after some centuries art and poetry will have become pure atavisms, and will no longer be cultivated except by the most emotional portion of humanity—by women, by the young, perhaps even by children" (543). Loy, who read Nordau's *Degeneration* (1892), might be taken at face value when she has the speaker of "In Maine: Green's Colony" assert that she finds herself compulsively interested in a "race of dithering imbeciles supporting, clothing, protecting themselves without a keeper" (*BM* 40; *SE* 54). This same fascination marks the legacy of Loy's decadent precursor, Rachilde, aka Madame Baudelaire, who wrote as compellingly and audaciously as Loy about sexuality and gender. Of Rachilde, the Nicaraguan poet Rubén Darío argued: "One can only believe . . . that atavistic forces afflicting this delicate being with generations-worth of perversity have inspired in her the awakening, discovery, or invention of ancient sins" (427). As is Rachilde's, Loy's is an atavistic avant-gardism, reaching back into reviled or suppressed pasts with Bergson's "upspringing of a new form of consciousness" always in view. As we will shortly consider, Loy's fascination with past modes and mores drives her interest in sacrifice, a practice that "test[s] the point at which culture most sees itself reflected in barbarism": one that illuminates "the atavistic traces in our minds" and cultures (Hughes 274).

Loy knows that her peers often considered her the very dithering "imbecile" by which she was so preoccupied. In "Woman and Language" the French Symbolist Remy de Gourmont describes his ideal woman:

> The form of her body makes her breathing a language. The rhythm of her bosom betrays the state of her soul and the degree of her emotion. No speech finds a man more sensitive . . . . With her eyes, with the varied curves of her mute mouth, woman can express her inmost thought. The eye pales or kindles, lifts or lowers its look, and spells desire or disdain, anger or promise—so many pages understood by man the moment he has an interest in reading them. To these gleams and these movements, the play of the eyelids adds its value. This play is affirmative, negative, interrogative. It utters a short and decisive yes, or a yes of languor and abandon. It questions the tone of anger or of complaining. It refuses with a half-abrupt closing of the pupil, which veils the eyes without closing them. But how many other shades there are, and how rich in speech the smile is, also! The whole woman speaks. She is language incarnate. (128–9)[53]

So visibly, palpably embodied is this woman that she has no need for verbal expression; she is pure, legible intuition, ready for colonising. Her breath, the rising and falling of her breasts, her sinuous, shuttered mouth, her downcast eyes say all that a man needs to, well, *see*. It is precisely this misogynistic sentience that Loy's resolute intellection rejects. And the motivation is clearly delineated in Loy's unfinished 1930s roman à clef, *The Child and the Parent*. Womankind's "is a long plaint, resistant as is negation", writes Loy, adding that while woman remains "unaware of her own meaning" – claims first made in Loy's 1914 "Feminist Manifesto" – "the average man fits his significance to himself." Unabated and "unanswerable", woman persists: "Her echoing indignation flows on and the sentient wreckage in its wake is absorbed by sanatoriums and asylums with the connivance of official discretion which never listens behind closed doors" (*CP* 19: 15). Loy's satire rails against the generation of still more sentient wreckage, even as it deploys self-conscious, perceptive, and nuanced feeling to effect this very attack. Still further, and in contradistinction to her predominantly male forebears: shared sentience – contact, proximity, love – is Loy's satiric goal.

Notes

1. For examples of Loy's claim to hyperaesthesia, see folders 24 and 25 of Loy's *Esau Penfold* (c. 1910s/20s).
2. Ample evidence exists of Loy's need to integrate abjection with the sacred, inviolate, or pure. In "Ignoramus" (1923), "boiling your soul down" leaves "a greasy residuum"; more prosaically, "the chopper board" in the kitchen of Loy's poem "The Effectual Marriage" (1917) exudes a "[g]reasy cleanliness" (*LoLB* 45, 39). As I discuss elsewhere, Loy's recognition of herself as a marginalised figure – female, Jewish, vanguard – facilitates her reclamation of the base (Crangle, "Mina Loy").
3. Feminist biologist Lynda Birke affirms this supposition and its terminology, noting that for her, knowledge required dismemberment: "The experiments I read about involved the 'sacrifice' of untold numbers of sentient animals, so that humankind could learn a little more, perhaps, about how animal bodies work" (9).
4. When an art student in Munich in 1900, Loy strolled through the streets smoking "a clay pipe adorned with an albino fly" (*BM* 60); in "Parturition", Loy likens the birthing woman, so proximate to death, to bluebottles seeking sustenance from a carcass (*LoLB* 7). Loy's "Ignoramus" (1923) is "Caged with the love of houseflies / The avidity of youth / And incommensuration"; her Venice is "an over purpled peach / swarmed by the flies of dusk" (*LoLB* 45, 101). The fly is similarly pervasive and ineradicable for Bataille, who uses it as evidence of the animal's originary, replete, and total immersion in its world: "No doubt the individual fly dies, but today's flies are the same as those of last year . . . . The flies remain, equal to themselves like the waves of the sea" ("Hegel, Death" 15). We will return to the fly at the end of the next chapter, where it literally dances through Loy's "Songs to Joannes" and 1930s ballet "Crystal Pantomime".
5. Jerome McGann sources Stein's rhythms in "the eighteenth century, when poetic writing began to explore the languages of the 'feelings' and the 'heart'—languages that sought to expand their expressive range by developing their non-semantic and transconceptual resources" (3–4). Although his turn to the corporeality of Stein's prose resonates, McGann underplays the philosophical complexity of her syntax. By contrast, Paul Douglass generatively relates Stein's style to

Bergsonian temporality, writing: "Stein's art focused on the *resistance* lurking in every vital impulse, and the struggle to renew the living language" (119).

6. For "cymophanous sweat" and "[e]tiolate body" see poem 28, "Songs to Joannes"; "homophonous hiccoughs" arise in poem 29 (*LoLB* 64–5). "The cuirass of the soul" appears in the 1922 "Apology of Genius" (*LoLB* 78).

7. While Loy follows Bergson in valuing a combination of intuition and intelligence, the latter category can be downplayed by scholars eager to illustrate that Loy spiritedly resurrects "primitive" or "feminine" discourses of embodied intuition. For example, Ellen McWhorter writes eloquently about Loy's suggestive, perceptive semantic deployments whilst arguing that Loy sets herself apart from rational science, or the "long history of treating humans as animated corpses, as things to be dissected and analysed rather than understood in their totality" (2, 8). Yet Loy the satiric anatomist challenges and avidly participates in scientific discourse, as Peter Quartermain attests in his discussion of her blending of colloquialisms with arcane, technical discourse ("Love Songs" 80).

8. Periphrasis refers to roundabout or loquacious speech; macrology, to the use of redundant words or phrases; pleonasm delineates superfluous terms or phrases rendered with the aim of greater clarity.

9. Henry James theorised "reflectors" or "centres of consciousness providing vantage points on the storyworld" (Herman 243).

10. Against this critical commonplace, David Herman argues for an "enactivist" reconsideration that foregrounds "the tight coupling between mind and world, the nexus between intelligent agents and the environments they seek to navigate" (264). For Herman, inner and outer realities are unpredictable and indeterminable, meaning that heightened interaction, not insularity, is the basis of modernist streams of consciousness. Given its combined origins in the psychological, the felt, and the polemical, Loy's sentience arguably aligns with to Herman's reworking.

11. Loy discusses the gait of the mentality in "Modern Poetry" (*LoLB* 157). In "History of Religion and Eros" she articulates "[t]he snap-back of human consciousness from the take-off of inspiration", noting that "the *stretch* of consciousness into the imperceptible still depend[s] ... on the contemporary stage of evolution in the *concrete world*" (*SE* 245). In the final chapter of *Elevated Realms*, I discuss further Loy's motif of the "incalculable tonnage" or "onerous animation" of gravity or consciousness upon the sentient being (*LoLB* 94; *SE* 37, 142, 244).

12. In "Brancusi's Golden Bird" (1922), Loy's speaker admires laboriously produced smoothness, but the urge to roughen surfaces, to revel in textual texturing, dominates Loy's writing. In "Transfiguration." (c. 1917–20s), Loy writes: "The flesh of the Mexican woman's face was

baked onto the bone and must jar inhumanly to the touch" (*SE* 142). This play between an anticipated yielding and provocative resistance recurs in Loy's satire "The Pamperers" (1920), when the Houseless Loony asks Diana, the "polished, sequestered . . . hermetically sealed" heroine, "what would happen if one scraped some of the nap off you?" (*SE* 171). Diana's social smoothness and impenetrability are thus exposed as a soft, raised surface that longs to be stroked in a specific direction.

Loy's haptic preoccupation accords with Santanu Das's claim for the resilience of modernist "tactile experience . . . [that] stubbornly adheres to the flesh" (6). It runs counter to the articulation of Loy as an emblematic cold modernist, who, by Jessica Burstein's terms, neglects the abject, interiority, and the disruptive in favour of modish, smooth continuities between contemporaneity and the past, as well as between self and world. Yet Loy reveres baseness, champions "[t]he introspector", and wilfully coarsens surfaces she encounters (*SE* 278).

13. A good example of this critical discourse on Loy arises in Ryan Bishop and John Phillips's *Modernist Avant-Garde Aesthetics and Military Technology: Technicities of Perception* (2010). These authors situate Loy within a larger vanguard embrace of the slow or backward, which they describe as "the decelerant logic of the avant-garde, which reverses [technological] processes that gather momentum throughout the twentieth century". In an express counter to the Futurist or Vorticist embrace of technology, some vanguardists – Duchamp, Kandinsky, Loy – opt out of "equating the power and aim of speed with *becoming faster*" and paradoxically, find that through slowness they "gai[n] a surprisingly firmer hold on this future to which everyone else is racing . . . than could have been rationally expected" (73–4). As Bishop and Phillips assert, Loy effects this process by "indulg[ing] in older – forgotten – idioms", offering as a prime example her use of the Italian Renaissance love lyric in "Songs to Joannes" alongside her satiric mockery of contemporary feminism, science, and experimentation (70–2). That Loy cleaves to ancient, "primitive", or antiquated discourses is similarly a mainstay of this *Anatomy*.

14. Loy is alert to the losses that modernism represents and overlooks. In her 1929 essay on Stein, for instance, Loy asserts that "the spiritual record of the race" is marked by "nostalgia for the crystallisation of the irreducible surplus of the abstract", meaning that in the absence of mystic or religious faith, "the evolution of consciousness has devolved upon the abstract art" (*LaLB* 297).

Loy's statement is triply retroactive: whilst sensitive to the mourning associable with the fading of some religious tradition, she takes one step forward and another back by suggesting that the novelties of contemporary art will act as salve for the resultant spiritual decline. This suggestion validates modernist aesthetics even as it potentially reinforces the perception that amorality and alienation are inevitable outcomes of an increasingly secular world. Loy's troubling if typical use of the phrase "the race" suggests that she is quite prepared to leave others behind in these new forms of consciousness. As Loy herself so frequently attests, backwardness has its blind spots.

15. In a diary entry dated 21 August 1947, Cornell describes this process as follows: "<u>This part of my journal</u> is the most profuse and overflowing . . . cluttered in memory received with endlessly unfolding experience" (146). Another example from 26 November 1947 reads: "One of those days which can be ordinary routine but in which a circumstance or so can start the unfoldment of an endless interplay of significant relationship" (151).

16. Charles Altieri tells us: "where there is an avant-garde, there must be an *arrière-garde*." Furthermore, "where there are such binaries, there will be ego formations that have a great deal at stake in maintaining the relevant distinctions", thereby "facilitat[ing] a far too easy contempt for what one has projected as in the rear (or in arrears)" (633). Altieri is sceptical of this ease, and of the implicit and explicit ways that vanguardism pretends to counter capitalist or mainstream views, whilst often unselfconsciously perpetuating the same; vanguard narratives of progress and endless novelty are among his readiest targets. In an alignment that resonates with my own suggestion that Loy's vanguardism is learned and filtered through satire, Altieri points out that "satire is the easiest genre in which to test how social identifications are formulated" (647).

17. At one juncture, Loy narrates how, as a child, she was akin to a "paralytic soldier at a military review", segmented into stasis by her conflicting Christian and Jewish heritages (*GI* 28: 42).

18. Carolyn Burke considers "New York Camelio" a fictionalised account of Marcel Duchamp, and the evening in question the Blind Man's Ball of 1917 (*BM* 239).

19. Less harmoniously, a like primeval substance is found in the same organs in "Pazzarella": staring into the eyes of Loy's titular protagonist, Geronimo discerns "a putrefying mass, a turbid residuum lying at the bottom of their wells", one containing "the decaying remains of an embryonic spirit" (*SE* 91). In other words, Loy repeatedly insists that intellectual illumination – often equated with sight, the most venerated sense – is sourced in the primordial.

20. Or, as Torgovnik puts it: "gender issues always inhabit Western versions of the primitive. Sooner or later those familiar tropes for primitives become the tropes conventionally used for women" (17).

21. Bataille nuances and intermingles his sexual categories, observing: "Human sexual activity is not necessarily erotic but erotic it is whenever it is not rudimentary and purely animal" (*E* 29). Bestiality is a key aspect of Bataille's theorisation of sex. He writes: "*Animal nature*, or

sexual exuberance, is that which prevents us from being reduced to mere things", whilst noting that "*[h]uman nature . . .* geared to specific ends in work, tends to make things of us at the expense of our sexual exuberance" (*E* 158).

22. "The Widow's Jazz" uncritically conflates women's marginalisation with that of African Americans. Loy does the same in an undated variant draft of "The Library of the Sphinx." where the "solution" to woman's nebulous status and her failure to attain satiation – figured as the answer to the feminised Sphinx's infamous riddle – is a jazz that "keep[s] on jumpin'!" (*SE* 392). This link is excised from later drafts, but the turn of phrase resurfaces, as discussed above, in "Lady Asterisk."

23. The relationship between Eros and primitivism is also discussed in the first chapter of *Elevated Realms*.

24. An archived typescript of this poem is dated 25 August 1940 next to the title and 27 August 1940 after Loy's concluding signature ("Loy, Mina: To Julien Levy and Joella Levy: Poems, 1940, undated").

25. Elsewhere, Loy deploys "aboriginal" to denigrate her enemies: in "Apology of Genius" (1922), the censorious masses are said to possess "smooth fools' faces / like buttocks bared in aboriginal mockeries" (*LoLB* 77).

26. In this typescript draft, the last three lines of the second stanza recur in the finished poem. But in the final version, these same concluding lines affirm, rather than interrogate, America's superiority. Consider:

> While you, as erst you instrumented ease,
> create for conquest
> in the wink – of – a – world's eye;
> sowing this hemisphere
> with dragon's teeth
> of defence, blooming overnight,
> lavishly
> as your predecessors
> cast their seed,
> you amaze mankind
> with the dimensions
> of your achievements. (*LaLB* 231)

27. In "America * A Miracle" Loy writes:

> Today,
> in spirit,
> those your pioneers
> salute the miracle America they made
> for that which currently arises in their wake;
> the complementary miracle of her safeguard.
>
> The very wind blows on your stars and stripes
> the gale of their laudations. (*LaLB* 230)

By contrast, the draft text reads:

> To – day –
> The spirit of your Pioneers
> Stirs in repose
> To sound the Miracle   –   America they made
> For what should logically have risen in their wake
>
> The complementary miracle of her Safeguard
>
> The very wind blows on your Stars and Stripes
> The gale of ~~your~~ their interrogations. (*EP* 24)

28. The published poem makes no mention of Americans fighting with the Allied powers in World War II; this reference in Loy's draft dates the poem to 1941–5, or after the USA militarily entered the Grand Alliance. Two pages of typescript draft are randomly inserted in *EP* 24, while a partial manuscript exists in *EP* 25.

29. If we follow Hal Foster's model, we might say that Loy replicates and appropriates primitivism like a Cubist, uses it as a disruptive tool in Surrealist fashion, but unlike poststructuralists and second-wave feminists, does not actively deconstruct or theorise it ("Unconscious" 65). I say "if" because I remain unconvinced that the Surrealists were as ideologically distanced from or conscious of their use of the primitive as Foster suggests.

30. Loy identifies the poem as "Cannibalistic Love Song"; as published in the little magazine *Gargoyle*, "Song" is plural, and I defer to this spelling. My heartfelt thanks to Eric White for his assistance in locating the original.

31. There are two volumes of *The Variation of Animals and Plants under Domestication*. Throughout this chapter, all citations refer to the second volume.

32. In "The Sacred Prostitute", the character Futurism states: "women are only animals, they have no souls" (*SE* 199). Extending its precepts to male and female alike, "One O'Clock at Night" makes a virtue of this insult.

33. A similar aversion surfaces in Loy's 1914 "Feminist Manifesto", where women are discouraged from "adapt[ing] themselves to a theoretical valuation of their sex as a <u>relative impersonality</u>" (*LoLB* 154). Rather than conform to what Loy posits as a lifelessly neuter state, women are urged to pursue an essential, individualised femininity.

34. In *Esau Penfold* (c. 1910s/20s), the protagonist couple have a child blessed with "exquisite wrists" that create "shadows on the wall". This grace is sourced in Esau's distant Hindu ancestor, reputed to have been a dancer. Throughout this text, Loy is by turns interrogative or scathing about Esau's bloodlines. But when oriental genes facilitate artistry, atavism is a triumph. And at one comical juncture, Loy deploys orientalism to diminish occidental educational privilege, satirically listing

the causes of Esau's supposed "atavisms" as "the East, nursery and public school and Cambridge" (*EP* 24).

35. Pointing out that "the ruling class" is "secure in the assent of the mass of the population", Bataille links its power to "primitive peoples [who] tend to reserve polygamy for their chiefs" (*E* 160). Although he proclaims his Marxist allegiances, Bataille remains wedded to the excesses of royal life and other forms of unearned authority.

36. For instance, Bates's proud heteronormative desire to parent is slyly skewed by the narrator's assertion that the "innate" maternal instinct is as random as it is volitional (*SE* 130). In addition, the narrator labels Bates a "mono-maternalist", indicating that her will to care has clear limits, and is neither defining nor all-consuming (*SE* 133).

37. I refer here to Coventry Patmore's celebration of female docility and domesticity, "The Angel in the House", published in parts in 1854 and 1856, and repeatedly revised and reissued thereafter (Patmore, Introduction, n.p.). This long narrative poem became a touchstone of Victorian gender relations.

38. The first of these comics was reproduced in an album published by *Harper's Weekly*; the second was part of an 1863 collection, *The Origin of Species, Dedicated by Natural Selection to Dr. Charles Darwin* (Browne 501–3).

39. Levine states that Darwinian sexual selection had little "influence on Victorian culture", yet he details how Darwin's opponents and acolytes wrestled in print and public with the unnerving prospect of female reproductive choice (189–91). Levine and John Holmes agree that contemporary psychologists and cognitive scientists are increasingly reattuned to sexual selection, a resurgence Holmes expressly aligns with the popularity of this subject in the "decades after Darwin himself published *The Descent of Man*" (189).

40. In one poem in "Evolutional Erotics", a Darwinian scientist churlishly wonders if sexual selection can be true when the woman he admires falls for an "'idealess lad'". Ultimately, Darwin's might is maintained: although the woman privileges a stupid boy over a genius, the scientist decides that she predictably succumbed to his powerful display of dancing. In her essay "The Evolution of the Sense of Beauty" (1885), Naden mocks Darwin's gendered anthropomorphism, by which, for instance, female birds become "brides" as if avian "mating . . . took place in a Victorian ballroom" (Holmes 191–3).

41. In "Universal Food Machine", Loy argues that "atavistic ferocity" causes war (*SE* 291). Writing during World War II, Loy's opposition to this aggression reads sincerely, but also evokes her valuation of the genetic reversion evident in creative individuals whose "atavistic ferocity" might catalyse the generative bellicosity of the avant-garde.

42. I take my cue about Loy's anti-psychoanalytic peers from Tamara Beauchamp's excellent *Enemies of the Unconscious: Modernist Resistances to Psychoanalysis* (2014), a dissertation that includes a chapter on Loy. For Beauchamp, Lawrence shares Loy's ambivalence toward Freud, whereas Lewis and Pound are more openly hostile.

    After completing the second volume of this *Anatomy of Mina Loy*, I was reassured to locate Beauchamp's work and see that our readings dovetail and diverge on some key points. Beauchamp argues that Loy resists psychoanalysis from feminist and transcendental perspectives but does not undertake a full-fledged critique on these fronts. The second volume of this study, by contrast, argues that as an active, life-long esotericist, Loy enacts a feminist visionary rereading of Eros that takes psychoanalysis into especial account. The workings of this Eros are particularly prevalent in the late, unfinished romans à clef that are not part of Beauchamp's focus. Where I argue that Loy's critique of Freud inflects her entire oeuvre and is emergent in her earliest writings, Beauchamp begins in 1918 and ends with *Insel*, a novel drafted by 1936.

    Beauchamp importantly argues that Loy challenges Freud by turning to the second-generation psychoanalytic theorist Roberto Assagioli. While I discuss Assagioli's psychosynthesis in *Elevated Realms*, I do so with a view to showing that it is specifically Freud's fragmented theory of the psyche, alongside psychoanalytic misogyny, that prompt Loy's resistance to Freud. As a consequence, she develops stronger intellectual relationships with mystically inclined or coalescent readers of mind, soul, body, and cosmos that pre- and post-date Freud's prominence, a group that includes not only Assagioli, but Frederic Myers and Sandor Rado, as well as contemporaneous feminist psychoanalysts such as Karen Horney.

43. A perfect example of Loy's proclivity for psychoanalytic terms, coupled with her disregard for the same, arises in a letter to her daughter Joella written in the early 1950s. Ostensibly apologising for failing to write, Loy states that she has not done so because "subconsciously I must have been _too_ upset" given that the cape Joella presumably sent as a gift "was twice my width." Loy's offence-taking about her daughter's overestimation of her figure enacts Freudian parapraxis. Yet, on the page that follows, Loy writes that she has strongly discouraged Joella's son from undertaking a course of psychoanalytic treatment ("Loy, Mina to Joella Bayer and Julien Levy, circa 1950–1954"). Loy's ambivalence has a discernible impact on her descendants, a truth to which they appear to be attuned. In an interview in May 1989, Loy's grandson, Jerrold Levy, told biographer Carolyn Burke that Loy "did admire Freud, thought him a genius" (Jerrold Levy, "Interview with Burke").

44. Alexandra Owen writes: "Bergson's philosophy spoke to an esoteric understanding of a reality beyond the purview of 'modern science'" (136–7). For Owen, his was an "'occult' philosophy" that appealed to modernist radicals who often linked the anti-status quo of the esoteric with their own avant-gardism, be it artistic or political (135). These links are discussed further in *Elevated Realms*.

45. Bergson's contemporaries who shared his view on reality and the intellect include Alfred North Whitehead, William James, F. R. Bradley, and Bertrand Russell (Burwick and Douglass 3).

46. The link between vitalism and impersonality was forged during Romanticism, which shares with modernism "an appeal to various forms of defamiliarization" and the creation of "concepts and languages to manage and diminish the forceful chaos of existence." Obscure art is said to direct attention to the hidden spirit of creativity behind the aesthetic process, productively detracting from authorial presence (Colebrook, "Queer" 88–9; see also Lehan 310–11).

47. Published under her married name, Eva Amendola, Kühn's "Futurist Occultism" was published in *Senza veli* in 1920. A translation of this brief article is appended to Matteo D'Ambrosio's 2018 "Notes on 'Esoteric Futurism'".

48. The ellipses in this quotation are Loy's own.

49. Schuster claims that "Parturition" betrays a longing "to achieve a feeling of organic redemption", arguing that Loy evokes the trope of woman as timeless origin to avoid "conceding the terms of [vitalist] evolution to male stereotypes" (118, 120–1). Her lifelong striving toward ephemeral Bergsonian moments of transcendence notwithstanding, Loy's "Parturition" – consistent with so many of her writings – generatively foregrounds the abject, agonised, and anatomised body first and foremost. In turn, the redemptive conclusion of Loy's poem is wryly attuned to the patriarchal limitations imposed upon women as static (read: passive, undeveloped) site of origin. As such, Loy critiques masculinist vitalism and the feminine stereotypes which keep that hyperbolic vitalism aloft.

50. Loy presents an intelligent sensorium as an ideal in her 1925 "Modern Poetry" (*LoLB* 157–61). In "Mi & Lo", Loy argues: "Morality can only be attained through a perfect understanding, domination and utilisation of the senses" (*SE* 277). In Loy's later, mystical prose works, she maps a desire to "transcend the restrictions of [man's] overt senses" via Eros (*SE* 239, 250).

51. Loy is often aligned with the decadent movement her vanguard peers so roundly trounced (see Kouidis, "Rediscovering" 50, 116; Januzzi, "Mongrel Rose" 415; Roberts 141; Burstein 155).

52. I discuss the relationship between avant-gardism and manipulative emotional display in Crangle, "Phenomenology and Affect".

53. Through de Gourmont's reputation, and his links with Loy associates Ezra Pound (an admirer), Giovanni Papini (an idoliser), and Natalie Barney (who moved in the same French pre-World War I literary circles), Loy was assuredly familiar with de Gourmont's work (*BM* 162, 330). Marissa Januzzi states that Loy appreciated de Gourmont's writing, but this claim goes uncited ("Mongrel Rose" 417).

Chapter 2

Bodies Sacrificial and Intimate

As an atavistic vanguardist, Mina Loy is a strategically split self, divided between an informed adherence to the past, both recent and ancient, and a need to journey relentlessly forward, pushing persistently at the cutting edge of artistic and social custom. This split extends to her responses to the status quo: ever keen to foreground the affective being, Loy returns continuously to a formulation of inner life that privileges feeling alongside intellection, be that by affirming sentience or the feminist compassion underpinning her replications of the modes and motifs of the eighteenth-century Cult of Sensibility. But the Loy who cares deeply and uninhibitedly is never far afield from the scabrous Loy who attacks the concepts or individuals Western patriarchal society reveres, the Loy who complicates our understanding of the "primitive" or unevolved, the Loy who discerns and disarms the sexist expectations of an otherwise liberating vitalism. These literary aggressions impressed those too long and too reductively credited with fashioning modernism in its entirety, among them Ezra Pound, who gave Loy the greatest compliment he could muster, praising her for refusing to indulge in sentimentality, in mawkish or manipulative feeling.[1] Pound recognises Loy as a fellow combatant, a strategist prepared to machete verbiage free from tentacular materiality and clinging affect. And Loy was assuredly Pound's avant-garde companion-in-arms, standing alongside him at the front line of twentieth-century aesthetics. But she was also an unabashed satirist, a role consistent with the atavistic proclivities that formed our focus in Chapter 1. For Loy engages in and extends a wittily bellicose heteronormativity understood to have catalysed the very origin of satire over two and a half millennia before she began to write her first poems.

"Bodies Sacrificial and Intimate" is a chapter that reaffirms the emotionality of Loy's corporeality, and furthers our exploration of the bodily feeling and risk presented in her writing. I begin by demarcating the systematics of the modernist economy of sentimentality, one by which feeling is a measurable value to which the privileged have greatest access. Such are its constraints and denunciations that the modernist affective economy is a de facto anti-sentimentalism. Loy deploys this economy, but also reworks its more misogynistic terms. Where leading modernist figures – Baudelaire, Wilde, and Marinetti, among others – restricted or censured emotionality, Loy resists their evaluations, instead calling attention to their neediness and to the brute violence at the heart of their own sentimental circulations. Her refusal draws on resolutely atavistic terms, is commensurate with her use of ancient tactical aggressions: sacrifice and satire. Deliberately wasteful, inherently irrational, sacrifice challenges the neat logic of any productive economy. Sacrifice undertakes harm in order to retain or restore an optimal state of affairs, even as it is a fundamental social ritual blind to the truth of the daily renunciations made by the marginalised. In her writing, Loy foregrounds overlooked female sufferance, recognising within women's effacement a model for a universal human proximity that privileges the communal over the self. By these proclivities, Loy predates Bataille, who argues that sacrifice restores humanity to a divine intimacy "because it is not compatible with the positing of a separate individual" (*TR* 51). Sacrifice matters to Bataille, as it does to Loy, because, "[i]n his strange myths, in his cruel rites, man is *in search of a lost intimacy*" (*AS1* 57). By these proclivities, Loy challenges fellow modernists such as D. H. Lawrence, or he who anxiously rallies his reader to "[r]ouse the old male spirit again" by evading self-revocation, the horror by which men risk "soften[ing] and soften[ing] in self-sacrificial ardour" until they become "white worms" ("Education" 658). It is to this very self-revocation, for all human beings, that Loy aspires.

From sacrificial intimacy, we turn to satire, which is posited here as literary sacrifice, a form of verbal violence that actively aims to harm and eviscerate, thereby mimicking malediction in raising questions about aggression and proximity. Traditionally, satire aggresses to distantiate author or speaker from enemies real or perceived, as well as to inflict shame upon or hex those very enemies. But as Charles Altieri argues, satire can be "less a vehicle of judgement than it is a vehicle for the deep pathos that emerges when we meet the enemy and find out that we are inseparable from it" (648). From its inception, satire has been unmistakeably intimate, originating with what the seventeenth-century English poet John Dryden (1631–1700) called "conjugal dialogues". Ironically, too much intimacy is said to have killed it: satire is believed to have come to a long, slow, modern demise courtesy of its feminisation, a process the Anglo-Irish writer Jonathan Swift (1667–1745) began decrying in the eighteenth century. Loy does not accept this history, returning the genre to its ancient roots with her understanding that the divide between women and men epitomises "the enmity of the exploited for the parasite, the parasite for the exploited" (*LoLB* 154). This enmity drives Loy's satire, is Thanatos to her Eros. For Loy, love must be freighted with lampoon, the beloved the locus of sparring comedy. Having lain the ground for Loy's twinning of hostility and affection, this chapter turns to Loy's feminist rewriting of the sacrificial modes that are crucifixion and virginity. A Christian Scientist and believer in Jesus as the Son of God, Loy is also keen to democratise his history and teachings, and as such, repeatedly transposes Christly death, resurrection, and transformation to her female characters. While many critics have discussed Loy's infamous resistance to treating the virgin as a commodity, Loy is also attuned to classical rituals of virgin sacrifice. Therefore, this chapter concludes with a close reading of her 1930s ballet "Crystal Pantomime", where Loy grossly, wilfully exaggerates the sentimental economy of fairy-tale love, the uniting of prince and virgin, to expose its unacknowledged and ancient sacrificial underpinnings.

"Passional Compromise": Modernist Sentimental Economies

In a review of 1918, Ezra Pound emphatically countered any plausible association between Loy and late eighteenth-century sensibility, finding her poems "neither simple, sensuous, nor passionate" and in possession of "no emotion whatever". Pound's gendered definition by negation implies that when an author is identified as female, the reader expects histrionics to ensue. Instead, Loy gives that reader "logopoeia", a self-reflexive poetic form tautologically "akin to nothing but language", a mode, according to Pound, with roots in the Augustan period that preceded sensibility, a time when literature in English was dominated by the likes of Alexander Pope (1688–1784) and Jonathan Swift ("'Others'" 57). Thanatos wins out over Eros in Loy's poetry, and Pound clearly approves. As Carolyn Burke puts it, Pound respected Loy's "refusal to traffic in sentiment" (*BM* v).

Traffic is commerce, and Pound's resistance to treating emotion as a transportable, and too readily available, commodity is not original; a version of this claim surfaces as early as Baudelaire's seminal modernist essay "The Painter of Modern Life" (1863). For Baudelaire, "money is indispensable to those who make a cult of their emotions" (27). But not, Baudelaire insists, money that is earned; the ideal occupation is dandified idleness, which in turn fosters a privileged and admirable love. At first blush, this is a curious position to uphold for the lauded father of modernism, the prescient iconoclast and harbinger of the *fin-de-siècle* rise of avant-gardism. That labour blights affectivity was in fact a pervasive belief of the Age of Sensibility, where the true pleasures of refined feeling were regularly ascribed to the gentry alone. In that period, the proof of one's anti-capitalism lay in having enough money to *give* away, but that money should fall miraculously unsullied into one's lap, thereby ensuring that "'the exquisite luxury of a feeling mind'" remained an upper-class indulgence (James Cobb, *The First Floor* [1787]; qtd. in Todd 13). Or, as Patricia Meyer Spacks puts it, in the literature of sensibility, "Money and tears take care of everything" (505). The widespread advocacy of "sentimental commerce" threatened some conservatives, who complained that the circulation of emotion between diverse demographic groups was potentially too democratising (Nagle 833). Given his notoriety as a dissolute, indebted spendthrift, Baudelaire's confident claim of access to the most refined and valuable passions might serve as their vindication.

Come modernism, charges of affective indulgence are levied at those who cheapen emotion by stealing it or underestimating its true value. In *De Profundis* (1897), Oscar Wilde writes:

> a sentimentalist is simply one who desires to have the luxury of an emotion without paying for it .... Even the finest and most self-sacrificing emotions have to be paid for. Strangely enough, that is what makes them fine. (639)

Quite likely a rewording of a quotation from George Meredith's *The Ordeal of Richard Feverel* (1859), this passage is written by Wilde in jail, when he is being forced to repay what was erroneously perceived to be his own moral debt to society (Dickson 33).[2] For Wilde, common individuals borrow emotions from circulating libraries, sullying them whilst refraining from paying for them outright, either due to incapacity or unwillingness, meaning that they will never know feeling of the highest quality. Wilde asserts that those who traffic in the degrading artifice of borrowed sentiments are cynics, and cynicism is "the perfect philosophy for a man who has no soul" (640). Traditionally, Cynics were among the intellectual descendants of Socrates, renowned for resisting the wealth Wilde, like Baudelaire before him, considers crucial to the experience of refined emotion. But more commonly, a cynic is a sneering fault-finder not far removed from a satirist, a role at which Wilde excelled. Wilde's arguments undermine his own literary legacy, and equally vexatiously, apply capitalist parameters to human sentience, a strange move for the author of "The Soul of Man under Socialism" (1891). Or perhaps Wilde's connection is logical, given that according to Gayle Rubin, Marx left unclarified the "'historical and moral element'" of the "'determination of labour power'", meaning that the exigencies of unpaid affective, feminised labour went overlooked in his revolutionary theories. For Rubin, the pre-modern histories and moralities to which Marx only alludes underpin women's displacement within capitalism, and the entrenched undervaluing of a social contribution of incessant, domesticated compassion and care ("Traffic" 164). Women, in other words, laboured long and hard at the very feeling that Wilde argues can be bought for a neat and tidy monetised sum. Implicitly, Wilde's theory acknowledges the unsung value of affective work. Explicitly, it consigns that labour to the estimation and disposal of the empowered. The logical conclusion of this thinking is the resolutely anti-sentimental sex trade to which the next chapter turns.

Wilde's commodification of feeling resurfaces in the work of many of his peers and descendants, quite literally finding a purchase in the writings of modernists including G. K. Chesterton, Wyndham Lewis, Gertrude Stein, and Walter Benjamin. G. K. Chesterton's "The Sentimentalist" (1910) extends Wilde's metaphoric terms from emotion to intellection, characterising the "type" in question as "the man who . . . will not see that one must pay for an idea as for anything else . . . . [H]e seeks to enjoy every idea without its sequence, and every pleasure without its consequence" (124–5). Lewis's issue with the same is levied at the wealthy: "At the most the moneyed crust of our time affects a pedantically cynical wildness that is often whorish enough, but so overlaid with a sweetening of sentiment (just as its rendering of childhood will run essentially to the insipid) that its representative is able to rival in repulsiveness the [M]iltonic prude" (*Lion* 60). Always saccharine, artificial, and unearned, Lewisian sentiment exposes the luxury whereby the upper classes dabble in the morally reprehensible whilst pretending at uprightness. Stein too dovetails the sentimental with the British upper classes. Since the Elizabethan age, Stein asserts, words "were used to accept everything as being there in the daily living they accepted their being there to tell something or to make everything have emotion have sentimental feeling or to be soothing" (*Narration* 11). Stein values American over British English because Americans privilege excitement and "moving" – action – over quotidian, staid feeling (*Narration* 6). For Stein, the hard-earned affectivity and ethos of the American dream is preferable to British gentrification and its luxurious, enervated emotions.[3] But in "One-Way Street" (1928), Benjamin effects a critique of the capitalist sentimental economy that he situates, *contra* Stein, in the American dream, in the equation of popular, purchasable culture – the hyperbolic, overwhelming optics of advertisement and cinema – with the lost authenticity of emotion. For Benjamin, the spectacle of modern life teaches "people whom nothing moves or touches any longer . . . to cry again", even as, for the average citizen, "it is money that affects him in this way, bringing him into perceived contact with things" (476). Benjamin's critique undoes the equation of emotion with leisured ease whilst affirming the ubiquity of Wilde's sentimental economy.

Wilde's most famous descendant remains James Joyce, who has Stephen Dedalus reiterate the terms of the modernist sentimental economy in a telegram he sends to the irrepressible Buck Mulligan in *Ulysses*: "The sentimentalist is he who would enjoy without incurring the immense debtorship for a thing done" (550–1). From the perspective of a twentieth-century vanguardist like Joyce, this metaphor appeals because it equates emotionality with difficulty, effectively asserting that proper modernist feeling, like proper modernist literature, ought to be rigorous, demanding, the discernible reward of hard intellectual labour. Furthermore, it turns ephemeral, unquantifiable states into something that can be levied and gauged based on an agreed-upon, if privileged, currency. By reassuringly quantifying the unquantifiable, its resonance is logical to Joyce's Stephen Dedalus, a character who grieves his recently deceased mother – once propagator of his own domestic comfort – and who now strains to repress his own overwhelming desires, be they intellectual, aesthetic, platonic, or sexual. But from this same art historical standpoint, this economy of sentiment is inescapably misogynist and homophobic, an anxious virile modernist fear of being contaminated by femininity, or the currency of *fin-de-siècle* vanguards celebrated for their deployment of the impassioned and the queer, Symbolism and Decadence among them. Containing and delimiting sentiment, this economy is in fact anti-sentimental, a means of censuring emotion.

Its privileged legacy reverberates well beyond modernism. It is evoked and countered, for instance, by Audre Lorde as late as 1984, when she contends that in order "to go beyond the encouraged mediocrity of our society" we must not yield "to the fear of feeling", as that *fear* "is a luxury only the unintentional can afford, and the unintentional are those who do not wish to guide their own destinies" ("Erotic" 54). Keen to be the emotionally courageous individual Lorde espouses, and never fond of systematic or masculinist restraints, Loy's participation in the modernist affective economy is complex, and occasionally complicit. But within it, we witness Loy demonstrate how male partners and artists extend a "serpentine whine through subterranean sentimentalities" and by extension, mistreat women who supposedly "ow[e]" their masculine counterparts "immeasurable amends" (*EP* 24). Revaluating and recognising women's underestimated affective labour, atavistic avant-gardist Loy turns to pre-capitalist, sacrificial economies by way of disrupting the modernist circulation of emotion.

Through the Futurists, Loy is given an opportunity to purchase vitriol against feeling wholesale, a topic that arises repeatedly in *Brontolivido*. "I'm a healthy man – ", Marinetti asserts, adding: "there's no sentimentality about me – I don't pander to women's pretensions – I go straight – for what I want – & there's only one thing woman's any use for" (*B* 6: 8). Hardly the best way to beguile a feminist, yet Loy evidently finds his bluntness refreshing, as the next line reads: "So he escorted her home". But Loy then determinedly undermines Marinetti's masculinity, describing how he "fla[pped] his passion about on the nocturnal air", "pranced", and "pursed his tidy little harlot's mouth" (*B* 6: 8–9). Loy's terms reduce the proudly potent Futurist leader to an "objectional" rent boy (*B* 6: 8).[4] Along the way, Loy exposes the truth behind Marinetti's disdain for feeling, his desire that she see "how miserably sentimental" he really is "under the hard exterior [he has] assumed to fight the world with" (*B* 9: 10). In return for his honesty, Marinetti hopes that Loy will smile for him, will make him at ease with his own vulnerable feeling, thereby restoring his confidence through the emotional succour from which he pretends to be immune. Marinetti's request is a cliché: as Sara Ahmed writes, "not smiling" can be an act of protest because "smiling is a requirement for women and for those understood as serving others through paid or unpaid work" (*Living* 254). Loy enacts this protest by informing Marinetti that she is already smiling, a statement that points to the yawning abyss of male emotional need: she is asserting her awareness that she can never smile enough to satisfy him (*B* 9: 10).[5] As Marinetti's Futurist peer, Papini simi-larly struggled to recognise the value of female emotion in an essay he wrote about a former lover whose passion he calculated via the time, number of pages, and postage costs of the 453 letters she sent during their relationship. Papini maintains this sentimental archive, yet identifies himself as existing at a hyper-rational remove from the affectivity it contains (Hofer 223–5). Unlike Loy, the Futurists remain unable to "recogniz[e] the senses, affect, and thought as fun-damentally interrelated processes" (Hofer 223). As Loy poignantly affirms in *Insel*, "'the sentiment of one generation is the neurosis of the next'" (*I* 151).

One of the things Loy admired about Arthur Cravan was that he defended the sentimentality other modernists "despised", charging them with lacking the requisite "sense to feel anything" and telling Loy "laughingly": "'One has to be <u>monumentally intelligent</u> to <u>be able</u> to love anything'" (Loy, "Promised"). Yet, through alternate recollections of Cravan, Loy shows herself capable of reinforcing masculinist modernist sentimentality. For there is no small echo of Oscar Wilde in Loy's description of his nephew: "When he was thirty-one Tenderness awakened in him; and tenderness in a strong man is always a deluge, because it is a luxury which the weak can not [*sic*] afford" (*LaLB* 321). This sentimentality *costs*. In Cravan, it is superior, expensive, rarefied. But where modernist iconoclasts like the Futurists called for an art that was strong and unemotional, Loy identifies the receptive affectivity intrinsic to the privileged male artist's body.[6] In so doing, Loy arguably returns to what Jerome McGann deems the origin of sensibility, the "self-conscious appro-priation of the wisdom of the body, the knowledge that comes through sympathetic understanding" (170). Figured as tenderness, Loy's sentiment has specific consequences for the exclusive individ-ual, but it is also autonomous, its own initiator, a form of sentience intrinsically, potentially housed within all creative selves, be they male or female. For Loy, women are artists of the quotidian, taught to perform certain affects, so that their "faces [can] express familiar-ity with sensations their bodies may never have known." Loy's prime concern in this instance is sexual satiation, but she couches the lack of this experience for women as a burden facilitated by their undue investment in sentimental narratives, be they marriage, domestic-ity, caregiving, childbearing. "[S]entimental women", asserts Loy, "bea[r] the ardent load of their passional compromise as lightly as it were a sigh." But these same women also seek escape from this affec-tive economy by which they are so evidently trapped. After religion and inebriate addiction, love is the best means of calming "the dynamic inquietude of our sensibility which is never entirely consumed in our struggle for existence, but subsists as a surplus potency to foment our ideals and our dreams" (*CP* 18: 62–3). As for Loy's tender male artist, love has a generative energy defined by, yet beyond, costly sentiment.

Loy seeks to change modernist sentimental economies. But she is not consistently critical: throughout her writings, Loy can be seen complicatedly mingling modernist and eighteenth-century affective approaches. In her 1914 "Feminist Manifesto", Loy razes the chaste, sensibilious woman as a luxurious role the contemporary female can no longer afford. Equating women's "desire for comfortable protection" with their sentimentalisation of sex and love, Loy aims to de-luxuriate, virilise, and thus modernise femininity by making it more masculine, more discernibly modernist (*LoLB* 156).[7] Pound's praise notwithstanding, Loy assuredly traffics in sentiment in "Auto-Facial Construction" (1919), her manifesto-cum-advertisement that offers her services as a guide to mastery of one's "facial destiny" with a view to preserving the ageing man or woman's waning "expression of sentiment" (*LoLB* 165). Blatantly self-serving and capitalist, the tract nevertheless places value on the nuances of sentimental communication. Just as earnestly, Loy's "Modern Poetry" (1925) denounces contemporary poets for being "entirely anti-human in their fear of sentimentality", barring E. E. Cummings, who maintains his "rich compassion ... for common things" (*LoLB* 159). According to Loy, Cummings is ahead of his time for partaking in an eighteenth-century economy of emotion; his is an extensive benevolence that echoes Loy's, reaching back to propel one forward. Finally, within the confines of the single poem "Lady Laura in Bohemia" (1931), Loy satirises the "sentimental slobber" of her fraught female subject, even as the final line asserts: "She is yet like a diamond on a heap of broken glass" (*LoLB* 100). Unlike Eliot, the guru of modernist impersonality, Loy can insist that, however sloppy, feeling can shore up the ruins of the self. Bergson writes: "disinterested art is a luxury, like pure speculation", and these affective and creative scepticisms permeate Loy's resolutely affective sentience (*CE* 33).

Loy's contrariness makes a truth of this statement: "Modernism developed its antisentimentality into a contemptuous treatment of women, who had to struggle both internally and externally with that contempt" (S. Clark 5). For Suzanne Clark, meta-sentimentality maintains an undiscussed yet definitive hold over modernism, so that the period's most fundamental, revolutionary aesthetic claim – that language and art can change reality – can itself be perceived as an affective fantasy.[8] Clark's incredulity notwithstanding, the modernist economy of sentiment soldiers on. In *The Female Complaint: The Unfinished Business of Sentimentality in American Culture* (2008), Lauren Berlant does not expressly reference this modernist lineage, yet deploys its financial lexicon, describing sentiment as an unpaid debtorship. Instead of proclaiming sentiment as a luxury either too easily accessed by the privileged or desultorily borrowed by the masses, Berlant argues that the sentimental debt is, by its very nature, *unpayable*:

> the unfinished business of sentimentality – that 'tomorrow is another day' in which fantasies of the good life *can* be lived – collaborates with a sentimental account of the social world as an affective space where people ought to be legitimated because they have feelings and [those feelings], if . . . listened to, could make things better. (2)

Like capitalist accumulation, Berlant's sentiment works off our hopes of progress, of a replete, fully functioning democracy, of affirmations micro and macro; its future is perpetually unattainable (and desirable) because idealised. While these arguments evoke a stupefying complicity, Berlant importantly differs from her modernist precursors by actively refusing to blame the impoverished sentimental consumer. In Berlant's formulation, that consumer is predominantly female and stands at the centre of "the emotional service economy" (19). From this key vantage, womankind enacts the daily complaint of Berlant's title, namely, that "women live for love, and love is the gift that keeps on taking" (1). Berlant's claim resists Loy's view of love as "surplus potency", whilst returning us to the combative eroticism of Loy's "pink-love", or, perhaps more accurately, her "enmity of the exploited for the parasite, the parasite for the exploited". By Berlant's coordinates, sentimentality cannot be vanguard à la Loy, because it fears nothing more than existing beyond the parameters of the cultural status quo. And as "gendered and sexual normativity" generate aesthetic convention, Berlant, like Clark before her, addresses writers who are more mainstream than experimental (211).[9] At the heart of this comfortably uncomfortable state of affairs is "the sanctified, sacrificial death" of idealised femaleness, a death literal or figurative, "encompass[ing] woman's labour, emotion, or sexuality" (Berlant 20–1).

A vanguardist, Loy nevertheless expertly deploys the economy Berlant identifies, one reliant upon the sentimental heroine defined by "a sacred aura . . . complete with sacrificial death" (Berlant 41).

Loy's writings document a litany of such sacrifices. Where Loy's male peers place feeling within an economy in which they remain the victors, Loy attacks as cursed the social infrastructure that generates complacency about ritualised violence against women, emphasising its destructive intentions over the systematic, emotional ease it pretends to propagate. Perceiving this violence for the threat that it is, Loy responds in aggressive kind, eschewing fairy-tale endings in favour of brutal, and often brutally comic, portrayals of gendered violence and its severest consequences. For Frye, humour offers a "rigidly stylised" world in which

> certain things, such as a picture of a wife beating her husband in a comic strip, are conventionally funny. To introduce a comic strip in which a husband beats his wife would distress the reader, because it would mean learning a new convention. (225)

In fact, this convention is neither new nor exceptional; making it funny certainly is, and that is the inverse, unexpected joke Loy tells, one that stretches to incredulous breaking point the predictable incongruities of humorous discourse in a bid to "break up the lumber of stereotypes [and] fossilized beliefs" (Frye 233). In Loy's literature, people are tortured, assaulted, incarcerated, driven insane, intellectually and emotionally deadened. As just some examples of these sacrificial modes, we might consider: lunacy in "Pazzarella" and "The Effectual Marriage" (1917); persecution in "The Agony of the Partition"; imposed confinement in the domestic poems "Italian Pictures" (1914) and "Virgins Plus Curtains Minus Dots" (1915); the martyr's crucifixion in "Parturition", "Songs to Joannes", and "Transfiguration." (post-1917); self-destructive infatuation in "Monde Triple Extra" (late 1910s/early 1920s) and "Piero and Eliza."; "the involuntary sacrifice" of Jew to Gentile in "Anglo-Mongrels and the Rose" (*LaLB* 114); domestic violence in *Esau Penfold*; the abused daughter of *The Child and the Parent* and *Islands in the Air* (c. 1925–35); the torturous spiritual death of "An Aged Woman" (late, undated); and the ambiguous survival of "love's . . . rich suttee" in "The Widow's Jazz" of 1931 (*LoLB* 96). Best known among these examples is Loy's advocacy for the systematic self-sacrifice of woman's "'<u>virtue</u>'" through "the <u>unconditional</u> surgical <u>destruction</u>" of girls' hymens at puberty in her "Feminist Manifesto". The express goal is to free the female sex from the "fictitious value" placed upon her, one conflated "with her physical purity" (*LoLB* 154–5).

In each of these works, Loy exposes the gendered violence upon which the sentimental economy relies, yet she does not shy away from partaking in that very violence. While Loy does not waste time blaming the sentimental consumer, she does openly attack those who unquestionably accept the sentimental status quo, be they victims, perpetrators, or the author herself. The adulated male celebrity Jove Ivon Corvon in Loy's "Monde Triple Extra" is sought after by a breathless harem of devoted women though he is a notoriously terrible lover. As Loy's narrator brittlely notes, "in view of women's disposition towards self-sacrifice and reform work" Corvon's narcissism and disregard are "not the least of his advertisements" (*SE* 59). Corvon is akin and opposed to Arthur Cravan, in whom Loy admires a blasé refusal of the en masse sacrifice that underwrites First World War conscription. She quotes him as follows: "'If [other men's] collective insanity suggests to them that they must sacrifice their lives for my sake, I will not trouble to stop them'" ("Colossus" 112). But simultaneously, in "Gloria Gammage" – a lampoon of Mabel Dodge Luhan – Loy wholeheartedly admires a willingness to "blo[w one]self up for a voluntary ostracism" (*SE* 27). As Loy knew all too well, demonstrative, attention-seeking self-immolation is foundational vanguard practice. Thus, Gammage's hyperbolic, self-styled outcast becomes aesthetic mandate in "Apology of Genius" (1922), where Loy's vanguard peers are "Ostracised . . . with God" – "A delicate crop / of criminal mystic immortelles" standing as ever-ready sacrificial victims "to the censor's scythe" (*LoLB* 77–8). In turn, these self-same vanguardists are ever ready to immolate. In her 1929 *transatlantic review* essay on Stein, Loy scrutinises and praises a passage from *Tender Buttons* (1914) that refers to "'the force of sacrifice'", likening its power to Old Testament evocations of Job, an archetypal sacrificial victim (*LaLB* 296). And "[i]n [Loy's] *Insel*, as in Surrealism, the Surrealist artist demands flesh sacrifice . . . that costs women their dignity, personal security, and financial resources" (Hayden 155). An atavistic avant-gardist, Loy returns to sacrifice by way of disrupting the modernist economy of sentimentality. Maledict, she victimises in turn, becoming a satirist who understands that it is sacrifice, and not derided, gendered, and costly emotionality, that sustains the universal need for affective intimacy.

"Surplus Potency": Sacrifice

Sacrifice is common to all cultures, remaining "fundamental to the human mind", conscious subjectivity, and linguistic cliché

(Hughes 151; Mizruchi 6, 23). At its most literal, sacrifice refers to ritualised deaths that are foundational to modern civilisation and capitalist statehood (Hughes 2).[10] Attributed first and foremost to gods and kings who nobly immolated themselves, sacrificial victimhood was then transposed to soldiers and labourers.[11] As willing victims became harder to find, the practice was thrust upon "social deviants and unfortunates" whose "very criminality or debility grew out of this sacrificial necessity" (Mizruchi 70). In the eighteenth century, the Christian ethos of self-sacrifice reinforced the feminine suffering presented in narratives of sensibility; come the nineteenth century, atonement – a Christly giving up of one's life for others – was crucial to the pursuit of moral perfection, often forming the climax of the novels of Charles Dickens, Elizabeth Gaskell, and George Eliot (Schramm 8, 15). This is the Son of God Loy inherited from her Protestant mother, namely "Christ as sacrificial prototype", which, as Keith Tuma argues, is not to be confused with "the idea of Christ as mankind's saviour" ("Mina Loy's" 195). For the vanguards of the early twentieth century, woman became a ready scapegoat, a repository of conservative tradition who must be sacrificed so that an autonomous male vanguard could be born anew.[12] For Pound, woman was "the conservator, the inheritor of past gestures ... not inventive" ("Introduction" xvi). Recognising and resisting a trajectory of female sufferance, Loy importantly identifies within that received aggression a bid for intimacy that encompasses and exceeds gender affiliation. In this regard, Loy's model of sacrifice precedes and dovetails with that of the transgressive philosopher Georges Bataille, who argues that recognising sacrificial modes can revolutionise the economies – material *and* affective – of the status quo. As Bataille writes: "In his strange myths, in his cruel rites, man is *in search of a lost intimacy*" (*AS1* 57).

In Bataille's view, society has succumbed over time to an ethos of servility, so that fulfilled humanity is seen to be humanity at work, never enjoying the fruits of its labour, consigned to a too utilitarian or restrictive economy (*AS1* 46). Simultaneously, however, all sentient beings – plants, animals bipedal or otherwise – always produce more than they need, and this surplus is the basis of Bataille's alternative, general law of economy. For Bataille, it is surplus and not instrumentalisation that determines the very warp and weft of civilisational fabric: "The surplus is the cause of the agitation, of the structural changes and of the entire history of society" (*AS1* 106). In our modern world, to foreground excess is to transform:

> Changing from the perspectives of a *restrictive* economy to those of
> a *general* economy actually accomplishes a Copernican transforma-
> tion: a reversal of thinking – and of ethics. If a part of wealth ...
> is doomed to destruction or at least to unproductive use without
> any possible profit, it is logical, even *inescapable*, to surrender
> commodities without return. Henceforth, leaving aside pure and
> simple dissipation ... the possibility of pursuing growth is itself
> subordinated to giving. (*AS1* 25)

A like desire for circulatory change permeates Loy's work.
Expansively consistent with Bataille's general economy, Loy writes:
"Looking back on my life I can observe one absolute law of physics –
that energy is always wasted" (*LaLB* 313). Recall that for Loy the
gift of love is a "surplus potency", falling beyond the strict modernist economisation of sentiment. Tellingly, of all the things Loy loved
about Arthur Cravan, it was his superabundance that she admired
most: the "extravagant" legends he evoked, the luxuriousness of his
clothing (entirely inconsistent with his lived penury), his massive
physique and "extreme leisure" ("Colossus" 104, 112). After their
first night together, Cravan congratulated Loy on procuring a lover,
then asked, a mite anxiously, if she regretted it. Loy's reply? "'I never
regret wasted time'" ("Colossus" 110). Thwarted, Bataille's surplus
can be squandered as lost energy, in detritus or war. Allowed to
grow freely, it manifests as luxurious consumptions subjective, intimate, or spectacular: ceremonies, festivals, carnivals (*AS1* 106). As
for Loy, for Bataille, ideal "love is a kind of immolation" (*AS2* 119).

To be truly free of commodification, Bataille asserts that we need
seek out the opposite of production and objectification, deliberately
pursuing wastefulness, be it material, spiritual, or emotive. Religion
is a key surplus expenditure for Bataille. Although ultimately too
externally oriented and imposed, religion is Bataille's pre-eminent
example of how we feel the personal loss of intimacy in our resolutely utilitarian society. By expressing and condoning intimate
feeling, wilfully irrational religion counters the drudgery of labour
(*AS1* 130–1). Unrestrained and excessive individual feeling also has
a part to play: effusion overrides our productive drive, our sense of
ourselves as autonomous, knowledgeable, or reasonable, thereby
returning us to an originary, archaic sovereignty, an inner experience in which the world and its inhabitants open up anew, urgent,
uncontained. These experiences arise through dance, drunkenness, childhood magic, the sacred, the playful, disgust, and "every
art form involving tragic, comic, or poetic aspects" (*AS3* 230).
Cruelty is another possibility, one Loy foresees, turning toward the

heightened aggression of sacrifice from her earliest writings. In articulating sacrifice, Loy validates extreme emotion as a defining aspect of subjectivity, thereby undermining the controlled circulation of modernist affective currency. For Loy and Bataille, the sacrificial victim is the ultimate surplus: consumed profitlessly, destructively, it is an accursed share that exceeds enterprise whilst ensuring the well-being of the community at large (*AS1* 59). As such, this curse is also a blessing: removing the victim from the servile, degraded relentlessness of positivist profane existence, it is gloriously excessive and inutile, magnificent and maledict (*AS1* 60; *AS2* 133). Aiming to extend some of that social recognition, even glory, to the sacrificed female, Loy positions sacrifice as a condition of intimacy with the potential to supersede gender. Likewise, Bataille articulates the transferability of the indescribable "inner torrent" of subjectivity, communicable through emotion, excess, and "a sensible, emotional contact" (*AS2* 203, 242).

Crucially, sacrifice illustrates the limits of consciousness: sacrifice occurs because we long for intimacy and self-consciousness, and for pleasure and pain, or what Loy considers the two poles of sentience. In pleasure, we recall, Loy believes the body is attracted to soul; in pain, the body moves away from the soul; "The struggle of life is a battle between these two attractions" ("Miscellaneous"). Bataille feels this struggle keenly, arguing that as self-consciousness involves a distancing objectification of the self, it returns the individual to the spectre of thinghood. Thus, sacrifice – awash in anguish, complicity, "measureless violence" – points to the very impossibility of a totalising self-consciousness, of clarity, challenging our sense of reality and our drive for an illumination that might surpass it (*TR* 57, 100). Bataille emphasises the value of dissolute yet adamantly sentient states: the proximations of the bestial, the self-negations of sexual climax, the violent extremities of laughter and tears are when we are most liberated from our subjectivity, yet most sovereign. ("[I]t made me ache and laugh in the same breath", says the sentry who finds Antigone, and knows she is destined to be sacrificed by Creon; as Sophocles knew in the fifth century BCE, "It's pure joy to escape the worst yourself", even as "it hurts a man to bring down his friends" [81, ll. 484–9]). For Bataille, irresolvable, resistant oppositions, internal and external, are constitutive: "The thought that comes to a halt in the face of what is sovereign rightfully pursues its operation to the point where its object dissolves into NOTHING, because, ceasing to be useful, or subordinate, it becomes *sovereign* in ceasing to be" (*AS3* 204). ("I don't even exist—I'm no one. Nothing", states Creon after his future daughter-in-law, son, and wife immolate themselves in obeisance to his sacrificial law [126, ll. 1445–6]). The combativeness of violence and desirable proximity – nowhere greater than in sacrifice – offer us our fullest experience of our foundational sentience. Intimacy relies upon the consciousness it inevitably exceeds (*AS1* 136, 189).

For those of us not caught up in Bataille's ecstatic self-immolations, deathly generativity is an irrefutably limited triumph, one that may only result in affirming, as Jean-Luc Nancy asserts, that mortality is sacrifice, an incessant giving over to the world that is neither volitional nor directed, a "de-subjectification" that, when theorised, reveals only an irresolvable fascination with transcendence or otherness (35–7).[13] Dismissive of logical resolution by design, Bataille's theory nevertheless offers a way out of the modernist sentimental economy, one that remains resolutely systematic in the metaphors Wilde and his peers use to shore up their resistance to the uncomfortable, illogical vagaries of feeling. This affective instrumentalisation is evident as early as Hume, for whom sensibility is a priority because it is *useful* to a functioning society. Bataille effects his escape through an extremist pursuit of the intimacy foundationally integral to Loy's thinking, and through the evocation and estimation of the sentient dissolution of NOTHING that is a refrain through his work. With these terms, Loy is in perfect accord, as "Songs to Joannes" articulates. Awash in paradox, poem 27 moves from a nothingness of inconceivability and "Insentient repose" to the following:

> The contents
> Of our ephemeral conjunction
> In aloofness from Much
> Flowed to approachment of — — — —
> NOTHING
> There was a man and a woman
> In the way
> While the Irresolvable
> Rubbed with our daily deaths
> Impossible eyes (*LoLB* 64)

This escape from servility is an erotic, unsustainable proximity, one that exceeds the rational and contains the violence of death. It also illustrates Loy's belief that ire is integral to desire, that a "wholesome hostility" drives heteronormative intimacy (*EP* 25). But, for Loy, men and women are only ever mutually, generatively embattled in the sexual embrace. In almost all other contexts, Loy perceives woman as victimised by a quotidian, pervasive sacrificial economy. While Bataille's resistance to drudgery and servility applies to men and women alike, he too reserves special mention for how the institution of marriage presents women as fecund sites of labour, as objects (*AS2* 49). Marriage, Bataille argues, is not mutual, but the act of the "'giver'" – the bride's father – who offers his daughter to another man; her objectification diminishes his guilt about his exploitation of her sovereignty, labour, and sexuality (*AS2* 126, 139).

Bataille's interests in female autonomy are not altruistic. He frets that "the economic value of the transferred woman tends to minimise the erotic aspect of the [marital] transition . . . dulling desire and reducing pleasure to nothing" (*AS2* 127). In later work, he continues to define woman as the erotic victim, man the sacrificer (*E* 18).[14] In this unexamined masculine privilege, Bataille is assuredly consistent with most theorists and historians of sacrifice. When sacrifice is era-defining, it is male; when overlooked, female. For instance, in league with Loy, Freud recognises that conventional morality imposes excessive and pointless sacrifice on humanity, but in *Totem and Taboo* (1913) formal sacrifice is always parricide (Rubin, "Traffic" 201). Desired (because prohibited) totemic women are incidental to the main Oedipal event, by which the father is killed and deified, while the violent male horde enjoy the ensuing fellowship of consumption, complicity, and catharsis. This male-defined "heritage of emotion", Freud claims, is the origin of contemporary religion, morals, art, and society ("Totem" 159).

As is Bataille's, Freud's sacrificial formulation is dependent on modernist sociologists and anthropologists – Marcel Mauss (1872–1950), Henri Hubert (1872–1927), James Frazer (1854–1941) – echoes of whom reverberate through the work of Loy's Futurist associates, Marinetti and Papini. In "The Foundation and Manifesto of Futurism" (1909), Marinetti welcomes the avenging male generation that will eviscerate him when he inevitably becomes *passéiste* (16). In *The Failure* (1913), Papini describes how he and his peers devour their fathers and then "recognise the [ensuing] vomit as our own" (261). Sacrifice, Papini argues, is glorious precisely because it is absurd, but he is careful to valorise his engagement in this irrational, unreasonable ritual by asserting: "I feel that I am strong enough to waste my strength" (319). The privileged pleasure of this sacrificial model can be discerned as late as René Girard's *Violence and the Sacred* (1972). Regrettably characterising violence as a seminal fluid that impregnates on contact, Girard announces, as if it were news, that "[i]n many cultures women are not considered full-fledged members of their society" (31, 13).[15] And "yet", writes Girard, and his conjunction does protest too much:

> women are never, or rarely, selected as sacrificial victims. There may be a simple explanation for this fact. The married woman retains her ties with her parents' clan even after she has become in some respects the property of her husband and his family. To kill her would be to run the risk of one of the two groups' interpreting her sacrifice as an act of murder committing it to a reciprocal act of revenge. (13)

For Girard, as for Bataille, woman cannot attain the status of divine sacrificial victim, because she is an object of exchange. As Gayle Rubin writes in "The Traffic in Women" (1975): "If women are the gifts, then it is men who are the exchange partners", and "[t]he relations of such a system are such that women are in no position to realise the benefits of their own circulation" (174).

Woman is object, not subject. Strictly speaking, sacrifice proper is ceremonial ritual, not daily, cumulative renunciation, even as the two have been conflated since Euripides (Hughes 273). Eliding domestic sacrifice from the equation assuredly skews the results. The stereotype is as follows: man's instinct is for property, accumulation; women's is for maternal self-immolation, renunciation. This binary drives venerated artworks, among them the Wagnerian operas that became a touchstone of modernist aesthetics; it also affirms our ongoing disregard toward the quotidian, incessant labour of female parents (Hughes 185–200; Staples 125). As if in anxious response to the first wave of feminism and its resistance to this archetype, modernists D. H. Lawrence and T. S. Eliot write fictions in 1925–6 and 1949 respectively that centre on a woman who actively seeks out sacrifice and is "rewarded" with her ritualised death.[16] But Girard's preposterous assertion notwithstanding, Lawrence and Eliot merely take their place in a centuries-long Western literary lineage that attends to the pervasiveness of women's immolation. "I stand for sacrifice", states Portia in *The Merchant of Venice* (Shakespeare 3.2.57). So too do Demeter, Sophocles's Antigone, Shakespeare's Lavinia, Aphra Behn's Imoinda, the Marquis de Sade's Justine, and Bram Stoker's Lucy. Needing victims, blood sacrifice encourages marginalised outsiders, is in fact an exercise in shoring up social categorisation. In the late nineteenth and early twentieth centuries, sacrificial victims included African Americans, "degenerates", and women (Mizruchi 7, 63). As Luce Irigaray tells us, to avoid the continuation of this fate: "women must learn how they relate both to gender and to kinship" precisely because women are always subject to patriarchal rules regarding reproduction and property (*Sexes* vi).[17] When faced with the irresolvabilities of gendered experience, Irigaray writes, "many men and women start talking about *love*" (*Sexes* 4). Loy certainly does. But how can there be love, Irigaray wonders, when there is ingrained, institutionalised subservience? This very question pulses through Loy's literature, driving her desire to enlist men in a sacrificial economy that involves real self-risk, but also, pivotally, greater recognition of self and other, the catharsis of shared emotionality.

Recalling Loy's resistance toward relentless male expectations of the "hospitalities of modest little women", Irigaray describes woman's unpaid labour as a censorship of her own desire to trade or amass property, a censorship to which women – as charitable volunteers, as parents – too willingly acquiesce (*I* 7). For Irigaray, to enter implicitly or directly into the institution of motherhood is to yield to "a system of values that prizes sacrifice above all, a system in which children and women have value as commodities that can be relied upon to remain relatively stable, regardless of fluctuations in currencies and economic regimes" (*Sexes* 85).[18] Loy agrees, offering her newly pregnant first-born this key piece of parental advice: "Avoid making a sacrifice of ~~your child~~ your self for your child"; as the redaction suggests, child and woman are interchangeable, and their renunciations equally unacknowledged.[19] This domestic economy Loy punctures with satiric, feminist sacrifice, calling attention to what Irigaray considers women's crucial role in "the dual foundation of social functioning – the united contribution of both mind and nature working at their highest level" (*Sexes* 86). Nature nourishes and destroys, and Irigaray believes that the contemporary civilisational technocracy seeks out violence to recover that lost aggression, cathartically sacrificing woman-as-nature along the way. While Loy is not as reverentially bucolic as her feminist successor, Irigaray's "nature" has affiliations with Loy's foundational sentience: both states of being are unabashedly atavistic, and re-establish a baseline of feeling and experience which, coupled with consciousness, becomes a democratic principle upon which life in all of its manifestations can be recognised, respected.[20] For Irigaray, "future sacrifice sacrifices all powerfulness" and social pretence to "narcissistic self-sufficiency" (*Sexes* 87). Foregrounding an absolute equality, this proposition is an impossibility, as power-laden violence remains integral to its realisation. As a strategic ideal, however, it resonates.

Loy's anatomical project is a dismemberment with a symbiotic coherence in view. In its corporeality, it foresees the *écriture féminine* of the satirically incisive Irigaray and her feminist peers, among them Hélène Cixous and Julia Kristeva, all of whom sought to give heightened visibility to the specificities of women's embodied experience. Loy's feminine sacrifice is greater and lesser than that invoked by the paternalistic theories of Bataille, and exceeds what Kristeva recognises as the originary, symbolic "matricide" that maintains Freud's Oedipal paradigm, a theme central to the final chapter of this volume, which focuses on the accursed muse (Bronfen, *Over* 132). A passing Derridean speculation may best encapsulate Loy's ideology: in *The Gift of Death* (1992), Derrida suggests that within our contemporary sacrificial economy, woman may be the eternal ironiser, presumably because she is the figure who calls attention to the disparity between sacrifice as celebrated, exceptional, purificatory ritual and derided, embodied state (77). Loy understands this duality and liminality, knows that women are sacrificed as impossible ideals – virgins, saints, madonnas, as the epitome of ephemeral, unattainable forms of beauty – but also as whores, mothers, wives, and shrews, immolations often more incessant, integral, and invisible. In "Giovanni Franchi" (1916), Loy writes about the extremities of Futurism, a movement whose hyperbolic masculinity she takes as symptomatic: "He would kill a woman / Quite inconspicuously it is true" (*LoLB* 30).

Loy determines to make the murderous sacrifice of women unavoidably palpable, as when men confide in the narrator of her undated story "In Maine: Green's Colony" about their love for local sweetheart Lucy, a sacrificial victim who one man "clasped [by] her beautiful throat[,] press[ing] her head down,—(nearly)—into the glowing embers of the hearth" (*SE* 49). Loy sardonically "excuses" this activity, thereby interrogating our presumptions about rural life, testing our latent fidelity to the belief that, because he is uncultured, this man's roughness might be forgiven.[21] Her forgiveness exacerbates and extends the blame to "superior" reader, presumptuous narrator. And of course, Loy's satiric exposure of complicity cannot exclude our author. For as Mauss and Hubert argue, in sacrifice we find "a protective sanctity, a means of redressing equilibriums that have been upset"; it is a ritual that briefly redeems the victim and restores the sacrifier – the priest who sacrifices – to the community (102–3). Girard takes this argument further, pointing out that sacrifice is a social safety value, "an act of violence without risk of vengeance" (14). For Girard, "violence permeates all human relationships", and these impulses are redirectable toward any immolated subject, be it actual or figurative, animal or human (291). As societies became organised by legal systems, the law continues hiding the truth of vengeance behind ritual, a trick it learned from sacrificial practice. Brutalities sacrificial and legal forestall emulation of the violent act, and reprisal for that act (Girard 27, 92). Knowing this, Loy describes the impervious upper classes as among the greatest ingesters of sacrificial victims. Tucked away in one of Loy's romans à clef is an early manuscript draft of Loy's epic poem about the development of the child Ova, "Anglo-Mongrels and the Rose". This archived fragment is titled "The Quadrate Rose":

> The god of antiquity demanded an eye for an eye
> But these have staked the soul of a people against a tea-cup
> The tea-cup is garlanded with rosebuds
> these are the symbolistic rosy wounds of the sacrifice
> And on the immaculate prongs and blades of their knives and forks
> they have impaled life.
> The tongue wags and the tongue tastes – wags to the rhythm of
> the imagined indulgences of others
> it tastes – the sweat of the human sacrifice
> The parasites who have clawed labour to shreds – and in his
> generation each – creator – and chewing the cud of their words –
> for years and years Ova had heard these creatures chewing the
> cud of dead minds
> – and this they accredited to themselves as their culture – – – (*EP* 24)

Above the law, morality, and labour physical or intellectual, these members of the gentry enact a diminished, self-affirming vestige of the ancient art of sacrifice, now reduced to a tempest in a blood-stained teacup. Genius and manual work alike are digestifs feeding only unearned cultural superiority, meaning that the privileged sit too comfortably in their clan-defining judgement. Later in the same archived file, Loy extends this rumination to those for whom human desire – "an activity from within calling for fulfilment to some activity without" – is submerged in the insulating, expensive civilisation of clothing, homes, and bric-a-brac, so that "human flesh is the living sacrifice to their fetishes" (*EP* 24).[22]

If Girard's socially sanctioned sacrifice is starting to sound eerily similar to the satiric attack that runs expertly amok through "Anglo-Mongrels" entire, it should: like the sacrifier, the satirist has a series of assaultive techniques that announce his or her formidable status whilst safely evading the immediate physicality of the kneejerk response.[23] Sacrifice, then, inoculates, and as a sacrificial satirist, Loy knowingly deploys its techniques to evade paternalistic contagion. As she writes in "Parturition" (1914): "I must traverse / Traversing myself" (*LoLB* 5). A similar self-immolating principle is at work in the conclusion of "The Effectual Marriage" (1917), where Loy authoritatively describes the protagonist wife as hysteric, thus taking up the position of privileged, presumptuous male diagnostician, even as the same postscript insists on the likeness between that wife and the author (*LoLB* 39). By satiric self-dissection, Loy proves eminently capable of keeping herself at one remove from her authorship, if always intimately, often abjectly, in view of her audience. And Loy seems to vaccinate herself against Girard's contagious male violence when she points her weaponry at wilfully suffering womankind. In the conclusion of the undated "Transfiguration.", Loy's narrator remarks that woman willingly plays the role of pack mule in a desperate bid for sainthood, behaving always "as if assured of a transcendental sanction." Well aware that this absurd hagiographic bid is women's lived truth, Loy remains at pains to denounce it as a "preposterous fantasy" (*SE* 147). Scapegoating – even of the self – distinguishes Loy from the complicities of victimisation, and perhaps also from the external aggressions of revenge. Nor can Loy's desire for power be denied. But both as aware victim and satiric sacrifier, Loy's assaults ultimately rest on the longing for proximity, or the intimacy that Bataille cogently theorises.[24] And in this regard, she draws on a long satiric legacy.

"The Instigatory Caress": Satire and Intimacy

The intimacies with which Loy is most preoccupied are heteronormative and familial, and these same gendered, domestic battles propelled the rise of satire as a genre (Sullivan 24). In his sixth satire, later titled "Roman Wives", the first-century satirist Juvenal holds forth on the improper enthusiasms of his female fellow citizens, taking especial aim at sensual women who play at battle. These women might remind us of the sporting vanguardist Loy: "What sense of shame can be found in a woman wearing a helmet, / who shuns femininity and loves brute force? (In spite of it all, though, / she'd hate to become a man—our pleasure is so much fainter.)" (45). To some degree, Loy agrees, writing in 1959: "'[T]he best way to conquer is to wear as helmet: *a smile*'"; under this bemused protection, Loy asserts that any individual can "[c]hange from *Persona non Grata* to PERSONA GOOD GRINNER" (qtd. in J. Williams xiv). According to Juvenal, unwelcome females most require modes of defence: weak in combat, strong in lust, "Woman" is mockable and enviable, a force, but one overcome by shared male laughter. Written between 110 and 130 CE, "Roman Wives" is Juvenal's longest satire: in it, he devotes some 661 lines to razing the opposite sex. In *A Discourse Concerning the Original and Progress of Satire* (1693), Dryden acknowledges that "Roman Wives" is too declamatory to be properly good, yet he cannot resist praising Juvenal's wit and judiciousness. Ultimately, Dryden concludes that if there is a fault with *Satire* 6, it does lie not with Juvenal: while it may "see[m] only an arraignment of the whole sex of womankind, there is a latent admonition to avoid ill women, by showing how very few who are virtuous and good are to be found amongst them" (79). What is more, in Dryden's view, the discerning ancient Juvenal remains superior to a recent surfeit of incompetent lampoonists who make women "their most ordinary theme" and are unduly severe to "the best and the fairest" (61). Yet even as Dryden implies that, good or bad, satire is consistently, aggressively masculine, he pivotally designates the origin of the genre in a surprisingly mutual gendered combativeness:

> If we take satire . . . as it is used in all modern languages, for an invective, it is certain that it is almost as old as verse; and though hymns, which are praises of God, may be allowed to have been before it, yet the defamation of others was not long after it. After God had cursed Adam and Eve in Paradise, the husband and wife excused themselves by laying the blame on one another, and gave a beginning to those conjugal dialogues in prose which the poets have perfected in verse. (33)

Satire begins with God's curse on humanity, for which Dryden unusually refrains from blaming womankind, ample historical precedent notwithstanding. Damned, both Adam and Eve rail in turn, and their exemplary domestic bickerings are the catalyst for satiric verse. Dryden will mollify this example as "not much to the honour of satire" because it emerges from depraved nature, rather than considered art (33). Nevertheless, his canonical essay implies that woman is integral to satiric assault: not only its victim, she is its more than capable perpetrator.[25]

History sustains Dryden's suggestion that satire originated in "conjugal dialogues". In the seventh and eighth centuries BCE, satire began with ancient fertility rituals, transitioning into iambography, or personal abuse in verse. Consistent with their origin, iambographic recitations were awash in curses of the beloved, bawdiness, obscenity, and anxieties about "lost potency" (Keane 50; Elliott 7).

The "Omphale archetype" is as old as satire itself, and rests on the "comedy" by which a woman bullies a man (Frye 228–9). This source of humour Loy refuses to consider "innocuous" or funny, raising nagging to the level of a malediction with the literal power to kill (*IA* 68: 135; *SE* 34). In so doing, Loy participates in a lengthy history of taking women's condemnatory power seriously: the female satirists who appear in the Old Testament and ancient Irish literature were disparaged as scolds, liars, and trollops (Elliott 17, 24–5). Oral and literary histories, in other words, affirm that strife between the sexes and female authorship are satiric traditions that precede one Mina Loy by some twenty-six centuries.

Combative, Loy works toward an intimacy that has also been celebrated as a determinant and an outcome of the Augustan period, or England's golden satirical age. Eighteenth-century politics were more familiar and localised than contemporary, creating a widespread interest in, and knowledgeable audience for, satiric discourse that focused on the personal affinities of "[c]ompeting narratives, violated contracts, broken pledges, insincere vows, and foresworn seductions" (Elkin 155; Alliker Rabb 49). In turn, that satire sought to enhance intimacy. The most renowned Augustan satirists actively campaigned against the public sphere and its markets whilst generating a confidential tone in their literature that exemplified stated preferences for small, close audiences, as in Swift's infamous desire to "laug[h] with a few Friends in a Corner" (Swift, *Intelligencer* 22; see also Thorne). But *in extremis*, this self-same intimacy is credited with bringing the great satirical period to an end. Satire, it has been pervasively argued, was slowly killed by kindness well before the Age of Sensibility. During the eighteenth century, a move away from Juvenalian railing toward a more Horatian raillery meant that witty, refined insult overtook the jolly aggression of outright abuse. Expressly favouring Juvenal, Dryden's *Discourse* nevertheless demonstrates the origins of this transition. The most-cited quotation from his essay praises the use of a delicate, inoffensive satirical touch:

> a witty man is tickled, while he is hurt in this manner; and a fool feels it not. The occasion of an offence may possibly be given, but he cannot take it. If it be granted that in effect this way does more mischief; that a man is secretly wounded, and though he be not sensible himself, yet the malicious world will find it for him; yet there is still a vast difference betwixt the slovenly butchering of a man, and the fineness of a stroke that separates the head from the body and leaves it standing in its place. (70)

Secret aggression, imperceptible wounding, superb exaction: Dryden's is an apology for open satiric rage, strategically duplicitous in generating the illusion that maiming or killing has not actually taken place. In a woman, this same behaviour might be considered capricious. Far too alert to death by a thousand cuts, no matter how well executed, Loy is not of Dryden's persuasion, arguing: "the woman who scratches her face will feel pain" while "the woman who gets her head blown off does not" (*SE* 259). Unlike Dryden, Loy wants to confront the political and social truths of chronic suffering. Intrepid beheadings are not her style.

Dryden catalyses an antipathy to violent and unseemly language ultimately strengthened by a surfeit of affable, domesticated, and immensely popular writing of the type propounded by influential newspapermen Joseph Addison and Richard Steele in the early eighteenth century. Swift labelled this literary style "fair-sexing", a term Claude Rawson defines as an *"embourgeoisement"* of "old chivalric codes and lordly ethos" (*Satire* xi). The attendant loss of aggression Rawson considers the movement by which satire went "from weapon to artefact", becoming, by about 1750, less homicidal threat than mummified corpse ("Introduction" viii). If we agree with Rawson's forensics – and many do – we might wonder at how satire is birthed and murdered by womankind, whose bloody-minded curiosity sparks the first curse and its invectives, and whose too-great capacity for feeling smothers its requisite antagonism.[26] But even as Swift laments this trajectory, he is witness to the rise of a modern feminist satire promulgated by his peer, Lady Mary Wortley Montagu (1689–1762). Montagu turned the assured tone and belligerence of the genre on the male reader, and her repertoire of attack persists in the work of our more immediate contemporaries, from Loy to Kathy Acker to Fran Ross. Montagu's techniques include hyperbolic assertions of female inferiority, in which passivity, vanity, and parasitism are key stereotypes; comic challenges to male potency and heroism; and the furious but artful listing of female dissatisfactions, be they sexual, intellectual, social, or professional, frequently with documented examples to hand. Often, a male perspective is adopted and lauded until the bitterly comic concluding exposé; often, that perspective will belong to a thinly disguised real-life combatant. These are tactics that risk redounding upon the female author, a risk mitigated by the satisfying stupidity presumed of a male reader considered perpetually prey to self-aggrandising prejudices. That said, masochistic misogyny also surfaces, both controlled and inescapably socially ingrained.[27]

On closer examination, this feminist satire may simply extend a genre in which the starkly drawn relationship between "masculine" satiric attack and "feminine" affective victimisation has always been uneasy. Hence Swift partook in the very fair-sexing he decried, and Mary Wollstonecraft justified women's victimisation, arguing that, because uneducated, women were inevitably satirised for their weak, undiscerning sensibility (Rawson, "Introduction"; Wollstonecraft 117). This gendered divide continues to define and dog criticism about satire, where presumptions abound that satire drowned in the deluge of Victorian sentiment, or that twentieth-century satire lacks rigour because it is not a heroically dominant genre.[28] When discussed – and until recently, it rarely has been – modernist or contemporary satire is denigrated for emerging from or perpetuating a prose tradition, rather than formal or epic (read: masculine) verse.[29] But where in this critique lies Petronius' fantastic, eminently novelistic *Satyricon*, or prose written in the first century CE and held up as a paragon of satiric practice ever since? And how might these arguments square with the prosodic formality of T. S. Eliot's anxiously feminised "The Love Song of J. Alfred Prufrock" (1915) or Loy's long satiric poem "Anglo-Mongrels and the Rose"? Of late, welcome reconsiderations of satire as "an increasingly prevalent cultural mode" do little to dispel "the assumption that satire is primarily" a male domain (Greenberg 43, 92).[30] For example, Emmett Stinson's well-conceived argument regarding the non-instrumentality of twentieth-century avant-garde satire, which he describes as a self-reflexive mode that foregrounds aesthetics, rather than ethics, is rooted in his belief that this genre is "overwhelmingly [dominated by] white men" (23). Yet, in addition to the formally experimental, interrogative satires of Rachilde or Leonora Carrington, among many others, Loy's widely available *Insel* is, as Hayden comprehensively argues, a scabrous critique of Surrealist mores (129–59). The taint of fair-sexing is proving difficult to scrub away.

The contortions needed to maintain these gendered, satiric binaries are visible in Loy criticism. Thom Gunn's essay on H. D., Moore, and Loy is keen to reassure us that Loy "writes as a woman", unlike Moore, who adopts what Gunn paradoxically perceives as the male privilege of writing in a non-gendered voice. Fairly straightforwardly, Gunn admires Loy's "unforced indignation at the comedy of male complacency", her authorial capacity to attack her subjects whilst eliciting emotion, and her attentiveness to the body (46–7). But Gunn's admiration is also bewildering. "For all her aggressive modernism and feminism", Gunn states, "[Loy] identifies with a traditional genre more easily than her great contemporaries – that of satire" (47). Gunn's distinction jars: his essay was written when high modernism and feminism had been admired and trounced for decades precisely because of their unabashed aggression, their didactic (and often witty) scorn for social mores. Yet for Gunn, neither movement can be satiric. Why not? Cribbing Pound's 1918 estimation of Loy in *The Little Review*, Gunn then reinforces this distinction by suggesting that Loy's readiest influences are eighteenth-century men: "The controlled anger and indignation of [Loy's best satire] make it the equal, to my mind, of the best of Pope or Swift."[31] As further ballast, Gunn adds: "Loy is a tough writer, and sentiment in the usual sense is seldom present in her work."[32] By the end of his essay, Gunn clarifies that emotion may arise *from* a reading of Loy's writing, but it is not locatable *within* the work itself; although he finds her satires moving, Gunn wants to convince us that she is a proper satirist, "hard, pure, unrelenting" (51). Gunn's vagaries are partly true – Loy's sentiment is singular – but also comically vacillating. His allegiances are emphatically high modernist: for Gunn, as for Wilde and Joyce before him (and Lauren Berlant after him), sentimental writing must be bad or middle-brow, labels that do not apply to Loy's oeuvre. By these terms, Loy's virile writing is shorthand for her modernist literary credibility, and to be satirical is to be masculine, impersonal, in possession of the clarity and perspective wrought by distance.

But Loy is disinvested in tracing out selves demarcated by inviolable contours. As Maeera Shreiber argues: the real object of mourning in Loy's celebrated "Songs to Joannes" is not any individual partner, but "a culture which is actively hostile to love." For Shreiber, Loy's resistance to outdated bourgeois mores or *passéisme* is matched only by her "distres[s about] the intensification of isolation accompanying the modernist estrangement from social experience" (88). With these concerns in her sights, Loy attacks to bring her enemies closer. These enemies include identificatory anxieties. As Laura Scuriatti observes, critics who examine "Loy's relationship to national and racial identity" tend to foreground a distantiation "expressed as irony, detachment, or rejection" (226).[33] Cravan recognised this first: "'All your irony is assumed'", he said to Loy by way of courting her, adding: "'my one desire is to be so very tender to you that you will smile without irony'" ("Colossus" 108). For Loy, intervals cannot be maintained, must cede to proximity. Hence the cosmopolitan Loy actively sought out ever-shifting, "localized stanc[es]" geographical and experiential (Scuriatti 226). And Loy presents solitude as a curse. The reptilian protagonist of "The Crocodile without any Tail" (c. 1920s) islands himself in a river, but when his hunger for companionship exceeds his need for nourishment, we know he has evolved. More harrowingly, Mr Bundy of "Hush Money" succumbs to dementia, a too-sentient "buri[al] under constantly dissolving currents of semi-lucid mud" (*SE* 33). Because sincere, Loy's fear of estrangement is palpable, horrific. It is also the catalyst for satire. In "The Pamperers" (1920), protagonist Diana is "made of the instigatory caress". Named after the goddess of the hunt, Diana aggressively goads, incites, and provokes, but her willingness to dote is reassuringly constitutive. Diana is Loy's hyperbolically ideal helpmeet: an "elusion that coo[s]" to man's "adolescent isolation", the embodied "reciprocal quality" providing inspiration and "laudatory discrimination" whilst attending to every minor male need (*SE* 169). Diana's "power" lies in her forfeiture of self, or her readiness to acquaint herself with what Loy describes in "Songs to Joannes" as "the intimacies" of the male lover's "insolent isolation" (*LoLB* 67). Presented as virile and independent, in Loy's work, masculine self-alienation is constantly remediated by the sacrifice of feminine autonomy. Striving to reverse this dynamic, Loy's characters often find themselves irretrievably enmeshed in its machinations. As Mrs Jones puts it in *Insel*: "I noticed how I was keeping my distance in my effort to 'get at him'" (*I* 24).

Loy's isolation anxiety teeters vertiginously on the banal: after all, the alienated subject is the literary inspiration *par excellence* of the modern age. And satirists actively court this alienation: they are renowned for deploying naked aggression, repugnance, or self-absorbed petulance to maintain distance between themselves and their nemeses. Consider, for instance, this emblematic passage dissecting the author–reader dynamic from Thomas Carlyle's *Sartor Resartus* (1833–4), a satire we know Loy read:

> of the innumerable multitude that started with us, joyous and full of hope, where now is the innumerable remainder, whom we no longer see standing by our side? The most have recoiled, and stand gazing afar off, in unsympathetic astonishment, at our career: not a few, pressing forward with more courage, have missed footing, or leaped short; and now swim weltering in the Chaos-flood. ... afflicted rather than instructed by the present Work. (204)

What pleasure Carlyle palpably takes in keeping his audience invisible, distant, wounded! Familiar with these conceits, Loy actively exposes the longing at the core of satiric assault, a longing embedded in the very etymology of its correlate, sacrifice, which is founded in a desire to communicate with gods: "[i]n biblical Hebrew, the root term [of sacrifice] is *korban*, 'to bring near'" (Mizruchi 26). Bataille argues similarly that sacrifice restores humanity to a divine intimacy "because it is not compatible with the positing of a separate individual" (*TR* 51). Like coordinates arise in the work of pioneering sociologist Georg Simmel, who states that unbalanced renunciation is integral to all human interaction, but "most frequently in erotic relations" defined by "reserve, indifference, or repulse" that "spu[r] us to efforts and sacrifices" (586). This spur is exceptionally protrusive in Loy's drama "The Sacred Prostitute" (c. 1914–16), where Futurist aggression and love are gendered and personified, alternately boxing or showering one another with affection. What Loy delineates literarily, Bataille affirms philosophically: presenting love as the coinciding of two equal, overpowering desires "perceived in the transparence of an intimate comprehension", Bataille hastily adds: "Of course . . . without repulsion the desire would not be boundless" (*AS2* 113). Repulsion is love's fertile ground.

In like manner, Loy's undated satiric memoir "Colossus" holds courtship in bemused disdain. Loy doggedly insults the man considered the love of her life, poet-pugilist Cravan. On first seeing Cravan's photograph in 1917 in the American art journal *The Soil*, Loy professes herself certain of his homosexuality. The comic strategy of Loy's claim is intensified by the interview accompanying the photograph, in which Cravan provides a thoroughly macho play-by-play of his well-publicised fight with the first African-American world heavyweight boxing champion, Jack Johnson, in Barcelona in 1916 (D. Jones 226). When she meets Cravan in the flesh, Loy finds him akin to a farmer, "dull and square in merely respectable tweeds" (104). At a ball, his touch disgusts her; he is monstrous, revolting, a pleasure to leave. As she begins to see more of him, sitting next to him at Walter and Louise Arensberg's era-defining New York Dada soirees, Loy continues to perceive him as "an indolent mountain" or an inert, brainless mass (107). Throughout this litany of assault, reader and lover alike are held at one remove, suspended by Loy's repulsion and fascination. As Loy writes: "Man's intrigue for a woman lies in his preposterous relationship to herself" ("Colossus" 104). Elsewhere, in a tattered archival fragment, Loy likens Cravan to the giant Gargantua, with a laugh that detonates "like the optimists' end of the world" (*B* 4: 6). In "Colossus", she clearly aspires to be his Rabelais.

Even Loy's reluctant admission of Cravan's attractiveness is freighted with lampoon:

> It was on my second meeting with him that I perceived him as beauti-
> ful. But his huge bulk, his empty stare, only called up a comparison
> with that still more unwieldy beauty of Grecian feature, *il gigante*
> Ugo, the light of whose eyes had also fallen petrified upon his reason
> and who, like a towering statue of animated stone, had swayed
> lethargically above the spectators in the side-show of a circus in Italy.
> ("Colossus" 104–5)

Battista and Paolo Antonio Ugo were the most photographed giants
in the world at the turn of the twentieth century. Seven and a half
feet tall, they earned their living from circus performing, a career that
included a tour with Barnum and Bailey; Loy may have been among
their Italian audiences (De Herder 30). By Loy's description, Cravan
is as much aberrant sideshow as he is a "beauty of Grecian feature"
or the Colossus of Rhodes, a sun-god statue erected to honour
military triumph famously among the Seven Wonders of the Ancient
World. Unable to extricate herself from or commit to this vexatious
man, Loy knowingly risks her audience projecting her ambivalence
back upon her. Eventually, Loy acknowledges that Cravan exceeds
standards physical *and* intellectual. His brutishness is mitigated by
his perceptiveness for "every degree of height and depth", his willingness to spend hours examining "splinters of quartz" ("Colossus"
111). But we cannot trust Loy's perspective, as she herself acknowledges. "It is impossible, or at least dangerous, to remember Colossus
after he left New York, for by this time I had magnified his being to
such proportions that all comparisons vanished, which is the trick
of falling in love" ("Colossus" 112). To suit our own needs and
perspective, a deliberate toying with proportion is as integral to intimacy as it is to satirical discourse: in love, as in lampoon, "reduction
and magnification go together" (Kernan 47). Writing well after the
crisis that was Cravan's disappearance in 1918, Loy does not yield
wholesale to nostalgia, but remains committed to the foundational
repulsions, aggressions, and affections of their relationship.

That injury is fundamental to intimacy is writ large in Bataille,
and approaches tired supposition in the deconstructed binaries of
contemporary theory. "[H]ate and love are intimately tied together,
in the intensity of the negotiation between presence and absence",
claims Sara Ahmed (*Cultural* 50); a key ingredient of intimacy is
aggression, states Lauren Berlant ("Intimacy" 1–2); "O violence in
love!", apostrophises Gillian Rose (97); love "is always a boundary violation", write Adam Philips and Leo Bersani (90). Better
yet, given its commensurability with our purposes here, consider
Slavoj Žižek's "love without cruelty is powerless. . . . The underlying

paradox is that what makes love angelic, what elevates it over mere unstable and pathetic sentimentality, is its cruelty itself, its link with violence" (173). While Loy is far more open to sentimental potentialities than Žižek, a like combination of Eros and Thanatos informs her circumvention of the privileged modernist sentimental economy. Loy remains renowned for an unabashed, explicit reconsideration of erotic intimacies: in "Songs to Joannes" alone, lovers collide, knock sparks off one another, beg to be shoved around. But Loy's Eros is an expansive category that includes the desire to create, "the condition of intimate friendship", and the rethinking of intimacies heteronormative, parental, and filial (*SE* 27).[34] Loy's Eros ascends into the mystical and esoteric. *Insel* traffics in intimacies "uncanny" and "ultra"; in précis, the novel might be considered an investigation of affinities "on the unexplored frontiers of consciousness" (*I* 15, 135). By extension, Insel is Loy's über-sentient creature, or the zenith of her lifelong bid to confront the limits and possibilities of conscious feeling. This dovetailing of artistic sentience and proximity is foregrounded in Loy's 1929 *transatlantic review* profile of Stein, where she writes admiringly: "so intimate is the liaison of her observation with the sheer existence of her objective, that she invites you into the concentric vortex of consciousness involved in the most trifling transactions of incident" (*LaLB* 295).[35] The range of Loy's intimacies is matched by her attentiveness to aggressions micro and macro, workaday and cataclysmic. But in fact, Loy's close attentiveness has always been central to satiric onslaught. Consider, from Loy's associate Wyndham Lewis: "*your* face, *your* character, *your* behaviour – all that is most intimately *you* – is what the satirist takes for his target" ("Satire Defended" 42).

Satire is effective precisely because it is as personal as it is public; it genuinely wounds. To succeed, satirists must know our inmost thoughts and feelings, and communicate their disregard or outright dislike of the same via language, a medium both intimately familiar, and by Jean-Jacques Lecercle's account, intrinsically violent. Lecercle does not directly address satire, but his theory suggests that its violence precedes intentionality. In his *The Violence of Language* (1990), language is not a system, but a battleground in which interrogation is figured as intrusion, and speech is unstable, never innocent of assaultive potential or consequence. Language is riven by its own paradoxes: it frees and constrains expression; it permits mastery, but also unbidden slippage and meanings; it is abstract, yet "material and even corporeal". For the violence Lecercle describes is not figurative, but literal, affecting the individual subject and the world entire. "My words emerge out of this body", writes Lecercle, "other people's words penetrate it" (105). Screams, loud music, violence are expressions of violent affect that inscribe, and this is because:

> Words do not only *do* things; they *are* things. Language cannot be a simple representation of the world; it is also an intervention within it, to be analysed in terms of positions, advance and retreat, territorial markings, and deterritorialization. We are moving here from the body of the individual to the body politic. The non-autonomy of language opens up to the social. Language is an institution with a vengeance. It suffers the fate of all institutions: it is a locus for the exercise of power, and a target for rebellious attacks. As such, it can be revolutionised. (48–9)

For good or ill, language is a forceful entity that demands recognition, as proven by the efficacy of the curse, from which, once uttered, even the most self-avowedly reasonable among us struggle to remain immune (234).

Lecercle's conviction that the curse succeeds is shared by Denise Riley in "Malediction", a chapter in *Impersonal Passion: Language as Affect* (2010) where she discusses how difficult it can be to rid ourselves of insult or accusation, as "the tendency of malignant speech is to ingrow like a toenail" (10). Reworking Lacanian terminology, Riley names the corporeal, lived reality of harsh words "extimacy".[36] Noting that the psychic and the linguistic are inextricable, and only artificially kept separate by "discursive convention", Riley maintains: "if there is a linguistic love which is drawn outward to listen, there's also linguistic hatred, felt by its object as drawn inward. A kind of 'extimacy' prevails in both cases" (10, 13). Via extimacy, language penetrates the individual, either shoring up the self or causing internal bleeding. This very belief system underpins iambography, or the ancient recitation of personal abuse believed to be the precursor to contemporary satire. If satire is an ill-tempered cursing disruptive to the status quo, its faith in language is notably not too far afield from the sentimental modernist fantasy whereby the frequently aggressive incursions of vanguard literature and art are believed capable of changing the world.

Language can intervene against power, but can also sustain it. As Lecercle states:

> The standard version of English is the dialect of cultured, white, European, heterosexual, urban, adult males. This reads like the converse of a list of the victims of comedians' jokes: women, peasants,

> [non-white foreigners] of all descriptions, trade unionists, lunatics.
> It is almost the same list, which means that the major dialect is
> the embodiment – and its adoption the practice – of relations of
> power. (50)

Lecercle's list of comedic victims is readily aligned with the marginalised figures that populate Loy's poems, fictions, and drama. Loy makes manifest what Lecercle considers the symptomatic anxiety of standardised English, namely "that the oppressed may speak in their turn". If minor dialects threaten major, women, for instance, "may forget that silence is golden" (50).

The term "New Woman" was coined in 1894, as Loy was coming of age. Encapsulating an energetic, independent resistance to the Victorian norms of femininity, this *fin-de-siècle* fervour laid ground for the violence of revolutionary feminist discourse (Felski, *Gender* 146–7, 165). Feminist aggression confronts what Riley identifies as the "stock formulas" of supposedly "idle sexism" (20); it magnifies and scrutinises the daily, articulated sacrifice of female autonomy. Inevitably, this challenge to the powerful paternalism of "standard" English was, and is, perceived as threat. A product and beneficiary of this proto-feminist age, Loy devises a satire that draws on the tradition whereby malediction effects pains intellectual, affective, and material. A revolutionary mandate inspires these inflictions, which are both macro-economic – against injustice and gendered injustices writ large – and micro: attentive to individual, damning words. Loy's early poem "Costa Magic" (1914) is an homage to victims of male violence: in it, a father doses his daughter with a malefic because he has taken against her betrothed. The speaker is witness to this crime and to the mumbling invectives of her own embittered husband, meaning Loy's lines "Malediction / Incantation" apply to both men (*LoLB* 13). Loy's "Lady Laura in Bohemia" (1931) offers "kisses and curses" at the bar she frequents (*LoLB* 98). These affectionate, drunken insults speak to Loy's determination to juxtapose intimacy with language that aims to wound, to attend to manifestations of "the instigatory caress". The curse retains its authority as late as Loy's undated boarding-house tale "The Agony of the Partition", where within the proximities of shared housing, invective and hexes prove all-determining. Intimate, extimate, loving, murderous: Loy remains attentive to the power of language and its sacrificial victims throughout her career. Hence her fascination with crucifixions and virgins.

"Transpierced Parts" and "Salvation": Crucifixions

"Jesus whose thorny majesty / with transpierced parts / Salvation ensures". So writes Loy in "Jesus and Eros.", an unpublished, undated encomium of Christian and classical deities that calls for a mingling of prayer with flirtatious play. According to Loy, "Love's wand of sorcery / Much honoured in Pompeii" has been mercilessly anchored to Jesus's cross, and this Christian usurping of love saddens even Jesus himself, who recognises it as a global loss. In this instance, Loy is drawn toward ecstatically "transpierced hearts" caused by combative "quiverful[s] of fun" ("Jesus and Eros."). But Loy can and does take Christ's sacrifice seriously, seeing in his corporeal suffering for a transcendent good – the sacred redemption of fallen humankind – a model of possibility for her disenfranchised contemporaries. As she argues in "Involution" (1914), "the last chains" can "forge the first freedom", just as the final ruler of any "crucified kingdom" might "[d]estroy himself to find his brother" (*LoLB* 223). Loy's Christ is more democratised peer than deity, as Loy is alert to the self-effacement linking female experience to a Messiah born to redeem others. "The christian era is the woman's period", Loy notes wryly in *Goy Israels*, leaving no time for our incredulity to set in before adding scabrously: "Nature may continue to impose upon her; but there is no doubt about it the christians have cleaned her up" (*GI* 28: 48). Loy knows that traditional Christianity relegated womankind to the margins, even as it is a religion ostensibly born of reverence for the persecuted. Hence she is amused and annoyed by what she calls Arthur Cravan's "'Christ motive'", or his easy masculine identification with the Son of God. On one of their extended rambles around New York, Cravan sings "an old song" reaffirming how Christ died on the cross for everyone. But Cravan's otherwise sonorous voice "forbade appreciation", because in it, Loy hears this "corrective": "He was really singing, '*I* am pure as a little child – *You*, lascivious woman at my elbow, partake not of the little Jesus'" ("Colossus" 111). A Christian Scientist and a feminist, Loy resists this exemption.

The effeminised, sacrificed Christ is transposed variously through Loy's work. In "The Prototype" (1914), the speaker is "the only follower in Christ's foot-steps" in the Florentine Duomo on Christmas Eve, alone in longing for the "pink & white" health of Mary and Jesus's likenesses "on the high altar" to be gifted to the sore-covered baby she espies in the congregation (*LoLB* 221–2). Christ's revered uniqueness is again transferable in "The Dead" (1919), where Loy resurrects the sacrificed soldiers of World War I in a sacrament in which the masses "swallo[w the] irate hungers" of corpses to prepare themselves for the "bread-breaking" that honours this global loss (*LoLB* 72). By this conceit, each fallen soldier becomes a furious Messiah, a martyr whose mortal righteousness hangs on no sanctified or sanctifiable cause.[37] In her later years, Loy transfers her Christ palimpsest from pointlessly destroyed soldiers to people needlessly impoverished, seeking models for a portrait of Jesus among the homeless men of New York's Bowery District.[38] The first such deific muse appears in Loy's "The Three Wishes", where a distinctly Christ-like "poor, bare man, sagging on his staff" is the focus of a life-drawing class (*SE* 136). The iconoclastic artist of the class cannot bring himself to depict this decimated figure, instead hanging garments from a hastily erected clothesline by way of capturing "'the contours of collapse'" (*SE* 138). This same conflation of holy mien with dull domestic labour recurs in Loy's collage work, "Christ on a Clothesline" (1955), which depicts Jesus hanging from that same prosaic tool by oversized, Frankensteinian arms, his eyes closed, cheeks gaunt, and palms supplicating, behind him a run-down cityscape absent of humanity. Again, a quotidian household chore reconfigures a sacrificial figure deemed divine. Loy's collapsing contours might be read as bathos, or as an elevation of domesticity to the saintly, that which, with recognition, can be canonised and renewed. Resurrection interests Loy.

Proffering babies, soldiers, and the homeless their Christly due, Loy also satirises and democratises the Eucharist, symbol or substance of Christ's self-renunciation for the atonement of fallen sinners. Hence an alcoholic bohemian in one of Loy's poems "presides" over "Jazz-Mass", lubricating herself all the while with "gin-fizz eucharist", a supposition that recurs in a roman à clef, where Loy insists that "transubstantiation" – the conversion of bread and wine into the body and blood of Christ – is "most likely to take place" within the confines of a pub or bar (*LoLB* 98; *CP* 18: 63). Hence Joyce can make word flesh, is "Christ capitalised" by the press (*LoLB* 89). And if Christ's perfectibility is consummated in his death and resurrection, Loy's "Aphorisms on Futurism" (1914) extends this propensity to all mankind: "in the Future, by inspiring the people to expand to their fullest capacity, the great man proportionately must be tremendous—a God" (*LoLB* 150). Loy's dig at the infinite Futurist ego reinforces long-held beliefs that ingesting the figurative body of Christ lends the individual Messianic stature. We ritualise Christ's sacrifice, writes Dennis King Keenan, to acknowledge that we too are comprised of suffering; in imbibing otherness, we direct life away from the self, toward love (186–7). Keenan echoes the terms of Loy's Christian Science, in which believers are exhorted to engage in "constant self-immolation" in emulation of Jesus's martyrdom, one so considerable "as makes us admit its Principle to be Love" (Baker Eddy, *Science* 23, 26). This privileging of love and only love through sacrifice, replicated through eucharistic ritual, is what church founder Mary Baker Eddy considers a foremost distinction between Christian Science tenets and those of "priest or rabbi affirm[ing] God to be a mighty potentate, who loves *and* hates" (emphasis added). Unlike Christian Science, Baker Eddy maintains: "The Jewish theology gave no hint of the unchanging love of God" (*Science* 42). There are echoes of Baker Eddy in the work of George D. Herron, the Christian Socialist activist whom Loy met in Florence. For Herron, society was en route to an "infinite love" through the adoption of Christly ways, and particularly Christ's embrace of sacrifice, which attested to "the unity and continuity of life" through "the surrender and offering of self" (18, 169). As in Loy's atavistic avant-gardism and sacrificial satires, so too in her faith: transpierced parts equal transpierced hearts, cruelty augurs love.

Taken into the self, the Eucharist is an embodiment that denies separation between divine and profane, teetering vertiginously on the sacrilegious. Its roots are discernibly pagan: the sociologist Emile Durkheim (1858–1917), who Loy is believed to have read, describes how, within totemic clans or tribes, the group's self-definition is maintained and rejuvenated by killing the sacred animal and "tak[ing] a little of the flesh of this same animal into [one's] own body from time to time" (*Elementary* 338).[39] Part sacrilege, part revivification, this ritual proves that "when a sacred thing is subdivided, each of its parts remains equal to the thing itself" (*Elementary* 228). Vestigially, this ritual recurs in Jewish Passover, when, under God's instruction, a lamb was slaughtered, its blood smeared on doorways, and parts of its body consumed. Hebraic affinity was established, salvation ensured. The links between Passover and the Eucharist that mark the death of Jesus, Lamb of God, are often remarked upon, including by one Mina Loy. Working against the history by which Christians hold Jews accountable for Christ's death, and with the equation of Jewish identity and "the model of sacrifice presented in the Gospels", Loy argues: "The crucifixion of the Christ at long distance is the persecution of the Jew—" (Gilman 19, 21; Loy, "Fragments"). Furthermore, Loy claims that "Christ was the concretion of the Jew's capacity for superseding himself" ("Fragments"). Sacrifice destroys, sacrifice unifies.

The historic ritualisation of the crucifixion has long been open to interpretation. For Catholics, Mass is transubstantiation; by it, host and wine are consecrated, literally becoming Christ's flesh and blood. For Protestants, as Sophie Read argues:

> Christ's single, historical sacrifice on the cross is sufficient to expiate human sin for all time, and does not need to be reiterated; if the priest is believed to be offering the sacrifice again, as would be the case if Christ were really present on the altar, this would both derogate from the sufficiency of the crucifixion, and imply that human effort might have a place in the economy of salvation. (15)

Emphasising language rather than corporeality, "Protestant sacramentalism privileges the figurative" and treats the liturgy as "a model for rhetorical expression" (Read 38). This "doctrinal foundation of fissure and flexibility" emerges with the Reformation and paves the way to further contestations and elaborations (Read 29). Nietzsche describes Christ's sacrifice – to his debtor, for love – as an absurdity that merely achieves a revocation of the basic principles of exchange, while others insist that Jesus's crucifixion is not a sacrifice at all, as "its carnality is mitigated by the survival of the victim" (Mizruchi 43; Hughes 50). Christ's death is made sinless through celebratory ritual, Bataille argues, lamenting this figurative, sanctioned, affectless violence with its failure to make "the faithful . . . responsible for desiring the sacrifice" (*E* 89–90; 120). Jean-Luc Nancy reads Christ's death, alongside that of Socrates, as a clear indicator that Western culture is founded upon and determined by sacrifice (21). Debates over "real presence in the Eucharist" and "eucharistic sacrifice" remain live (Hunsinger 10–12). But like sacrifice itself, the Eucharist symbolises binaries of presence and absence, death and life, and Loy understood the rhetorical value of these appositions. Loy's unpublished prose "The Revolution in Revelation", for instance, bemoans the loss of the spiritual in an increasingly secular world, and turns to Christ as a saviour not of the sinner, but of a "unique dual-consciousness" that "associat[es] with the world in an intercommunicative co-identity of the visible and invisible universe."[40] For Loy, Christ's "consummate comprehension enabl[es] Him, uniquely, to function under a dual law of interrelative abstract and concrete." Consummated sacrifice is inextricable from the binaries of embodied feeling and perception, or the key ingredients of Loy's foundational sentience.

Loy recognises the bloody Hebraic roots of the Eucharist, its emphatically embodied suffering. But consistent with turn-of-the-twentieth-century Christian Science, for Loy, Jesus's "blood *symbolizes* Life" and the host represents not flesh, but "communion with God, for [Jesus] acknowledged no other Life or Substance than God (Spirit)" (emphasis added, Ziller n.p.). Straddling corporeal and figurative readings of the Eucharist, Loy persistently uses it as a metaphor for women's suffering. "'All my life I seem to have been the eternal 'innocent-accused'", states Mrs Nome to the Irishwoman who shares the boarding-house setting of Loy's undated fiction "The Agony of the Partition". Her interlocutor agrees: "'I have seen the psychic mark of the cross on your poor forehead'" (*SE* 8). "Sacrificial blood . . . is a concentrate of the power to do away with sins", and Loy's women bleed figuratively and incessantly to wash away male impropriety and violence (Kilpatrick 25–6). One Loy protagonist is martyr to a lover who wanders through her flat after assaulting her, positioning himself as "[t]he Parish Priest accompanied by his acolyte visiting the houses of the devout at Eastertide to asperse their rooms with holy water" (*SE* 68). Another woman is the object of sacrificial fantasy by which she becomes the vessel for sanctified blood, her "'body . . . a vase of fairest alabaster" that men "had longed to break" in order to "sprinkle the ruby wine of 'her' warm young life on the altar of eternity—" (*SE* 49). The quotes around the feminine pronoun set this violent longing at one remove, making the desire symbolic, historicised. Consequently, the woman in question becomes every female lamb brutally slaughtered at the hands of sadistic, unwitting, brutish mankind. Arguing that the "transubstantiation of the communion altar is not unique", Loy points out that women can inflict this same paternalistic violence on each other. From Loy's perspective, there is little difference between the Eucharist and "the cakes and sandwiches laid on occasional tables" for women's tea parties. The sacrificial subject in this instance is "the fallen woman", an invert resurrected being who, instead of ascending to God, attains the divine, mysterious pleasures of sexual satiation unknown to the average Victorian married lady (*CP* 15: 41). Loy resents the immolation of this figure on the altar of propriety, but in some of her writings, the post-1917 "Transfiguration" in particular, she discernibly participates in this violence.

In "Transfiguration," Loy satirises God's miraculous affirmation of Christ's status as sacrificial redeemer, with a "fallen" Mexican woman playing the part of Messiah, and Loy's speaker as her follower. In the transfiguration that occurs in the New Testament,

Christ ascends a mountain to speak with past prophets and God himself, his being and clothing illuminated throughout with a light so pure that it frightens his disciples Peter, James, and John. In Loy's parody of the same, she watches the gradual descent of her fellow traveller from self-proclaimed chaste puritan to the debased love interest of an all-consuming man whose rapaciousness transforms her otherwise "mummified face": "Her shrapnel eyes had softened into a velvet tranquillity and from the battered pores of her skin a warm disclosing radiance flowed" (*SE* 147). Where Christ on a mountaintop is a divining rod conjoining terrestrial and celestial, "Transfiguration." foregrounds a primeval landscape from which the Mexican woman cannot extricate herself, even as she believes herself saved, "tamed", and resurrected by her "fly-by-night amour with a stranger" (*SE* 147). There is no shortage of racism on show in Loy's presentation of this sudden coupling: the woman is, sardonically, "a virginal tiger lily" who dissembles; diminished as "the spawn of the Latin races", her Latinx lover is begrudgingly "suave and somewhat entertaining" (*SE* 142–3). Nevertheless, as the story opens, the Mexican woman presides over the procurement of salt for Loy's speaker's eggs, a Last Supper that is named sacrament and comically defined by the organs of female fertility. Throughout, the first-person narrator acts as moral and practical guide to the precarious journey at hand; taking place in 1917, it is framed by the violence of the Mexican Revolution. Pretending at loyal capitulation, she emerges as a wearily triumphant judge of womankind writ large, who "undeniably behaves in all contingencies as if assured of a transcendental sanction" (*SE* 147). Transfigured, Jesus's external being radiates; transfigured, the Mexican woman's "consciousness" is "coated . . . with a final filth" (*SE* 147). This sacrifice of sentient self redeems nothing but tired patriarchal cliché. The potentiality is evident, however, as Loy does not condemn the sexual liberties taken, but rather the woman's willingness to succumb to a man through whose negligible privilege she aims at resurrection. By the terms of Loy's "Feminist Manifesto", this woman will not "[l]eave off looking to men to find out what [she is] <u>not</u>", and thus sacrifices herself in vain (*LoLB* 154).

More reverentially, Loy's "Songs to Joannes" rewrites Christ's crucifixion as the experience of the devout, long-suffering female. Loy inverts the Mexican woman's sullied transfiguration in poem 28, where the speaker emerges purified, whitened, after ascending an infinite column of white steps to seek a sign from the lover who defines her faith:

Smelt   to synthetic
Whiteness
Of my
Emergence
And I am burnt quite white
In the climacteric
Withdrawal of your sun
And wills and words all white
Suffuse
Illimitable monotone (*LoLB* 64)

In this version of Christ's transfiguration, the mountaintop is a ziggurat, the deific figure is absent, and the radiance that follows painful. Recalled, the lover's "[e]tiolate body" and "New Day / Shu[t] down" the speaker, for whom this experience is both sufferance and liberation (*LoLB* 65). In the Catholic mass, Luce Irigaray points out, Christ's injunction that host and wine are his body and blood obliterates the truth that "woman bleeds". Woman bleeds not only menstrual or post-natal blood, but also from the perpetual wound that is her excision from the Trinity, and from the ritualisation of Christ's sacrifice and heavenly ascension. By foregrounding God the Father and Christ the son, woman "is being offered in partial oblation, she who manages the communion between them and among the other men and women present" (*Sexes* 26). In place of a Eucharist reliant upon what Irigaray considers an unacknowledged, feminised tradition of sacrificing the fruits of the earth, Loy offers a "profane communion table / Where wine is spill'd on promiscuous lips" and resurrection is enacted by a butterfly "With the daily news / Printed in blood on its wings" (*Sexes* 27; *LoLB* 54). Nature is restored to the heart of sacrificial process, albeit imprinted by the technocracy that Irigaray conflates with patriarchy, or the very origin of sacrificial civilisation. The body wears and announces its sacrificial status, a truth repeated in Loy's painting *Untitled (Surreal Scene)* (c. 1935), where the exposed innards of the female figure who dominates the canvas are comprised of flowers in place of mammary glands and ovaries, sheaves of wheat for organs or ribs, and a chalice of red wine as a uterus. Pagans imbibed a part of their totem as a mark of respect and affiliation; in this image, Loy's woman embodies sacrificial goods ancient and Christian. Her female biology is earthly fruit and Christly body, eliding any divide between self and sacrificial object. Woman is immolation.

Throughout "Songs to Joannes", Loy's communions are many and various, encompassing not only the Christian Trinity of Father,

Son, and Holy Spirit, but any prosaic grouping: "Where two or three are welded together / They shall become god" (*LoLB* 58). To aim for love is to fantasise the other into deity. But in truth, "Two or three men   looked only human" and even the most "Superhuman" among them possesses not life-giving, sanctifying blood, but a "weak eddy" of "drivelling humanity" (*LoLB* 59). These consummations are physical and spiritual. Defined by longing and aggression, they relentlessly "[p]rob[e] wounds for souls", a turn of phrase invoking the infamous action of the sceptical disciple Thomas on Jesus's abjectly embodied return from death (*LoLB* 55).[41] The communion of "Songs to Joannes" breaks the self rather than symbolic bread, a break irredeemably resurrected through the three crucifixions of poem 31:

> Crucifixion
> Of a busy-body
> Longing to interfere so
> With the intimacies
> Of your insolent isolation
>
> Crucifixion
> Of an illegal ego's
> Eclosion
> On your equilibrium
> Caryatid   of an idea
>
> Crucifixion
> Wracked arms
> Index extremities
> In vacuum
> To the unbroken fall

Loy's is a trinity of proposed redemptions – each resolutely cut down – within an enclosed, unbalanced dyad. Woman desires intimacy, but is consigned to gossipy irritant. Woman's ego is emergent, new-born, illicit; seeking legitimation, it is sacrificed to a paradoxically all-powerful equilibrium to which it remains "caryatid" or structural support. Woman is broken and punished, the very protrusions of her body retracted into a "vacuum", her fall from grace perpetual (*LoLB* 67). In "Songs to Joannes", Loy's sacrificial lamb – womankind – remains overlooked, infantilised, and outcast, unable to move past her role as "elemental substrate of life". Yet "Songs to Joannes" proclaims women's fundamental place in the resurrection, and in the consummation of life itself, thus articulating the unspoken truth Irigaray considers central to the celebration of the Eucharist: "the body that gives life never enters into language" (*Sexes* 46). Or, as Loy writes in "Aid of the Madonna" (1943), women constitute the "Omitted omen of Calvary! / Uncarved crucifixion!" (*LoLB* 115). As a satirist, Loy carves space for unspoken truths, prophetically insists upon the restoration of the female, and anticipates Irigaray's fury at the elision of women as religious officiators (*Sexes* 78). Loy's confidence as self-reflexive sacrifier emerges in "Parturition" (1914), where the birthing speaker is a "crucified wild beast" whose agony is overwhelming, transcendent, an affirmation of her Christly "superior Inferiority", her "infinite Maternity", and "cosmic reproductivity" (*LoLB* 5–7). This experience sanctifies this "woman-of-the-people" who now bears "[a] ludicrous little halo", taking her rightful place next to the often ludicrous paternalistic God who is the foundation of the Judeo-Christian tradition that has so effectively usurped her centrality. Loy's message is clear: the biology by which women are immolated also has the capacity to resurrect.[42]

"'Inordinate Chastity'": Virgins

"It is the body and blood especially of virgin women that are being sacrificed to . . . intermale society", writes Irigaray (*Sexes* 47). In response to this long-recognised truth, Loy presents virginity as resurrectable, a site of eternal return, thereby eradicating its over-valued prototypicality. Loy habitually restores virginity to the post-coital woman, whose *petite mort* is a transcendent return to innocence, a revivified purity.[43] At the end of "Transfiguration.", Loy writes that her Latinx protagonist "glow[s] and blossom[s] with that essential virginity of the spirit which women reconquer only in the arms of those illusions that they call their lovers" (*SE* 147). Like Bataille, Loy attributes a brief, unsustainable immaculacy to the immolated, even as she knows that her female victims are reborn into a world poised to besmirch them anew. In its ceaseless iterations on the individual body, this process recalls Demeter's perennial sacrifice of Persephone, whose solitary victimisation and return supplants the need for a limitless, cyclical supply of mortal victims. With its singular onus and sustaining purity, Loy's approach to virgin sacrifice also recalls the story of Jesus. In the year-long Christian liturgy celebrating his immolated life, Jesus's immaculacy remains constant: even as fallible, embodied human he is chaste bridegroom, a legacy to which Loy alludes in the first of her "Songs".[44] Purity and sacrificial preparedness define Christ and womankind, but where Jesus's malediction is world-altering spectacle, women's immolations are as unending as they are minute: death by a thousand cuts. As a result, Loy must account for the exigencies of a dismissible, circadian sacrificial rhythm. In "Songs", the lascivious speaker, having attained sexual Nirvana, brings "the nascent virginity" of herself to her lover on another day, a day that is, like Loy's approach to virginity, "[e]verlasting   passing   apparent imperceptible" (*SE* 147). This claim is discernibly romantic, sentimental: in each act of lovemaking, the lover is born anew, seen anew. It also provokes, presenting virginity as a malleable valuation of the modest, devout woman that is only as powerful or destructive as we allow. To bring this chapter to a close, I will consider how Loy relates virginity to subjective transcendence and social sacrifice, culminating in a close reading of her 1930s ballet "Crystal Pantomime", where Loy hyperbolically interrogates the mythology of domestic bliss predicated on female purity.

Loy considers virginity as fictional as an "incubus", a "literary bathos" personified as a "head-hanging female, creeping alone forever in the shameful shadow of a rainy wall, [existing] on the outside of human confines" (*EP* 22). Virginity can be easily excised, as in the ritualised flick of the scalpel across the hymen in Loy's "Feminist Manifesto". But the damage of this mutilation is considerably diminished if virginity can be reinstated whenever it is asserted or desired, if the hymen is simply another body part, like an appendix, that can be removed without moral or economic repercussions. And by Loy's measure, virginity is an anatomical dismemberment performed at will, replete with rejuvenating capabilities, not unlike Bataille's celebration of bodily excisions (teeth, fingers, foreskins) as "rupture[s] of personal homogeneity" that are "linked to ... debaucheries openly evoked by the ceremony marking the entry into adult society" ("Sacrificial" 68). The orthodox Jewish boy's entry into mature subjectivity is marked by the wearing of phylacteries that reiterate the covenant with God that began with his circumcision, his ceremonial mutilation. Can it be a coincidence that Loy, who writes extensively about her Jewish patrilineage, inscribes the female body at the onset of puberty in her "Feminist Manifesto"?[45] For who better to expose as maimed than the girl-woman, the unsung sacrificial victim in perpetuity? As sacrifice is so pointedly, irrationally aimed at the female subject, so too, Loy defiantly asserts, might woman's resurrection be subjective, a perception granted to the satiated or besotted. Just so does Marinetti, himself capable of "virginal reactions" to all he encounters, admire Loy's post-coital expression, her eyes emanating an "'inordinate chastity'" (*B* 9: 18; 2: 4). Just so does Geronimo perceive in the lovelorn Pazzarella a "virginity of spirit" exceeding that of any female who has yet to experience sex (*SE* 72). Just so does Loy's Jove Ivon Corvon, a swooned-after celebrity, fall head over heels for a grey-haired, heavy-set cleaner who "appear[s] to him" – quite improbably – "in the light of a virginal visitation" (*SE* 72, 62). This experience Loy extends even to the abused wife of *Esau Penfold*, whose "face . . . had freshened as is the way with women who have come in contact with the male vibration" (*EP* 22). With requisite faith, Loy suggests, all "fallen" women might be resurrected as was Christ, who took after his "virgin" mother in this regard.[46]

Many critics have discussed the relationship between Loy's preoccupation with the fiction of the virgin and the vestiges of a Western marriage market whereby women are valued for housing a "commodity" – their intact hymen – that can be sold only once.[47] But virginity is also central to Loy's sacrificial ritualisations and methodologies, her attempts to step outside the economics of marriage, to resuscitate female subjects disfigured or slaughtered. Ancient dramatists were fond of chronicling the immolation of maidens, and Loy is a liberal user of classical references: her work is populated by proper nouns such as Adonis, Apollo, Bellona, Demosthenes, Eros, Hades, Lethe, Olympus, Orpheus, and Persephone, as well as allusions to the "Hermes of Praxiteles" and "The Birth of Venus"; the Egyptian Osiris also surfaces. While the truth of human sacrificial practice in Greco-Roman cultures remains indeterminate, scholars agree on the part played by virgins in the immolating narratives these cultures produced (Garstad 1998). Cultural ritual gave families – and elite families in particular – opportunities to overcome the paradox by which virtuous females were meant to remain out of the public eye, yet were required to be profitably married to someone outside of their household. By displaying their daughters within a socially sanctioned rite, families solved this conundrum.

As a consequence, ancient religious festivals became a plot device in which "erotic possibilities" emerged from the happy "accident" of young, available women being espied by desiring young men as they took part in honorific or celebratory processions (Scodel 112). This is the role played by the ten virgins in the New Testament parable referenced in Loy's "Songs to Joannes": these maidens "[t]ri[m the] subliminal flicker" of their lamps in anticipation of a bridegroom, and of their ceremonial part in his wedding cortège (*LoLB* 53; Matt. 25.1–13). Opportunities to display daughters in public fora mitigated a pronounced sense of urgency: "The virgin was an ephemeral being. A man had to hope that his daughter would be his only briefly" because "only daughters were simultaneously inessential and precious" (Scodel 113–14). Loy affirms this paradox in "Virgins Plus Curtains Minus Dots" (1915), where sequestered maidens watch the world pass by, knowing that "Love is a god / White   with soft wings", and that they need someone to "shou[t] / Virgins for sale" on their behalf, because "Somebody who was never / a virgin / Has bolted [their] door" (*LoLB* 22). Britishly punning on masculine inconstancy, this "bolter" must be a man, a being never defined by his virginity who is now vexed by incommensurate needs to keep the maidens of his household safe whilst flogging them as available wares. How else will the arrows of the soft-winged Greek Eros or Roman Cupid reach these young women, who have no coins or gold, and who are swaddled in curtains, armed only with nails to scratch at the fortress of their fate?[48] Memorialised in an increasingly secular period, Loy's virgins are in dire need of religious ceremony.

If marriage rites permit direct exchange between parents and prospective suitors, they are complicated by virgin sacrifice, a practice that rode roughshod over the precepts of piety and women's social utility alike. The virgin immolation is the apotheosis of Bataille's sacrificial economy: to eviscerate one's daughter is luxurious expenditure of an exemplary kind, an "overconspicuous consumption" that does away with instrumentalisation in favour of "excessive display of the virgin's body" (Scodel 112). This is objectification at its most lethal. The young man sacrificed to war retains a shred of autonomy: he may outwit or flatten his opponent, may luckily escape battle unscathed. But while he risks immolation, the maiden who gives herself or is offered in sacrifice will assuredly die.[49] In return for her ritual murder, she might bring eternal honour to her family, as when her name was linked to the *tyche* or goddess of fortune who secured a city's fate (Roselli 130). Alternately, her corpse could be buried in the corner or foundation of a building to ensure its prosperity, a process known as "the walled-up wife" and bleakly prescient of the living matron's eternally supportive, suppressed fate (Garstad 95, 112). To be chosen for sacrifice, the woman in question must be virgin as the ideal sacrificed animal need never have been; she must be virgin as the bride of god or spirit that she promises to become; and of course, she must be virgin to increase the erotic-to-pornographic fascination with her violent, sexualised end (Garstad 105, 114).

This inescapably gruesome history forms the climax of Loy's 1930s ballet about a youth and a sacrificed maiden, a subject Loy insists possesses universal appeal, mockingly describing it as "rich in possibilities as all simple eternal subjects are" (*SE* 153). Generically, "Crystal Pantomime" is legibly comedic: a young man desires a pretty blond female and finds himself opposed; as the resistance dissipates, a communal ritual should ensue. But instead of a festival, Loy places her "maiden bound" atop a pyramid, a ziggurat or pyre (*SE* 160). Where comedy should scapegoat an irrelevant character, Loy prepares to sacrifice a protagonist. Although she is presented as inert and replaceable, the maiden manages to avert death, and on the surface, comedy metamorphoses into heteronormative romance, as love and reproductivity – a honeymoon, a baby – prevail. Importantly, the marriage ceremony is implied, but never seen: for the viewer, the threat of sacrifice actively supplants that celebratory communal rite. And throughout, Loy satirically turns love's triumph into bathos as she moves toward a resolution that does not overturn or affirm, but doggedly, pointedly reinforces a deficient status quo. Within this narration, we find another manifestation of Loy's life-long claim to a "genius for evoking the aesthetic from the ridiculous" (*B* 8: 23).[50] In "Crystal Pantomime" Loy tells us that her over-sized props, including shuttlecocks and battledores, offer "a little of the ridiculous that lends so much charm to ancient art" (*SE* 154). The ancient art in question is virgin sacrifice, and in this instance, it is a ritual calling attention to reader or audience complicity in the plot's sentimental economy.

In "Crystal Pantomime", the curtains open upon a maiden and witch looking into a crystal ball. Modulated, gentle, Loy's voice is nevertheless laced with satire: "Only, as this maiden lived in the times when maidens waited at home while the youths went out into the world, it is rather the adventures of the young man that she will eventually marry . . . that the maiden will see" (*SE* 152). Consistent with this chafingly tidy immolation of the maiden's future, the scenes that follow underscore male freedom and action, including the youth's dance of the wild oats, which presages his erotic dances with a married woman, amorous mermaids, and a fairy queen (also, less explicably, jellyfish). The initial scene, however, takes place on the village green,

> where little girls are dancing skipping rope and little boys are playing marbles while mixed groups play shuttlecock and battledore . . . . The crystal shuttlecocks of bright colours are enormously big and the curves of the glittering skipping ropes are a great addition to the attitudes of the dance.

> The shuttlecocks afford color motion up in the air—and the equally enormous glass marbles of the playing boys, a balance on the ground . . . . The subject of the ballet will appeal to everyone because, being so simple, the high-brows will enjoy it with that humorous compassion they afford for the souvenir sentiments and the general public will 'get it' without effort. (*SE* 152–3)

As in "Songs to Joannes", shuttlecocks are elevated above battledores, even as Loy strives for equality in the binaries of gender and class. Highbrows, Loy suggests, will reduce the ballet to a modernist affective economy that gratifies their sense of superiority, while lowbrows will readily comprehend its express message. Loy propounds as a virtue, then, what Wilde and his peers proclaim as a vice: the democratised pleasures of accessible, ready sentiment. These feelings are a luxury for which no class has to pay, and are not, therefore, Wilde's "finest and most self-sacrificing emotions" ("De Profundis" 639–40). While Loy is never immune to the appeal of tinting her own spectacles with the very pinkest of "pink-love", in "Crystal Pantomime" she will take this emotionality to extremes that are deliberately oppressive, patently unsustainable. As such, Loy's promise of universal audience satisfaction becomes anxious chorus: her ballet will offer an unequalled "impression of ethereal beauty" and an "evanescent dream world so irreal and tenuous" it will leave the audience breathless (*SE* 152). This clichéd, oneiric beauty is compounded by references to enchantment and charm, almost as if Loy has lost her satiric way.

Almost, but not quite, as the overwrought romance on the village green is disrupted by combat. The infatuated youth snatches a blue hair ribbon from the maiden; she scoffs, and he offers her a marble as recompense. The scene sets the stage for the gendered battling and affection that will ensue: the boy's marble and the girl's winding ribbon will take on overbearing proportions throughout the remainder of the ballet, becoming, respectively, a looming ball that dances through "the hour of sentiment" when maiden broods over the youth, and a tenacious reminder of the youth's conscience that weaves its way, weft-like, through his desire-laden dances with a series of women (*SE* 155–6). As these suffocating symbols indicate, both male and female are haunted by heteronormative fantasy throughout "Crystal Pantomime". Loy registers resistance to these gendered norms in wilful disproportions linguistic and material, in romantic props and clichés that are cumbersomely exaggerated, literally oversized: prettiness grown unwieldy and crudely self-promoting.

As Loy writes "Crystal Pantomime", she is also drafting *The Child and the Parent*. Chapter 7 of this roman à clef, "Ladies in an Aviary", bears similar coordinates to the ballet: women of pouty breast and tremulous ribbons are entrapped in a gilded cage, having eaten addictive lumps of unsatiating, saccharine romance from the hand of a "great strong man" (*CP* 15: 39). "[O]ver-carved, over-draped, and over-stuffed", their imprisoning aviary is a set complete with a curtain drawing each day to a close (*CP* 18: 37). In turn, the woman's beplumed selves are micro-stages over which lacy bustles fall, occluding "the jewel of the[ir] body" which "God hung . . . upon breath" (*CP* 15: 44, 46, 36). Popping by to give the ladies their daily dose of treacle, the great strong man intones: "'Here is Love . . . 'tis woman's whole existence.'" Loy's narrator sees it differently, satire at the ready: "It is so sweet this sugar, the sugar of fictitious values" (*CP* 15: 35). In the 1930s, Loy ramps up her war with the misogyny of Victorian romantic fairy tales.

This war suffuses "Crystal Pantomime", which refutes legends associable with marriage and reproduction, the generation of the human homunculus among them. A quaint dance becomes assault when a homunculus appears on the stage at the outset, "with propeller-like wings . . . like a blue bottle or a striped wasp". Presumably the longed-for foetal outcome of the fecund maiden's anticipated marriage, this nascent being enacts "the motion of quadrille", which Loy compares to the movements of the common housefly and considers "one of the finest rhythms observable" (*SE* 151). The carrion-eating fly is for Loy a life-long affirmation of the rudiments of existence, our sentience.[51] Loy's readers have witnessed this veneration of entomological quadrille before:

Leading astray
Of fireflies
Aerial quadrille
Bouncing
Off one another
Again conjoining
In recaptured pulses
Of light (*LoLB* 61)

A dance of violence and love, quadrille originated in Europe as a display of skilful might in equestrian competitions or military parades; by the eighteenth century, it was popularised as a set dance involving four couples. Elegant flies are consistent with Loy's high estimate of abjection, a revaluation furthered in a scene in her ballet where the youth is propositioned by "crass glass colored light ladies" who conduct "the insect quadrille – exactly as [Loy has] observed it outside a shady hotel in Paris" (*SE* 156). Hardly a skilled, formal interaction, this quadrille embodies the rhythms of street trade, prostitution, a subject to which we will return in the next chapter, and yet another means by which, as Loy recognises, women are co-opted by the sentimental fiction of fidelity. By juxtaposing the "Crystal Pantomime" homunculus with prostitutes and insects, Loy reduces the fully formed, miniature version of the male parent that, since Aristotle, it has been believed that the foetus will become, to a social irritant whose power is limited and limiting.[52] Resisting the presumption that offspring inherit nothing from the Aristotelian fallow ground that is the mother, Loy cedes the homunculus persistence and grace, then pronounces it negligible: as the maiden peers determinedly, her crystal ball expands to encompass the stage entire, and the subsequent demise of homunculus is marginal, parenthetical: "(the homunculus disappears)" (*SE* 152). Homunculus is derisorily overtaken by world-making crystal ball; in turn, ball tells the story of the maiden's future, itself overtaken by that of the youth. Over-determined, Loy's stage is continually defined by conflict between the raw, ugly propaganda of the sex war and the consoling, smothering currencies of heteronormative sentimentality.

A proper fairy prince, our youth enjoys a fantastic sexual adventure, certain that he will find a virgin ready for the taking when the time comes. And just before he does, Loy assesses the value virginity retains in this saccharine, enchanted world. Having been whisked to a moonlit wood by Venus, the goddess of love, the youth nearly stumbles over "a clump of white thorn bushes", where he discovers a fairy ring comprised of "a group of exquisite marionettes [that] dance beside a black glass pool surrounded by very luminous arum lilies". Hawthorn symbolises purity and marriage; arum or calla lilies combine virginity and desirability. Legend has it that Venus was so incensed by the beauty of the lily that she gave it a protracting, phallic pistil to diminish its radiance. In "Crystal Pantomime", the sight of these wantonly pure flowers prompts the youth's movement, alongside a dryad, in a reverential "slow dance of admiration" (*SE* 159). Earlier in the ballet, the youth's extensive sowing of wild oats was catalysed by a distinctly Surrealist "large, lashy, luminous eye" winking at him from the darkness of the stage; now, prompted by "luminous" lilies, virginity is briefly honoured (*SE* 156). This scene in the woods, replete with fairy marionettes, resonates with Loy's "Magasins du Louvre" (1914), a poem in which dolls and maidens stare each other down in a shop, prompting the refrain: "All the virgin eyes in the world are made of glass" (*LoLB* 17–18). In Loy's ballet, marionettes dance among unsullied foliage around a dark glass pool that is as ominous as the all-seeing glass eyes of Loy's virginal dolls. "They alone have the effrontery to / Stare through the human soul / Seeing nothing" (*LoLB* 17; see also *LoLB* 64). Again, the reader witnesses Loy anticipate Bataille, whose ideal sentience is a thinking that "pursues its operation to the point where its object dissolves into NOTHING, because, ceasing to be useful, or subordinate, it becomes *sovereign* in ceasing to be" (*AS3* 204). This is a nothing that bespeaks felt autonomy, that makes sense of the irrationality of sacrificial desire, its insistence that destruction can exceed calculable gain. Writing "Crystal Pantomime" more than two decades after "Magasins du Louvre", in her ballet, Loy continues reducing virginal machinations to a puppetry that is equal farce, equal exposé.

The youth's experience within the glade of purity, and his idealisation of this virgin terrain, does not prompt a conversion: for him, yet another sexual entanglement ensues. It does, however, signal the sacrificial return of the maiden, resplendently aloft on the "towering column of narrow glass steps" that is her altar, temple, or pyre (*SE* 160). On either side of the maiden hang the sun and moon respectively, suggesting her proximity to the gods and the limitless temporality of impending death. Emphasising the maiden's virginity, "[t]he scene is terrifically cold and pure in line and whiteness". "[R]ound her feet curves the first curve of a dragon, with flames—tiny flames—darting from its tongue". Maintaining chivalric illusions, the youth attacks, sporting "an enormous yellow gilt shield, sword, helmet and winged sandals like Mercury", or the god of commerce, thievery, gambling, and communication with the divine (*SE* 160). Our maiden is a commodity the youth is prepared to claim for his own. Loy's attentiveness to the complicity cementing the maiden's fate is curiously complicated by modernist aesthetics:

> At last [the youth] strikes the dragon— The pinnacle of stairs falls apart—giving an amusing cubistic pattern of white oblongs in the air at different angles to each other between the falling-apart blocks. The maiden descends, floatingly, to earth while the dragon falls apart to reveal nothing but the maiden's mother holding up her lorgnette— The maiden flies into the youth's arms—and after embraces he takes her blue ribbon out of his pocket— The scene fades. (*SE* 160)

Loy considers Cubist art a "clairvoyance" that has much to tell us about the paths and "travel of our being alive" (*CP* 20: 11).

Cubist in form, the destruction in "Crystal Pantomime" echoes Loy's fascination with the term *casser*, or French for "to break", that is embedded in Picasso's name (*SE* 230). Cubism, then, is prescient and revolutionary, and in "Crystal Pantomime" its incursion brings to a close the medieval scene of dragon, pyre, and available maiden. Yet the dragon is a nesting doll containing yet another mythical beast, the monster that is the mother.

In one of her romans à clef, Loy intones: "According to the etiquette of mythology, the will must encounter a dragon", noting that in the "toy-like stage" of childhood, the parental "counter-will" fulfils this purpose (*CP* 13: 29). For Loy's balletic maiden, the mother remains the simultaneous source of protection and betrayal. This ambivalence is echoed by her attire: this mother carries an old-fashioned lorgnette – a noun infused with the French verb *lorgner*, or "to cast sidelong glances" – even as she wears a daringly front-less skirt and a pork-pie hat, a millinery style popularised in the 1930s.[53] Her garb is as ambivalently old- and new-fashioned as the ballet itself, one replete with magic lanterns and Surrealist eyes, quadrille, and Nijinsky's *The Spirit of the Rose*, a fairy tale first performed in 1911 and imbued with a New Woman scepticism toward matrimonial tradition, particularly monogamy.[54] And so it is that the fierce, protective dragon-mother approves a marriage that sees her daughter, all-too-tellingly, embark on a honeymoon on "a white china horse which gallops but never moves", an emphatically static start to a journey into shared adulthood (*SE* 160). The ballet concludes with "a crystalline baby tumbling over and over itself swiftly out of the sky, while the blue ribbon, in momentous curves, with, as in old story books, 'The End' written upon it, rises up to receive the baby as it falls" (*SE* 161). Though the maiden's symbol is given the last word, the end in question is as much hers as ours; she will embark on a lifetime of servitude to a privileged man, the the traditional "ever-after" that fairy tales always elide. That said, we are still looking into a crystal ball at the end of this draft of "Crystal Pantomime"; sentimental and sacrificial, Loy's prophecy remains a self-conscious fiction.

In this fictive vein, we can't forget the maiden's ability to "descen[d], floatingly, to earth", a super-human capacity vertiginously echoed by her tumbling, bathetic baby, and one foreshadowed by "a large wicker perambulator" ineffectually "showered" upon a struggling family by "some goddess" in one of Loy's early prose pieces (*LaLB* 82). Women, children, and baby accessories thus fall magnificently to their respective fates. But while insisting on the spectacle of this sentimental production, Loy presents it as troubling. In *Insel*, the novel she wrote in the 1930s alongside "Crystal Pantomime", Loy's protagonist Mrs Jones speaks to the titular protagonist about composing a ballet. As the studio where they sit flickers with light, Jones fixates on her translucent sets and other prospective staging difficulties:

> 'It is the story of a maiden seeing her life in a crystal— .... Yet as in the days when there were maidens they had no 'life,' what she sees is her future spouse sowing his 'wild oats.'
>
> 'All dancers are terribly ponderable after Nijinsky—yet once I came across one who possessed a dual *equipoise* which threw him into a huddle with himself. That is how my youth would dance, with the wild oats springing up to the moon around him, whichever way he turned— But I should have to do maquettes—animated maquettes of the choreography—and *I* can't make *anything* grow out of the floor,' I said deferentially.
>
> 'Of course he makes love to everything. A cocotte's eye. The woman in the litmus petticoat forecasting the weather. A rainbow,' I continued, seeing Insel entranced ....
>
> 'Always at the crucial moment the youth is intercepted. There comes floating in between him and the object of his concupiscence, a—' I stopped, as Insel, seemingly relieved by the frustration of a rival, closed his eyes, and waited till he came to. 'Over and again I drop the idea in despair. Over and over again I find a solution so simple it constantly slips my mind. I have only to make some little people about five inches high and tell them what to dance.' Insel nodded comprehendingly. 'Yet whenever I get to work I come upon some fundamental obstacle. It takes me *hours*,' I complained to Insel, 'to remember it cannot be done.' (*I* 84–5)

Jones elicits envy in the heart of her listener, or the quasi-Surrealist, emaciated, toothless Insel, who longs to be the protagonist of a ballet about a young man sowing wild oats (""I dance divinely"", he comically coaxes Jones [85]). But read straight, this sentimental ballet cannot be brought to fruition: though pleasingly romantic, it is so mired in fairyland that it resists becoming even a performable fiction. Striving for nothing but artifice, Jones is resisted by her own over-wrought sentimental souvenirs. The very scenes Jones acknowledges as impossible – the wild oats springing from the floor, the fairy ring (led by their queen, mounted on a reined tiger) – remain in the text of "Crystal Pantomime".

The typescript is full of Loy's attempts at realistic plausibility: the wires of the fairy ring, she writes, "can be manipulated by a sitting figure" (*SE* 159). Plans surface for streams of "water" that run from mermaids onto the youth (strings of transparent sequins), as do practical means of making fishy mermaids dance (doubled tails). A crossed-out portion at the typescript end envisions a balloon seller chased by a child hovering on a wire, figures necessarily stiff "like the ones in 'Cartesian' bottles", as if Loy's crystal ball set might be filled with water, the dancers offered as proof of the principle of buoyancy (*SE* 359). But other improbabilities – growing oats, cubistically disintegrating sets, floating maidens – are left with their pragmatics undescribed. The ballet script is edited, typed, clean, polished, and worked over; it deliberately remains a curious mixture of fantasy and dispassionate intervention, cloying affectivity and unabashed aggression. But in juxtaposing the maiden's imminent virginal sacrifice with her ambivalent "rescue", Loy places the struggle between sex war and sentimental norms in the hands of the viewer, who is encouraged to enjoy the romantic sport that leads to a relentlessly immolated life, even as the hyperbolic symbolism of the very props, sets, and machinations of "Crystal Pantomime" interrogate those assumptions apace. As Judith Roof acknowledges, we might like to believe that gender is a self-conscious, autonomously driven performance, but "[o]ur ideas of subjective choice . . . are alibis for the ways individual dispositions [are] part of the systematic operation, determining and determined by complex sets of interrelations that flow through and beyond will and consciousness, but where will and consciousness (such as they are) are parts of the system" (26–7). Loy remains perpetually fascinated by these sentient, individual responses that elude yet importantly define analysis, critique, and replication.

For the reader or viewer, the fascination of "Crystal Pantomime", as elsewhere in Loy's writing, lies in its genuine struggle to jettison typical feminine desirability and the happiest of heteronormative endings, where pretty blue ribbons offer ready safety nets that inevitably ensnare. "'It takes me *hours*,' [Jones] complained to Insel, 'to remember it cannot be done.'" Loy's relationship with the sentimental is not always the "ironic appreciation" ascribed to Joyce in the wonderfully syrupy "Nausicaa" episode of *Ulysses* (Bell 161). Loy's appreciation can be embattled and vicious; it can also be surprisingly sincere. Loy considered her wedding to Arthur Cravan the culmination of "the formal dream of my life, a marriage of love" ("Colossus" 118). In a draft of this text, before "formal" Loy wrote, then pencilled out, "conventional"; her traditionalism troubles, exposes an anxiety about the truth that, by convention, "marital debts are reckoned in female flesh" (*EP* 25; Rubin, "Traffic" 182).[55] Loy is well aware, as she articulates elsewhere, that marriage can be a moralising, paternalistic imposition.[56] But her autobiographical statement bears repeating: the constitutive essence, the foremost goal of Loy's sentient existence was love recognised and sanctified by ritual. (So too, it has been argued, at the heart of Bataille's work, lies "a longing for union" [Traylor 151]).

In Loy's late, undated poem "There is No Love Alone", love is shiny, valuable, and ecstatic. "[L]ove is not of the body", asserts Loy, "love is of bodies" (*LaLB* 233). As ever where Loy's Eros is concerned, these bodies are sentient, material, intimate, and rhythmically attuned to an esoteric "cosmic duet" (*LaLB* 233). And yet, Loy prided herself on having found a partner she likened, rapturously and mockingly, to a backward dullard, an effeminate outsider who insisted that love be a "constant carnival" ("Colossus" 118; Rose 131). In other words, Loy's atavistic proclivities extend from art to life and back again, fulfilling the avant-garde dream to conflate the prosaic and the aesthetic by way of circumventing art as alienated institution. "His companionship", Loy rather placidly sums up, "was at times an antagonism, his consciousness pulling away from me, 'the mistress presumptive'" ("Colossus" 112). But this enmity is constitutive, consoling: in her early draft novel *Brontolivido*, Loy has her female protagonist say to a male lover: "'I respect you – because I recognise in you an enemy worth understanding'" (*B* 5: 3). The poems, fictions, and autobiographical writings that follow this novel speak to Loy's perpetual struggle to maintain a Nijinksy-like *equipoise* between sentiment and satire, shuttlecocks and battledores. On its own, sentiment is for Loy unperformable, unrealisable, and impossibly fundamental. Conscious, wilful violence animates it; pink-love needs its blood-red battlefields, its attentiveness to the excesses and proximities of sacrifice. But exposing the social complicity in the immolation of femininity – the martyrdoms and resurrections Christly or classical, the ritualised murders literal or figurative – is fundamental to the satire that results from this conflict: this exposure is assertive, unceasing, and on occasion, self-accusatory. Nevertheless, bound maidens invariably invoke Loy's scabrous, sidelong glances. And in Loy's writing, linguistic intimacies and assaults combine with affective and intellectual drives that aim for Loy's version of the modernist epiphany, or the "flash of attainment to infinite sentience" (*SE* 250). Bodies collide to stay aloft. Shuttle-cock, battle-dore.

Notes

1. I refer here to seminal works of modernist criticism that defined the period through a Poundian lens, most tellingly Hugh Kenner's *The Pound Era* (1971).
2. Another source preceding and possibly influencing Wilde is Sir Leslie Stephens's *English Thought in the Eighteenth Century* (1881), where sentimentalism is "'the name of the mood in which we make a luxury of grief'" (qtd. in Todd 7). That said, the origin may appear still earlier: in Thomas More's *Olla Podrida* (1787), only men with large estates are given permission to weep (Todd 13).
3. Stein similarly equates sentimentality and outmoded British literature throughout her 1935 essay, "What is English Literature".
4. In relation to one of Marinetti's sojourns to London to promote Futurism, Loy effeminises him again, describing his "[b]oasting of a fantastically inflated conquest of [the city] – his eyes bleeding sentiment" (*B* 5: 6). Marinetti lectured in London in 1910, 1912, 1913, and 1914; while the last series failed spectacularly, he claimed every tour as a Futurist victory (see Rainey). Loy's description suggests that Marinetti's body betrays an unresolved internal conflict between vanguard bravado and the requisites of lived, and in this case, staunchly repressed, feeling.
5. So overwhelming is Marinetti's need for compassion that when he finally acknowledges the painful truth of his deep feelings for Loy, she remains unconvinced. Her earned suspicion outrages Marinetti, who exclaims: "*Per Dio*, she calls me theatrical when I'm suffering the abject tortures of sincerity!" (*B* 2: 29).
6. For one among innumerable examples, see Marinetti and Christopher Nevinson's jointly authored manifesto, "Futurism and English Art" (1914), which rails against the soft, sickly, feminised, conservatism of Wilde and England, favouring in their stead strength, virility, and sport: in short, "a powerful advance guard" (197).
7. In the unpaginated manuscript "Promised Land" (1937), Loy similarly, uncomfortably identifies one woman's need to associate with "wealthy jews who were to afford her a haven in lush sentimentality".
8. Michael Bell echoes Clark's thinking, stating: "the attack on sentiment is deceptive. Remembering that the original meaning of sentiment was not simply feeling, but feeling justified by a moral idea, then modern ideological passion is actually the truest avatar of moral sentimentalism" (165).
9. Among Berlant's foci are the Hollywood movie-musical *Show Boat* (1927/51), and popular writers Dorothy Parker and Fay Weldon. Perhaps because she is working against male vanguardists, or the most emphatic denunciators of sentiment, Clark similarly attends to

well-known female writers or activists, including Edna St. Vincent Millay, Alice Walker, and Emma Goldman. Experimentalists who propound sentiment are mentioned only in passing: Clark's list in this vein includes Loy, Gertrude Stein, and Djuna Barnes (38).

10. On the fundamental relationship between sacrifice and financial exchange, Loy's contemporary Georg Simmel writes: "the economic system of the world is assuredly founded upon an abstraction, that is, upon the relation of reciprocity and exchange, the balance between sacrifice and gain" ("Chapter" 580). For Simmel, this macro-economic truth is sourced in the microcosm of the self, where "the give and take between sacrifice and accomplishment, within the individual, is the basal presumption, and at the same time the persistent substance, of every two-sided exchange" ("Chapter" 583; see also Mizruchi on capitalism and sacrifice, 26–7).

11. In relation to the 1853–6 Crimean War, Jan-Melissa Schramm writes:

    > Self-sacrifice was seen as crucial to public discourse in this period, both of individual male soldiers, who were willing to die 'on behalf of' those at home, and of women who, like Florence Nightingale, felt called by God to 'embody' Christian charity and nurse the fever-ravaged troops abroad at considerable risk to themselves. (3)

    Against Schramm's lineage, Hughes insists that World War I was the first in which the soldier was pervasively considered a sacrificial victim (218).

12. Cinzia Sartini Blum writes: "The role of women in the [Futurist] manifestos is comparable to that of the scapegoat in ancient myths and rituals: the scapegoat becomes the repository of all the effects of sacrificial crisis, which can thus be represented in a reassuring version and exorcised" (37). In *The Gender of Modernity*, Rita Felski argues that woman "functions as a sacrificial victim exemplifying the losses which underpin the ambiguous, but ultimately exhilarating and seductive logic of the modern" (2). In sum, modern innovation remains wholly reliant on the archaism that women sacrifice themselves and are sacrificed in turn.

13. So thoroughly immured is existence within the void at the heart of sacrifice that, for Nancy, it ultimately becomes "unsacrificeable" (37).

14. On occasion, Bataille comes tantalisingly close to recognising the harms and complicities of a gendered double standard. Consider, from *The Tears of Eros* (1961), his claim that human sexuality "went astray" between prehistory and antiquity – an era identifiable as the fomenting of patriarchal culture – because of the development of war and slavery (59). Noting that, as ancient civilisations developed, marriage secured a place for procreation, Bataille argues that "[t]his place was rendered all the more difficult in that from the beginning the freedom enjoyed by males tended to let them stray from the house" (60). For Bataille, "Today, even now, humanity has hardly got out of

this rut" (60). The rut is the failure of a more ecstatic, liberated sexuality; the cause is civilisation *tout court*. Throughout, patriarchy writ large goes unnamed.

15. Girard acknowledges that women are objects of exchange in kinship negotiations, and critiques the gendered implications of transferring the blame for social violence onto women via menstrual taboos; furthermore, he resists the Oedipal mythology whereby male interactions alone are rooted in violence (281, 318–20, 39, 53).

16. I refer to Lawrence's "The Woman Who Rode Away", a short story published in *The Dial* in 1925, and his novel *The Plumed Serpent* (1926). Eliot's play *The Cocktail Party* was first performed in 1949.

17. On further links between Loy and Irigaray, see Roberts on their mutual engagement in a critique of misogynist discourse (139) and Hilda Bronstein, who relates Loy's marginal vanguard positionality to Irigaray's call for a different mode of hearing to grasp the female voice.

18. Less critical than Irigaray, and nowhere near as feminist, Bataille to some degree concurs, pointing to childbirth as "a rending process", a sacrifice that denies established order, yet nevertheless continually feeds the "transition from nothingness to being, being to nothingness" (*E* 55).

19. Loy continues: "The child <u>belongs</u> to its own generation – and will only think what an ass you were!" (Letter dated 7 January 1928, Loy to Julien and Joella Levy, Box 30, Folder 8, 1928).

20. Irigaray proposes an improved "economy of consciousness" against the still-accepted contemporary sacrifice of women who retain the status of the "'primitiv[e]'" (*Sexes* 88).

21. Loy's complete quotation reads as follows: "These things are difficult for such as do not read the smart set to understand" (*SE* 49). An early twentieth-century American literary periodical, *The Smart Set* was subtitled "A Magazine of Cleverness" and published leading authors of the day, among them Joyce and Pound. Loy's satire is directed at her reader, who is almost irrefutably a member of the journal's target audience, and at the political limitations and snobberies of the cultural elite, who disdain the behaviour she describes as if they do not perpetuate it.

22. In the original, "fetishes" reads "fetishes" (*EP* 24).

23. Seidel alludes to this link between sacrifice and satire, arguing that "Girard holds that what was once unthinkable becomes, after a fashion, legal. The satirist maintains that what is represented as legal is really unthinkable" (22). By extension, the satirist returns us to the sacrifier: both openly acknowledge the accepted pervasiveness of violence.

24. Replete as it is with palpably aggressive sexual desire, this goal sets Loy apart from her peers. Olive Schreiner, for instance, believes that we can and ideally should evolve away from the need for sacrifice, yet considers the movement from barbarousness to civilisation

contingent upon men taking up the burden of conscious self-sacrifice (264, 234).

25. Contrary to my own assessment of *Discourse Concerning Satire*, Melinda Alliker Rabb argues that Dryden's "answers to th[e] questions" of what constitutes satire "peremptorily brush women aside" (117). Alliker Rabb details feminist readings that locate a phallic female and/or homosocial desire in Dryden's essay.

26. Rawson credits the rise of progressive, revolutionary, and liberalising rhetoric at the end of the eighteenth century with satirical demise ("Introduction" viii). P. K. Elkin's work similarly links the loss of European male privilege with the erasure of satire, equating twentieth-century celebrants of that privilege – Wyndham Lewis, Roy Campbell – with the maintenance of a true satiric legacy (1973). Critics discussed further below implicitly agree with these conservative, masculinist readings of the genre.

27. I draw here from my reading of Montagu's *Essays and Poems and Simplicity, a Comedy* and *Romance Writings*.

28. As the work of Gary Dyer, Marylin Butler, and Barbara Everett attests, ample evidence exists that satire remained a prevalent genre through the first half of the nineteenth century and beyond.

29. For examples of this argument, see Rawson, "Introduction" ix; Everett 242; Quintero 220; Engell 233; and Steele 434–45.

30. Of the eleven authors this strong text considers, only two are women; furthermore, Greenberg's identification of a female satirical voice, rather than methodology, teeters uncomfortably on essentialism.

31. Pound's assertion that Loy's writing embodies "logopoeia" or "a dance of the intelligence among words and ideas" is often cited in Loy studies. Rarely does any critic quote the sentence that follows: "Pope and the eighteenth-century writers had in this medium a limited range" ("'Others'" 57). Dunn also aligns Loy with the long eighteenth-century satiric tradition, likening "Anglo-Mongrels and the Rose" to Carlyle's 1833–4 *Sartor Resartus* (102).

    Loy references Swift's *Gulliver's Travels* in "Crab Angel" (1923), a poem about a circus performer she dubs "Helen of Lilliput" (*LoLB* 86). In *Insel*, Loy refers to her protagonist's tendency to speak in a manner that combines John Gay's 1728 satirical "*Beggar's Opera* and oratorio" (48). There is a discernible Swiftian influence in Loy's dialogic satires, a category that includes Futurist spoofs such as "The Sacred Prostitute" and, still more particularly, the undated "Lady Asterisk.", which pretends at high-society niceties whilst lampooning the same, thereby echoing Swift's wonderfully titled *A Compleat Collection of Genteel and Ingenious Conversation, According to the most polite Mode and Method, now used at Court, and in the best Companies of England* (1738).

32. Kenneth Fields echoes Gunn in this regard, writing that, at her best, Loy holds aloft the hard-boiled and the clichéd with exceptional

equipoise: "Frequently with great brevity, she handles many of the sentimental stereotypes which had been too easily accepted for some time" (604, 599).

33. As evidence, Scuriatti draws on Loy criticism undertaken by Marjorie Perloff ("English as a 'Second' Language"), Cristanne Miller (*Cultures of Modernism*), and Matthew Hart (*Nations of Nothing but Poetry*).

34. Loy consistently associates the ecstatic with the orgasmic. But her stark categorisation as an erotic female poet may betray our preoccupations as critics. In theorising a multifaceted Eros, Loy challenges "modern assumptions about the centrality of sexual desire to all human contact and feeling" (Kosofsky Sedgwick, *Touching* 17). This challenge is one half of my own critique of human longing in *Prosaic Desires: Modernist Knowledge, Boredom, Laughter, and Anticipation* (2010), which examines modernist literature and philosophy with a view to nuancing human desire by theorising longings beyond entrenched, dominant preoccupations with sexuality and power.

35. Later in the same essay, Loy speaks of Stein's "projection of the intellect into the intimacy of the inanimate" (*LaLB* 296).

36. Lacan discusses "extimacy" in seminar 9, where it is defined not as the opposite of intimacy, but as the possibly unconscious difficulty of accepting otherness when in direct proximity to one's neighbour (see J. Miller).

37. Reverberations of the bleak parody that is "The Dead" recur in "Der Blinde Junge" (1923), where Loy describes the fallen youth of war as "'Kriegsopfer,' a German term combining the word for war (*das Krieg*) with the word for offering or sacrifice (*das Opfer*)" (Prescott 156).

38. On 16 May 1951, Loy writes her daughter Joella about locating "the most doleful creature in the world" on the Bowery streets. But when offered payment to sit for Loy, the man in question becomes "the most happily twinkling human one could imagine!" "So there for the moment goes my Bowery crucifixion", Loy states resignedly ("Loy, Mina to Joella Bayer").

39. In her dissertation, Tamara Beauchamp argues convincingly for a direct line of influence between Durkheim's notion of "collective consciousness" and Loy's 1918 manifesto "International Psycho-Democracy" (265).

40. "The Revolution in Revelation" is part of the archival folder "Notes on Metaphysics" that Sandeep Parmar "dat[es] from the late 1920s to the 1940s" ("'Unfinishing'" 72). Unlike the disparate work the folder contains, this three-page commentary on religion, evolution, and contemporary culture is titled and neatly written, if largely unedited.

41. Thomas refuses to believe in Christ's resurrection and ascension into heaven until he has placed his finger in the stigmata, or the wounds caused by the nails driven through Jesus's hands during crucifixion; he is encouraged to do precisely this when Jesus appears among the disciples eight days after his death (John 20.24–9).

42. See also "'Cosmic Force': Vitalism", the concluding section of Chapter 1. In brief, in the closing lines of "Parturition", crucified woman takes her place next to God: "—Man and woman God made them— / Thank God" (*LoLB* 8). As Joshua Schuster argues, this figuration puts man at one remove, while reproductive woman is seated at God's side, Messianic at last, both absurdly and "sublimely" (Schuster 130).

43. Connectedly, but far more drastically, Loy extends this metaphor of woman reborn by *petite mort* to the sacrificial victims of pogroms, whose mass martyrdom she strives to resurrect in "Photo after Pogrom" (1961), writing: "Corpses are virgin" (*LoLB* 122).

44. The much-discussed first poem of "Songs" replicates Loy's motif whereby sexual liaisons generate purity. Beginning with a visceral sowing of "wild oats", Loy then moves to the speaker's commitment to living in a lantern, "Trimming subliminal flicker / Virginal   to the bellows / Of Experience" (*LoLB* 53). Her reference is to the parable of the wise and foolish virgins, by which Jesus's followers are taught readiness for the Day of Judgement, when they will be reunited with their virtuous saviour (Matt. 25.1–13). In this tale, virgins, the resurrected dead, and Christ are cyphers for a chasteness that is extended to the otherwise wanton speaker of Loy's poem. For Christians, Jesus's "essential virginity" is only strengthened by the sacrifice that marks his marriage to the people of God, the believers sanctified by his resurrection.

45. I discuss this link between the "Feminist Manifesto", anatomy, and Loy's Jewish heritage at greater length in "Feminism's Archives: Mina Loy, Anna Mendelssohn, and Taxonomy" (251–4).

46. In addition to Loy's "Aid of the Madonna", Mary appears in "The Costa San Giorgio", which Tara Prescott interprets as a parody of the "Hail Mary" prayer. Rather than asking Mary to "'forgive us our trespasses'", Loy implores her to "'preserve . . . mistresses'" from perceiving the woebegone truths of their male lovers. Prescott also considers "The Black Virginity" (1918) Loy's homage to a Madonna statuette Loy sent Gertrude Stein (25).

47. In this regard, see Burstein 156; Prescott 22–3; and Hayden 73–91.

48. The source for the scratching virgin may arise in *Brontolivido* (c. 1913–20), where Loy describes a fight between two teenagers for F. T. Marinetti's affections. Marinetti reads love letters aloud at a public gathering, presumably from one individual of this pair, who then finds her face gouged by the other girl. Denouncing his performance as "'bad form'", Loy wonders how "'a man can love the sort of women who scratch'"; Marinetti claims that the 15- or 16-year-old's behaviour was beyond her control due to "'the intensity of irritation'" at stake (*B* 2: 8).

49. The equation of soldier with sacrificial maiden is sourced in antiquity and continues (Roselli 142).

50. This quotation surfaces in Loy's *Brontolivido*, where the female protagonist awaits a lover and endeavours to lend appeal to her meagre domicile. In a 1917 interview for the New York *Evening Sun*, Loy asserts that becoming "'modern'" involves being "'very frank with yourself and [not] mind[ing] how ridiculous anything that comes to you may seem'" (*BM* 8–9). In that same year, Loy will describe "Art" as "*The Divine Joke*" (*LaLB* 285).

51. Loy's relationship to the fly is discussed in Chapter 1, "'Being Alive': Sentience".

52. Teresa Brennan and Elizabeth Grosz discuss the persistence of Aristotle's misogynistic reproductive theory (Brennan 89–90; Grosz, *Volatile* 206). For Grosz, contemporary men continue to "regar[d] their sexual organs on the model of the homunculus, a little man within the man, with a quasi-autonomy of its own" (*Volatile* 200).

53. Tim Armstrong writes about how, at the outset of the twentieth century, independent women like Loy sought to "assert their distance from the moral purity of the Victorian mother . . . the *bête noire* of Modernism" (126). In like spirit, Susan Rubin Suleiman's *Subversive Intent: Gender, Politics, and the Avant-Garde* (1990) argues that avant-gardism developed over the prone bodies of women, particularly mothers.

54. *La Spectre de la rose* clearly influenced Loy's "Crystal Pantomime": it features a young girl who attends a ball, returns home with a rose, and is visited in her bedroom by the rose's spirit, first danced by Nijinsky. Souvenir sentiment and romance grace this ballet as they do Loy's, even as *La Spectre de la rose* was renowned for a simplicity evidently lacking in Loy's interrogative, satirical, and complexly performed rereading of its nostalgic themes.

55. As Gayle Rubin discusses, the kinship systems at work in society since Palaeolithic times have reinforced a division of labour that emphasises the difference between male and female whilst presenting women as objects of exchange. For Rubin: "If biological and hormonal imperatives were as overwhelming as popular mythology would have them, it would hardly be necessary to insure heterosexual unions by means of economic interdependency" ("Traffic" 180). In turn, economic interdependency is reinforced by the social, religious, and legal strictures of the formal marriage Loy idealises.

56. In "Notes on Religion" Loy elliptically but also doggedly argues against a controlling, capricious Christian moral order, noting that, when it occurs, virtuousness is erratic, eluding system, and that under this religious regime, "Marriage is the arduous maximum of 'unity' imposed by the ironical levity of the moralist upon rudimentary beings" (15).

Part II

Chapter 3

Feet, Legs, Genitals: The Pornographies of Loy's Punctuation

> While the sphinx retains her secret, who shall reveal the unconsummated significance of the asterisk—
>
> Notwithstanding that the secret of the sphinx is not conveyed in words—the asterisk is an assumption that the secret is possessed by each of us and therefore need never be mentioned—
>
> the asterisk is the signal of a treasure which is not there. (*SE* 253)

Radiating a mysterious propriety, Loy's asterisk is a sign untouched and ambivalent, censorious and explicit. Over-valued, Loy tells us, the asterisk is a commonplace, an empty cypher. Yet still it divaricates, demands attention. Asterisks are deictic connectives, *signes de renvoi*, diminutively pointing beyond the main event to its margins; asterisks mark omissions and emissions, divisions and redactions; they boss, interrupt, belittle their audience.[1] I will "perform childishly", asserts the satirist Kurt Vonnegut, drawing an asterisk in felt-tip pen as evidence of his immaturity (Fig. 3.1). Noting its likeness to our rearward orifice, Vonnegut justifies this rendering as a means of "clear[ing] his head of all the junk in there—the assholes, the flags, the underpants" (5). Rectums, star-spangled banners, genital coverings; Vonnegut takes pleasure in rubbing our noses in the workings of the asterisk, incorporating the private and patriotic in his gleeful return to the child's anal phase.[2] Loy chastises two male contemporaries with a like retentiveness, albeit more fulsomely eroticised: John S. Sumner, Executive Secretary of the New York Society for the Prevention of Vice from 1915 to 1950, and Owen Reed Smoot, Utah senator from 1903 to 1933 and infamous censorship campaigner. For Loy, Sumner and Smoot are "[t]he worst kind of sex

Fig. 3.1 Asterisk, Kurt Vonnegut, *Breakfast of Champions* (1973).

maniac": overwhelmed by "canine affinities—they can only sustain their sexual potentiality by sticking their noses into their neighbour's ———" (*SE* 225). Concealment reveals, as Loy illustrates; it is as public as flags that stand for governance and law, as public as dogs unabashedly examining each other's rear passages. "There is no secret to be kept when 'all' are in the secret", Loy reasonably maintains; why censor what everyone already knows (*SE* 225)?

What do we all come to know indefatigably? Of a heteronormativity that aspires to "[t]he normal sexual aim . . . the union of the genitals in the act known as copulation, which leads to a release of the sexual tension and a temporary extinction of the sexual instinct—a satisfaction analogous to the sating of hunger" (Freud, "Three Essays" 149). "A coitus in the normal position" is neither from nor within the behind (Freud, "Infantile Neurosis" 45). Post-Enlightenment, Caucasian women were said to lack "carnality" and its aggressive passions, and Freud's heteronormative sexuality affirms their passivity, objectification, and dissatisfaction (Bland 49, 52). At the turn of the twentieth century, women remained unable to locate the source of their pleasure: "'in their ignorance of anatomy, women often look upon the vagina and womb as part of the bowel and its exit of discharge'", confusing urethra with the vagina, "'vulva with the anus'" (Ellis, *Studies* I 52–3). Herself a censored articulator of women's sexual desire, it is not "pornographic literature, distributed under the rose" – privately, confidentially – to which Loy objects.[3] Instead, "it is" the fact that "that very pornographic literature— . . . has exposed— / The secret—that the sphinx does not know her own secret—" (*SE* 253).

Where Wilde insists that women are sphinxes without secrets, Loy is concerned that women have no idea of what might constitute subjectivity beyond sentience, a selfhood conversant with satiation. Celebrated monumental mystery, the sphinx stands for the individual in pursuit of gratification in Loy as in Bataille, who worships this ancient hybrid monster – half woman, half lion – and longs to become her. "From time to time," writes Bataille, "a decisive passion, an accidental irruption: torpor follows, the immobility of the sphinx, deaf to every resolution, eyes empty, absorbed in its own enigma", replete "with animal wisdom … more capricious and sure of itself than any other" (G 12).[4] Loy's sphinx is more consciously capricious: a passive, long-silent venerator of "womanly modesty" and the "lo-o-o-vely!" romance of erotic modernist literature who remains painfully aware of her own unmet desires (*SE* 253–4). In the fragmented, parenthetical phrases of "Library", the sphinx "who never gave a sign" is marked by the asterisk, subtext on show (*SE* 254). For men, this subtext is scarcely submerged queer desire. For women, it is anatomical and mystical: in a mid-1930s roman à clef, Loy details the sphinx's secret at long last, a secret to which she begins referring in her writing in the 1910s. Women, Loy argues, treat orgasm as esoteric knowledge, "play[ing] the Sphynx" to satisfy male "concupiscence". For Loy, when women access sexual pleasure, they become adepts, attaining the elect stature of "the satisfied", aware at last of the secret their bodies possess, so long undiscussed, so perpetually and personally unrecognised (*CP* 18: 67). Few women attain this elevating carnal knowledge. Loy's asterisk, then, signifies a transcendental truth inseparable from an orgasmic physical pleasure, is a combining of spirit and soma central to Loy's esoteric Eros, the focus of the second volume of this *Anatomy of Mina Loy*. As site of sodomy or ecstatic gnosis, Loy's starry, anal punctuation reorients our attention away from Freud's "normal sexual aim", toward sexualities relegated to the margins.

Feminine or feminising, Loy's asterisks effect a queer challenge to paternalistic articulations of the sexual, as the first section of this chapter discusses more fully via a closer look at "The Library of the Sphinx." and associated writings. Loy's rendering of the asterisk echoes descriptions of punctuation as womanish, helpmeet, hysteric, or prude. Ellis, for instance, tells us that, along with the dash, the asterisk comes into its own in the eighteenth century, marking "a new ardour of modesty", a "sudden reticence", a "quality of literary prurience" (*Studies* I 65). Building upon conventions established in that century's literature of sensibility, Loy posits punctuation as a cartography of the feeling, longing, rhythmic body, its movements and transit. Defined by omission and tangential reference, Loy's "Lady Asterisk." *is* her radiant mark; likewise, Insel's "very personality take[s] the form of a question mark", as does the last remaining "scraped nerve" of Loy's father, a figure reduced to "an interrogation mark tied in a knot" (*I* 25; *IA* 68: 136). But punctuation is an ambivalent form, given to double meanings, as in the asterisk that censors and points to that most derided of human orifices, a queerness that sidesteps reproductivity and other worn and wearing narratives, among them the fallen woman or the self-effacing mother. Loy has long been recognised as a writer with a resolute incapacity "to rest satisfied", one who "bal[ks] before she utters" and seeks "a more provocative mark of position" (Wilkinson 162). Resistant to the closed, unbroken circumference of the full stop, Loy's defining marks, her hyperpunctuations, give voice to restlessly desirous bodies. The feminised body has a specific place in Loy's stigmeology: silenced, overlooked, forced into mute gesture, the female body moves furtively and speculatively, escaping or redrawing the well-worn routes of masculinist logos and legibility.

Loy's punctuation perforates male privilege, wanders wilfully, mapping the coordinates of the as-yet-unknown secret of the sphinx, as well as new desire lines. Emerging in the early twentieth century, "desire lines" is a phrase I borrow from designers and city planners that refers to anarchic trails of longing that are officially or systematically unrecognised. In Loy's hands, punctuated desire lines become counter to the constrained paths of the public female, historically conflated with the streetwalker. As the comma lies low upon and crosses the line, so will what follows interrogate base corporeality: significantly, toes, feet, legs, and genitals anatomise Loy's satiric, spatial, punctual interrogations of gendered desire. Uniquely deployed punctuation is Loy's graffitied signage; with it, she challenges dead-ended perceptions of women's sexuality, and particularly, the unsentimental economy of prostitution, one that near-comically, certainly ironically, brings to fruition the outdated, anti-emotive affective reckonings of the modernist avant-garde. Defence of the forced women is the foundation of Loy's feminism, as it was for so many women raised in the *fin-de-siècle*. But Loy differs from her peers in recognising that a sexual explicitness that includes the pornographic is not inherently oppositional to women's freedom. Instead, Loy promotes a non-censorious approach to sexual exploration and satiation, a wilfully open-ended wandering through the intimacies of self and other. As a direct consequence of this sex-positive militancy, Loy envisions a sexuality that is sacrificially risky and in turn, inevitably intimate, for men and women alike; her excessiveness exceeds utilitarian economies of financialised affect and proximity. Along the way, Loy posits her male modernist peers as flimsy, unwitting imitations of the ancient institution that is the sacred prostitute, caricaturing them as self-regarding, beatified gigolos. In turn, she delineates how, as things stand, we are all – regardless of sex or gender – fallen beings, teetering vertiginously upon the horizon line of being, porous marks in need of interpretation.

✱ : Queer Pleasures, Women's Pleasure

In the 1920s and 1930s, Loy embarks upon a series of essayistic, roughly drafted manuscript fragments discussing women's precarious, unsatisfying realisations of their sexuality and reproductivity in the context of legal and moral prohibition. Alongside "The Library of the Sphinx." – our focus in this section, and a work Loy began drafting alongside "Apology of Genius" (1922), her defence against the obscenity charges lobbed at Joyce's *Ulysses* – these writings include "Censor Morals Sex.", "Havelock Ellis", "Lady Asterisk.", and "My Catholick Confidante".[5] Implicitly, these writings address the after-effects of post-1850 censorious legislation triangulating obscene literature, sodomy, and prostitution.[6] Twice Loy calls upon the sexologist Havelock Ellis (1859–1939), whose multi-volume *Studies in the Psychology of Sex* (1897–1928) detailed sexual impulses in men and women; Ellis's *Sexual Inversion* (1897) was the first English medical textbook to treat homosexuality as neither crime nor disease (Bland 262). At the outset of "Library", Loy quotes Ellis's assertion that women resigned to dissatisfaction in marriage get "*'nothing'*" in return, a statement Loy evidently heard in person in 1920 (*SE* 235, 254).[7] The sphinx's library is filled with texts by authors censored for obscenity whose erotic proclivities have failed, in Loy's opinion, to include what remains the most illicit subject: "the disappointments of the hymen as an accepted fact". Rather than opening a conversation about this underdiscussed topic, self-styled vanguard modernists continue to capitulate to the status quo: "The primary phenomenon of our new 'liberated' literature—is the superiority complex of the male as regards his intimate relationship with the female." "Practically the whole of our psychological literature written by men might be lumped together as the unwitting analysis of the unsatisfied woman", Loy writes exasperatedly (*SE* 257). Redacting truths deemed obscene, asterisks expose truths in absentia. In "Library", Loy satirises her male peers as more interested in hindquarters than female satiation. Her mockery is interpretable as homophobic, a queering of her stoutly heteronormative peers that participates in and reinforces their sexual anxieties. But as readily, Loy's methods can be read as transgressive, a recognition of the shared stature of those who participate in non-reproductive sexual practices dubbed perverse, effeminately receptive, debasing, or enclosing. In this regard, the more asterisks, the better: in a letter written in 1928, Loy openly mocks a friend of hers for having a love life that "could be written with one asterisk" alone (Undated letter, Loy to Julien and Joella Levy, Box 30, Folder 8, 1928).

Importantly, the asterisk speaks to Loy's own self-censoriousness, as she discernibly struggles toward the very openness and female sexual recognition she advocates. Witness Loy's inability, in the first instance, to convey the whole truth of Italian Futurist F. T. Marinetti's public pronouncement of the integrality and decency of the word "vagina". In her *Brontolivido* (c. 1913–1920) manuscript, Loy writes: "<u>Woman</u> [Marinetti] blazed is a <u>wonderful</u> <u>animal</u> – & when I print any part of her body I choose – it is in purist appreciation – I do not admit – that I can write about a fondant which gives me some pleasure – & not about a vagina which gives me infinitely more" (*B* 7: 7). Referring to herself, Loy continues: "[H]e had said one word – utterly unaffectedly – & it had broken down the barriers of her subconscious reactions in prudery, that divided self-truthfulness from self-expression" (*B* 7: 8). And yet, when she initially puts pen to page, Loy reduces the liberating word in question to a pronoun that she only belatedly clarifies (Fig. 3.2). Although she ultimately redacts her censoriousness, Loy's manuscript text illustrates how psychosocial barriers take time and conscious effort to dismantle.

Loy does not shy away from ascribing a "vaginal clairvoyance" to women astute about the truth of their place in heterosexual

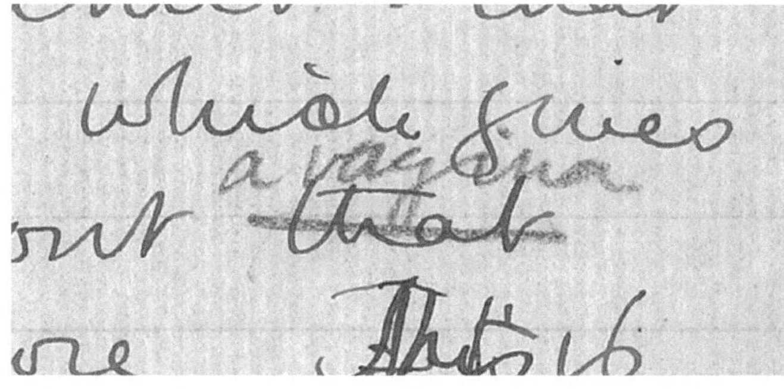

Fig. 3.2 Mina Loy, *Brontolivido* (c. 1913–20), manuscript details (7: 7). Mina Loy Papers. Yale Collection of American Literature, Beinecke Rare Book and Manuscript Library. Permission granted by Roger Conover.

intercourse: by this genital insight, women come to recognise that men have greater access to sexual pleasure than they do, are confirmed in their suspicion that women are objectified even in their most intimate relationships (*CP* 18: 65). Yet, in passages devoted to the articulation of female desire in her late künstler-romans, Loy is wont to discuss "the latent tactile impulses of a satin-lined Venusberg" rather than an aroused vagina (*CP* 17: 55). This inhibition extends to her correspondence: in a comical comment on a regretted misprint of the word "tuck" in a publication overseen by her son-in-law, Loy censors her short, explicit poem responding to his misfortune:

little duck
try your luck
at a s——

or a f——
with a buck
in the muck ——

(Undated letter, Loy to Julien and Joella Levy,
Box 30, Folder 10, 1930)

Similarly, in an interview given in her eighty-second year, Loy spoke proudly of her poetic reputation whilst confessing "I always feel I'm going to blush when I read my poems" ("Mina Loy: Interview" 214).[8] Two steps forward, one step back. Loy's is a complex reticence from which even the almighty Marinetti was evidently not immune: according to Loy, he was in possession of "his own little look of potted prudery" that arose alongside an unwillingness to voice aloud "blennorrhagia", a word referring to genital discharge usually caused by venereal disease (*B* 7: 11). By contrast, Arthur Cravan boasted to Loy that male youths in Paris equated manhood with an experience of "'blennorrhagia'"; admiring his resilience, Loy tells him that, in truth, she doubts he could calmly sustain any blemish on his "'alabaster flesh'" (*EP* 25). Ever aware of ruptured purity, Loy turns to the passive assertiveness of an asterisk that identifies without naming, that modestly refrains whilst acting as guiding star to Loy's excoriation of male modernist renderings of women's pleasure in "The Library of the Sphinx."

The Swiss psychiatrist Carl Jung considered the final episode of Joyce's *Ulysses* an unnervingly accurate portrayal of "'the real psychology of a woman'"; second-wave feminists denounced Joyce for equating women with the primitive and natural; Joyce himself argued that the "'greatest revolution in our time [is] the revolt of women against the idea that they are the mere instruments of men'" (qtd. in R. Ellmann 629; qtd. in R. Brown 94). Loy's "Library" recognises the importance of the "introspective finale" of *Ulysses* – the "Penelope" episode, or Molly Bloom's monologue – whilst reading it as a list of unslaked female desires. Central to this litany is Molly's reluctant yielding to cunnilingus in which Bloom "does it all wrong . . . thinking only of his own pleasure" yet is feebly excused because "his tongue is too flat" (*SE* 254; Joyce, *Ulysses* 919). According to Loy, "Mrs. Bloom" makes a "sacrificial suggestion", permitting her husband to "'retire' on [her] 'bases'" in the hopes of receiving a greater beneficence in return (*SE* 254). Loy is alert to the anal truth of the matter, which is that Bloom's lust, like that of Freud's Wolf Man, satiates itself upon "the female nates", be it the pleasing sight of the "moving hams" of a woman exiting the butcher's in the morning of 16 June 1904, or the back view of the Bloom's erstwhile servant Mary, who "padd[ed]" out her false bottom to excite him" (Freud, "Infantile Neurosis" 56; Joyce, *Ulysses* 71, 873). Better to smell prostitutes on his clothing, Molly states, than witness this perversity. But as sado-masochistic penance for her adultery, Molly tells herself that when next "he wants to kiss my bottom Ill drag open my drawers and bulge it right out in his face as large as life he can stick his tongue 7 miles up my hole as hes there my brown part then Ill tell him I want £1 or perhaps 30/" (929). This wife's willingness to "let him do it off on me behind provided he doesnt smear my good drawers" is, for Loy, a self-immolation too far (Joyce, *Ulysses* 930).[9] Selling anilingus to her husband might reinstate Molly's wifely submissiveness, her willingness to participate in a transgressive variant of the socially sanctioned economy of marital prostitution. But it is also an assertion of vaginal autonomy, as the Marquis de Sade understood: his Justine allows her asterisk to be consummated to "giv[e] some ground" while "preserv[ing] what seemed to be the most essential of things" (33). Unconvinced by the salacious pleasure with which Molly relays her penitential fantasy, Loy leaves open the possibility that "on more propitious days of the month [the Blooms] may have" (*SE* 254). Sexual pleasure is implied, but here Loy's sentence ends, aposiopesis unresolved.

With unedited abruptness, Loy's "Library" "mak[es] the absolute descent from [the] Parnassus" of Joyce's *Ulysses* to the acerbically identified "opus par excellence" of Frank Harris (1856–1931), a man Loy considers an ass, full stop (*SE* 254). Leaving the text unnamed, Loy's focus is Harris's *My Life and Loves* (1922–7), an autobiographical, four-part tome that Harris, and Harris alone, considered in the same league as Joyce's 1922 tour de force (520).[10] Irish-born, British-educated Harris became a naturalised American, attaining recognition as editor of *The Fortnightly* and *The Saturday Review* among other popular journals, and by ingratiating himself with a host of notables, including King Edward VII. Like Loy, Harris opposed the social "condemnation of the body and its desires" as "idiotic" and unduly punitive; like Loy, he felt that most men and women "cannot lose their souls, for they have never found them" (Harris 7, 9).[11] Yet for Harris Loy reserves what may be the most vicious critique of her archive:

That little x x x x tuber Frank Harris—cun-T INKER
   How minutely he describes the geographical aspect of the Venusberg—it was not given to him to witness Vesuvius in eruption—the spasimal larva – – – – –

> So he absolves his manhood with the 'love juices' of expecta-
> tion – – –
> Frank Harris who entered the seventh heaven with a syringe in his
> pocket— (*SE* 254–5)

Harris's autobiography was first privately printed, then reproduced in 1931 by Obelisk Press, a publisher renowned for circulating work banned, as was *My Life and Loves*, in England or the
USA.[12] Harris believed his autobiography sold only about fifty
copies in France, but Loy clearly had access to its first volume, in
which he improbably presents himself as an itinerant sexual crafts-
man of remarkable prowess from earliest adolescence, deflowering many a reluctant, if ultimately grateful, virgin, receiving
gushing praise for his stallion-like stamina from more experienced conquests. While Loy's broken "T INKER" objectionably
combines Romany and Irish slurs, Harris is irrefutably an inker
of female genitalia: his text is awash in "hot slit[s]", "cunt[s]",
"cunn[ies]", "puss[ies]", "tickler[s]", and "Mount[s] of Venus"
that "enchant", even as he piously renders "damn" as "d . . n".[13]
This linguistic duplicity extends to the ladies Harris favours, to
whom he swears undying love, yet imagines striking if they reject
his advances. Painfully aware of his own physical unattractiveness,
he nevertheless scrutinises his lovers' bodies with a perfectionist's
eye, constantly finding inadequacies in their hips, vulvas, and other
body parts. The ultimate figure of female sacrifice to patriarchal
culture – Antigone – Harris considers "the prototype of the new
woman for all time" (138).

Countering this male "compensation phobia", in "Library", Loy
acts as predator Harris's detumescent, redacting his cock/sureness
with four telling "x's"; parodying what he reverentially labels his
"man-root" as diseased outgrowth or inert, vegetal "tuber"; positing
as phallic prosthesis the "syringe" that Harris did indeed have at
the ready at every sexual encounter, his constantly inconstant birth
control (*SE* 255; Harris 134–5).[14] Loy's metaphors of impotence
oppose Harris's epic account of innumerable well-wrought heteronormative orgasms, even as her brief critique gestures to the
unavoidable queerness of *My Life and Loves*. Primarily narcissistic
and misogynistic, Harris's autobiography is also openly homosocial, discussing men in conversation about their "pricks", wet
dreams, and onanism; public school fagging and forced frigging,
anal sex and rape.[15] Throughout, Harris delineates his unswerving
devotion – pre-, during, and post-sodomy-trial – to Oscar Wilde.[16]

The "Vesuvius" whose eruptions Loy insists Harris never sees is associated with the *über*-masculinity of Jupiter, Hercules. The eruptions in question may be Harris's or other men's; their twinning with "spasimal larva" suggests nascence, immaturity, the pre-genital. And Loy's totalising insistence that Harris "absolv[e] his manhood" may direct us to penetrative sex between men that was, in Harris's time and long before, perceived as using another man as a woman "by means of the bowel" (Kosofsky Sedgwick, *Epistemology* 98; Freud, "Infantile Neurosis" 79).

Harris's queerness is respite for the reader beleaguered by his tirade of sexual aggression couched as generosity, a transition from misogyny to homosexuality that Loy repeats as she brings "Library" to a close. Moving from modernist fictions to age-old mythologies, Loy argues that with the sex trade, and its *filles de joie*, the male self-congratulatory lie by which women are invigorated by penetration in any guise is at its most "repugnant". "In Germany—the nearest [the prostitute] comes to joy—is when she can while away an hour of leisure in the, *from her inevitable point of view*, purifying atmosphere of a pederasts' café" (emphasis added, *SE* 258). When sparring with Futurists, Loy argued on behalf of "'pederasty [as] the highest and noblest form of love'"; her daughter, who considered Loy more masculine than feminine, believed Loy "had great, great feelings for the homosexuals" (Burke, "Interview with Joella Bayer", 65–6).[17] Yet Loy quietly qualifies the sex-trade worker's adherence to a similarly non-heteronormative view, oscillating between consummating and "unconsummat[ing] the significance of the [anal] asterisk" (*SE* 253).

A queer, feminist diatribe, Loy's "Library" wanders from one modernist purveyor of masculinist sexual fictions to another, determinedly countering the "interminable procession—of ladies 'possessed' in floods of delight". D. H. Lawrence is critiqued for portrayals of "maidens [tumbled] on the banks of a river" minus "the civilized safeguards of the toilet in the love nest of clay" (*SE* 256). The "anxiety" caused by this public sex fantasy is no "cantharide", a term evoking the aphrodisiac and the diuretic, the excremental leaving its lingering odour. Gabriele D'Annunzio, Aldous Huxley, and T. S. Eliot are likewise chastised for their "instantaneous beatification[s] of the female by the (always) condescending male" (*SE* 256).[18] Instead, female characters are forced "to intellectualise a content for the vacuum of their sensation", leaving men assured of their superiority in all intimate matters (*SE* 255–6). Is Loy wrong? "The activity, the orgasm was his, all his; she could strive for herself no more", thinks Lady Constance Chatterley, berating herself about her sexual encounter with Oliver Mellors until, evidently, "[h]er tormented modern-woman's brain had no rest" (Lawrence, *Lady* 121). "[A]verage intercourse" is for Loy "most accurate[ly] present[ed]" in Evelyn Scott's hard-bitten satire *The Narrow House* (1921), where one wife masochistically acquiesces to her husband's infidelity until she reaches senescence whilst another longs only to diminish her estranged husband, a minor sacrifice to women like herself, forced "to be weak to the whole world" (*SE* 257; Scott 66). In "The Three Wishes" (n.d.), Loy describes faded matrimony as the heterosexual status quo: couples "lov[e] and respect each other for having done a dirty thing"; wife reveres and fears husband; both parties "seemed only with the years to be scrupulously washing themselves away" (*SE* 135–6). The adult counterpart to the infantile anal phase, Freud tells us, is a will to order and cleanliness, a near-obsessive rejection of once-appealing excrement. Fittingly, Loy's next sentence in "The Three Wishes" resurrects the anality of our starriest punctuation: "Like millions and millions of us, they were living off a literature that has worn down to asterisks" (*SE* 136). In long-standing heteronormative love, only the censorious nub of a once-radiant asterisk survives, prurience overtaking pleasure.

"*To be penetrated is to abdicate power*", writes Leo Bersani; giving way to another, the asterisk loses the force of its redactive closure (212). But perhaps, Bersani muses, "the rectum is the grave in which the masculine ideal (an ideal shared – differently – by men *and* women) of proud subjectivity is buried" (222). Loy's unconsummated asterisks are cyphers for her real target, the deflation of phallic avant-garde privilege. After lambasting peers seated too comfortably upon a cutting edge whetted by self-serving shock tactics, Loy incises in turn, noting that only "third rate Parisian erotico-comic papers ... prepared exclusively as popular excitants to lubricity" exhibit an awareness that women do not share in ecstasy's deluge (*SE* 256–7). The popular press is more sexually astute, more perceptive, than the masculinist avant-garde: Loy's is no small provocation, even as her claim lends credibility to the satiric lineage from which she herself descends.[19] And she extends this truth to a draft, high-society dialogue in which the Irish novelist George Moore (1852–1933) is haltingly propositioned by Loy's otherwise silent, eponymous host, "Lady Asterisk":

> It was about the time that George Moore—
> Said dear lady—Asterisk
> I should so much like to have you – – –

   'No?'—
  – – – well perhaps another cup—thank you!
  This stirred the London intelligentsia up—"So *brilliantly*
    casual – –" (*SE* 44)

Personified as a respectable "Lady", the asterisk appropriately redacts the need for difficult, intimate conversations, skating calmly over rejection and insinuation toward propriety. Like Harris, Moore wrote a censor-provoking kiss-and-tell autobiography. Moore, Loy goes on to report, "knows that he knew how to write . . . and then he stuffed all his mistresses with 'literature'—" (*SE* 44). But for Loy, the vagina is not Moore's preferred orifice. Having committed untold improprieties with many women, Moore's lasting satiation, according to Loy, is rectal: he "himself lies buried in the last Bustle—" (*SE* 26, 44). Perhaps Moore rejects Lady Asterisk's advances for fear of revealing his rearward proclivities.

Moore is far from alone: Sumner and Smoot are derisible for habitually "sticking their noses into their neighbour's ———", but Loy assures us repeatedly that they share these "canine affinities" with the avant-garde artists they long to silence (*SE* 225). Loy's Houseless Loony, instantaneously notorious vanguard convert, bestially sniffs at the approach of "Woman"; in "Sacred Prostitute" (1914–16), Futurism intones "There is nothing in life that is not best apprehended by the presentment of the nose!" (*SE* 168, 194). Sniffing "*like a GOD*", Futurism calls for a dog to "prov[e] the infallible superiority of animal instinct over human reason" (*SE* 194). These dramas precede or are written alongside the first poem of "Songs to Joannes", where a "rosy snout" snuffles toward a "startopped" or asterisked plant "sown in mucous-membrane"; so begins a poem sequence awash in "suspect places" where reproductive and non-reproductive sexual desires continually clash (*LoLB* 53). The human body houses its plethora of mucous membranes, as we see in Loy's "Lion's Jaws" (1920), when a Futurist disciple kisses his leader "full on his oratory" in a poem liberally sprinkled with asterisks (*LoLB* 48). But the specifically "erotic" nature of the "mucous membrane of the bowel" is a truth increasingly acknowledged by sexologists in Loy's day (Freud, "Infantile Neurosis" 84).[20] To be suspect, subversive, places must first be observed.

Or demonstrated, as Marinetti evidently did for Loy. "[W]ith cockeyed assurance his head on one side he pursed his tidy little harlot's mouth", writes Loy, reducing Marinetti to a prostitute before detailing his proud proclivity for conducting *feuille de rose*, a French phrase that literally translates as rose leaf or bud, but is also slang for anilingus:

> ... – – – and this is 'feuille de rose' he announce[d], flapping her about on the bed like a busy fishmo[nger] slapping a dab on a marble counter.
>
> His caresses in his native tempo had the rapid staccato of a sewing machine.
>
> 'Do you enjoy doing that' she enquired 'I shouldn't.'
>
> 'Because' he said disparagingly 'you are not a man – (*B* 2: 3–4)

Throughout *Brontolivido*, Loy is Marinetti's fish, repeatedly "rising to the bait" of his misogyny; "gasp[ing] to his touch ... with ~~forced~~ pretty little ripples of delight"; swimming upstream against his sexual antics as he states openly he has "'not conduced [her] to the ultimately spasimal'" (*B* 2: 8; 8: 18; 4: 16). Note Loy's edit from "forced" to "pretty": for Loy, feigned pleasure is workaday self-immolation, a cunningly conducted performance her language relates to craft, to aesthetics: "this <u>is</u> the reality of pleasure – on the altar of her self-sacrifice to artifice" (*B* 8: 19). Loy yields willingly, if at a knowing remove, to Marinetti's sexual experimentalism, his pursed orifice exploring hers. For her too-rational querying of his intimate motive, she is paradoxically dismissed as unmanly, lacking carnal knowledge. So far does Marinetti take this metaphor that he thereafter praises "the inordinate chastity of [Loy's] eyes" whilst telling her that "'it's all nonsense looking as though you were in a church when you're only in Bed'" (*B* 2: 4). Marinetti is pleased to be perverse experimenter to Loy's pristine ascetic. Relaying this scene a few times in her drafts of *Brontolivido*, Loy deploys the revealing French slang, *feuille de rose*, on this occasion only.

In an alternate variant, Loy describes Marinetti pitying her for living too much in the past, speaking "to her eyes which had hardly extricated themselves from the amoresque 'au Delà' ——." Loy has yet to return from an intimacy that resembles love, an "au delà" or beyond suggesting, as does the asterisk itself, either transcendence or rearward sexual anatomies. The latter meaning is sustained by the sentence that follows: "Through the night of invoked voluptuary – its only intimacy being that she played perforce – – two parts to his demon" (*B* 8: 7). Invocation, playing: note the prevalence of the performative in Loy's phrasing. To become voluptuary, Loy pretends at sexual gratification, at being a sybarite, a term referring to the ancient Greek city Sybaris, legendarily home to a population effeminised by its hedonism, wealth, and luxury. Doubling as sexual insatiate and chaste maiden, Loy might represent an alternate pairing for the demon Marinetti: gay and heterosexual lover. A final Loy variant confirms this queering: here Loy leaves a "gulp[ing]" Marinetti interrogated by Loy, a Marinetti who continues to berate Loy for not being a man, thereby "appropriating in his assurance the whole of his side of a licentious absolute!" (*B* 8: 19). Loy will not receive any sacrificial recognition, even as Marinetti's repeated dismissal posits desire: does he wish she were a man? Does she? The verso of this manuscript page offers evidence that Loy was drafting poem 19 of "Songs to Joannes" as she reconsidered this episode. It reads: "Nothing so conserving / As cool cleaving / Note of the 'qhu – / Qhu / Done" (*B* 8: 20). "QHU" remains in the complete poem, a referent perpetually eluding Loy scholars and readers. Is it code for the unmentionable events – the exposure of Loy's rearward cleft, conserving because not reproductive – both intimated in and censored out of this draft roman à clef? First recorded in 1894 in a letter by the Marquess of Queensberry, the father of Wilde's lover Lord Alfred Douglas, "queer" – its sound tantalisingly in tune with Loy's syllable – is not used to directly refer to homosexuality in Loy's oeuvre. Indirectly, however, it is: the "'queer death'" of a heterosexual love affair is followed by speculation upon the likelihood of an ensuing lesbian relationship (*SE* 305).[21]

Another possibility: first published in 1917, shortly after Loy met Marcel Duchamp, might "QHU" predate or influence his famous goateed parody of Da Vinci's *Mona Lisa* (c. 1503–6), titled *L.H.O.O.Q.* (1919)? Duchamp's altered postcard of *La Giaconda* superimposes masculinity upon the world's most famous female portrait. When the letters of his acronym are read aloud in French, Duchamp's title reads *"elle a chaud au cul"*, a slang expression implying a woman's sexual desire whilst literally meaning "she has a hot ass"; in sum, Duchamp's work is a legibly queer misogynistic parody of art, sexuality, desire.[22] These ties resonate with the anti-heteronormative anality of Loy's sexual experience with Marinetti that appears on the recto of her poem 19 draft. Yet these intimations remain contextually and historically unproven, possibly – although not *im*possibly – too skewed to be verifiable, factual. Nevertheless, this *Brontolivido* anecdote illustrates that Loy knows whereof she speaks when she references the asterisk as cypher for an unattained female sexual satiation matched by a circuitously explored if unacknowledged male vanguard anality. Reflecting her own sexual forays, Loy's asterisk transgressively resists the sexual status quo.

Like Loy, Bataille deploys corporeal baseness to challenge and extend his reverence toward his intellectual influencers. Springing from a critique of Nietzsche's sublimities, Bataille's writing tracks human evolution via the asshole, from its "obscene blossoming . . . bald hal[o]" in our ape forebears, to its "seclu[sion] . . . deep within the flesh, in the crack of the buttocks" (Biles 51; "Jesuve" 76–7). With this "inversion of the anal orifice", writes Bataille, humanity experiences "the decisive reversal of animal existence" ("Pineal" 89). All that we consider noble in humanity – our dignity, so visible in our faces – Bataille perceives as a disruption of our need to be provocative, dissolute ("Jesuve" 78). Bataille insists that we must continually erupt like the earth's volcanic anuses, and that we regularly do so from our faces, with the laughter and tears that manifest the inevitable contradictions of rationality: "the practice of intellectual scatology requires the excretion of unassimilable elements, which is another way of stating vulgarly that a burst of laughter is the only imaginable and definitely terminal result . . . of philosophical speculation" ("De Sade" 99). As his essay title suggests, Bataille longs to conflate the anus with our most radiant star, the sun, which, with its "fecal eye . . . has torn itself from . . . volcanic entrails" to express its "anal maternity" ("Pineal" 85). Perverse, yes; singular, surprisingly not.

At the end of the meandering manuscript of Loy's late, undated philosophical dialogue "Mi & Lo", there are "Notes." on topics so disparate and all-encompassing that they might be the basis of a *Gesamtkunstwerk* involving religious disquisitions, poetry, philosophy, and a comparison of Dada with ancient Greek art. Making oblique reference to Loy's associates Duchamp and Picabia, this latter "Description of Dada Statue." concludes: "The eye of the anus perceives divinity – / Excrement and the solar system keep greenwich time. / Women and cows have the same coiffeur" ("Mi and Lo"). To resist defining humanity with sheer utility, Bataille's "The Solar Anus" (1931) situates the transcendental in the rectum, thereby resurrecting our lost attachment to religious transport and the lowest of bestial lows. Loy's claim is similarly oppositional: observing the Dada arrangements of "broken sewer-pipe" and the mechanised female forms for which both Duchamp and Picabia are well known, she points out that where Grecian women were "chiselled in . . . pure marble", contemporary women are excremental vessels. But Loy's reading elevates the anal eye of these replicated females to the solar; their baseness determines the temporality of earth and universe. Animal they may be, but they are not at one with nature:

domesticated, both cows and ladies are nurtured into likeness, sharing the same male hairdresser, surely a lampoon of the male artist's "mastery" over the female form. In "Apology of Genius" (1922), Loy will depict the "smooth fools' faces" of the censorious as "buttocks bared in aboriginal mockeries" (*LoLB* 77). In this fragment from her "Notes." to "Mi & Lo", Loy bares "female nates" in an age-old act of "defiant scorn", but also, plausibly, as a request "for tenderness that has been overtaken by repression" (Freud, "Infantile Neurosis" 56; "Anal Erotism" 173). As Loy acknowledges, we must "clear the drifts of spring / Of our forebear's excrements"; the past must manure our "subconscious archiv[e]" so that life can flourish anew (*LoLB* 71). In the process, Loy, like Bataille, reveals the divine baseness of the starry-eyed asterisk, its gnostic and somatic transcendence.

The Unsentimental Economy of Prostitution

"The division of labour by sex can ... be seen as a 'taboo' ... against the sameness of men and women, a taboo dividing the sexes into two mutually exclusive categories, a taboo which exacerbates the biological differences between the sexes and thereby *creates* gender" (Rubin, "Traffic" 178). In Westernised societies, that division allocates affective labour – a category including relatability, a winsome attitude, unlimited caretaking, domestic attentiveness, and intimacy – to the feminised, the marginalised, the under- or unpaid. As discussed in the previous chapter, modernist writers considered the best, truest human emotion for sale at a premium, earnable through purchase. From Baudelaire to Wilde to Chesterton, we find variations upon the assertion that the "sentimentalist is simply one who desires to have the luxury of an emotion without paying for it" (Wilde, "De Profundis" 639–40). On the one hand, this commodification underscores the truth that feeling is often the product of labour. On the other, these same modernists distanced themselves from that labour, envisioning authentic feeling as something available to them because of their privilege: leisured, monetised ease and comfort, masculine authority. In this latter sense, modernists participate by extension in what Gayle Rubin, borrowing her phrase from anarchist Emma Goldman (1869–1940), calls "the traffic in women" that long preceded capitalist "traffic in merchandise". By this foundational "sex/gender system", female beings and feminine skills are considered convertible, tradeable, at the disposal of paternalistic system. "Women are given in marriage, taken in battle, exchanged for favours, sent as tribute, traded, bought, and sold", argues Rubin, who notes that men are also trafficked – "but as slaves, hustlers, athletic stars, serfs, or as some other catastrophic social status, *rather than as men*." By contrast: "Women are transacted as slaves, serfs, and prostitutes, but also *simply as women*." For Rubin, women have been perceived as intrinsically "sexual semi-objects—gifts—for much of human history" (emphasis added, "Traffic" 175–6). By this political economy, the male client of a female prostitute is arguably admirable, as he is no sentimentalist, never failing to "enjoy without incurring the immense debtorship for a thing done" (Joyce, *Ulysses* 550–1). If not immensely, this client has historically paid more for sexual pleasure than, say, a man employing a woman to cook and clean for his comfort. In the nineteenth century, it was understood that men paid for sexual servicing on the streets whilst receiving near-gratis moral and domestic servicing in the home (Bland xviii). In the wake of World War I, Italian Futurist Marinetti expressed concern that "Sentimentalism" – unearned emotion – was being transposed to men becoming nothing more than "useless wom[e]n" in societies where women were evidentially increasingly valuable, working in and outside of the home ("Against Marriage" 309, 312). Pointedly confirming Marinetti's fears, Loy mocks the Futurists as participants in the reversal of gendered labour they decry, wielders of a "rather dilapidated duster, used for flitting [their] uttermost liberties . . . about the eyes of the public" (*B* 7: 4).

Inseparable from the traffic in women, prostitution nevertheless challenges the sentimentalised economy of domesticity, exposing the male privilege behind the supposedly honourable desire to pay for feeling. As Luce Irigaray argues in "Women on the Market" (1978), the prostitute blurs the lines between use value and circulation in the patriarchal economy by which woman is traditionally objectified and commodified; she is *"usage that is exchanged"* (186). Refusing altruism and self-sacrifice, the prostitute charges outright for affective labour. As Anne McClintock wryly observes: "'Society demonises sex workers because they demand more money than women should, for services men expect for free'" (qtd. in Bernstein 11). The prospect that a woman might volitionally charge for intimacy distressed and distresses still. Following in the footsteps of male reformers, nineteenth- and twentieth-century feminists remained blind to the liberating possibilities of payment for sex, re-entrenching prostitutes as passive, poor, golden-hearted women "seduced" by evil men into a trade from which they longed to be saved, or as unrepentant, lascivious aberrations of proper womanhood (Bland 118). Both sides of this tainted coin are visible in *Prostitution Considered in its Moral, Social, and Sanitary Aspects in London and Other Large Cities* (1857), where William Acton asks:

> 'Who are these painted, dressy women flaunting along the streets and boldly accosting the passersby? Who those miserable creatures, ill-fed, ill-clothed, uncared for, from whose misery the eye recoils, cowering under dark arches and among bye-lanes?' (qtd. in Walkowitz 44)

Volition is absent from Acton's description, yet, as Judith Walkowitz attests, in the nineteenth century, prostitution was the female equivalent to running away to sea. Asked direct questions about prostitution, women spoke – then as now – about how sex work facilitated autonomy, freedom, and a higher standard of living than most feminised unskilled labour (21).[23] Entrenched gender hierarchies irrefutably maintain women's dominance at the front lines of the sex trade, but where they retain some control over their destinies, female sex-trade workers arguably undermine both sentimental freeloading and long-standing presumptions that women are mere conduits in the transactional femininity upon which Western paternalism is based.[24]

These arguments are not meant to overestimate the potentially revolutionary challenge the prostitute effects upon the status quo. As Audre Lorde writes: "Poor women and women of Colour know there is a difference between the daily manifestations of marital slavery and prostitution" precisely because, for them, prostitution is not at one remove from their daily lives: it is their daughters who are far more likely to line the streets of red-light districts ("Master's Tools" 112). But as men continue to exchange women, sex-trade workers continue to insist upon their right "to realise" at least some benefits from "their own circulation" (Rubin, "Traffic" 174).

From childhood onward, Loy was informed that "'a girl who mislaid her maidenhood was promptly let out on the streets'"; for her parents' generation, prostitution was both widely accepted and considered "the Great Social Evil", a contagion infecting all walks of life (*IA* 69: 151; Walkowitz 32). Alertness to this ideological duplicity and its social and legal history runs through Loy's writing, perhaps most directly in "The Library of the Sphinx.", where she gestures to her knowledge of Emma Goldman's activism against prostitution – Loy and Goldman were correspondents – and makes specific reference to French and British sex-trade laws.[25] Loy describes the sex worker's need to "brib[e] the police" or endure "examin[ation] in indescribable circumstances for venereal disease" (*SE* 258). The English Contagious Diseases Acts of 1864, 1866, and 1869 demanded that streetwalkers residing in garrison towns or ports be officially registered; once tallied, these women became subject to regular genital examinations as their clients were not, rendering the invasive procedures wholly ineffectual. Police used this authority to subdue and humiliate any woman in public deemed suspect and, by extension, as an excuse to examine the anus of any man thought homosexual with a venereologist's "sphincteromete[r, an instrument used] to identify sodomites by millimetres of [rectal] dilation" (Wolf 254). Similar laws in France were levied at prostitutes and, to a lesser degree, their clients (Corbin 335). The successful repeal campaign that followed effectively inaugurated twentieth-century liberal feminism, but legal measures to control prostitution – in England, never ban – continued apace, so that, in 1885, women were forced from the relative protection of the newly criminalised brothel to urban streets, where, until 1914, severe penalties were imposed for street solicitation (Weeks 90; Walkowitz 211, 252).[26]

In Paris, few of the *maisons de tolérance* established by Napoleon survived the post-World War I economic downturn and the subsequent crackdown on brothels in the early 1930s, meaning more women were, as Loy puts it, "threatened into supporting a *maquereau*" or pimp (*SE* 258). The Parisian brothels that survived catered for an elite male clientele, offering theatre screenings and literature alongside sex (Corbin 338). One such brothel was *Le Sphynx* of Montparnasse, of which Loy's son-in-law, Julien Levy, was a regular patron in or around 1932, as he details in his *Memoir of an Art Gallery*:

> At the Sphinx there was a basic costume of a transparent white peplum that could be lowered from one shoulder to expose a breast or hiked up on one hip to expose the private parts. Each girl wore a band around her forehead which was built up into a fantasy headdress expressing a little of the girl's own creativity: flowers, feathers, sequins, or whatever she might invent. The atmosphere was half-nude, very carnival, pretty and amusing. The artists in the neighbourhood had developed a habit of coming to the Sphinx at aperitif time in the late afternoon, just for the pleasure of having a glass of wine and chatting in this rather unusual atmosphere. The girls were not at all averse to this, enjoying being treated to a drink by the artists and having a chat before their professional clients came in, usually later in the evening. This became a habitual indoor café for the 'in'

group. It was nice, and clean, and fun, and the girls were pleasant and pretty, something rather unusual for the everyday, or rather everynight cathouse in Paris. (143–4)

The women are dressed in white; the hour is tame; the exchange is mutual. Writing nearly a century after Acton's condemning description of streetwalkers, Levy nevertheless propitiates Victorian ideologies. Evidently, Levy's consumption is not driven by uncontained sexual desire, just a longing for good company. Acknowledging his voyeuristic tendencies, he reassures the reader that he and his fellow artists engage in activities one might undertake at any pub or restaurant. Hence the tripartite blandness of his assertion: "It was nice, and clean, and fun". Affirming his vanguard associations, Levy strives to realise the autonomy of the women working in the brothel, lingering over their pleasure and their diminutively realised creativity. Levy's celebrated feathers and sequins overtly patronise. By stark contrast, Loy's "The Library of the Sphinx." turns briefly at its end to the untold stories of abused and prostituted women, implying the prospect of an alternate artistic canon. Attuned to the laws, social narratives, and specific locales by which sex-trade workers are defined for their survival, Loy indicates that while these women may titillate educated men, they have untold stories of their own to write, libraries to fill.

Loy's approach to the sex-trade worker is not free of Victorian moral *pudeur*, an insistence that prostitutes are by and large stricken with a countenance of "profound inferiority" (*SE* 258). But Loy recognises prostitution as labour, as an income-generating venture that forgoes pleasure and security. By including sex-trade workers in an essay on renowned modernist literature, Loy gestures to the elevation of prostitute to artist famously rendered in Baudelaire's era-defining "The Painter of Modern Life" (1863). Baudelaire celebrates women "elaborately dressed and embellished by all the rites of artifice" as "having received at birth a spark of [the] sacred flame" that inspires "true artists" (34–5). Half-devil, half-goddess, Baudelaire's prostitute is all-seeing, all-knowing, a cruel, unpredictable moral compass who is "provocative" and "barbaric":

She is a perfect image of the savagery that lurks in the midst of civilisation. She has her own sort of beauty, which comes to her from an Evil always devoid of spirituality, but sometimes tinged with a weariness which imitates true melancholy. She directs her gaze at the horizon, like a beast of prey; the same wildness, the same lazy absent-mindedness, and also, at times, the same fixity of attention.

> She is a sort of gipsy wandering on the fringes of a regular society, and the triviality of her life, which is one of warfare and cunning, fatally grins through its envelope of show. (36–7)

Levy's anodyne celebration of the adorned workers of *Le Sphynx* is etiolate allusion to Baudelaire's pyrotechnically sublime whores who entreat, embody, and expunge the exorbitant guilt, pleasure, and violence of European "civilisation". Baudelaire reinforces ground taken up by Manet in *Olympia* (1865) and Picasso in *Les Demoiselles d'Avignon* (1907), by which racist presumptions of "dangerous black sexuality [were] often incorporated into the image of a white prostitute" (Foster, "Scenes" 79).[27] For Baudelaire, the most elite white prostitutes can become artists: as courtesan is to actress, so actress is to poet; the courtesan, replete with "soul" and "genius", remains at one remove from the artist, whereas the "poor slaves of those filthy stews" cannot embellish themselves, cannot bring their artistry to bear ("Painter" 37).

Decades later, Bataille repeats Baudelaire's terms, idealising the transgressive prostitute and particularly, the courtesan's power over rich men, her capacity for "extravagant expenditure and ornaments that ma[ke] her more desirable" (*E* 132). Note that the courtesan's potentially liberating income is used to titillate her clients still further, so that her excesses are co-opted into a resolutely masculine economy. Like Baudelaire, Bataille distinguishes high prostitute from low: the courtesan remains elusive and coquettish, igniting and keeping at bay the shame and risk requisite to male lust; by contrast, the working-class prostitute is too inured to disgust, "fall[ing] to the level of the beasts", too complicit in her own sordid condition (*E* 134–5; 138). Bataille's oeuvre is indefatigably opposed to the forfeiting of human intimacy for labour and utility, the degrading, willing turning of the subject into object (*AS1* 57). Yet Bataille does not consider prostitution at risk of instrumentalisation, because he follows Baudelaire in refusing to consider it work: for Baudelaire the prostitute is lazy, for Bataille, "idle" and as such, ideally feminine, outside the capitalist economy, a cypher of self-sacrificing excess (*AS2* 142, 146–7).[28] Redacting the integral value of women's intimate labour upon which capitalism continues to rely, Baudelaire and Bataille nevertheless contradictorily categorise prostitutes by their earnings, participating in a modernist affective economy whereby the wealthiest prostitute engenders and experiences the most luxurious feelings. Along the way, they elide the autonomy afforded trafficked women.

The sacred prostitute appears to offer a way out of this monetised affective impasse. For, like Baudelaire's, Bataille's thinking on the sex trade takes a distinctly religious turn:

> The sacred or forbidden aspect of sexual activity remained apparent in [the prostitute], for her whole life was dedicated to violating the taboo. We must look for coherence between the deeds and the words describing this vocation; we must see the ancient institution of sacred prostitution in this light. [Before] Christianity, religion, far from opposing prostitution, was able to control its modalities as it could with other sorts of transgression. The prostitutes in contact with sacred things, in surroundings themselves sacred, had a sacredness comparable with that of priests. (*E* 133)

Unscorned and reserved, this sacred prostitute is in command of the fear Bataille claims women must exhibit to satisfy the male desire to violate. Drawing on James Frazer's influential text *The Golden Bough* (1890), Havelock Ellis describes the tradition to which Bataille alludes:

> [I]t would seem that the origin of prostitution is to be found primarily in a religious custom .... The typical example is that recorded by Herodotus, in the fifth century before Christ, at the Temple of Mylitta, the Babylonian Venus, where every woman once in her life had to come and give herself to the first stranger who threw a coin in her lap, in worship of the goddess. The money could not be refused, however small the amount, but it was given as an offertory to the temple, and the woman, having followed the man and thus made oblation to Mylitta, returned home and lived chastely ever afterwards. Very similar customs existed in other parts of Western Asia, in North Africa, in Cyprus, and other islands of the Eastern Mediterranean, and also in Greece. (*Studies* IV 229)

Unlike Baudelaire and Bataille, Ellis separates the prostitute's artistry from her sanctity, even as he recognises that "she is a mistress of the feminine arts of adornment", with an appealing, even vanguard, tendency to snub all that is "conventional and established", including modern humanity's "withering atmosphere of artificial thought and unreal sentiment" (*Studies* IV 299–300).

In "The Traffic in Women" (1910), Goldman cites Ellis while arguing on behalf of the long-standing links between the sex trade and creativity, noting that religious prostitution was thought to have "developed ... out of the belief that the generative activity of human beings possessed a mysterious and sacred influence in promoting the fertility of Nature" (136). Goldman and Ellis look to ancient, esoteric history to explain the contradictions and persistence of the twentieth-century sex trade, one historically condoned by the patriarchs of the Christian church. For Bataille, transgression enhances the appeal of prostitution; for Ellis, it is its very cause, as it is only in societies where marriage is delayed and rigidly monogamous that prostitution arises (*Studies* IV 224, 227).[29] In other words, prostitution is not the world's oldest profession or a "consecration in the first place" (*E* 132); by conventions ancient and Christian, a prostitute becomes sacred only by virtue of renouncing her profession after performing reparation, be it by payment to a temple or begging forgiveness for past "misdeeds", a trope famously evinced by Mary Magdalene of the New Testament.[30] Where Bataille's brothel is his "true church", his activist modernist peers condemn the church for sanctifying the prostitution of all women in marriage, an argument made by such unlikely bedfellows as Emma Goldman, Olive Schreiner, F. T. Marinetti, and Mina Loy, whose "Feminist Manifesto" informs women that they must choose between domesticated "Parasitism, & Prostitution —or Negation" (*G* 10; *LoLB* 154).[31] This is an equation Ellis roundly rejects, strictly defining a prostitute as "a person who makes it a profession to gratify the lust of various persons of the opposite sex or the same sex" (*Studies* IV 225–6). Ellis pragmatically insists on skill, repetition, and a variety of income sources as mainstays of the sex trade.

Marriage may not be prostitution for Ellis, but he acknowledges that prostitutes are sacrificed to maintain its sacrosanct status. Gesturing to a long line of this thinking, he quotes Balzac's statement that prostitutes "'sacrifice themselves for the republic'" (*Studies* IV 281). Schopenhauer uses the highest diction to extrapolate upon the "human sacrifices" of the lowest-regarded profession: "'She remains, while creeds of civilisations rise and fall, the eternal priestess of humanity, blasted for the sins of the people'" (qtd. in Ellis, *Studies* IV 281–2). This is the sacred prostitute neither forgiven nor newly chaste, but decimated entire to maintain the purity of the community. "[M]oralists are prepared to sacrifice one-half of the human race" to hold aloft the institutions of marriage and family, writes Goldman, for whom prostitutes and wives alike jostle for space on the altar of patriarchy (141). In *The Great Scourge* (1913), suffragette Christabel Pankhurst extends this sacrificial argument to both sexes, arguing that men waste energy and health in brothels, while women are needlessly sacrificed on the altar of the double standard (Weeks 164). The ancient origins of Pankhurst's argument are discussed by Foucault, who notes that prostitution has long been perceived as "negative value" for men and women because the sex trade facilitates "the useless discharge of sperm, its waste, without the benefit of the offspring the woman can provide." Etymologically, "the brothel is designated by a word [favourably] signifying shop or workshop (*ergastērion*), [but] it is also called, like a cemetery, 'a place for everyone,' 'a common place'". In the ancient world, these associations explained "why going to prostitutes, can, in a dream, portend death" (Foucault 19). Bataille, that great lover of wasteful expenditure, draws joyously and self-excoriatingly upon these ancient associations when he writes:

> I know that I descend alive not even into a tomb, but into a common pit, without either grandeur or intelligence, quite nude (as the woman of pleasure is nude). Would I dare to affirm: 'I will not yield—in no case will I extend my confidence and allow myself to be buried as if I were dead'? (*IE* 67)

Longing to be overwhelmed and detesting any impetus to save his abject self, Bataille reinterprets Rimbaud's famous "Je est un autre" as "Je est un fille de joie"; his self-immolation falls under a subtitle that asserts: "I WANT TO CARRY MY PERSON TO THE PINNACLE" (*IE* 66). To ascend in Bataille's general economy, one must first debase the self, and there is no better self-sacrifice for this modernist male, no better way out of the strictures of unearned sentimentality, than to sanctify himself as the lowest low, the "woman of pleasure" stripped bare by philosophical ecstasies, willing to die for the cause of non-useful expenditure.

Avant-garde writing is expenditure that refutes market value by design, positioning itself beyond the filth of mass appeal and its attendant financial gain. Vanguard authors consider themselves sacrificial victims who live and die by their intimate thoughts, their vulnerable novelties, offered to a public that uses, berates, or ignores them in turn by way of retaining a too-sacrosanct status quo. So it is that resolutely masculine members of the twentieth-century avant-garde, men deeply opposed to the femininities strategically embraced by their decadent forebears, identify with the sacred prostitute, juxtaposing the generativity of this revered, exceptional courtesan against the commonplace textual exchanges of the urban street, implicitly and explicitly likening popular, readily consumed literature to the affordable, ever-available streetwalker. In the nineteenth century, George Moore fatuously affirms his admiration for a male artist as follows: "by thy holy example didst [thou] save us from all base commercialism, from all hateful prostitution"; this man is labelled "our high priest", rather than consecrated whore (108). Come the twentieth century, the self-debasing feminisation intensifies. "[A]dvertisement and poster work" may democratise, argues Wyndham Lewis, but this street art calculates, reinforces the cumulative costs and passing minutes by which we obsessively measure and reduce life ("Politics" 118). At its greatest, art allows us to exceed the limits of our constrained subjectivity, an access Lewis believes threatened because:

> The sacred prostitutes, the artists, are being disbanded and dispersed, whatever may be said to the contrary. The notion of vicarious experience is bitterly assailed, in the name of freedom. This disintegration is a great human event, and it should not be hushed up, for more than the private experience of the artist is involved. ("Politics" 119)

Mass culture unites the crowd, but divides and conquers pre-eminent artists. Loy is aware of this anxiety, using it to mock esteemed writers George Shaw and Bernard Wells in an alternate draft of "The Library of Sphinx.", likening them to embodiments of the marketplace, authorial prostitutes.[32] By contrast, pre-eminent artist Lewis counts himself among the sacred prostitutes, valiantly defending the transcendentalism so many modernists were loath to abandon completely, a metaphysics always more palatable when registered in a mythical or ancient context.

Although diametrically opposed to Lewis's politics, Walter Benjamin offers similar arguments in "One-Way Street" (1928), deploring how, for his contemporaries, "money stands ruinously at the centre of every vital interest" (451–2). Against this avarice, Benjamin calls attention to "the ancient custom of the libation", to rituals and incantations by which humanity honours deities, rather than being relentlessly on the take, digging our "sacrificial shafts . . . in Mother Earth" (455, 486). As part of his peripatetic critique of capitalist modernity, Benjamin deplores the crowd-pleasing book, likening mainstream literary culture to contemptible whore. Applauding Mallarmé's *Un Coup de dés* (1897) as "the first [poem] to incorporate the graphic tensions of the advertisement in the printed page", Benjamin feels this typographical experiment has gone too far, does not endure as well in, say, the Dada art that follows. For Benjamin, the avant-garde cannot be too cautious against complicity in the history of textual prostitution:

> Script – having found, in the book, a refuge in which it can lead an autonomous existence – is pitilessly dragged out into the street by advertisements and subjected to the brutal heteronomies of economic chaos. This is the hard schooling of its new form. If centuries ago it began gradually to lie down, passing from the upright inscription of the manuscript resting on sloping desks before finally taking itself to bed in the printed book, it now begins just as slowly to rise again from the ground. (456)

Where books were yielding lovers gloriously perused in the private autonomy of the home, Benjamin aligns the vertical reading of billboard, film, or newspaper, cultural texts imbibed in public, with urban contagion, lowly streetwalkers. Against these "[l]ocust swarms of print", Benjamin longs to retain the poet's exalted status, but fears that, in this proliferating literary economy, "experts in writing" will be reduced to generating "statistical and technical diagrams" (456–7). Gesturing provocatively to the modernist vanguard's utopian desire for a universal language so eloquently delineated in Benjamin's "The Task of the Translator" (1921), this "international moving script" is satiric dystopia, a world where "all the innovative aspirations of rhetoric" – aspirations dictating Benjamin's own elevated form and style – "will reveal themselves as antiquated daydreams" ("One-Way" 457). Countering this harlot's progress, Benjamin posits an ideal: a conflation of book and courtesan defined by generative insatiability, precious ephemerality, the pretence of possessing knowledge carnal and otherwise that will "vanish before [it] expire[s]" (461). This venerable book has links to the sacred prostitute, a truth confirmed by the Mallarmé quotation prefacing this section of Benjamin's essay: "'The tight-folded book, virginal still, awaiting the sacrifice that bloodied the red edges of earlier volumes; the insertion of a weapon, or paper-knife, to effect the taking of possession'" (460). Lasciviously immolated, for Benjamin, the exemplary book as prostitute is a ritual victim to literary sanctity, a metonym for the "great writers" who give their lives to ensure a future cultural prosperity, who "perform their combinations in a world that comes after them, just as the Paris streets of Baudelaire's poems, as well as Dostoevsky's characters, existed only after 1900" ("One-Way" 447).

In modernist equations of print and prostitution, the good book is an oblated courtesan, the esteemed male author a sacred prostitute, the female author a common whore. In *Woman and Labour* (1911), Loy's peer Olive Schreiner, not unlike Benjamin, critiques modern parasitism, her term for endless consumption unmatched by productivity; Schreiner's acclaimed text is assuredly the basis of Loy's argument that women must choose between parasitism, prostitution, or negation in her 1914 "Feminist Manifesto" (*LoLB* 154). Women are dependent in contemporary economies, writes Schreiner, because their labour is either "forced or ill-paid"; as evidence, Schreiner points to vocationless pampered wives, prostitutes who yield to "disease and death", and female fiction writers (91, 98, 104). The last group she justifies as follows:

> [As] modern fiction . . . [is] the only art that can be exercised without special training or special appliances, and produced in moments stolen from the multifarious, brain-destroying occupations which fill the average woman's life, [women are] driven to find this outlet for their powers as the only one presenting itself. How far otherwise might have been the directions in which their genius would naturally have expressed itself can be known only partially to the women themselves . . . . Even in the little third-rate novelist whose works cumber the ground . . . may lie buried a sound legislator, an able architect, an original scientific investigator, or a good judge. (159)

Evidently unable to attain the highest standard of this chronically disreputable art form, women novelists expend wasteful energy, are no better than streetwalkers or, as Schreiner attests, typists who "fin[d] outlets for their powers in the direction of least resistance" (159). This association between public female author and prostitute similarly undergirds Emily Dickinson's "Publication – is the Auction / Of the Mind of Man –", in which the male intellect is sold to stave off poverty while a feminised mind and body remain pure by refusing the appeal of solicitation and its nefarious consolations. The poem continues:

> Possibly – but We – would rather
> From our Garret go
> White – Unto the White Creator –
> Than invest – Our Snow –

For Dickinson, the "Corporeal illustration" of God-given thought – the printed text – cannot be honourably subjected "To Disgrace of Price –" (Poem 709, 348–9). Bound page, bound body: both are preserved unmarked for Dickinson, who remains steadfastly, if defensively, unsullied by market aggressions and diminishments. Pure, she commits to an anonymous life and recognition in the hereafter; as an encapsulation of Dickinson's own legacy, this poem is prophetic. But as literary history shows, whether women publish or not, their language is inextricable from their sexuality: the young virgin desirably mute, "'ignoran[t] of sexual commerce'"; the vociferous wife a nag or shrew; the female author who sells words just another brazen hussy (qtd. in Brooke-Rose 14). The woman who demands to be heard as well as looked over, evaluated, put to use; the woman with opinions that threaten fluid trafficking: this woman is worthless commodity, a supply without demand.

Feminist Pornographies

Against these stereotypes, Loy asserts her right to "She[d] . . . petty pruderies" and "sidle up / To Nature / – – – that irate pornographist" (*LoLB* 63). The circulation of illicit sexual literature surged in the generation before Loy's birth, and the speaker of poem 26 in "Songs to Joannes" recognises nature as author of the same (Weeks 20–1). The term "pornography" emerged in Europe as a reworking of a Greek referent for writing about selling sex; from the early nineteenth century, "pornography" referred to treatises on prostitution. As the century unfolded, "pornography" was applied to sexually explicit artefacts uncovered from the ancient world, and came to categorise private collections of erotica usually owned by educated, wealthy men (Rubin, "Misguided" 261). Continually referencing prostitution in her poetry, fiction, essays, and romans à clef, Loy is assuredly heir to a pornographic lineage of literature about the sex trade. But in her resistance to censorship and her feminist sex positivity, Loy anticipates Gayle Rubin's arguments against perceiving pornography as "intrinsically antithetical to the interests of women" ("Misguided" 256). In one roman à clef, Loy asserts: "'While I am very empty—I can't sustain myself on any man's pornography'".[33] The concessive first clause is juxtaposed against the assertively delimiting masculine qualifier in the second; Loy's phrasing leaves open the question and prospect of a satiating female pornography. Against the violence and misogyny often associated with the erotic, Loy expressly "dream[s] an unformulated dream", striving to locate the intimacy that might generatively sustain the hollowed-out female sexual self (*B* 5: 3). Rather than adopting an expressly anti-pornography stance, Loy most resists sexual ignorance and incompetence, the overloud "buzz" caused by an "innocuous pornographic darkness" that fails to recognise sex as central to existence, or female sexuality at all (*IA* 67: 109).

Nature is Loy's less-than-sacred creator of the erotic, a monolith humanised by her irascibility and proximity. Is it the suppression of sex positivity that makes Nature so irate? The monetisation of sex? Its dependency on the traffic in women that continues to underwrite the very term "pornography"? Loy's treatises on prostitution constitute a pornography evincing similarly various, complexly interpretable approaches to this topic. Wilfully inconstant, often feminist, Loy's critique of the modernist unsentimental economy of prostitution is complicated by fascination, reverence, complicity, reformatory desires. In her *romans à clef*, Loy demonstrates how, when confronted by sexual solicitation, young middle-class women at the *fin-de-siècle* are uncomprehending naïfs, as when newly married Sophia gawks "with a devastating wonder" at "a soldier mauling his *fille*" on the *Impasse de L'Enfer,* or the disreputable Montparnassian street named for baseness, hell on earth. A mutualised desire inflects and deflects this judgement: both parties "stumbl[e] under grasping limbs through the thick summer dusk[,] their eyes blinded with a liquid incandescence" (*EP* 22). The risk of becoming the fallen woman was a personal threat wielded by way of controlling burgeoning sexualities.

But as Loy shows, that threat made eroticism synonymous – often tantalisingly – with a mysterious, occluded transgression: "For in those days . . . . [t]he streets were the unknown; the track on which the erotic revelation paced." By extension, "Pleasure elusive is become furtive, only to be picked up at the street corner, where decent women dare not venture lest they be mistaken for—" (*CP* 15: 41). Forbidden, the street entices, is pathway to sexual freedom as well as castigation. Loy identifies women as the most harsh judges of sexually active females, ironically participating in a blanket distaste for her own sex on these very grounds. As a youth Loy recalls asking a woman working the London streets for the time, and finding herself overwhelmed by seeing hell in the woman's eyes. Reflecting on this exchange, she blames women – not male procurers – for allowing their peers to work in the sex trade. Loy includes herself in this estimation, considering this incident an epiphany that catalyses in her an "enigmatic sex-class culpability toward that woman in Piccadilly" (*IA* 69: 142–3). In Loy, prostitution usually prompts feminist empathy and responsibility.

More precisely, Loy's *romans à clef* reveal that both sexual coercion and her own experience of being prostituted are foundational to Loy's stature as both a sex-positive, anti-censorious feminist and in turn, a vanguardist. Attending Munich's *Künstlerinnenverein,* or

Society of Female Artists' School, in 1900, Loy lodged with a family who, unbeknownst to her, advertised her charms to prospective male guests in a local paper. It was their hope that 18-year-old Loy would have her virtue compromised and be sent home in shame before her parents discovered that her German caregivers had fraudulently spent the money sent to them from England expressly for Loy's use. Comprehending the duplicity at stake, Loy struck a bargain with her guardians, offering to refrain from reporting the truth to her parents in exchange for freedom to wander the streets of Munich unchaperoned. When an octogenarian, Loy continues to recall this incident as foundational, struggling to understand both the willingness to exploit her (she speculates that the woman of the family was herself "the daughter of a prostitute"), and how she managed to come out unscathed after lengthy, unaccompanied exposures to men ("Mina Loy: Interview" 222, 234–5).

For Burke, it is because of this experience that Loy garners a newfound independence protected by her cultivation of an eccentric vanguardism of manner, appearance, habit, and coterie (*BM* 60). On a personal level, to be a vanguard young woman was to project unfemininity, to be unappealing, but also on the defensive: labouring to hold the male gaze and body at bay. Loy smoked a pipe, moved in artistic circles. She also became politicised. In Loy's own words, her brush with prostitution generates a direct kinship with women forced to participate in sexual activities that fall outside the strict confines of Victorian purity. "Inwardly I was evolving a weird strictly personal form of feminism of which the militant aspect consisted in being 'peculiarly benign' to any woman who had been 'pushed'" (*IA* 69: 150). A surface knowledge of the history of feminism indicates that Loy's affinities are neither odd nor singular; prone and manipulable, the "fallen women" became the ground upon which one strand of feminism took its initial steps in the *fin-de-siècle*. The Social Purity movement was a feminism that proclaimed women's superiority based on their morality, whilst denying their sexuality; it was countered by the free love movement and feminist sex radicals who proclaimed the strength of women's sexual desire (Blau Duplessis 52). Gravitating toward the latter position, Loy's feminism emerges as historically situated, its individuality lying less in its polemic than in its duration, expansivity, passion, and the singularity of her avant-garde expression.

Elsewhere in Loy's treatises on prostitution, she adopts a variety of stances on the sex trade. In Loy's "The Three Wishes", Jacky Sider sees through Baudelaire's eyes: "when certain women passed him in the street" he is struck by a "strange convulsion of his breath" caused by "[t]heir powder and their rouge [that] seemed only the scintillating pulverescence in the radius of an arc-light", their "flesh ... iridescent substance" (*SE* 125). In "Library of the Sphinx.", Loy critiques the "literary hoax ... of the *gros gaillard*" or "[t]he big strong man as the best lover", chiding the male drunkard who wakes up to "congratulate himself on joy he has erotically administered to a *fille de joie*" (*SE* 259). But in other writings, Loy cheerily forgives the same: "I love the story of his parading down *Unter den Linden* with four of these girls on his shoulders – tremendous muscles, exuberant with adolescence, his face singing out from among their laces" ("Colossus" 115–17). For his spectacularly literal elevation of prostitutes, Loy's husband Arthur Cravan was barred from the streets of Berlin, but not before robbing one sex-trade worker of her handbag, only to give it to another with whom he spent the night. Brought before a magistrate, Cravan's theft was dismissed as "a practical joke played by the son of respectable parents" ("Colossus" 114–15). Bypassing the fortitude of the prostitutes who charged Cravan, Loy praises his deftly manipulated class and gender entitlement. In *Insel*, Loy's Mrs Jones is bemused by Insel's failure to access the same privilege, chiding him for his mismanaged pimping of "two negresses" who go pointedly unnamed: "'Whoever heard of a *maquereau* without any money!'" (*I* 71). In "Alda's Beauty" Loy similarly satirises the sex trade whilst observing neither john nor pimp, but prostitute. On a passenger ship to New York in 1916, Loy encounters an "[e]xtremely popular" sex-trade worker, and this scabrous disquisition follows:

> My concern for prostitutes being the same as for all other people, it seemed illogical that this sociable person should embody, for me, exactly the figment a maniac puritan brain would create out of what it supposed a prostitute to be. She seemed so rich in filth, her glance left a stain. (7)

Loy has an altercation with this woman, and notes with some satisfaction that she is prevented from disembarking in the United States. But while she recognises this worker, in distinctly Victorian parlance, as an "unfortunate", Loy's admiration remains palpable, both for the woman's unabashed embrace of her abjectification, and for her adoption of an intimidating mien that transcends social expectation at every turn ("Alda's" 7).

As has been persuasively argued by Susan E. Dunn, Loy interrogates and insists upon women's right to occupy public space whilst showing us how women are co-opted into models of desire and consumerism, a trafficking acknowledged through her late poems, "Mass-Production on 14th Street" (1942) and "Chiffon Velours" (1944) inclusive.[34] In notes for "My Catholick Confidante" (c. 1939), Loy argues: "In an ideal Society prostitutes would be [appreciated] as the kind ladies – – –" but also proposes that "prostitution might disappear". Like Ellis, Loy presents censoriousness as the cause of the sex trade, arguing on behalf of a "christianly clarification" whereby "'Sex' would be consecrated by the church—", thus making sacred prostitutes of us all, turning every brothel into Bataille's church (*SE* 372). Why this career-defining panoply of approaches to the sex trade? Keen to maintain the transcendent place sex holds in the human psyche, and to allow women overdue, unrestricted access to its transport, Loy restlessly circles the legend of the sacred prostitute, trying to make sex and religion as interchangeable "as Freud infers"; this linkage will become the substance of the esoteric Eros that comes to define her oeuvre (*SE* 226). Moreover, the sacred prostitute underscores how, as ever for Loy, the aggressions and reverent immolations of sacrifice are inseparable from intimacy, a truth she wants recognised for all people, regardless of gender. Elevated, critiqued, the prostitute is cypher for the urgent need to redefine the sexual status quo.

Consistent with the inseparability of sacrifice and prostitution, violence and intimacy, Loy's sacralisation of the sex trade regularly succumbs to satire. Female sacred prostitutes are scattered through Loy's oeuvre: from the beatified Pazzarella (c. 1914–17), who tremulously vows to become the prostitute who will "cleanse" the defiled soul of the "great man" who is her lover, to the "demi-rep angels / in tinsel bordels" of "Jules Pascin" (c. 1930), to "Lady Laura in Bohemia" (1931), an "abbess-prostitute", "gin-fizz eucharist" in hand, "bill-poster eyes" on show, awash in the "sentimental slobber" of her desire for "'di-vi-ne'" intercourse (*SE* 89; *LoLB* 104, 98–100). And in the autobiographical "Anglo-Mongrels and the Rose" (1923–5), Loy posits herself as a product of twinned enterprises: sex trade and church. Newly arrived in England, Loy's paternalistic stand-in, Exodus, is at loose ends on

> Sundays   when
> England closed   the eyes of every
> commercial enterprise
> but the church   and spewed
> her silent servants   out of her areas

> in their bi-weekly 'best'   to
> 'Ow get along with you'   their lurching lovers
> along the rails of parks
> The high-striped   soldiers of the swagger stick
> tempting the wilder flowers of womanhood
> to lick-be-quick ice cream
> outside the barracks (*LaLB* 116)[35]

With the convenient aversion of the nation's eyes, young female servants prostitute themselves to strutting, tripping soldiers, returning hastily performed, partly public sexual favours for petty luxurious purchases. Quick consumption is key. Loy rolls out historically recognised truths: dollymops, as Henry Mayhew calls them in *London Labour and the London Poor* (1851–2), were women sustained by modicums of loyalty and expenditure from soldiers and sailors (487).[36] Amidst this free-flowing sexual economy, Exodus remains convinced of his Jewish superiority, which Loy reduces, in the next stanza, to "an aristocracy   out of currency" (*LaLB* 116). If aristocracy it ever was: as Sander Gilman writes, Jews have long been seen as nomadic contaminants, syphilitic outcasts, as debased as the streetwalker: "both Jew and prostitute [are perceived to] have but one interest, the conversion of sex into money or money into sex" (122–3). Contagiously feminine, too, writes the Austrian thinker Otto Weininger in 1903, his anti-Semitism neatly dovetailing with his homophobia (329). Satirising these prejudices, Loy duly ensures that Exodus is "'all dressed up'" with "'nowhere to go'", stood "upon the corners of incarcerate streets", a veritable prostitute confined to a beat (*LaLB* 116).[37] From prostitute, Exodus is promoted to pimp, an itinerant "parasite" upon the working-class, Christian English Rose who will become Loy's mother, whom he evidently begs to "come be a 'Lady in the City'" (*LaLB* 119, 124). Jews are urban creatures with deadened emotions, avers sexologist Krafft-Ebing, and although Loy assures us that Exodus reads Proverbs to "mak[e] sharp distinction / between the harlot / and the Hausfrau" he appears desensitised to this distinction (qtd. in Gilman 31; *LaLB* 125). Couched in religious and racial terms, the foundational "disequilibrium" of this doomed couple will stamp their child, monstrous descendant of a resolutely unholy prostitution, with "unmentionable stigmata" (*LaLB* 148). Stigmata tattoo, brand, bruise, and imprint to identify animals or slaves; historically, the vast majority of stigmatics are women (Szendy 4). Thus marked, Loy will turn to stigmeology, the art of punctuation, to map out the maligned terrain of the sexual woman, and the routes by which she might escape her own trafficking.

The Traffic in Men: Punctuating the Sacred Gigolo

Loy's satire unearths what remains implicit in the sanctification of the courtesan from Baudelaire to Bataille: her occasionally glorified sacrificial status aside, the female sex worker as figured by the male artist or philosopher remains deeply entrenched within a modernist economy of feeling, tethered to the capital of male desire, a currency nonconvertible into feminine recognition or satiation. Loy openly mocks the agonistics of the supposedly prostituted male vanguardist, his wares trafficked against his will, presenting him as a gigolo inevitably co-opted by his own affective economy, putting his feet to the martyr's pyre in the hopes of purifying himself from the mire he unwittingly creates; the next chapter contains still more of this performative self-immolation. I use "gigolo" with an awareness of its inadequacies. Referring to an escort or kept man, a gigolo is not necessarily someone who makes a living by having sex for payment with strangers or an established clientele; as traditionally used, "gigolo" lacks the precarity, vulnerability, or transitoriness of the streetwalker. But there are few readymade terms sufficient to the cause of male sex worker: the cumbersome adjective "male" points to how the male prostitute, like the male nurse, midwife, or model, is the exception in feminised trades.[38]

A rare, direct Loy reference to the gigolo emasculates: arguing that we should never be deceived by individual good looks, Loy points out that "often the most adorable girls are impassive to erotic stimuli, just as the gigolo who looks like a static of rapture is frequently subject to Ejaculator [*sic*] Precox" (*CP* 18: 62). Next to this association of the gigolo with the impotence of fruit ripening before its time, Loy places an asterisk; at the bottom of the page, she justifies her observation via her knowledge of the German psychiatrist Richard von Krafft-Ebing (1840–1902), presumably of his landmark *Psychopathia Sexualis* (1886). Loy's recall of the gigolo's supposed tendency to premature ejaculation runs counter to the more common stereotype of his virility, and adds an extra layer of insult to Loy's satires of her male vanguard peers as figures associable with the sex trade. This thematic begins in *Brontolivido*, where Marinetti is derided as "'a magnificent cocotte'" by his peers, and by Loy herself, who describes him as her escort, "flapping his passion about on the nocturnal air as he pranced" alongside her through city streets, thereby reducing him to a showy streetwalker (*B* 6: 3; 8: 2). Where Marinetti declares himself "'a God'", Loy tells him sternly that he "'share[s] with the Olympians a totally disgusting promiscuity . . . raised to a sublimity that escapes the crowd'" (*B* 2: 12). Given that promiscuity is usually repugnant in women only, Loy reduces and deifies Marinetti simultaneously in this instance, thereby establishing the coordinates of her unique sacred gigolo.

While Loy's language effects strong satiric critique of the gloriously debased male, her punctuation calls attention to his unarticulated counterpart: the unrecognised female self and her desires, or the sphinx's secret that continues to fall outside of the modernist male's affective circulation. A telling example: the Futurist veneration of "agamogenesis" – asexual reproduction that excises women's reproductive role – Loy parenthesises as follows:

> .   .   .   Insurance
> of [male] spiritual integrity
> against the carnivorous courtesan
> .   .   .   (*LoLB* 47)

These lines are alert to the male fear that even the most debased woman, the woman paid for sex, is enjoying emotions whilst being paid, when she should pay for any inadvertent pleasure she receives. Against the modernist affective economy, Loy places this anxiety between two hyperbolic ellipses that undermine misogynist certitude. Punctuation is inseparable from the corporeal, the gestural, limbs and muscles in motion: genuflecting index fingers are quotations; the back of a hand raised to the corner of the mouth is dramatic parenthetical aside; the arched brow echoes the question mark, itself a tonal indicator like its rigidly exclamatory sibling (Lennard 94). Underscoring the embodied nature of any text, punctuation generates textual affect, writes Jennifer DeVere Brody; in turn, the reader "react[s] viscerally" to its pictorial communication, which "stages an intervention between utterance and inscription, speech and writing, activism . . . and apathy" (7, 9). Liminal by design, punctuation is marginalised, feminised, a truth Loy indirectly acknowledges in a riposte to the English poet John Rodker's review of the 1919 *Others* anthology, where she maintains that his "critique" of female contributors frequently amounts to "Lola Ridge ! ! !" or "Evelyn Scott ! ! !" ("'Others'" 56). Satirising his review entire, Loy saves particular ire for his presentation of femininity and women authors, writing: "never mind what the women want . . . well, most of them must content themselves with exclamation marks, according to Mr. Rodker" ("John Rodker's Frog" 59).

This categorical gendering goes unidentified in theories of punctuation, yet remains a constant, unstated theme. Consider this quotation from a 1953 punctuation guide:

> 'When punctuation was first employed, it was in the role of the handmaid of prose; later the handmaid was transformed by the pedants into a harsh-faced chaperone, pervertedly ingenious in the contriving of stiff regulations and starched rules of decorum; now, happily, she is content to act as auxiliary to the writer and as guide to the reader.' (qtd. in DeVere Brody 2–3)

Outdated? Not yet. Figured as body, punctuation is the undervalued hieroglyphic correlate to masculine mind and logos, to Western phonetic script. As one of Loy's über-masculine characters attests: "I launched myself on a philosophical argument . . . which my [female] companion punctuated with occasional gleams of intelligence" (*SE* 66). Used excessively, emotive punctuation, which should be prudently deployed, is often considered hysterical affront to clear, rational text. From a psychoanalytic perspective, punctuation is fundamentally ambivalent, rule-bound but wilfully, unpredictably subjective, duplicitous to capriciousness, entrenched in a symbiotic but dependent relationship with the paternalistic authority of language which it reveres but continually challenges.[39] While language strives for objective authority, punctuation is subjective, a "personal matter" (Parkes 5). With still more feminine specificity: the hyphen is hesitant, stuttering counter to the solid autonomy of the singular term; the full stop conjures a frivolous polka dot, and as period, insists upon its inextricability from women's cycle (DeVere Brody 36, 55). Punctuation is domestic: it coheres, eases, tidies, attends to the infinitesimal; "buttress" or "prop" (Carlyle 24).

Rarely standing alone, punctuation is afterthought, both in textual history and the act of writing itself. Its very genesis is lapsarian, disrupting the reign of *scriptio continua* and the "privilege" by which a reader could "punctuate to his or her satisfaction" (Lennard 2). Loy's friend Gertrude Stein felt this fall keenly, describing punctuation as "servile", and resenting the comma for "helping you along and holding your coat", thereby "keep[ing] you from living your life as actively as you should lead it". "[P]ositively degrading", Stein concludes, forgoing a mark of exclamation with admirable consistency ("Poetry" 220). Loy became evidence of the efficacy of Stein's stigmeological methods: in *The Autobiography of Alice B. Toklas*, Loy is celebrated for reading a manuscript of *The Making of Americans* and "understand[ing] without the commas" (145). But just as Beckett became spartan, pared counter to Joyce's logophilia, so Loy is overpunctuator to Stein's resolutely nonpictorial prose.[40] Where Stein critiques punctuation, Loy empowers its nethered, ignoble forms to critique the hyperbolically self-martyring, privileged male body, using it to map out the sidelined female corpus.

As secondary, abjectified body, punctuation is an upstart, its arbitrariness a challenge to standardised language, itself a display of nationalistic might, as attested by Robert Bridges, founder of the Society for Pure English in 1913: "'Defence of the language became an indirect and intellectually respectable way of defending the borders'" (qtd. in DeVere Brody 15). Hyphenated surnames and identities give voice to submerged, complex lineages, undermining patriarchal possessiveness and the xenophobic dissolutions of the melting pot.[41] Against contemporary forgetfulness or repression, the hyphen can insist on the contemporaneousness of past traumas, discords, diversities.[42] Manuscript variants of Loy's "Joyce's *Ulysses*" (1922) deploy dashes analogously, chinking the armour of the British empire and occidentalism writ large. As published, the poem praises the Irish author's imperialist attacks, mock-respectfully cordoning off the borders of his resistant colony's self-designated, domineering parent country:

> Phoenix
> of Irish fires
> lighten the Occident
>
> with Ireland's wings
> flap pandemoniums
> of Olympian prose
> and satirise
> the imperial Rose
> of Gaelic perfumes
> —England
> the sadistic mother
> embraces Erin—   (*LoLB* 88–9)[43]

One undated draft of this poem credits Joyce with "rip[ing] the occident / With [h]is sibilant satire – – – –" ("Joyce's *Ulysses*: Fragment"). In another, the dash effects this destruction. Under the heading "The cur of destiny" Loy's rough manuscript reads:

> Lashed capitalized creatures
> through the incontinent streets

into the hole and corner of their necessity –
   temples of duplicity
  The sun's avid advertisement
   Virile smells
   Sonorous coinages —
biological relationship —
   To the omnipotent —
And ri – ip the occident
or tear the occident
with this sibilant
   ri – ip of satire —
   laid the steamy entrails
of the living man
   in volvulous patterns
   of vertiginous rhythms —[44]

Advertisement cheapens language, Benjamin and Lewis tell us, and Loy's "capitalized creatures" summon up punctuated words, exploited urban masses. But for Loy, commercialisation is as long-standing, as pervasive, as the very sun: the exalted has always had its stench. Similarly, Joyce's honed mellifluousness is complexly aural: a sonorous, sibilant sheen over rank malodorousness, clandestine and base exchanges, decimating disembowelments. In turn, Loy's punctuation is unduly rowdy, when, by the demands of her native tongue, it should be discreet, silent. To dash is to bespatter, cast down, ruin; verbally, we dash "[t]o strike with violence, so as to break into fragments" (Denham 32). Woolf derided Joyce's method as a formulaic "cutting out [of] the explanations", a mere "putting in the thoughts between dashes" (99). By contrast, Loy's "ri – ip" embodies Joyce's tearing the veil off the world divided, takes boisterous pleasure in the gashed, obstructed, and turned innards of occidental entitlement exposed by the deceptively smooth surface of his "Olympian prose". This dashwork enacts Peter Szendy's "punchuation", or the overlooked, generative aggression of minor marks.

We are taught to think of punctuation as attuned to the rhythmic body, a breathing space, a blink providing respite from eye-watering textual demands. When Loy begins writing, she punctuates her poetic lines with blank spaces that she called the "'fallow-lands of mental spatiality'" or rhythmic, necessary gaps of respite (*BM* 169). Against this harmoniousness, Szendy argues that we must take seriously the violence of stigmeology's root in stigmata, respecting its latent capacity to break the skin of language, to sting and jab, and its homophonic connection to the punch. "Punchuation" is a "doubling blow . . . the singular flash or clap that, remarking what happens, allows us to have and inscribe an experience of it" (Szendy 4). Punchuation is a forceful epiphany, directly rendered. Szendy's rich, difficult theoretical work is stylistically and contextually indebted to a modernist vanguard lineage: emphasising the oppositional, pugilistic power of punctuation; viewing the self as alienated, martyred, "stitched and nailed to itself" to satiate the need to be marked, "truly stopped, anchored somewhere" (9). Yet his pursuit of "allegories of the punctuated structure of experience" exceeds periodicity: escalated sensation does facilitate memory, does collage otherwise infinite, subjective fragments. "Pinch me, I'm dreaming; punctuate me so that I feel" (3). For Szendy, "the point" is "the figure par excellence of gathering into unity with the self" even as it is "immediately destined to be dispersed and multiplied" (9). Stammering, stuttering, flickering, this self is unstable and unfixed, what Hegel calls "'the *pulsating point* of selfhood'" (qtd. in Szendy 63).

For American philosopher Eugene Gendlin, this indeterminate *punctum saliens* is best rendered serially, as ellipsis: perceiving before language, before conceptualisation, Gendlin's "self-sentien[t]" human being is "the . . ." ("Primacy" 344–5). The body continuously senses itself, knows a past, feels what lies unseen behind its back, recognises its emotive life, physically in the moment whilst implying future movement and interaction. All is not culturally determined, Gendlin argues; instead, the body directs us to the new and perplexing, as when a poet senses the immanence of an unwritten line or phrase, or when we sit in a room of people, awaiting a turn to speak, only to be unable to articulate our thoughts when that turn comes, "something which a . . . . . somehow implicitly knows" ("Assertions" 32; "Wider Role" 199). Demarcated as ellipses, Gendlin's self-sentience undergirds and upholds the subject, directing, intuitively analysing, palpably countering the Cartesian divide and theoretically endless, random evolutionary variants ("Wider Role" 203). Gendlin's ". . ." asserts itself, feels its way toward recognition of its own needs and desires, in a manner consistent with Loy's pursuit of the asterisked sphinx's secret. In her satires of the male avant-gardist as sacred gigolo, Loy is attuned to the emphases of Szendy's punchuation. But in her dramas "The Sacred Prostitute" (c. 1914–16) and "The Pamperers" (1920), Loy's excessive ellipses move from rows of dashes to dots that approximate Gendlin's primordial figurations, that clamour for the dynamic, gender-astute "being alive" to which Loy perpetually aspires, her unique variant of Bergson's élan vital. In Loy, ellipsis is assertive critique.

Loy's manuscripts and typescripts are awash in a slapdashery that marks thoughts incomplete, perhaps unworthy, connected yet detached: "In the dash, thought becomes aware of its fragmentary character" (Adorno 304).[45] Overused, dashes are said to "create a jumpy or breathy quality in writing" (*Little, Brown* 434). Form and content snubbing this very maxim, Loy insists that "there is no renaissance without breath— / The breathing upon of the logos—" (*SE* 262). Nor does Loy go in fear of nervous panting: in "Gloria Gammage", the wealthy protagonist's consistently inconsistent "accesses of surfeit" are matched by the profusive, inconclusive dashes by which the vast majority of her clauses end; notably, be-dashed Gloria is particularly adept at "keeping the secret—of the Sphinx" (*SE* 25, 28). Loy's prose dialogues are similarly marked, as in the posturing anxieties of "Lady Asterisk.", where the sentences are superficial, combative, and aposiopetic by repetitive design. A "sign of suspension", dashes hover, gesturing to words perceived intellectually or morally unsayable (Parkes 56). Both inarticulacies surface in Loy's "All the Laughs in One Short Story by McAlmon", where, amidst elliptical lines of dashes and laughters brittle, drunken, penetrating, adorable, hysterical, unbearable, and taunting, a young woman "smile[s] sphinxly", briefly attuned to her own mystery, its silent appeal (*SE* 219–20). Elsewhere in Loy, demarcations of the unsaid mark a child's "[q]uivering with a dashed out laughter"; a crocodile's magnificent song: "– – – – – –"; obliterative male confusion: "– – – – – ?"; hesitation over the unpalatable prospect that a boy may be genetically predisposed to criminality; the slow turning pages of a photo album; and the all-consuming fear at the dropping of the atom bomb: "– – – – – anxiety . . . ." (*IA* 68: 135; *SE* 23, 82, 122, 132, 287). "[W]hy dash a line where the eyes should be . . . Where was the beauty in that?", asks adolescent Loy in her first days at art school (*IA* 67: 103). As a writer, she would continually promote the aesthetic value of imperfectly formulated, fragmentary occlusions. And at their most sublime, Loy's punctuated lines mark the divide between vertiginous affective drops and transportive desire.

Loy punctuates experiences that evade resolution or ready turns of phrase, experiences discerned intuitively, affectively, corporeally. Loy's is a hieroglyphic demand that the unremarked sentient body have its say: she is an overpunctuator, self-reflexively illustrating "the leap or bounce of pulsation, elasticity", the "freedom at once *in* and *from* matter—where the possibility of phrasing, vocalizing, begins" (Szendy 104). At its most poetic, consciously crafted, Loy's punctuation points to "a new period or limb in the speculative phrase of thinking", but it is also wilfully hyperbolic, "a hyperpunctuation that, by dint of detailed articulation, atomizes, pulverizes, and granularizes phrases and forms" (Szendy 104). Hyperpunctuation prevails in "The Sacred Prostitute", or the drama that is Loy's most overt, sustained riposte to the unexamined contradictions at the heart of the modernist affective economies that traffic in maintaining the subjugated uncertainty that is "Woman!?! . . ." (*SE* 189).[46] This ejaculation is emitted by a character in Loy's play, the male Idealist, and retrospectively punctuated by our female author. Loy surrounds the Idealist's interrogative with affective exclamations – of outrage? of long-suppressed silence? – that subside into ellipsis, the mark of the easily disregarded sentient being. "Woman must exist—", the Idealist patronises resignedly, only able to envision her existence as possession (*SE* 189). The almighty male Futurism labours harder, proposing to fellow protagonist Love that she and he try "Just – – – BEING" (*SE* 212). Sat close to one another, temple to temple, this couple is silently, communally alive, ecstatically sentient, as Love affirms: "I never knew how wonderful it is that hearts can beat" (*SE* 213). Respite is brief. Overtly about the sex war, "The Sacred Prostitute" is founded upon a diametric opposition of sacrificial and unsentimental economies of desire, of violence versus commerce as conduits to intimacy. From Loy's theatre of war, Futurism emerges as a sacred gigolo seeking recognition as a martyr to his own affective economy. But as his story unfolds, we watch as Futurism uneasily straddles untenable positions of aggressive immolation and a fully paid-up love that, his financial commitment notwithstanding, remains feminised because unsatiated, an elusive sphinx's secret.

"The Sacred Prostitute" opens on a group of educated male clients in the brothel the world has become, debating their participation within a system of circulation where sex is purchased through cunning, guile, and hard-lost expenditures of money and affective labour. Parodying their relentless misogyny toward the category Woman, the men are dismissible types: an immature Youth, an Idealist, a Don Juan, a Victorian "Tea Table Man", and a blatantly inconsequential trinity of "Some Other Man", "Another Man", and "A Man". Resisting *"over-valuation"*, this group deliberately underestimates woman as commodity, as battered possession of "bully" or pimp; as undeserving, unpaying recipient of male chaperonage in public spaces; as consummate purchaser of like luxurious frivolities and capricious withholder of her only asset: sex (*SE* 192, 189–90, 191). Futurism arrives on the scene, insulting all and sundry with the oblique expression: "Tango Tout!" (*SE* 193). Marinetti wrote a diatribe against the fashionable tango, posited as "masturbated waltz" that failed to achieve climax: a single insufficient knee between a woman's legs; all rub and no penetration ("Tango" 132–3). If a tout sells indirectly, profits off another's labour, for Loy's character Futurism, these men neither pay for their feelings, nor get to the point; instead, they showily overperform, too eagerly selling themselves to their female subordinates. But Futurism is equally prey to the exigencies of a modernist affective economy, debasing sentimental love itself as "'Greed' with a capital 'G'" and therefore "female", remaining cloth-eared to Nature's denunciation of men as overeaters who need to learn self-control (*SE* 197, 206–7). "[T]he value of sex is fictitious", insists Love, telling Futurism – age-old female plaint – that he moves too fast for her pleasure (*SE* 202). His reply is typical, dismissively impatient, unwittingly comical: "Too quick! When my love is eternal and my train leaves in fifteen minutes—" (*SE* 201). Loy's punch is a double hook: in his best-selling *How to Seduce a Woman* (1917), Marinetti reports that his promotion of rapid lovemaking in wartime garnered a woman's complaint that he treated the female sex like railway stations (Re 106). For Loy, Marinetti/Futurism is intimate sell-out to the rapidities of capitalist "progress", and authorial sell-out to the mass market: he traffics his own masculinity.[47] Serially published at the same time as Loy was writing "The Sacred Prostitute", *How to Seduce a Woman* was standard issue to Italian soldiers throughout World War I; as Lucia Re discusses, it is less concerned with wooing than with "alleviat[ing] the male fear of betrayal" (96). Loy monetises this fear in "The Sacred Prostitute", where any emotional attachment is posited as a risky investment in a potentially vacuous or rapacious sentimental economy, even as everyone is prostituted, citizen to the global brothel that is her drama's set. As the presiding Procuress indicates at the play's end: "We haven't succeeded in balancing accounts yet—You see, it is not yet decided whether the demand creates the supply, or the supply the demand" (*SE* 215).

Against precariously financed feeling, Loy posits sacrificial aggression. As women are madonnas or whores, Loy typifies men as either powerful economists of "civilised", remunerated feeling or "primitive" brutes who take by force what they can't afford. Resolutely aspiring toward type one, the Tea Table Man recognises the appeal of type two, "confess[ing]" that this divide "results in a double personality" (*SE* 191). Pretending at polite sexual disinterest whilst shopping with women for their undergarments, the Tea Table Man seethes within, scarcely repressing "a vision of [him]self clubbing a naked women over the head in a virgin forest" (*SE* 192). Equally mired in modern economies, Futurism does not hesitate to entertain his "savage" desires, dragging Love across the floor by her hair to "'finish her off'" (*SE* 198).[48] Juxtapositions of contemporary and ancient economies continue apace: a powerful "*prophet*", Futurism is a "conjuring commercial traveller" who "speculat[es]" on what lies ahead (*SE* 195). Rejecting parasitic "emotion of vague sentimentality", Futurism is nevertheless disinclined to pay for fine feelings, preferring love that is "atrociously carnal", consummation by force (*SE* 195, 199). Love Futurism calls a "divine little woman", presumably as sacrificable as his previous mistresses and womankind, whom he hopes to obliterate by mastering procreation (*SE* 201–2; 205). Attuned to this carnage, Love plays her ritualised part, pronouncing herself willing to join Futurism's harem or "be burnt alive on [his] corpse" (*SE* 213–14). But Futurism sees only his own self-immolation: "I am sacrificing myself to make things new—", he asserts, adding: "and only succeeding in making them *louder*" (*SE* 205). By his own admission, Futurism possesses a "bombastic voice that has a meretricious ring in it" (*SE* 210). Etymologically, "meretriciousness" originates with the stereotyping of prostitutes as gaudy, false, lacking in value or integrity. Excising and exercising himself to regenerate culture, sociality, and sexuality, Futurism is indistinguishable from a common prostitute.

Futurism's bombast is full of contradictions easily resisted or revoked, but his performance is as complexly gestural as it is dogmatically verbose. As the stage director's voice attests, Futurism's "*every gesture propounds vulgarity intensified to Divinity*", embodying the substance of Bataille's sacrificiality, whereby the profane becomes deific through ritual expulsion (*SE* 197). Master of commandeering sleights of hand and body, Futurism plucks prospective time from thin "*air with a superb gesture [holding] it invisible between an eloquent thumb and finger*" before pronouncing: "Gentlemen ———— The FUTURE" (*SE* 195). A spatial and temporal marker, Loy's long dash connects and divides this male audience from the progress assumed to be theirs, affirming whilst undermining their quasi-deific superiority, so easily transvalued into victimhood. Equally nuanced is Futurism's supercilious gaze upon Love, "*looking unutterably sentimental*"; Love returns this bodily artifice in kind, "*throw[ing] her arms round his neck with a gesture of surrender*" (*SE* 198, 203). Neither feeling nor capitulation goes unqualified; both are tainted by knowing performance, expiate themselves to the gendered status quo. A charlatan of words, Futurism's body language is porous, multivalent, lending plausibility to his promise to Love that he "shall reach [her] soul though the medium of [her] body" (*SE* 199). But, ultimately, Futurism is the comic mascot of Loy's most integral precept, one she shares with Bataille and a host of contemporary thinkers, namely, that "love without cruelty is powerless" (Žižek 173). This truth is almost too obviously evident in the climactic, infamous boxing match Futurism stages with Love, heart-shaped gloves at the ready. Body language confirms this pugilistic allegory: this is a couple that *"glare[s] at each other amicably"* (*SE* 209). And yet: foregrounding the body, aspiring to the divine, Futurism's gestures punctuate ambivalently, falling cataclysmically, if generatively, short of the satiating mark. Remembered for his indefatigably innovative performances, in his experimental writing, Marinetti longed to "'burst the sentence's steam-pipe, the valves of punctuation'", and is often said to have influenced Loy's stigmeology (qtd. in Bartram 20).[49] But where Marinetti graffitis constraining linguistic convention, Loy's marks underscore affectivity, irresolvability, and the identificatory, often degrading, stigmatic.

Punctuation co-opts Futurism into the role of everyman, or, by the terms of Loy's "The Sacred Prostitute", a common gigolo. Hovering between exasperated participation in a modernist affective economy that eschews sentimentality and the consuming aggressions of ancient sacrificial ritual, the male actors of this drama speak, by and large, in incomplete phrases. Their aposiopetic dialogue "interinterrupts", disrupting its own hesitations and inconclusivities, "bursting the punctiformity of the point" (Szendy 25, 35). Interinterruption mocks authority and pretensions to authorial clarity alike; in Loy's play, it lends a breathless, improvised open-endedness to the paternalistic didacticism of her typified males. Finality evades even the machine-gun oration of Futurism: asked by the Procuress to sit still for a moment, he exclaims, outraged: "I—dynamic—plastic—velocity—stop—!" (*SE* 204). This arrest seeps, is undone by the reverberating affective waves of the sudden, exclamatory break by which Futurism's phallic command is reduced to buttressed comedic mark. By the terms of Loy's punctuation, Futurism is irrational hyperbolist, as when he begs Love in a hyphenated rush: "Will-you-love-me-will-you-love-me-will-you-love-me-love-me-love-me-love-me-me-me-ME—???" (*SE* 200). Mocking Futurist masculinity and its punctuating aesthetics simultaneously, the reversion to the "me-me-me-ME" of the demanding male self functions as Futurism's deferred, de facto response to the Idealist's "Woman!?! . . .". Both phrases end in excessive, emphatic, anxious aposiopesis.

This taut suspension recurs when Futurism gives inaudible voice to his desire, an ineffable, amorous intensity Loy transcribes as follows:

FUTURISM. To be faithful to me—while I am never there – – – – –
– – – – – – – – – – *(Silence)* – – – – – – – – *Now* do you believe me?

LOVE. Nearly.

FUTURISM. *(with passionate sincerity)* You can – – – – – you can – – – – you do – – – – you

LOVE. *(transfigured)* "Lord now lettest thou thy servant depart in peace."

FUTURISM. – – – – do!

LOVE. Good God. What am I doing— What am I saying?— Who am I talking to? *(quotes Futurist tirade against women)*

FUTURISM. *(imploringly)* You can't hold me responsible for anything I said last week – Believe in me – – –

LOVE. I ask nothing better than to believe in something— You – – – – – or myself.

FUTURISM. *(briefly, his eyes blazing through her)* Do you – – – – – – – in yourself?

LOVE. Sssssssssssh – – – – – – – if anybody's listening, this will end in a draw. *(SE* 211–12*)*

As indicated by the stage direction "*(Silence)*" in the middle of his dashed line, Futurism's ellipses mark inarticulable, occluded, or self-censored speech, while Love pauses within otherwise continuous phrasing. Futurism's punctuation is logos, Love's is corporeal, is "the signal of a[n unlocatable] treasure" (*SE* 253). Responding to Futurism, Love paraphrases a New Testament passage in which Jesus's disciple Luke asserts that he can die in peace, having encountered deific salvation through complete acquiescence to God (Luke 2.29). If Love isn't being sarcastic, Loy assuredly is: Love alludes to a final uncoupling of body from spirit, an ecstatic transport wrought by Futurism's affection, even as Futurism enacts a parody of the marriage ceremony, where the performative commitment – "I do" – becomes a badgering: "You do!" Both seek a satiating finality undone by the plethora of dashes; of these, typically, manic Futurism has the lion's share. Regarding Lawrence Sterne's similarly excessive dashwork in *Tristram Shandy* (1759), Szendy writes: "By stretching the sentence like an elastic strained to the point of breaking, each dash is *on the point* of cutting as it retraces with its mark the very continuity of the statement" (20–1). So too do Loy's dashes reveal and withhold, suture and maim, remaining incontrovertibly incomplete whilst circumscribing the "monumental phallic power to puncture" (Szendy 29). These dashes suspend economies of desire sacrificial, economic, and as-yet unexperienced: between Futurism's disavowal of last week's circulated diatribes and his abiding need for belief lies a row of anticipatory, inaudible dashes, a traversable link between humanity and "——— The FUTURE" (*SE* 195). But this future has become less declamatory than humble, more fragmented trestle than erect monument: according to Artemidorus, "to dream that one becomes a bridge signifies that one will be a prostitute . . . 'allow[ing] many to go over'" (qtd. in Foucault 27). Chastened by self-debasement into genuine feeling, Futurism momentarily forgets himself. His recognition of Love, his asking about her self-belief, prompts a sole instance of shared feeling, the wonder of hearts beating slowly, sentiently, marking an intimate silence.

"I am measured by the silence of inspiration", announces Diana, huntress-cum-manageress of geniuses of Loy's "The Pamperers" (1920), the sister text that followed "The Sacred Prostitute". In the earlier play, the female inmates of the world brothel remain in the background, near-uniformly silent. The only identified female among the cast of "The Pamperers", Diana is an ideal female, "tuned to a laudatory discrimination . . . made of the instigatory caress [. . .] the woman who understands" and who is always "*still more preparedly posing*" (*SE* 169, 176).[50] Absorbing the madonna/whore complex without demur, Diana gives silent comfort in turn: touches, pleases, listens, makes pretty. Perpetually situating herself in relation to others, Diana is irresistibly drawn to the Houseless Loony, a nomad free of spatial or mental fixities, the direct opposite of Diana's sidekick Ossy, whose name evokes stagnant rigidity, ossification. A "great Vitalist", the Loony pursues and generates a levitous "*Life*" that exceeds deific creation because it amuses; thus elevated, he deflects fatuous Diana as one of "the submerged" (*SE* 181, 170–1). Diana longs to accompany the Loony on his "'miraculous ambulance in spatial mystery'", but he sees no way of including her in his apostleship "of Fraternity", his brotherhood of "secluded coward[s]" with narrow sympathies (*SE* 171–2). This male coterie, the Loony asserts, will "slight" Diana: "Your most fervid conversation would lose itself as an impertinent silence among the debonair rumble of our caste" (*SE* 172). The silence by which Diana is evaluated is inspired; in unequal turn, her every utterance is read as silence. Elsewhere in Loy's oeuvre, quiet negates or terrifies.[51]

By comparison, Diana's "impertinent silence" jars, is as impudent as it is irrelevant; dismissed yet oppositional, it demands acknowledgement. A keening quietude is refracted though "The Pamperers", a play perforated by ellipses that mark the rhythmic rumble of the body beneath the intellectual and aesthetic posturings of Diana's male vanguard peers. The ". . ." takes centre stage, even as a curiously unattributed **"SILENCE"** – does Diana say this? is it bellowed stage direction? – re-escalates Diana's gendered diminuendo (*SE* 180). **"SILENCE"** marks a narrative turn: following this resounding non-utterance, Diana garners control over her Loony, who is thereafter acquiescent to her every diktat on how to participate in the vanguard she controls (*SE* 180). A feminised sentience, it seems, is unobtrusively in charge.

The elliptical lifebeat of "The Pamperers" is far steadier, far more constant, than the erratic breathlessness, the prostrate, hyperbolic dash-bursts of "The Sacred Prostitute". And this punctuated affirmation of the play's beating heart feeds its sacrificial conclusion. For where "The Sacred Prostitute" closes with an ambivalent recognition of a modernist affective economy still being accounted for, our inevitable situatedness in the weary exchanges of a perpetual global brothel, "The Pamperers" concludes with this apocalyptic stage direction: "THE END OF THEM ALL" (*SE* 182). Again, this is neither stage direction nor direct utterance, but authorial intervention: having delineated the Loony's conversion to Houston Loon, master vanguard dissembler, Loy steps in to execute not a ritual "THE END", but her entire cast. This desultory victory is the outcome of the play's battle between sentimental and sacrificial economies of feeling and desire, a thematic repeated from "The Sacred Prostitute", as is its love awash in cherished aggressions.[52]

In fact, "The Pamperers" satirically commodifies Christ's crucifixion. The catalyst of the Passion is reduced to "the forty gold pieces of a manicure set"; Jesus's agony on the cross is rendered in "Dresden china 15th century" (*SE* 163–4). Christ's immolation is the raw material of technological reproduction, but like rituals reverberate through the machinations of Diana's vacuous coterie. Wilfully vague characters – "SOMEBODY", "SOMEBODY ELSE", "1ST FRIEND", "2ND FRIEND" – celebrate "'the virginity of white carpets'" over which the Loon is carried from the stables he inhabits on a throne, revered lamb ready for the slaughter as Diana's "virgin eyelashes" are proffered to the Loony's "predatory eye" (*SE* 166, 168, 165, 163). Against these expiatory urges, Diana has imbibed Futurism's love of speed, progress, and financial exchange, upon which she sets her luminous watch, yearning to stay abreast of the ever-shifting ground of vanguard novelty; embodying a "reciprocal quality", she facilitates the perceived need to "serve [the genius] directly to the consumer" (*SE* 167–9). By turns courtesan and madam, Diana is a purveyor of sacred gigolos, a trafficker in avant-garde men. But if "The Pamperers" is the story of the Loony's recruit, it also hones Loy's critique of sacred prostitution, a critique in which the vanguard male is suspect because he believes himself insufficiently sanctified *or* degraded.

With his passion for "picking up cigar ends", the Loony is a streetwalker, a near-perfect replica of Baudelaire's ragpicker:

> One comes upon a shaking ragman, who
> Staggers against the walls, as poets do,
> And disregardful of policeman's spies,
> Pours from his heart some glorious enterprise.
>
> Swearing his oaths, he dictates laws he's made
> To vanquish evil, bring the victims aid,
> And there beneath the sky, a canopy,
> Grows drunk upon his own sublimity. (*SE* 163; *Flowers* 217)

Just as the Loony will be hoisted upon his throne by "Picked People" who worship his aesthetic daring, so too is this ragman a revered king by the poem's end (*SE* 162). The Loony, too, responds to the refined elitism of his worshippers with garbled maxims, as if "drunk upon his own sublimity". At its most palpable, the Loony's manifesto consists of the tautological proclamation that he is "going to make *Life* out of cigar-ends / *Life*"; near-metaphysically, he will "shed [the] transcendental showers of ideo-fags" and collect "battered finger-posts" that represent "ideal / Ashy quotas in Balance of / The easier equilibrium of Life" (*SE* 170, 174). His is a philosophy of detritus, an aestheticising of what was once the lowest form of street vending. In the nineteenth century, Henry Mayhew categorises "street-finders" as those who gather dogs' dung, refuse, and "cigar-end finders, or 'hard-ups'", who "collect the refuse pieces of smoked cigars from the gutters, and having dried them, sell them as tobacco to the very poor" (7). A cigar-end finder and creator, the Loony considers his artworks "A tear of absolution / For the weak" mired in pagan beliefs, yet he recognises that the greatest among us, himself included, are subject to life's "common call": "Fourpence for dinner, sixpence for love" (*SE* 175). Debased streetwalker begging absolution, his intimacy for sale, the Loony is another of Loy's sacred gigolos.

The Loony prides himself on his spatial mastery – "the grand man is able to pick up anything he is able to see" – and fears most "diminished elasticity": "The most expansive / Periodically contract / Can it be possible I am getting narrow?" (*SE* 171, 176). Countering Futurism's hyperbolic, overstretched dashes and hyphens in "The Sacred Prostitute", the Loony and his community contract into the condensed terrain of ellipses figured as silent, feminised body to masculine vanguard posturings. Prey to Diana's hypnotic insistence that "when you're not holding forth you must be like us . . .", the Loony is swayed by her offers of cigar boxes entire, her claim that "Here the Grand is the infinitesimal . . .". But the persistently impertinent silences of "The Pamperers" disrupt Diana's affirmations of "the ethics of property", her injunction that the Loony treat any Duchess "as if she were a prostitute" (*SE* 180). Loy's hyperpunctuation gives pause to sentience, to the knowing body that resists staged complicities, to the beating vanguard hearts that will be sacrificed to narrative nous at the play's end.

In "The Pamperers", Picasso, who "stack[s]" unpredictable masterpieces is praised for using "all sorts of odds and ends" (*SE* 163). Elsewhere, Loy celebrates Picasso as "our greatest aesthetic interpreter", master of "distances of space", challenger of "pauper aesthetic[s] that fall to the stacking" (*SE* 260–1). Loy's critique of the vanguard, its propensity to elevate and debase itself as a form of sacred prostitution, discerns and selects. Juxtaposed against Picasso's skill, the Loony is pure charlatan, his impoverished aesthetic on the tumble, his rows of dots evoking the Greek origin of ellipsis, "falling short"; he is, as Loy will write in a late poem, one among endless "shampooed gigolos" who "prowl to the sobbing taboos" (*LoLB* 95). "It is the unrepresentable in presentation that causes it to exceed replica—", Loy asserts, again in praise of Picasso; similarly, the unrepresentable sentient body pulses within the ellipses of "The Pamperers", ready for the execution that will purify art that neither proselytises nor prostrates itself to money or fame, that exceeds the confines of any affective economy (*SE* 261). Where "The Sacred Prostitute" pokes at Futurism's self-sanctification, pointing to its complicit debasement within patriarchy's prostituted world, "The Pamperers" recreates the self-prostituting vanguard coterie as faction sacrificed to its deific author. In both plays, punctuation illustrates a vertiginous meta-narrative, an all-too-human propensity to collapse into a foundational prostration. This ever-proximate baseness underwrites Loy's oeuvre, and is anatomised in her approach to the body's lower half: the assholes and vaginas with which this chapter began, but also feet and legs.

Collapsing, Soaring: Transcendent Fallenness

Gauged, evaluated, and propelled by her lower half, the female streetwalker emblematises Loy's atavistic aesthetics: early criminologists called attention to the prostitute's "physical and mental stigmata", punctuating her with the marks of so-called savagery, among them misshapen ears, skulls, "protruding jaws" (Bland 76; Horn 24). Albeit euphemistically, the "streetwalker" is defined by bipedalism, or "'the salient point that differentiates the forebears of man from other primates'"; as walkers, we could carry provisions, domesticate land, animals, women (Mary Leakey qtd. in Solnit 44; 37). Through walking, men evolve; "the typical modernist novel ends with someone walking away solitary and disenchanted, his problems unresolved but free of social or domestic obligations" (Eagleton, *How* 168). Note how, in this quotation, "someone" becomes a liberated, autonomous "he"; a Paul Morrel, a Stephen Dedalus, but not a Clarissa Dalloway who remains reassuringly fixed in time and space at the end of her narrative.[53] Female walking is suspect. In public, any mobile, hubristically erect woman can be judged too free, on the brink of a fall or in need of a good shove (Bland 119). Preyed upon by "routine harassment" that reconfirms unequal citizenship, women come "to think like prey" (Solnit 240–2).

Always related to the perambulations of the mind, male walking is also sexual freedom, as modernists Baudelaire, Whitman, and Breton knew well, conflating the love of the city with a lust "for the passer-by" that was consummated on the streets, turning walking into sex (Solnit 207). Loy knows these injustices: her sexually suspect females "tram[p]"; her besotted women "long to run against the blowing wind" with their lovers; enlarged pelvis attendant, her birthing women scale "distorted mountain[s] of agony" as their male peers run away lightly, irresponsibly, or with "a gait of urgent enterprise" (*SE* 52, 84; *LoLB* 5; *EP* 24). Where her first husband continually strews his belongings about, obstructing her path and necessitating her adoption of a downward, submissive gaze, Loy finds an ideal lover in Arthur Cravan, a man "whose nature it was to walk straight on – over everything . . . unconcernedly"; with him, Loy's life "consisted entirely in wandering arm in arm through the streets . . . tap[ping] the source of enchantment" (*EP* 21, 25).

Recognising, as does Bataille, that eroticism is assumed to begin with male pursuit of the female, Loy looks for what he calls the "vicissitudes" where desire can "move away from its essence", away from nostalgia, outdated continuities, "sneaking aside along [alternate] paths" (*E* 130, 146). Yet Loy remains enamoured of the "rough, dirty magic" of city streets, their democratising, oppositional possibilities; shared protest, yes, but also individual wandering, "intrepid pilgrim[ages]", the blissfully remapped self (Solnit 176, 217–29; *SE* 95). Working appositively with narratives of maligned or malignant streetwalkers, the traversable street is the filthy base from which Loy achieves sublime transport; from its stony stones, its prohibitions and curtailments, she draws her own desire lines. Along the way, she transvalues the lower half of the body, punctuating her revelatory ecstasies with its baseness.

In its broadest conceivable sense, streetwalking captivates Loy: from Florence to Paris to New York, the life – especially the low life – of city streets is endless fascination, one monumentalised in "Modern Poetry" (c. 1925), where "the baser avenues of Manhattan" generate era-defining poetic rhythms (*LoLB* 159). Where Benjamin finds contemporary "script" co-opted "by advertisements" and "the brutal heteronomies of economic chaos", Loy remains fascinated by how "poets' work [can be identified] by the gait of their mentality", their reaction to "the spontaneous tempo" of modern life (*LoLB* 157–8). Bataille shares Loy's reverence for an ambulatory tempo neither rational nor regular: in "'abandoning a lucid gait'" we transcend the limitations of language and discourse, returning ourselves to the generatively devolved state of our distant ancestors (qtd. in Heimonet 235). Bataille's inversion of this proposition reads as follows: "When man's meditation upon himself and the universe attains its extreme limit, it recovers the blind, unerring gait of those undistracted by the complexities of reason" ("Sacrifice" 64). In "International Psycho-Democracy" (1918), Loy likewise foregrounds the need for "*a new social rhythm*" that will reroute evolution, consciousness, and militarism, or the "*[r]hythm of national popular enthusiasm*: the march, the band, parade." In the wake of World War I, the synchronised movement of the crowd risks perpetuating the damaging, "*belligerent masculine* social ideal" (*LaLB* 281–2).[54] "Most movements", Loy asserts, "have a fixed concept towards which they advance, we move away from all fixed concepts in order to advance" (*LaLB* 278).

Like her sacred prostitutes, Loy "proceeds recedingly"; to her pronounced resistance to the rectilinear we will return in the second volume of this *Anatomy* (*LoLB* 98).[55] Against narratives of sustained longevity, upward mobility, and linear progress, Loy portrays haggard side streets where "the human . . . race" is "altered to irrhythmic stagger", where limbs flail, sail, wobble, and sway (*LoLB* 133).[56] Loy's love of the lurch extends to aesthetic form, including the "jerk[s] of beauty" skewing Stein's prose; when she praises Marianne Moore as a poet whose "writing so often amusingly suggests the soliloquies of a library clock", we know this is satire (*LaLB* 298; *LoLB* 160). As for Dickinson before her, Loy's critics have often deemed her writing clumsy, shod in granite, unbalanced, inebriate, hesitant, floundering. Even Pound's oft-cited diktat that Loy's "poetry . . . is a dance of the intelligence among words and ideas" is countered by his overlooked, subsequent claim that her logopoeia is "the utterance of clever people . . . hovering on the brink of despair" ("'Others'" 57–8).[57] Loy's elegance threatens to collapse at any moment. Or, as Loy puts it: "I go / Gracelessly / As things go" (*LoLB* 62). At stake in this wilful bathos of form and content is Loy's sense that we are all, universally, as fallen as any prostitute.

Fallen, because irrecoverably weighed down: standing and walking are continual deferrals of collapse, our erect "column of flesh and bone always in danger of toppling", our "proud unsteady tower" unique within the animal kingdom (Solnit 33). Loy feels this workaday miracle keenly, is attuned to the "essence of drooping", our constant fight to shore up "inner support" against a weighty ontological sentience long figured in her work as an infinite "universal tonnage" always at the ready to crush the human self (*SE* 138, 268–9). Like Loy, Bataille is interested in the oscillations between grounding and destabilisation; within disequilibrium, both perceive illumination, the potential for transcendence. Reversing Genesis, Loy's and Bataille's falls are epiphanic, sublime, as in Loy's "ridiculous little incident" of 1919. Walking in Geneva with Emily Balch, a prominent member of the Women's International League for Peace and Freedom, Loy nods whilst laughing, and feels her skull dislocate from her spine. Having lost contact with the universal energy running from her head to her feet, Loy enters a void, until:

> Very gradually, very low down, on an horizon in profundity, a faint, dark light began to penetrate the nothingness; a sombre luminousness I compared to the bluish base of a steel J nib that had fascinated me in childhood.
>
> My ease became absolute, transcending any ease of the body, as if I had entered an ultimate safety-zone, I looked forward with placid curiosity, to the different gamut of experience I *knew* awaited me. I felt no concern for the world I was lately involved with. (*SE* 37)

Outside of her body, Loy positions herself within a suitably decumbent "safety-zone": reminiscent of a "bluish base", profundity notably emerges from "very low down". A click signals Loy's return to animacy: "Suddenly, a shaft of rushing 'force', with an impact-potential of incalculable tonnage descended from above" (*SE* 37). Fearing that she will be crushed, Loy finds instead that her electricity resurges and reanimates, meaning that the full implications of her revelation disappointingly evade her. Seeing her consciousness return, Balch urges her to lie down, but Loy resists: "in the middle of a public square!" (*SE* 39). Opposed to literally embodying the fallen woman, Loy is nevertheless confirmed in her sense that "being alive" means becoming a "magnet" to an always mysterious "universal electricity" (*SE* 39). Aleatory, epiphanic, servile, "Incident" affirms Loy's mystic vitalism, just as a collapse in the street proved epiphanic for Mary Baker Eddy, founder of the Christian Science church of which Loy was a life-long member; to these visionary propensies we will return in the second volume.[58]

Bataille, too, has his urban revelation at "the crossing of the rue de Four", a vertiginous clash with "the 'impossible'", a "shipwreck of reason" by which he becomes "'Nothingness'". Alone in the Paris night, Bataille is freed of constraints literal and figurative, "rush[ing] into a sort of rapture", divine laughter attendant, eradication on the supine horizon: "the extreme depth of each thing opened itself up—laid bare, as if I were dead" (*IE* 34). Thus unsteadied, Bataille extends this experience to humanity writ large: "*Are we not plunging continuously? Backward, sideward, forward in all directions? . . . . Are we not straying as through an infinite Nothingness?*" (*IE* 152). To be fully autonomous is to embrace destabilising excess, the self-sacrifice that falls willingly "into the void"; sovereign thought begins with an abrupt, immediate descent that "destroys the world that reassures" (*BR* 82; *AS3* 381). "It is when I collapse that I have a start", writes Bataille; we aspire to the angelic in order to reach fallen Lucifer, mired in the integral depths (*AS3* 381). Attuned from an early age to "the physiological myths of Rise and Fall", Loy sought out her own atavisms as a child: "spurts of primeval magic", an "intellectual acumen" indistinguishable from "a fallen angel become a savage" (*CP* 13: 25). Paradoxically, "perfect equipoise" is achieved by decimating the durable foundation of familial heritage and its defining Victorianism (*CP* 13: 27). In recreating oneself as "optimistic throwback", seeing joyously through a lens of regressive collapse, autonomy emerges triumphant: "So while I was as yet nothing but a bud of animation . . . in falling after a rubber ball I decided to conquer the world" (*CP* 13: 29).

Derouted Soles, Phraseless Parentheses: Feet and Legs

For Bataille and Loy, debilitating downfall is never far from "the longed-for swoon"; "the disequilibrium of love" is marked by the fearful desire for losses of self and balance, "squander[ing] all one's reserves until there is no firm ground beneath one's feet" (*E* 240–4). Feet are intended to "giv[e] a firm foundation to the erection of which man is so proud", writes Bataille, tidily conflating phallus and figure ("Big Toe" 20). Indispensable, the feet are nevertheless despised. Doggedly rooted, they emblematise our continual oscillation from low to high and back again, our inability to attain "permanen[t] elevation . . . into pure space" ("Big Toe" 20–1). For Bataille, "we have a sexual organ and feet in a very animal way": the foot is indistinguishable from mud, darkness, evil, and the taboo, and as such, our "secret horror" of our lowest point turns feet into a site of deviance, "sexual uneasiness" (*E* 151; "Big Toe" 21).

With like disquiet, in the immediate aftermath of the rape conducted by the man who will become her first husband, Loy's abject description of his frantic manner, contorted features, and "purple mat" of hair is broken as she casts about for something positive to say, praising his foot as "the most perfect [she had] seen on any human being – outdoing the epitome of Greek sculpture in that evanescent supremacy of being alive" (*EP* 24). This ambivalence recurs in Loy's "The Pamperers", where the foot is simultaneously degraded and cherished, an indulged body part. Admired for her "perfect toes . . . pedicured on a diamond footstool", Diana woos the Loony by playing the part of *"precocious trump taking off one shoe and stocking"* (*SE* 164, 178). The Loony rewards this prostitution of Diana's toes with a sleepy recounting of "This Little Piggy Went to Market". But Diana's perversity prompts the Loony's own, and he soon finds himself next to her, both *"minus one shoe and stocking"*, wriggling their toes *"thoughtfully up and down"* (*SE* 178). "You see after all they're very much alike", Diana comments; similar soles, similar souls (*SE* 179). Uncovering another person's feet is an act of sexual possession, as ritualised by the public removal of a bride's stocking or garter (Ellis, *Studies* III 23). Realising his susceptibility to the sexually charged ethos of Diana's coterie-cum-brothel, the Loony angrily replaces his footgear. He is too late: the podiatric seduction has done its work, reversing the Loony's love of the plodding foot, the pride he took in keeping his "feet in mud but [his] hea[d] more or less in the light"; his spouting of dull metric feet; his distaste for padded soles and plush carpets that eschew the "spiritual explorer's / Footprints" ("Big Toe" 20; *SE* 176–7, 173). By the play's end, the Loony willingly gains entry to a "rotting soft" group who liken their "intellects" to "walking about" on a double-pile rug, who "resolve" the sex question by asserting women's right to wear silk stockings (*SE* 166, 163).

Between 1916 and 1917, Loy was a regular attendee of the New York salon of Walter and Louise Arensberg. One evening "a young Frenchwoman" was found lying on the sofa, her body parts – from foot to knee, midriff to head – reverently stroked by male devotees, Marcel Duchamp among them (*BM* 218). In "The Pamperers", Loy rewrites this spectacle as an exchange initiated by a madam exerting control over a persuadable male artist. Masculinity and value are challenged on a global scale: the soft-footed Pamperers are enjoined by the Loony to "[t]hink of that mud . . . that bloody awful mud" that covers and coats the foot (*SE* 173). Mud that infiltrates the human body, becoming permanent attire and domicile, is a dominant narrative of the trench life that defined World War I, or the conflict that rages as the Pamperers coalesce and digress, flippantly gossiping about love and fashion; the foot was the most-discussed body part of that same conflict, as it was often "the only [discernible] vestige of exploded bodies" (Das 35–72; M. Ellmann 257). Unlike mired or splintered soldiers, the Pamperers are – to paraphrase Joyce's Stephen Dedalus – too busy paring their toenails like impersonal, deific creators to be sacrificed to any worldly cause.[59] No matter how exalted, the foot is never far from ground: Friedrich Engels deemed the Irish "dissolute, unsteady"; as Loy acknowledges, Jews were said to possess "anomalous legs" and feet flattened by endless migration; on this basis, as Sander Gilman writes, they were excluded from conscription and contemporary citizenship; Lombroso and his criminologist peers felt that most women possessed feet "'prehensile'" and "'unshapely'".[60] An exploitable marker of migrancy or marginalisation, the foot is commodifiable: "Every prostitute of any experience has known men who merely desire to gaze at her shoes, or possibly to lick them, and who are quite willing to pay for this privilege" (Ellis, *Studies* IV 23).[61] With their reverence for beautifully pedicured feet ensconced in deep pile, the Pamperers transcend common ground while aligning themselves with perverse predilections and privileges.

Within this supposed perversity, Loy discerns democratising opportunities. In "The Artist and the Public", an essay written as the "The Pamperers" gestated, Loy claims that the artist can see newly, purely, and without preconception. Education, she argues, sceptically and unnecessarily divides "jolly" artist from "jolly" audience; both seek comic succour in "Art" or *The Divine Joke* so readily understood by all (*LaLB* 285). While educators systematically dismiss the democratic origins of art,

> *The Public* knows better than this, knowing such values as the under-inner curve of women's footgear, one factor of the art of our epoch. It is unconcerned with curved Faun's legs and maline-twirled scarves of artistic imagining or with allegories of life with thorn-skewered eyes. It knew before the Futurists that life is a jolly noise and a rush and sequence of ample reactions. (*LaLB* 285)

What Loy describes are features common to the avant-garde: the fetishisation of women's body parts; ancient predilections (mischievous, roving fauns, faun-like satyrs, satire itself); the intertwining of technology and art ("maline" refers to machine-made lace); self-immolation, martyrdom, or sacrifice; joyous shock. Because innately understanding, the public Loy depicts "is unconcerned" – does not care, is not bothered – by critical declamations of contemporary art; artist and audience find common ground in humour, and in their shared attraction for the filthy sole of Woman. The avant-garde may be paternalistic, but it is not inaccessible.

But before "The Artist and the Public", Loy had already experimented in using the foot to stamp out the perceived grandiosity or elitism of twentieth-century avant-gardes. In "Giovanni Franchi" (1915), "minor Giovanni" Franchi sits at the feet of "major Giovanni" Bapini, "picking the philosopher's brains" (*LoLB* 29). Giovanni is a doubled self, and the speaker is a female trinity, a "threewomen" occupying a dress patterned with "falling ferns", or a *"Divine Joke"* awaiting her comic descent (*LoLB* 27). The way to truth is not through the brain, but the toes, declares this fulsome "she". Philosophy and science have been "an expression of human subordination", writes Bataille; both fail to adequately represent humanity as "a moment of a homogeneous process—of a necessary and pitiful process—" ("Pineal" 80). What better way to treat philosophy as "a beast of burden" than to conflate it with the toe, or that which Bataille considers "the most *human* part of the human body" (because least correspondent to the anthropoid ape), and the most ignoble: "fingers have come to signify useful action and firm character, the toes stupor and base idiocy" ("Pineal" 80–1; "Big Toe" 22). Loy shares Bataille's fascination: of the ethereal genius that is "major Giovanni", it is his toes her speaker pursues near-metaphysically, recognising them as the epiphanic fragments of a great podiatric site of unknowing:

> She made a moth's-net
> Of metaphor and miracles
> And on the incandescent breath of civilisations
> She chased by moon-and-morn light
> Philosopher's toes (*LoLB* 31)

The self-same toes are envisioned as virginally unblemished; unworn, their nails clear of "'white marks'", they are essentialised: "All quicks and cores", they are verdant, restorative life, the heart of the matter. Materially insubstantial, "they fluttered to her fantasy"; leadenly descending, they "[f]ell into her lap" (*LoLB* 31). Unreliable foundations, these toes are the bathetic key to Giovanni Bapini's mysteriously pneumatic reputation. These little piggies resist the market round-up; despite numerous attempts, neither the speaker nor Giovanni-the-Small can accurately establish their number. "[T]uned to the tops of trees", mired in "the fallacious nobility" of his flopping trousers, "major Giovanni" is strung up by his glorious feet for our inspection, our reverence strategically undercut by the demoralisation of his inverted hanging (*LoLB* 27).[62] But, for Loy, this sordid public exposure is imperative: filthy soles and fragmented toes are the foundation of art and philosophy, resting as they do on shared ground.

In "Giovanni Franchi", we are asked to admire how a leader's toes are free of leukonychia, or those marks that score and punctuate the nail bed; by contrast, "minor Giovanni" is "[d]amned by scholiums", or marginal notations (*LoLB* 32). To be punctuated is to be irretrievably marked by feminisation, a truth underscored by Giovanni's discourse on "women ————————" (*LoLB* 30). Among Loy's longest aposiopetic dashes, this is overpunctuation at its most hyperbolically diminutive, grandiosely redundant. What might it mean, then, to describe a story about cursed women sharing a boarding house as "a tragedy" of "phraseless parentheses, episodes indefined"? (*SE* 6). Pure punctuation, the obliquely rendered experience of the women of Loy's "The Agony of the Partition" defies rational language and certitude, even as it presupposes lowness, proximity to foundational horizons: "Curses always indicate a downward motion, directed to the ground, the legs, the buttocks" (Bakhtin 166). Hexed heroine Cassandra is bracketed by two maternal figures who uphold different versions of her recent "tussle in cupidity": one idealised ("'I have . . . been audience to The Most Beautiful love-affair'"), one pragmatic ("'What she *wanted* was to get him away from the other girl'") (*SE* 15–16, 11). Impregnated by her lover, Cassandra is jilted in favour of a previous girlfriend the day before their planned marriage comes to pass. Soon after, romantic Mrs Nome finds her "'lying upon her incomparably betrayed bed of a bride'":

> 'Like those corpses excavated from Pompeii, who in lightning overthrow, sheathed in the lava of Vesuvius, retain the rounded contours of bodies erect, seem to be bounced upon the horizontal, she appeared not to flatten on her mattress; but unsupported, to be stretched out rigid on the axis of her contractile agony. A centripetal demolition of despair, defiant of gravity as if she were too heavy to fall, endowed her with an insane levitation of sorrow become lead.
>
> 'On her lovely long body, the facing curves of the inner thighs whispered like marble to the instinct for form. The corner of a sheet she had, in an inalienable reflex of modesty, wafted across her midst, also incompliant to the planes of its location, traversed her as a fallen bar of folded stone.
>
> 'Vertical her derouted feet stood to the air, the mounds prominent on the sole as if released from treading further. (*SE* 12)

Erupted into an instantaneously ossified, monumentalised grief, Cassandra becomes a mark of suspension, a dash that will not yield to the bottom line, but hovers just above it, "as if released" from gravitational force and ground. The tension between her body's linear fixity and the circular swirl of her emotions holds her aloft. But corporeal "rounded contours" ripple from Cassandra's "centripetal demolition of despair": her hilly soles, "the facing curves of the inner thighs" that "whispe[r] like marble to the instinct for form" (*SE* 12). These thighs *are* "phraseless parentheses", pure punctuation awaiting their defining text, grounding linearities.

In her late romans à clef, Loy describes coming into consciousness – recognising her fall into this cursed world – via a pain in her leg caused by the too-tight lacing of a boot; with this all-encompassing sensation, child Loy realises she is inextricably tied to materiality (*IA* 60: 15–16). Loy's thighs often signal nascence, be they the landing place of the newborn, the child's restricted view of the adult body, adolescent or underdeveloped, in need of "herculeanization" (*LoLB* 6, 81; *SE* 255).[63] The modern-day "virgin leg", writes Loy in a sentence connecting legs to an ever-elusive female genital pleasure, "is bred to be brittle and fleet as a Derby mare's to race excitement to the winning-post" (*CP* 18: 68). The phallic "post" suggests that the elation in question remains male.[64] Wandering, Loy's legs parenthesise the overlooked and undiscussed: "Between bandy legs / Jerk patches of street" (*LoLB* 11).[65] Brackets enclose digressions from goals stated or unstated, as when the streetwalker "parenthetically introduces her offers" (Ellis *Studies* IV 262).[66] In "Piero and Eliza.", Loy has a bachelor recount a similarly parenthesised vulvic goal:

> '———— ———— she invited the young attachés to dinner ————— a shaft leading from a trap door in the ceiling to the roses banked in the centre of the dinner table ——————— and down slid Lady Pink ————— but *only* Lady Pink ———— .'
> The bachelor wafted his hands from his flanks, invoking Eve—but his gestures displayed the anomaly of an allusion to his own graces rather than hers. As of life so of art, they spoke with an unintentional aloofness, as those who speak in the language of signs to the deaf and dumb. (*SE* 101)

We need not be familiar with Marinetti's homage to "the pink sacred vulva . . . of humid rust and rotten rose", his paean to the "pink Vulva perfumed by the breath of the Stars!" to grasp the unsubtle euphemism of Lady Pink's moniker ("Sensual" 30–1). Deploying a gestural language, this bachelor draws a line from thigh to crotch, inadequately evoking the female genitalia at the heart of his story. His dash-laden narrative is genuinely suspensive: he is mystified by his female protagonist, from whom he wants to remain at one remove, but he also prolongs his climax, performatively delaying the rose's arrival into rose bed. We assume the pink lady in question is satisfied by the resolution of her spectacle, a fate Loy's Cassandra does not share. For if there is a secret whispered by "the facing curves of [Cassandra's] inner thighs", it is the story of a botched back-street abortion, one her romantic mother figure considers a "hideous carnality, a "prenatal murder": nascence truncated (*SE* 12, 14). But the termination of Cassandra's pregnancy is genuinely parenthetical to Loy's "Agony of the Partition", which focuses, narrative incredulity at the ready, on Mrs Nome's denial of her daughter's sexuality. Female sexual freedom is this Cassandra's unheard prophecy, the digression lying between curvaceous legs that should be allowed to wander at will. For Loy, it is only by exploration, redrawing extant maps and boundaries, that woman can assert the centrality of a desire key to the realisation of their volition. Loy's lower limbs democratise, refute the fetishised co-optation of "the under-inner curve of women's footgear", the fragmentation of female anatomy and autonomy (*LaLB* 285).

●, — — —: Puncta and Desire Lines

As a child, Loy recalls: "the legs of furniture . . . pillared so much of my adventure", were the structural support of a hidden world of playful narrative, a site of pleasure (*IA* 60: 16). "I don't care where the legs of the legs of the furniture are walking to / Or what is hidden in the shadows they stride", writes Loy in "Songs to Joannes". If giving something legs sets it in motion, these generative limbs possess an exponential volition, even as they bracket the unknown and inarticulable, still more "phraseless parentheses". "Heavy on her knees", her mouth a "round vacuum", her breath "[d]ilating", this speaker has been viably interpreted as performing fellatio or receiving an illegal abortion (Quartermain, "Love Songs" 78; Shreiber 102). Either act rejects the strictures of procreative sexuality in a poem where the fragmented body proliferates perversely, nomadically. This is the heteronormative vulvic goal bypassed, a punctum evaded in a refusal of domesticated intimacies. Decades later, Loy takes this refusal to the street with the homeless man of "Hot Cross Bum" (1950), who is depicted "pounding" the pavement "with caressive jollity", all trousers and no phallic pleasure, his shady activities digressive, parenthesised by em dashes, if unavoidably on show:

> decorously garbed
> he's lovin'up the pavement
>
> —interminable paramour
> of horizontal stature
> Venus-sans-vulva— (*LoLB* 144)

Where Futurism loves rapidly, reconfirming "the disappointments of the hymen", this lover reduces sexual ardency to tedious masturbation (*SE* 257); where Baudelaire and Whitman consummate their metrophilia with the passer-by, this man makes impotent love to urban concrete. Like Cassandra, victim to Jupiter's explosive Vesuvius, this homeless man is sexually insatiate, laterally suspended, at the mercy of the gods. Unrequited, missing its satiating point, one-sided love is infinitely open to dissatisfaction and disapprobation. But in "Songs to Joannes", Loy redirects and elasticates the tautologous full stop, refusing its apparent satiation, its finality, its very puncti-formity. In the process, she draws desire lines that reroute modernist affective economies whilst actively transforming the public, wandering woman. This punctuation is a variant of the "'pure language'" Loy claimed to aim for, her riposte to the tainted logos that is English (qtd. in Quartermain, "Love Songs" 77). Loy's punctuation reroutes outdated sexual thinking, relaying how "there is <u>nothing</u> <u>impure</u> <u>in</u> <u>sex</u>—except the mental attitude to it" (*LoLB* 156).

Loy's puncta terminate, penetrate, and radiate, affirming hard stops, but also an emanation beyond themselves. In "Songs to Joannes", Loy's lonesome or broken-hearted figures long to "coupl[e] / In the bed-ridden monopoly of a moment"; many have "broken flesh with one another / At the profane communion table" (*LoLB* 54). Circular, the Eucharist is the punctum that marks Christ's mortal full stop, which Loy conflates with the orgasmic *petite mort*, then sacrifices upon a surface she cannot quite bring herself to call an altar. To assuage our sense of ourselves as "a point in empty space", Bataille attests, "love" must be "a kind of immola-tion" (*IE* 37; *AS2* 119).[67] The period is counterpart to the phallic pen, a momentary penetration of the page, a powerful declaration of an end; it is also a suturing stitch, a mark of completed cycle, a single cell, a building block; needles, mosquitoes, and pools of conscious-ness take on these manifestations in Loy's writing (DeVere Brody 32, 61, 47).[68] Loy's full stops have auras: just as "—a moment is Time surrounded by itself—", a resonant end point scaffolded by suspen-sive, dispersive parentheses, so too does the most distant "instant" evoke "[t]he unsurpassable openness of the circle" (*LoLB* 115, 73). The circle leaks, ripples outward. We recall Szendy's argument that the point "gather[s] into unity" even as it is "immediately destined to be dispersed and multiplied" (9). In Szendy, this dispersal is akin to the systolic and diastolic movements of the beating heart; in Loy, it is the work of the desiring heart: in love, we long to "[d]isorb inviolate egos", to dishevel circumferential contours (9; *LoLB* 58). Loy's "blot[s]" are "tepid" or "[f]luidic", her "Nucleus   Nothing / Inconceivable concept" (*LoLB* 10–11, 63). Bataille concurs: life "passes rapidly from one point to another"; reduced to "a stopping point", the individual will "radiate arms, cry out, set itself ablaze" (*IE* 94–5; 118). We can only "slip toward the point", writes Bataille, as it is fundamentally ungraspable, "a furtive, bewildered flight toward night" (*IE* 126).

Modernists are renowned for pursuing orgasmic full stops, yet few want to be "contracted . . . . to the size of a point" (Bataille,

The Impossible 143). "Bergson compares our 'whole psychical exist-ence' to 'a single sentence, continued since the full awakening of consciousness, interspersed with commas, but never broken by full stops'" (Douglass 111).[69] This is the era of May Sinclair's "woman's sentence", a period-free utopia infamously evinced by Joyce's loqua-cious Molly Bloom, who, like Stein and Baroness Elsa von Freytag-Loringhoven, yields begrudgingly and only infrequently to end points. This context feeds the ambivalence of Loy's "The Ineffectual Marriage" (1917), where dissatisfied "Gina's world would have been at an end" had partner Miovanni's disregard altered. "[W]ith no axis to revolve on", Loy writes, Gina "[m]ust have dwindled to a full stop" (*LoLB* 39). If Loy's stoppage refers to long-sought sexual climax, this diminishment indicates a momentary, desirable loss of a self that is otherwise too grounded in the performance of a pleasing domesticity. But if stoppage gestures toward an outright refusal to yield, this full stop portends the end of servility, and a concomitant plunge into the unknowns of self-identification. Speaking a paternal discourse of female negation, Loy's anticipation of Gina's demise in Miovanni's absence is duplicitous: closely scrutinised, lessening never looked so moreish.

A similar reversal of paucity is at work in "Virgins Plus Curtains Minus Dots" (1915). Suspended in a surfeit of empty time, con-strained by poverty and tradition, unmarried women watch as the world passes them by, recognise that they are believed parasites who "take a walk" while the men outside their home-cum-prison "are going somewhere", are externally driven by purpose and goals (*LoLB* 21). Etiolate, these females discern that, beyond their door, "Fleshes like weeds / Sprout in the light . . . Wande[r] at will"; unlike "the legs of the legs" in "Songs to Joannes", this proliferating "flesh" is less perverse than historically euphemistic, having stood for sexual intercourse since the fifteenth century (*LoLB* 22). Superficially, these women embody desire as Freudian dearth: they lack *la dot*, the French phrase for dowry, and in turn, the full, expansive stop of sexual satiation. But they are not without ellipses, are attuned to the "Flutter . . . . . flutter . . . . flutter . . . ." of their anticipatory hearts, "Throb[bing] to the night" (*LoLB* 22). Before their mirrors, they punctuate time, self-reflected and self-reflexive. Their giggles are wasted on cloth-eared men who respond only to the crescendos of finance; nevertheless, they glean that the "secret well kept" by the sphinx, "[m]akes the noise of the world" (*LoLB* 22). Loy's title posits an equation: "V + C − •". Replete with just audible, persistent beats of sentience, her poem is its strategically ambivalent solution:

"V + C – • = ...". Like Gina of "The Ineffectual Marriage", Loy's virgins "dwindle to a full stop" that is porous, a potentially quenching trickle. While Loy admired the pleasure Marinetti took in public roars of "vulva" and "vagina", "V + C – •" must surely counter his mathematised words-in-freedom, his "'VIRILE MEMBER = deflowering – vulva – fecundation – kisses blood, etc.'" (*BM* 166; Marinetti qtd. in Sartini Blum 42).[70] By Marinetti's formulation, women's hole is stopping point wholly overshadowed and circumscribed by male desire. This absolutism is consistent with his desire to abolish "the question mark, which fixes its atmosphere of doubt too arbitrarily on a single point of consciousness" and replace it with mathematical formulae that "leave the imprecise behind" ("Numerical" 94). Against Marinetti's drive toward precise geometrical splendour, his belief that using the mathematical symbol in literature can "express the maximum of vibrations and deep syntheses of life", Loy posits rows of indeterminate *punctum saliens*, a line denoting a self-sentience the precedes conscious conceptualisation ("Sensibility and Wireless" 88).[71]

Countering Futurist circumscriptions, Loy envisions alternate penetrations, discharging fissures. In lieu of marital dots, she advocates slicing the hymen with the surgeon's knife (*LoLB* 154–5). In lieu of receiving the phallus or emitting the child, she envisions a female character who "stuff[s] everything into her vulva" in an act of (pro)"creative modification" that foresees Carolee Schneemann's *Interior Scroll* (1975), a performance piece in which a roll of language emerges from the vagina, reasserting "the deep connection between gestus and punctum" (*SE* 26; DeVere Brody 147). Recall that Gloria is an adept familiar with the sphinx's secret, knows that "[t]he plum" or sumptuous, replete end point that she desires is buried well beneath the pie crust of life, and is not averse to plunging her fingers into this confection (*SE* 26). And where, historically, woman is the leaky vessel, emanating that most taboo substance, menstrual blood, Loy focuses on male bodily fluids, a subject that remains consigned to gay or pornographic literature and media, even as it surfaces as early as Horatian satire, where "scenes from a dirty dream spatte[r]" a speaker's "nightshirt and stomach" (24). Semen maintains an oddly pervasive cultural sacrality commensurate with the need to preserve the ideology of the autonomous, contained subject, a concept theoretically neuter, but masculine in practice (Grosz, *Volatile* 192–206). "[Y]ou alone / Superhuman", Loy writes in "Songs to Joannes", an inflation immediately qualified by: "apparently / I had to be caught in the weak eddy / Of your drivelling humanity" (*LoLB* 59). Seemingly superhuman; evidently appealing; absolutely neither watertight nor cataclysmic. If the eruption of male semen is the perceived pinnacle of intercourse, Loy actively sullies the monumentality of that flow, reducing it to "an ocean / Whose rivers run no fresher / Than a trickle of saliva" (*LoLB* 53). For Loy, abjection oozes both ways, is shared – "*our* ephemeral conjunction . . . . Flow[s]" – and originary: "Proto-plasm was raving mad / Evolving *us* – – –" (emphasis added, *LoLB* 64, 67). And the exalted spermatozoon is but a tailed full stop, an ambitious atavism that comes to rest in the fulsome, fluid circularity of the feminine, "the milk of the Moon" (*LoLB* 56). Dependent upon women's despised viscosity, Loy's men leak: not only physically, but emotionally, by blushing, raging, begging; spiritually, by casting seeds of "satyric squander" (*SE* 59; *LoLB* 105).[72] Assaying the precise, contained patriarchal figure, one civilised enough to contain his body, to command traces of the "most heinous of infant misdemeanours", Loy keeps an ear cocked for his punctuating, punctured "SPLOSH" (*IA* 65: 61; *LoLB* 12).[73]

In "Songs to Joannes", rather than come to a full stop, "[t]he contents" of brief intimacies, "our daily deaths", "[f]lo[w] to approachment of — — — —" (*LoLB* 64). Eschewing destination or end point, they are an irresolvable dilemma "[r]ubbed" with "[i]mpossible eyes", circular body parts ineffectually, even horrifically, approximating the punctum's place (*LoLB* 64). "When matter becomes elastic ... the punctiformity of the point is no longer" (Szendy 66). Can bodies elasticate? Can affect? Against the round closure of the familiar punctus, Loy's lines of dashes throughout her writings – aporetic, anticipatory, divisive, disruptive, suturing, perforating, extensive, rhythmic – map desire lines, ascendant cartographies. A road or path is "a prior interpretation"; to follow it is to accept its construal (Solnit 68). Marking the well-worn grooves of those who deviate from paved or cordoned off routes, "desire lines" are identified in the early twentieth century as a means of signifying the mute resistance to or failure of urban planning (Norman 126).[74] Easily observed in parks, campuses, grassy or snowy roadsides, these alternate paths are illicit, wayward, and must recur to be seen. Like the cracked book spine, the dog-eared recipe, the frayed stretch of carpet, the desire line is a social signifier of "pure human purpose" that is often unintentional, occasionally ambiguous or misleading (Myhill 301; Norman 93, 108). It wanders wilfully off-piste, like Derridean language, "'a process, completed by innumerable half-steps, half-consciously made'" (qtd. in Moses 152). Desire lines express sentience: the walking body "does not only perceive the hard resistance of the ground", is not moving "just as a displacement between two points in empty space", but strives and strides "to answer 'the call of things'", articulating its '. . .'" (Merleau-Ponty qtd. in Gendlin, "Primacy" 345). Often shortcuts, these foot lines may also express a longing for contemplation, slowness, appealing alternatives (Furman 27). "[E]xpressions of free will or 'paths with a passion'", desire lines are the work of "'foot anarchists'" (Nichols 650, 647). Mapped, footpaths are often indicated with dotted lines that emulate the lift and fall of the foot. Irrational desire Freud also draws dottily, while rational desires are solid lines.[75] And a contemporary social geographer renders the Western model of desire thus:

> YOU   II ---------------------------- II   ME"
> to proximity (being together as 'us')
> IIII
>
> (Thien 192)

This model of ever-greater proximity escalates to a fusion that is only possible when "'a couple [can] bracket off the material, economic, and social aspects of their relationship'" (qtd. in Thien 194). Minus this utopian bracketing, the heterosexual couple is assumed comprised "of selves that are constant, stable, self-enclosed . . . gendered only in that the feminine forms the other half of the masculine same" (Thien 201). It is this inflexible model that Loy's desire lines aim to elasticate, reroute.

When ambulatory – and they often are – the dash ellipses in Loy's writings map paths untried, destinations unknown.[76] In "The Three Wishes", the Siders's rag-and-bone shop is frequented by working men whose "boots had worn down to their arrival"; pursuing paid work, they must first replace their footgear, as "[b]oots are the civilized man's last foothold in society, without boots – – –!" (*SE* 110). While Loy's phrasing is sympathetic to socially pre-determined routes, her dashwork wanders away from prescription toward open-ended possibility. What is the alternative to the worker's daily plod? One answer might be the foot anarchy that underpins "In Maine: Green's Colony" (c. 1920s/30s). Deciding she will walk to a nearby colony of "degenerates" to sate her curiosity, Loy's protagonist eschews numerous warnings against contact with this community, but admits: "I did take a very stout walking stick to beat them off a little—in case – – – –" (*SE* 54). Defined by oppositionality, the speaker's subsequent relaying of her deviant journey is marked with a spate of aposiopetic phrases detailing a surprisingly beautiful path where "the very dust was like a carpet in heaven—" (*SE* 55). Against all expectation, "[n]obody start[ed] out of the hedges – – –", and the anticipated view of hovel-dwelling inbreeds is eviscerated as the speaker stumbles upon a pastoral idyll where an individualistic old couple lives off the land, home-school their grandchildren, and keep their "toes . . . out in the sunlight" (*SE* 55–6). A disapproved-of per-ambulation culminates in basking bare feet, a life free of civilisation's boots.

Maps of defiant escapades, Loy's dashes also signal escapes: in "Monde Triple-Extra" (c. 1910s/20s), Jove Ivon Corvon falls head over heels for a charwoman; lost in a reverie, "reflecting that here was a super-woman good fortune had trailed across his path", he is suddenly "aware that she evaded him ———— was fleeing away from him!" (*SE* 61). Refuting his gawping idealisation of her self and livelihood, this woman expertly draws Corvon a humble path, her mop "jerking . . . with lightning dexterity among his feet ————" until he is knocked unconscious (*SE* 61). Uprooted, unmanned, Corvon's grounding signals her freedom.

Loy's ambulatory dashes reinforce bodily sentience, movements of limb and intelligence, as in her description of a mystic whose "mind wandered – – – –" and who, in meditation, found that "his breath subsided – – – –/– – – – ––[. . .] his body [was] sustained no longer by air but by something comparable to the ether" (*SE* 240–1). Loy's desire lines move from body to soul, three dimensions to four. They can delineate the material boundaries of the text, as when they map the passage of time or a changed perspective in "Incident" and "Pazzarella" (*SE* 39, 97). But they also direct us to the sublime, to the way, for instance, that Brâncuşi's sculpture cap-tures the foundation of form, "so elemental – – – –/ that it actually connives with the atmosphere in any attainment of / a prolongation of its direction" (*SE* 222). This motif is repeated in Loy's assess-ment of how William Carlos Williams's artistic texts reach beyond materiality to infinity, his "unexpected marriages of words – – – – – – giving his verse the enduring individuality" (*SE* 294). Loy's dashes direct us from the page to "the writer — — —", "the lover — — —" and back again, as in the resounding close of "Songs to Joannes": "Love — — — the preeminent litterateur" (*LoLB* 129, 68).[77] This close to Loy's best-known poetry sequence is fitting, as its very structure is determined by her profound sense that it is from the fullest articulation of the base body – a body mired in its bestial-ity, consuming need, and the filth of the grounding earth – that we can draw new desire lines that soar beyond the material plane. A body, in other words, of slapping feet, wandering legs, and oozing genitals, foetidly longing.

Suspicious of urban and pastoral cartographies alike, "Songs to Joannes" establishes an underground market within the modernist affective economy: the female speaker is a "prig of passion — — — — / To your professorial paucity", stealing feeling from a dogmatically imposed dearth rendered masculine (*LoLB* 67). The poems reinstate the male artist/lover as the sacred prostitute, a catalyst for "Little lusts and lucidities / And prayerful lies", catching "tricks" with his "street-corner smile" (*LoLB* 62).[78] "Silting the appraisable" to see what new affective values might rise to the surface, the speaker grinds herself into the very filth and degeneracy by which she is surrounded: "suspect places" where eroticism is rubbish, water stagnant; where societal institutions – the news, the church – are openly vulgar and violent; where generativity is rerouted by non-normate genetic heritage, where even the most angelic child is permanently stained by the dirt of poverty (*LoLB* 53). Nothing can be cleaned or healed: instead, wounds are "[p]robe[d] for souls"; the broken body is the threshold of a phallic invasiveness that interrogates individuality, damaging it still further (*LoLB* 55). This speaker realises she is among the faceless crowd that is marginalised and feminised by her male modernist peers; knows that the public street is defined by a paternalistic ethos in which she cannot be heard, no matter how hard she clamours: "My pair of feet / Smack the flag-stones / That are something left over from your walking" (*LoLB* 55). At home, she firmly closes the shutters to the judgement of passers-by; late at night, her lover "got home to [him]self—first" as she falters en route, "undecided" and unsure of her direction, "which turning to take" (*LoLB* 55). The street is his: the "scum" kicked up from his passage is inhaled into her being; his bleached body whitewashes her movements, her feelings, the literal or figurative steps she climbs; the skyline is his too: "Unthinkable   that white over there / — — — Is smoke from your house" (*LoLB* 55–6, 64–5). Amidst "the jostling of aspirations" and "the jolting of the crowd" he is set apart by an "insolent isolation" in which she is reverently complicit, and against which she feels a burgeoning resistance bordering on aggression (*LoLB* 57–8, 67).

How to remap these dead ends? If the city belongs to men, feminised Nature might offer a viable alternative, a "Breath-giving / Pollen smelling / Space" of drinkable water, edible haulms, dancing fireflies (*LoLB* 60–1). Yet this "flowered flummery / Breaks" against the speaker's "silly shoes", those necessary if constraining tools of civilisation within which she proceeds recedingly, effecting her graceless walk (*LoLB* 62). Some believe they have transcended nature, turned machine, in sync with progress, erect, bipedal, as high as plains' grasses, "Cutting [a] foot-hold / With steel eyes" (*LoLB* 63).[79] Against this complicity, Loy's speaker imagines impossible possibilities: residing within river-light, "apple stealing under the sea", insubstantial games of hide and seek "in love and cob-webs", soothing music emanating from raucous kitchen utensils (*LoLB* 59). This is a world of articulable fantasy.

Yet there is an alternate realm that defies enunciability, that is marked by dashes oppositional and suspensive, awaiting its unformed future, an intimate terrain that Loy wants to map personally, locally, globally: "Let meeting be the turning / To the antipodean / And Form   a blurr" (*LoLB* 65). The solution to "simple satisfaction" is an orgasmic, earth-shattering clash of tectonic plates that will unleash its force as far as the frozen, persistent moon, to a limitless "Mediterranean — — — — —" (*LoLB* 66–7). Against this utopian, universal oppositionality, Nature is but a "raving mad", blind or green-eyed monster, evidently irritated by its allocation as pornographer, and by the "[i]mmodifiable plastic" of the human species (*LoLB* 67). Evolutionary development be damned; Loy's speaker longs for a post-Babel, fallen populace that "jibber[s]" incomprehensibly and mysteriously, that is reduced to an atavistic perplexity that might facilitate new perspectives (*LoLB* 65). In poem 30, Loy's desire lines actively resist evolutionary progress and repetitions: the "Prenatal plagiarism[s]", "Foetal buffoons", "archetypal pantomime[s]", and the very "proto-form" of our superficially moral species. In their stead, Loy posits lines of contradiction, a cartography of alternate routes that disrupt each stanza of this poem, tracking their way through and against the text, brazenly perforating the width and heft of their respective stanzas: "— — — — —"; "— — — —"; "— — — — — — — — — —"; "— — — — — — —" (*LoLB* 66–7). Against Nature's repetitive "purity", Loy posits reproductive urban waste: inhaled by the speaker, the scum unearthed by male passage through streets becomes: "Exhilarated birds / Prolonging flight into the night / Never reaching— — — — — — —" (*LoLB* 56). Upended by feet, greasy residue is enlivened by contact with the speaker's innards; her sentient body propels this reborn being into the night sky, effecting what Loy describes elsewhere as "a gravitation upward – – – – a sublime buoyancy" (*SE* 243).

This soaring works with and transcends the modernist affective economy via an illicitly sentimental style indebted to eighteenth-century literatures of sensibility; "summon[ing] the material resources of the page" – its gaps, its punctuation marks – Loy calls attention to the "insufficiency of words to express feelings" (S. Clark 22).[80] This is a sentimentality that refuses indebtedness, that is disinterested in indemnity. Working outside the strictures of the modernist affective economy, Loy's dashes incise, steal, transform, and redirect; porous, impenetrable dash trails are given lines of their own. In "Songs to Joannes", these lines are often boundary trails marking a divide between negative and potentially transcendent affect, as in poem 8, which reads in full:

> I am the jealous store-house of the candle-ends
> That lit your adolescent learning
>
> —————————————
>
> Behind God's eyes
> There might
> Be other lights (*LoLB* 56)

The beloved's intellectual past is a source of antagonism, a past remnant illuminated by a worthless, miserly collection of candles almost ready for disposal. Approximating a deific all-seeing eye, the speaker sees poorly, her vision occluded by eminently mortal envy. Her path of dashes walks its way out of this dead end, toward alternate sources of irradiation, properly transcendent. Inverted, this pattern repeats itself in poem 13:

> Where two or three are welded together
> They shall become god
>
> ————————
>
> Oh that's right
> Keep away from me   Please give me a push

This poem oscillates wildly, repeatedly, from the transcendent to the base and back again. It begins with a promise of an unidentified "[s]omething taking shape", replete with a set of novelties: "a new name", "new dimension"; "new use"; "new illusion" (*LoLB* 57–8). But this invisible, inaudible, highly anticipated something quickly devolves into affective violence, in turn prompting the orgasmic blending of self and other quoted above, or what Loy will label the "ELECTRIFICATION OF BLISS" that "cours[es] alongside the avenues of Eros", a subject to which we return in *Elevated Realms* (*SE* 251).[81] For Loy, bliss extends beyond itself, must perambulate, jostle through pressing crowds, "tumble together" as poem 13 concludes, "Into the terrific Nirvana / Me you — you — me" (*LoLB* 58). These final dashes mark a reciprocal indistinction, a "Form" that as "blurr" neither calculates nor evaluates (*LoLB* 65).

Sacrificing personal integrity does indeed prove deific, sublime, as Loy will reassert in poem 21, which returns to the hoarding and negative affect of poem 8. In its entirety, it reads:

> I store up nights against you
> Heavy with shut-flower's nightmares
>
> — — — — — — — — — —
>
> Stack noons
> Curled to the solitaire
> Core of the
> Sun (*LoLB* 61)

Famous for his articulation of wasted, malign flowers – the stuff of nightmares – Baudelaire believed that "those who make a cult of their emotions" tend toward material accumulation ("Painter" 27). Replacing financial with temporal accumulation, Loy wallows briefly in this modernist affective economy, then draws a path above and beyond, toward the transcendent sun. To "[s]tack noons" smacks of accounting, stockpiling, until we recall that Loy praises Picasso on more than one occasion for his artistic prowess, his legendary ability to stack masterpieces (*SE* 163, 260–1). And high noon, as Nietzsche's Zarathustra well knew, is the traditional time for meditation and revelation. These noons are sacrificed to a greater cause, a higher deity, time writ large and looming, the marker of night and day, the astral body from which the "Tongue of Dawn" will emerge to "[i]nterfer[e] with our eyelashes" in poem 25 (*LoLB* 63). Ostensibly attesting to our sense of ourselves as sentient, cognisant, bipedal beings, poem 25 is also marked by a boundary trail of ambulatory dashes: below Loy's perforating punctuation lies the delusion of evolution; above it, the infinite sun, parentally licking into visuality the puncta of our blinking, nascent lids, starting afresh, looking into distances unknown, destinations unreached.

Loy's desire lines actively transform the public woman, associable with the downtrodden prostitute, to a cartographer of stratospherically ecstatic proportions. Dissatisfied with geographies – pastoral or urban – that accept or reject women based on an evaluation of their sexual purity, Loy instead affirms a universal baseness that is the foundation of an equally universal and, to her thinking, attainable transcendence. Like many of her female peers,

Loy is a modernist who resists the dictates of urban mapping; her cartographer speaker is akin to the modernist *flâneuse*, "the more consciously adventurous", if less leisured, counterpart of the *flâneur* (Parsons 15, 42).[82] In Woolf's *Night and Day* (1919), Mary Datchett enjoys her morning walks through the city to work, as they offer "a paradoxically suspended time period in the consciousness" (Parsons 117). Loy is similarly interested in the rejuvenations of sentience, of accessing the "[s]omething *prior to language and concepts*, and *not-yet-formed*, [which] is still now constantly provided by the body" (Gendlin, "Primacy" 347). But this ambulatory generativity, this pedestrian, integral syncing of mind and body, this access to a foundational "..." is also, for Loy, "where new thinking happens", the base of an affective, feminist sublime, a visionariness to which the next volume of this *Anatomy* will return (Gendlin, "Primacy" 351). Or, as Loy puts it in a late künstlerroman, womankind remains cognisant of a desirous, integrated life because she possesses "a sort of vaginal clairvoyance" – a capacity to foresee, through knowing genitals, the route to an as-yet-unexperienced satiation (*CP* 18: 65). While Bataille shares Loy's belief that pleasure resides in refuting final steps and stops, in embracing a sacrificial desire that can never reach its destination, the woman's body is the terrain upon which he maps his contradictory impulses "toward excess on the one hand and respect of the boundary on the other" (*E* 141; Suleiman 82–3). Woman as terrain, terrain as woman: Marinetti describes Venice as whore, as lascivious, available woman, a vaginal haven for his perusal: a "pink city" of "sensual walls", replete with "goddess's hips / that spill into hills" and a "horizon / where the city wishes to tuck her pretty feet" ("Sensual" 28).[83] It is against this conflation of ground with women's lower halves that Loy stamps impatient feet, exclaiming: "Some think [Florence] is a woman with flowers in her hair / But NO   it is a city with stones on the streets" (*LoLB* 30). These well-trodden trails are what Loy's desire lines strive to remap and transcend.

"Stigmergy" is a phenomenon found in the natural world, whereby "the trace of . . . previous activity constrains and directs . . . future activity" (Norman 92). Beaver dams, bees' nests, chemical trails, footprints are marks that map where animals have passed and perhaps transformed a landscape; future generations implicitly recognise these passages and activities, and will fall in line with past behaviours in a way less systematic than sentient. For Loy, the modernist affective economy, the male model of feeling and desire, is stigmergic: survivalist, repetitive, performance driven rather than processual, "[m]onumentally the same", a form of path dependency (*LoLB* 39). Against stigmergy, Loy deploys stigmeology, a different kind of marking, sets of desire lines that are inutile, open-ended, elasticated, incisively blurred. This is Loy's depiction of finding herself on a boat headed to New York during World War I, watching as unidentifiable "[b]reasts of battleships" strive to protect their respective nation states:

> Incessant ray – – regal ride of search-light – – of ships – – converging in a methodic measure of a marine gavotte – – rhythm of defence – – of advance – – rhythm of dominion — — —
>
> — — — — — — — — — — — — — —
>
> — — — The beacon extends a royal wink, indicating this wondrous searchlight as the eye of Neptune risen from the Wave to watch over that Empire on which the sun – – – – . ("Alda's" 6)

Every claim to naval constancy, security, and might; every reassurance that this is a combative dance imbued with measurable, predictable rhythm sought out by the understandably anxious Loy is undermined by the awful truth that no militaristic way is foreordained, no preparation for aggressive eventualities sufficient. Loy's dashes express geography and heightened fear; the lines of long dashes she draws onto the typed page are uneven, skewed, uncertain. These lines embody the assertion she makes against her detractors that her poetic punctuation is meant to represent the "'fallow-lands of mental spatiality'" – spaces uncharted, unknown, prospective (qtd. in *BM* 169). Loy's punctuation is excessive, hyperbolic, an irrational riposte to rational or theorised desires. Throughout her oeuvre, Loy overpunctuates to call attention to what is taken for granted, the way that overlooked marks support and sustain our masculinised logos, the stigma attached to Woman and the feminine writ large. Her punctuation has many roles: it expresses the inexpressible, the censurable, the bodily gesture, and for her, most significantly, the affective unknown of woman's sentience and her pleasure, that yet-to-be articulated Sphinx's secret:

In 1956, Bataille writes his own tale of sacred prostitution, of a whore repeatedly acknowledged to be "GOD". Fearing collapse in the magisterial, bestial presence of Madame Edwarda, the narrator just manages to follow her up the stairs of her brothel and through the city streets; in her wake, he feels himself "hung strangely suspended" (135). Their sex is sacrificial, marked, as is the pig cupidity and vestal virginity of Loy's first song to Joannes, by bestiality and ritual, its base sublimity rendered punctually:

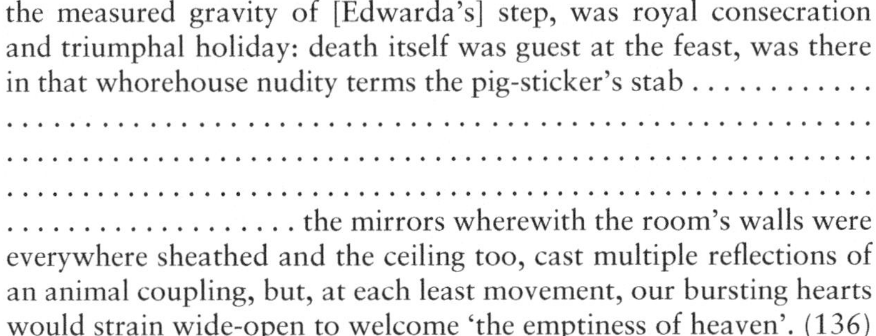

> the measured gravity of [Edwarda's] step, was royal consecration and triumphal holiday: death itself was guest at the feast, was there in that whorehouse nudity terms the pig-sticker's stab . . . .
> . . . .
> . . . .
> . . . .
> . . . . the mirrors wherewith the room's walls were everywhere sheathed and the ceiling too, cast multiple reflections of an animal coupling, but, at each least movement, our bursting hearts would strain wide-open to welcome 'the emptiness of heaven'. (136)

Willing sacrificial victim, Edwarda's step is consciously in thrall to Loy's "universal tonnage", the ontological gravity that weighs down upon us all. Her eyes dead after sex, Edwarda inspires the narrator to contemplate "sell[ing him]self to meaninglessness, nonsense", the deadly nothing at the heart of mortality (142). Bataille's "I" earnestly aspires, in other words, to the status of sacred gigolo, or the very role Loy satirically identifies with her male vanguard peers, F. T. Marinetti and Giovanni Papini among them. He does so secure in the knowledge that "'[t]he activity, the orgasm, [will remain] his, all his'", blissfully disregarding the truth that it is the woman's lot, as Loy puts it in "The Library of the Sphinx.", "to intellectualize a content for the vacuum of their sensation" (Lawrence, *Lady* 121; *SE* 255). Loy's oeuvre is, in large part, a bid to deduce women's unrecognised, unfelt sensations, their tendency to "liv[e] off a literature that has worn down to [censorious] asterisks" (*SE* 136). To be penetrated is, as Leo Bersani attests, to abdicate power; for Loy, this position of supposedly base servility is an ideal vantage from which to rethink its perpetuation. As Bataille writes: "It is when I collapse that I have a start"; fallen, "everything right up to the likelihood of the world is dissipated"; sunk low, we enter a necessary not-knowing, breaking with the status quo (*IE* 153).

Like Loy, Bataille has a fondness for empty spaces and extended lines of punctuation that wilfully fragment the materiality of his texts; his ellipses are said to mutilate, to echo the violence that his texts contain, and in "Madame Edwarda", the resolute lines of full stops underscore the deathliness of the ritual to hand, the pleasure taken its stabbing satiation, its throbbing, dissolute full stop (Cokal 92). Loy's punctuation can aggress, horrify: Alfred

Kreymborg, editor of *Others*, the journal that published Loy's "Songs", was said to have found her unusual spacing and marks as practically problematic as they were intellectually and aesthetically fascinating (*BM* 5).[84] And Loy's marks can punch, as the overpunctuation of "The Sacred Prostitute" attests. But if Lawrence Sterne's was a "poetics of punctuating interruption", Loy's poetics – the very language of her poetry and prose – can appear to interrupt her dominant punctuation, as in the sentient lifebeats that run through her play "The Pamperers" or the soaring dash lines of "Songs" (Szendy 25). Where Bataille's punctuation repeatedly erupts into or echoes a predictable violence, Loy's retains an ambivalence, her "phraseless parentheses" pointing to "episodes indefined" (*SE* 6). Unmarked toes, parenthetical legs, seeping full stops – vulvic and phallic – ground the body transcendent, dotting it with their "unmentionable stigmata" (*LaLB* 148). In "Songs", Loy's desire lines impossibly map the unknown, gesture to destinations that Loy herself cannot discern, perforate and puncture whilst guiding and aspiring. They are a Baedeker to a utopia possibly less attainable than the moon, a travel guide to the esoteric proclivities, the gnostic, that will be the focus of *Elevated Realms*.

"'Paradox, scandal and aporia are themselves nothing other than *sacrifice*'", argues Derrida, "'the revelation of conceptual thinking at its limit, at its death and finitude'" (qtd. in Ptacek 594). Filled with the paradoxical reliance of the sublime upon the base, the scandal of sexuality frankly addressed and centralised, and the perplexing difficulty of the "sex question", Loy's sacrificial "Songs" resist this death and finitude with aposiopetic lines of dashes that infinitely extend and prolong, even as the poem pitches its sacrificial economy of intimacy against a modernist affectivity that is reduced to financial exchange. Love without cruelty is powerless, but Loy remains alert to the blotches, discolorations, and imperfections that humanise intimacy's grandeur. As Benjamin writes in "One-Way Street":

> [M]oles, shabby clothes, and a lopsided walk bind [the lover] more lastingly and relentlessly than any beauty. This has long been known. And why? If the theory is correct that feeling is not located in the head, that we sentiently experience a window, a cloud, a tree not in our brains but rather in the place where we see it, then we are, in looking at our beloved, too, outside ourselves . . . . feelings escape into the shaded wrinkles, the awkward movements and inconspicuous blemishes of the body we love, where they can lie low in safety. And no passer-by would guess that it is just here, in what is defective and censurable, that the fleeting darts of adoration nestle. (449)

Benjamin's is a body that proceeds recedingly, that awkwardly transcends and sublimely inhabits its base materiality, that is recognised by the lover attuned to pervasive, sentient ephemeralities and lasting stigmata. A body desirable marked by its own well-worn desire lines, tottering along in a fallen world, awaiting the puncta of love's darts. Defective, censurable, yet adored: this is the corporeal terrain to which Loy's asterisks, parentheses, and dashes give voice.

Notes

1. See M. B. Parkes on the medieval origin of the asterisk, and its evolution (57–9). Via William Cobbett's 1823 *Grammar of the English Language*, John Lennard delineates the asterisk as "interrupter" (143).
2. Vonnegut is not alone in directing the reader's attention toward the similarities between asterisk and anus. Consider this diagram, from Andreas Hejnol and José M. Martín-Durán's "Getting to the Bottom of Anal Evolution" (2015):

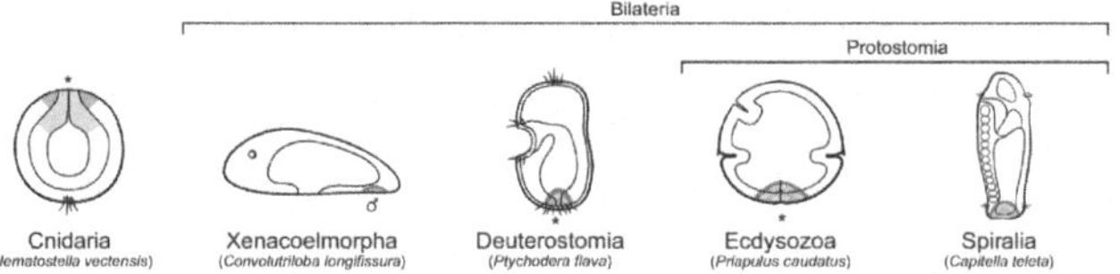

Depicting the slow, unsteady evolution of the anus from the "sack-shaped gut" by which food was once consumed and waste expelled from the same entry point, the explanatory note for the diagram reads: "the asterisk denotes the position of the blastophore", or the opening from which the anus develops (Hejnol and Martín-Durán 64).
3. The first of the two books Loy published in her lifetime, *Lunar Baedecker* (1923) was produced by Robert McAlmon's Contact Editions. Recalling this Paris-based venture, McAlmon observes that he was poor at collecting monies owed to him by bookshops, and that "great portions of each [publication were] confiscated at the docks" when exported to the United States. His list of books so treated includes Hemingway's *Three Stories and Ten Poems* (1923), Gertrude Stein's *The Making of Americans* (1925), and Loy's volume of poetry (*Being Geniuses* 305).
4. The first successful modern excavation of the Sphinx began in the 1930s. While research increasingly confirms this world-famous statue's role as a monument to Pharaoh Khafre built around 2600 BCE, the original name, purpose, and history of the Sphinx's construction, use, and renovations continue to be debated (Hadingham).

5. Evidence for this claim rests in Loy's archive, where a single note-book page shows her drafting key, replicated terms from "Apology of Genius" (1922), and the as-yet-untitled "The Library of the Sphinx." ("Joyce's *Ulysses*": fragment, n.d.).

6. England's Obscene Publications Act (1857) made it possible to censor literature considered remotely suspect; the Offences Against the Person Act (1861) re-entrenched laws against abortion and reduced the sentence for "buggery" to life imprisonment; from 1533, it had been capital punishment.

7. Loy's reference to the "womanly modesty" of the sphinx may allude to Ellis's "The Evolution of Modesty.", which appears in the first volume of his *Studies in the Psychology of Sex* and details the biological and social factors behind women's "coquettishness" and resistance to sex.

8. Loy attributes this embarrassment to hearing of "some female poet" who "said that [she] was the most immoral creature that ever lived"; her unnamed reference is likely Amy Lowell ("Mina Loy: Interview" 214).

9. Molly's rectal vision is the culmination of an established history of marital anality in *Ulysses*. As we see in "Ithaca", Bloom likes to sleep head to toe with Molly, his nose near her rump; she also tells us that he habitually kisses and ejaculates upon her "bottom" (873–4).

10. A fifth part of Harris's autobiography was published posthumously in the 1950s, or after Loy writes "The Library of the Sphinx."

11. An outspoken opponent of censorship, Harris lamented Victorian puritanism and "the domination of girl readers" over the increasingly literate public (2).

12. Harris's explicit biography was deemed obscene by Mr Justice Levy of the New York Supreme Court, and was ultimately charged with "an outrage on good morals" in France (Harris 517, 834).

13. These phrases occur on 27, 19, 44, 133, 121, 145, 71; 141 includes an expurgated "damn". These are just a few examples from an autobiography approximating 1,000 pages.

14. An avaricious reader of medical texts, Harris often "educated" his ladies on their sexual parts and cycles. After sex, Harris instructed each lover to "'get up immediately and syringe [themselves] with water thoroughly; water kills my seed as soon as it touches it'" (121).

15. Harris's queer proclivities may fulfil Freud's assertion that "a person's love of his own penis, which is in other respects narcissistic, is not without an element of anal erotism" ("Infantile Neurosis" 84).

16. Admirably, Harris published a praising biography of Wilde in 1910, when the stigma of the trial remained severe.

17. Roger Conover cites Loy's correspondence with Carl Van Vechten as evidence of her pro-pederasty sparring with Giovanni Papini. Conover attests that, for Papini, the accusation of homosexual proclivities could only be anathema, hence Loy's decision to queer the Futurists in her scabrous 1915 poem "Giovanni Franchi" (*LoLB* 183). Recent

scholarship by Laura Scuriatti complicates this perception: evidently, Papini's journal *Lacerba* presented homosexuality as appealingly anti-woman and anti-bourgeois (27–9).

18. Lawrence's *Lady Chatterley's Lover* (1928) and Huxley's *Brave New World* (1932) were banned directly after publication. T. S. Eliot is the only figure in Loy's essay to have evaded legal censorship. But as an editor at Faber and Faber, "Eliot performed a precarious balancing act between supporting authorial freedom, exercising his own aesthetic and moral judgement, and protecting his firm from possible prosecution" (Potter 85). Loy might have been aware of Eliot's King Bolo poems, or his infamously pornographic literature detailing sodomy and rape that he shared within a male literary circle that included Loy's associates Lewis, Joyce, and Pound. A close friend to Djuna Barnes, Loy may have also been aware that Eliot supported the publication of *Nightwood* (1937), but heavily censored its language, including its references to anal sex (Potter 85).

19. Loy's archived "Biography of Songge Byrd" (1952) – partly published in *The Last Lunar Baedeker* – opens with references to *Le Rire* and *Simplicissiumus*, popular humorously scabrous publications that began in 1894 in France and 1896 in Germany respectively. Loy also mentions the innovations of "newspaper cartoonists" when trumpeting the aesthetic value of "the fundamental time-is-money idiom of the United States" in "Modern Poetry" (*LoLB* 158). *Punch, or the London Charivari* – a satiric British journal running from 1841 to 2002 – is also referenced in "Anglo-Mongrels and the Rose" as a deflator of too-pristine Britishness (*LaLB* 130). Loy was clearly fond of caricature and lampoon throughout her life, reading comic strips into her late years (*BM* 396).

20. Drawing upon the work of Alison Hennigan, Lucy Bland points out that the sexology of Loy's era "was a fusion between heterosexual observations and homosexual information – a 'two-way traffic' between sexologists' theorizing and inverts' lifestyle." Bland considers these ideas influential pre-World War I, but still more widespread in the lead up to World War II, or the period when Loy appears to have written her asterisked and anal-oriented essay fragments on women's sexuality (257–8).

21. I refer here to a draft of "The Agony of the Partition", where Loy describes the loss of the beloved as "'a queer death'" in a conversation ruminating upon the possibility that her lovelorn protagonist Cassandra has become intimately devoted to a female friend. Cassandra and Martha are often seen physically entwined, "'l[ying] all over each other on the divan'", talking and touching, and spending most nights together, prompting speculation that they might be "'lesbian'" (*SE* 305–6). "Lesbian" is a term Loy rarely uses, even as many of her associates identified as such, Stein, Barnes, and Natalie Barney among

them. In "Agony", the demise of a cataclysmic heterosexual love lends itself to a homosocial – possibly homosexual – relationship.

22. My thanks to Sam Ladkin for suggesting that I pursue the possibility of a Duchamp lineage in relation to Loy's "QHU".

23. Walkowitz's excellent study on nineteenth-century prostitution discusses how working-class women entered the sex trade in response to limited and/or demeaning employment opportunities. Careers were brief and subject to fluctuations in the male leisure economy, but in *fin-de-siècle* England, the sex trade was managed by women who often banded together to deal with difficult clients or police officers, financial hardship, and illness (15, 20, 25–7).

    Contemporary studies argue that Victorian mores against the sex trade remain entrenched. Some present-day feminists continue to posit its workers as victims of patriarchy, and demand the outright elimination of sex commerce, rather than "radical regulationism" and decriminalisation (Shrage 82–9). "[S]eek[ing] to complicate the view that the commodification of sexuality is transparently equatable with diminished intimacy and erotic experience", Elizabeth Bernstein details how women continue to enter the trade for economic, social, and geographic mobility, as well as for affective pleasures including empowerment and attraction (21, 8, 46, 184–7).

24. In "Thinking Sex: Notes for a Radical Theory of the Politics of Sexuality", Gayle Rubin discusses how women remain on the front lines of the sex industry because they continue to be excluded from larger networks of production and consumption (308). Felski argues that the prostitute is simultaneously consumer, producer, and product, thus becoming "the ultimate symbol of the commodification of eros, a disturbing example of the ambiguous boundaries separating economics and sexuality, the rational and irrational, the instrumental and the aesthetic" (*Gender* 19).

25. Acknowledging that Loy had "sympathy" for Goldman, Burke argues that "their acquaintance did not develop into friendship" (*BM* 315). Yet Loy's daughter recalls Goldman visiting Loy in Berlin in the early 1920s with Alexander Berkman, and expresses dismay over the loss of the Loy–Goldman correspondence (Burke, "Notes by Carolyn Burke": notes dated 6/8/89 and December 15–16, 1979 respectively).

26. In a nationwide bid to end the "'instrumental rape'" of streetwalkers by the medical and legal professions, thousands of women and men joined the National Vigilance Association and the Ladies' National Association from 1870 to 1876, when the Contagious Diseases Acts were finally repealed (Walkowitz 57, 2).

27. Loy enacts a like racism in "Library", where her conclusionary discussion of abused women posits their violent partners as "Apaches" From this reductive "primitivisation" of troubling male sexuality, she then pivots to workers in the Parisian sex trade (*SE* 258–9). See also endnote 48.

28. As Bataille writes: "Not every woman is a potential prostitute, but prostitution is the logical consequence of the feminine attitude", one he conflates with a willingness to objectify the self. By this reasoning, the objectifier – the aggressive, desiring male – is hapless victim to women's charms (*E* 131).

29. Ellis argues that the Christian prohibition of the orgy, a once-accepted social ritual and cathartic release, led to "the high tension, the rigid routine, the gray monotony of modern life" that catalysed the sex trade (*Studies* IV 222–4). Ellis maintains that censoriousness breeds illicitness: France, he suggests, has the longest, harshest history of banning sexual commerce, yet is the nation where "prostitution has played [the most] conspicuous part" (*Studies* IV 240).

    For Bataille, only common prostitution complements the Christian ethos, as both practices pretend to exalt the lowly in a manner that worsens oppression and hopelessness (*E* 137).

30. Contemporary theorists agree with Ellis that prostitution is a distinctly urban phenomenon predicated upon the disruption of pre-modern kinship systems that had permitted a more casual system of barter and exchange (Bernstein 23).

    Mary Magdalene's coordinates recur in a Christian story of a beautiful, wealthy sex worker who lived in Antioch in the fifth century. Shunned by all, she was baptised by a forgiving Bishop Nonnus, who renamed her Pelagia, or Pearl, a rite that reinstated her purity. This tale counters the biblical teachings of Jerome, who asserts that "'though God can do all things, he cannot raise up a virgin when she is fallen'" (Salisbury 102). It also chimes with Loy's authorial capacity to resurrect the sexual purity of fallen female characters discussed in the previous chapter.

31. Goldman writes: "It is conceded as a fact that woman is being reared as a sex commodity" and that it is perfectly acceptable for her to "sel[l] her body" in wedlock, "while any other union is condemned and repudiated" (138). Schreiner goes further in her 1911 *Woman and Labour*, likening any sexually active female to a prostitute, given the "necessitous acceptance . . . of material good in exchange for the exercise of [women's] sexual functions" (245). In "Against Marriage" (1919), Marinetti argues that, for women, the family "is born out of a buying and selling of body and soul [that] becomes a masquerade of hypocrisies or else a façade of good sense, behind which a legalized prostitution, with a dusting of moralism, is played out" (310).

    Jessica Burstein demonstrates how Loy's poetry explicitly and implicitly equates virgin with prostitute by way of the New Woman, who remains prey to the marriage market even as she is "remade as the mobile female", always a cypher for the streetwalker (169).

32. "Shaw and Wells", writes Loy, are "turning themselves into Pantechnicons", are movers of "middle-class conceptions", ideal exhibitions for Britain's "Inanity Fair" ("Joyce's *Ulysses*: Fragment").

"Pantechnicon" refers to a bazaar or marketplace that sells a range of items, particularly the "exotic"; in keeping with the sexual and satirical impetuses of "Library", these authors' wares are mocked for titillating only base consumers.

33. The pornography in question is Marinetti's. In *Brontolivido*, Loy argues that the Futurist is less a vanguard prophet than a pornographer whose literature is so transgressive "even Paris refused to swallow it" (*B* 8: 10; see also 7: 6).

34. Dunn illustrates how, in the nineteenth century, the department store was seen as a place where women might fall prey to the lure of prostitution. In turn, in "Mass-Production on 14th Street", Loy presents "the city as a distorted garden of Eden, with products in windows leading women into temptation"; by contrast to the typical view of the streetwalker, in "Chiffon Velours", Loy challenges the affluence and well-being of feminised consumerism by presenting an aged, destitute woman "at rest against the corner-stone / of a department store" (Dunn 111, 114; *LoLB* 119).

35. The second and third stanzas of Loy's "The Costa San Giorgio" (1914) replicate a similar scenario, albeit with an expressly adulterous rather than an implicitly prostituted sexualised economy. Both poems reference barracks, churches, eager and fertile women, the enthusiastic licking of ice cream, and boots that traverse unevenly and provocatively (*LoLB* 10–11).

36. Engels similarly details how urban-based soldiers lure young women from the countryside in *The Condition of the Working-Classes in England* (44). One outcome of this economy arises in "Perlun" (1921), where Loy describes "the syphilitic sailor / on . . . death bunk" (*LoLB* 75).

37. The need to stand fixed to a particular spot, usually whilst scantily clad and in all weathers, is often cited as one of the more gruelling aspects of streetwalking. The specificity of sex-trade territory is long-standing and defining: Corbin lists the many names attributed to women who worked particular areas of the city in twentieth-century Paris, among them the *chandelles* or candles who stood nightly in hotel doorways, the *échassières* who solicited from bar stools, and the *amazones* who worked from cars (355).

38. Euphemistic options for "male prostitute" include "rent boy" or "call boy", which imply youthful appeal or idealisation. Alternately, the gigolo can be known as a "Casanova" or "Don Juan". These latter terms affirm the sex trade as an extension of the male prerogative to "sow wild oats" widely, even as it condemns women for the same.

39. According to Freud, the homosexual or feminised male is deemed irrevocably ambivalent, whilst woman is believed inherently capricious ("Infantile Neurosis" 26–8). As logos is authority, it ascribes to Freud's theory of powerful people – rulers, parents – who generate ambivalence in their followers ("Totem" 49).

40. Peter Quartermain argues that Stein impacted Loy's "avoidance of normalized punctuation"; if so, Stein influenced invertedly ("Love Songs" 76).

41. DeVere Brody's "Hyphen-Nations" is a brilliant chapter on misogynistic, xenophobic American resistance to wilfully bipartite self-identifications, including double-barrelled surnames and the phrase "African-American" (85–107).

42. For Bergson, the hyphen is the ideal mark of human evolution, "impl[ying] a real persistence of the past in the present, a duration which is, as it were, a hyphen, a connecting link" (*CE* 22). A modernist in tune with pasts atavistic and recent, Loy echoes Bergson's formulation, often deploying hyphens to associate archaic with modern diction.

43. In "Apology of Genius" (1922), a poem written in the wake of the obscenity trial for Joyce's *Ulysses*, Loy will, with a like scepticism in view, parenthetically cordon off the revered artistic ideal that is "—the Beautiful—" (*LoLB* 78).

44. This draft of "Apology of Genius" (1922) exists in a file in Loy's archive devoted to her long, unpublished poem on Isadora Duncan; it is located on a manuscript page headed "Words and fragments discarded from poems" ("Biography of Songge Byrd").

45. Fragmentary, and as Strunk and White have it, casual: "A dash is a mark of separation stronger than a comma, less formal than a colon, and more relaxed than parentheses" (9).

46. This ellipsis is Loy's own.

47. Deaf to Nature's scolding, Futurism continues "*taking* [LOVE'S] *measure with a masterful eye*", reducing sex to "a game of advantages" devoid of "fair play". Beholden to the daily, competitive grind of technological and informative efficiency, Futurism measures his intimacy by train schedules, and wraps Love in newspaper. Even the domineering Don Juan expresses approbation when Futurism insists that men "identify . . . with machinery!" (*SE* 207, 203–4).

48. A like scenario arises in *Woman and Labour*, where Schreiner decries "[t]he ignorant savage, whether in ancient or modern societies, who violates and then clubs a female into submission" (232). In "Library of the Sphinx." Loy describes identical actions as "'garnitures'" of Apache "social status" (*SE* 258). See also endnote 27.

49. For instance, Koudis discusses how Loy's earliest poems utilise gaps rather than formal punctuation in a nod to Futurist influence and mores (*Mina Loy* 49–50). This typographical spacing recurs throughout Loy's life and oeuvre, as in "Anglo-Mongrels and the Rose" (1923–5) and "Time-Bomb" (1961).

    Similarly, Loy's long lines of dashes are discernible in Futurist works, among them Aleksai Kruchenykh's *Explodity* (1913) and Francesco Cangiullo's *Fumatori* (1914) (Bartram 37, 119). Most significant for the final portion of this chapter, Futurists set precedents for using dash-work as cartography: Amando Mazza's "Marinetti" includes a Futurist dance of war involving vertical lines of dashes, and Lucio Venna's "Equestrian Circus" mimics the movements of a rider in a ring with a circular broken line (Bartram 147–8).

50. Unbracketed ellipses in quotations from "The Pamperers" are Loy's own.

51. A widow mournfully "searches / the opaque silence / of unpeopled space"; "Silence bleeds" from a suicide's "slashed wrists"; Victorian mistresses "belonged to the generation of women who suffered in silence"; Maine's residents curtail conversations with a "deadly silence"; the "treacherous invitation" of a night-time jungle is a "sibilant silence – – –" (*LoLB* 97, 104–5; *SE* 44, 53, 141).

52. In "The Pamperers", the integral relationship Loy draws between violence and intimacy is reasserted in the conversation between two friends titillated by a recollection of a mutual fight between lovers, black eyes and splintered furnishings attendant, garnering the pat, insouciant summation: "Life can be very beautiful with a lover" (*SE* 165).

53. Terry Eagleton makes this observation in two different books; in *The Event of Literature* (2012) he attributes it to Raymond Williams (173).

54. Loy's "Sketch of a Man on a Platform" is her most obvious razing of a sturdy masculine leg. It opens as follows:

> Man of absolute physical equilibrium
> You stand so straight on your legs
> Every plank or clod you plant your feet on
> Becomes roots for those limbs (*LoLB* 19)

Standing on his own two feet, this man grows the very roots he longs to avoid with velocity and his embrace of constant change, key tenets of his Futurist agenda. Troubling patriarchal perambulations recur in Loy's critique of priests with their "[r]hythm of redemption", and in narrative suspicion toward Insel's "gliding gait" (*LoLB* 42; *I* 24).

55. To proceed recedingly is to acknowledge a flawed mortality that lives and breathes but inevitably wanes; for Loy, only the metaphysical realm permits constant advance (*SE* 281). "[M]y desire / receded / to the distance of the dead", asserts the speaker of "The Widow's Jazz" (1931); similarly, in Loy's "Lady Asterisk.", Mrs Birthright "never faded— / but receded—somehow—ceremoniously— / Behind her regal presence" (*LoLB* 97; *SE* 42).

56. In this spirit, Loy admires a silly or implausible tread: "Messianic mites tripping" through public gardens; cactuses resembling "[v]egetable cripples of drought"; "[w]alking the ceiling" (*LoLB* 43, 74, 72).

57. In 1926, Yvor Winters suggests that Loy struggles to conquer "the clumsiness which one can scarcely help feeling in her writings", adding: "She moves like someone walking through granite instead of air"

("Mina Loy" 496). These claims continue through the ebbing of Loy's reputation from the 1930s until the 1980s. "Ugly, clumsy, brutal" are Samuel French Morse's adjectives for Loy's writing in 1961 (19). Contemporary variants on this theme include Roger Conover's description of Loy as a poet akin to "a naturally balletic dancer with inebriate tendencies" or John Wilkinson's suggestion that Loy's writings "gather their positions and stages in an uneasy coexistence" ("Introduction", *LoLB* xvii; Wilkinson 147).

For Elisabeth A. Frost, Loy ironically adopted "strategic overwriting: an overdoing of poetic technique to the point of parody, an overdeterminacy of meaning in verse saturated with polysemy, alliteration, inflated diction, punning, bathos, and ironic rhyme" (*Feminist* 32). The involved, expansive literary edifice Frost catalogues seems destined for a tumble of the sort articulated by Peter Nicholls: "it was precisely Loy's achievement to push [Pound's] 'logopoeia' to a boisterous extreme, where even the ironist's pretensions to aloof superiority would ultimately fall victim to the 'humid carnage' of bodily life" ("'Arid'" 64). Nicholls argues that Loy's "Modern Poetry" (c. 1925) is a riposte to Pound. Nicholls is interested in Loy's suggestion that "'one can recognise each of the modern poets by the gait of their mentality'", observing:

> It is hard not to feel that this last phrase—"the gait of their mentality"—is a calculated reformulation of Pound's "dance of the intelligence." If it is, it's a telling one, with Loy substituting for the stylish symbolist dance the more deliberately mundane figure of walking (a "gait" is also something a horse has). ("'Arid'" 160)

This substitution of bestial, eminently grounded walking for ethereal dancing is commensurate with Loy's commitment to the lowest echelons of pedestrianism, prostitution among them. The next chapter includes a discussion of Baudelaire's affinity for the era-defining gait, another possible influence on Loy's diction.

As for Loy, clumsiness is a term that has maintained critical currency in Dickinson studies. Dickinson's most avid modernist American exponent, Conrad Aiken, described her verse as in 1914 as "a delicate bombardment of parable and whim which she perfectly knows will stagger" (11). In 1938, Yvor Winters considered Dickinson heavy-handed, careless, blundering, "lack[ing] lightness and grace" ("Dickinson" 39). In an echo of Pound on Loy and logopoeia, in the same article Winters likened Dickinson to a figure on the brink. Winters was not the first to make this claim: in 1915, a critic had already described her as "'acute as the edge of a precipice, as lambent as a meteor cleaving the night'" (qtd. in Wineapple 42). A more recent exponent of Dickinsonian imbalance argues that she is a poet who establishes elaborate metaphors that promise to support and explicate one another, only to ultimately refuse the reader any tidy, self-evident affinities or systematic pleasure. In Dickinson, then: "figural correlation becomes figural slip-page" (Wolosky 130).

The slipping, tripping body is key to Loy's celebration of an abjecti-fied sexuality more present in her work than in Dickinson. That said, both writers use intensely cerebral language to demarcate the visceral, and both evince a tendency to promote the fallen body as a conduit to the spiritual, be it the visionary, ecstatic, or transcendent.

58. In a chapter entitled "The Great Discovery" in her autobiography *Retrospection and Introspection* (1891–2), Eddy details how she spent two decades attempting "to trace all physical effects to a mental cause", a conundrum resolved by an injury incurred when she took a tumble on a winter night's return home from a temperance meeting. For Eddy, this accident "was the falling apple that led me to the discovery how to be well myself, and how to make others so." From a position of lowness expressly aligned with Genesis, Eddy becomes a woman who makes a considerable mark on the Western world (n.p.).

59. By way of concluding his theory of artistic impersonality, Stephen Dedalus tells his friend Cranley:

> 'The personality of the artist, at first a cry or a cadence or a mood and then a fluid and lambent narrative, finally refines itself out of existence, impersonalises itself, so to speak . . . . The mystery of esthetic like that of material creation is accomplished. The artist, like the God of the creation, remains within or behind or beyond or above his handiwork, invisible, refined out of existence, indifferent, paring his fingernails.' (*Portrait* 181)

60. See Engels 104; *LaLB* 116; Gilman 40, 45; Lombroso qtd. in Horn 52–3.

61. The erotic symbolism of the foot is widely acknowledged by Loy's contemporaries. Streetwalkers tell Mayhew that if they have good feet, they "always parade them" (490–1). Ellis considers the foot one of the most fetishised parts of the body, noting that women who show their feet in public have been mistaken for prostitutes since ancient Rome, and pointing out that his sexologist peer Richard von Krafft-Ebing makes similar observations in *Psychopathia Sexualis* (*Studies* III 21–38).

62. From the Middle Ages onward, public hanging by the feet – either to torture or kill – was a sentence meted to the most marginalised crimi-nals; in some parts of Europe, this punishment came to be reserved for Jewish thieves (see, for instance, Glanz).

63. In the portions of her romans à clef devoted to childhood, Loy describes adults as "people in the concrete" who "extended no further than the waist", expressing fascination for her mother's "subordinates" hidden under a Victorian skirt, and her father's "two tubes rattling coins in their summits" (*IA* 61: 19). Loy refers to "adolescent thighs / draped / in satirical draperies" in her 1923 "Lunar Baedeker" (*LoLB* 81).

As Hilda Bronstein argues, this reference may well be a riposte to the despised "'Moon with her lovely warm thighs'" in the anti-symbolist and misogynist "Second Futurist Proclamation: Let's Kill Off the Moonlight" (Marinetti 28).

By Loy's treatment, legs are also signs of troubled or troubling childishness. A man with dwarfism who performs in a circus is an aspirant crustacean, his bowed, bandied limbs parenthetical, atavistic, making comical the "manly . . . stamp" of his small foot (*LoLB* 85). And legs signal childish disobedience in "Anglo-Mongrels and the Rose", where the young Ova is punitively "pulled out by her leg" for being so base as to crawl on her belly under the furniture (*LaLB* 142).

64. Loy extends this leg metaphor still further into the term "arabesque", one that implies complex form and balletic pose. In *The Child and the Parent*, she argues that men inhabit an "interstitial arabesque" that comprises their universe, while women are expected to become "a composite monster set on a revolving platform": "a troupe of female acrobats" culminating in "metaphysical arabesques", "tentacular facility" always at the ready (*CP* 19: 6; 18: 68–9).

65. Loy will repeat this motif and perspective decades later in "Mass-Production on 14th Street", where, in the undertow of the "[p]edestrian ocean" "the rosy scissors of hosiery / snip space / to a triangular racing lace // in an iris circus of Industry" (*LoLB* 111). These legs frame an ever-shifting industrial terrain.

66. These associations are long-standing: consider, for instance, John Marston's Jacobean play *The Malcontent* (1603), in which lunulae, or rounded brackets, are used to signify bandy legs, "a copulatory thrust", and possibly, to "stylise the vagina" (Lennard 41). Barthes likens parentheses to a miniature death, reconfirming the link with the *petite mort* of orgasm (qtd. in DeVere Brody 4). Furthermore, the *fin-de-siècle* legislation directed at the sex worker's livelihood was originally called "Contagious Diseases (Women) Act" (Walkowitz 70). Another variant of this euphemistically titled legislation: "Contagious Diseases (Not Concerned with Animals) Acts". In both parenthetical asides, women's sexuality is the deferred, evaded target.

Loy's sexualised, phraseless parentheses recur throughout her oeuvre. In "Magasins du Louvre" (1914), for example, two women in a doll shop are cocottes whose respective facial expressions resemble parenthetical dash or bracket: "the solicitous mouth of one is straight / The other curved to a static smile". They "surpris[e] a gesture that is ultimately intimate" and "[s]eek each other's surreptitiously"; both gesture and goal go tellingly unarticulated (*LoLB* 18).

67. This is the lust parodied in Loy's "Pazzarella", where Geronimo rapes the protagonist, only succeeding in resurrecting in her "a contemptible beatitude" in which she taunts him to make her *really* die of love next

time (*SE* 67, 82). Geronimo's full stop does not cessate. This incident is discussed more fulsomely in *Elevated Realms*.

68. Loy's penetrative puncta are not always orgasmic: in her poems, "Wanton Italian matrons / Discuss the better business of bed-linen / To regular puncture of needles" (*LoLB* 9). In her fiction, "drowsiness [is] punctured by the sting of a mosquito", and a cloying home life is a series of bottomless full stops, "black pools of unconsciousness punctuating [the] hurry of life"; strung together, these pools might be sentient ellipses (*SE* 144, 126).

69. Paul Douglass points out that Stein attended Bergson's Parisian lectures, and that her own written style was indubitably influenced by Bergson's theory of life as a long, unbroken sentence. He cites *The Making of Americans* (1925) alone as evidence, a text predominantly written in the first decade of the twentieth century, or shortly before Loy met Stein in Florence (118).

70. Equally stereotypical in sentiment, if not in rendering, is this quotation from Marinetti's "Dunes" (1919): "dunes of pride / + smell of vulva / speeding" (103). For the most part, Marinetti posits the vagina as a vehicle that serves or rewards physical, power-laden, amatory male desires. As he writes on the eve of World War I: "See the furious coupling of war, this enormous vulva inflamed by the lusts of courage, this shapeless vulva that splits wide open to offer itself more easily in the terrible spasm of imminent victory!" ("Second Futurist" 31). In an unwitting parody of the mythology of the *vagina dentata*, for Marinetti, vulvic parentheses are didactic or wounding: they can embody directions, "(fast) (faster) (slow down) (double time)", or slice words or sounds in half ("Typographic Revolution" 89).

    A counter to this bombast appears in Marinetti's love poems to his wife Benedetta Cappa – works of extraordinary sentimentality, dated between 1920 and 1938 – in which he likens himself to "one of the two lips of the wound" of their separate selves; that the resolutely phallic Futurist Marinetti compares himself to one portion of a vulva is clear by the poem's ending, in which he "plunge[s] in Her Infinity / Infinity hot burning wound" ("Poems to Beny" 135, 137).

71. That said, barring her essays "Conversion" (c. 1920s–30s) and "The Logos in Art." (n.d.; both in *SE*), Loy rarely takes up Marinetti's clarion call to intersperse language with mathematical symbol. And, in "Virgins Plus Curtains", Loy spells out her pluses and minuses.

72. See Michael Argyle on blushing as emotional leakage (81).

73. In her autobiographical writings, Loy articulates the anxieties associated with managing bodily flows, processes fundamental to the rearing of "civilised" children. The epiphanic passage of "Anglo-Mongrels and the Rose" wherein child-Loy overhears a nurse describing her infant sister's green diarrhoea in hushed tones is often considered a crucial turning point in Loy's aesthetic development, given that she exoticises

the curiously named bodily flow in question to an "orb of verdigris", one that becomes foundational to her aesthetic of "excrements and physic" (*LaLB* 140–3).

Less discussed is a similarly formative incident in which Loy recalls needlessly confessing, when a young girl, to having left "a remarkably tidy turd" in her bed. Her nurse sympathetically reassures her that the brown mass is in fact the remains of a leaking linseed poultice. Anxiously informing her reader that this "misdemeanour was not at all of [her] habit," Loy's childhood eagerness to admit guilt prompts a moral epiphany: she realises that by virtue of growing up in a Christian household, her "mind had already begun to conform to a rhythm of recurrent culpability" (*IA* 65: 61).

74. The origin of the term is contested. Carl Myhill insists that it arose with urban planning, but J. M. Barrie refers to a similar phenomenon in his *Peter Pan* (1911), describing, in a rural context, "'Paths that have Made Themselves'"; furthermore, alternate terminology for the same includes "pirate paths, social trails, *kemonomichi* (beast trails), *chemins de l'âne* (donkey paths), and *Olifantenpad* (elephant trails)" (Myhill 293; Bramley). Many of these terms are distinctly pre-urban. Credit for the coinage is often given to Gaston Bachelard's *The Poetics of Space* (1957), where he is said to discuss "'Les chemins du désir' . . . to relate to the beautiful instance of making pathways that are instinctive, habitual, and work on an emotional level in direct opposition to moving in lines inscribed onto a city that operate as . . . offsets from property lines" (Furman 27).

75. In an essay published in 1917, or the same year as Loy's thirty-four part "Songs to Joannes", Freud draws a diagram of the relational transition from anal erotism to the castration complex (in boys) and penis envy (in girls): in it, irrational desires – for a penis, for instance – are represented by a dotted line, while rational desires – such as a girl's mature sexual desire for a man – are signified by solid lines ("Transformations" 132).

76. This Loy motif extends to the ambulatory conversation in her contribution to the second number of *The Blind Man*, "O Marcel - - - Otherwise I also have been to Louise's" (1917). Labelling this short text a compilation, Loy collages overhead conversation among her vanguard associates at the Dada-esque Blind Man's Ball held in New York on 25 May 1917. Throughout, Loy uses elliptical dashes to indicate how languages trails off, unevenly transitions from one speaker or subject to another, or gestures toward the obscene, as most obviously in the segment reading: "I will have a tongue sandwich – you must suck it – – – Censorship!" (15).

77. Examples are rife of Loy's desire-line dashes reaching beyond the third dimension. Consider: "But Eliza by dint of horoscopes and seances was reaching a higher plane ———— some plane on which psychic phenomena, like orgasms, so tantalisingly suggest themselves" or "It is the oil

in the machine to which the mystics referred as the Holy Dove ————"
(*SE* 102, 285).

78. "Tricks" is first published in relation to prostitution in a 1926 novel by Loy's close friend Carl Van Vechten. The gestation of Loy's "Songs" precedes this print reference by a decade, but Loy may have heard "tricks" used in this context, and its relation to theft and deviousness is originary.

79. Scientists have long maintained we evolved from tree-hanging apes, dwelling in forest and jungle, to bipedal creatures of the plains, tall enough to see into the distance, our newly erect bodies less exposed to the powerful sun. Describing the strength of the sun's "shining" and the ascent to the "cool plains", Loy's poem 25 appears to allude to a similar theory (*LoLB* 63).

80. As Janet Todd writes, lacunae, asterisks, and dashes pepper works such as Richardson's *Clarissa* (1747) to demonstrate emotion and call attention to the ineffectualities of language; Todd considers meandering punctuation a means of rerouting the reader, forcing her to respond to conveyed emotion whilst failing to connect to individual characters (6). A similar argument is made about Austen's use of punctuation as a means of heightening indeterminacy between narrative and character voice (Rawson, *Satire* 271). Todd's punctual motility is also discussed in relation to Sterne's *A Sentimental Journey through France and Italy* (1768), where "expressive typographic dashes . . . punctuate the history of [Yorick's] travels" (Nagle 829).

81. Sexual bliss is a "terrain" Loy feels Freud has occluded in his "infinitely extensible maze of introversion in search of Eros – – – the little man who isn't *there* – – – – –" (*SE* 251). Again, the dashes mark out unmapped and potentially transcendent affect.

82. For Parsons, Loy's speaker in "Songs" is more vagrant than *flâneuse*; she argues that the poem presents the "artist as outcast elegiacally mourning a beloved urban wasteland, and a belief in the role of the artist to create a vision of 'everyday life'" (182). Without discounting the cogency of this reading, some of Loy's later writings (published after Parson's excellent monograph) indicate that Loy's dash-laden sublimities remain a constant throughout her writing, acting as ballast against the otherwise relentless lows and degradations explored in "Songs".

83. For Marinetti's likening of Venice to a brothel, see "The Battles of Venice" (1910).

84. Harriet Monroe, the editor of *Poetry: A Magazine of Verse*, indirectly critiqued Loy's "telegraphic" writing for its lack of correct punctuation by acerbically asking Loy's forgiveness for using "a few" presumably more conventional "punctuation-marks" in her review of the 1923 *Lunar Baedecker* (*sic*) (100–1).

Chapter 4

"Upon Bossed Bellies": Loy and the Accursed Muse

If the celebrity artist is "the creative self sacrificed to its image", what sacrifice is undertaken by the celebrity muse (Steiner 48)? Written at the close of the first quarter of the twentieth century, Loy's "Monde Triple-Extra" asks this question through the posturing and impostured body, one that achieves recognition in the determining set of a pelvis. Our protagonist is Jove Ivon Corvon, who, though poorly raised, has "heaved himself into the highest society", achieving far-flung fame (*SE* 57). The talent driving Corvon's reputation goes unclarified. He may be an artist, but Loy's descriptions best befit a model: his prized skill is the irresistible "certain little lift" that arises in "the left corner of his mouth when he smiled"; superficiality and sumptuousness emerge in his "idyllic overcoat" and fantastically embroidered dressing gown (*SE* 57, 58–9). The vacuity of Corvon's celebrity is confirmed when one Mina Loy enters the story, channelling the authoritative, all-determining voice of deific creator to progenitorial model. Asked by Corvon how to live, Loy replies: "'he who cannot live on his smile, lives not at all'" (*SE* 57). With this prophetic message, Corvon's fate is sealed: he is reduced to his capacity for appeal. In turn, Corvon's home is graced by a harem of "women of fashion" who sculpt and adorn themselves, are both muses and artists, a complexity reinforced by a noted member of their throng, the "Duchesse de Da Da". Beauties contrived and innate, these women are prized for, and pride themselves upon, their attentiveness to Corvon (*SE* 58–9). Unimpressed by their assiduity, Corvon entertains himself by posing: like Dante Gabriel Rossetti before him, he combs the streets for working-class women, bringing them home to flout his "ignored exasperated crowd" of cultured women before disappearing with the chosen one behind closed doors. His most egregious object choice is a muddied kitten stroked so sensuously before his "uninvited seraglio" that the group swoons. Asked how he can reconcile his kindness to this animal with his cruelty to women, Corvon pointedly replies that the feline's appeal lies in its aversion to his desire (*SE* 58). As artist or model, Corvon courts resistance from his muses and his audience, all of whom become strays to corral and coax at his errant whim. Corvon's proclivities are distinctly vanguard.

Believing himself a prototype, Corvon finds tedious the models who throw themselves before him. They are mannequins, just so many identical, self-immolating corpses strewing his venerable halls each morning. And then he meets his match:

> Of a new shape, refreshing to his eyes, the full curves of her bust meandered into the folds of a skirt revealing only her feet (so much larger than the insignificant little things he was so weary of—). And her loose slippers flapped rhythmically to and fro as she walked.
>
> In her hands she held a great sceptre or wand decorated at its lower extremity with a mass of soft wisps matted together like a mermaid's hair and the colour of twilight.
>
> This she was waving about in mystical arabesques upon the tessellated pavement, driving before her a shallow flood of beautiful water.

Corvon's latent powers now come to fruition: from a state of boredom, he transforms a heavyset, ill-dressed, middle-aged char-woman into a breath-taking being originating from a world of enchantment, her mop a wand, her grey hair "made of light ... purely argent" (*SE* 60).

This muse has her prototype, and she is Maritornes, the Asturian servant who works at an inn that Cervantes's Don Quixote, true to form, elevates to a castle. Maritornes is "broad-faced, flat-headed, and saddle-nosed, with one eye squinting, and the other not much better." Possessed of some grace, she is nevertheless "not even seven hands high ... and her shoulders, which burdened her a little too much, made her look down to the ground more than she cared to do" (Cervantes 111). Like Jove Ivon Corvon's "vision", Maritornes is all torso, all trunk. Imagining her the comely heir descendant of the innkeeper-cum-king, Quixote welcomes Maritornes into his bed that evening, sustaining his illusion against overpowering odds:

> Presently he fell to feeling her smock, which, though it was of canvas, seemed to him to be of the finest and softest lawn. She had on her wrist a string of glass beads; but to his fancy they were precious oriental pearls. Her hairs, not unlike those of a horse's mane, he took

for threads of the brightest gold of Arabia, whose splendour obscures
that of the sun itself. And though her breath, doubtless, smelled of
last night's stale salt fish, he fancied himself sucking from her lips a
delicious and aromatic odour. (114)

Loy's "Monde Triple-Extra" emulates Cervantes's canonical narrative model by naming its author, and in its plot machinations and
characterisation. Further, Loy pilfers chivalrous etiquette and fervent
turns of phrase from that picaresque novel, so that Corvon, precisely
like Quixote before him, pronounces his transmogrified ideal the
"'rarest of women,'" offers his life to her, and thanks "Good Fortune"
for allowing her to cross his path (*SE* 60–1). As does Maritornes,
Corvon's alarmed muse struggles violently to free herself from the
clutches of an amorous protagonist, understandably resistant to the
aggressions of a deranged male infatuated with his own atypicality.

In "Monde Triple-Extra", the battle that ensues between Corvon
and his lady reveals Loy's engagement in ancient sacrificial economies,
and her esoteric understanding, commensurate with Bataille's, that
in everyday resistances and excesses, "life [can slip] from one person
to another in a feeling of magical subversion" ("Laughter" 61).
Fearful that his "vision w[ill] evaporate", Corvon launches his most
attractive weapon, bestowing upon this woman his poised smile,
and "wait[ing] for it to take effect." The charwoman offers him her
stock pose in return: she "planted one hand on her hip —— a powerfully archaic gesture —— and cried in a voice unlike other voices
'Lookit the guy!'" (*SE* 60). Rather than clichéd scold, the gravitas of
this feminine hip-hold is sourced in ancient history, a temporal heft
emphasised by formal diction and extended parenthetical dashes.
Corvon's all-too-easy smile is efficiently trounced in favour of an
atavistic aesthetic that arguably grounds the entirety of Loy's satirical, contemporary narrative. For the "powerfully archaic" is hard
at work in Loy's ironic title: this "Monde Triple-Extra" is awash
in hyperbolic, high-society vogueries whilst remaining mere model
to the prototype that is the "extra-monde" or parallel universe that
was an ancient metaphysical or religious ideal, a universe that preoccupied Loy throughout her life, and is intensively addressed in the
second volume of this *Anatomy*.

Jove Ivon's name is a composite of Jupiter, king of gods and
sky, and Ivon, affiliated by Celtic tradition with the yew tree,
symbol of dreams and magic. Strangeness of mythical proportions
seems likely to ensue.[1] Corvon's devotees are similarly ethereal,
inhuman "[m]agical slips of women" (*SE* 58). Their modishness

notwithstanding, these women fall prey to Victorian mores in their intimate lives, as Corvon is "notoriously the worst lover in the world, which in view of women's disposition toward self-sacrifice and reform work was not the least of his advertisements" (*SE* 59). Accursed, these enchanted muses remain socially accountable, embracing self-martyrdom as the all-defining source of their influence. By presumptuous extension, Corvon proves thrilled to have a "matutinal charwoman" assault his feet with her "mop of matted twilight", chanting all the while in phrases he hears as ritual, spell:

'Young manile
Aveyouno
asima lidy
Iāmm' (*SE* 62)

Read slowly, this quatrain is merely fragmented English spoken by a woman fobbing off an assault: "Young man I'll— / Have you know— / As I'm a lady— / I AM!" There are echoes here of Fanny Cornforth, a working-class model remembered for chiding Dante Gabriel Rossetti with the phrase: "'Oh, go along Rissetty!'"[2] Like his precursor, Corvon magically converts his "lidy's" resistance into a language of assent, one confirming his place in a ritualistic order: "elated with these Eleusinian mysteries incident to his introduction to the favours of his super-woman, [Jove Corvon] hopped in and out of the beautiful water with ecstatic alacrity" (*SE* 61). Improbability reigns supreme: the voluntary harem long to give up their idealised bodies to an adolescent fumbler, and Corvon imagines himself an initiate of an ancient agrarian cult celebrating the return of Persephone to her mother Demeter, goddess of fertility. Both harem and Corvon embrace the sacrificial, a truth compounded by Corvon's belief that his aged ideal comes "to him in the light of a virginal visitation", ready for the slaughter (*SE* 62).

Resolutely grounded, the charwoman challenges and reverts this economy of female oblation. As unprepossessing copy of an unprepossessing model, her surprisingly desirable archaism compromises Corvon's otherwise resolute pursuit of novelty, his unquestioned belief in his embodied creativity and authority. And this critique begins with her grasp of her own pelvis, fingers encasing her thick trunk, directing the eye to her heavy belly and womb, a gesture as old as the foundational site of biological existence it points toward. In what follows, the charwoman "purifies" Corvon with filthy water; thus "'made holy'" – the very definition of sacrifice – Corvon is mopped off his feet, and the story concludes over his unconscious body (Hughes 10). Within Loy's narrative resolution lies yet another trace of Cervantes: after his encounter with Maritornes, Don Quixote, too, is "quite senseless" and believed dead (116–17). But where Quixote openly models himself on past knights errant, Corvon is a self-proclaimed prototype unaware that he is an emulator, a parody of a parody whose sole purpose is sacrifice of self and others. Loy's satire operates on multiple levels: historically speaking, the act of sacrifice refutes the prototypicality Corvon espouses. As James Frazer observes in *The Golden Bough* (1890), immolation affirms the mimetic: sacrificial ritual occurs precisely because human beings fundamentally and persistently swear allegiance to the irrational belief that imitation makes things happen, that the sanctioned murder of one enervated life or life cycle can elongate or resurrect another.[3] In "Monde Triple-Extra", Loy deploys a sacrificial satiric model to critique the hubris of an artist-creator, even as her own muse is an individual narcissistically and blindly invested in the impossible singularity of his originality.

Throughout her life, Loy variously occupied the positions of sitter or muse, and was an artist who paid people as models or created malleable characters.[4] As a youth living abroad and unsupervised, she relied on her "perspicacity" when asked to pose for male artists, testing their intentions by informing them that she was not "'allowed to sit for [her] portrait without a chaperone'" (*IA* 68: 125). Many failed, tellingly losing interest in Loy after realising they could not be alone with her. A graduate of art schools immersed in vanguard coteries throughout her life, Loy's engagement with the dynamics of modelling was politicised and philosophical. Some fifty years before Laura Mulvey famously articulated the expectations and satiations driving women's "'*to-be-looked-at-ness*'" (11), Loy developed her own theory of the male gaze:

> The expression of the most popular beauty is a 'still' of some evanescent reaction associated with the orgasm: her eyes are always turning up for the spasmodic oncome, so that men may plunge a preliminary gaze into this seeming promise that their senses have come upon something to share. (*CP* 18: 61)

The implicit predatoriness of this visual dive notwithstanding, Loy promotes these genital-stirring representations of the female face as a plausibly rapturous association between art and sexuality: "The sensory scale of the erotic symphony must in some way accord with the unknown laws of proportion in beauty, as if perfection in art induces in the intellect a consummation comparable to that with which the harmonies of a human face crown some aesthetic craving in the genitals" (*CP* 18: 62). This sentence affirms Loy's lifelong theorisation of an esoteric Eros that includes the artistic desire for beauty, one reliant on an understanding of ecstatic "erotic symphon[ies]". Idealised, Loy's esoteric Eros is feminist and aspirational. As things stand, however, Loy realises that male confidence, autonomy, and sexual potency – powers readily extendible to the artist with his muse – "conjure up" images of womankind that reflect their own desires (*CP* 18: 65). A man, Loy argues, can "catch an eye in the full of its lustreless pretence" and "polish it with his lubricity until it dazzles him in the very radiance he induces" (*CP* 18: 65). This generativity is as sexual – intimate, attentive – as it is artistic. By it, woman remains reduced to her appearance and oxymoronically occluded, a just-perceptible layer in a male-defined palimpsest.

Loy realises that ocularity and embodiedness have distinct ramifications for women perceived and perceiving, for the woman whose instinctual self may recognise that it lacks what it wants, even as "she, herself, so often fails to find out" (*CP* 18: 62). For Loy, contemporary women can neither take dominion nor create. Reiterating and questioning the gendered biblical mythologies that begin with Genesis, Loy argues that man is the model, the prototype, to which woman has had "to conform", leaving outstanding the question of "where woman begins and where woman ends". Loy speculates that if women had been created first, she might "have run like melted wax" over the earth, overcome by her all-consuming, all-defining inertia.[5] Loy then envisions man arriving on this female-suffused planet and matching his "tread" to women's, recognising her preestablished presence "as his perfect foot-print" (*CP* 18: 66). Passive woman is ground for active man. So entrenched is this gender divide that Loy clearly struggles to imagine a world where woman leaves her mark on the world. As culturally rendered, Loy writes, woman's "very beginning was of an initial secondariness that left her the whole gamut of development, except the creative impetus or starting point" (*CP* 18: 66). Loy the artist-muse finds galling this loss of female creative originality, this definitional absence of a thing never yet possessed.

Within the muse, Loy locates women's creative power. In artistically narrating and theorising the position of the model, Loy labours to challenge the muse's diminution, her mishandling as mere sentient tool, her presumed fate of volitionlessness and violation. Loy's is the feminist work of re-evaluation and recreation, an insistence on her right to critique old mythologies, reorient their foci, and thereby render them anew. In so doing, Loy knowingly draws on a long, scarcely recovered history of the accursed muse, one that continues to distort the history of women models who were often artists in their own right, women who often died too young or too tragically, their intelligence and personal achievements obscured by their affiliations with renowned "masters" content to eschew these women or further their ignominy. Loy's ire feeds an undiscussed motif of her writing, whereby the reproductive or digestive body actively circumvents traditional renderings of artistry, the inspired gut overtaking aesthetic soul or genius mind. Where the muse is traditionally reduced to an inert body, Loy insists that the woman's torso has a language – gestural, vociferous, critical – that takes part in its recreation, that asserts itself beyond the sexual and reproductive capacities for which it has been valued. In the process, Loy's writing is immersed in a dialectics of artistic autonomy and represented subject matter, positioning each perspective as worthy of our attention, if often opposed. Where artistry retains its masculine connotations, Loy contrasts her predominantly female models with male muses who are either feminised or powerfully resistant to their abjectification. Throughout, the belly, increasingly recognised in the twenty-first century as the body's visceral brain, is the place where Loy's considerations of generativity, influence, and legacy ferment.

Lending the pelvis this autonomy is not novel: since Plato's *Timaeus* was written in the fourth century BCE, women's wombs have been afforded lives of their own, wandering at will, often damaging the body they inhabit. A paternally sanctioned womb is one that produces not trouble but people, thus fulfilling women's destiny as self-sacrificing maternal figures. Against this paradigm, Loy's wombs remain barren, yield evolutionary atavisms, or voice outrage at their mistreatment. These wombs are not downtrodden hysteric victims, but register their resistance to the patriarchal disregard for the woman's body. Loy critiques and reworks essentialised femininities and maternalities, responding to the charges she attributes to Futurist leaders that woman is born with a """"prurient"""" or "rapacious" womb (*B* 9: 8; *SE* 80). These same commentaries counter and uneasily engage in the avant-garde's continual return to the female parent, a return Susan Rubin Suleiman posits as "a confrontation between an all-powerful father and a traumatized son, a confrontation staged across and over the body of the mother" (Suleiman 87). Countering Suleiman, Loy's mothers tend to be more fortress than doormat. While Loy's resistance to living "under the law of thy mother" can take on the guise of tedious critique in her romans à clef, her resistance to paternalistic familial hierarchies feeds her interrogation of all origins, prototypes among them (Proverbs 1.8). In this regard, it is noteworthy that modelling, a topic that fascinates Loy, has been likened to parenting. "The model engages in a self-sacrifice in which she 'births' a creation that displaces her"; hence "[w]omb and matrix are archetypes of feminine modelling – moulds that generate copies" (Steiner 15). Loy acknowledges and refutes this configuration, winnowing away at woman's relegation to vessel for prototypes, or mere copy.[6] Ironically, her female muses repeatedly fail to innovate in no small part due to the lack of a good model to emulate. In the process, Loy reconfirms that there is no gestational monad to which only the privileged (male) few have access. Instead, originality – and vanguard originality in particular – is as contingent on antecedents as it is on external inspiration. Put simply: Loy's interrogation of the artist's model might be read as an extended critique of Pound's modernist mantra: "make it new".

In her reconsideration of the feminised muse, Loy insists upon the muse's autonomy, extricating her from her sacrificial role as mere sentient being on the artist's altar, revered in near-obliterative absentia. Loy's muse is in league with her friend Djuna Barnes's insistence that the contemporary model should be viewed as an artist in her own right:

> In the old days a model was simply a model; she broke men's hearts but not his [*sic*] traditions; she stood for hours upon the model stand, saying nothing, while the painter measured and planed her and got her down upon canvas for the autumn Salon.
>
> But times have changed. The model is no longer the monopoly of him who deals in colours. Musicians, yes, and writers have fallen under the sway of the 'personal and living enchantment' of the models themselves . . . .
>
> It has even gone so far that a group of the four arts calling themselves 'Super Realists' have sworn to lay aside their inspiration forever unless it comes to them through the '*belles femmes*,' and in turn the model demands her long subordinated personality, she will no longer be the *decor*, she will be the actor too. ("Models" 16)

Writing in a 1924 issue of *Charm*, the same journal that would publish Loy's "Modern Poetry" (1925), Barnes recognises Kiki of Montparnasse, or Alice Prin, as the prototype of this new model, one who evidently shucks none of the paradoxes of the old: she "is superbly irrelevant, magnificently disconnected, triumphantly trivial" (91). Barnes's "The Models Have Come to Town" openly lampoons the deific status of the inspired vanguard artist whose muse remains in the background. In model Kiki's case, the artist in question was the photographer Man Ray, with whom both Loy and Barnes associated. Elevating Kiki's stature to match her contemporaneous popularity, Barnes suggests that the figure best disposed to conflate art and life, that now-infamous vanguard diktat, is the much-maligned muse: "For the Montparnasse model is everywhere you are and are not" (92). Barnes champions the neglected perspective of the female model, who occupies spaces and positions from which artist and audience are exempt, even as creativity and spectatorship are, for her, familiar terrain.

Like Loy's many contemporaneous writings on the artist's model – written throughout the 1920s and beyond – Barnes's focus is undergirded by historical change: the model's fortunes are revolutionised in the *fin-de-siècle*, an era renowned for its cataclysmic reconsiderations of gender and sexuality. Alongside the rise of the New Woman surfaces a concomitant, begrudging respect for the model's creativity. Simultaneously, burgeoning vanguard movements, among them Decadence and Symbolism, co-opt femininity, a move evident in their willing self-martyrdom, their ecstatic claims of failure, fragmentation, and wretchedness. (The associated vanguardist belief in their own vulnerability to the prostitution of institutionalised art and rapacious audiences forms a central focus of the previous chapter.) These same movements evince a fury against the female muse driven in no small part by her newly stubborn unwillingness to enact the endless yielding and caregiving ascribed to the maternal, a "mothering" demanded of female parents, servants, siblings, associates, and lovers alike. A satirist, Loy is attuned to this invective; a politicised female artist and writer, she takes umbrage with the relegation of women to passive model, pliant muse, perpetual mother. The accursed muse that preoccupies Loy is antonym and equal to Paul Verlaine's *poète maudit*, a self-martyring typology of the literary genius that comes into prominence in the early nineteenth century and informs vanguard sacrificial thinking into the twentieth, Bataille's inclusive. While "accursed poet" has become a colloquialism or well-recognised stereotype, considered critical attention to its origin and legacies has yet to occur. My formulation of the "accursed muse" latent in Loy's work is a descendant of the accursed poet lineage, as well as a neologistic phrase that establishes its feminist ramifications. Where the artist's model can be any sentient or insentient being, the accursed muse is as knowingly abject, marginal, and neglected as the accursed poet, but her doom is perpetual, her legacy unassured: the accursed muse is profoundly, painfully aware of the lived truth of her sacrificial status, of the malediction that embeds itself as felt entity within her corporeal, affective being. In league with this muse's unwillingness to yield to imposed misogynist ideals, Loy's satires draw the reader's gaze to a sentient womb, from which – or from whom – generative understanding emanates. This chapter will consider Loy's lampoons of the myth of singular male creativity in works archived and published, among them the as-yet-unpublished "Static" (c. 1920s) and "Pygmaleon and Galatea" (n.d.), short stories including "Piero and Eliza." (1921), and Loy's late romans à clef. Given that Loy's ongoing speculations regarding the generative pelvis of the muse are most fulsomely realised in her story "The Stomach" (1921), I conclude with a close read of its relationship to the controversial American portraitist John Singer Sargent and his abdominally overdetermined accursed muses. Within this story the model's stomach takes centre stage, asserting itself as an aesthetic authority. This midriff is not hysteric, but genius.

The Accursed Poet

Why, precisely, is the muse accursed? Edgar Allen Poe grasps the excised heart of this matter in "The Oval Portrait" (1842), a story centred on a painting of "a maiden of fairest beauty" who transfixes the narrator with her "immortal" good looks. The portrait is fantastically executed, its success predicated on an "absolute *life-likeness* of expression" (189). As this uncanny admixture of mortal metaphors portends, the woman's fate is tragic. Her husband is a bigamist, already married to "his Art", a rival she comes to hate, even as she "meekly", predictably, consents to becoming his model (189–90). Plant-like, the woman becomes etiolate in the turret that is her husband's studio, withering in its meagre light. No visitors are allowed, and the painter does not discern her demise: "wild with the ardour of his work", he "turned his eyes from the canvas rarely, even to regard the countenance of his wife." On completing the portrait, he declares: "'This was indeed *Life* itself!'" He then looks, for the first time in weeks, at the ostensible subject of his art. We never know how he responds. Instead, the narrator intervenes, intoning: "*She was dead!*" (190). So concludes "The Oval Portrait". Teetering vertiginously on bathos, Poe's story addresses well-worn art historical conundrums: the impossibility of absolute realism, the privileging of artifice over reality, and the power ceded to the human gaze.

Narrator and painter gain experientially and aesthetically from this fecundly egg-shaped portrait, whose subject dies just as she is "ripening into womanhood", poised for reproductive self-sacrifice. Poe is renowned for blurring womb and tomb, for conflating women with the inert objectification of death; hence Loy's "Poe" (1921) celebrates his "lyric elixir" that "embalms / the spindle spirits of [his] hour glass loves" (*LoLB* 76). Framed by the womanly tasks of spinning wool or fate, these adored beings are femininely curvaceous, emphatically mortal. But in "The Oval Portrait", Poe unusually foregrounds the suffering of the female model over that of the angst-ridden male artist, a focal shift foreseeing the preoccupation with the model that would emerge in the era following Poe's own.

Portraits have never been objective representations. But in the latter half of the nineteenth century, stylisation veered toward acute psychological investigation, partly as a counter to the stark realism of the burgeoning technology of photography. Just before twentieth-century abstraction turned this subtle truth into a clarion call, "realistic" portraiture enjoyed a burst of *fin-de-siècle* popularity. Artist's models were in high demand, and with their growing professionalisation came an ambivalent acknowledgement of their role in artistic production, one nascently alert to how models had historically been effaced, or sacrificed, to sustain the mythical singularities of artistic inspiration and reputation. Risibly melodramatic though it may be, Poe's "The Oval Portrait" encapsulates what I am calling the accursed muse, a phrase countering and correlating to the accursed poet who is its precise forebear. *Les Poètes maudits* was a coinage that successfully entered literary vernacular courtesy of Paul Verlaine's volume by that same name (1884/8). By express design, *The Accursed Poets* is a gallery of condemned rogues, among whose number Poe, via Baudelaire, is a revered influence. Its ancient model is *homo sacer*, its modern Alfred de Vigny's *Stello: A Session with Doctor Noir* (1832), a novel structured as a triptych of portraits of eighteenth-century poets doomed to ignominy and early death.[7]

"'Portraits'", Doctor Noir tells his eager acolyte Stello, "'make one's heart beat faster, and when that one heart no longer beats, they should be destroyed" (Vigny 164). For the viewer, the portrait is an always available sacrificial victim. This aggressive stance is typical of psychiatrist Noir, who undertakes treatment of the idealist poet Stello, or he who believes poetry can change the world. Noir aims to cure Stello of his all-encompassing malaise: sentimentalism. Asked why he is a poet, Stello sighs deeply and intones: "'there exists in creation nothing beautiful, nothing grand, nothing harmonious which does not send a prophetic quiver through me, which does not make itself felt in my very bowels, and fill my eyes with divine and mysterious tears'". Rambling on, Stello assures Noir he is driven by prescience, sympathy, love, and inspiration. In reply, Noir tells him flatly this proves nothing other than the goodness of Stello's heart (19). The modernist resistance to sentimentality discussed in the previous chapters thus shows itself as emergent roughly five decades before most vanguardists were born. Anti-sentimentalists are meant to be hard of heart and tough of stomach, a truth of which the gastrically inclined Loy was all too aware. Via Noir, young Stello is instructed that poets are necessarily social pariahs sullied by affiliation with the mediocrities of waged labour, popular reception, and most emphatically, politics. Noir focuses on poets Nicholas-Joseph-Laurent Gilbert (1751–80), Thomas Chatterton (1752–70), and André Chénier (1762–94), but they are a select few amongst his gallery of "melancholy phantoms", a collection that includes Cervantes, Milton, and Dryden (170).[8] Amidst the litany of advice Noir offers Stello is the injunction to "[k]eep ever present before your mind these portraits, representing a thousand others" (Vigny 181).

"I have remarked that every age had its own gait, glance and gesture", writes Baudelaire in "The Painter of Modern Life" (1863). Seven decades later, Baudelaire's revelatory perambulation saunters through Loy's assessment of the modern poet, a figure "recogniz[able] . . . by the gait of their mentality" (*LoLB* 157). Where Loy "verif[ies] this proposition" by presenting a gallery of wandering poets, Baudelaire prescribes a jaunt through "some vast portrait-gallery, such as the one at Versailles" ("Painter" 13). Baudelaire remains an exemplary accursed poet, replete with proclivities for outcasts, failures, opium, impoverishment, suicide, and literary portraiture of like figures (Starkie 1–11). His biographical essay on Poe honours his antecedent as an autodidact of alcoholism and a vocational suicide whose "method of work" was "drastic and fatal . . . but suited to his passionate nature" ("Poe" 89). It is Baudelaire who is said to have inspired the titular phrase of Verlaine's collection, which intersperses previously published essays on his contemporaries with long tracts from their various works.[9] Published in 1884 and expanded in 1888, the final roll call of accursed poets includes Tristan Corbière, Arthur Rimbaud, Stéphane Mallarmé, Marceline Desbordes-Lalmore, Villiers de L'Isle-Adam, and Pauvre Lelian (an anagram of Paul Verlaine), with Baudelaire as the absent presence at its heart.[10] Leading us from one essayistic portrait to the next, Verlaine celebrates each poet's heroic capacity to withstand aches, injustice, and rejection.

Less prescriptive than Vigny, Verlaine's work is more hagiographic, more willing to court paradox; his poets are "exquisitely perverse, ravishingly chaste" (46); they do not need publications or audiences, but as Mallarmé has both, Verlaine dismisses these worrying tokens of success as "enormous minor detail[s]" (59). Misunderstood experimenters, sweet martyrs all, Verlaine's poets are "[a]bsolute by imagination, absolute in expression . . . . But cursed!" (12). Volition is crucial to their miserable fates: when poor, they reject money; when rich, they shun an easier life; desperately in thrall to their art, they nevertheless command. Verlaine demonstrates how, as we approach the twentieth century, sacrifice is increasingly posited as a conscious, authenticating individual choice rather than a societal ritual. With a nod to Vigny, he asks: "is it not true that . . . the sincere poet will see himself, will feel himself, will know himself *damned* by the rule of any faction, o Stello?" (79). Against this glorified outlaw autonomy is the curious truth that Verlaine deliberately objectifies his heroic comrades, turning them into muses.

Verlaine's "About the Following Portraits" introduces his poets via extensive physical descriptions. Given that they became lovers, Verlaine lingers predictably over Rimbaud's "sensual" lips, his "handsome dimpled chin" and "proud mop of hair", but Villiers de L'Isle-Adam is similarly reduced to "magnificently dreamy eyes" (10, 116). Manet's portrait of Mallarmé is relayed with like adoring detail (10). Verlaine will not be dismissed as fatuous or infatuated; instead, he insists that bodily contours correspond to poetic forms and lineages:

> But looking at them again, just as the verses of these dear Cursed Ones are very steadily written . . . . even their features are calm, like bronzes from decadent Rome . . . or like polychromed marble statues . . . . [L]ong live the pure, stubborn (but no less amusing) line that communicates so well, through the material structure, the incompressible ideal!
>
> There is something impassive about these strange and handsome faces – take a good look – that irrevocably validates the peerless verses one is about to read. (11)

These poets write as they appear; their fineness as muses facilitates their musings. And this mixing of categories – are they models or artists? – is compounded by Verlaine's decision to foreground a sample from Corbière's "Epitaph". Drawn from his 1873 collection, *Les Amours jaunes*, "Epitaph" is a veritable portrait of the *poète maudit* as a suicidal, indolent young man who longs to be his own mistress, acquiesce to chance, and pursue disgust. At its end, Corbière assures us of the authenticity of these desires: "'Not a poseur, –" he proclaims; instead, his subject is "posing as the *unique*'" (Verlaine 18). Corbière's is an anxious paradox by which the accursed poet is a derivative prototype who actively represses the impossibility of his originary individuality.[11] His very heroism is synonymous with martyrdom, his exalted genius inextricable from the lowest social strata: brothels, filthy penury. Worse still, as Verlaine confirms, the *poète maudit* is mere model to a genre that occupies a subordinate place within artistic hierarchies: portraiture.

The modernist artist aims to be prototype, not copy; origin, not descent. We witness this drive in the "Crisis of Verse", where Mallarmé claims that his renderings of flowers realise "what is absent from every bouquet" (210). By this account, the distilled essence of the model yields more than the sum of its parts, and more than all other models – all those other bouquets – that came before, currently exist, or have yet to come. Ironically, Mallarmé's wilful manipulation of prototype and copy, of influence and generativity, causality, chronological time, and the limits of what can be seen or known is itself an emulation. Consider the terms of Baudelaire's description of his relationship to Poe:

> 'Well! They accuse me – me! of imitating Edgar Poe! Do you know why I translated Poe so patiently? Because he resembles me. The first time I opened a book by him, I was terrified and ravished to find not only topics I had dreamed of, but phrases, my own thoughts, written by him twenty years before.' (qtd. in Symons 167)

Baudelaire will not be copy to his prototype. Extending this meta-*mise-en-abyme*, this quotation is drawn from Arthur Symons's *The Symbolist Movement in Literature* (1899/1919), an English imitation of Verlaine's *Les Poètes maudits*. Like Vigny, Baudelaire, Mallarmé, and Verlaine before him, Symons generates a series of essay portraits of the poets he wishes to celebrate, all of them intense individuals who suffer "a long vagabondage" of excess punctuated by misunderstood and under-acknowledged genius (34). Under Symons's gaze, Verlaine is imitated in style and substance: he is presented as a model whose bodily form determines his poetics: "a face all character, full of somnolence and sudden fire, in which every irregularity was a kind of aid to the hand" (42). Verlaine the portraitist now becomes portrait, his original work just one component of a series. And like most models, *Les Poètes maudits* is more famous for its name than an interrogation of its substance: Verlaine's volume remains underdiscussed by literary critics.[12]

Portraits of the damned artist continue into the twentieth century. Witness Antonin Artaud's extension of *poète maudit* to *peintre maudit* in "Van Gogh: The Suicide Provoked by Society" (1948), an essay that rehearses familiar themes: "No one has ever written, painted, sculpted, modelled, constructed, or invented anything, except in order to extricate himself from hell" (48). Satisfyingly, this hell is inescapable. Bataille, too, turns to Van Gogh as exemplar, using the painter's experience to drag the self-sacrificial mode of the accursed poet from its back-alley haven into the light of philosophical validation. Van Gogh's famous self-mutilation Bataille reads as a marvellous synecdoche of his disengagement with the world entire, a succinct measure of the artist's capacity to rush headlong into the abyss of cultural alienation: "in our day, with the custom of sacrifice in full decline, the meaning of the word, to the extent that it remains a drive revealed by *inner experience*, is still as closely linked as possible to the notion of a *spirit of sacrifice*, of which the automutilation of madmen is only the most absurd and terrible example" ("Sacrificial Mutilation" 67). The wound left by Van Gogh's self-sundering is a defining feature of Bataille's philosophical landscape. Treating the sacrificial victim as foundational, Bataille magnifies Verlaine's terms, describing ours as an accursed age par excellence (*AS2* 78; *G*: 7). Not only are we freighted by obsessions with work and woefully ignorant of the sacred, we also long acutely for a natural world that we relentlessly transfigure. Nature remains estranged courtesy of our heightened consciousness, our artifice; art lifts yet reinforces the curse upon humanity (*AS2* 78).

This curse defines the poet, artist, philosopher, mystic, and lover, or anyone consumed with conceptual boundaries, anyone aiming at the "disruptive nonknowledge" that results in sacrifice, be it of the body, the profane world, or language (Arnould 87). For Bataille, salvation lies in becoming as Van Gogh's discarded pinna to the socio-economic body:

> The victim [of sacrifice] is a surplus taken from the mass of *useful* wealth. And he can only be withdrawn from it in order to be consumed profitlessly, and therefore utterly destroyed. Once chosen, he is the *accursed share*, destined for violent consumption. But the curse tears him away from the *order of things*; it gives him a recognisable figure, which now radiates intimacy, anguish, the profundity of living beings. (*AS1* 59)

Freeing the victim from servility, accursedness provides near-transcendental insight; in its clarity and originality, it is the ground of enlightened individuals more acted-upon than active (*IE* 60). In turn, philosophers or authors aggressively transgress in a state of torment and delirium; Bataille acknowledges that, although "condemned" to write poems, "even a 'damned' poet is eager to possess the moving world of images" (*IE* 147–9). Poetry in particular, Bataille argues, restores the sacred to language. The poet detaches words from the rational, punctures the artificial patina of communication, taking us from the known to the unknown. Bataille considers poetry the path humanity takes to redress the abuse heaped upon language in quotidian, ends-driven discourse; poetry *is* redemptive sacrifice (*IE* 135–56).

For Jean-Luc Nancy, Bataille uses art "to relay or to sublat[e] the impasse of sacrifice"; thus, his goal is not death, but an awakened sensibility that reinforces the very instrumentality he claims to loathe (30). Bataille is alert to this conundrum: "Good was always the ultimate end of sacrifice, so the whole process was really mutilated, was almost a failure" (*LE* 58). As art or ritual murder, Bataille's immolating liberations remain as short-lived as festival; his reworked sacrificial model continually risks collapsing in upon itself. This irresolvable collapse reappears in another twentieth-century portrait of the *poète maudit*, Asger Jorn's "Guy Debord and the Problem of the Accursed" (1964):

> Paradoxically, the general sympathy toward modernism since the turn of the [twentieth] century, and especially since World War II when it was proclaimed that 'the accursed artist no longer exists,' represses these creative forces even more radically. The reality of social malediction is wrapped in a tranquilising and antiseptic appearance of emptiness: *the problem has disappeared; there never was a problem.* At the same time, the journalistic label of 'accursed' becomes, on the contrary, an immediate valorization. It is enough to get yourself cursed, to be all the rage. (157)

Artists are now condemned only to be appropriated, writes Jorn, sourcing this process in ancient sacrificial ritual. He qualifies: "Today, since we must be more civilised, we no longer literally sacrifice; we curse. There is no more mystery, and the shrewdest form of sacrifice is sanctification by praise" (159–60). Like his high modernist forebears, Jorn fears the reverential, the positive, the potentially sentimental. Jorn's portrait of yet another founding figure of a vanguard movement – in Debord's case, the Situationist

International – apes Verlaine and Vigny in its pretence that malediction is preferable to valorisation, as if to exempt the portraitist from the charge of fatuousness. Nor is Jorn's alignment of accursedness and immolation new. As Vigny's Noir tells Stello in 1832, expiation has existed since ancient times, and "[t]he bloody sacrifice of a few men for many will continue until the end of the world'" (132). Come the close of *Stello*, it is clear that the poet remains among the most extinguishable of victims:

> 'The Poet bears a curse upon his life and a blessing on his name. The Poet, apostle of the ever-youthful truth, is a source of perpetual umbrage to the man of Power, apostle of an obsolete fiction; for the one is inspired, the other has at best some power of concentration or some ingenuity of mind. The Poet leaves behind him a book in which the judgement of both public actors and their actions will be read; and at the very moment when these actors disappear forever in death, the author begins his lasting life.' (181)

Contemporary sacrifice may be condemned to a Sisyphean life of mimesis, of repeating its own terms, in thrall to the immolation that is its own impossibility, "a gesture that can no longer distinguish between its reality and its simulacrum, between a real death and its poetic rendition" (Arnould 95). But artists and geniuses will consider this a risk worth taking, know that genius – inseparable from art – always lowers more than it uplifts. Artists and geniuses remain prepared, as is Bataille, to think and write "in order not to know of any method of being better than a cloth in tatters" (*IE* 82, 66). To transcend mortal confines, one must accept a brief life heroically redeemed by future regard or disgrace. Even the imprecation of the untrustworthy masses bests invisibility. But what then of she who is consigned to the servitude, obscurity, and suffering sacrifice is meant to overcome? The destiny of the accursed muse is considerably less liberating, heroically self-determined, or, in the hands of satiric portraitist Loy, earnest.

The Accursed Muse

Loy is not immune to the value of the curse, or unaware of how it is, as Jean-Jacques Lecercle describes, a bewitchingly "illicit performative" by which an articulated aggression can garner long-term, perceptible consequences (234, 236).[13] This cycle of malediction is short-circuited by the accursed poet, who masochistically makes of

Denise Riley's "extimacy" an internalised feedback loop, thus disrupting a literary history of cursing that begins with iambography and culminates in satire.[14] Along the way, the silenced accursed muse proves formative. In the sixth century BCE, Hipponax was rewarded for his abusive verses with a sculpture that caricatured perceived deformities and deficiencies of his physique. His riposte was so venomous that it was said to have prompted the two artists responsible to commit suicide (Elliott 13). The protagonist of Petronius's first-century CE *Satyricon* is an accursed muse: Encolpius's hapless, relentless narrative quest is prompted by the fury he elicited in Priapus, the phallic god of regeneration, in a blundered ritual homage. As Dryden states, the finest satire is written by "'[t]he best good man" accompanied by "the worst-natured muse". Given that good writing must be written by those possessing "good nature[s] – the most godlike commendation of any man", the very vitriol of satire must originate, by default, in an ill-tempered and usually feminised other (13). From Eve's originary disobedience to the contemporary euphemism for menstruation, women are inextricable from cursing; there is nothing particularly noteworthy or exceptional in Dryden's pairing. In Loy's era, this generalised accursedness is extended to an understanding of the limitations applied to the feminised muse, a figure self-reflexively presented in fine art from Gustave Courbet onward, and in the literatures of Loy's predecessors and peers, from the Pre-Raphaelites to Wyndham Lewis.

In 1903, Austrian philosopher Otto Weininger published a bestseller, *Sex and Character*, in which he argued that womankind has no sense of her destiny, and will never overcome her continual association with the sexualised, hysterical body. In fact, Weininger believes women's efforts to do so are feeble and flimsy by capricious design:

> at the last moment [women] will kiss the man who ravishes them, and succumb with pleasure to those whom they have resisted violently. It is as if women were under a curse. At times she feels the weight of it, but she never flees from it. Her shrieks and her ravings are not really genuine, and she succumbs to her fate at the moment when it has seemed the most repulsive to her. (279)

"The curse, which was said to be heavy on women, is the evil will of man", states Weininger, an acknowledgement promptly decimated by the caveat that "nothing is only a tool in the hand of the will for nothing." Woman is culpable for her innate plasticity, a malleability that makes artists of all mankind: "Man created woman, and will always create her afresh, as long as he is sexual" (299). The accursed poet knows his destiny: belated but near-certain recognition of his genius. The accursed female's fate is volitionlessness and violation. Weininger's peer and influence, the German neurologist Paul Julius Möbius, agrees. Author of the popular pamphlet *The Mental Inferiority of Women* (1900), Möbius avers that if woman "'fails in her duty to the species and insists on living her individual life for herself, she is struck as if by a curse'" (qtd. in Sartini Blum 119).

Loy counters these ruling misogynies with a generalisation of her own: although she perceives in her second husband, Arthur Cravan, the qualities of the accursed poet – he is poor, combative, resistant to the "arbitrary condemnation" of social prescriptions, military conscription included – she points out that he merely makes good use of the "dual role" played by any man, "the one apparent which curses his earthly status – & the other divine" (*LaLB* 318–19). By contrast, Loy's accursedness is less binary than continuum. Witnessing her father procuring marked-down pictures from the Royal Academy, Loy characterises these purchases, and her own attendance at art school, as risible oblations to her parents' overpowering upward mobility. In the 1890s, Loy argues, "[t]he artist [is] butt to the bourgeoisie": both a target to be achieved and a figure of derision. Aspirational purchases of photogravure aside, Loy recognises that, in turn, she is the butt of her parents' domestic joke: "just as martyrdom was instituted as a pastime for a crowd", Loy, as fledgling artist, can "congratulate herself that the only laughter ever heard in that disheartened home is raised by herself" (*GI* 29: 144). As misunderstood genius, Loy momentarily counts herself among the ranks of accursed artists. But to be an accursed female artist is to disproportionately escalate an already prescribed state. Aiming at tragic inspiration, Loy is instead considered comically incongruent.

Against the baseness of embodied accursedness, to be identified as a muse is high praise, is to receive the artist's acknowledgement of the model's "generative power, physical or psychological" (Steiner 12). As Wendy Steiner argues in *The Real Real Thing*, the model "is a relational concept through and through . . . . giv[ing] rise to something else—a product, a work of art, a 'creature'" (12). In the main, artists' models are sentient tools, conduits to sought-after aesthetic truths. Their intellection is not required; they need only be vital, sensing beings, ready for the artist's execution. Sacrificial, generative. Secondary to artist, artwork, and audience, they passively, hopefully await the bestowal of an aleatory recognition. Where a portrait sitter commissions, controls, and determines the titling of their own representation, a model is replicated without acknowledgement, represents another, or becomes anatomised fragment to a composite ideal (S. West 37–8). Historically, when artists referred directly to individual life models, it was to deride their impudence, tardiness, drunkenness, or financial desperation. Autobiographical accounts of modelling only appear in the twentieth century. This disregard for knowing and understanding individual models is tempered by the occasional begrudging admission that some are possessed of ineffable qualities that exceed practical requisites of stamina, alertness, punctuality, pliancy, and physical appeal (Borzello 59–62). Like prostitution, modelling paid more than menial labour, thereby attracting all genders and the working classes. In nineteenth-century European art schools, women generally earned more than men for posing. The additional income was intended to mitigate the social stigma, the risk of encountering lascivious male art students, and the potential loss of above-average earnings in the brothels from which they were sometimes recruited (Borzello 19).

As students, women were debarred from art schools until the *fin-de-siècle*, and even then were prohibited from drawing nude models, an experience familiar to Loy, an adolescent attendee of St John's Wood School of Art in London from 1897 to 1899 (*BM* 40). Loy's pupillage dovetailed with the high-water mark of the artist's model as a profession, which then experienced a steady decline, along with life-drawing instruction, between 1910 and 1945. The late Victorian clamour for models was exacerbated in part by the burgeoning middle-class aspirations evinced by Loy's family of origin: the desire to master aesthetic knowledge through formal education and by the ownership of original artworks. This same clamour was furthered by a concomitant popularity of realist and narrative painting (Borzello 26–7). But where Loy was a figure who engendered mockery within her own staid Victorian home, in the well-circulated journals of the time such as *Punch, or the London Charivari* (1841–2002), it was artists' models who became stock figures, ripe for lampoon. Advertisements proliferated for models who met specific, desirable characteristics and typologies; a formal model register emerged, belatedly, in the 1912 *Art Chronicle* (Borzello 48). The model's success was confirmed in England by purity campaigners who published chilling narratives of vulnerable, attractive women forced into posing for money by pitiable, unavoidable circumstances. This fresh spin on the age-old tale of the fallen woman garnered a wide readership that reached its peak in Loy's infancy. It was propagated by women's organisations, Christian churches, and male artists who swore allegiance to its pathos by way of combating allegations or insinuations of their own complicity in licentiousness.[15] This self-same narrative was also used as a stick to beat the three daughters of the Loy household. Writing in the first person, Loy recalls her long-nurtured hope of earning her own living by way of countering her parents' "threats of the period" to disown their children, "with the inferential concomitant – that all we could do would be 'go to the dogs' – which rather naturally led . . . to envisaging the lowest employments such as dish-washer – or desperately; 'Artist's Model'" (*EP* 24). Victorian moral sanctions furthered the anxious fiction that artistry is masterfully, heterosexually masculine, whilst modelling is submissively if narcissistically feminine.[16]

With professional recognition came changes in the artistic presentation of the model, who becomes increasingly astute, defiant, unignorable. Gustave Courbet's *The Painter's Studio: A Real Allegory Summing Up Seven Years of my Artistic and Moral Life* (1855) is an early indicator of this transition. Courbet's oil painting depicts an artist working at a canvas in a room of two dozen onlookers, all of whom are clad excepting the female model positioned directly behind the painter, a sheet loosely and ineffectually held to her sternum, leaving her breasts, back, and hindquarters on show. We are invited to condemn her nonchalant, gratuitous nudity, but also to observe her absorption in the act of creation, her alert proximity to the artist. His head tilts left, hers right as they scrutinise the work before them, and she quite literally has his back, leaving her own exposed as she stands protectively behind his seated form.

Where the model need only be sentient, consciousness and skill are integral to the accursed muse, and these capacities are ambivalently, begrudgingly recognised by her male peers. Among Courbet's envisioned fraternity is his associate Baudelaire, who is depicted at the far right of *The Painter's Studio*, evidently immune to the noise of the audience, or the appeal of art or naked model, as he sits engrossed in a book. "My wretched muse", writes Baudelaire, "what does your morning bring?" The quotidian subject of Baudelaire's "Sick Muse" is defined by madness, horror, nightmare, and illness, or the very sources of the poet's inspiration. Recognising his dependence upon her, Baudelaire affords her just enough autonomy to shoulder the blame for his impieties and obscenities. Tongue firmly in cheek, he self-servingly wishes her health, great thoughts, and "Christian blood" that "flow[s] in waves that scan" (*Flowers* 25). In "The Venal Muse" Baudelaire announces his possession of this feminised other, attributing to her a base need to "put up . . . charms for sale" like a whore, clown, or altar boy singing empty songs of praise to "never present gods". Baudelaire's muse prostitutes herself inadequately: her skin is mottled, her "purse and palate" parched. Miserable, weary, she strives to "bring amusement to the vulgar crowd", freeing Baudelaire to reject the same from a self-reflexive and controlled distance (*Flowers* 27). Baudelaire's sonnets are homages to and perpetuations of the abject exaltation offered the muse, whose curse does not, in Bataille's sacrificial terms, "tea[r her] away from the *order of things*", but ensnares her as object within the artist's order (*AS1* 59). Branded, servile, her freedom to create or illuminate is constrained by the artist's frame.

"In patriarchal ideologies of art the role ascribed to the feminine position is either as art's object, the model, or as its muse by virtue of a romantic affiliation with an artist" (Pollock, *Vision* 136). To Griselda Pollock's tidy summation, we might add the following experiences as constitutive of the accursed muse: an upbringing marked by subjugation, opprobrium, and/or penury; a fateful chance meeting with an artist on the cusp of recognition; an immediate turn to modelling for that artist; a vexed public reception of her representation; and lastly, a tragic, early death. At no juncture should the accursed muse's mental or creative abilities be acknowledged without first establishing their use for the male artist. When these circumstances do not occur, the accursed muse's biography should be posthumously altered, as was that of nineteenth-century painter, poet, and artist's model Elizabeth Siddall. Historicised as "Siddal" because her husband Dante Gabriel Rossetti preferred this spelling of her name, Siddall is said to have been seven years Rossetti's junior.[17] As legend has it, he rescued her from work in a millinery, and they had a brief, perfect romance truncated by her premature death from consumption. But Siddall's birth certificate indicates that she was only Rossetti's junior by twelve months, and no proof exists that she worked as a hat-maker. Rather than a being wife on the receiving end of perfect love and devotion, Siddall was said to have been wracked by Rossetti's infidelities. What's more, she died in 1862 from an overdose of the laudanum to which she had become addicted (Bronfen, *Over* 172, 176).

Siddall's narrative coincides with that of many women involved with the Pre-Raphaelite Brotherhood, a group of male artists who repeatedly sought "out working-class women as models, lovers and wives . . . . [and] subjected them to a programme of drastic re-education requir[ing] . . . an induction into that social role and psychic condition called femininity – silence, pleasant experience, deferential manners, self-sacrifice" (Pollock, *Vision* 148). In Rossetti's portraits of Siddall, she is typically positioned with downcast eyes, her identity subsumed into the mould of a pronounced style that, by his own admission, overwrote the individual features of every one of his female models (Pollock, *Vision* 159–60, 182–3). To this career-long litany of alteration, Elizabeth Bronfen adds that Rossetti's brushstrokes embellish one of the few surviving photographs of Siddall (*Over* 177). Rossetti buried some of his original verses in Siddall's coffin, then exhumed her seven years later so that he could recover the lines she had inspired when ill; he claimed her corpse was lovely to behold, a veritable portrait all aglow (Bronfen, *Over* 176–7). Even in death, Siddall remained Rossetti's aestheticised mannequin.[18] Siddall's treatment is prophesied in Rossetti's influential "Hand and Soul" (1850), a story in which a muse magically appears before an artist. Speaking on behalf of the gods, she tells him he must sacrifice himself to his art, and promises him that, by painting her, he will create a complete vision of his own soul. Not just a feminine ideal, this muse is man transparent to himself, briefly sanctified – set aside as holy – only to be assimilated into a narcissism posing as self-immolation. As Loy avers, a man can "catch an eye in the full of its lustreless pretence" and "polish it with his lubricity until it dazzles him in the very radiance he induces" (*CP* 18: 65).

Siddall was a creator: she exhibited her visual art, and her poems were published posthumously in 1906 in and amongst the reminiscences of her brother-in-law, William Michael Rossetti (Bronfen, *Over* 169–70; Siddal 233, 235). These poems reveal how Siddall was anything but an acquiescent feminine ideal. Consider "Love and Hate" (1857), which begins with the furious injunction: "Ope not thy lips, thou foolish one, / Nor turn to me thy face" (233). In addition to not wanting to be spoken to, or have "thy shadow" on "my path", the speaker repeatedly resists being looked at:

> Turn thou away thy false dark eyes,
>   Nor gaze upon my face;
> Great love I bore thee: now great hate
>   Sits grimly in its place. (234)

Gall rises under the scrutiny of the beloved. A creator and model among artists, Siddall's rendering of focused perception is inevitably multivalent. Incensed and maligned, Siddall's poetic speakers posit subjectivity precariously. "Early Death" (c. 1862) actively welcomes its titular demise. In "At Last" (1861), the speaker begs her mother, not her lover, to carry out the final wishes by which she will remain unknown and unlocatable for eternity: "when the sun has set", she implores, "carry me through the dim twilight / And hide me among the graves" (237). While the self-effacement on offer is commensurate with Rossetti's depictions of Siddall as modest lady with bowed head, what emerges, paradoxically, is a desire for a legacy of totalising anonymity so forcefully articulated in verse that it raises questions about strategies rooted in vengefulness, fear, perhaps both. A catalogue of Rossetti's "portraits" of Siddall shows a like defiance. Amidst the timorous elegant fictions of Rossetti's oeuvre is a sketch dated September 1854. In it, Siddall is seated with legs tucked beneath her, hands folded, head against chair back. Reclining, Siddall is far from prone: her chin is elevated, and her eyes, enlarged through artistic fancy or real-life gauntness, stare forcefully at Rossetti. For a moment, Siddall is less accursed than accusatory, a muse taking ruthless stock of the artist as she occupies her allotted place (Surtees, n.p.; Fig. 4.1).

Fig. 4.1 Gabriel Dante Rossetti, *Untitled Sketch of Elizabeth Siddall* (1854). Private collection; included in *Rossetti's Portraits of Elizabeth Siddal*, edited by Virginia Surtees (1991).

Eyes often expose the accursed muse's oppositionality, her habitually occluded self-consciousness. Of Manet's *Olympia* (1865), T. J. Clark writes that hers "is a gaze which gives nothing away, as the reader attempts to interpret its blatancy; a look direct and yet guarded, poised very deliberately between address and resistance" ("Preliminaries" 34). Victorine Meurent's eyes embody what Clark considers Manet's art historical achievement: his rendering of an expression of "palpable and frank inconsistency" integral to what is delineated here as the plight of the accursed muse (*Painter* 11). For Clark, *Olympia* encapsulates 1860s discourse on womankind, which was dominated by an "obsessive rehearsal" of the relationship between woman, the nude in fine art, and the prostitute ("Preliminaries" 23). Manet offers his viewers a model laid out for sale, but with her dignity as on show as her wares, thus turning male fantasy into "real, uncomfortable, dominating and dominated form" ("Preliminaries" 38). Giving nothing away, Olympia's novel gaze demands reciprocity, recognition.

Predictably, acknowledgement arrived as disapprobation: *Olympia* was widely condemned on numerous grounds, including the perception that her hand, poised above her pubis, was "'shamelessly flexed'" ("Preliminaries" 23). Female nudes were expected to cover their genitals, a modesty compounding and lessening the viewer's complicity in the power imbalance between audience and model. "Shamelessly flexed", this hand exposes the audience's desire and the creator's artifice. For the prototypical hand in question was not idly beautiful, but grafted for a living: immortal, triumphant *Olympia* was working class.[19] She was also a recognised artist. Meurent had hands that played music and painted, earning Manet's infamous model four opportunities to exhibit at the Paris Salon and, in 1903, membership in the *Societé des Artistes Français*. A pioneering female student at the *Académie Julian* from 1875 to 1876, Meurent was gainfully, if not easefully, employed throughout her life, and supported her ailing mother in old age (Lipton 57, 164–6). Historical accounts of Meurent tend to emphasise her promiscuity, alcoholism, and premature death in 1892. Unearthed, her death certificate reads 1928 (Lipton 90). Meurent of the famously challenging stare was personally, historically subsumed by the mythology of the accursed muse.

By the end of the nineteenth century, authors discernibly wrestle with the burgeoning status of the model: Zola's *The Masterpiece* (1885) reiterates the terms of Poe's forward-looking "The Oval Portrait"; Henry James publishes "The Real Thing" (1893), a story in which models of all classes override the male artist's genius, his presumption that his subjects can be treated as bestialised or racialised others, "animals on hire or useful blacks" (46). Come modernism proper, superficially reverent or anxious responses to the model-cum-muse would become "suspicion and hostility", affects sourced in the growing respect for the autonomy of the artwork and abstraction (Steiner 29). Evidence of this response can be seen in Eliot's and Pound's respective lady portraits, apostrophic lyrics that anonymise, patronise, and dismiss their striving subjects.[20] Trouncing portraiture and lamenting the constraints of commissions, in 1922, their peer Wyndham Lewis similarly reserves his greatest vitriol for the model:

> She is an exploitable figment of the crowd's mind . . . . The artist's wife, or the model, has to be imbued with an audacity and brilliance probably foreign to her. Somewhere between the reality (the model) and the figment . . . . the painter will lose the little bit of truth that might, in a painting from nature, have redeemed his work. ("Credentials" 69)

Where the artist's model-as-lover is usually considered his muse, Lewis acknowledges this distinction only to dismiss it. Rather than a conduit to an aesthetic truth, Lewis's model is a siphon whose draw the artist must actively resist. Mastery and artifice are all; Lewis rejects the avant-garde conflation of life and art that might credit the model's role in the creative work.[21]

In Lewis's *Tarr* (1918/28), historical opposition between artist and model comes to violence when Bertha Lunken, having reluctantly posed nude for artist Otto Kreisler, asks to see her portrait. In response, Bertha watches as he "grow[s] more male every moment, his eyes settling down 'masterfully' into her" just before he rapes her (177–8). In the immediate aftermath of this assault, Bertha views the room as a series of portraits in which each stage of her visit is compartmentalised, framed, observing that it is "[t]he monotony and silence of the posing" that facilitates the clarity of these compositions. One of her visions aptly sums up the latent aggression of any assumption of mastery, the brutality underpinning presumptions of creative licence and nous: "She saw side by side and unconnected, the silent figure engaged in drawing her bust and the other one full of blindness and violence" (178). Bertha leaves Kreisler's flat "bent awkwardly" and "sp[itting] out the usual epithets for the occasion" (*Tarr* 175). Validating Victorian cautionary tales about modelling whilst reasserting the male artist's power, Lewis nevertheless lends Bertha a painterly eye, a narrative incursion that gestures toward the model's awareness and aesthetic ability. This painterly eye offers Bertha a survivalist distance on the rape that she has just experienced, even as it cements her position as accursed and cursing muse, conscious of her victimisation to her violated core.[22]

Voicing Damnation: Loy's Muses

In life and art, Loy had intimate knowledge of the accursed muse. Loy was close to Gwen John, sister to Augustus, whose artistic talent many believe Gwen surpassed. John modelled for her lover Rodin in the pre-World War I years during which Loy and her first husband were regulars in his circle. Rodin's mistreatment of John is now legendary, and her belated posthumous recognition was prompted by this association (Borzello 11). Friend and model to the vanguard photographer Man Ray, Loy would surely have socialised with his muse, Kiki of Montparnasse, an artist who died young, possibly struggling with addiction, certainly poor. Loy was variously resident in Munich, New York, and Paris in the same years as writer, artist, and model Baroness Elsa von Freytag-Loringhoven. Perhaps the modernist avant-garde's most successful conflator of life and art, the Baroness is the readiest prototype for the "Duchesse de Da Da" of Loy's "Monde Triple-Extra", even as their knowledge of one another remains critically under-discussed.[23] The Baroness died prematurely, impoverished, and in circumstances that do not rule out suicide, but these brutal coordinates notwithstanding, her insistence upon her artistic autonomy makes her more *poètesse maudite* than accursed muse (Gammel 382–4).

Alongside these biographical coordinates, Loy was a portraitist in poetry, art, and prose, one fascinated by exchanges between models, muses, and artists. This interest reflects her lived experience as one of the most photographed women of modernism who willingly served as muse and portrait sitter from her earliest romances and affiliations, a career that began with the rudimentary photography of the *fin-de-siècle* and extended to her son-in-law's forays into Surrealist film.[24] And Loy was not averse to generating accursed muses: her nine-page typescript "Alda's Beauty" lingers protractedly, microscopically for three pages over the features of Loy's lightly fictionalised eldest daughter before announcing that all Loy recalls of leaving her pre-pubescent children to travel to New York "is the portrait of Alda framed in the window of the railway carriage". Alda remains still, innocent, and beautiful, preserved as a lifeless object of aesthetic nostalgia for her portraitist's anxious parental posterity, as, beside her, her unnamed and otherwise overlooked brother "stomp[s] out a dance of excited farewell" ("Alda's" 3).

In the late 1910s and early 1920s, Loy produced a series of short fictions predating Djuna Barnes's 1924 *Charm* article prophesying how contemporary models would reject the status of ornament for actor. These fictions include "Static" (c. 1920s), "Piero and Eliza." (1921), "The Stomach" (1921), and to a lesser extent, "The Three Wishes" (c. 1920s). None of this work was published in the twentieth century. Archived variants on this theme include the undated poetic squib "Pygmaleon and Galatea", and chapters or passages from Loy's draft romans à clef *Esau Penfold* (1910s/20s), *The Child and the Parent* (c. 1932–6), and *Islands in the Air* (1940s–50s). Loy's posthumously published *Insel* (1933–6) also incorporates the model. Incomplete, this list nevertheless conveys the extent of Loy's engagement with the muse's experience.[25] Loy's willingness to give voice to the accursed muse is prescient, foreseeing what Steiner considers a twentieth-century rejection of "the model referent" that crystallised in the 1960s with Warhol's promotion of Edie Sedgwick (93). Like her nineteenth-century antecedents, Sedgwick died the early death of a severe addict. Nevertheless, Sedgwick catalyses the treatment of the model as celebrity – by artists, by adoring fans – that lays the ground for a second-wave feminist reclamation of the sentient artistic subject as a conscious creator in her own right. Linking female creativity with the biological capacity to reproduce, Loy's literatures foresee this turn, showing how women's artistry, like their bodies, is unduly stifled by reproductive expectations that, viewed differently, might enhance their creativity. With this reconsideration in view, Loy anatomises and foregrounds bellies, torsos, and wombs.

As did the Pre-Raphaelite Brotherhood before her, Loy reworked the mythology of Pygmalion and Galatea, and was familiar with Ovid's first-century account of the same. Ovid describes a Galatea born of Pygmalion's revulsion for "the many faults which nature has implanted in the female sex". Pygmalion's misogyny is narratively justified on the basis that the women of his native Amathus (a Cypriot city) irreligiously fail to give Venus her proper recognition. As punishment, Venus condemns them to "prostitut[e] themselves in public", a mythology that conveniently places the blame for the sex trade on females terrestrial and celestial (232). Rather than interact with these "wicked" women, Pygmalion deploys his "marvellous artistry" to make an ivory statue lovelier than any real woman. Needlessly, he then fervently woos the inert creature he names Galatea, all the while wishing for a wife as beautiful, passive, and ideal. Come her annual festival, Venus grants his wish: Galatea grows pliant under Pygmalion's touch, but remains steadfastly pure, blushing and "timidly" raising her eyelids only when she needs to "see her lover and the light of day" (Ovid 232). Less model than ideal prototype, Galatea's story ends when she successfully generates copies by reproducing with the man who is simultaneously her God, mother, and husband.

Galatea's eyes remain averted in two series of paintings devoted to her by the Pre-Raphaelite Edward Burne-Jones (1868–70; 1878), an artist Loy revered in adolescence (*BM* 41–2). Burne-Jones's peer Robert Buchanan also reinterprets this classic story, initially in "Pygmalion the Sculptor" (1864), where he creates an artist cursed for appropriating deific powers. This guilt evaporates in Buchanan's later version of the same, "Artist and Model: A Love Poem" (1866–70), where a muse pines for a creator devoted to illuminating and consecrating her beauty. This transcendent goal falls by the wayside when the artist in question suggests that "the touch of [the model's] hand" mightn't go amiss (298). The Pre-Raphaelite fascination with Pygmalion homage may originate with Rossetti's "Hand and Soul" (1850), which nods to Ovid in taking place on a feast day and involving a supernaturally enlivened muse. From her youth to her death, Loy admired Rossetti as both painter and poet.[26] But where these Pre-Raphaelite variants reinterpret only to retain and augment Pygmalion's superiority, Loy's early unpublished ballad "Pygmaleon and Galatea" gives voice to the women Ovid and his descendants silence.[27]

As in Ovid, Venus "tak[es] pity / on the sorrowful young" Pygmalion in Loy, and the first two quatrains of her squib stick to the typical narrative of a young, talented sculptor forming and adoring "the loveliest statue / that ever had been seen". But Loy's Pygmalion is not a censorious, craven bachelor. Instead, he is a lascivious husband:

> Galatea had nothing on her
> as everybody knows
> and so one night Pygmaleon
> had to prig his wife's old clothes
>
> And while all day he sighed to think
> The vision had no life
> he could not eat or sleep or drink
> to the annoyance of his wife

In Loy's "Songs to Joannes" (1917), passion "prig[s]" the "professorial paucity" of the male lover; here, prigging is material, pragmatic, and confirms the proximate forms of the wife and her idealised stone competitor (*LoLB* 67). Coupled with the wife's disposability, this female interchangeability is a misogynist tenet that Loy deploys to diminish Galatea's status as ideal prototype. Furthermore, by indicating that Pygmalion was married before he creates Galatea, Loy makes Venus complicit in infidelity, her transformative work catalysing not idealised romance, but adulterous strife. And Pygmalion's wife is disinclined to quietly accept the state of this affair:

> But his wife consulted Slater
> the fun was growing hot
> and midst visions of Sir Francis Jeune
> Galatea was soon forgot

Pygmalion's wife forcefully, strategically excises Galatea from her husband's mind and their shared household. Refusing easy replacement, she turns to *A Manual of Moral Theology* (1906), or the first English translation of Catholic moral teachings, conducted by the Reverend Thomas Slater (1855–1928).[28] In this text, the sixth and tenth commandments, regarding sexual fidelity, are given extended due. While Slater upholds the principle that "[t]he wife becomes by marriage subject to her husband", he offers the proviso that she "is not the slave or servant of her husband, but rather his companion" who "should be treated with love, consideration, and deference, and consulted in what concerns the family affairs" (185). A woman who consults Slater, in other words, gains recognition of her authority to be consulted; if she is not treated deferentially, the precepts for divorce are conveniently spelt out in the same volume.

Loy's allusion to Slater, then, is both apt historic allusion and aptonymic lampoon of Pygmalion's hubris: an exalted sculptor of stone is decimated by a figure whose name refers to a worker who quarries and lays tiles for a living. Earnest labour grounds inflated aesthetics. In turn, the effectual reading of Slater leads to "visions of Sir Francis Jeune". Whose visions? If Pygmalion's, they may be born from the fear of going before the President of the United Kingdom's Divorce Court. If they are his wife's, they may twin a desire for divorce with sexual fantasy, as the charismatic Sir Francis – a *fin-de-siècle* household name – was reputedly "THE HANDSOMEST MAN ON THE BENCH".[29] Pygmalion is confronted by a partner who may well share his rejection of domestic, monogamous mundanities. As such, Loy's reworking of Ovid ascribes to a stock figure – the overlooked, clapped-out housewife – the overwhelming desires of her artistic husband. Muse and artist blur.

Loy's final stanza extends her affirmation of women's autonomy:

> But Galatea did not weep and turn to stone again
> As tradition would have you know
> She became a living picture
> And joined the Folly show.

The tradition by which Galatea is re-petrified is unfamiliar to a contemporary reader more likely to recall the sentient sculpture's fate as a fairy tale lived happily ever after. Loy may refer to Franz von Suppé's *Die schöne Galathée*, or *The Beautiful Galatea*, a German operetta that toured Vienna, New York, and London between 1865 and 1872. In this comic version of the Ovidian myth, Galatea does not come to life as a tremulous innocent, but as a scheming, capricious woman who privileges her wealth and sexual satisfaction above all. Ascertaining that Galatea will never be his alone, Pygmalion asks Venus to return her to stone. When the goddess complies, it is Galatea who is prostituted, rather than the irreligious women of Amathus: she is sold to King Midas, whom Galatea earlier extorted in exchange for tolerating his open licentiousness. This satire razes artist and model alike, but Loy is not content with its outcome, instead awarding her Galatea the temerity and nous to generate a steady income. As part of a *tableau vivant* – a living picture by which actors or models pose in costume, often theatrically lit, for public entertainment – Galatea is no longer strictly a muse or a portrait. Instead, she takes her part in what was a craze at the turn of the twentieth century, reminding us of Lily Bart posing in like performances in Edith Wharton's *House of Mirth* (1905), albeit, in that instance, with a view to attracting a specific man, a future husband. Loy's conclusion is knowingly risqué, salaciously comic: an undercurrent of eroticism drove this voyeuristic entertainment, one that could be performed in a state of undress. The *tableau vivant* also underscores what Steiner deems "the ontological paradox" by which "[t]he model is . . . real and at the same time artificial" (5). Determining to escape her creator's controlling gaze and hands, Loy's Galatea chooses an alternate, self-sustaining modelling economy where she actively watches her audience, who perceive her in real time. In this immediacy lies autonomy, even fleeting (if constrained) creative opportunity. Loy may have drawn inspiration from Robert Browning's "The Lady and the Painter" (1889), another poetic squib in which a woman challenges the gendered power imbalances at work in the artist–model relation. But as the over-long first line of her final stanza suggests, Loy's editorial hand was lightly applied in "Pygmaleon and Galatea". Although she took pains to type this long-saved manuscript, the poem is more pleasurable ferocity than literary triumph. Nor is it indicative: in Loy's writing, models rarely escape as unscathed as her variation on Galatea.

Instead, in Loy, modelling is an exercise inextricable from the destructive and creative powers housed within the female torso, and particularly its inner organs: the stomach, the womb. This motif gestates in the partial manuscripts and typescripts of *Esau Penfold*, a text Burke places within Loy's "portrait gallery of [Florence] residents" that includes sketches of Mabel Dodge Luhan and gay male expatriates who fled England in the wake of Oscar Wilde's 1895 conviction (*BM* 109).[30] Like Vigny and Verlaine before her, Loy has her gallery of rogues. Misleadingly titled with the pseudonym Loy uses for her first husband, Stephen Haweis, *Esau Penfold* centres upon a variously named female protagonist, with Sophia being the moniker to which Loy reverts most.[31] Sophia's is a portrait of the artist as a young woman, first as a student at the Parisian Académie Colarossi (c. 1900–3), and then as a Florentine resident, socialite, and observer of a fledgling Italian vanguard (c. 1907–10). Artistically ambitious, Sophia is riddled with anxieties about her unworldly background and gendered prohibitions.

She is also twice cursed: firstly, marked by a "scarlet star X" that appears in her white underwear the day after Esau – then a recent acquaintance – rapes her in her sleep. Satirising heteronormativity and the mythology of the wanton fallen woman, Loy describes how the portentous red letter "ascend[s] into heaven to guide [Sophia] on her way" toward a pregnancy necessitating a mutually wary "puppet marriage" between herself and the abusive Esau (*EP* 22).[32] The second hexing manifests itself as a red square on Sophia's cheek. "[A] brand yet not a burn", this mark appears as she awakens from a dream "arrested by a total black out" (*EP* 24). Sophia believes herself "'touched upon'" by a group of British expatriates who dabble in black magic, among them Esau's former lover, who admits to having jealously directed her destructive necromancy at Sophia's beautiful face (*EP* 24). As per Lecercle, cursing has perceptible consequences, not least that the recipient incorporates its enmity. Esau elicits a "half-materialised hatred" from those around him, and Sophia bears the palpable brunt of this malice on her body and in her daily interactions. The more she associates with Esau, the more "oppressive" she finds the Colarossi studio, which appears "capitated with evil fearful faces". This vexation feeds Esau's "soporific infelicity", a phrase suggesting that Esau casts others into sleep with his improprieties and tales of woe (*EP* 24). This aligning of hypnosis and misfortune recalls Esau's first imprecation, his rape of the unconscious Sophia, who was lulled to sleep by his monotonous verbal barrage.

Loy's Esau is neither muse nor artist but uncertain model. His liminality consigns him to an abjection that, unusually for Loy, goes unmitigated and unredeemed. In "Songs to Joannes", Loy triumphantly presents a comic Pig Cupid who pulls at weeds "sown in mucous-membrane"; in *Esau Penfold*, she lingers with palpable disgust over her protagonist's "'rose lip'" that exposes a "tiny expanse of mucous membrane" relentlessly "caress[ed] with his third finger" (*LoLB* 53; *EP* 22). Esau is derided in ableist, effeminising terms: he is microcephalous, dwarfish, small-handed. Whiny-voiced and attired in the "'little dresses' he tended with a pre-Raphaelite economy", he is an outdated, sexually ambiguous decadent who lacks the command or privilege of that vanguard movement. Where Dorian Gray amasses rarefied collections of jewels, perfumes, and textiles, Esau venerates worthless inheritances, among them his mother's bustle and the ashes of his aunt's pug (*EP* 22). Loy aligns this affinity for collecting with a failed generativity: "Esau like old maids whose wombs are unfurnished – hoarded scraps – his mind – his home – he stored with ragtail – trifles" (*EP* 21). A barren spinster, Esau surrounds himself with a "seraglio" of like "untalented old maids" who are audience to his onanistic creativity (*EP* 24). As artist Esau is "inter-identically virile – virile unto himself" or "impotent" (*EP* 21).[33] Loy's assaults measure Esau against the sexualised mythology of the male artist. Although she shares Esau's femininity, Loy clearly finds it deplorable in individuals with ready access to masculine privilege. Flaunting himself as "the ever[-]mysterious artist", Esau is a talentless "dilletante who confound[s] art with opportunism" (*EP* 22, 24). Most tellingly, Loy considers him a "civilised simulacrum": "His real and his ideal nature ignored each other socially - - the daily game of culture sidestepping the actual" (*EP* 22).[34] All posture, Esau's indefinite subjective core demands multiple rewrites. Awakening from his assault, Sophia sees Esau's physique "of exaggerated modelling" and mentally declares: "Tremendously muscular – Esau Penfold had no body!" With a prejudicial nod to his remote Indian ancestor, Loy describes Esau as a Eurasian "squatted in serpentine contortions", fraught with "uncomfortable poses [that] slipped into a cul-de-sac of aesthetic intention". She proclaims: "Esau Penfold, centrifugal - - had no centre".[35] Ever wily, Esau is not consigned to this dead end: "when [he exhausts his] stock of intriguing postures", he pushes Sophia into the foreground, basking in her more "certain notoriety" (*EP* 22). As captive muse-cum-maternal substitute, Sophia must "hea[l] the eternal wound of Esau[']s] predestined failure", a description recon-firming his porosity, his life of empty affectation (*EP* 21).

Abject simulacrum, Esau inspires in Sophia equal parts fascina-tion, disgust, and fear, affects manifested in the torsos she sculpts and draws, and within her own abdomen. Loy's rendering of Esau reveals that she is prepared to use misogynistic and racist tropes to shame others, a process that exposes her own unreconstructed Victorianism as well as the masochistic urges often ascribed to the marginalised. But Esau is also an assailant, an aggressive man who strategically parades a sham weakness that goes unreplicated in his intimate life, where he regularly co-opts Sophia's artistry and reproductivity alike. Before they become a couple – an affiliation formalised through marriage only because Esau assaults and impregnates Sophia – Esau appears to be the absent subject of a chilling art school encounter that Loy drafts repeatedly. "One night", Sophia "wander[s] into an upper studio in search of a better ~~model~~ body" – "body" superseding the pejorative "model" – and her "eyes swept the formation of stu-dents common to sketch classes everywhere". Students in graduated seating encircle an enthroned model; in dusty air, easels and stools conjoin in "a timber maze of carpentry". And then Sophia's "eyes stopped dead" before "something incomparable" and she is "struck with horror" (*EP* 24). The source of this alarm remains indescribable and undescribed, but elsewhere, Loy identifies Esau as "the 'horror' of the night class" (*EP* 25). Within this spate of art school musings, Loy drafts a rare fragment about creating art. "Handling clay for the first time", Sophia struggles to "thro[w] more 'swing' into the torso" of her sculpture whilst keeping up with the prescribed half-hour turns of the model before her. Replication of the trunk evades her, and the initially enthused praise of her teacher – "the master" – subsides (*EP* 24). This uneasily rendered torso foregrounds Loy's ongoing preoccupation with the relationship between modelling and midriffs.

Loy draws a redacting line through this passage, but a related anecdote linking creativity, torsos, and a first afternoon with Esau remains intact. Having agreed to split the costs of a privately hired model with an English "Maddy" (in life, Loy had a friend named Madeline Boles), Sophia is discomfited as Esau arrives at the studio

(*BM* 80). Sophia alone proves unable to "make good use of [her] share in the model" due to an "instilled" and pervasive "flux of terror-stricken shame".[36] Wracked with self-consciousness, Sophia longs to take a "'plunge' so to be done with it once and for all." Again, Loy sexualises creativity, conflating Sophia's virginity with ignorance aesthetic and experiential. To abate her unease, Sophia self-deprecatingly, jokily begs God's forgiveness "'for Being Alive'", both by way of acknowledging Esau and Maddy's afternoon-long parody of the liturgy, and to relieve the "strange pain . . . that functioned according to some cerebration of its own in the abdomen" (*EP* 25). Not her abdomen, but a sentient, separate life within her body: *the* abdomen. Engulfed as she is by the mantle "Creator", Sophia finds that her language and body articulate yearnings and discomforts resident within, or associable with, her generative anatomy. Loy's diction is telling: "abdomen" encompasses "womb" and pelvic cavity as "stomach" does not. Concomitantly, "the 'horror' of the nightclass" presides over torsos that Sophia fails to replicate, contain, or comfortably inhabit.

The draft sketches of *Esau Penfold* reassert a pervasive tenet of Loy's writing by which the reproductive body occludes female artistry. Critics have justly celebrated Loy's "Parturition" (1914) for its presentation of an epiphanically transcendent labouring woman who demands a recognition typically ceded to the baby to whom she is meant to be vessel and vassal. "Parturition" fantastically satirises the generative male artist who gains prominence through "birthing" masterpieces, a widely used metaphor that co-opts woman's fertility whilst furthering her invisibility. By the starkest conceivable contrast, Loy's *Esau Penfold* paints a picture of a female artist doggedly, exhaustingly at odds with heteronormative demands. Where "Parturition" lays proud claim to the reproductive woman's indistinguishability from the bestial, in *Esau Penfold*, pregnant Sophia is overcome by shame and disgust, affects exacerbated by the abject Esau. ""The indecency of those unflinching alien eyes presiding over the daily swelling of her womb and breasts exploded in her sensibility", writes Loy, adding: "To carry her loaded hips among the swarming social receptions with this ever[-]strange man's nose so near her fruit was an offence so monstrous!" When Sophia resists public forays, Esau beats her with her clothing until she yields (*EP* 22). This debasement extends to the newborn whose parentage they share, or, in Loy's terms, the "massacred incubus twitch[ing] as the foetal fats were rasped from its body by the sponge". Watching this removal of vernix, Sophia dreads the return of Esau with "his strange stale smell" and is pleased to have "ridden her body of his accidence". The baby is unremitting parasite to detumescent host, who frankly recounts "the new airiness of her flaccid abdomen – rolling like clouds of relievement from flank to flank as she shifted her pelvis". During this post-partum examination of her torso, Sophia desires "to stride with the new nothingness in her particular womb . . . . out into a life without relationship" (*EP* 25). The free womb is the free woman and, in this case, the free woman artist. But, for Sophia, jettisoning familial gestation for artistic is untenable: she is bound by law to Esau and by financial dependence to a father who will only support her if she plays traditional wife and mother.[37]

The nadir of recreative and reproductive abjection is reached in *Esau Penfold* shortly after Sophia watches Giovanni Papini sit for his portrait in the chapter entitled "Geronimo". If ever there was a sitter who commanded an artist, it is Papini: asked to stand next to his rendering, the "great Geronimo" does not demur, but "mov[es] with an attractive unbending slouch to reach the canvas, where, throwing back his shoulders, he set up his face as its own criterion" (*EP* 23: 1–2).[38] Geronimo is not model, but prototype; not sacrificial victim, but a sacrificer at powerful ease, marked by "ancient weariness" and "the torturer's complacency", his mouth "an impertinent gamin in readiness to deride" (*EP* 23: 2). Studying him, Sophia is fascinated, attracted, sourcing his confidence in an ugliness that is *jolie-laide* and synaesthetic, yet compellingly autonomous. Sensing Sophia's interest, Esau is prompted on their return home to toy with his "companionate pistol", menacing his pregnant wife as she ineffectually draws. "The beauty that struggled to germinate in the past had withered under the ugly psychic shadows falling between my mind and its modest visions" (*EP* 23: 6).[39] Moving from idealised male muse to failed female generativity, "Geronimo" culminates in a sinister description of the foetus Sophia carries:

> The night brought forth the weirdest sensations. When my body lay down, it was given up entirely to the growth of invasion. The intermittent roll and stress of a blind invader endeavouring to unbundle itself from the tissues unfolding it, to thrust further with its steadily animating limbs the extensile confines of the cavern in which it lay, making room for a sure augmentation on the morrow.
>
> In this comatose insistent motion like a progressive stir of life through evolutional stages—swimming—spasmodic—undulative as a thing borne by a wave—taut in the incipience of a leap—a fist would land its muffled blow, an aimless foot as if to walk through the flesh, raise a hard excrescence upon the abdominal wall.

> Lastly, this entrammelled marauder seemed to push upward against the heart to stop its beat. Choking, I would creep to the window to inhale air. (*EP* 23: 8–9)

Not-yet-sentience attacks sentient being in a battle where corporeality is cognate, autonomous: Sophia's body lies down of its own volition; the distancing definite article presides over her womb, heart, flesh, and tissues; the aggressive foetus is at the mercy of evolutionary process. Less parasite than combatant, this foetus threatens to kill its overstretched host. So too does the host's husband: after a night she likens to a "long semi-asphyxiation", Sophia arrives at the breakfast table to find Esau "crouched over the pistol", his gaze and gun sharing "an identical abortive intention" (*EP* 23: 10). Sophia is sacrificial victim to fertile, intelligent bodies – her husband's, her own – that stifle her creative and subjective freedom.

Loy's title, *Esau Penfold*, reinforces Sophia's relegation to muse, even as she is a recognised artist, a member of the prestigious Parisian *Salon d'Automne* as Esau is not.[40] In like sacrificial fashion, accursedness, abjection, and the abortive repeatedly vex Loy's aspirational female models. In "Piero and Eliza." (1921), Piero is "drop of arsenic" on Eliza's "clay", and both "hanke[r] after the arts as a social outlet" (*SE* 98–9). Longing for a lover, the sexually naïve Eliza competes with Piero's seraglio of queer "expatriated bachelors" who she posits as disciples to his Jesus, "guardians of some holy bread", keepers of mysterious rituals (*SE* 101). Creators all, these men turn women into maternal muses. Piero "wanted a mother" and finds one in Eliza, who darns his socks and buys his suits, facilitating what Loy satirises as a "transcendental family life" that is otherworldly because unconsummated and childless (*SE* 99). With another "intimate artist", Piero designs costumes for Eliza as she stands "like some marionette" or, more precisely, "like a mummy resuscitated with a fictitious breath of flattery" (*SE* 100). With monkey fur, striped crêpe, and "expensive silken hose", this effigy is adorned for her slaughter, her status falsely elevated to satiate the gods.[41]

While Eliza stares at wallpaper roses, beset by an uneasy feeling that life and love elude her, Piero has a dalliance with "the poet who has written of 'The Immaculate Vermin of the Sugar Dove'" (*SE* 100, 103). Piero's secret lover parodies the Virgin Mary, reducing her biblical sacrifice – two turtledoves in thanksgiving for Jesus's birth – to the work of a sweet-loving reprobate or pest.[42] In turn, Eliza is incessantly, implicitly mocked for her own guise of sanctified motherhood. Lacking offspring, she turns to the occult, determining to make herself a spiritual vessel "against the loaded mystery of Piero and his bachelors" (*SE* 102). Yet Eliza's mediumship is distinctly barren: her aura is "a garden of unscented flowers"; attaining a higher plane, her body is hollow, her blood staunched. This experience is a crisis, a battle combining frustrated sexual desire with "savage ancestry and the Christian devil"; at its apex, "a hand and forearm 'materialize' from out her abdomen" (*SE* 102). Misused, infertile muse, Eliza produces a partial, ephemeral being. In the second volume of this *Anatomy* we will consider the performative occultist successes, in Loy's work, of avant-garde males. Juxtaposed against their resonant, powerful mesmerising powers, Eliza's mediumship appears especially solitary, compensatory, and fragmented. Eliza has her double in Loy's eponymous Insel, another medium whose "abdominal void" produces an "unclenching fist."[43] Capable of "the most lamentable dupery", Insel nevertheless finds recognition by positioning himself as an accursed artist, a figure starved of sustenance emotional and material. Unlike the overtaken Eliza, Insel's abdominal fist is his own, and is extended in a performance of dire, impoverished want duly met by Mrs Jones's "alarmed compassion" (*I* 27–9). No such faith or nurture greets Eliza's perverse generativity.

The accursed muse is universalised at the outset of the unpublished, undated story "Static", where Loy insists that the individual is always "a mannikin, in the distorted posture of an outward accident."[44] Everyone, Loy asserts, "fall[s] from the mother's womb to their particular attitude. Stricken statues unto death." Bearing marked similarities to Loy's undated poem "Portrait of a Nun", "Static" describes the life of Marjolaine Battement, "[t]hat palliated prostitute, an artist's model", who is raised in a convent, "[h]er virginity . . . furled in the purity of linen sheets".[45] Consistent with Loy's fascination with women's daily, domestic self-immolation, these sheets are the nuns' sacrificial offering "to Life". From their "immaculate white world of ghostly flax [Marjolaine's] womanhood proceeded in a black interrogation." Thus narratively cursed, Marjolaine travels to Paris as a young, poor woman, securing the "dangerous work" of modelling, submitting to the role of housekeeper and the "farmyard caresses" of a painter. She is soon pregnant, abandoned, and starving. When she miscarries her malnourished foetus, she takes it in a napkin to the hospital. "In my memory", Loy writes, "she remained with that gesture, of offering up something virginal or abortive in white linen—". This unrealised life is the defining metaphor for the socially consigned women of "Static", who are sacrificial by definition and in act; swaddled in purified mantles, they swaddle in turn. By the terms of Loy's fiction, Marjolaine survives as a serial muse, roving from one artist to another, but ending up as self-described "mother, devoted nurse, [and] faithful friend" to a painter who has neither moved nor spoken in nine years. Marjolaine's unnamed artist is powerful counterpart to the meekly anonymous unheard muse of Poe's "The Oval Portrait", a figure deathly in life, more cypher than individual. "[R]ais[ing] her eyes like the Mother Mary", Marjolaine recounts to Loy's narrator how her "permanent gesture of destiny" continues as she maintains him like a baby in a crib, his sheets spotless. Too repletely immolated, Marjolaine's offerings do not replenish.

Marjolaine's fate is shared by most of Loy's muses, who tend to become objects of barter within male artist kinship groups. Resistant Sophia is battered by Esau; martyred models Eliza and Marjolaine fail to regenerate spiritually or physically. Truncated generativity is inseparable from abject or aborted maternality, a contagion infecting even the "virile and intransigent" Ian Gore of "The Three Wishes", a vanguard artist who rejects his parents' desire to "offer [him] on the altar of society" (*SE* 135, 115). Like Loy's Jove Ivon Corvon and Geronimo, Ian is a self-proclaimed prototype, committed to creating an as-yet-unmade world (*SE* 135). At art school, he is confronted by a woeful life model, an "unproud", "lamentable being" who is incoherently fragmented, burdened by a "leaning torso" that "sagged into the pelvis" (*SE* 135–6). This surfeit of abjection sullies Ian's masterful gaze, prompting thoughts of that most universally reviled figure, the leaking, clinging, disgusting female parent: "It was as if his mother in her chaste dress momentarily in his vision, foundered" (*SE* 139). Consistently for Loy, a model, midriff, and mother undercut Ian's prototypical triumph. But, curiously, Ian's exemplar is Loy herself. In *Islands in the Air*, Loy describes her first experience going to evening life class at art school in precisely the same terms as she uses in "The Three Wishes":

That was where I came upon the poor bare man with the eyes of a lizard who had known no sun. Because the studio dust was somehow similar to the jaded hair on his body, that body seemed fearfully deprived of a divine right, while the professor cocked his eye at a plumb-line appraising the perpendicular of a lamentable being who hardly seemed able to hold together. I heard him discourse on sensing the bony structure beneath the masses, noting how the leaning torso sagged into the pelvis. All that was clear to me was how the excrescences of the model's unproud knees confounded his symmetry.

> Not being sufficiently developed intellectually to guess that knowl-
> edge can be 'adapted', requiring Adonis, I repudiated the model.
> (*IA* 67: 103)

Loy lingers extensively over male inadequacies, abjectifying as she
goes along. A narrative sadistic pleasure may be detectable in the
female dismissal of a male body, senescent or otherwise, for its
failure to live up to an ideal. However qualified by self-deprecating
gestures to immaturity, this passage affirms Loy's understandable
desire for power, her longing to be artist to an accursed muse, prototype to a male artist, determiner of "leaning torso[s]" that "sa[g]
into the pelvis".[46]

As the *Islands* anecdote continues, it becomes clear that as an art
student Loy partakes in Ian's ambition to "'frighte[n] good form
to death'": she challenges the conventions by which she is asked to
create, thereby setting herself apart from her classmates. But this
Loy variant shares more than Ian's plans: her full name is Linda
Gore, suggesting that she is a fictional blood relative of Ian Gore.
Given that Linda and Ian are respectively modelled on the real-life
Loy and Cravan, Loy establishes a potentially incestuous narrative relationship, a perhaps unwitting, if curiously deviant, break
with heteronormative convention. But while they share a surname
and a vocation, Linda Gore refuses to be derailed, as is Ian, by an
"unformed" model (*SE* 115). Ian's vision of a buttoned-up maternal
collapse reinforces how his own vanguard pretensions lurch beneath
the weight of ingrained Victorian morality. Ian is a weaker version
of Linda/Loy, a watered-down derivative, less inured to social pressure and the abject: sagging bodies, trussed mothers. Critique of the
impenetrable male artist is assuredly embedded in this portrayal, a
critique fully in keeping with Susan Rubin Suleiman's suggestion that
the masculinist vanguard was forged over the prone maternal body.
Implicitly, Loy appears to suggest that women artists are attuned to
generativity in all of its guises: artistic, reproductive. What is more,
courtesy of her positioning in the world, the female artist is more *au
fait* than the male with corporeal excess and disgust, the abjection
that fine art so often labours to conceal, to mask with the ideal. In
"The Three Wishes", Ian Gore purges himself of his exposure to a
too-explicit taint via uttered oaths and epithets, spitting, and performed rebellion. We sense that Ian's own visionary stumble will be
short-lived. This will not be the case for Virginia Cosway of Loy's
"The Stomach".

The Stomach

In "The Stomach" (1921) we revisit Loy's accursed muse, but as her title suggests, the torso is the protagonist of this story, eclipsing model and artist with its organic cognisance, discernment, and ambition. On the manuscript of "Piero and Eliza.", Loy writes: "The Stomach – Sargents [*sic*] portrait of – – –". Beneath this incomplete statement reads, in a lighter and possibly different hand: "Isabella Stewart Gardner?" (*SE* 344). The artwork goes uncertified. This elision furthers the possibility that in her portrait of Virginia Cosway, Loy executes the artistic privilege of anatomising the model, who is a discernible collage of three of Sargent's most notorious muses. Of the famous American portrait painter, John Singer Sargent (1856–1925), the German-born British painter Walter Sickert (1860–1942) writes: "The problem of turning out satisfactory likenesses with a certain brilliant allure, and the little touch of piquant provocation that respectable women are always so anxious to secure, has seldom been solved by an abler hand or a juster eye" (57). Scabrous. But Sickert makes this cutting observation in 1910, or more than two decades after the scandals associated with Sargent's early portraiture, their infamy usurped by his late-career reputation as an excessively remunerated darling of the bourgeoisie. A celebrity artist, his "creative self sacrificed to its image", Sargent became a figure who Loy might have found appealing precisely because his once-vanguard mastery became feminised, marketised for ready consumption (Steiner 48).[47] Loy's direct awareness of Sargent is irrefutable: his notoriety aside, they shared London exhibition space on two occasions, and moved in similar circles.[48]

Sargent's first offence-generating painting was *El Jaleo* (1882; Fig. 4.2). "Jaleo de Jalez" refers to a frenzied, sexualised Romany dance; on its own, "jaleo" means ruckus or hubbub, and proved a prophetic encapsulation of the minor outcry the painting elicited (Prettijohn 18). Exhibited in the Paris Salon of 1882, this twelve-foot canvas disoriented by combining epic scale with ephemeral, impossible movement. Critics were intrigued, but the public, and Sargent's friend Henry James, dismissed it as an ugly, perverse, and flagrant approximation of sexual climax (Farebrother 102). Importantly, *El Jaleo* catalysed Sargent's career-long preoccupation with "splendidly clad women control[ling] space and exert[ing] a powerful allure with stretching, twisting, leaning, or vamping gestures" (Farebrother 106). The opprobrium sparked by *El Jaleo* set the stage

Fig. 4.2 John Singer Sargent, *El Jaleo* (1882). Isabella Stewart Gardner Museum, Boston. 2016©Photo SCALA, Florence.

for the best-known Sargent outrage, the vexed reception of *Madame Pierre Gautreau* (1884; Fig. 4.3). Later known as *Madame X*, this painting was exhibited in the 1884 Paris Salon, and provoked widespread scorn commensurate with responses to Manet's *Olympia* two decades previous (Farebrother 75). Gautreau amazed for her powdered, lavender skin, her resolute profile that taunted and shunned the viewer, and her revealing black dress that stood aloof from her torso. In the original painting, one dress strap was damningly fallen, pressed taut against her strangely mottled arm.[49] The hand resting on the adjacent table was fantastically torqued, emulating the wilful, unnatural strain imposed upon Gautreau's body. Artifice dominates the entirety. Unlike Olympia, Gautreau is not languorous sex-trade worker but "[upper-class] commodity for window-display" or "professional beauty" overtly deploying her looks for social advancement (Lubin 92; Prettijohn 25–6). After the exhibition opened, Gautreau realised that she had been used to satirise the upward mobility of the *nouveau riche*, and asked Sargent to remove her portrait from the salon. He refused, and found himself left with an unsaleable canvas that many considered the pinnacle of his career. Sargent was 28.

Four years later, a third scandal erupted over Sargent's commissioned portrait *Isabella Stewart Gardner* (1888; Fig. 4.4), which was exhibited at Boston's Saint Botolph Club. The wealthy socialite that

Fig. 4.3 John Singer Sargent, *Madame X (Madame Pierre Gautreau)* (1883–4). Metropolitan Museum of Art, New York. 2023@Photo SCALA, Florence.

Fig. 4.4 John Singer Sargent, *Isabella Stewart Gardner* (1888). Isabella Stewart Gardner Museum, Boston.

is its subject approached Sargent because she admired and aimed to rival *Madame X* (Hall Tharp 131). Gardner stands in front of an ornately papered wall, the design of which enhaloes her head. Against her black dress, two strands of pearls fall in a curve under her tightly cinched waist, beneath which her hands are loosely clasped. Corset, plunging neckline, and posture push her midriff into a foreground echoed by the concentric rings of arms and gems. Gardner modestly considered this painting the height of Sargent's achievement, but it merits next to no mention in Sargent studies, and had the briefest airing in Boston (Hall Tharp 134–5). Because a muse is always presumed a mistress, rumours circulated that Sargent and Gardner were lovers, and Gardner's husband summarily removed *Isabella Stewart Gardner* from public view, thereby inflaming recollections of its subject matter, which was, in absentia, misremembered as nothing short of obscene.[50]

Public disgrace was the immediate consequence of Sargent's presentations of females in brazen poses. These portraits arguably delineate an increasing recognition of the model's autonomy, beginning with the unnamed, exuberant dancer of *El Jaleo*, moving to the defiant, upwardly mobile *Madame X*, and culminating with Gardner, the sitter who commissions her own work and conspired with Sargent to generate her own publicity. But equally, this lineage might articulate diminished autonomy: the Romany dancer is a sensualised racial and sexual stereotype; Gautreau and Gardner aspire to an art historical legacy that falls prey to gendered limitations. The women's incontrovertible embodiment raises questions: in the first two paintings, gaze and expression are occluded by severe profile, forcing the interpretive eye toward corporeal dramatic pose. Full face, Gardner's body language nevertheless conveys eagerness, acquiescence, uncertainty. The forward tilt of her pelvis exacerbates these affects: she leans toward the viewer, an unspoken assertion resting intimately, hesitantly on her just-open mouth. Gardner's biographer suggests that her portrait is not as hard, glossy, or arrogant as most of Sargent's renderings of society beauties (Hall Tharp 133). But her skewed torso is a noted feature of Sargent's female subjects, among whom "emaciated body types and seemingly instantaneous poses" nervously, alertly prevail (Prettijohn 46).

A well-sat woman keeps her "stomac[h] indrawn from the table", notes Loy of Florence socialites (*EP* 24); in art, indiscernible waists are associated with the working classes, a stereotype Loy evokes with the heavyset charwoman of "Monde Triple-Extra" discussed at the outset of this chapter.[51] Where thin uprightness is customary among renderings of the upper classes, Sargent's affinity for the tilted lady jars. His love of the leaning body has been sourced in Manet's portrait of Mallarmé slouching in an armchair over a book and cigar, the weight of his upper body resting on a single buttock, or the same portrait that sent Verlaine into a swoon in *Les Poètes maudits* (Prettijohn 15). But *Stéphane Mallarmé* (1876) is a candid snapshot of a self-contained intellectual at ease, his slightly protruding midriff offset by comfortably crossed legs and a hand pocketed in a loosely buttoned jacket, authoritatively Napoleonic and studiedly casual. Sargent's three disreputable women evince none of this calm mastery: they awkwardly, unsustainably jut pelvises into a foreground enhanced by reflected light, ornament, and drapery. By the terms of Loy's "The Stomach", they possess insubordinate abdomens, projections "outswung" and clamouring for attention.

Modelling appears thrust upon the protagonist of Loy's story. "Years ago", Loy's narrator intones, "a sculptor had chosen Virginia Cosway as a model for *La Tarantella*, had taken her fingers between two of his own and slid them further apart on her hip; then with accurate gesticulations he had inspired her with "'the pose'" (*SE* 105). The sculptor's manipulation controls and acquiesces: the inspiration is partly Cosway's, and the final, determinate movement belongs to her entirely. The pose evokes "the momentary momentous projection of the stomach in the *danza Española*" (*SE* 105). Twenty-five years ago, Cosway convincingly represented a dancer; we meet her in middle age, still performing her "Hispano-abdominal ceremony" on command: "at *les vernissages*, the private views, auctions of the Hôtel Drouot and the birthdays of new movements; it served as a bass accompaniment to her spoken verdicts." Art is for sale; woman's body is for sale. Ties to Sargent abound: in Cosway, we see the Andalusian dancer with levitating pelvis of *El Jaleo* and the "authoritative and challenging gesture" of *Madame X* (*SE* 107). Virginie Gautreau strains her empurpled self before her viewer, and so too is her plausible namesake, Virginia Cosway, attractively deformed: the sculpture of Cosway is "over-lengthy on its pedestal", complete with a "small head with its arched eye-brows sneer[ing] with a simultaneous invitation and repulse" (*SE* 105). And where Isabella Stewart Gardner's oddly provocative pose prompts rumours that she has engaged in compromising positions with Sargent, Cosway has also "accumulated her mythology": "[c]allous women deprecated her shortsightedness on the occasion of [the sculptor's] proposal", while "[e]lderly bachelors pointed her out as the great man's guiding star" (*SE* 106). Both rumours prove true, but Loy presents the clichéd artist/model liaison as a calculated competition in which Cosway gambles to win greater stature. She fails: "Only too early after she had refused him the sculptor had leapt to a rare and official celebrity, and Virginia found herself powerless to cap him with a husband of greater distinction" (*SE* 106). Rejecting the strictures of marriage, Cosway finds herself defined by the sculptor regardless, "hammered . . . into a posture in which she was to become fixed for life" (*SE* 107). Galatea to her Pygmalion, the pose is Cosway's fate, her brand, her "tag of identity"; by her pelvis, she is "familiar to the whole of Europe" (*SE* 106).

But the mercilessness of Virginia's constraining pose is not all-defining. "The Stomach" makes a case for the model as source, site, and generator of creation, refusing to reduce her to the artist's malleable prop. Cosway adopts her generative pose publicly, unceasingly: "under the arc of the handshake, with a brief undulation of the hip, and the adjustment of a forefinger, the stomach outswung to its notable attitude, as if enticing aesthetic culture into her womb to be reborn for her audience" (*SE* 106). Like Baudelaire's wretched muse, Cosway must play to her crowd, but by investing her womb with artistic mastery, Loy undermines the stereotype that women reproduce human beings, while men generate artistic and intellectual genius. The womb dominates Cosway's rendering: tourists who visit her most famous statue find themselves face to pelvis, and are studiedly dismissive or open-mouthed. Vexing her audience as much as any groundbreaking artist, Cosway's celebrity remains rooted in her "lifelong" affiliation with "the Master" (*SE* 106). Loy's nomenclature similarly inflates and deflates: "Virginia" suggests newness, prototypicality, but is inextricable from gendered expectations of sexual purity; "Cosway" homophonically evokes roads elevated and well trodden. By withholding her artist's proper name, Loy ascribes to him the model's traditional anonymity, even as her repeat invocations of "the Master" reinforce his superiority. As Pollock contends: "There is no equivalent term of value and respect for great *mistresses* of art comparable to the old *masters* who form the very substance of the canon" (*Differencing* 24).

Cosway's celebrity is sustained and compromised by said Master's art historical dominance: to maintain it, she continues consorting with her "erstwhile suitor", whose invitations are spurred by her reliable loyalty and "intima[cy] with some of his wealthiest clients". Like Gautreau, Cosway is a professional beauty, her status reliant on highly constructed public appearances, including the maintenance of an entourage of "women of greater age and hereditary prestige".

But for all her upward mobility, Cosway's stomach and its gesture transcend her, "attain[ing] to insolence" as she ostensibly presides over "well-attended inquisition[s] of the muses." Having "become an arbiter of aesthetics", her belly prevails, increasingly conscious and well informed, even pompously assured (*SE* 107). Birthplace of her legacy, Cosway's torso becomes her destiny.

Bakhtin tells us that, like the genitals, the belly grounds and degrades (21). More than the contentious wombs of Loy's Sophia and Marjolaine Battement, Virginia Cosway's stomach is an organ denoting not only exalted reproduction, but also consumption, rumination, and feeling, associations that populate Loy's writing and that of her modernist peers. Nourishment is equated with thinking in poem 22 of Loy's "Songs to Joannes" (1917):

Green things grow
Salads

For the cerebral
Forager's revival
Upon bossed bellies
Of mountains
Rolling in the sun (*LoLB* 61–2)

Loy's regenerative diction connects nutrient for the mind with the "bossed" – swollen, projected, rounded out – abdomen. The sentience in question is intellectual and physical, cultured and natural, as integral as it is superfluous aesthetic frippery, given that "bossed" can refer to ornamentation. As in her poem "Hot Cross Bum" (1949), Loy has "alimentary fun" with the abdomen and its multivalence, countering masculinist presumptions that bravery involves a strong stomach, a refusal of squeamishness.[52] As a World War I nurse, Loy boasted of her own capacity to watch a stomach operated upon without anaesthetic (*BM* 187).[53] Loy makes this claim just as the female digestive organs became a site of controversy in Britain, as suffragettes, imprisoned for militant activism, began hunger striking for their cause, only to find themselves forcibly fed by medical and prison authorities. Loy's inevitable awareness of this campaign may underpin the undated "Gloria Gammage", where her eponymous protagonist's survival of a suicide attempt to "pay the debt of threatened honour" is reduced to "a commotion of the intestines" (*SE* 28). This diminishment mocks the sincerity of Gammage's emotion, yet also speaks to a woman's capacity to endure (*SE* 28). This reversal of gendered expectations continues in "Anglo-Mongrels and the

Rose" (1923–5), where feminised tailor Exodus courts the business of gentlemen who sport masculine "clothes / with an easy air / of debonaire / inevitability". In turn, "He is despised / this ostracised / fancier of travestied torsos" (*LaLB* 174–5). That men require the disguise or protection of the uniform, linear suit is evidence that women are not alone in fretting about their abdominal bearing.[54]

In Loy's oeuvre, no stomachs are as decimated as those of the corpses of World War I: in "The Dead" (1919), Loy depicts viscera forced to imbibe the "irate hungers" of global attack that continue "digesting" the ravaged cities of wartime. Supernatural, prescient, these stomachs give collective, cohering voice to anatomised remains and foresee the multifarious "remorses" that the future holds (*LoLB* 72–3). This poem indicates how Loy's torsos contemplate, taking in more than food: in one roman à clef, she describes "the diaphragm" as a bodily electric socket to "physical fear", correlate to the "psychic fear" channelled by "the nape of the neck" (*GI* 28: unnumbered leaf ii). A like pairing can be discerned in Loy's undated drafts of *Colossus*, where the stomach draws the self toward the very essence of being alive, acting as gastric counterpart to the transcendently dislocated spine and nerve centre of Loy's 1919 "Incident" (*SE*). Starving in Mexico in 1917, Loy feels herself overtaken by a universal "Life-Ray" or "animation", leading to "a clear hallucination of [her] oesophagus, extended, opening out of [her] mouth as an enormous funnel". Loy's body has become a battle site in a war of air and food: "Between the spasmodic gripes of the ravenous organ closing upon it, and the avid funnel sucking at it lest it abandon the body, in influx and reflux the animating principle boomed (for my hyperaesthesia) with an infinite pulsation" (*EP* 25). This all-encompassing peristaltic abyss is binary to the "punishment bread" a governess meted out – one slice per factual error in schoolwork – to child Loy. Forced to eat "tremendous slabs" of mass-produced bread under the governess's watchful eye, Loy recalls: "Aridity absorbs saliver. My throat contracts. My stomach becomes delirious as the tawny pulp expands its way down, tedious as an inverted parturition" (*IA* 65: 67). Influx, reflux: Loy's stomach absorbs vital and aggressive energies, then emits affect in turn, becoming the blurred, anxious site of tomb and womb, the barometer of mortal atmospherics. And immortal: Loy argues that in the fusty, fussy population of 1880s England, "sermons were bombastic as . . . bric-a-brac" and "stomachs" took on "the shape of their souls" (*CP* 15: 37).

Loy's anatomised, abject accounts of starvation and forced eating counter the fetishised and euphemised female bellies of her precursors and contemporaries. For the fetishist, the youthful female stomach signifies woman reassuringly fragmented, her generativity limited or untapped. "'[T]he most beautiful belly of all Christendom'" is discussed by gossipy men in D'Annunzio's *Pleasure* (1889), who liken an unnamed woman's abdomen to a reflection of their own desires: hers is "the belly of an infertile Pandora, an ivory bowl, a radiant shield, *speculum voluptatis*" (219). This same propensity to admire "the belly of a girl in bloom" arises in F. T. Marinetti's poem "The Sensual City" (31). For the euphemisers, the stomach is a usefully capacious category permitting indirect reference to sexual desire and non-reproductive generativity. In Gertrude Stein's "Lifting Belly" (1915–17), the opaque titular phrase is relentless refrain.[55] Lifting belly, Stein insists, is strong, bold, beautiful, kind, nice, pleasing, astonishing, and soothing; it is both a regular habit and a sublime site of power, unmistaken and all-knowing. Often diametrically opposed, Stein's countless adjectival categories wilfully cancel themselves out. But the practice in question is persistently intimate, a togetherness: "Lifting belly is full of love" (92). Stein courts and refuses the gastric and the reproductive: on the one hand her lifting belly is "Representative . . . Of the evils of eating"; on the other, "Lifting belly means me . . . . I do not say a mother" (66, 78). That this intimacy fuels artistic generativity is clear from the final line: "In the midst of writing there is merriment" (115).

While the complex joyousness of lifting belly is key to Stein's artistry, a different type of hilarity is at work in Nina Hamnett's autobiography, *Laughing Torso* (1932). Widely known as the "Queen of Bohemia", Hamnett made a living selling her artworks or teaching, achieving some recognition as an artist (she participated in Roger Fry's Omega Workshops) and considerable notoriety as a well-connected socialite, often moving through similar institutions and networks as Loy.[56] The title of her autobiography is a reference to Henri Gaudier-Brzeska's marble sculpture of Hamnett's trunk, *Female Torso* (1913). Hamnett claims to have reluctantly modelled for the first time for Henri Gaudier-Brzeska because he was too poor to hire anyone. Recognising Hamnett as an artist, he returned the favour unasked. Hamnett's unrequited romantic feelings for Gaudier-Brzeska are presented as tangential to the narrative, yet her titular homage suggests that her acquaintance with a man now considered among the great twentieth-century sculptors was not only formative, but all-defining.[57] Its risibility remains ambiguous. Is the torso's laugh triumphant? Sardonic? Self-pitying? Hamnett's tragic death – struggling with alcoholism, she fell from a window in circumstances that remain unclear – gives further ground to the supposition that she is yet another accursed muse. *Laughing Torso* concludes with Hamnett awkwardly holding a friend's squalling infant on a train en route to London, "wondering what my exhibition and the future would bring forth" (322). As in "Lifting Belly", artistic generativity takes precedence over reproductivity. But Hamnett's legacy is now jettisoned in the annals of modernist history, even as her bestselling *Laughing Torso* takes its place in the era's pervasive associations between female sexual embodiment and creative desire, an association in which the midriff frequently becomes an anatomical cypher for woman at her most idealised or marginalised.

In *Insel*, Loy demonstrates her awareness of the female torso as a site of beauty and desire, sourcing Mademoiselle Alpha's appeal in her stomach:

> Her whole body was impudent with a slightly crass adolescence; it centred in her little tummy, which dared to be round.
>
> A hard young apple—it was immediately plain to see, how, had one been on the other side of the fence of sex—one would have wanted to bite into it. (103)

Unlike the waifs of "Monde Triple-Extra", or Sargent's thin ladies, this belly dares to be bossed, to occupy its fecund symbolism as originary, feminine temptation. And as Loy's narrator attests, anyone can be overcome by a desire to consume the site of consumption itself. In Loy, this ideal is starkly opposed by the expansive torsos of the reproductive female. Loy recalls her mother as a "Briton colonising the alien attributes of her marriage", a process engendered by the donning of "rich gowns" as her children wear the garments "of the refugees of an orphanage". Attired in superiority and lush fabric, this mother glides through the domestic sphere like a ship: "abdomen fore she moves in majesty among her subjected children" (*GI* 28: 52). As part of this imperialising mission, the mother will not hear that her daughter does not want to wear a marked-down, ill-fitting housemaid's skirt that "'billows out over [her] tummy'". With pre-marital fattening-up in view, the daughter is dismissed: "'You're too slim; a little stomach will improve you'" (*GI* 28: 54). Recognising that "expectant mothers modestly disappeared from circulation" in her childhood, Loy maintains an ingrained revulsion toward any distended or enlarged belly, including that of her Munich host of 1900, the Baroness whose "inflation was trompe-l'oeil", an illusion of pregnancy that Loy soon learns is an irremediable condition. Often forced to accompany the Baroness in public, adolescent Loy is awash in embarrassment, and Loy's adult narrative self similarly makes "the belly" metonymic of the woman entire (*IA* 69: 149).

The Baroness reduced to "the belly" has her idealised precursor in Loy's "The Stomach". In title and plot, Loy's "The Stomach" may be indebted to Enif Robert's *Un Ventre di donna* (1919), a text endorsed by Marinetti, who signed its preface.[58] Variously translated as *A Woman's Womb* or *A Woman's Stomach*, Robert's story is about an ambitious writer – a widow and reluctant mother – whose genius interferes with her reproductive organs (Gomez 158–9). Corrective surgery and a concomitant conversion to Futurist "surgical" language do not diminish the self-loathing she feels toward her female biology, or her regret at being unable to fight in World War I (Sartini Blum 116). At one juncture, Robert's narrator states: "'How disgusting to be a suffering uterus, while all the men are fighting in the war! To think that I don't even have the courage to face injections!'" (qtd. in Scuriatti 48). Throughout, Robert equates her personal gynaecological struggles with heroised war sacrifice, as in: "'The womb of the land has an immense surgical wound of trenches'" (qtd. in Gomez 157). Sharing Robert's anatomised attentiveness to the quotidian renunciations of the creative, intelligent woman, Loy's "The Stomach" lays the blame for failed generativity at the feet of her protagonist's misguided Victorian self-immolation.[59]

Virginia Cosway has an ailing mother whose care is "sacred duty" and sacrifice (*SE* 107). It is by this familial responsibility, and not her artistic legacy, that Cosway's story is introduced:

> There sat the mother.
> Where the flesh should have been there was shawl—the wits of the aged go wool-gathering, dutiful relatives knit them into frowsty comforter for the blinking, twitching, wheezing forgetter of many delights.
> Her blind eye floated like a decaying fish in the dregs of her lucidity [. . . .]
> Delicate and decent however were the appointments of the sitting-room, the cleared and garnished tabernacle for this bundle of human garbage. (*SE* 104)

Resembling the swaddled beings of Loy's "Static", this woman is mummified, at one with her wrappings, in thrall to the vestiges of a long-diminished consciousness. She is in a tabernacle, a tomb filled with the promise of resurrection, the transcendent legacy of a humble, self-sacrificing Christ. And Cosway makes a great show of worshipping this human vestige, citing her mother's ill health as the rationale for her marital and social unavailability. In fact, Cosway's biography chimes with a tale of a young woman "'of almost irreproachable character . . . offer[ed] employment as a naked model'" recounted in an 1885 issue of *Seeking and Saving*:

> The girl had a very perfect figure; the pay per hour was considerable, and she was told that she would have many hours in the day at her own disposal. The girl's wages in her situation were comparatively small; she thought it an opening which would enable her to better support an aged and dying mother, entirely dependent on her, for a year or so, when she could resume her life as a servant. Surely the only safe advice to be given would be 'refuse the offer,' as God's blessing could not be asked on such an occupation. (qtd. in Borzello 74)

Having entertained the prospect of modelling, this young woman is already besmirched: while her figure is "very perfect", her character is qualified as "almost irreproachable". Her decency is reaffirmed by impoverishment and her support of a female, infirm relative. The girl is safely maternal, a victim of circumstance with an ideal body, a gift from God that may prove a curse. In "The Stomach", Loy satirises the hyperbole of these sorts of purity campaigns: Cosway's dying mother is rubbish, and her derided career is consciously chosen: "Virginia Cosway employed her leisure with the Arts" (*SE* 105). To wealthy associates, Cosway describes herself as "'a prisoner to [her] affections'" (*SE* 107). But no affection transpires between this familial pair. Instead, this accursed muse garners popularity through a well-performed show of daughterly devotion.

Trapped by social and aesthetic posturing, Cosway imprisons her mother in turn. "Gr[owing] daily colder in her woollens", her mother complains about the pose, which is, for her, a visual torture:

> The old woman rolled her surviving eye on the stomach of her attendant daughter and only one of all the visitors distinguished among the wheezing and rumbling these words like exhausted thunder.
>
> 'If only she would take it out of my way —— even for a day. If only I could be left alone.' (*SE* 107)

Cosway ignores this plea, "remain[ing] at her post", which is inseparable from her pose, meaning "[a]rtistic polemics prowled [always] beyond the mother's doors" (*SE* 108). When the mother dies, Cosway tells the friends who attend the funeral that she will not bury her dead. Where Antigone's loyalty is staked on her determination to give her brother burial rites against Creon's decree, Cosway's vexatious devotion refuses to let her mother lie in peace. Antigone may be the prototypical self-immolating female, but Loy mistrusts the sincerity of Cosway's "disposition toward self-sacrifice" (*SE* 59). "[B]ereft of [the] excuse" of her now-dead mother, Cosway is forced to confront her unconventionality as a model who rejects her master, and the less-than-fertile consequences that refutation invokes:

> She gave forth sighs for her past sacrifice, which floated among her cultured acquaintances like whiffs from that protracted maternity of *outre-tombe*.
>
> The stomach in its age was become fibrous and rigid.
>
> And as it proceeded towards me, I could have sworn I could see, set in the wrinkled lids of its navel ——————————— a calculating eye. (*SE* 108)

From beyond the grave, the mother spectrally disrupts Cosway's self-aggrandising, fractured grief, divided between parent and personal past. Cosway's once-creative womb is now an ossified space haunted by a regressive heredity, the deviant rebirth of her mother's disapproving eye from within her navel, united by the umbilical cord of Loy's perversely long dash.[60] Because eye-organ emerges alongside the speaker's "I", the narrative voice is implicated in this disfigurement. This navel is not "a pure seal of grace, an eye that is blind but more splendid than a star" (D'Annunzio 219). It well exceeds the uncanny, maternal merging of self and other, overdetermining the suggestion that the navel is "the mother's mark of mortality" (Bronfen, *Over* 190, 132). Nor is it just a mark of menopause or spinsterhood, an Emily Dickinsonian anxiety about the "transformation of womb into tomb" (Gilbert and Gubar 88). Instead, this navel eye melds the sentient, fragmented organs of two generations: belly-aching mother overtakes the belly of her daughter, her stern gaze intact.

How, precisely, to read this eye? Or, perhaps more accurately, how to stop reading this eye? It may be another nod to Sargent's *Madame X*, in that Virginie Gautreau was said to be sexually voracious, intensely fertile, and to have housed her unborn twin within her own womb, a discovery made by the famous gynaecologist Dr Samuel John de Pozzi, who was also the subject of a Sargent portrait (Syme 140). Alternately, Darwin theorises just such an eye in his discussion of metagenesis, or spontaneous, atavistic inheritance. In metagenesis, a lizard might lose a tail and regain a double tail, a crustacean may develop an antenna from an imperfect cornea, or "an eye, for instance, may be developed at a spot where no eye previously existed" (*Variation* I 388).[61]

Metagenesis corresponds with the "primal creation" that is Cosway's notoriously outswung pelvis, and with Loy's delight in atavism as a harbinger of productively deviant aesthetics (*SE* 107). Or perhaps this eye is "a queer life form" not unlike "'the fearful and sterile burden'" that is the army of silenced "inverts" who clamber through Stephen Gordon's otherwise "'barren womb'" at the close of Radclyffe Hall's 1928 novel *The Well of Loneliness* (Ahmed, *Promise* 102).

Then again, Cosway might take her place in the long history of hysteria, whereby the sufferer is mistrusted model and artist, continually posturing and narrating a symptomology for an audience of family, friends, and medical professionals.[62] Since Hippocrates's *On the Diseases of Women* (500–400 BCE), hysteria has been located in a womb gone rogue, othered: bestial and wilful, this "unhooked" organ wanders hungrily about the bodies of women sexually inexperienced and/or lascivious (Bronfen, *Knotted* 103–5). During the European inquisition, hysterics were believed possessed by the devil; come *fin-de-siècle* psychoanalysis, the hysterical body was possessed by past experience, imposed mental construct, or imagined voice, usually familial (Bronfen, *Knotted* 107). As Freud recounts in his study of Dora, hysteria can result in displaced responses to negative affect moving from one part of the body to another, a process he labelled conversion ("Fragment" 53). Is Cosway's eye a hysteric displacement from one body to another? Hysteric blindness reimagined as monstrous Cyclopean sight? After all, Loy titles an alternate reading of eyes and navels, one that references Freud, "Conversion" (c. mid-1920s). In this essay, she claims that D. H. Lawrence "has dangerously damned his own creative flux with a theory, and [regards] the polarised navel of the infant Jesus through the eye of his pen" (*SE* 228). Loy satirises the raving male hysteric whose writerly tool, his pen/penis, becomes an absurd "channel for [the] discharge" of an epiphanic conversion (Freud, "Fragment" 53). Lawrence himself argued that his "pseudo-philosophy" or "'pollyanalytics'" – writings that engage and resist the Freudian unconscious – emerged from the "novels and poems that come unwatched out of one's pen" (*Fantasia* 15). Self-proclaimed vessel or blind seer, Lawrence thus poses as an effortless Tiresias of artistic inspiration. Toying with patriarchal origins religious and psychosexual, Loy scoffs at Lawrence's proudly asserted freedom from paternal constraints or influence by telescoping the phallic eye/I and redirecting the male gaze toward the navel that marks that most famously occluded mother, the Virgin Mary.[63] In so doing, Loy confirms Lawrence's unwitting entrapment within a misogynist Oedipal economy where desire for the mother is fundamental yet dismissed.

In this Oedipal regard, it is significant that the mother of "The Stomach" was a father until the final typescript. The rationale behind Loy's resolute change of the gender of Cosway's ailing parent is undocumented, but within the manuscripts of *Esau Penfold*, Loy takes express issue with the censorious male gaze. In "The Stomach", the mother rolls her one functioning eye across her daughter's offending body part; in *Esau Penfold*, it is the eye's role to keep an intellectually, socially, and sexually vivacious young woman in check: "Esau's eye, so sullenly moronic … boded something even worse than when my father had accused me of gestures he was 'observing' in a fit of delirium tremens" (*EP* 24). Another variant replicates the quasi-occultist terms of "The Stomach" and, by extension, "Piero and Eliza." It reads:

> Esau … looked me over as a knife resolving where to cut out [the] first slice.
>
> An accusatory eye swam up to the surface of my deep anxiety – it was my father's eye again – probing me as he taught me the adage
> 'Give a dog a bad name – – – – '
> For a while as I gazed at the floor I saw in the patch of glow from the stone an evil head as it grew from the ground of my childhood nightmares. After so many years it began to admonish me – (*EP* 24)

Like the disapproving gaze, this spectral head conflates Esau with Sophia's father, finding both wary and chastising. And like Cosway's mother, the head is fragmented relic, damning vestige. Reputational anxiety drives all disapprobation. Patriarchal success hangs on Sophia's performance of chaste demureness: hence Esau's desire to dissect and disable; hence her father alludes to the English proverb "give a dog a bad name and hang him". In *Esau Penfold*, Sophia's father's accusatory eye swims to the surface just as in "The Stomach" the offending eye "swum into infinity" (*SE* 108).

Mobile, adaptive, powerful, and eternal: there is arguably more father than mother in Cosway's navel eye, particularly when we consider Loy's description of the "dumbfounded women's eyes" that peeped over crinolines in the Victorian "age of patience and plenitude" (*EP* 25).[64] But Sophia's mother does not go narratively unscathed: "With the petty fuming of Esau my subconscious became as involved as with my mother's hysterics. His person was hardly less repugnant to me than her avenging abdomen" (*EP* 24).[65] The mother's malign womb is counterpart to the father's malign gaze:

"Alone my subconscious linked Esau's louring pupil with my father's ~~neurotic~~ condemnatory eye; identified my horror of him with that 'protestation' of my whole being my parents had laboured so direly – perhaps successfully, to overcome."[66] In early variants, "The Stomach" unites aggressive womb with phallic eye/I – a gaze implicating the artist Master – within the thinking, feeling, all-consuming bowl of Cosway's otherwise "transcendental anatomy" (*SE* 105). The female child is doomed to reproducing parents whose gendered censoriousness embeds itself in her very organs.

Loy's shift from father to mother replicates Freud's self-correction in his study of Dora, where he focuses upon a male economy of exchange between Dora's father and his friend Herr K., within which Dora is trafficked commodity, sacrificial victim. By now, it is old news that Freud's Oedipal triangle demands a relinquishment of the maternal in favour of the father, to whom the female subject will continue to defer in marriage, her husband a foreordained father substitute. Lacking phallus, woman is relegated to lack. Freud's story of Dora persists with this misogynistic bias: only in a belated footnote does Freud acknowledge that he failed to give due deference to Dora's defining relationship with Frau K., which, by psychoanalytic strictures, would prioritise mother over father as the object of desire.[67] Where Freud considers Dora a duplicitous *poseur*, feminist scholars reinterpret her evasions and silences as resistance. Given the centrality of the patriarchal family unit from the eighteenth century forward, Bronfen reads the prevalent nineteenth-century "hysteric" as the female family member who "uses her body, knotting together strife and gender, to articulate the difference at the heart of the family. She vacillates between accepting and questioning the paternal metaphor as the law dictating her being" (*Knotted* 120). Hysteria "performs an illness in and of the family"; by extension, "the deepest level of meaning of hysterical symptoms is . . . a breakthrough of the prohibited desire for the mother" (Bronfen, *Knotted* 131; Moi 69).

If Loy's Cosway is hysteric, she remains in a truly ambivalent state: she identifies with the symbolic father in running her household, but plays the dutiful daughter in conversations with other women. Her desire for artistic mastery goes unfulfilled, and her relationship with her mother is openly antagonistic. Ultimately, the mother remains the most despised figure of Loy's story: bereft of audible speech, she asserts herself through a judging gaze, a malignant communication that dwells within Cosway even after her death. Cosway experiences Denise Riley's extimacy, discussed earlier in this volume, by which hateful communication is drawn into the besmirched individual, generating a foreign body that lodges within the self.[68] In this case, the foreign body is eerily familiar: muse Cosway's abdomen houses her mother's evil eye, her curse, which lodges itself in the navel, or the site marking loss and irrevocable physical bond (Bronfen, *Knotted* 55, 81). Situated in the omphalos, this curse returns us to origins biological and parodic, recalling how satire began in ritual denunciations of failed generative powers, of impotence and infertility. In "The Stomach", these reproductive expectations prompt perverse somatic alteration: an incestuous, partial, hysterical pregnancy that is nightmare rather than catharsis.[69] As such, Cosway, famous muse, is doubly cursed: from without by a patriarchal legacy that perceives her barren womb as embodied lack and is equally dismissive of her creativity; from within by a mother whose enmity prevails over Cosway's ambitions and her innards, felt and constraining.

Consistent with her own ambivalent relationship to Freudian psychoanalysis, Loy may have turned father into mother precisely to avoid an Oedipal reading of "The Stomach", a story in which sexuality is incidental to the larger conundrum of female self-invention.[70] At the outset of "Conversion", Loy derides "psychoanalytic literature" for "offer[ing] no escape from the post-natal womb of the Eternal Mother" (*SE* 227). In keeping with this premise, "The Stomach" appears less a story about hysteria than a satire of its presumed causes and its hold over the Western psyche. By this reading, the extraordinary sentience of Cosway's abdomen rewrites hysteria as the locus of artistic genius rather than madness.[71] Loy's roman à clef *The Child and the Parent* corroborates this postulation: in it, Loy argues that bodily organs possess their own consciousness, a genius that "subsist[s] from generation to generation, [having] acquired a sort of eternalness through transmission" (*CP* 19: 2).[72] In chapter 11, "The Outraged Womb", Loy's theory comes to fruition, as she ascribes to the uterus an ability to access cosmic sentience through pleasure, and then internalise that feeling in the "finite receptacle" of the self (*CP* 19: 5).[73] Loy carefully points out that, even if the womb is not literally fertilised, its genius "never ceases to ideate the concussion of ecstasy which is the sole content of its consciousness" (*CP* 19: 6). As in "The Stomach", the womb can ideate – imagine, conceive, form ideas, think; it is not just a womb, but a "womb-brain" (*CP* 19: 7). This theory is not without its offences: throughout, Loy considers reproduction woman's destiny, suggests that the genius of male organs is more coherent than that of females, and argues that the generations-long genius of the womb preserves the sanctity of the (white, European) race.[74] But in this chapter, we also witness Loy subverting the nineteenth-century obsession with hysteria, jettisoning pathology to emphasise mental well-being through an eminently attainable womb happiness. Loy discerns how woman is paradoxically perceived as existing at the mercy of her "natural" body – highly strung, decimated by parturition – whilst being constantly subjected to impossible levels of artifice, "painted to look as much like a bon-bon as possible" (*CP* 19: 9). Females know artifice, then, as they know generativity; key terms of artistry emerge in Loy's critique, affirming women's acumen as creators.

Ironically for a modernist deeply invested in originality, Loy argues in *The Child and the Parent* that what woman needs most – artistic women included – is a viable prototype with whom they might identify. Where Freud suggests that hysteric reactions can appear exaggerated because of their unknown origins, Loy asserts that Woman entire is inseparable from the strictures of wilful (mis)representation (Freud, "Aetiology" 217). As such, both her brain and her womb have always been tossed "onto the discard area of unconsummated things", even as the uterus "aspir[es] to have its dream confirmed" (*CP* 19: 12–13). Patient to a fault, the womb can be roused from its apathy, Loy warns, to locate a "torrential indignation":

> Women's reprisals are uttered behind closed doors. Her 'incantation for laying the blame,' like malefic secret rites of destructive magic, strikes undertones in our social symphony omitted in orchestration . . . . It is a long plaint, resistant as is negation. For she is unaware of her own meaning while the average man fits his significance to himself. Hers is an empty tirade which, as if her desperation were as unreal as her argument, never wears her out. She persists: unanswerable. Her echoing indignation flows on and the sentient wreckage in its wake is absorbed by sanatoriums and asylums with the connivance of official discretion which never listens behind closed doors. (*CP* 19: 14–15)

Acknowledging the profundity and fellowship of Freud's "semitic acumen", Loy replaces his theory of irrational hysteria with a legitimate outrage sourced in a womb that thinks and speaks from within its maligned body.[75] If that outrage mystifies, it is only because womankind lacks the definition historically, continually on offer to men. In other words, Cosway's failure as model-artist lies in the absence of a predecessor to emulate. And in women's "'incantation for laying the blame'" we might even find absolution for Cosway's mother, whose gendered exclusion plays its part in the curses she wreaks upon her daughter. Against the limitations of hysteria, women will prevail: woman's "is a long plaint", but it is as "resistant as is negation", and in its wake it leaves a sequestered, institutionalised, but consciously oppositional debris. Accursed and cursing, woman is nevertheless aware that she deserves more than a lifetime of immolation. Loy's repeat articulations of the muse make a truth of the premise asserted in James Frazer's *The Golden Bough* (1890): sacrifice occurs because human beings believe that imitation is a catalyst, that the ritualised loss of one individual – a criminal who resembles a beloved king; an individual acting as proxy for a god; a child for a parent – can elongate a valued life or lives (Frazer 264–93). Repetitive, performative, self-reflexive, Loy's musings on the muse demand recognition of the losses at stake with a view to increasing the status of the models of the future.

Loy universalises the need to reconsider the muse. Recall that, in her story "Static", Loy insists that all human individuals "fall from the mother's womb to their particular attitude", becoming "[s]tricken statues unto death". Accidents of birth and families of origin define our pose, form the works of art we will become. In *The Child and the Parent*, Loy focuses on how this global accursedness particularly affects women. In a chapter entitled "Ladies in an Aviary", Loy represents woman as a flock of over-plumaged birds, lured into their golden cage by "the sugar of fictitious values" (*CP* 15: 35). Captive, overcrowded, and trained to over-moralise, these women are indistinguishable from one another. Against this domesticated flock, Loy juxtaposes the model of Johannes Vermeer's *Girl with a Pearl Earring* (1665), a figure positioned against "the shadowy plush of a wine-red curtain to hang a pearl in her ear" as the hand that arranges the jewellery is "loaded with invisible chains, securing her at once to something within herself, and to something beyond conjecture." Woman, Loy argues, "has been decorating herself eternally, to camouflage the vehicle of a primary inertia to which all creation has recourse for replenishment, the female principle in nature" (*CP* 15: 36). Denied advancement, woman's body has comfortingly sustained, nourished, and pleased others, meaning that she is perpetually "hanging a pearl in ear", adorning herself in lieu of being able "to invent herself", plasticly conforming "to any shape Society considers plausible" (*CP* 15: 37). Woman yields to a fashion and surface refashioning considered frivolous, but Loy does not want us to underestimate this endeavour.[76] Loy's "Ladies in an Aviary" are haunted by "the nacreous figure of the woman with the ear-ring, and even she is becoming blurred" (*CP* 15: 42).

The beautiful pallid youth of Vermeer's painting is presented as an ideal, one at risk, if gendered expectations do not change, of losing the "amphoral pose" of self-adornment, her leisured, stylish positioning of ornament replaced by "stuffing fingers in her ears to muffle the cry of hunger from multiplying mouths" (*CP* 15: 43). Needy stomachs will take priority over self and beauty, enacting a "cruel metamorphosis" by which "the hand that suspended an orient" will "clutc[h] hold of a wooden stirrer, to rotate with hectic monotony in the midst of a column of steam" (*CP* 15: 43). Loy's message is clear: by participating in the generative beauty of art – including as bedecked model – women can avoid being defined, potentially exhausted, by their reproductive wombs. Loy's thinking is consistent with Ida John, wife to the revered artist Augustus, who, when pregnant in 1904, wrote a friend lamenting how her "Belly" kept her from socialising, travelling, and sitting for a portrait. "I would rather lose a child than the power of sitting", wrote John, adding: "The longer I live the more subordinate do all things become to that old monster Augustus Edwin – the monster" (172). For John as for Loy, to be the malleable, overwritten focal point of the male creator is better than not participating in art at all. However accursed, the muse continues to orbit the generative, defining herself by possibility rather than the practicalities of inhabitation and consumption.

As Ida Nettleship, John attended the Slade School of Art, where she met her husband. She died in 1907 following the birth of a fifth child. A self-described avid reader – of Dostoyevsky and Empson, among others – John struggled to accept the demands of full-time parenting; it "cost [her] much pain to give [painting] up" (John 178, 248). A typical accursed muse, John yields to her torso's autonomy in a manner matched by the discerning authority of Cosway's pelvic pose. While feminists have long and understandably resisted the essentialising of gendered bodies, recent research affirms the gut as a cognitive organ, one that ruminates, deliberates, comprehends, and yes, can feel depressive, can evince habitual, irrational, pathological responses to troubling mental and emotional stimuli. Not roving, not hysterical, but certainly in possession of a mind of its own, as Elizabeth A. Wilson argues in *Gut Feminism* (2015), a book that asks how feminists might reintegrate biology into their understanding that culture overpoweringly constructs femininity (17). For Wilson, ingestion, digestion, and peristalsis are significant parts of the psychic landscape one inhabits and, in turn, are ways of reading female desire, aggression, and masochism – all crucial aspects of envisioning or realising a more equal gendered world (22). Consequently, Wilson advocates on behalf of a deeper study of the viscera, a "critical splanchnology". Given that the stomach takes shape from what it ingests, as well as from its own internal organs – the diaphragm, the intestines – it is "an organ uniquely positioned, anatomically, to contain what is worldly, what is idiosyncratic, and what is visceral, and to show how such divisions are always being broken down, remade, metabolized, circulated, intensified, and excreted" (43). The stomach integrates and rejects and, according to Wilson, might be heard uttering "organ speech" strikingly commensurate with Loy's indignantly vociferous womb (76). Like Loy, Wilson labours to give the female body voice, to hear how it withstands surfeits of aggression and hostility, to attend to the hormonal complexities and reproductive organs of female bodies pressured to conform, procreate, and be quietly, perpetually resilient, no matter how badly maligned as the weaker sex.

Writing *The Child and the Parent* as she moves toward senescence, Loy theorises womb outrage. Recall that Loy was impregnated through a rape that was among her first sexual experiences; that she witnessed the deaths of two of her four children; that she was abused by her first husband, and lost her second just as she recovered from starvation, having recently discovered that she was pregnant with her fourth and final child. Given the paucity of recognition afforded the womb, Loy might justifiably feel "an echoing indignation" that "flows on" even as she exits the fertile menstrual economy by which women's stock and value have always been measured, what Loy calls that "eternal river of blood" that is "so successfully deviated from the social landscape that even advertisements for Kotex less than remind us of it in pictures of pale clients whose appearance of super-carnal delicacy suggest their being, slightly, disgusted with God." Loy makes this statement in and amongst a call for us to acknowledge that we cannot "sort out th[e] woman of crude reality from among the multiple reality of the 'social surface'" (*CP* 19: 10–11). What Wilson advocates for contemporary feminists is implicit and explicit throughout Loy's oeuvre: Loy recognises that biology and feminism share a generative vertiginousness, each undoing and reanimating the other (Wilson 172). All body, all reproduction, Loy's accursed muse, too, has her animating propensities.

Critiquing Victorian hysteria, Loy's "The Stomach" is nevertheless not without a vexed relationship to what Mary Jacobus calls "the maternal imaginary", or "the fantasmic mother who may or may not possess reproductive parts, nurturing functions, and specific historical or material manifestations; but who exists chiefly in the realm of images and imagos" (iii). The maternal imaginary is a constitutive facet of the accursed poet, for whom the infant's gradual renunciation of the primary caregiver fails, so that she becomes emblematic of his unsustainable rejection of readership, the femme fatale, or otherness writ large. This motif arises as early as Vigny's 1832 *Stello*. Slowly coming to terms with the good Doctor Noir's lesson, Stello asks, "'Are we [poets], then, the eternal Pariahs of society?'" The Doctor replies:

> 'Be you Pariahs or Gods . . . the Multitude, while carrying you in its arms, looks askance on you as it does on all its children, and from time to time will throw you on the ground and trample you under foot. The crowd makes a bad mother.' (165)

The bad-enough mother is the subject of the first poem of Baudelaire's *Les Fleurs du mal*, "Benediction", where the very night of his conception is cursed by a mother ashamed of his poetic vocation and "eager to blaspheme" God for saddling her with an incomprehensible offspring (11).[77] She will recur in Mallarmé's portrait of Verlaine, where the latter is praised as a hero who embraced his destiny, a man who "showed himself to his Mother, whoever she was, a lady veiled, the crowd, inspiration, life; in any case she stripped the poet bare, and he remained loyal, sensitive, imbued with honour" (63). The only woman included in Verlaine's *Les Poètes maudits* is Marceline Desbordes-Valmore, whose ambivalently "true albeit feminine talent" is defined by "maternal tremblings!" (87). Desbordes-Valmore's poetry is full of good, hesitant mothers who know their marginal place, and express horror about their occasional outbursts at their sons (89, 91, 103). Where peers tellingly assert that "[i]t took a strong digestive apparatus" to read Loy's work, Desbordes-Valmore's genius consists of a palatable, carefully contrived self-effacement that does little to stem the tide of *maudit* maternal blame, a current discernible as late as Artaud's insistence, in 1947, that Van Gogh's work illustrates "the suffering of the pre-natal" (Kreymborg, *Singing* 488; Artaud 48). The accursed poet forms in the womb and effectively stays there, maintaining his originary narcissism; Loy's rendering of Cosway's inhabitation by her dead mother might parody or reclaim this intractable maternality.

For accursed poets, entanglement in mother's apron strings produces a tormented, perverse originality, a spurning of daunting, exhausted patriarchal aesthetic traditions. For the accursed muse, the bond with the mother betokens the fixity for which Loy's tale of Marjolaine Battement is named, "Static". Rather than advancing, the accursed muse is mired in the still Sargasso Sea to which Pound likens the subject of his "Portrait d'une Femme" (1912). And little separates Battement, "palliated prostitute", from Baudelaire's "Venal Muse", whose "charms" are also "for sale".

At the end of his portrait of Poe, Baudelaire praises the American writer's surrogate mother, his maternal caretaker Mrs Clemm, who "tireless[ly] minister[ed] to [Poe's] genius" and became the dedicatee of Poe's posthumously published work: "His glory will embalm the name of the woman whose love could dress his wounds and whose image will forever float above the martyrology of literature" ("Poe" 81–3). Clemm is a champion every cursed poet would like to have, and a reassurance every accursed muse needs. The second volume of this *Anatomy* will discuss how Loy was cursed by her own mother; in turn, Loy too longed for an *"eternal comforter"* and encouraged her daughters to play this role. This was a lesson taught at length and in absentia: a letter written in 1921, or the same year that Loy produced the archived typescript of "The Stomach", reveals how her eldest child Joella, then 14, was rocketed into adulthood, taking care of the family finances in both parents' absence.[78]

It is not difficult to comprehend the appeal of an ideal and idealising, ever-present nurturing figure who shores up one's artistic legacy, particularly one who poses no direct threat to one's creative autonomy. "The Stomach" acknowledges that appeal, but articulates its impossibility for the aspirant female model: like Loy's Marjolaine and Eliza, Cosway fails to become a prototype, fails to escape from the plight of the accursed muse, whose job it is to be generative for others, artistically and domestically. Although unrecognised for their artistry, Loy's muses reject presumptions of their passivity, not unlike the dolls and mannequins displayed in Loy's shop poems, plastic females who "have the effrontery to / Stare through the human soul" or "jolt" aggressively "to their robot turn" (*LoLB* 17, 112). A similar effrontery marks Frau Ferlein of *Insel*, who is diminutively, deceptively introduced as Mrs Jones's "little model", only to become Jones's confidante, a canny feminist colluder who corroborates Jones's denunciation of Insel's "approach" toward women as one defined by "continent rape" and incontinent expenditure (*I* 3, 72, 116). As for Gertrude Stein, a prototype Loy took as her own model,

Loy's portraiture recognises "that each one is themselves inside them", pursuing what is "intrinsically exciting" within the model by "find[ing] out what is moving inside them that makes them them" ("Portraits" 173, 183). Loy and Stein instate the model's world view, recognising and meeting the defiance in her gaze.

But before Stein was Dante Gabriel Rossetti, as attested by Loy's juvenilia about the Pre-Raphaelite portraitist: "you concocted in your poesy so powerful an emetic of the spirit as to relieve a middle-class visionary of her adolescence and cloy the gorgeous rubber corps of your wide-eyed women stricken with fried hair" (*IA* 67: 106). Rossetti's portraiture provides curiously gastric revelation: it empties Loy's stomach, purging her of youthful innocence and fervour, whilst simultaneously sickening her with the feminine artifice on offer. "Tipped off as it were" by her favourite artist, Loy writes: "I discovered that if my powers of concentration flagged with a model before me, I could draw anything I longed to see provided I had nothing to look at." In turn, "much that is learned from the study of models", Loy avows, "seemed to have registered on some unsuspected plane of memory" (*IA* 67: 107–8). Through Rossetti, Loy comes to recognise the flimsy causal relationship between model and portrait, claiming herself an inspired fashioner of prototypes.

"I say: a flower!", states Mallarmé in 1897, "And out of the oblivion where my voice casts every contour . . . there arises, musically, the very idea in its mellowness; in other words, what is absent from every bouquet" ("Crisis" 210). Stein echoes Mallarmé in her famous aphorism: "Rose is a rose is a rose is a rose", she writes in the first of many publications in 1913, a teleological banality elevated in this instance by the line that follows: "Loveliness extreme" ("Sacred Emily" 187). In an age of venerated vanguard novelty, emulation anxiety runs deep. In many ways, "The Stomach" is a fable about that anxiety, an experience Cosway shared with the accursed poets, who acknowledged themselves as models and muses, and who adopted a feminised pose that became integral to twentieth-century art and theory. In 1917, Dadaist Hugo Ball anticipated that "the pose will become serious", envisioning its future as "a struggle that will take over our innermost organs" (110). Six decades later, Susan Sontag would declare that we live in an age where "[t]o live is also to pose" (qtd. in Steiner 2). Courtesy of second-wave feminism, the model's perception and generative, referential symbolism have become full-fledged artistic preoccupations, as the renowned artists Cindy Sherman, Sherrie Levine, and Kathy Acker attest (Steiner 93). Empathy and respect for the represented subject grows, inflecting the social sciences, where modelling is increasingly integral to an affect economy driven by the labour of "interaction and human contact" in order to "'elicit 'intangible feelings of ease, excitement, or passion'" (Wissinger 240). The accursed muse is related to these paradigms, phylum to its kingdom.

Historically, the negation of the muse is intensified by the threat she represents: the accursedness of the poet is partly attributable to the knowing if ephemeral power of the female subject he longs to master. Indirectly, begrudgingly, the muse's intellect is recognised throughout accursed poet literature: in Vigny's *Stello*, Doctor Noir tells the eponymous protagonist that the poet's destiny is determined by the muse's hold over the base of his heart, a muse initially more comprehending than her artist (172). In Verlaine's *The Cursed Poets*, the artist registers resignation and veneration toward a muse who shares his rejection of patriarchal authority: "The Muse (Oh well! Long live our fathers!) . . . strikes all the notes, plucks all the harp strings, strums all the guitar's gut cords and caresses the bend of the agile bow" (32). For her troubles, the muse is treated disloyally, dismissed, jinxed; she is a better mistress than wife, as Noir quotes a powerful man stating (Vigny 60). Yet, like her male, accursed poetic peers, the accursed muse interrogates the sacred, intimate realm for which Loy, like Bataille after her, palpably longs. And as in Loy's extimate curses, Bataille turns to communicative fundamentals to define the ingrainedness of this loss.

Maintaining that language and representation unduly civilise and possess experience, Bataille holds up art, and poetry in particular, as the vertiginous zone that sacrifices ends-driven communication in the always dashed hopes of attaining some sovereign, all-possible, ideally immoral realm that inevitably exceeds our meagre mortal existence. To access sacrificial extremes, Bataille writes, is to willingly succumb to that which supersedes us; this succumbing he considers fundamentally feminine (*IE* 40). Poetry, too, is feminine, because to write is to be acted upon (*IE* 60). But, for Bataille, the truest sacrifice of all, the one that most evades the instrumentalisation of discourse, is silence. Thus, he presents for emulation the accursed poet Rimbaud, who, by famously renouncing poetry altogether, lets go of "feminine evasiveness . . . [and] uncertain, involuntary expression" in favour of a decisive, virile response to the possible, to the lived world (*IE* 40). In silencing himself, Rimbaud brings the accursed poet full circle: "abandoning [poetry]", he "make[s] sacrifice complete, without ambiguity, without reserve" (*IE* 148). Bataille recognises the ironic jest, the self-satire, involved in naming and honouring a resolutely non-formulating intelligence in a prose he cannot stop himself from writing (*IE* 67–8). Yet his admiration for Rimbaud's silence remains palpable. Bataille's terms are as implicitly misogynist as Verlaine's; these are thinkers who appropriate and venerate the very terms of womankind's marginalisation – her silencing, abjections, and martyrdoms – whilst failing to recognise the truth that Loy describes, that woman's is a "long plaint, resistant as is negation". But with an irony that escapes Bataille, his theory makes of Rimbaud an ideal accursed muse: a witting model of constraint and sacrifice, a revered "sentient wreckage". And in so doing, he merges model and artist in a manner that Loy's work so persistently interrogates.

Notes

1. Ivon has numerous ancient associations: in Norse, "Eivind" evokes "warrior" or "winner". In Welsh, "Owen" means "warrior" or "well born", and Irish and Scottish Gaelic variants of "Eógan" connote noble origins. The French male name Corvon is also uncannily akin to Cravan, the French surname of Loy's second husband. By the terms of Loy's undated draft text *Colossus*, Cravan resembles the fictional Corvon in his womanising and avant-gardism.
2. Cornforth was Rossetti's muse in his final years (Pollock, *Vision* 156). A working-class woman, she refused to keep demurely silent and still as her body was displayed for the benefit of Rossetti's guests. She is recalled chiding the artist, giggling, and performatively "'spreading her ample charms upon a couch'" (qtd. in Borzello 43).
3. Frazer's highly influential modernist text is considered the first to ably and expressly conflate Christian ritual with ancient sacrifice (Hughes 7; 212–13). Loy frequently conflates the same, as evinced by the baptism and Eleusinian mysteries of "Monde Triple-Extra".
4. Francis M. Naumann's *Daughters of New York Dada* is said to be the first publication to define Loy as a model (Steiner 97). As will be discussed further below, the anonymous artist's model and the commissioned sitter are distinct entities, and Loy consistently falls into the latter category. That said, Loy did not hesitate to encourage her daughter Fabienne to work as a mannequin in a shop window, and supported her in modelling for *Harper's Bazaar* in 1936 (Bayer, "Letter dated Monday 18th").
5. Stagnation is a quality ascribed to Loy's Insel, and appears to underscore his unpredictable oscillations between an overpowering masculinity and a cowering femininity. Early in the novel, Jones describes finding Insel wild-eyed on the street, anxious from the realisation that he has "too lately thrown off an unguessable inertia" (*I* 53). As Insel

contemplates his artistry with Jones at end of the novel, he describes the process of creation and inspiration as a journey of a thousand directions. Jones believes she can see this "map of immanent direction" hanging above Insel's head, "endless lines across a limitless canvas" (150). This "map of inertia" exhibits "[i]ndefinable lines of cerebral nerve", mimicking the affectivity of a decadent artist, the twists and turns of a prone nervous system. Insel's abandonment of inertia is as problematically delayed as its manifestation.

6. Jessica Burstein identifies an "[a]nxiety about copying" in Loy, focusing on her entrepreneurship and the need to maintain patents for the sale of her own inventions, but also extended, in ways that bear relation to my argument about Loy's muses, to how Loy posits the prostitute as a cheapened copy of the virgin (191).

7. In ancient Roman law, a *homo sacer* was an individual banished from the state whom anyone had permission to kill, excepting by sacrificial ritual. The *homo sacer* thus sits with the gods in transcending immolation, but in all other regards is at the mercy of humanity, utterly accursed (Girard 293). Vestiges of this configuration run through Bataille's thought, as when he writes: "The curse is the necessary path for true blessing" (*LE* 21).

8. Chénier, for instance, voluntarily joined the French Revolution only to be denounced by Robespierre as an anti-Jacobite. Executed in 1791 before he attained a readership, Chénier's legacy was recovered by his subsequent influence on French Romanticism.

9. Baudelaire's influence is circuitous. The phrase "accursed poet" arises once in the 1868–70 edition of Baudelaire's works, where the poem "Sépulture" appears as "Sépulture d'un poète maudit", a title attributable to editor Charles Asselineau that is not commensurate with Verlaine's usage, given the lack of a poetic or male subject in the poem. Verlaine owned this Baudelaire publication, and uses the expression "*poète maudit*" for the first time in a letter of 1883 (Burch 754–5).

10. Desbordes-Valmore, L'Isle-Adam, and "Pauvre Lelian" were added to the second edition.

11. Implicitly, Verlaine and his reader understand as much: *Les Poètes maudits* is, after all, a compiled series.

12. "*Les Poètes maudits* is among the most frequently cited literary studies of its period", writes Burch, but his brief, expert article remains one of the few critical sources in English wholly devoted to Verlaine's text (753).

13. While recognising that contemporary Western culture rejects the power of witchcraft, Lecercle will not acquiesce to this dismissal, arguing that, once an individual is condemned – as possessed, as hex recipient – they inevitably enact their curse, and find their worst fears corroborated by their immediate community (234–6).

14. For further discussion of Lecercle, Riley, and the power of language, see Chapter 2 of this volume.
15. The aesthetic purity campaign included letters to *The Times* insisting that nudes be removed from galleries, the public chastisement of models' male relatives, and the demand to restrict attendance at life modelling classes (Borzello 76–83).
16. This stereotype consciously inflects Steiner's feminist *The Real Real Thing*, where she uses the female pronoun for the model throughout, a decision justified in a footnote acknowledging how "this gendering may occasionally play into misogynistic traditions" (194). This gendering has not held true through the ages: in the early modern period, male models were preferred because they could be represented in a wider range of roles (women tended to be consigned to allegories or victims), and because their more pronounced muscles and tendons were said to afford a desirably higher degree of relief for the artist (Borzello 21; S. West 148–53).
17. Throughout the text of this chapter, I will refer to her as Elizabeth Siddall, but the references to her poems will defer to the published spelling of her surname.
18. Siddall continues to be sidelined: in a Tate Britain exhibition of the Pre-Raphaelites in the 1980s, two of the 250 works available for viewing were by Siddall, the only woman represented (Pollock, *Vision* 161).
19. Pollock furthers understanding of the legibility of Olympia's hand gesture by pointing to the history of bourgeois discourse contemporaneous with her portrait; by it, woman is the heart of society, man the head, and the working classes the hands and body parts associated with filth and sexuality (*Differencing* 50).
20. I refer to Pound's "Portrait d'une femme" (1912) and Eliot's "Portrait of a Lady" (1917). Neither poetic subject is ceded a speck of originality or vitality: Pound's woman possesses "Nothing that's quite [her] own" (*Poems* 35); Eliot's female is, like her tragic forebears, a docile lamb led to the slaughter, her domestic space emitting "[a]n atmosphere of Juliet's tomb" (*Poems* 18).
21. Another variant on this theme surfaces in *Time and Western Man* (1927), where Lewis takes umbrage with the Futurists for liking women better than their representations, meaning that the adored females in question fail to sufficiently revere either their portraits or artists (204).
22. It is not my aim to mitigate the pronounced narrative misogyny at stake in the rendering of this incident. Kreisler's rape is foreshadowed by his admiration for another painter, who is gratified at not having "to apologise for his brutal behaviour as an artist". This same painter "flung a man or woman on to nine feet of canvas and pummelled them on it for a couple of hours, until they promised to remain there, or were

incapable of moving" (*Tarr* 75). In general, the ideal model of Lewis's writings is not creative accomplice but willing victim.

23. Beyond their geographical and aesthetic linkages, Loy and the Baroness were both close to Djuna Barnes, shared Peggy Guggenheim's patronage, and published in *The Little Review*; furthermore, Loy references the Baroness's writing and name in a 1920 *Little Review* exchange between herself and the British writer John Rodker (Gammel 374, 454).

24. Quoting Susan E. Dunn, Linda A. Kinnahan claims that Loy was "'one of the modernist avant-garde's most photographed women'", before offering an impressively comprehensive history of Loy's modelling for photography pioneers Stephen Haweis, Man Ray, Julien Levy, George Platt Lynes, and Joseph Cornell, among others (*Mina* 28–35).

25. For instance, this chapter could justifiably encompass Loy's play "The Pamperers" (1920), in which protagonist Diana is both muse and matron of the arts, or Loy's poems about women on display, among them "Magasins du Louvre" (1914) and "Mass-Production on 14th Street" (1942).

26. In her teens, Loy's father bought her a complete set of Rossetti's writings (*BM* 40). In 1966, the year she died, Loy was interviewed by the Colorado newspaper *The Aspen Times* and proclaimed Rossetti her favourite poet, noting that she continued to admire his paintings (Loy, "Loy, Mina: Records, documents, and addresses").

27. Loy uses the unusual variant spelling "Pygmaleon". This poem is undated. On the typescript, Loy writes: "written eons ago". Its earliness in her oeuvre is further confirmed by its range of historical reference, which is, as will be discussed, contemporaneous with individuals and events that were noteworthy at the outset of the twentieth century (Loy, "Pygmaleon and Galatea"; all subsequent quotations are drawn from the same reference).

28. Editions were available in Latin, and in European languages such as French and German, but Slater's work was pioneering in making this material available to an English readership for the first time. Initially published in 1906, the text went into half a dozen editions by 1931. Slater's work is believed to have led to a greater democratisation of the interpretation of Catholic law. For more on this topic, see James F. Keenan, *A History of Catholic Moral Theology in the Twentieth Century* (2010) and specifically the first chapter, "Moral Pathology and the Manualists".

29. British-born Sir Francis Jeune (1843–1905) was divorce court president from 1881 to 1903. An obituary dated 1905 in the *New Zealand Herald* confirms that he was enviable both for his appearance and his adjudicating abilities. Not only did Sir Francis garner widespread admiration, "socially he was immensely popular" ("Death of Sir Francis Jeune").

30. See, respectively, "Gloria Gammage" and "Piero and Eliza." (both *SE*); in Loy's portraits, Florence is "Palms".
31. Esau Penfold reappears in Loy's "Anglo-Mongrel and the Rose", where his childhood is described in terms that parallel Haweis's biography (see *LaLB* 133–5 in particular). Loy's drafts of *Esau Penfold* are incomplete and disorderly. Loy's female protagonist is alternately named Sophia, Dinah, Ova, and Linda, suggesting overlaps with the female protagonists of *Brontolivido*, "Anglo-Mongrels", and *Islands in the Air*. Esau too has more than one moniker: "Paddy" is another variant of his first name, and his surname alternates between Ambrose and Penfield.
32. In an alternate draft of this incident, the red letter betokens "[t]he corpse of the future l[ying] heavily on the sky" (*EP* 22). Although immediately visibly aged and devoid of aspiration, Sophia remains momentarily unaware that she has been assaulted, or that her hymen might be torn. Previously, Esau suggested that he was a hermaphrodite, a biological inheritance Sophia equates with impotence, a not-uncommon view in the late nineteenth century (Reis n.p.). By extension, Sophia presumed she could safely spend time unchaperoned with Esau. See also subsequent endnote.
33. Loy offers numerous descriptions of Esau's pitiful artistry, describing him as a poor plagiariser of Aubrey Beardsley and a hapless painter who "exploited the accidental with - - - his infeasible impotence" (*EP* 24). Loy's suggestion that Esau is "virile unto himself" as an artist appears to extend his claim that he was a hermaphrodite. In Loy's era, medical professionals sought to confirm whether hermaphrodites were capable of solo penetrative sex and/or procreation (Reis, n.p.). See also previous endnote.
34. With greater sympathy, Loy will also acknowledge how Esau embodies the "endless paradox" that is the "scission between the poor broken organic individual and the cultivated personality" (*EP* 22).
35. Elsewhere, Loy describes Esau's face as a protrusive "wedge" with "huge meticulously carved features". This hyperbolic visage culminates in yet another confirmation of Esau's absent presence: "Tremendous unfeature – – – Esau Penfold had no face!" (*EP* 25).
36. Perhaps because of its gestational links to Loy's "Anglo-Mongrels and the Rose", Burke attributes Sophia's shame to her hybrid background, a supposition that assumes that this fictional character shares Loy's Anglo-Hungarian ancestry, which does not merit protracted mention in the text itself (*BM* 81). Instead, *Esau Penfold* is more overtly preoccupied with Esau's Eurasian forebears, a claim staked on a single Indian relative and problematically used to further claims of his abject indeterminacy.
37. The drafts of *Esau Penfold* oscillate without clarification between Sophia's first pregnancy (via Esau's assault) and her second by a man

with whom she has an affair. With the second child, the story becomes increasingly complex: on the one hand, Esau, who knows the truth of the gestation, supports Sophia's "overladen belly" through the night with his thigh, an empathetic gesture Loy diminishes by suggesting that it "assuage[s] his anxieties about this child that would mix its roots with his own" (*EP* 25). On the other hand, whilst pregnant, Sophia feels trapped in a "shell of hyperaesthesia", "deprived of the hovering male solicitude and solace that [was hers] by right of nature" and "the ethical foundation of the familial covenant" (*EP* 24). Sophia is exhausted by the drain of the "extra-egoist Being" on her "female vitality" and by Esau, her "willing jailor", a man who threatens her physically and insists that she continue to play the part of wife in full (*EP* 24). Fathers elect and biological fail the restless, sensitised Sophia through her untraditional pregnancy, as does the patriarchy writ large: in this mutually unconventional, non-monogamous marriage, Sophia is aware that she risks the greater stigma.

38. Unlike most drafts of *Esau Penfold*, this chapter is a paginated typescript.

39. The gun is ultimately, aimlessly fired at Sophia's head by a friend whose portrait she attempts, just skimming her temple. Rather than expressing concern for Sophia, Esau is furious that another man enacted his long-cherished fantasy (see also *BM* 114–15).

40. Burke details how, after submitting fine art annually to the Salon from its inception in 1903, Loy was asked "to become a *sociétaire* of the drawing section" in 1906 (*BM* 101). Stephen Haweis contributed similarly, but was not extended the same invitation, and their uneven Salon reception evidently became another flashpoint within an already acrimonious marriage (*BM* 97–104).

41. Via the French sociologists Marcel Mauss and Henri Hubert (both discussed in Chapter 2), Susan L. Mizruchi describes how sacrificial victims were often decked out in false crowns and elaborate dress (80).

42. Forty days after Jesus's birth, Mary and Joseph journey to the temple in Jerusalem to sacrifice two turtledoves or pigeons (Luke 2.24). The Christian symbol of the Holy Spirit, the dove also represents regeneration – hence the dove-shaped cakes or cookies of Christian feast days and rituals, among them Easter and weddings – or peace, as in Loy's World War II poem "Omen of Victory", in which uniformed women observe "a dove's feather / fallen in the sugar" (*LaLB* 214).

43. In "Anglo-Mongrels and the Rose", this extrusion from the stomach is repeated and inverted. Having emanated "spiritual   tentacles of vanity . . . . towards   the culture / of his epoch", Exodus finds no means of attaching himself, nothing with which to make "contact". He therefore retreats "to fumble among his guts" (*LaLB* 119).

44. Cataloguers at the Beinecke Rare Book and Manuscript Library date "Static" at 1944, but Loy writes this number at the end of the text to

indicate a final word count, rather than the year of composition; with similar intent, "1900" appears earlier on the same page. Alongside uneven attempts at page numbering (1–5, 7–8, and, unusually, L, M, N, O), Loy maintained an accumulative and precise word count throughout her most complete draft of "Static". The first page is typed, the remainder handwritten. More than one draft exists of some portions.

A sketch of Loy's poem "The Widow's Jazz" appears in the same notebook. Loy read "The Widow's Jazz" at Natalie Barney's Paris salon in 1927 and published it in 1931. Short portions of "Static" appear elsewhere in Loy's archive (see "Passivia" and "In Maine: Green's Colony"). Like "Hush Money" (c. 1917–22) and "The Three Wishes" (undated; both in *SE*), "Static" is formatted with the use of a centred "+" to indicate narrative breaks.

45. In "Portrait of a Nun" the purity of the subject's starched clothing and diminutive gestures – crossed hands, downward gaze – conceal, first, "a mystic conception" or hidden pregnancy of uncertain parentage and, second, "a cloth coffin" (*LaLB* 260). In "Static", where the legacy of the nuns prevails, white linen will similarly be a sacrificial motif, both as daily domestic task and as shroud.

46. In a later chapter, Loy will recall showing her adolescent friends "a 'study' of the model [she] had first deplored, his ~~pudenda~~ virility crammed into a linen bag" (*IA* 68: 124). The correction here is interesting, as pudenda can refer to any externalised genitalia, but more commonly refers to the vulva. Even as she elicits incredulity and humour from her friends with this portrait, Loy's edit reinforces the masculine prowess of her beleaguered model.

47. American-born, raised in Europe, Sargent exhibited annually at the Paris Salon between 1877 and 1886 before moving to a London residence proximate to Rossetti's former studio (Prettijohn 9, 13, 29). Barring forays into landscape painting and murals, Sargent's oeuvre was defined by portraiture, and critics continue to debate the merits of his emphatic focus on the fashionable and elite; that he was one of the early proponents of French art in England is often forgotten (Farebrother 9, 7). While Sargent insisted that he attended to the surface and not the psychology of his subjects, his portraits are continually interpreted contextually and ideologically (Farebrother 153).

48. In 1910, Loy's drawings were included in a summer exhibition curated by the New English Art Club; Sargent was among its renowned participants (*BM* 126). In 1912, Loy had a one-woman show at London's Carfax Gallery, a space that had previously exhibited Sargent (*BM* 137–8). Whilst in London for her exhibition, Loy attended the bohemian salon of the American socialite Muriel Draper, a friend Loy knew from Florence (*BM* 139). Draper's regular guests included

Sargent, who painted and sketched Muriel's sister-in-law, Ruth Draper, a well-known performer of monologues, and possibly Muriel herself (Watson 94). But Loy's awareness of Sargent may have begun in her adolescence, as the American painter was a well-known supporter of Augustus John, whose reputation dominated London's Slade, the art school that Loy longed to attend (*BM* 45).

49. This fallen dress-strap sparked such vitriol that Sargent allegedly begged the Salon committee for permission to repaint it. His request was denied, presumably to deliver a stern lesson on the risks of aesthetic provocation. Post-Salon, Sargent altered his original depiction (Farebrother 75).

50. The romantic linking of Sargent and Gardner was conducted circuitously. When the portrait was exhibited, a scandal sheet observed that "'Sargent had painted Mrs. Gardner all the way down to Crawford's Notch'" (Hall Tharp 134). Crawford's Notch was a popular local resort, and Crawford was also the surname of a listless, dispossessed author and heir to a fortune, Frank Crawford, with whom Mrs Gardner had "chandeliered" or showily dominated ballrooms through the winter of 1881–2 (Hall Tharp 74, 68). Gardner was said to have been Crawford's inspiration, or to have influenced his first two novels. By becoming Sargent's very public muse, Gardner inadvertently reignited past rumours of illicit affiliation (Hall Tharp 80–1).

    Burgeoning scholarship on Sargent's closeted homosexuality sustains the ever-present likelihood that Gardner and Sargent shared a purely platonic relationship; see, for instance, Alison Syme's wonderful *A Touch of Blossom: John Singer Sargent and the Queer Flora and Fauna of Fin-de-Siècle Art* (2010).

51. As Pollock observes: "The body of the bourgeois woman was disciplined from childhood by both whalebone and convention not to bend"; her rigid costume furthered "the masquerade of a decorporealised femininity." By stark contrast, the working-class woman's uncorseted body moves, yields, and is exposed by the rolled sleeves or short skirts that facilitate labour (*Differencing* 47). Pollock argues that working-class women's torsos stoop beneath or toward material burdens, as in Millet's *Peasant Women with Brushwood* (c. 1858) and Van Gogh's *Peasant Woman Binding Sheaves* (1889).

52. Examples of this precept that Loy may have encountered include Marinetti's "The Pope's Monoplane" (1912), in which the protagonist counsels his belly: "Stomach, my flying stomach / don't be squeamish! / You'll have to pay for your trip with a little nausea". He then advises that the male pilot vomit on the feminised earth by way of managing his anxiety and disorientation (44). Similarly, in an issue of *Others*, a journal in which Loy published, William Carlos Williams's "Belly Music" likens unthinking critics to fearful soldiers: they "prefer the safe belly posture when the shrapnel is bursting." Against the hordes

beholden to their viscera, Williams asserts: "Any man can lead the world if he have the courage, the insight, the brains" (29).

53. Burke discussed Loy's stomach in interviews with her daughter Joella at the end of the 1970s. On 10 February 1978, Joella recalls how Loy "had a strong stomach on bandaging" the wounded in World War I (Bayer, "Interview, Burke and Bayer" 55). In her later years, Loy suffered from gastric ulcers, and on 15–16 December 1979, Joella told Burke that she believed her mother died due to "a stroke to the stomach" (Bayer, "Interview, Burke and Bayer" 28).

54. Susan E. Dunn offers a good reading of these lines by way of the nineteenth-century invention of the man's suit as a bourgeois norm from which Loy's Exodus, as othered Jew, is exempted (104).

55. Virgil Thomson introduced Gertrude Stein's "Lifting Belly" (1915–17) by declaring it "a hymn to the domestic affections" whilst candidly admitting that he did "not know the meaning of the title" (64).

56. Like Loy, Hamnett attended art schools across Europe; at different times, they were both students at the Parisian Académie Colarossi (Hamnett 181). Throughout *Laughing Torso*, Hamnett identifies associates also linked with Loy, among them James Joyce, Nancy Cunard, Jules Pascin, Walter Sickert, and Aleister Crowley. In *Being Geniuses Together: 1920–1930*, Loy's friend and publisher Robert McAlmon describes early 1920s Paris in great detail, and includes Loy and Hamnett within his circles of association (37, 49).

57. According to Hamnett, she and Gaudier-Brzeska were close for a brief period. One evening, Gaudier-Brzeska confessed that the woman he had described as his sister was his mistress; Hamnett notes that she "choked down some sobs" as their dinner calmly resumed (41). Following Gaudier-Brzeska's death in World War I, Hamnett journeys to visit his partner Sophie for a fortnight. At one juncture, the eccentric Sophie shouts up the stairs to Hamnett to ask her if she would have "'gone off with Henri'" had he asked her to do so. Hamnett bellows back in the affirmative, and again, the revelation goes without further discussion (94).

58. As no complete English translation exists, my précis is based on critical quotation and description. The preface, co-authored by Robert and Marinetti, is available in *Futurism: An Anthology* as "**COURAGE + TRUTH**".

59. Laura Scuriatti's linking of Loy and Robert in *Mina Loy's Critical Modernism* surfaced after this chapter was drafted. Serendipitously, Scuriatti's work provides additional evidence for my supposition that these two writers drew upon the experiences of the female reproductive body as an indicator of women's fitness for creative work, effectually reversing the essentialism that excluded both writers from masculinist avant-gardes.

    In this regard, Scuriatti juxtaposes Loy's "Parturition" (1914) with Robert's *Un ventre di donna* (1919). By this comparison, Loy leans toward the generative, integrative aspects of female reproductivity, Robert to what Scuriatti calls the "castration" that "forever maims her possibility to become a mother" (49).

By contrast, this chapter argues that Loy focuses widely and repeatedly on the torso and its abortive or uncanny capacities in a sustained critique of the presumptions about the ease of female regeneration, and with a view to recognising the hidden depths and repressions of women's creative impulses that emerge for models and artists alike.

60. For the observation that the dash is akin to an umbilical cord, I am indebted to a student in Maud Ellman's seminar on reading Freud and visual culture that took place at the University of Chicago, 30 October 2018.

61. Darwin attributes the incongruities to the way that gemmules – his term for free-floating reproductive cells – "unit[e] with wrong cells or aggregates of cells during their nascent state" (*Variation* I 391).

62. Freud foregrounds the narrative impulse in "The Aetiology of Hysteria", asserting: "*no hysterical symptoms arise from a real experience alone*" (197). In his famous study of Dora, Freud repeatedly insists that his patient adopts dissembling poses, learning, for instance, how strategically useful it can be to claim illness or feign forgetfulness ("Fragment" 38, 57).

Via Juliet Mitchell, Bronfen more sympathetically describes "the hysteric as a creative artist of sorts, telling tales and fabricating stories, 'particularly for doctors who will listen'" (*Knotted* 332).

63. The paternal authority of Lawrence's phallic eye/I is further undermined by long-standing associations between eyes and women's sexualised anatomy. Pollock argues that, in art, the eye is often believed suggestive of female genitalia (*Vision* 185). Citing Magritte's *Rape* (1934) as evidence, David M. Lubin writes of the likeness shared by breasts and eyes, noting: "The metaphor suggests itself naturally, given the geometric similarities: dark rounded forms concentrated in the centre of substantially lighter rounded forms" (34).

64. "Plenitude" is difficult to decipher.

65. That Loy perceives the midriff as maternal terrain is underscored by her recollection of starving in Mexico and hearing her mother's voice "recriminat[ing]" her for "[e]very remnant of edible matter . . . ever left on a plate, every dreg in the bottom of a bowl" (*EP* 24).

66. In *Esau Penfold*, Loy conflates Esau and Sophia's father with mastery. Gazing at Geronimo, Sophia states that "[i]n obedience to ~~my father~~, the master" she felt she "should challenge this . . . fellow" (*EP* 23). Similarly, Esau is said to have "found [Sophia] ripe for the imprint of his peculiar mastership" (*EP* 24).

67. The infamous footnote arises in the postscript to "Fragment of an Analysis of a Case of Hysteria", written four years after the text was first drafted. In it, Freud admits that he "failed to discover . . . that

[Dora's] homosexual (gynaeocophilic) love for Frau K. was the strongest unconscious current in her mental life" (120).

68. See "'The Instigatory Caress': Satire and Intimacy" in Chapter 2 of this volume.

69. False pregnancy is a noted outcome of "the [hysterical] conversion of unconscious sexual desire into physical symptoms" (Jacobus 29).

70. Burke maintains that Loy's story "Hush Money", which she expressly asked Freud to read, is about a dying father, a powerful mother, and a son who is a thinly disguised Loy (*BM* 248, 313). If Burke is correct, Loy may have reversed sexual ascriptions on more than one occasion in a bid to rewrite the Oedipal narrative. Loy's complex relationship to psychoanalysis is discussed in Chapter 1 of this volume of *An Anatomy of Mina Loy* and is an express focus in Chapters 1 and 2 of the second volume.

71. Loy's redetermining of bodily organs and function has precedent in Futurist and Dada writings. In "Extended Man and the Kingdom of the Machine" (1910) Marinetti advocates turning the heart into the "stomach of the brain" so that it can be "fed systematically [and] the spirit can embark on action" (87). Similarly, in 1914, Arthur Cravan avers that "genius is nothing more than an extraordinary manifestation of the body" (7).

72. On this front, Loy may have taken inspiration from D. H. Lawrence, who wrote numerous tracts delineating a human consciousness that originates in the belly and the solar plexus, insisting that "[m]ental activity, final cognition, ideation, is only set up secondarily from the perfect interaction and inter-communication of the primary affective centres, which remain all the time our dynamic first-minds" ("Education" 620).

73. Loy's "The Outraged Womb" furthers her links to Enif Robert's aforementioned *Un Ventre di donna*, which includes a chapter entitled "The Struggle of Women's Wombs". Here "the female protagonist mentally strips female passersby and elaborates a feminine typology in the form of a classification of wombs: the hysterical womb of the *passéiste* intellectual, the tired womb of the matron, and the happy womb of the beautiful figurine" (Sartini Blum 116–17).

74. Loy's racial referencing exposes her susceptibility to nineteenth-century mores by which "[t]he female reproductive system came to be seen as a sacred trust, so delicate and temperamental that a woman must constantly work to preserve it in the interest of the race" (Stage 463). See also the consideration of Loy and primitivism in Chapter 1 of this volume. Loy's relationship to the racialisations of Theosophy is addressed in Chapter 3 of *Elevated Realms*.

Loy manages to personalise her offensive uses of the "womb-brain" in her archived tract "Promised Land" (1937). Describing the discomfort of living with her daughter Joella (named Alda) as she divorced from Julien Levy (Aaron), Loy writes that at one emotional juncture, Joella insisted that when Loy had initially proposed their marriage, Joella "'wept for hours on [Loy's] neck <u>begging</u> [her] not to let me marry <u>that man</u>!'" In a particularly distasteful resistance to what she will later in the same tract describe as Joella's "lie" or "feint", Loy writes:

> Alda's bolts from the blue always gave me a strange sensation of the brain in my cranium being about to burst with sanity: the while the womb-brain writhed in the treachery of a belated afterbirth. Monstrously this afterbirth flounced out of the room. ("Promised Land")

Loy is wholly dependent on Joella at this juncture, both emotionally and financially. As discussed in this chapter, she has a remarkable capacity to romanticise and portraitise Joella when she considers her inherited good looks and learned docility (see "Alda's Beauty"). But when confronted with Joella's uncomfortable recollection, Loy adopts and contorts the paternalistic terms of Victorian hysteria discourse, proclaiming herself as the ultimate rational being whose womb-brain is unjustly in thrall to its own horrifically abjectified creation.

75. As is evinced by "Anglo-Mongrels and the Rose" (1923–5), Loy can favour Hebraism over Christianity, a heritage she shares with Freud. But Loy's customary ambivalence toward psychoanalysis recurs in this chapter: after praising Freud, Loy states that she is interested in the "prenatal cavern of his theory" from which emerges "an intelligible voice" that mercifully supersedes the "throng of neurotic minnikins" we anticipate issuing from Freud's mouth (*CP* 19: 1).

76. As Tim Armstrong argues with reference to "Auto-Facial Construction" (1919), Loy "invents her own bodily reform movement, but stresses the element of performance and self-commodification in her technique . . . introducing *décor* into physical culture" (129).

77. My phrase "the bad-enough mother" reworks the well-known formulation of "the good-enough mother" first conceived by the British paediatrician and psychoanalyst D. W. Winnicott (1896–1971).

    The maternal imaginary has a secure purchase even in contemporary criticism on *les poètes maudits*, as when Richard D. E. Burton unquestioningly accepts Baudelaire's hyperbolic assertion that his "whole life" could be framed "in terms of maternal rejection and vilification" (2).

78. The letter from Joella begs Loy for more money on the grounds that prices have escalated since Loy resided in Florence (Bayer, "Letter dated 18 July 1921"). In an interview with Carolyn Burke on 10 February 1978, Joella described receiving no money from Stephen Haweis after he left the family, first for New York, and then, in or around 1914, for the Bahamas (Bayer, "Interview, Burke and Bayer" 56; *BM* 189).

Bibliography

Adamson, Natalie, and Toby Norris. "Introduction." *Academics, Pompiers, Official Artists and the Arrière-Garde: Defining Modern and Traditional in France, 1900–1960*, edited by Natalie Adamson and Toby Norris, Cambridge Scholars Publishing, 2009, pp. 1–24.

Adorno, Theodor W., and Sherry Weber Nicholsen. "Punctuation Marks." *The Antioch Review*, vol. 48, no. 3, 1990, pp. 300–5.

Ahmed, Sara. *The Cultural Politics of Emotion*. Edinburgh UP, 2004.

—. *Living a Feminist Life*. Duke UP, 2017.

—. *The Promise of Happiness*. Duke UP, 2010.

Aiken, Conrad. 1914. "Emily Dickinson." *Emily Dickinson: A Collection of Critical Essays*, edited by Richard B. Sewell, Prentice Hall, 1963, pp. 9–15.

—. *Scepticisms: Notes on Contemporary Poetry*. Alfred A. Knopf, 1967.

Alaimo, Stacy. "Trans-Corporeal Feminisms and the Ethical Space of Nature." *Material Feminisms*, edited by Stacy Alaimo and Susan Hekman, Indiana UP, 2008, pp. 237–64.

Alcoff, Linda Martín. *Visible Identities: Race, Gender, and the Self*. Oxford UP, 2006.

Alliker Rabb, Melinda. *Satire and Secrecy in English Literature from 1650 to 1750*. Palgrave Macmillan, 2007.

Altieri, Charles. "Avant-Garde or Arriere-Garde in Recent Contemporary Poetry." *Poetics Today*, vol. 20, no. 4, 1999, pp. 629–53.

Argyle, Michael. *Bodily Communication*. 2nd ed., Routledge, 2007.

Armstrong, Tim. *Modernism, Technology, and the Body: A Cultural Study*. Cambridge UP, 1998.

Arnould, Elisabeth. "The Impossible Sacrifice of Poetry: Bataille and the Nancian Critique of Sacrifice." *Diacritics*, vol. 26, no. 2, 1996, pp. 86–96.

Artaud, Antonin. "Van Gogh: The Suicide Provoked by Society." *Horizon*, vol. 17, no. 97, 1948, pp. 46–50.

Baker Eddy, Mary. 1891, 1892. *Retrospection and Introspection*. First Church of Christ, Scientist, Project Gutenberg, www.gutenberg.org/files/16734/16734-h/16734-h.htm.

—. 1875. *Science and Health with Key to the Scriptures*. Boston, MA: Trustees under the Will of Mary Baker Eddy, 1934.

Bakhtin, Mikhail. *Rabelais and his World*. Translated by Hélène Iswolsky, Indiana UP, 2009.

Ball, Hugo. 1914–21. *Flight Out of Time*. Translated by Ann Raimes, edited by John Elderfield. The Documents of 20th-Century Art, edited by Robert Motherwell et al., Viking Press, 1974.

Barnes, Djuna. 1927. "Dusie." *Americana Esoterica*, introduced by Carl van Doren, Macy-Masius, 1927, pp. 75–82.

—. 1928. *Ladies Almanack*. Dalkey Archive Press, 1992.

—. "The Models Have Come to Town." *Charm*, vol. 2, no. 4, 1924, pp. 16, 91–2. YCAL MSS 778, Box 5, Folder "*Charm* [undated]." Carolyn Burke Collection on Mina Loy and Lee Miller. Beinecke Rare Book and Manuscript Library, Yale University, CT, USA.

Bartram, Alan. *Futurist Typography and the Liberated Text*. Yale UP, 2006.

Bataille, Georges. 1949. *The Accursed Share: An Essay on General Economy*. Vol. 1. translated by Robert Hurley, Zone Books, 1991.

—. 1949. *The Accursed Share: An Essay on General Economy*. Vols 2 and 3, translated by Robert Hurley, Zone Books, 1993.

—. 1929. "The Big Toe." *Visions of Excess: Selected Writings, 1927–1939*, translated by Alan Stoekl et al., edited by Alan Stoekl, U of Minnesota P, 1985, pp. 20–3.

—. 1957. *Erotism: Death and Sensuality*. Translated by Mary Dalwood, City Lights Books, 1986.

—. 1944. *Guilty*. Translated and introduced by Stuart Kendall, State U of New York P, 2011.

—. "Hegel, Death and Sacrifice." *Yale French Studies*, translated by Jonathan Strauss, vol. 78, 1990, pp. 9–28.

—. 1962. *The Impossible*. Translated by Robert Hurley, City Lights Books, 1991.

—. 1930. "The Jesuve." *Visions of Excess: Selected Writings, 1927–1939*, translated by Alan Stoekl et al., edited by Alan Stoekl, U of Minnesota P, 1985, pp. 73–8.

—. 1954. "Laughter." *The Bataille Reader*, edited by Fred Botting and Scott Wilson. Blackwell Publishers, 1997, pp. 59–63.

—. 1957. *Literature and Evil*. Translated by Alastair Hamilton, Penguin, 2012.

—. 1956. "Madame Edwarda." *My Mother, Madame Edwarda, the Dead Man*, translated by Austryn Wainhouse, Penguin Books, 2012, pp. 121–44.

—. c. 1930. "The Pineal Eye." *Visions of Excess: Selected Writings, 1927–1939*, translated by Alan Stoekl et al., edited by Alan Stoekl, U of Minnesota P, 1985, pp. 79–90.

—. "Sacrifice." *October*, translated by Annette Michelson, vol. 36, spring 1986, pp. 61–74.

—. 1930. "Sacrificial Mutilation and the Severed Ear of Vincent Van Gogh." *Visions of Excess: Selected Writings, 1927–1939*, translated by Alan Stoekl et al., edited by Alan Stoekl, U of Minnesota P, 1985, pp. 61–72.

—. 1931. "The Solar Anus." *Visions of Excess: Selected Writings, 1927–1939*, translated by Alan Stoekl et al., edited by Alan Stoekl, U of Minnesota P, 1985, pp. 5–9.

—. 1961. *The Tears of Eros*. Translated by Peter Connor, City Lights Books, 1989.

—. 1973. *Theory of Religion*. Translated by Robert Hurley, Zone Books, 1989.

—. "The Torment." *The Bataille Reader*, edited by Fred Botting and Scott Wilson. Blackwell Publishers, 1997, pp. 64–91.

—. 1929/30. "The Use Value of D. A. F. de Sade (An Open Letter to my Current Comrades)." *Visions of Excess: Selected Writings, 1927–1939*, translated by Alan Stoekl et al., edited by Alan Stoekl, U of Minnesota P, 1985, pp. 91–102.

Baudelaire, Charles. 1856. "Edgar Allen Poe: His Life and Works." *The Painter of Modern Life and Other Essays*, translated and edited by Jonathan Mayne, Phaidon Press, 1995, pp. 70–92.

—. 1857. *The Flowers of Evil*. Translated and edited by James McGowan, introduced by Jonathan Culler, Oxford UP, 1998.

—. 1863. "The Painter of Modern Life." *The Painter of Modern Life and Other Essays*, translated and edited by Jonathan Mayne, Phaidon Press, 1995, pp. 1–42.

Bayer, Joella. 1926–36. "Bayer, Joella to Mina Loy, 1926–1936". YCAL MSS 778, Box 1, Alphabetized Folder, Carolyn Burke Collection on Mina Loy and Lee Miller. Beinecke Rare Book and Manuscript Library, Yale University, CT, USA.

—. n.d. "Interview, Burke and Bayer." YCAL MSS 778, Box 2, Folder "Transcripts, 1978–1981, 1989." Carolyn Burke Collection on Mina Loy and Lee Miller. Beinecke Rare Book and Manuscript Library, Yale University, CT, USA.

—. 1921. "Letter dated 18 July 1921." YCAL MSS 778, Box 3, Folder "Family, 1911–1949." Carolyn Burke Collection on Mina Loy and Lee Miller. Beinecke Rare Book and Manuscript Library, Yale University, CT, USA.

—. n.d. "Letter dated Monday 18th." YCAL MSS 778, Box 1, Folder ""Bayer, Joella to Mina Loy and Fabienne Loy [*sic*], 1917–1948". Carolyn Burke Collection on Mina Loy and Lee Miller. Beinecke Rare Book and Manuscript Library, Yale University, CT, USA.

Beauchamp, Tamara. *Enemies of the Unconscious: Modernist Resistances to Psychoanalysis*. 2014. U of California, Irvine, PhD dissertation. *eScholarship*, escholarship.org/uc/item/50m6k9xw.

Bell, Michael. *Sentimentalism, Ethics, and the Culture of Feeling*. Palgrave, 2009.

Benjamin, Walter. 1928. "One-Way Street." *Walter Benjamin: Selected Writings*, vol. 1: *1913–1926*, translated by Edmund Jephcott, edited by

Marcus Bullock and Michael W. Jennings, Belknap Press of Harvard UP, 1996, pp. 444–88.

—. 1921. "The Task of the Translator." *Walter Benjamin: Selected Writings*, vol. 1: *1913–1926*, translated by Edmund Jephcott, edited by Marcus Bullock and Michael W. Jennings, Belknap Press of Harvard UP, 1996, pp. 253–63.

Berghaus, Günter. "The Foundation of Futurism 1909." *F. T. Marinetti, Critical Writings*, translated by Doug Thomson, edited by Günter Berghaus, Farrar, Straus, and Giroux, 2006, pp. 9–10.

Bergson, Henri. 1907. *Creative Evolution: An Alternate Explanation for Darwin's Mechanism of Evolution*. Translated by Arthur Mitchell, CreateSpace, 2014.

Berlant, Lauren. *The Female Complaint: The Unfinished Business of Sentimentality in American Culture*. Duke UP, 2008.

—. "Intimacy: A Special Issue." *Intimacy*, edited by Lauren Berlant, Chicago UP, 2000, pp. 1–8.

Bernstein, Elizabeth. *Temporarily Yours: Intimacy, Authenticity, and the Commerce of Sex*. U of Chicago P, 2001.

Bersani, Leo. "Is the Rectum a Grave?" *October*, vol. 43, Winter 1987, pp. 197–222.

Biles, Jeremy. *Ecce Monstrum: Georges Bataille and the Sacrifice of Form*. Fordham UP, 2007.

Birke, Lynda. *Feminism and the Biological Body*. Edinburgh UP, 1999.

Bishop, Ryan, and John Phillips. *Modernist Avant-Garde Aesthetics and Contemporary Military Technology: Technicities of Perception*. Edinburgh UP, 2010.

Blanchard, W. Scott. "Renaissance Prose Satire: Italy and England." *A Companion to Satire: Ancient and Modern*, edited by Ruben Quintero, Wiley-Blackwell, 2011, pp. 118–36.

Bland, Lucy. *Banishing the Beast: Feminism, Sex, and Morality*. Tauris Parke Paperbacks, 2001.

Blau Duplessis, Rachel. "'Seismic Orgasm': Sexual Intercourse and Narrative Meaning in Mina Loy." *Mina Loy: Woman and Poet*, edited by Maeera Shreiber and Keith Tuma, National Poetry Foundation, 1998, pp. 45–85.

Borzello, Frances. *The Artist's Model*. London: Junction Books, 1982.

Bramley, Ellie Violet. "Desire Paths: The Illicit Paths That Defy the Urban Planners." *The Guardian*, 5 October 2018, www.theguardian.com/cities/2018/oct/05/desire-paths-the-illicit-trails-that-defy-the-urban-planners.

Brennan, Teresa. *The Transmission of Affect*. Cornell UP, 2004.

Bronfen, Elizabeth. *The Knotted Subject: Hysteria and its Discontents*. Princeton UP, 1998.

—. *Over her Dead Body: Death, Femininity, and the Aesthetic*. Manchester UP, 1992.

Bronstein, Hilda. "'Intermittent — Unfinishing': Mina Loy and the Elusive Text as Resistance." *How2*, vol. 1, no. 5, 2001, n.p., www.asu.edu/pipercwcenter/how2journal/archive/online_archive/v1_5_2001/current/in-conference/mina-loy/bronstein.html#back24.

Brooke-Rose, Christine. "Woman as a Semiotic Object." *Poetics Today*, vol. 6, nos. 1/2, 1985, pp. 9–20.

Brown, Bob. *You Gotta Live*. Desmond Harmsworth, 1932.

Brown, Richard. *James Joyce and Sexuality*. Cambridge UP, 1985.

Browne, Janet. "Darwin in Caricature: A Study in the Popularisation and Dissemination of Evolution." *Proceedings of the American Philosophical Society*, vol. 145, no. 4, 2001, pp. 496–509.

Buchanan, Robert. 1866–70. "Artist and Model: A Love Poem." *The Pre-Raphaelites: Writing and Sources*, vol. 1, edited by Inga Bryden, Routledge, 1998, pp. 294–8.

—. 1864. "Pygmalion the Sculptor." *The Pre-Raphaelites: Writing and Sources*, vol. 1, edited by Inga Bryden, Routledge, 1998, pp. 299–309.

Buffet-Picabia, Gabrielle. 1938. "Arthur Cravan and American Dada." *The Dada Painters and Poets: An Anthology*, edited by Robert Motherwell, Wittenborn, Schultz, 1951, pp. 13–17.

Burch, Francis F. "Paul Verlaine's *Les Poètes Maudits:* The Dating of the Essays and the Origin of the Title." *Modern Language Notes*, vol. 76, no. 8, 1961, pp. 752–3.

Burke, Carolyn. *Becoming Modern: The Life of Mina Loy*. Farrar, Straus, and Giroux, 1996.

—. 1978. "Interview with Joella Bayer, February 10, 1978." YCAL MSS 778, Box 2, Folder 1: "Transcripts, 1978–1981, 1989." Carolyn Burke Collection on Mina Loy and Lee Miller. Beinecke Rare Book and Manuscript Library, Yale University, CT, USA.

—. "Introduction by Carolyn Burke for Mina Loy: Interview with Paul Blackburn and Robert Vas Dias." *Mina Loy: Woman and Poet*, edited by Maaera Shreiber and Keith Tuma, National Poetry Foundation, 1998, pp. 205–9.

—. n.d. "Loy, Mina: Lampshades." YCAL MSS 778, Box 6, Carolyn Burke Collection on Mina Loy and Lee Miller. Beinecke Rare Book and Manuscript Library, Yale University, CT, USA.

—. "Notes by Carolyn Burke, 1978–1981, 1989." YCAL MSS 778, Box 2, Carolyn Burke Collection on Mina Loy and Lee Miller. Beinecke Rare Book and Manuscript Library, Yale University, CT, USA.

—. c. 1978. "Paris in the 1920s." YCAL MSS 778, Box 6, Carolyn Burke Collection on Mina Loy and Lee Miller. Beinecke Rare Book and Manuscript Library, Yale University, CT, USA.

—. "Supposed Persons: Modernist Poetry and the Female Subject." *Feminist Studies*, vol. 11, no. 1, 1985, pp. 131–48.

Burstein, Jessica. *Cold Modernism: Literature, Fashion, Art*. Pennsylvania State UP, 2012.

Burton, Richard D. E. *Baudelaire in 1859: A Study in the Sources of Poetic Creativity*. Cambridge UP, 1988.

Burton, Robert. 1651. *The Anatomy of Melancholy*. Edited by Holbrook Jackson, New York Review of Books, 2001.

Burwick, Fred, and Paul Douglass. "Introduction." *The Crisis in Modernism: Bergson and the Vitalist Controversy*, edited by Frederick Burwick and Paul Douglass, Cambridge UP, 1992, pp. 1–14.

Butler, Judith. 1990. *Gender Trouble: Feminism and the Subversion of Identity*. Routledge, 2007.

Butler, Marylin. "Satire and the Images of Self in the Romantic Period: The Long Tradition of Hazlitt's *Liber Amoris*." *English Satire and the Satiric Tradition*, edited by Claude Rawson, Basil Blackwell, 1984, pp. 209–25.

Carlyle, Thomas. 1833–4. *Sartor Resartus*. Edited by Kerry McSweeney and Peter Sabor, Oxford UP, 2008.

Caselli, Daniela. "Novitiates, Saints and Priestesses: The Unreadable Pleasures of *Ladies Almanack*." *Textual Practice*, vol. 20, no. 3, 2006, pp. 463–89.

Caws, Mary Ann. "Joseph Cornell as Seen by Others." *Joseph Cornell's Theatre of the Mind: Selected Diaries, Letters, and Files*, edited by Mary Ann Caws. Thames and Hudson, 1993, pp. 21–7.

Cervantes, Miguel de. 1605. *Don Quixote*. Translated by Charles Jarvis, edited by E. C. Riley, Oxford UP, 1991.

Chesterton, G. K. 1910. "The Sentimentalist." *Alarms and Discursions*. Methuen and Co., 1924, pp. 124–7.

Chrisler, J. C., and I. Johnson-Robledo. *Women's Embodied Self: Feminist Perspectives on Identity and Image*. American Psychological Association, 2018.

Clark, Suzanne. *Sentimental Modernism: Women Writers and the Revolution of the Word*. Indiana UP, 1991.

Clark, T. J. *The Painter of Modern Life: Paris in the Art of Manet and his Followers*. Princeton UP, 1999.

—. "Preliminaries to a Possible Treatment of 'Olympia in 1865.'" *Screen*, vol. 21, no. 1, 1980, pp. 18–42.

Cokal, Susan. "Wounds, Ruptures, and Sudden Space in the Fiction of Georges Bataille." *French Forum*, vol. 25, no. 1, 2000, pp. 75–96.

Colebrook, Claire. "The Joys of Atavism." *Understanding Bergson, Understanding Modernism*, edited by Paul Ardoin, S. E. Gontarski, and Laci Mattison, Bloomsbury Publishing, 2013, pp. 282–96.

—. "Queer Vitalism." *New Formations*, vol. 68, 2009, pp. 77–92.

Conover, Roger. 1982. "Introduction." *The Last Lunar Baedeker*, by Mina Loy, edited by Roger Conover, Carcanet, 1985, pp. xv–lxxix.

—. 1996. "Introduction." *The Lost Lunar Baedeker*, by Mina Loy, edited by Roger Conover, Carcanet, 1997, pp. xi–xx.

—. "(Re)Introducing Mina Loy." *Mina Loy: Woman and Poet*, edited by Maaera Shreiber and Keith Tuma, National Poetry Foundation, 1998, pp. 245–59.

Corbin, Alain. *Women for Hire: Prostitution and Sexuality in France after 1850*. Translated by Alan Sheridan, Harvard UP, 1990.

Cornell, Joseph. *Joseph Cornell's Theatre of the Mind: Selected Diaries, Letters, and Files*. Edited by Mary Ann Caws. Thames and Hudson, 1993.

Crangle, Sara. "Feminism's Archives: Mina Loy, Anna Mendelssohn, and Taxonomy." *The New Modernist Studies*, edited by Douglas Mao, Cambridge UP, 2021, pp. 246–77.

—. "Mina Loy." *A History of Modernist Poetry*, edited by Lee M. Jenkins and Alex Davis, Cambridge UP, 2015, pp. 275–302.

—. "Phenomenology and Affect: Modernist Sulking", *Handbook of Modernism Studies*, edited by Jean-Michel Rabate, Blackwell, 2013, pp. 323–42.

—. *Prosaic Desires: Modernist Knowledge, Boredom, Laughter, and Anticipation*. Edinburgh UP, 2010.

Cravan, Arthur. 1914. "Exhibition at the Independents." *The Dada Painters and Poets: An Anthology*, edited by Robert Motherwell, Wittenborn, Schultz, Inc., 1989, pp. 3–12.

Crowley, Aleister. 1969. *The Confessions of Aleister Crowley: An Autohagiography*. Edited by John Symonds and Kenneth Grant, Routledge and Kegan Paul, 1979.

D'Ambrosio, Matteo. "Notes on 'Esoteric Futurism': Marinetti and the Occultist Circle in Milan." *International Yearbook of Futurism Studies*, vol. 8, 2018, pp. 294–324.

D'Annunzio, Gabriel. 1889. *Pleasure*. Translated by Lara Gochin Raffaelli, Penguin Books, 2013.

Darío, Rubén. 1896. "Rachilde." *Selected Writings of Rubén Darío*, translated by Andrew Hurley et al., edited by Ilan Stavans, Penguin Books, 2005, pp. 424–9.

Darwin, Charles. 1871. *The Descent of Man, and Selection in Relation to Sex*. Princeton UP, 1981.

—. 1872. *The Expression of the Emotions in Man and Animals*. Edited by Paul Ekman, Oxford UP, 1998.

—. 1859. *On the Origin of Species*. Edited by Gillian Beer, Oxford UP, 2008.

—. 1868. *The Variation of Animals and Plants under Domestication*. Vol. 1, Cambridge UP, 2010. https://doi.org/10.1017/CBO9780511709500.

—. 1868. *The Variation of Animals and Plants under Domestication*. Vol. 2, Cambridge UP, 2011. https://doi-org/10.1017/CBO97805117 09517.

Das, Santanu. *Touch and Intimacy in First World War Literature*. Cambridge UP, 2006.

"Death of Sir Francis Jeune." *New Zealand Herald*, vol. 42, no. 12871, 20 May 1905, Papers Past (National Library of New Zealand), paperspast.natlib.govt.nz/newspapers/NZH19050520.2.84.14.

Denham, Kamilla. "Emily Dickinson's Volcanic Punctuation." *The Emily Dickinson Journal*, vol. 2, no. 1, 1993, pp. 22–46.

Derrida, Jacques. "*Différance.*" *Margins of Philosophy*. Translated by Alan Bass, Harvester Wheatsheaf, 1982, pp. 1–28.

—. *The Gift of Death*. Translated by David Wills, U of Chicago P, 1992.

—. *The Margins of Philosophy*. Translated by Alan Bass, Chicago UP, 1982.

DeVere Brody, Jennifer. *Punctuation: Art, Politics, Play*. Duke University Press, 2008.

Dickinson, Emily. *The Complete Poems of Emily Dickinson*. Edited by Thomas H. Johnson, Back Bay Books, 1976.

Dickson, Jay. "Defining the Sentimentalist in *Ulysses*." *James Joyce Quarterly*, vol. 44, no. 1, 2006, pp. 19–37.

Dodge Luhan, Mabel. *Movers and Shakers*, vol. 3: *Intimate Memories*. Harcourt Brace and Co., 1936.

Douglass, Paul. "Bergson, Vitalism, and Modernist Literature." *Understanding Bergson, Understanding Modernism*, edited by S. E. Gontarski, Bloomsbury Publishing, 2013, pp. 107–27.

Dryden, John. 1693. *Discourses on Satire and on Epic Poetry*. Tredition Classics, 2012.

Dunn, Susan E. "Fashion Victims: Mina Loy's Travesties." *Stanford Humanities Review*, vol. 7, no. 1, 1999, pp. 101–17.

Durkheim, Emile. 1912. *The Elementary Forms of the Religious Life*. Translated by Joseph Ward Swain, George Allen Unwin, 1971.

Dyer, Gary. *British Satire and the Politics of Style, 1789–1832*. Cambridge UP, 1997.

Eagleton, Terry. *The Event of Literature*. Yale UP, 2012.

—. "Foreword: Modernism, Time and History." *Historical Modernisms: Time, History and Modernist Aesthetics*, edited by Jean-Michel Rabaté and Angeliki Spiropoulou, Bloomsbury Publishing, 2021, pp. xix–xxvii.

—. *How to Read Literature*. Yale UP, 2013.

Eisenstein, Sergei. 1935. "Film Form: New Problems." *Film Form: Essays in Film Theory*, by Sergei Eisenstein, translated and edited by Jay Leyda, Harcourt Brace, 1977, pp. 122–49.

Eliot, T. S. 1949. "The Cocktail Party." *The Complete Plays of T. S. Eliot*. Harcourt Brace and World, 1967, pp. 123–213.

—. *Collected Poems, 1909–1962*. London: Faber and Faber, 1963.

—. "Observations." *The Egoist*, vol. 5, no. 5, 1918, pp. 69–70.

—. 1919. "Tradition and the Individual Talent." *The Sacred Wood: Essays on Poetry and Criticism*, Methuen, 1960, pp. 47–59.

Elkin, P. K. *The Augustan Defence of Satire*. Clarendon Press, 1973.

Elliott, Robert C. *The Power of Satire: Magic, Ritual, Art*. Princeton UP, 1960.

Ellis, Havelock. 1894. *Man and Woman: A Study of Human Secondary Sexual Characters*. A. & C. Black, 1930.

—. 1897–1928. *Studies in the Psychology of Sex*. Vols 1–4, Random House, 1936.

Ellmann, Maud. "More Kicks Than Pricks: Modernist Body-Parts." *A Handbook of Modernism Studies*, edited by Jean-Michel Rabaté, Wiley-Blackwell, 2013, pp. 255–80.

Ellmann, Richard. *James Joyce*. Oxford UP, 1983.

Engell, James. "Satiric Spirits of the Later Eighteenth Century: Johnson to Crabbe." *Companion to Satire Ancient and Modern*, edited by Rubin Quintero, Blackwell Publishing, 2011, pp. 233–56.

Engels, Friedrich. 1842–4. *The Condition of the Working Class in England*. Oxford UP, 1993.

Esbester, Mike. "Nineteenth-Century Timetables and the History of Reading", *Book History*, vol. 12, no. 1, 2009, pp. 156–85.

Everett, Barbara. "The New Style of *Sweeney Agonistes*." *English Satire and the Satiric Tradition*, edited by Claude Rawson, Basil Blackwell, 1984, pp. 243–63.

Farebrother, Trever. *John Singer Sargent: The Sensualist*. Yale UP, 2000.

Feinstein, Amy. "Goy Interrupted: Mina Loy's Unfinished Novel and Mongrel Jewish Fiction." *Modern Fiction Studies*, vol. 51, no. 2, 2005, pp. 335–53.

Felski, Rita. *The Gender of Modernity*. Harvard UP, 1995.

Fields, Kenneth. "The Poetry of Mina Loy." *The Southern Review*, vol. 3, 1967, pp. 597–607.

Foster, Hal. "'Primitive' Scenes." *Critical Inquiry*, vol. 20, no. 1, 1993, pp. 69–102.

—. "The 'Primitive' Unconscious of Modern Art." *October*, vol. 34, 1985, pp. 45–70.

Foucault, Michel. *The Care of the Self*, vol. 3: *The History of Sexuality*. Translated by Robert Hurley, Penguin, 1988.

Frazer, James. *The Golden Bough: A Study in Magic and Religion*. Wordsworth Editions, 1993.

Freud, Sigmund. 1896. "The Aetiology of Hysteria." *Early Psychoanalytic Publications*, The Standard Edition of the Complete Psychological Works of Sigmund Freud, vol. 3, translated and edited by James Strachey and Anna Freud, Hogarth Press, 1962, pp. 191–221.

—. 1908. "Character and Anal Erotism." *The Standard Edition of the Complete Psychological Works of Sigmund Freud*, vol. 9, translated and edited by James Strachey et al., Hogarth Press, 1959, pp. 169–75.

—. 1905/1901. "Fragment of an Analysis of a Case of Hysteria." *A Case of Hysteria: Three Essays on Sexuality and Other Works*, The Standard Edition of the Complete Psychological Works of Sigmund

Freud, vol. 7, translated and edited by James Strachey et al., Vintage Books, 2001, pp. 3–124.

—. 1914/18. "From the History of an Infantile Neurosis." *The Standard Edition of the Complete Psychological Works of Sigmund Freud*, vol. 17, translated and edited by James Strachey et al., Hogarth Press, 1957, pp. 3–123.

—. 1917. "On Transformations of Instinct as Exemplified in Anal Erotism." *The Standard Edition of the Complete Psychological Works of Sigmund Freud*, vol. 17, translated and edited by James Strachey et al., Hogarth Press, 1957, pp. 127–33.

—. 1905. "Three Essays on the Theory of Sexuality." *A Case of Hysteria: Three Essays on Sexuality and Other Works*, The Standard Edition of the Complete Psychological Works of Sigmund Freud, vol. 7, translated and edited by James Strachey et al., Vintage Books, 2001, pp. 125–247.

—. 1913–14. "Totem and Taboo." *Totem and Taboo and Other Works*, vol. 13, translated and edited by James Strachey et al., The Standard Edition of the Complete Psychological Works of Sigmund Freud, Vintage Books, 2001, pp. 1–162.

Frost, Elisabeth A. *The Feminist Avant-Garde in American Poetry*. U of Iowa P, 2003.

—. "Mina Loy's 'Mongrel' Poetics." *Mina Loy: Woman and Poet*, edited by Maeera Shreiber and Keith Tuma, National Poetry Foundation, 1998, pp. 149–80.

Frye, Northrup. *Anatomy of Criticism: Four Essays*. Princeton UP, 1957.

Furman, A. "Desire Lines: Determining Pathways through the City." *The Sustainable City VII: Urban Regeneration and Sustainability*. Vol. 1, edited by M. Pacetti et al., WIT Press, 2012, pp. 23–33.

Gaedtke, Andrew. "From Transmissions of Madness to Machines of Writing: Mina Loy's *Insel* as Clinical Fantasy." *Journal of Modern Literature*, vol. 32, no. 1, 2008, pp. 143–62.

Galvin, Mary E. *Queer Poetics: Five Modernist Women Writers*. Greenwood Press, 1999.

Gammel, Irene. *Baroness Elsa: Gender, Dada, and Everyday Modernity: A Cultural Biography*. MIT Press, 2003.

Garland-Thomson, Rosemarie. *Extraordinary Bodies: Figuring Physical Disability in American Culture and Literature*. Columbia UP, 1997.

Garstad, Benjamin. "The Tyche Sacrifices in John Malalas: Virgin Sacrifice and Fourth-Century Polemical History." *Illinois Classical Studies*, vol. 30, 2005, pp. 83–135.

Gendlin, Eugene T. "The Primacy of the Body, Not the Primacy of Perception." *Man and World*, vol. 25, nos 3–4, 1992, pp. 341–53. *Gendlin Online Library*, previous.focusing.org/gendlin/docs/gol_2162.html.

—. "Three Assertions about the Body." *The Folio*, vol. 12, no. 1, 1993, pp. 21–33. *Gendlin Online Library*, previous.focusing.org/gendlin/docs/gol_2064.html.

—. "The Wider Role of Bodily Sense in Thought and Language." *Giving the Body its Due*, edited by M. Sheets-Johnstone, SUNY Press, 1992, pp. 192–207. *The Gendlin Online Library*, previous.focusing.org/gendlin/docs/gol_2067.html.

Gilbert, Sandra M., and Susan Gubar. 1979. *The Madwoman in the Attic: The Woman Writer and the Nineteenth-Century Literary Imagination.* Yale UP, 2000.

Gilman, Sander. *The Jew's Body*. Routledge, 1991.

Girard, René. 1972. *Violence and the Sacred*. Translated by Patrick Gregory, Bloomsbury, 2013.

Glanz, Rudolph. "The 'Jewish Execution' in Medieval Germany." *Jewish Social Studies*, vol. 5, 1943, pp. 1–26.

Goldman, Emma. 1910. "The Traffic in Women." *Anarchism and Other Essays*. Filiquarian Publishing, 2005, pp. 131–47.

Gomez, Carmen M. "Gender, Science, and the Modern Woman: Futurism's Strange Concoctions of Femininity." *Carte Italiane*, vol. 2, no. 6, 2010, pp. 151–68.

Goody, Alex. "Empire, Motherhood and the Poetics of the Self in Mina Loy's *Anglo-Mongrels and the Rose*." *Life Writing*, vol. 6, no. 1, 2009, pp. 61–76.

—. "Ladies of Fashion/Modern(ist) Women: Mina Loy and Djuna Barnes." *Women: A Cultural Review*, vol. 10, no. 3, 2009, pp. 266–82.

Gourmont, Remy de. 1901. "Women and Language." *Decadence and Other Essays on the Culture of Ideas*, translated by William Aspenwall Bradley, Grant Richards, 1922, pp. 118–38.

Greenberg, Jonathan. *Modernism, Satire, and the Novel*. Cambridge UP, 2011.

Gross, Jennifer R., Ann Lauterbach, Roger L. Conover, and Dawn Ades, eds. *Mina Loy: Strangeness is Inevitable*. Princeton UP, 2023.

Grosz, Elizabeth. "Darwin and Feminism: Preliminary Investigations for a Possible Alliance." *Material Feminisms*, edited by Stacy Alaimo and Susan Hekman, Indiana UP, 2008, pp. 23–51.

—. *Volatile Bodies: Toward a Corporeal Feminism*. Indiana UP, 1994.

Guest, Barbara. "Note on Mina Loy." *Mina Loy: Woman and Poet*, edited by Maeera Shreiber and Keith Tuma, National Poetry Foundation, 1998, p. 497.

Guggenheim, Peggy. *Out of This Century*. Doubleday, 1980.

Gunn, Thom. "Three Hard Women: H.D., Marianne Moore, and Mina Loy." *Shelf Life: Essays, Memoirs and an Interview*, Faber and Faber, 1993, pp. 33–52.

Hadingham, Evan. "Uncovering Secrets of the Sphinx." *Smithsonian Magazine*, February 2010, www.smithsonianmag.com/history/uncovering-secrets-of-the-sphinx-5053442/.

Hall Tharp, Louise. *Mrs Jack: A Biography of Isabella Stewart Gardner*. Little, Brown, and Co., 1965.

Hamnett, Nina. *Laughing Torso: Reminiscences of Nina Hamnett.* Constable and Co., 1932.

Harris, Frank. 1922–7. *My Life and Loves.* Edited by John F. Gallagher. Grove Press, 1963.

Hart, Matthew. "Epilogue: Denationalizing Mina Loy." *Nations of Nothing but Poetry: Modernism, Transnationalism, and Synthetic Vernacular Writing.* Oxford UP, 2010, pp. 177–90.

Hayden, Sarah. *Curious Disciplines: Mina Loy and Avant-Garde Artisthood.* U of New Mexico P, 2018.

Heimonet, Jean-Michel. "Recoil in Order to Leap Forward: Two Values of Sade in Bataille's Text." *Yale French Studies*, translated by Joaniko Kohchi, vol. 78, 1990, pp. 227–36.

Hejnol, Andreas, and José M. Martín-Durán. "Getting to the Bottom of Anal Evolution." *Zoologischer Anzeiger*, vol. 256, 2015, pp. 62–74. Elsevier, bora.uib.no/bora-xmlui/bitstream/handle/1956/10848/PDF?sequence=3&isAllowed=y.

Herder, Wouter W. de. "Familial Gigantism." *Clinics*, vol. 67, no. 1, 2012, pp. 29–32.

Herman, David. "1880–1945: Re-minding Modernism." *The Emergence of Mind: Representations of Consciousness in Narrative Discourse in English*, edited by David Herman, U of Nebraska P, pp. 243–72.

Herron, George D. *The Menace of Peace.* Mitchell Kennerley, 1917. Internet Archive, archive.org/details/menaceofpeace00herr/page/n9/mode/2up?view=theatre.

Hobhouse, Leonard T. *Mind in Evolution.* Macmillian & Co., 1901.

Hofer, Matthew. "Mina Loy, Giovanni Papini, and the Aesthetic of Irritation." *Paideuma: Modern and Contemporary Poetry and Poetics*, vol. 38, 2011, 219–58.

Holland, J. Gill. "George Henry Lewes and 'Stream of Consciousness': The First Use of the Term in English." *South Atlantic Review*, vol. 51, no. 1, 1986, pp. 31–9.

Holmes, John. *Darwin's Bards: British and American Poetry in the Age of Evolution.* Edinburgh UP, 2009.

Horace. 1st century BCE. *Horace, Satires and Epistles and Persius, Satires.* Translated and edited by Niall Rudd, Penguin Group, 2005.

Horn, David G. *The Criminal Body: Lombroso and the Anatomy of Deviance.* Routledge, 2003.

Hovey, Jaime. *A Thousand Words: Portraiture, Style, and Queer Modernism.* Ohio State UP, 2006.

Hubert, Henri, and Marcel Mauss. 1899. *Sacrifice: Its Nature and Function.* Translated by W. D. Halls, Cohen and West, 1964.

Hughes, Derek. *Culture and Sacrifice: Ritual Death in Literature and Opera.* Cambridge UP, 2007.

Hume, David. 1777. *Enquiries Concerning Human Understanding and Concerning the Principles of Morals*. Edited by P. H. Nidditch, Clarendon Press, 1992.

Hunsinger, George. *The Eucharist and Ecumenism*. Cambridge UP, 2012.

Irigaray, Luce. 1987. *Sexes and Genealogies*. Translated by Gillian C. Gill, Columbia UP, 1993.

—. 1978. "Women on the Market." *This Sex Which is Not One*. Translated by Catharine Porter with Carolyn Burke, Cornell UP, 1985, pp. 170–91.

Jacobus, Mary. *First Things: The Maternal Imaginary in Literature, Art, and Psychoanalysis*. Routledge, 1995.

James, Henry. 1893. "The Real Thing." *Selected Short Stories*. Penguin, 1963, pp. 43–70.

Januzzi, Marisa. "Dada through the Looking-Glass, or: Mina Loy's Objective." *Women in Dada: Essays on Sex, Gender, and Identity*, edited by Naomi Sawelson-Gorse, MIT Press, 1988, pp. 578–612.

—. "Mongrel Rose: The 'Unerring Esperanto' of Loy's Poetry." *Mina Loy: Woman and Poet*, edited by Maeera Shreiber and Keith Tuma, National Poetry Foundation, 1998, pp. 403–42.

John, Ida. *The Good Bohemian: The Letters of Ida John*. Edited by Rebecca John and Michael Holroyd, Bloomsbury, 2017.

Jones, Amelia. *Seeing Differently: A History and Theory of Identification and the Visual Arts*. Taylor and Francis Group, 2012.

Jones, Dafydd. *The Fictions of Arthur Cravan*. Manchester UP, 2019.

Jorn, Asger. 1964. "Guy Debord and the Problem of the Accursed." *Substance: A Review of Theory and Literary Criticism*, vol. 28, no. 3, 1999, pp. 157–63.

Joyce, James. 1916. *A Portrait of the Artist as a Young Man*. Edited by Jeri Johnson, Oxford UP, 2008.

—. 1922. *Ulysses*. Edited by Declan Kiberd, Penguin Books, 2000.

Juvenal. 1st–2nd century CE. *The Satires*. Translated by Niall Rudd, edited by William Barr, Oxford UP, 1991.

Keane, Catherine. "Defining the Art of Blame: Classical Satire." *A Companion to Satire Ancient and Modern*, edited by Rubin Quintero, Blackwell Publishing, 2011, pp. 31–51.

Keenan, Dennis King. *The Question of Sacrifice*. Indiana University Press, 2005.

Keenan, James F. *A History of Catholic Moral Theology in the Twentieth Century: From Confessing Sins to Liberating Consciences*. Bloomsbury, 2010.

Kenner, Hugh. *The Pound Era*. U of California P, 1973.

Kermode, Frank. "Dissociation of Sensibility." *The Kenyon Review*, vol. 19, no. 2, 1957, pp. 169–94.

Kernan, Alvin B. *The Plot of Satire*. Yale UP, 1965.

Kilpatrick, George Dunbar. *The Eucharist in Bible and Liturgy*. Cambridge UP, 1983.

Kinnahan, Linda A. *Mina Loy, Twentieth-Century Photography, and Contemporary Women Poets*. Routledge, 2017.

—. *Poetics of the Feminine: Authority and Literary Tradition in William Carlos Williams, Mina Loy, Denise Levertov, and Kathleen Fraser*. Cambridge UP, 1994.

Kosofsky Sedgwick, Eve. *Epistemology of the Closet*. Penguin 1994.

—. *Touching Feeling: Affect, Pedagogy, Performativity*. Duke UP, 2003.

Kouidis, Virginia M. *Mina Loy: Modernist American Poet*. Louisiana State UP, 1980.

—. "Rediscovering our Sources: The Poetry of Mina Loy." *boundary 2*, vol. 8, no. 3, 1980, pp. 167–88.

Kreymborg, Alfred. "Lima Beans." *Plays for Poem-Mimes*, The Other Press, 1918, pp. 43–60.

—. 1929. *Our Singing Strength: A History of American Poetry*. Tudor Publishing Company, 1934.

—. *The Troubadour: An Autobiography*. Boni and Liveright, 1925.

Lane, Riki. "Trans as Bodily Becoming: Rethinking the Biological as Diversity, Not Dichotomy." *Hypatia*, vol. 24, no. 3, 2009, pp. 136–57.

Lauretis, Teresa de. *Figures of Resistance: Essays in Feminist Theory*. Edited by Patricia White. U of Illinois P, 2007.

Lawrence, D. H. 1936. "Education of the People." *Phoenix: The Posthumous Papers of D. H. Lawrence*, edited by Edward D. Donald, William Heinemann, 1961, pp. 587–665.

—. 1923. *Fantasia of the Unconscious* and *Psychoanalysis and the Unconscious*. Penguin Books, 1971.

—. 1928. *Lady Chatterley's Lover*. Penguin Books, 1980.

—. 1926. *The Plumed Serpent*. Penguin Books, 1973.

—. 1925. "The Woman Who Rode Away." *The Complete Short Stories*, vol. 2, William Heineman, 1958, pp. 546–81.

Lecercle, Jean-Jacques. *The Violence of Language*. Routledge, 1990.

Lehan, Richard. "Bergson and the Discourse of the Moderns." *The Crisis in Modernism: Bergson and the Vitalist Controversy*, edited by Frederick Burwick and Paul Douglass, Cambridge UP, 1992, pp. 306–29.

Lejeune, Philippe. *On Autobiography*. Translated by Katherine Leary, edited by Paul John Eakin, U of Minnesota P, 1989.

Lennard, John. *But I Digress: The Exploitation of Parentheses in English Printed Verse*. Clarendon Press, 1991.

Levine, George. *Darwin Loves You: Natural Selection and the Re-enchantment of the World*, Princeton UP, 2006.

Levy, Jerrold. May 1989. "Interview with Burke." YCAL MSS 778, Box 8, Folder "Bayer, Javan, and Jerrola [*sic*] Levy, 1982–1989." Carolyn Burke Collection on Mina Loy and Lee Miller. Beinecke Rare Book and Manuscript Library, Yale University, CT, USA.

Levy, Joella. "Levy, Joella Lloyd: To Julien Levy, 1926–1980, undated." Box 29, Folder 8, Julien Levy Gallery Records, Correspondence: 1857–1982. Philadelphia Museum of Art, Library and Archives, PA, USA.

—. "Levy, Joella Lloyd: To Julien Levy, undated." Box 29, Folder 9, Julien Levy Gallery Records, Correspondence: 1857–1982. Philadelphia Museum of Art, Library and Archives, PA, USA.

Levy, Julien. "Levy, Joella Lloyd: From Julien Levy, 1928, undated." Box 29, Folder 7, Julien Levy Gallery Records, Correspondence: 1857–1982. Philadelphia Museum of Art, Library and Archives, PA, USA.

—. "Loy, Mina: From Julien Levy: Dated correspondence, 1928–1954." Box 31, Folder 11, Julien Levy Gallery Records, Correspondence: 1857–1982. Philadelphia Museum of Art, Library and Archives, PA, USA.

—. *Memoir of an Art Gallery*. G. P. Putnam's Sons, 1977.

Lewis, Wyndham. 1937. *Blasting and Bombardiering*. U of California P, 1957.

—. 1922. "The Credentials of the Painter." *Creatures of Habit and Creatures of Change: Essays on Art, Literature, and Society, 1914–1956*, edited by Paul Edwards, Black Sparrow Press, 1989, pp. 66–76.

—. 1927. *The Lion and the Fox: The Role of the Hero in the Plays of Shakespeare*. Methuen and Co., 1955.

—. 1925. "The Politics of Artistic Expression." *Creatures of Habit and Creatures of Change: Essays on Art, Literature, and Society, 1914–1956*, edited by Paul Edwards, Black Sparrow Press, 1989, pp. 114–19.

—. 1934. "Satire Defended." *Enemy Salvoes: Selected Literary Criticism*, edited by C. J. Fox, Vision Press, 1975, pp. 41–9.

—. 1918. *Tarr*. Chatto and Windus, 1968.

—. 1927. *Time and Western Man*. Edited by Paul Edwards. Black Sparrow Press, 1993.

Lipton, Eunice. *Alias Olympia: A Woman's Search for Manet's Notorious Model and her Own Desire*. Thames and Hudson, 1993.

The Little, Brown Handbook. Edited by H. Ramsay Fowler et al. Harper Collins Publishers, 1990.

Lloyd, Fabienne. "Lloyd, Fabienne: To Julien Levy and Joella Levy, to Julien Levy and Muriel Levy, and to Julien Levy and Jean Levy, 1929–1974, undated." Box 30, Folder 6, Julien Levy Gallery Records, Correspondence: 1857–1982. Philadelphia Museum of Art, Library and Archives, PA, USA.

Lorde, Audre. 1979. "The Master's Tools Will Never Dismantle the Master's House." *Sister/Outsider*, Crossing Press, 2007, pp. 110–13.

—. 1978. "Uses of the Erotic: The Erotic as Power." *Sister/Outsider*, Crossing Press, 2007, pp. 53–9.

Love, Heather. *Feeling Backward: Loss and the Politics of Queer History*. Harvard UP, 2007.

Loy, Mina. 1916. "Alda's Beauty, autograph manuscript." YCAL MSS 778, Box 1. Carolyn Burke Collection on Mina Loy and Lee Miller. Beinecke Rare Book and Manuscript Library, Yale University, CT, USA.

—. 1952. "Biography of Songge Byrd." YCAL MSS 6, Box 5, Folder 130, Mina Loy Papers. Beinecke Rare Book and Manuscript Library, Yale University, CT, USA.

—. c. 1913–20. *Brontolivido*. YCAL MSS 6, Box 1, Folders 1–9, Mina Loy Papers. Beinecke Rare Book and Manuscript Library, Yale University, New Haven, CT, USA.

—. n.d. "Ceiling at Dawn, n.d." YCAL MSS 6, Box 5, Folder 83, Mina Loy Papers. Beinecke Rare Book and Manuscript Library, Yale University, CT, USA.

—. c. 1932–6. *The Child and the Parent*. YCAL MSS 6, Box 1, Folders 10–20, Mina Loy Papers. Beinecke Rare Book and Manuscript Library, Yale University, New Haven, CT, USA.

—. "Mina Loy's 'Colossus': Arthur Cravan Undressed." Edited and introduced by Roger Conover, *Dada/Surrealism*, vol. 14, no. 1, 1985, pp. 102–19.

—. n.d. "Designs." YCAL MSS 6, Box 7, Folder 184, Mina Loy Papers. Beinecke Rare Book and Manuscript Library, Yale University, New Haven, CT, USA.

—. c. 1910s/20s. *Esau Penfold*. YCAL MSS 6, Box 1, Folders 21–6, Mina Loy Papers. Beinecke Rare Book and Manuscript Library, Yale University, New Haven, CT, USA.

—. n.d. "Fragments." YCAL MSS 6, Box 2, Folder 30, Mina Loy Papers. Beinecke Rare Book and Manuscript Library, Yale University, CT, USA.

—. c. 1925–30+. *Goy Israels*. YCAL MSS 6, Box 2, Folders 27–9, Mina Loy Papers. Beinecke Rare Book and Manuscript Library, Yale University, New Haven, CT, USA.

—. 1932. *Goy Israels: A Play of Consciousness*. YCAL MSS MISC, Group 606, Item F-1. Yale Collection of American Literature Manuscript Miscellany. Beinecke Rare Book and Manuscript Library, Yale University, New Haven, CT, USA.

—. 1991. *Insel*. Edited with an afterword by Elizabeth Arnold. Newly edited and introduced by Sarah Hayden, Melville House Publishing, 2014.

—. c. 1940s–50s. *Islands in the Air*. YCAL MSS 6, Box 4, Folders 58–71, Mina Loy Papers. Beinecke Rare Book and Manuscript Library, Yale University, New Haven, CT, USA.

—. n.d. "Jesus and Eros." YCAL MSS 6, Box 5, Folder 141, Mina Loy Papers. Beinecke Rare Book and Manuscript Library, Yale University, New Haven, CT, USA.

—. "John Rodker's Frog." *The Little Review*, vol. 7, no. 3, 1 September 1920, pp. 56–7.

—. n.d. "Joyce's *Ulysses*: Fragment." YCAL MSS 6, Box 5, Folder 98, Mina Loy Papers. Beinecke Rare Book and Manuscript Library, Yale University, New Haven, CT, USA.

—. 1982. *The Last Lunar Baedeker*. Edited and introduced by Roger Conover, Carcanet Press, 1985.

—. 1996. *The Lost Lunar Baedeker*. Edited and introduced by Roger Conover, Carcanet, 1997.

—. "Loy, Mina, 1913–20, n.d." YCAL MSS 196, Box 24, Folder 664, Mabel Dodge Luhan Papers. Beinecke Rare Book and Manuscript Library, Yale University, CT, USA.

—. c. 1934–49, 1960. "Loy, Mina to Joella and Assorted Others." YCAL MSS 778, Box 1, Carolyn Burke Collection on Mina Loy and Lee Miller. Beinecke Rare Book and Manuscript Library, Yale University, CT, USA.

—. 1950–1954. "Loy, Mina to Joella Bayer and Julien Levy, circa 1950–1954." YCAL MSS 778, Box 3, Carolyn Burke Collection on Mina Loy and Lee Miller. Beinecke Rare Book and Manuscript Library, Yale University, CT, USA.

—. "Loy, Mina: To Julien Levy and Joella Levy, 1928." Box 30, Folder 8, Julien Levy Gallery Records, Correspondence: 1857–1982. Philadelphia Museum of Art, Library and Archives, PA, USA.

—. "Loy, Mina: To Julien Levy and Joella Levy, 1931." Box 30, Folder 11, Julien Levy Gallery Records, Correspondence: 1857–1982. Philadelphia Museum of Art, Library and Archives, PA, USA.

—. "Loy, Mina: To Julien Levy and Joella Levy, 1932." Box 30, Folder 12, Julien Levy Gallery Records, Correspondence: 1857–1982. Philadelphia Museum of Art, Library and Archives, PA, USA.

—. "Loy, Mina: To Julien Levy and Joella Levy, 1933." Box 30, Folder 13, Julien Levy Gallery Records, Correspondence: 1857–1982. Philadelphia Museum of Art, Library and Archives, PA, USA.

—. "Loy, Mina: To Julien Levy and Joella Levy: Poems, 1940, undated." Box 31, Folder 8, Julien Levy Gallery Records, Correspondence: 1857–1982. Philadelphia Museum of Art, Library and Archives, PA, USA.

—. n.d. "Loy, Mina: Records, documents, and addresses, undated." YCAL MSS 778, Box 8, Carolyn Burke Collection on Mina Loy and Lee Miller. Beinecke Rare Book and Manuscript Library, Yale University, CT, USA.

—. 1914–59. "Loy, Mina. Series 1. A–Z Correspondence." YCAL MSS 1050, Box 76, Folders 1082–3, Carl Van Vechten Papers. Beinecke Rare Book and Manuscript Library, Yale University, CT, USA.

—. *Lunar Baedeker and Time-Tables: Selected Poems*. Edited by Jonathan Williams, The Jargon Society 23, 1958.

—. n.d. "Mi and Lo." YCAL MSS 6, Box 6, Folder 166, Mina Loy Papers. Beinecke Rare Book and Manuscript Library, Yale University, New Haven, CT, USA.

—. 1965. "Mina Loy: Interview with Paul Blackburn and Robert Vas Dias." Introduced by Carolyn Burke. *Mina Loy: Woman and Poet*, edited by

Maaera Shreiber and Keith Tuma, National Poetry Foundation, 1998, pp. 209–44.

—. n.d. "Miscellaneous." YCAL MSS 6, Box 7, Folder 187, Mina Loy Papers. Beinecke Rare Book and Manuscript Library, Yale University, CT, USA.

—. n.d. "Notes on Metaphysics." YCAL MSS 6, Box 7, Folder 191, Mina Loy Papers. Beinecke Rare Book and Manuscript Library, Yale University, CT, USA.

—. "Notes on Religion." Edited by Keith Tuma. *Sulfur*, vol. 27, Fall 1990, pp. 13–16.

—. "O Marcel – – – Otherwise I also have been to Louise's." *The Blind Man*, vol. 2, May 1917, pp. 14–15.

—. Postscript, "To Mina Loy" by John Rodker. *The Little Review*, vol. 7, no. 4, 1 January 1921, pp. 44–5.

—. 1937. "Promised Land, autograph manuscript." YCAL MSS 778, Box 1, Carolyn Burke Collection on Mina Loy and Lee Miller. Beinecke Rare Book and Manuscript Library, Yale University, CT, USA.

—. n.d. "Pygmaleon and Galatea." YCAL MSS 6, Box 5, Folder 145, Mina Loy Papers. Beinecke Rare Book and Manuscript Library, Yale University, CT, USA.

—. n.d. (erroneously dated 1944). "Static." YCAL MSS 6, Box 6, Folder 177, Mina Loy Papers. Beinecke Rare Book and Manuscript Library, Yale University, CT, USA.

—. *Stories and Essays of Mina Loy*. Edited and introduced by Sara Crangle, Dalkey Archive Press, 2011.

—. n.d. "Street Sister." *That Kind of Woman: Stories from the Left Bank and Beyond*, edited by Brontë Adams and Trudi Tate, Virago Press, 1991, pp. 41–2.

—. 1921. "Would You Be 'Different'? Madame Loy Shows How." *Pittsburgh Press*, 3 April 1921. Reproduced in Kinnahan, Linda A. "Italian Retreats: Fourth Tour", *Mina Loy: Navigating the Avant-Garde*, edited by Suzanne W. Churchill, Linda A. Kinnahan, and Susan Rosenbaum, University of Georgia, 2020, mina-loy.com/chapters/italy-italian-baedeker/5-italian-retreats/.

Lubin, David M. *Acts of Portrayal: Eakins, Sargent, James*. Yale UP, 1985.

Lyon, Janet. "Mina Loy's Pregnant Pauses: The Space of Possibility in the Florence Writings." *Mina Loy: Woman and Poet*, edited by Maaera Shreiber and Keith Tuma, National Poetry Foundation, 1998, pp. 379–402.

McAlmon, Robert. 1923. *Post-Adolescence*. U of New Mexico P, 1991.

McAlmon, Robert, and Kay Boyle. 1938. *Being Geniuses Together: 1920–1930*. Hogarth Press, 1984.

McGann, Jerome. *The Poetics of Sensibility: A Revolution in Literary Style*. Clarendon Press, 1996.

McWhorter, Ellen. "Body Matters: Mina Loy and the Art of Intuition." *European Journal of American Studies*, vol. 10, no. 2, 2015, pp. 1–26.

Mallarmé, Stéphane. 1897. "Crisis of Verse." *Divagations*, translated by Barbara Johnson, Harvard UP, 2007, pp. 201–11.

—. 1897. "Verlaine." *Divagations*, translated by Barbara Johnson, Harvard UP, 2007. pp. 62–3.

Marcus, Laura. *Auto/biographical Discourses: Theory, Criticism, Practice.* Manchester UP, 1994.

Marinetti, Filippo Tommaso. 1919. "Against Marriage." *F. T. Marinetti: Critical Writings*, translated by Doug Thomson, edited by Günter Berghaus, Farrar, Straus, and Giroux, 2006, pp. 309–12.

—. 1910. "The Battles of Venice." *F. T. Marinetti: Critical Writings*, translated by Doug Thomson, edited by Günter Berghaus, Farrar, Straus, and Giroux, 2006, pp. 165–9.

—. 1913. "Destruction of Syntax—Untrammeled Imagination—Words-in-Freedom." *F. T. Marinetti: Critical Writings*, translated by Doug Thomson, edited by Günter Berghaus, Farrar, Straus, and Giroux, 2006, pp. 120–31.

—. 1914. "Down with the Tango and *Parsifal!*" *F. T. Marinetti: Critical Writings*, translated by Doug Thomson, edited by Günter Berghaus, Farrar, Straus, and Giroux, 2006, pp. 132–4.

—. 1919. "Dunes." *Selected Poems and Related Prose*, translated by Elizabeth R. Napier and Barbara R. Studholme, Yale UP, 2002, pp. 99–116.

—. 1910. "Extended Man and the Kingdom of the Machine." *F. T. Marinetti: Critical Writings*, translated by Doug Thomson, edited by Günter Berghaus, Farrar, Straus, and Giroux, pp. 85–8.

—. 1909. "The Foundation and Manifesto of Futurism." *F. T. Marinetti: Critical Writings*, translated by Doug Thomson, edited by Günter Berghaus, Farrar, Straus, and Giroux, 2006, pp. 11–16.

—. 1919. "Futurist Sensibility and Wireless Imagination." *Selected Poems and Related Prose*, translated by Elizabeth R. Napier and Barbara R. Studholme, Yale UP, 2002, pp. 87–8.

—. 1910. "The Necessity and Beauty of Violence." *F. T. Marinetti: Critical Writings*, translated by Doug Thomson, edited by Günter Berghaus, Farrar, Straus, and Giroux, 2006, pp. 60–74.

—. 1919. "Numerical Sensibility." *Selected Poems and Related Prose*, translated by Elizabeth R. Napier and Barbara R. Studholme, Yale UP, 2002, p. 94.

—. 1920–38. "Poems to Beny." *Selected Poems and Related Prose*, translated by Elizabeth R. Napier and Barbara R. Studholme, Yale UP, 2002, pp. 133–48.

—. 1912. "The Pope's Monoplane." *Selected Poems and Related Prose*, edited by Luce Marinetti, translated by Elizabeth R. Napier and Barbara R. Studholme, Yale UP, 2002, pp. 41–54.

—. 1909. "Second Futurist Proclamation: Let's Kill Off the Moonlight." *F. T. Marinetti: Critical Writings*, translated by Doug Thomson, edited by Günter Berghaus, Farrar, Straus, and Giroux, 2006, pp. 22–31.

—. 1908. "The Sensual City." *Selected Poems and Related Prose*, translated by Elizabeth R. Napier and Barbara R. Studholme, Yale UP, 2002, pp. 25–40.

—. 1919. "Typographic Revolution and Free Expressive Orthography." *Selected Poems and Related Prose*, translated by Elizabeth R. Napier and Barbara R. Studholme, Yale UP, 2002, p. 89.

—. 1911. "We Renounce our Symbolist Masters, the Last of All Lovers of the Moonlight." *F. T. Marinetti: Critical Writings*, translated by Doug Thomson, edited by Günter Berghaus, Farrar, Straus, and Giroux, 2006, pp. 43–6.

Marinetti, Filippo Tommaso, and Christopher Nevinson. 1914. "Futurism and English Art." *Futurism: An Anthology*, edited by Lawrence Rainey, Christine Poggi, and Laura Wittman, Yale UP, 2009, pp. 196–8.

Mayhew, Henry. 1851–2. *London Labour and the London Poor*. Edited by Victor E. Neuberg, Penguin, 1985.

Meyer Spacks, Patricia. "Oscillations of Sensibility." *New Literary History*, vol. 25, no. 3, 1995, pp. 505–25.

Miller, Cristanne. *Cultures of Modernism: Marianne Moore, Mina Loy, and Else Lasker-Schüler*. U of Michigan P, 2005.

Miller, Jacques Alain. "Extimity." *The Symptom*, vol. 9, 2008, www.lacan.com/symptomExtimity.

Miller, Nancy K. *Getting Personal: Feminist Occasions and Other Biographical Acts*. Routledge, 1991.

Mizruchi, Susan L. *The Science of Sacrifice: American Literature and Modern Social Theory*. Princeton UP, 1998.

Moi, Toril. "Representation of Patriarchy: Sexuality and Epistemology in Freud's 'Dora.'" *Feminist Review*, vol. 9, 1981, pp. 60–74.

Monroe, Harriet. "Guide to the Moon." *Poetry: A Magazine of Verse*, vol. 23, no. 2, November 1923, pp. 100–3.

Montagu, Mary Wortley. *Essays and Poems and Simplicity, a Comedy*. Clarendon Press, 1977.

—. *Romance Writings*. Clarendon Press, 1996.

Moore, George. 1887–1923. *Confessions of a Young Man*. Edited by Susan Marie Dick, McGill-Queen's UP, 1972.

Moore, Marianne. *The Poems of Marianne Moore*. Edited by Grace Schulman, Penguin Books, 2003.

Morrisson, Mark. *Alchemy: Occultism and the Emergence of Atomic Theory*. Oxford UP, 2007.

Morse, Samuel French. "The Rediscovery of Mina Loy and the Avant Garde." *Wisconsin Studies in Contemporary Literature*, vol. 2, no. 2, 1961, pp. 12–19.

Moses, Omri. *Out of Character: Modernism, Vitalism, Psychic Life.* Stanford UP, 2014.

Mulvey, Laura. "Visual Pleasure and Narrative Cinema." *Screen*, vol. 16, no. 13, 1975, pp. 6–18.

Myhill, Carl. "Commercial Success by Looking for Desire Lines." *6th Asia Pacific Computer–Human Interaction Conference (APCHI 2004), Rotorua, New Zealand, June 29–July 2, 2004*, edited by Masood Masoodian, Steve Jones, and Bill Rogers, pp. 293–304. Interaction Design Foundation, link.springer.de/link/service/series/0558/bibs/3101/31010293.

Naden, Constance C. W. 1887. *A Modern Apostle; The Elixir of Life; The Story of Clarice; and Other Poems.* Kegan Paul, Trench, & Co./Classic Reprints, n.d.

Nagle, Christopher. "Sterne, Shelley, and Sensibility's Pleasures of Proximity." *ELH*, vol. 70, no. 3, 2003, pp. 813–45.

Nancy, Jean-Luc. "The Unsacrificeable." Translated by Richard Livingston, *Yale French Studies*, vol. 79, 1991, pp. 20–38.

Nicholls, Peter. "'Arid Clarity': Ezra Pound, Mina Loy, and Jules Laforgue." *The Yearbook of English Studies*, vol. 32, 2002, pp. 52–64.

—. "Mina Loy and Lexicophilia." *Feminist Modernist Studies*, vol. 2, no. 3, 2019, pp. 263–73.

Nichols, Laura. "Social Desire Paths: A New Theoretical Concept to Increase the Usability of Social Science Research in Society." *Theory and Society*, vol. 44, 2014, pp. 647–65.

Nordau, Max. 1892. *Degeneration.* Translator unidentified, D. Appleton and Co., 1895.

Norman, Donald A. *Living with Complexity.* MIT Press, 2010.

Norris, Margot. "Doing Djuna Justice: The Challenges of the Barnes Biography." *Studies in the Novel*, vol. 28, no. 4, 1996, pp. 581–9.

Odlin, Reno. "Her Eclipse Endur'd." *The Antigonish Review*, vol. 59, 1984, pp. 53–63.

Ovid. 1st century CE. *Metamorphoses.* Translated by Mary M. Innes, Penguin, 1955.

Owen, Alexandra. *The Place of Enchantment: British Occultism and the Culture of the Modern.* Chicago UP, 2004.

Packham, Catherine. *Eighteenth-Century Vitalism: Bodies, Culture, Politics*, Palgrave Studies in the Enlightenment, Romanticism and Cultures of Print, edited by A. K. Mellor and C. Siskin, Palgrave Macmillan, 2012.

Papini, Giovanni. 1913. *The Failure.* Tranlsated by Virginia Pope and edited by J. E. Spingarn. Harcourt Brace and Co., 1924.

Parkes, M. B. *Pause and Effect: An Introduction to the History of Punctuation in the West.* U of California P, 1993.

Parmar, Sandeep. "Mina Loy's 'Unfinishing' Self." *Salt Companion to Mina Loy*, edited by Suzanne Hobson and Rachel Potter, Salt Publishing, 2010, pp. 71–98.

—. *Reading Mina Loy's Autobiographies: Myth of the Modern Woman.* Bloomsbury, 2013.

Parsons, Deborah L. *Streetwalking the Metropolis: Women, the City, and Modernity.* Oxford UP, 2000.

Patmore, Coventry. *The Angel in the House.* Introduced by Henry Morley, Cassel & Co., 1887. Google Books, www.google.co.uk/books/edition/ The_Angel_in_the_House/VqZbAAAAQAAJ?hl=en&gbpv=1&pg=PR3 &printsec=frontcover.

Perloff, Marjorie. "English as a 'Second' Language: Mina Loy's 'Anglo-Mongrels and the Rose.'" *Jacket* vol. 5, 1998. *Jacket 2*, jacketmagazine. com/05/mina-anglo.html.

Petronius. 1st century CE. "The Satyricon." *Petronius "The Satyricon" and Seneca, "The Apocolocyntosis"*, translated and edited by J. P. Sullivan, Penguin Books, 1986, pp. 37–208.

Philips, Adam, and Leo Bersani. *Intimacies.* U of Chicago P, 2008.

Pitts-Taylor, Victoria. *The Brain's Body: Neuroscience and Corporeal Politics.* Duke UP, 2016.

Poe, Edgar Allan. 1842. "The Oval Portrait." *Tales of Mystery and Imagination.* J. M. Dent & Sons, 1975, pp. 187–90.

Pollock, Griselda. *Differencing the Canon: Feminism and the Rewriting of Art's Histories.* Routledge, 1999.

—. *Vision and Difference.* Routledge, 2003.

Potter, Rachel. "Censorship." *T. S. Eliot in Context*, edited by J. Harding, Cambridge UP, 2011, pp. 83–92.

Pound, Ezra. 1926. "Introduction." *The Natural Philosophy of Love*, by Remy de Gourmont, translated by Ezra Pound, Neville Spearman, 1957, pp. vii–xvii.

—. "A List of Books: 'Others.'" *The Little Review*, vol. 4, no. 11, 1 March 1918, pp. 56–8.

—. *Selected Poems, 1908–1969.* Faber and Faber, 1977.

—. 1913. "The Serious Artist." *Literary Essays of Ezra Pound*, edited by T. S. Eliot, Faber and Faber, 1960, pp. 41–57.

Prescott, Tara. *Poetic Salvage: Reading Mina Loy.* Bucknell UP, 2017.

Prettijohn, Elizabeth. *Interpreting Sargent.* Tate Gallery Publishing, 1998.

Pryor, Sean. *Poetry, Modernism, and an Imperfect World.* Cambridge UP, 2017.

Ptacek, Melissa. "Sacrificing Sacrifice." *Theory and Society*, vol. 35, no. 5/6, 2006, pp. 587–600.

Quartermain, Peter, "'The Tattle of Tongueplay': Mina Loy's Love Songs." *Mina Loy: Woman and Poet*, edited by Maeera Shreiber and Keith Tuma, National Poetry Foundation, 1998, pp. 75–85.

—. "The Value of Scholarship: Mina Loy as Fact and Fiction." *PN Review*, vol. 27, no. 3, 2001, pp. 42–5.

Quintero, Ruben. "Pope and Augustan Verse Satire." *A Companion to Satire Ancient and Modern*, edited by Rubin Quintero, Blackwell Publishing, 2011, pp. 212–32.

Rainey, Lawrence. "The Creation of the Avant-Garde: F. T. Marinetti and Ezra Pound." *Modernism/modernity*, vol. 1, no. 3, 1994, pp. 195–220.

Rasula, Jed. "A Renaissance of Women Writers." *Sulfur*, vol. 3, no. 1, 1983, pp. 160–72.

Rawson, Claude. "Introduction." *English Satire and the Satiric Tradition*, edited by Claude Rawson, Basil Blackwell, 1984, pp. v–xiii.

—. *Satire and Sentiment: 1660–1830*. Cambridge UP, 1994.

Re, Lucia. "Futurism, Seduction, and the Strange Sublimity of War." *Italian Studies*, vol. 59, 2004, pp. 83–111.

Read, Sophie. *Eucharist and the Poetic Imagination*. Cambridge UP, 2013.

Reis, Elizabeth. "Perfect or Perverted?" *Commonplace: The Journal of Early American Life*, vol. 8, no. 2, 2008. commonplace.online/article/perfect-or-perverted/.

Rexroth, Kenneth. 1944. "Les Lauriers Sont Coupés." *Lunar Baedeker and Time-Tables: Selected Poems*, edited by Jonathan Williams, The Jargon Society 23, 1958, n.p.

Riley, Denise. *Impersonal Passion: Language as Affect*. Duke UP, 2005.

Robert, Enif, and F. T. Marinetti. 1919. **"COURAGE + TRUTH"**, *Futurism: An Anthology*. Edited by Lawrence Rainey, Christine Poggi, and Laura Wittman., Yale UP, 2009, pp. 458–60.

Roberts, Andrew. "'How to be Happy in Paris': Mina Loy and the Transvaluation of the Body." *The Cambridge Quarterly*, vol. 27, no. 2, 1998, pp. 129–47.

Roche, Hannah. *The Outside Thing: Modernist Lesbian Romance*. Columbia UP, 2019.

Rodker, John. "The 'Others' Anthology." *The Little Review*, vol. 7, no. 3, 1 September 1920, pp. 53–6.

Roof, Judith. *What Gender Is, What Gender Does*. U of Minnesota P, 2016.

Rose, Gillian. *Love's Work*. Vintage, 1997.

Roselli, David Kawalko. "Gender, Class and Ideology: The Social Function of Virgin Sacrifice in Euripides' *Children of Herakles*." *Classical Antiquity*, vol. 26, no. 1, 2007, pp. 81–169.

Rossetti, Dante Gabriel. 1850. "Hand and Soul." *The Pre-Raphaelites: Writings and Sources*. Vol. 3, edited by Inga Bryden, Routledge, 1998, pp. 7–17.

Roughgarden, Joan. "The Theory of Evolution." *Evolution's Rainbow: Diversity, Gender, and Sexuality in Nature and People*, U of California P, 2013, pp. 159–81.

Rubin, Gayle. "Misguided, Dangerous and Wrong: An Analysis of Antipornography Politics." *Deviations: A Gayle Rubin Reader*, Duke UP, 2011, pp. 254–75.

—. "Thinking Sex: Notes for a Radical Theory of the Politics of Sexuality." *Pleasure and Danger: Exploring Female Sexuality*, Routledge and Kegan Paul, 1984, pp. 267–319.

—. "The Traffic in Women: Notes on the 'Political Economy' of Sex." *Toward an Anthropology of Women*, edited by Rayna Reiter, Monthly View Press, 1975, pp. 157–210.

Sade, Marquis de. 1791. *Justine: or the Misfortunes of Virtue*. Translated, introduced, and edited by John Phillips, Oxford UP, 2012.

Salisbury, Joyce. *Church Fathers, Independent Virgins*. Verso, 1991.

Sartini Blum, Cinzia. *The Other Modernism: F. T. Marinetti's Futurist Fictions of Power*. U of California P, 1996.

Schramm, Jan-Melissa. *Atonement and Self-Sacrifice in Nineteenth-Century Narrative*. Cambridge UP, 2013.

Schreiner, Olive. 1911. *Woman and Labour*. T. Fisher Unwin, 1914.

Schuster, Joshua. *Modernist Biotopias: Organicism and Vitalism in Early Twentieth-Century American Poetry*. 2007. U of Pennsylvania, PhD dissertation. ProQuest, www.proquest.com/docview/304826424?pq-origsite=gscholar&fromopenview=true.

Scodel, Ruth. "Virigin Sacrifice and Aesthetic Object." *Transactions of the American Philological Association (1974–2014)*, vol. 126, 1996, pp. 111–28.

Scott, Evelyn. 1921. *The Narrow House*. Shoreline Books, Norton and Co., 1986.

Scuriatti, Laura. *Mina Loy's Critical Modernism*. UP of Florida, 2019.

Seidel, Michael A. *Satiric Inheritance: Rabelais to Sterne*. Princeton UP, 1979.

Shakespeare, William. 1605. *The Merchant of Venice*. Edited by George Lyman Kittredge and Irving Ribner, John Wiley and Sons, 1973.

Shrage, Laurie. *Moral Dilemmas of Feminism: Prostitution, Adultery, and Abortion*. Routledge, 1994.

Shreiber, Maeera. "'Love Is a Lyric/of Bodies.': The Negative Aesthetics of Mina Loy's *Love Songs to Joannes*." *Mina Loy: Woman and Poet*, edited by Maeera Shreiber and Keith Tuma, National Poetry Foundation, 1998, pp. 87–110.

Shreiber, Maeera, and Keith Tuma. "Introduction." *Mina Loy: Woman and Poet*, edited by Maeera Shreiber and Keith Tuma, National Poetry Foundation, 1998, pp. 11–16.

Sickert, Walter. "Sargentolatry." *The New Age*, vol. 7, no. 3, 19 May 1910, pp. 56–7.

Siddal, Elizabeth. 1857–62. "Elizabeth Siddal." *The Pre-Raphaelites: Writing and Sources*, vol. 1, Edited by Inga Bryden, Routledge, 1998, pp. 233–7.

Simmel, Georg. "A Chapter in the Philosophy of Value." *American Journal of Sociology*, vol. 5, no. 5, 1900, pp. 577–603.

—. 1903. "The Metropolis and Mental Life." *On Individuality and Social Forms*, by Georg Simmel, edited by Donald N. Levine. Chicago: U of Chicago P, 1971, pp. 324–39.

Slater, Thomas. 1906. *A Manual of Moral Theology for English-Speaking Countries*. Vol. 1, 5th ed., Burnes Oates and Washbourne, 1925. Internet Archive, archive.org/details/MN5034ucmf_1.

Snaider Lanser, Susan. "Speaking in Tongues: 'Ladies Almanack' and the Language of Celebration." *Frontiers: A Journal of Women Studies*, vol. 4, no. 3, 1979, pp. 39–46.

Solnit, Rebecca. *Wanderlust: A History of Walking*. Granta Publications, 2002.

Sophocles. c. 5th century BCE. "Antigone." *Three Theban Plays: Antigone, Oedipus the King, Oedipus at Colonus*, translated by Robert Fagles, introduction and notes by Bernard Knox, Penguin Books, 1984, pp. 55–128.

Spalding Gatton, John, translator and editor. "Mina Loy." *Adventures of the Mind*, by Natalie Barney, New York UP, 1992, pp. 159–60.

Stage, Sarah. "Female Complaints." *Women's Studies Encyclopedia*, vol. 1, edited by Helen Tierney, Greenwood Press, 1999, pp. 462–3.

Staples, David. "Women's Work and the Ambivalent Gift of Entropy." *The Affective Turn*, edited by Patricia Ticineto Clough, Duke UP, 2007, pp. 119–50.

Starkie, Enid. *Baudelaire*. Victor Gollancz, 1933.

Steele, Timothy. "Verse Satire in the Twentieth Century." *Companion to Satire Ancient and Modern*, edited by Rubin Quintero, Blackwell Publishing, 2011, pp. 434–59.

Stein, Gertrude. 1933. *The Autobiography of Alice B. Toklas*. Penguin Books, 1981.

—. 1926. "Composition as Explanation." *Selected Writings of Gertrude Stein*, edited and introduced by Carl Van Vechten, Random House, 1946, pp. 453–61.

—. 1915–17. "Lifting Belly." *Volume Three of the Yale Edition of the Unpublished Writings of Gertrude Stein*, edited by Carl van Vechten et al., Yale UP, 1953, pp. 65–115.

—. 1935. *Narration: Four Lectures by Gertrude Stein*. U of Chicago P, 1935.

—. 1935. "Poetry and Grammar." *Lectures in America*, Virago Press, 1988, pp. 209–46.

—. 1935. "Portraits and Repetition." *Lectures in America*. Virago Press, 1988, pp. 165–208.

—. 1913. "Sacred Emily." *Geography and Plays*, Dover Publications, 1999, pp. 178–88.

—. 1908–12. "Two: Gertrude Stein and her Brother." *Two: Gertrude Stein and her Brother and Other Early Portraits*, The Unpublished Writings of Gertrude Stein, vol. 1, Yale UP, 1951, pp. 1–142.

—. 1935. "What is English Literature." *Lectures in America*, Virago Press, 1988, pp. 11–55.

Steiner, Wendy. *The Real Real Thing: The Model in the Mirror of Art*. Chicago UP, 2010.

Sterne, Lawrence. 1768. *A Sentimental Journey*. Edited by Paul Goring, Penguin Books, 2001.

Stinson, Emmett. *Satirising Modernism: Aesthetic Autonomy, Romanticism, and the Avant-Garde*. Bloomsbury Publishing, 2017.

Strunk Jr., William, and E. B. White, *The Elements of Style*. 3rd ed. Macmillan Publishing Co., 1979.

Suleiman, Susan Rubin. *Subversive Intent: Gender, Politics, and the Avant-Garde*. Harvard UP, 1990.

Sullivan, J. P. "Introduction." *Petronius "The Satyricon" and Seneca, "The Apocolocyntosis"*, translated and edited by J. P. Sullivan, Penguin Books, 1986, pp. 11–36.

Suppé, Franz von. 1865. "Die schöne Galathée: The Beautiful Galatea." *The Guide to Light Opera and Operetta*. www.musicaltheatreguide. com/composers/vonsuppe/galathea.htm.

Surtees, Virginia. *Rossetti's Portraits of Elizabeth Siddal*. Scolar Press, 1991.

Sweeney, Carole. *Fetish to Subject: Race, Modernism, and Primitivism, 1919–1935*. Praeger Publishers, 2004.

Swift, Jonathan. 1738. *A Compleat Collection of Genteel and Ingenious Conversation, According to the most polite Mode and Method, now used at Court, and in the best Companies of England*. General Books LLC, 2012.

—. 1729. *The Intelligencer*. No. 3, A. Moor, St. Paul's and Booksellers of London and Westminster, Hathitrust Digital Library, babel.hathitrust. org/cgi/pt?id=uc1.b2837215&view=1up&seq=34.

—. 1729. *A Modest Proposal*. Penguin Classics, 2015.

Syme, Alison. *A Touch of Blossom: John Singer Sargent and the Queer Flora and Fauna of Fin-de-Siècle Art*. Penn State UP, 2010.

Symons, Arthur. 1919. *The Symbolist Movement in Literature*. Edited by Matthew Creasy, Carcanet Press, 2014.

Szendy, Peter. *Of Stigmatology: Punctuation as Experience*. Translated by Jan Plug, Fordham UP, 2018.

Taylor, Julie. *Djuna Barnes and Affective Modernism*. Edinburgh UP, 2012.

Thien, Deborah. "Intimate Distances: Considering Questions of 'Us'." *Emotional Geographies*. Edited by Joyce Davidson, Liz Bondi, and Mick Smith, Ashgate Publishing, 2005, pp. 191–204.

Thomson, Virgil. "Introduction" to "Lifting Belly." *Volume Three of the Yale Edition of the Unpublished Writings of Gertrude Stein*, edited by Carl van Vechten et al., Yale UP, 1953, pp. 63–5.

Thorne, Christian. "Thumbing Our Nose at the Public Sphere: Satire, the Market, and the Invention of Literature." *PMLA*, vol. 116, no. 3, 2001, pp. 531–44.

Todd, Janet. *Sensibility: An Introduction*. Methuen, 1986.

Torgovnik, Marianna. *Gone Primitive: Savage Intellects, Modern Lives*. U of Chicago P, 1990.

Traylor, Andrew D. "Violence Has its Reasons: Girard and Bataille." *Contagion: Journal of Violence, Mimesis, and Culture*, vol. 21, 2014, pp. 131–56.

Tuma, Keith. "Loy at Last." *Jacket2*, vol. 5, 1998. jacketmagazine.com/05/mina-tuma.html.

—. "Mina Loy's 'Anglo-Mongrels and the Rose.'" *Mina Loy: Woman and Poet*, edited by Maaera Shreiber and Keith Tuma, National Poetry Foundation, 1998, pp. 181–202.

Uexküll, Jacob von. 1934. *A Foray into the Worlds of Animals and Humans with A Theory of Meaning*. Translated by Joseph D. O'Neil, U of Minnesota P, 2010.

Untermeyer, Louis. *The New Era in American Poetry*. Henry Holt and Co., 1919.

Vail, Lawrence. "Cannibalistic Love Songs." *Gargoyle*, January–February 1922, pp. 34–6.

—. *Murder! Murder!* Peter Davies, 1931.

Van Vechten, Carl. *Peter Whiffle*. The Modern Library, 1929.

Verlaine, Paul. 1888. *The Cursed Poets*. Translated by Chase Madar, Green Integer Press, 2003.

Vigny, Alfred de. 1832. *Stello: A Session with Doctor Noir*. Translated by Irving Massey, McGill UP, 1963.

Vonnegut Jr., Kurt. 1973. *Breakfast of Champions*. Dell Publishing Co., 1975.

Walkowitz, Judith R. *Prostitution and Victorian Society: Women, Class, and the State*. Cambridge UP, 1980.

Watson, Steven. *Strange Bedfellows: The First American Avant-Garde*. Abbeville Press Publishers, 1991.

Weeks, Jeffrey. *Sex, Politics, and Society: The Regulation of Sexuality since 1800*. 2nd ed. Longman, 1989.

Weigman, Robyn. *Object Lessons*. Duke UP, 2012.

Weininger, Otto. 1903. *Sex and Character*. Translator unacknowledged, AMS Press, 1975.

Weiss, Allen S. "An Anatomy of Anatomy." *The Drama Review (1988–)*, vol. 43, no. 1, 1999, pp. 137–44.

West, Rebecca. 1928. *The Strange Necessity*. Virago Press, 1987.

West, Shearer. *Portraiture*. Oxford UP, 2004.

White, Eric B. *Reading Machines in the Modernist Transatlantic: Avant-Gardes, Technology, and the Everyday*. Edinburgh UP, 2020.

White, Hayden. "The Forms of Wildness: Archaeology of an Idea." *Tropics of Discourse: Essays in Cultural Criticism*, Johns Hopkins UP, 1982, pp. 150–82.

Wilde, Oscar. 1905. "De Profundis." *The Portable Oscar Wilde*, edited by Richard Aldington and Stanley Weintraub, Penguin Books, 1981, pp. 508–658.

—. 1891. "The Soul of Man under Socialism." *The Soul of Man under Socialism and Selected Critical Prose*, edited by Linda Dowling, Penguin Books, 2001, pp. 125–62.

Wilkinson, John. "Stumbling, Balking, Tacking: Robert Creeley's *For Love* and Mina Loy's 'Love Songs to Joannes'." *The Lyric Touch: Essays on the Poetry of Excess*, Salt Publishing, 2007, pp. 254–72.

Williams, Jonathan. 1982. "A Note." *The Last Lunar Baedeker*, edited and introduced by Roger Conover, Carcanet Press, 1985, pp. xiii–xiv.

Williams, William Carlos. *The Autobiography of William Carlos Williams*. Random House, 1951.

—. "Belly Music." *Others*, vol. 5, no. 6, 1919, pp. 25–32.

—. "Mina Loy." *Lunar Baedeker and Time-Tables: Selected Poems*, edited by Jonathan Williams, The Jargon Society 23, 1958, n.p.

Wilson, Elizabeth A. *Gut Feminism*. Duke UP, 2015.

Wineapple, Brenda. "The Politics of Politics, or, How the Atom Bomb Didn't Interest Gertrude Stein and Emily Dickinson." *South Central Review*, vol. 23, no. 3, 2006, pp. 37–45.

Winters, Yvor. 1938. "Emily Dickinson and the Limits of Judgement." *Emily Dickinson: A Collection of Critical Essays*, edited by Richard B. Sewell, Prentice Hall, 1963, pp. 28–40.

—. "Mina Loy." *The Dial*, vol. 80, no. 6, 1926, pp. 496–9.

Wissinger, Elizabeth. "Always on Display: Affective Reproduction in the Modelling Industry." *The Affective Turn*, edited by Patricia Ticineto Clough, Duke UP, 2007, pp. 231–60.

Wolf, Naomi. *Ecstasy or Justice? The Sexual Author and the Law, 1855–1885*. 2015. New College, U of Oxford, PhD dissertation, *Oxford University Research Archive*, ora.ox.ac.uk/objects/uuid:5eb 70130-f130-4c8f-8757-1f304d2ffb96.

Wolff, Janet. "Reinstating Corporeality: Feminism and Body Politics." *Meaning in Motion: New Cultural Studies of Dance*, edited by Jane C. Desmond, Duke UP, 1997, pp. 81–99.

Wollstonecraft, Mary. 1792. *A Vindication of the Rights of Woman*. Edited by Carol H. Poston. W. W. Norton & Co., 1975.

Wolosky, Shira. "Emily Dickinson: Being in the Body." *The Cambridge Companion to Emily Dickinson*, edited by Wendy Martin, Cambridge UP, 2002, pp. 129–41.

Wood, Clement. "Poetry's New Tools." *The English Journal*, vol. 22, no. 8, 1933, pp. 615–27.

Woolf, Virginia. *Congenial Spirits: The Selected Letters of Virginia Woolf*. Edited by Joanne Trautmann Banks, Pimlico Books, 2003.

Ziller, R. L. "The True Eucharist." *The Christian Science Journal*, October 1894, n.p. journal.christianscience.com/shared/view/rfjz7j7epc.

Žižek, Slavoj. *Violence: Six Sideways Reflections*. Profile Books, 2009.

Index

EU Authorised Representative:

Easy Access System Europe Mustamäe tee 50, 10621 Tallinn, Estonia

gpsr.requests@easproject.com

Printed and bound by CPI Group (UK) Ltd, Croydon, CR0 4YY

17/05/2026

02112410-0010